Arguments with Silence

Arguments with Silence

Writing the History of Roman Women

❧

AMY RICHLIN

The University of Michigan Press
Ann Arbor

Published in the United States of America by
The University of Michigan Press
Manufactured in the United States of America
⊗ Printed on acid-free paper

2017   2016   2015   2014   4   3   2   1

A CIP catalog record for this book is available from the British Library.

ISBN 978-0-472-11925-7 (cloth)
ISBN 978-0-472-03592-2 (paperback)
ISBN 978-0-472-12013-0 (ebook)

For Judith Hallett and Marilyn Skinner

comitibus

Contents

❧

Acknowledgments

This book takes a long look back over two decades that shaped several generations, and my debts of gratitude are many. My first thanks go to my parents, Samuel and Sylvia Richlin, who not only paid for my education with two lifetimes of alienated labor but gave me constant moral support, cheering me on. My father referred to my time on the job market as "going down by Heckerman's," a sympathetic echo of the neighborhood prostitute who, tormented by my father's boyhood gang, used to yell at them, "Go vay, ya doidy bums! I'm going down by Heckerman's to peddle mine hess." I owe him lifelong thanks for his perspective, and the love and faith behind it. The essay that now forms chapter 10 was dedicated to "S. V. R.": my father, who took "Vercingetorix" as his middle name, and went back to college at the age of seventy-six to major in Women's Studies. He died while *Feminist Theory and the Classics* was in press, but, in *Arguments with Silence*, his spirit lives on; right next to my mom's, who was the one who took me to the Met, and taught me to look at old things.

My teachers Jack Cundari, Sarah Smith, Jeffrey Henderson, Gordon Williams, and Jack Winkler started me out, and Elaine Fantham gave me her *imprimatur* at a time when I badly needed it, along with a lot of coaching, most of which I probably did not take in. James Tatum has been a constant friend and co-joker since my days at Dartmouth; Mary-Kay Gamel, with her usual magnanimity, welcomed me to beautiful Santa Cruz and into the world of ancient theater. My students over the years have been a source of joy and inspiration, and I particularly want to thank Ellen Olmstead for the bibliography on women writers of the world, Melinda de Jesus for the diskettes (because), Monica Rios for handing me her paper and a Spanish dictionary, David Fredrick for standing (and sitting) by me in San Francisco, Cindy Benton and Trevor Fear for grace under pressure, Philip Purchase for making me read Franco Moretti, Mark Masterson for travels in late antiquity, Rhiannon Evans for travels in geography, Siobhán McElduff for help with translation theory, and most recently Emily Selove for bridging trashy texts in Arabic and Latin, and Ellen Snyder for pushing me onward in feminist theory.

For this new collection of old things, new thanks are due. Ellen Bauerle prompted me to seek out her editorial help by the paper she gave at the 2011 APA meeting, a statistical survey of women publishing in the field of ancient history; she has boosted me through every chore. Grace Gillies, fresh from her MA work on Domitia Lucilla, spent the summer of 2012 checking references with meticulous care, funded by a generous grant from the UCLA Faculty Senate. For advice on new bibliography, I am grateful to Fanny Dolansky, Rebecca Flemming, Elizabeth Greene, Lora Holland, Sharon James, C. W. Marshall, Holt Parker, Elizabeth Pollard, and the anonymous reviewers for the Press. At UCLA, special thanks go to Christopher Johanson and John Papadopoulos for help with images, and to Kathryn Morgan and Mario Telò for many consultations. Appropriately, Judith Hallett and Marilyn Skinner plowed through the whole manuscript and greatly improved both the bibliography and the introduction—Marilyn, especially, reminding me to keep optimism in the picture. My dear husband, Lon Grabowski, has kept the home fires burning even during the throes of the editing process.

The volume introduction attempts to paint a picture of the sociology of feminism in Classics in the 1980s—an incomplete one, I know, because it is written specifically from the perspective of my own experience in writing about Romans, and textual Romans, at that. Along the way, two people above all have helped me learn more about theory: Sandra Joshel and Nancy Sorkin Rabinowitz, to whom I owe an ongoing debt. This book, meanwhile, is dedicated to the two scholars who were, and still are, my companions in thinking about Roman women and about why it matters to teach and write about them: Judith Hallett and Marilyn Skinner, two great teachers, two great scholars, two great women.

Introduction

In Search of Roman Women

੨੩

History-writing, in my book, is material—a history that thinks about events enacted by, experienced by, real people. Here are the tracks of two people like those I have in mind:

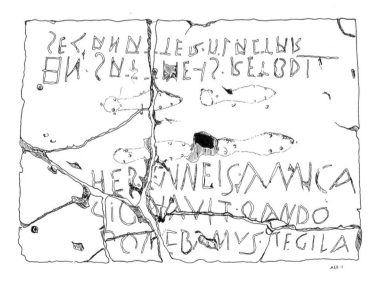

Fig. 1. Roof tile from Pietrabbondante, Italy, bearing the footprints and signatures of the two workers who made the tile. (Drawing Amy Richlin, after La Regina 1976: 285.)

Andrew Wallace-Hadrill describes this object in the context of the mix of cultures in Republican Italy (2008: 90):

> In the great sanctuary complex of Pietrabbondante . . . up in the roof of the temple, where nobody could see, a roof tile betrayed a bilingual reality. . . . Two workers in the tile factory "signed" their work by imprinting [it] with their footprints, and by incising their names and slightly different messages from opposite edges of the tile, one in Oscan, the other in Latin:

> > *hn. sattiieis detfri*
> > *seganatted. plavtad*
> > (Detfri slave of Herennius Sattius/ signed with a footprint)

> > *Herenneis Amica*
> > *signavit. quando*
> > *ponebamus. tegila*
> > (Amica slave of Herennius/ signed when/ we were placing the
> >   tile)[1]

These two slave women made a mark to show they were there, not only in words but in the flesh.

Finding Roman women is a challenge. In the ten essays here presented, I was following more elusive tracks through words mostly written by Roman men; from most ancient women we have only silence, hence the title *Arguments with Silence*, and the book's constant search for the women just out of hearing. Because my own early work was on Roman satire and invective, I picked up a trail running through the seamy, bodily side of women's experience: sex, procreation, body modification, medicine, cult practice, work, death. Because of the nature of these texts, the work made me think and write about the methodological problems of writing such history. The first nine chapters appear in the order in which they were published, 1981–2001, and trace a continuous arc of thought, a set of developing ideas, about Roman women and about how to write their history. As became evident when I came to consider the conditions under which these essays were produced, they also trace a history of ideas in a developing subfield of history-writing, "Women in Antiquity," now discussed in the introductions to each chapter; the new connective tissue here then deals not only with the theory of history, but also with the sociology of knowledge. The chapters themselves, though, are not of historic interest only, dealing as they do with issues in women's history that are still under-studied and too rarely juxtaposed; literature and history are still uneasy companions, and there are still a hundred readers of love poetry for every reader of invective. Everything in this book still seems to me to need explaining, teaching, and discussion.

The essays here included were published in a variety of venues: classical journals (chapters 2 and 4); collections of essays in Classics aimed at a feminist or gender-studies readership (chapters 1, 5, 8, and 10); collections aimed at a readership in disciplines other than Classics (chapters 3, 6, and 7); a Festschrift (chapter 9). I wanted to put them all together in a single volume, calling them together from their far-flung stations for the use of present and future seekers of Roman women. Making the collection and updating the bibliography have made me reflect on how venue determines audience: not just how hard it is for feminist classicists to reach a general Women's Studies audience, a big preoccupation of ours in the 1990s, but how unlikely it was that, for example, an essay on Roman women's religion published in a collection titled *Women and Goddess Traditions* would find its way to classicists. Reading and writing are social actions.

Because most of these essays had been produced before Microsoft Word—some of them, indeed, before the adoption of computers—all the text had to be retyped. I took this as an opportunity to tinker, and so the essays are retooled, not just for wording and accuracy but with new bibliography and expanded primary sources, particularly Plautine comedy. The essays you hold in your hand now address both the time of writing and the time of rewriting, already receding into the past even as I type these words. Historians of women must confront the perishable nature of women's lives, and our own are no different. So I write this to commemorate the lives of Roman women, whom I never knew, as well as the lives of the women I have known who have thought about Roman women.

This introduction, along with the chapter introductions, is written in the personal voice, not everyone's cup of tea; I still remember strongly what a liberation it was to me to use this voice for the first time, writing "Hijacking the Palladion" (1990), sitting in my tower room in Bethlehem, Pennsylvania, and throwing footnotes out the window. This practice was itself the subject of a volume of essays edited by Judith Hallett and Thomas Van Nortwick (1997), and of a three-year colloquium at the American Philological Association (APA) leading to a special issue of *Arethusa* in 2001; Nancy

Rabinowitz eloquently locates personal-voice writing in contemporary discourse and explains what it has to do with women and feminism.[2] I can only echo her conclusion that "the personal voice must be characterized as one committed to social change" (2001: 207). Moreover, I firmly believe, and try to teach my students, that the main thing in writing is to know why you do it; here I am putting my cards on the table.

So: why do I do it? I feel a sense of duty to the dead, to tell their stories as best I can; in telling women's stories, I am working toward a society that remembers women. But I have companions in the telling, all with reasons of their own. This project, now spanning thirty years, exemplifies the kinds of questions asked by the wave of women who entered the academy in the 1970s, and founded a new study of the history of women. We wrote in order to change the stories our culture tells about its past—to make women visible in that past, and to make gender visible as a major element in all cultures. We wrote in order to become scholars; we wrote in order to be heard ourselves; we wrote for a living; we wrote, like all writers, because it called us. Those of us coming from graduate programs in Classics wrote in partnership—sometimes we called it "sisterhood"—with women in other fields in the humanities and social sciences. In 1981, the year the first chapter in this book was published, we were still in the early stages. In 2012, as I write, we might be facing the end of the project in Classics—or maybe not; we can usefully reflect now on what we learned, what we taught, and what remains to be done. Work is still in progress.

Methodology: The Woman in the Table

In her novel *The Dispossessed*, Ursula K. Le Guin juxtaposes two societies, one on a planet, one on that planet's moon. On the moon live anarchists, committed to a completely egalitarian society; on the planet, a conventional hierarchical society holds sway. A physicist defects from the anarchy to the hierarchy; en route, on the spaceship, he is much surprised to find there are no women on the ship—his hosts feel that women do not belong there, that women could not handle running a freighter. Even so, the physicist begins to notice a sort of sensuous feel to the ship's fittings (Le Guin 1974: 15):

And the design of the furniture in the officers' lounge, the smooth plastic curves into which stubborn wood and steel had been forced, the smoothness and delicacy of surfaces and textures: were these not also faintly, pervasively erotic? He knew himself well enough to be sure that a few days without [his wife], even under great stress, should not get him so worked up that he felt a woman in every table top. Not unless the woman were really there.

The "K." in Le Guin's name stands for "Kroeber," and, as a writer of science fiction, she walks in the tracks of her father, the great anthropologist. Anthropologists, at least ideally, look at societies as whole systems, and in the twentieth century this began to seem like a good idea to historians as well. The study of history from below helped to enable the project of writing women into history, underscoring the fact that the history seen from the top had been so almost exclusively male, except for the odd queen. The problems with writing women's history, or a gender-inclusive history, stemmed from the same truths that caused problems with writing the history of the poor, or slaves, or children: these groups either did not themselves write, or what writing they did was not kept. To find what is hard to find is still a challenge much to the liking of many history-writers. The women were really there. Maybe we could find them in the table. Or maybe, if we search the corners, the kitchens, the laundry, we could hear them speak in their own voices.

Such a search is grounded in what I have called an "optimistic epistemology": the belief that past events are recognizable—that concepts travel, as Mieke Bal puts it (see chapter 10; Richlin 2013b). Suzanne Dixon deflatingly calls the idea that we could squeeze women out of that recalcitrant table "the Sleeping Beauty view of history" (2001: 5), but she continues to try; as the essays in this volume show, the project of hunting around for Roman women leads to some methodological tactics and principles. First, the whole project is filled with what historians call "lamppost problems," based on the old joke about the man who was looking for his keys under the lamppost because it was too dark in the alley where he'd dropped them. Would you like to know, from women themselves, about ordinary women's daily life, their relations to their families, their use of property? You can't look in Athens or Rome—try Egypt, where whole dossiers of papyrus letters are extant. Do you want to know about slaves, from their own perspective? Look in the graveyard—the library will not really tell you; the same goes for women's religious practice, especially their agency as leaders.

This strategy ties in with another issue: different kinds of sources tell different stories when asked the same question. As seen in chapter 1, the question "what happened to a man and woman caught in adultery?" has different answers in law, history, moral exempla, gossip, and satire; possibly, then, by asking as many different kinds of sources as possible we can arrive at a complex answer, closer to "what happened." The process of running these questions I long ago compared (1990: 181) to the scene in *Forbidden Planet* where the invisible monster is ambushed by a circle of men armed with laser cannons: they fire at the monster from their points on the circle, and with them we see the monster outlined in 3-D. For this purpose, from early on it came to seem crucial to me to look low as well as high; it was an intellectual blessing, if at times a professional curse, to have begun with a low theme (sexuality) in a low genre (satire) and its even lower relations (the *Carmina Priapea*, epigram, graffiti). In Rome, the same writers wrote both epic poetry and obscene poetry; classicists put the epic poetry and not the obscene poetry into the curriculum, but in the original culture the top and bottom made each other. To see the whole monster you really need a sphere and not a circle. The chapters that follow are full of cultural junk, and I only wish we had more of it.

Thus chapter 2, on invective, deals with the most harshly misogynistic texts in Latin—disgusting texts, texts that speak disgust—contemplation of which caused me to argue that such texts (counter to then-common readings) do not tell you directly about women, but they do tell you what women had to put up with. In taking these texts to have had a direct effect on contemporary women, I began an argument against what is now known as "persona theory," in which such texts are read as ineffectual through their very outrageousness (more on this below).

Chapter 3 in particular taught me another lesson about writing about Rome in particular that in turn should be useful elsewhere. The jokes about Julia, daughter of Augustus, preserved in Macrobius's *Saturnalia*, bear witness to (at least) two times: the time of their original production and the time when Macrobius put them into his book. Roman writers going back to Plautus are always writing about something else in order to write about now—it was a strongly marked cultural trait, and should sensitize us to the complicated nature of any writer's motivation (or, of any text's context). If meaning is made at the point of reception, we have to realize that we are usually dealing with something already at least once received, and that we ourselves need, then, to write accordingly: doubly, triply. The jokes are about Julia, but also about something—somebody?—else, and it turned out to be quite possible to find out what other women Macrobius might have had in mind. Similarly, as seen in the chapters on religion (7) and medicine (8), the same text can often be read in opposing ways: glass half empty, glass half full (see chapter 10). Rather than presenting possibilities as in a priamel, picking the best one (*egô de*), we might more usefully present each as equally valid, or each equally possible at different times (see Rabinowitz 1998 for an example of this technique applied to Greek drama). History-writers today cannot decide, based on the existing evidence, whether these jokes were really Julia's words or were made up about her; chapter 3 works out analyses based on both scenarios.

In writing "Julia's Jokes" and trying to establish an "historical context" for Julia and her jokes—two contexts, one in Augustan Rome and one in Rome around 400 CE—I ran into the *Forbidden Planet* problem again, since Roman narrative histories themselves are as constructed as the jokes are. The experience led me to the uncharacteristically pessimistic conclusion that Julia herself is unreachable to a history-writer. Others have arrived at a similar radical skepticism, notably Suzanne Dixon in *Reading Roman Women*, who comes to focus on how different genres go about their cultural work (2001: ix):

> Each text is designed to project ideology (e.g. of proper womanly behaviour) rather than circumstantial information about any given woman, even when it purports to record a specific, historicised woman. My own wish to recover the history of women has survived . . . but my initial confidence that the real Roman woman could be conjured up from a close reading of legal sources has dwindled.

Yet this downturn in confidence is not final (2001: 15): "Behind our sober statements and academic language lurks the passionate wish to see through the veils of representations and read the women obscured by them, even if the one thing on which we all agree is that we cannot."

Kristina Milnor defines a similar project (2005: 40–41):

> Ultimately, however, this is a study of representation rather than reality—although, in truth, I hope that the following pages will do something to challenge the conventional dichotomy between those two terms. . . . It is very difficult to write the 'real' history of women, slaves, working men, foreigners, and other marginalized groups, both because they often do not appear in ancient texts, and because, when they do appear, they are so clearly figments of an elite male author's imagination.

Dixon's "wish," Milnor's "hope," infuse the pages of this book as well; I can see the ideology ticking away, but ultimately hope to find, hope I have found, something about real women.

By the mid-1980s, feminists in other academic disciplines had moved toward work on writing by women, ransacking libraries and archives. What were we to do without any comparable body of texts? And what about the authors on the reading list—were we just to abandon them? Phyllis Culham's iconoclastic argument at the 1985 Women's Classical Caucus panel at the APA meeting insisted that no real women could be derived from the pages of Ovid, and that real women were our proper business. Culham spoke as an historian with a robustly optimistic epistemology, but most classicists are trained in literary criticism and not in history-writing. Her argument resonated with the material-culture scholars—some archaeologists, some art historians, some papyrologists; unlike text people, they can hold in their hands an object that once belonged to a Roman woman.[3] Some objects, indeed, say in large letters that they were paid for by a Roman woman; as Suzanne Dixon points out, "Naevoleia Tyche went to some trouble to ensure that we knew her name" (Dixon 2001: x, cf. ix, 97).

Chapter 4 deals with a Roman woman writer, Sulpicia the satirist, who is almost unknown, because all that remains of her work is a two-line fragment. She thus stands as a handy reminder of why it is important to read women writers: (1) they were there, and their first-person voice can tell what no one else can tell for them—in the case of this Sulpicia and her foremother Sulpicia the elegist, they tell not only their desire, but their desire for men, a great rarity in premodern literature; (2) their fragmentary state is a fact about them, and repays thought and inquiry. To have a woman satirist is a bonus, taking us back to questions raised by Julia's jokes and to questions about women and comedy in general, as in chapter 2. Moreover, chapters 2, 3, and 4 all incorporate testimonia from late antiquity; a great deal of work remains to be done on the persistence of the satirical and invective traditions in Christian ideas. Here Sulpicia also stands as a reminder that women talked back.

Whereas historians tend to accept that a large marble tomb, for example, was paid for by the person indicated by an inscription on that tomb, most scholars would not take a literary text at face value. Trends within the academy at large from the 1980s to the present have encouraged readers to abandon the idea of determinable meanings and authorial intent, along with any confidence that we can arrive at any knowledge of a reality outside the text, or see anything other than the text itself, or a set of texts in relation to each other, or analyze an alien text with our own system of ideas. This last poses a big problem for classicists, who cannot interview the audience after Ovid gives a reading. But it seems to me that the insistence on the radical difference of the past can border on a sort of exoticizing; the word "before" in a title now makes me think, "Cue tom-toms" (cf. Bennett 2006: 43 on the myth of the premodern as necessarily the opposite of all things modern). History-writers work to become conscious of the limits of their understanding, and write accordingly; the nature of the whole project demands, as Walter Benjamin says, a recognition of the past by the present as one of its own concerns. To continue with the "Theses on the Philosophy of History": "Only that historian will have the gift of fanning the spark of hope in the past who is firmly convinced that *even the dead* will not be safe from the enemy if he wins" (1968: 255).

The slipperiness of authorial intent inspires persona theory. In the United States, this approach owes a great deal to William S. Anderson's urgings, going back to the 1960s, that classicists should give up reading so naively and take a tip from our colleagues in the English Department (e.g., Anderson 1964). We should be conscious of how writers address each other in their writing, how self-conscious they are, how almost parodic. I wrote chapter 5 originally, in part, in indignant reaction to the thesis put forth by several of Anderson's former graduate students, who argue that the nasty jokes about rape in the *Ars amatoria* belong to a ridiculed character, not to Ovid himself, who in reality is showing this character up for the fool he is. Similar arguments have been made about Juvenal, and continue today. In reply, I would say that content is not erased by quotation marks. In "Reading Ovid's Rapes," looking at the *Ars amatoria*, *Fasti*, and *Metamorphoses*, I compared Ovid's style to "a bow on a slaughterhouse," and it is very interesting that the same kinds of cuing, like wrapping paper, are used on violent sexual fantasies like Ovid's and on crude jokes and invective (Juvenal, Martial, the *Priapea*). That is, each writer presents each reader with a beautiful style (the incomparable Juvenal), or an elegant package (the miniature perfection of an epigram), or a cool persona (Lucilius, Catullus, Persius). Theorists of humor write about the "cue" that tells you "it's just a joke," thereby disarming any anger, indeed preempting it; it seems that rhetoric, that style itself, can have the same function as "Three men walked into a bar . . ." The literary system works like a team of con men, with tragedy yelling "Help!" while comedy picks your pocket; people who love literature tend to divide into epic/tragedy people and comedy/satire people, and epic calls the shots. But to understand gender in history, it is crucial to read across these generic lines, and not be beguiled by the packaging.

"Making Up a Woman" (chapter 6) takes off from chapter 5, beginning with Ovid's didactic poem on women's cosmetics. Both essays use a set of tools developed around 1990 to analyze the pornographic—the way texts and visual media objectify bodies—including "gaze theory" and approaches to analyzing violent fantasy. It seems to me that this body of theory, so closely associated with its time, deserves to be kept in use, since the issues that inspired it are, if anything, more pressing than ever. In addition, both Ovid's rape stories and ancient texts about cosmetics relate both to the history of slavery and to the construction of gender through body modification: in antiquity, ideas about rape and the painted body affected not only all women, and not only all slaves, but also the spectrum of male sexualities (especially through rhetorical theory) and the development of an Orientalism whereby East/West was painted as effeminate/manly. Thus students being asked to read classical texts as canonical need gender theory in their toolbox, not only to denaturalize misogyny but also to help them see how similar ideas structure gender, ethnicity, slave/free status, and class.

Class, and a fortiori slavery, have historically been hard for the women's movement to deal with, and the same problem affects history-writers. Are women a class? Who are we talking about when we say "Roman women"? "Everybody with a vagina," as a student once said in my history seminar. But there is a long-standing tendency among scholars to mean "citizen women" when they say "women," and for slaves to be treated separately or just left out. Did women identify as women across class divides (for example, at the theater, at the Lupercalia, on the street, while weaving)? Chapter 1, in dealing with adultery, focuses on the citizen women by definition covered by the law, with only passing recognition of the ways in which slavery structured women's sexual experience within households. Chapter 7, written fourteen years later, is subtitled "Class and the Body in Roman Women's Religion," and comes to an understanding of Roman women's religion as fundamentally structured around class divisions related to control of sexual access to the body—goddess worship thus being liberating in no sense of the word. At the same time, following a good news/bad news approach that was becoming habitual, this chapter lays out the basic evidence for women's agency in religion, for the gender-integrated nature of Roman religion, and for the constant, active involvement of women in the Roman religious calendar at all levels, from state to home. (I emphasize this because you would not know it from current handbooks on Roman religion; see below.) Chapter 8, "Pliny's Brassiere," similarly looks for women's agency in their own medical treatment, visible even in a decidedly male-oriented writer like the elder Pliny. Just as we can reconstruct the daily lives of real women through the religious calendar, we can fill in part of their schedule with an eye to the health practices to which Pliny, however grudgingly, attests. Finally, the "emotional work" tracked in chapter 9 focuses on the figure of the *praefica*, the hired worker who led the funeral lament. The word *neniae* means both "lament" and "trivial things"; sticking to the theoretical principle that trivial things are telling, this essay considers the relation between class and loss in Roman thought.

The *praefica* stands in the midst of an elaborate funeral on the Amiternum relief, bringing us back to the two tile workers who began this introduction. If you look hard enough, you can see the woman in the table. Nine ways to look for her:

- The *Forbidden Planet* principle: use a wide range of evidence, from low to high.
- Think about how texts affect their audiences, but never take those audiences to be monolithic; look for ways in which different people talked back.
- Remember that all history is contemporary history, in the past as well as now, so that past history-writers wrote their own times, too, when they wrote the past: show this.
- When you have ambiguous evidence, write two possible solutions; indeterminacy is more accurate than a forced determinacy.
- Look for women writers; when they are fragmentary, read fragmentation. Get off the beaten path to look for them.
- Use old tools that, like gaze theory, stay useful.
- Think about the co-implications of gender, class, and ethnicity, and never forget that in the ancient Mediterranean there was no place outside the slave system. Do not say "Romans" when you mean "Roman men," and do not say "Roman women" when you are talking only about citizen women. Try not to talk only about citizens; where enslavement was a fluid experience, treat it as such.
- Treat cultural systems like medicine and religion as necessarily involving all kinds of people, including women.

- Make time to broaden your skill base: learn to read inscriptions, graffiti, papyri, writing tablets; learn another ancient language; go late, on into Byzantium.
- Don't take no for an answer. Argue with silence.

A Parenthesis on the History of Theory and Method

It must be conceded that the history I recommend writing, while I believe it will certainly be written, has checked a lot of baggage; the question "Who are we talking about when we say 'Roman women'?" didn't just pop into my head. By the mid-1980s, feminist theory as a whole was moving toward an extreme form of the "takes one to know one" stance, amounting by the early 1990s to a prevailing solipsism. The term "women" itself, as referring to any comprehensible group, was falling into such disfavor that the editors of the *Journal of Women's History*, in its inaugural issue (1989: 7), felt obliged to apologize for its title. This situation has only been exacerbated by the natural move, starting around 2000, to global feminism. Women's Studies survived the threat of submersion into Gender Studies in the 1990s only to find itself primarily involved with cross-cultural studies in which "women" could not comfortably be used as a generic term; the same rule, by this reasoning, applies to women who lived before the present (although the study of premodern history is now itself threatened with extinction). So the Iranian historian Afsaneh Najmabadi, writing in the *Journal of Women's History* (2006: 18):

> The more general question is how concepts travel and what happens to concepts as they travel. Let me briefly point to one such example. Remember the debates over the question, were there any lesbians (or lesbian-like women) in medieval Europe? Without replaying that discussion, I want to use it as a way of returning that question to gender: Were there any women in medieval Europe? Try asking this question in your classes and see what a great discussion you get! That we ask the first question with comfort and presume the ease of the answer to the second (well, of course there were women, but defined differently) works on the presumption of the naturalness of woman; that there have always been women. What does it mean that we do not have the same discomfort with presuming the possibility of existence of women in medieval Europe that we have about lesbians?

In other words, not only can we not find out what happened in the past, we don't even have a set object to look for. This cheery skepticism (Najmabadi's essay began as a keynote address to an audience of a thousand historians of women at the Berkshire Conference) takes a dig in passing at the patient work of Judith Bennett, who coined the term "lesbian-like" in order to hold onto a much-valued object of study (2000; cf. Bennett 2006: 9–10 on "women" as a problematic term).[4] It is certainly true that the targets of invective, as in the case of *cinaedi*, cannot be assumed to have defined themselves as they were defined by their attackers, or even to have self-identified as a group, especially when, like *cinaedi*, they have left no first-person statements about themselves as such (see Richlin 1993). But ancient women have left at least some statements about themselves as women.

What we might usefully do in the twenty-first century is think about the part those women played in the ancient Mediterranean viewed transnationally (or transculturally—across, say, the Roman empire), and how that set of gender systems carried over into late antiquity and the development of the Christian/Islamic world. We can talk to scholars who work on women in neighboring cultures, from Persia to China. As Uma Narayan argues (2000: 86):

> Antiessentialist feminists can counter [the] static picture of culture by insisting on a historical understanding of the contexts in which what are currently taken to be "particular cultures" came to be seen and defined as such. For example, while a prevailing picture of "Western culture" has its beginning in ancient Greece . . . a historical perspective would register that the ancient Greeks did not define themselves as part of "Western culture." . . .

A similar argument was made by Bella Vivante in comparing archaic Greek to Native American gender systems (Zweig 1993). We have a multiple set of cultures in the ancient Mediterranean, where the sex/gender systems varied quite a bit from east to west: differing practices in veiling, divorce, public presence, property rights—all coexisted side by side. Different how? And what did these institutions mean to women and men then, and afterwards, as Christianity and Islam took over, as Judaism went on? I will suggest below that what looks like an extremely male-dominated system might not have appeared so much so to the participants.

Nevertheless, to follow Narayan further (2000: 95):

> Insofar as versions of relativism subscribe to these colonial pictures of "essential differences" between cultures, relativism becomes a danger rather than an asset to feminist agendas. . . . Third World feminist political struggles are often painfully aware that there are a number of "master's houses." Some of these houses are owned not by "Western" masters but are part of the local real estate, while others have deeds so intricate that it is difficult to unravel how much they are the properties of "local" or "Western" masters.

Narayan here borrows a term from a famous essay by Audre Lorde, "The Master's Tools Will Never Dismantle the Master's House" (1984)—an essay that came home to Second Wave feminists in Classics, uneasily conscious that the master's house is our home. But all classicists are wont to look upon antiquity sometimes as foundational, sometimes as the before-time (see chapter 10). The cultures we study went through a major transition in late antiquity, and we might do some good by thinking about how it happened, as in Kathy Gaca's study of the range of relations between Christian and Jewish asceticisms and pagan philosophy (2003). The heavy history of the many receptions of the pre-Christian past is ours to tell.

Who are we talking about when we say "Roman women"? The answer to that question, too, has changed over time. In the 1970s women's history began with what lay to hand, focusing on what came to be described as "women worthies" —high-profile, elite women, familiar from the canonical texts everybody knew. For us, Cleopatra, Livia, there must be more . . . Caesar's wife, Cornelia-mother-of-the-Gracchi, Cleopatra, Messalina, and then the temptations of literature's paper dolls: Lucretia, Clodia/Lesbia, Cynthia, Delia, Corinna. As Judith Bennett notes in her overview of developments in the field of women's history (2006: 23–24), by the 1980s, feminist historians were looking for everyday women; the 1985 WCC panel centered on Phyllis Culham's insistence that everyday women's lives were not to be found in elite male-authored literature (see Culham 1990; Liveley 2006). Marilyn Skinner, in "Rescuing Creusa" (1987b: 4), hailed the arrival of an era in which canonical texts, the Reading List, were moving over to make room for the noncanonical, and, to the degree that this is so, it makes the everyday more available. Judith Hallett, in 1993, called for a move away from the canonical alley and over to that lamppost: get away from Athens and into Hellenistic Alexandria and the multicultural world of the Second Sophistic; deal with "Rome" as a multicultural empire; look away from the time periods narrowly defined as "golden." The more we work with scholars in the history of religion—who study the Christian and Jewish contemporaries of the women we study, our next-door neighbors—the better a picture we will have of women's lives in that long-gone world. The same goes for papyrology, which has always been the precinct of a very few highly specialized scholars; the work being done now by Roger Bagnall, Raffaella Cribiore, Maryline Parca, Jane Rowlandson, and Terry Wilfong takes us through more than a thousand years of women's history. Sarah Pomeroy herself began as a papyrologist. Lloyd Llewellyn-Jones's work on veiling (2003) shows what material culture can offer to the new questions we might ask.

Scholars now live in a world that incorporates human trafficking, but probably not on their street; we don't know what slavery feels like to slave or free. Tensions between owner women and slave women infused Roman households, and comedy suggests there were culture-wide issues between sex workers and married women. It is illuminating to track the hard-to-translate word *paelex* through the chapters of this book: it refers, from the wife's point of view, to another woman with whom her husband has sex, with strong implications of lower status and feelings of bitterness. As we move on in writing the history of ancient women, we need to keep the practices of enslavement in mind. Sandra Joshel and Sheila Murnaghan did pioneering work in their collection *Women and Slaves in Greco-Roman Culture* (1998b); ongoing work includes major projects by Kathy Gaca (rape and enslavement of women and girls in war) and C. W. Marshall (human trafficking as seen in New Comedy), by Sandra Joshel and Lauren Petersen (slaves in the built environment of the Roman villa), and by the group headed by Bernadette Brooten (below). It now seems to me that "Reading Ovid's Rapes" and "Emotional Work" need to be completely rethought in terms of the accounts of what was done to women and girls in the course of what Gaca calls "populace-ravaging warfare," and of the images of such women in Roman art (see Dillon 2006). The "structure vs. agency" debate (chapter 10) is blown open by the juxtaposition of Kyle Harper's analysis of Roman honor/shame norms as implicated in "systemic sexual exploitation" through slavery (2011), and Sarah Levin-Richardson's reclamation of women's agency in Pompeian sexual graffiti (2013). Horizons beckon: late antiquity, Byzantium, performance studies (dance, all drama genres), material culture. It's not just that there's more light under the lamppost than in the alley; there's more space.

Chapter 10 steps back to look at the process of theory-making itself, based on a passing remark by Marilyn Skinner about "pessimists and optimists," and divides history-writers accordingly, first at the level of epistemology (can we know about the past?) and then at the level of results (do we like what we find there?). In that essay, I felt obliged to identify myself as an essentialist, since I firmly believe that misogyny is a transhistorical and transcultural phenomenon; I agree with Judith Bennett that we have to deal with the question "Why and how has the oppression of women endured for so long and in so many different historical settings?" (2006: 28). But I also reached the relativist conclusion that people choose theory according to their temperament, and that the important thing is the dialogue itself—keeping the thing going, as Sojourner Truth once said. Ironically, a prevailing relativism in the academy has often become that oxymoron, a dogmatic relativism. I hope tolerance will prevail, for we have a lot to say to each other, and to the world. We have a history together.

Sociology: We Are Not Invisible to Each Other

> I'm down on the strike line with my children and we are not invisible to each other, to those who won't cross our lines, or to those who pass by us.
> *Donna Langston, "Down on the Strike Line with My Children" (1990)*

"We are not invisible to each other" explains what happened: women arrived in the academy in large numbers around 1970 and called for a new object of study. As Alice Echols makes clear in *Daring to Be Bad* (1989), the training in political activism women found in the New Left derived directly from the Civil Rights movement; so it might be said that women achieved critical mass in the academy as a by-product of the final (or temporary) ending of the institution of slavery in the West. It is abundantly clear that gender matters in determining what questions get asked, what counts as scholarship, what is worth studying. This book brings back some research I did between 1981 and 2001, and tells how it came to be written, not only for the sake of Roman women, but to argue with another kind of silence: the silence that falls over women's writing (ongoing—see Holland 2012: 213). I wrote about this in 1991 in "Zeus and Metis"; although I know now that most scholarly writing is forgotten, work by women still seems to me to have too hard a time getting into canonical reading lists. Yet extensive work on the history of scholarship has taught me that it is possible to leave a trail.

The story of the rise of the field known as "Women in Antiquity" has been well told by Barbara McManus (1997); see also comments by Suzanne Dixon, writing specifically as a Roman historian (2001: 3–15), and by Genevieve Liveley, writing from the perspective of the "Third Wave" of feminism (2006), and the special issue of the Women's Classical Caucus publication *Cloelia* from fall 2007.[5] I came in in the middle, getting involved with the Caucus in 1982 once I had my first tenure-track job, after spending five years in temporary positions. By then I was ready. My research had made me a feminist, even as I began to see what was happening to the women all around me on the job market and on the job. Before then, in college, in grad school, I had seen no need. Embodying a transition of which I was barely conscious, I spent my freshman year at Smith College and then transferred to Princeton, joining in 1970 the first coeducated class to start there. It wasn't just that women were new to Princeton; I walked the paths where not a lot of working-class students or Jews had walked in past decades, but suddenly there were plenty of us, and it was all fine (cf. Rabinowitz 2001: 197). The head coach who tried to block the founding of women's crew at Princeton fell to the juggernaut of Title IX, and we won the Easterns; I enjoyed being the only woman in my undergraduate classes, I started graduate school in 1973 with confidence in the future, I refused to join NOW, I had no children. All around me, other smart Jewish girls were shooting their mouths off; as a classicist and a jock, I was practically a conservative. At Yale in the spring of 1976 I took up a dissertation on "sexual terms and themes in Roman satire and related genres" almost casually—David Claus pointed out to me, in a two-minute conversation on a street corner, that the dissertation I was planning on colonialism as seen in Tacitus and other Roman historians might take me some years to write, and Jeffrey Henderson, encountered five minutes later in the library, suggested a study of the Roman lexicon like the one he had just published on Aristophanes. It sounded like fun. Down the hall, Jack Winkler was joining in Catharine MacKinnon's nascent activism around sexual harassment, and I did walk around New Haven wearing a pink triangle to show solidarity, but it took the *Carmina Priapea*, along with the total lack of notice in the scholarly literature that there was anything odd about this text, to make me think about what Engels called "the world historical defeat of the female sex." At Rutgers, in my first job (1977–79), I was just trying to survive under a four-four teaching load; at Dartmouth, starting to write *The Garden of Priapus*, I began to look around for explanations of violent sexual humor and bought a copy of *Take Back the Night* at the Dartmouth Bookstore. When I arrived at the NEH Institute on Women in Antiquity in the summer of 1983, after a year teaching at Lehigh, I introduced myself to the group as a feminist, and with some belligerence.

I was angry, and with good reason. School, national examinations, athletics, grad school, so far, in my (lucky) experience, had been more or less meritocratic. The job market was not. All around me I saw brilliant women barely hanging on in marginal jobs. Their work was judged, and often dismissed, by established colleagues, some of whom had published little themselves. They had no library (and this was long before JSTOR), no research leave, no research teaching load, usually no maternity leave, no graduate students. It remains a great sorrow that the flower of a generation has bloomed and gone, without descendants. The books they might have written, beyond the ones they wrung out of a grueling schedule, are lost to the grind of course overloads, of teaching gen-ed courses without a break, of waiting for summer to travel for a week to a good library, of tending families. Indeed, this is still the lot of many in the academy, men and women alike, but in the 1980s there were too many talented women out of place. This was the experience that made *A Room of One's Own* into a talismanic book for us.

There was an upside: we were not invisible to each other, we needed each other to talk to, and we did. Sandra Joshel and I met in our first semester of teaching, and team-taught a memorable mythology course at Rutgers (Froma Zeitlin's old course; she had moved on). Judith Hallett invited me down to speak to her class when she was still teaching at Boston University, an entirely characteristic act of outreach to a newcomer. I was still at Dartmouth and beginning work on *The Garden of Priapus* when I came across an article on Catullus that made me think someone else was on the same track; the writer was Marilyn Skinner, then at Northern Illinois University, and I wrote her a letter to find out. This was the start of a long epistolary relationship, bolstered by idea-packed conversations at the annual APA meeting that often sent me off on a new project. In 1987, speaking at Hamilton College at the invitation of a psychologist I'd met at the Dublin Congress on Women, I met Nancy Rabinowitz, who still periodically drags me onward in reading theory; on the same trip, I'd met Carlin Barton at a talk at Amherst. That same year, at Marilyn's behest, I organized a panel on pornography and representation at the APA, with papers by Robert Sutton, Terri Marsh, Molly Levine, and Madeleine Henry. The list of others met along the way whose work and ideas inspired me is a long one: the whole group at the NEH Institute, including Greg Daugherty, Shelley Haley, Barbara McManus, Alan Shapiro, Niall Slater, Bella Zweig (now Vivante), and our redoubtable teachers Helene Foley, Natalie Kampen, and Sarah Pomeroy, who trained us all to see ancient women and sent us back home to teach others, armed with a handbook we made together (NEH 1983); later in the decade, new collaborators joined the *Pornography and Representation* group—Shelby Brown (also ex-Dartmouth), Holly Montague, Holt Parker. Mary-Kay Gamel invited me to Santa Cruz, Barbara Gold invited me to Santa Clara and later to Hamilton; Diana Robin, out of the blue, invited me to stay with her as I drove from Bethlehem to Los Angeles in the summer of 1989. Suzanne Dixon I met by mail through Marilyn Skinner; Maria Wyke showed up at the 1987 Berkshire Conference at Wellesley, and through her I met Mary Beard, Helen Morales, and Jonathan Walters. In the 1980s we were all in the same boat. We spent endless hours on the phone and wrote long letters and, when we could, hosted each other, and we shared our own work and, through it, bibliography: Terri Marsh made me read Hélène Cixous and Toril Moi, Marilyn Skinner made me read film theory, Carlin Barton made me read Bataille, Sandra Joshel made me read everything.

And Judith Hallett made me apply my politics to the real world through the Women's Classical Caucus. Professional meetings meant a great deal to us; Marilyn Skinner and I once amazed a group of undergraduates by explaining how we both *shopped* for the APA every year. It was our chance to meet as a group, through the WCC, and to present papers; through 1985, the WCC's papers were double-juried, having to pass first the scrutiny of our own program committee and then the APA's, a situation that climaxed in the 1985 panel, which the APA refused to accept. This denial had practical repercussions, since many people could not get travel funding from their institution without documenting that they were on the program; at the meeting that year, we had to finagle a room in which to hold the panel, and advertise it through flyers (see figure 2, fortunately preserved because I took notes on the back of two flyers—notes that lead off with the head-count as of 9 AM: "72—SRO with people outside"). I served as WCC *Newsletter* editor from 1986 to 1990, and joined the steering committee in 1984, spending an exhilarating year as co-chair with Judy in 1987–88. We aimed to shake things up; Judy, whose information network is unsurpassed, collected injustices, and then aimed me at them like a cannon. Through the *Newsletter*, we ran the APA election questionnaire, and I started a blacklist of schools with no women faculty and did theme issues on "Survival" and "Is Classics Dead?" (see Richlin 1989). In those years, through the WCC, there were always multiple panels on ancient women at the Berkshire Conference, and the WCC always had a party; at the Wellesley Berks, Judy and I did a song-and-dance dressed in Lanz nightgowns as a tribute to Wendy Wasserstein's *Uncommon Women and Others*, with Hugh Lloyd-Jones in the audience. I don't know what he made of it.

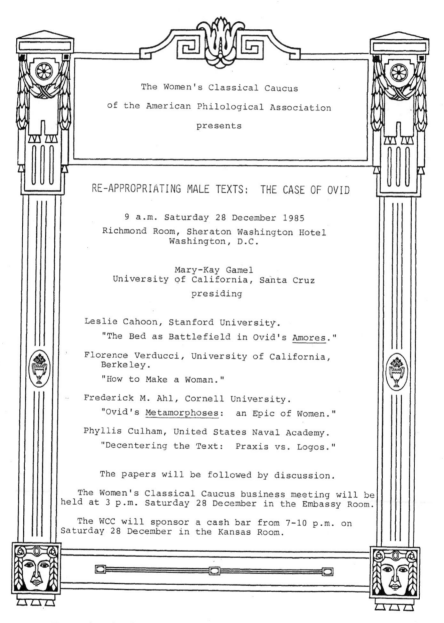

The Women's Classical Caucus
of the American Philological Association
presents

RE-APPROPRIATING MALE TEXTS: THE CASE OF OVID

9 a.m. Saturday 28 December 1985
Richmond Room, Sheraton Washington Hotel
Washington, D.C.

Mary-Kay Gamel
University of California, Santa Cruz
presiding

Leslie Cahoon, Stanford University.
"The Bed as Battlefield in Ovid's _Amores_."

Florence Verducci, University of California,
Berkeley.
"How to Make a Woman."

Frederick M. Ahl, Cornell University.
"Ovid's _Metamorphoses_: an Epic of Women."

Phyllis Culham, United States Naval Academy.
"Decentering the Text: Praxis vs. Logos."

The papers will be followed by discussion.

The Women's Classical Caucus business meeting will be
held at 3 p.m. Saturday 28 December in the Embassy Room.

The WCC will sponsor a cash bar from 7-10 p.m. on
Saturday 28 December in the Kansas Room.

Fig. 2. Flyer for the 1985 Women's Classical Caucus panel at the APA
meeting in Washington, D.C. (Author's collection.)

Women's groups were thriving in the 1980s, fueled by a general sense of need and consciousness of wrongs to be righted. Feminist activism in the academy was often centered on the academy itself, but some of us—Judy Hallett and Suzanne Dixon are outstanding examples—were active in the world outside as well.[6] Typically for the time, a feminist research group started at Dartmouth in the early eighties, and at Dartmouth I met the French historian Margaret Darrow, who first introduced me to the Berkshire Conference; the Lehigh Valley offered groups at every level from college to region, and the Feminist Research Group founded then is still going. At Lehigh I met a group of women in Religion Studies who influenced me profoundly, and introduced me, long-distance, to a new group in Los Angeles: Lydia Speller and Chava Weissler in Pennsylvania; Sheila Briggs, Karen King, Claudia Rapp, Michele Salzman, Teresa Shaw, Karen Torjesen in Los Angeles. They in turn got me to join the American Academy of Religion, and at AAR meetings I met yet more women actively involved in changing the thinking in their field. The flexible, big-tent structure of the AAR program made a big impression on me, and, like others, I took it back with me to the APA, where it inspired lasting improvements in the organization of the program.

In July, 1987, some of us capped the whole experience by attending the Third International Interdisciplinary Congress on Women, held in Dublin; Marilyn Skinner organized a classical panel with Eva Keuls and me. Bliss was it in that noon to be alive, and bliss radiates from the report I wrote for the granting agencies:

> I can hardly think how to convey to you the excitement and the joy of this meeting. The Congress centered on Trinity College, but events were scattered all over central Dublin. As we walked from venue to venue, we saw the Congress reported in every newspaper, heard news of ourselves on the radio and TV, and saw displays of women's books in every bookstore and of women's art in every gallery. The organizing committee had distributed bookbags with the Congress logo to all registrants, so we could recognize each other wherever we went—and we filled the streets of Dublin. People were extremely friendly and curious about the Congress, and discussions would begin on street corners. It was as if the university, and the universities of the world, had poured out into the streets, and the boundary between the academy and the world had become permeable.

A discussion on the history of the women's movement in Ireland . . . was held in the Round Room of the Mansion House, where the meeting that began the movement was held fifteen years ago. . . . One speaker told about the contraceptive train to Belfast. . . . And then a lesbian activist spoke on the old days, and about what it was like to say openly what no one had ever even mentioned before, and what it was like to be working all together: "We were tearing each other apart with jealousy and longing, but it was in a good cause." And then she said that she had felt recently a great falling off in consciousness and support, and she asked anyone who had ever loved another woman to stand up; and one by one and then in great waves the whole audience stood together. Everyone was in tears. And then individual women stood up in the audience to attest to the continuation of the miseries of Irish women: the shame heaped upon unwed mothers, the denial of abortion or even of pregnancy counseling, the loss of the divorce referendum, the oppression caused by the church, the denial of sexual freedom of choice, the lack of effective sanctions against rape, battering of wives, child abuse.

After my paper (on Ovid's "Rape of Philomela" in the *Metamorphoses*) there was a storm of discussion on the problem of teaching misogynistic texts . . .

There was a demonstration in front of the Ministry of Justice to protest the abolition of the women's clinics, which wound up in an impromptu march through the streets of central Dublin [that ended] in a sitdown in the huge main road in front of Trinity.

—Most vividly I remember how the women in the women's prison that lay along the road we took hung at the windows and waved and called to us through the bars.—

The third plenary session . . . took place at the Olympia Theater, a Victorian theater all in red plush with festoons of white carvings and caryatids and lamps in red silk shades. To look around that theater at the sea of women's faces, all ages, all shapes, all colors—all intent on the speakers, leaning forward in their seats, heads pillowed on fists all along the balconies—I tell you, it was remarkable. The speakers were frequently interrupted by cheers. . . .

Monique Wittig, in "One Is Not Born a Woman," imagines gender as an artificial mark, a set of political and economic categories, capable of suspension (1981). Surely at the Olympia Theater that day for the first time in my life I saw the mark of gender disappear in the faces of hundreds of women, now each a person, as in group portraits of the founding fathers: you see them as personalities, and so we were: clearly visible to each other, clear in my memory.

Thirty Years Later, How Are We Doing?

Today the WCC goes on, and a group has formed in Europe to bring together scholars working on gender studies (Réseau européen sur les Gender Studies dans l'Antiquité/ European Network on Gender Studies in Antiquity, EuGeStA); although there is still no European equivalent to the WCC, there is a surge in work on women's history and family history (see Kolb 2010), in which the students of Hildegard Temporini play a large part. At Brandeis, Bernadette Brooten put together a multiyear working group on ancient slavery and its impact on women, the Feminist Sexual Ethics Project (see Brooten 2010).[7] On related fronts, there has been a boom in research on women writers in the Renaissance, headed by Diana Robin.[8] The APA program now routinely has many papers on women and gender; the major journals have all had women editors, most graduate departments have women faculty (UCLA is 50–50), women are better represented among those getting jobs, there has been a recent run of women presidents of the APA (6 of 11 from 2000 to 2010, up from 6 of 30 from 1970 to 1999, up from 6 of 40 from 1930 to 1969, up from 1 of 60 from 1870 to 1929). I lost to Ruth Scodel in 2005, peacefully, whereas in 1991 the nomination of two women to run against each other for president impelled outraged APA members to put up a male write-in candidate who split the vote and won the election. The time of markedly unjust gender imbalance seems to have passed; the numbers presented by the Committee on the Status of Women and Minority Groups are less lopsided. Six women won the Goodwin Award, the APA's only book prize, in the years 1990–2009, compared with five in the years 1951–89: forward motion is perceptible, if only from 13% to 30%, which indeed is not much lower than the percentage women now constitute of the classical professoriate. We're still working on fifty-fifty.

Another group meeting that came out of the eighties was the series of "Feminism and Classics" conferences, the first of which was held in 1992 at Cincinnati under the leadership of Kathryn Gutzwiller and Ann Michelini—a leadership that marked Gutzwiller's successful court battle over her tenure decision (she would go on to win the Goodwin Award in 2000). A sense of accomplishment and energy came out of this meeting and those that followed it, although at this meeting and the subsequent one, organized by Judith Hallett and Janet Martin at Princeton in 1996, the final sessions focused on the field's continuing failure to address and incorporate women of color. With local and national committees now linked by e-mail, I organized FC3 at USC in 2000 to mark the new millennium with the theme "The Next Generation"; the talk I gave at FC2 had been titled "Revolution in the Middle Ages, or, What Became of My 'Take No Prisoners' Attitude." I was getting worried about keeping the thing going. And indeed at FC3 a whole new group arrived, then fresh out of grad school, now many with tenure: Joy Connolly, Jen Ebbeler, Kate Gilhuly carrying her new baby, Miriam Leonard with a group from England, Marsha McCoy with her daughter in a stroller, Kristina Milnor (whose book *Gender, Domesticity, and the Age of Augustus: Inventing Private Life* would win the Goodwin Award in 2006), Sarah Stroup, along with a raft of USC graduate student organizers including Cindy Benton, Rhiannon Evans, Mark Masterson, and Daniella Widdows. FC4, organized by Marilyn Skinner and Bella Vivante in 2004 at the University of Arizona, aimed at broadening the geographical scope of antiquity; FC5 brought us to Michigan in 2008 under the leadership of Ruth Scodel and at the urging of Bruce Frier, since co-chair of the Lambda Classical Caucus. FC6, organized by Fanny Dolansky, Allison Glazebrook, and Katharine von Stackelberg, took place at Brock University in St. Catherines, Ontario, in 2012, with the theme "Crossing Borders, Crossing Lines." I am proud to say that eight of my former students gave papers there: Sarah Blake, Del Chrol, Mark Masterson, Melinda Powers, Ellen Snyder, Chiara Sulprizio, Catherine Tracy, and Joanna Valentine. Four of them, though, were speaking on a panel they had put together on survival at the margins of the academy. I wish they did not have to fight so hard still, I am proud that they fight on.

The fact that these conferences are being held on campuses with PhD programs should mean that the study of women in antiquity has become established in the field; the involvement of scholars not previously best known for involvement in gender studies, like Ruth Scodel (see *Cloelia*, spring 2004, for her essay on combining scholarship with single motherhood), is a kind of endorsement by the classical establishment. In fact the (continuing) professional marginalization of the study of women matches a similar set of limits in thought, as manifested in curriculum and publication. Just as women in the 1980s found jobs (when they could) outside the North American graduate programs, and men and women using feminist theory likewise continued outside the graduate programs through the 1990s, so the topic of women has remained in a kind of intellectual ghetto.[9]

In the curriculum: Where is the course "Women in Antiquity" taught, and how do young scholars learn to teach it? Who takes it, and do they go to graduate school? This course has been taught on (some) campuses to undergraduates since the 1970s, and the basic sourcebook, *Women's Life in Greece and Rome*, now in its third edition (Lefkowitz and Fant 2005), has been making a neo-canonical set of primary sources easily available since 1982, indeed in its earliest form since 1977: most of the extant women writers, Lysias *On the Murder of Eratosthenes*, pseudo-Demosthenes *Against Neaira*, gruesome medical texts, hair-raising excerpts from Aristotle, Musonius Rufus on women's education, Pliny's letters to and about his wife, the prison diary of Perpetua, all very memorable.[10] Yet it is easy to find scholars who are completely unaware of any of this material. All of it except the poems of Sappho is noncanonical; most of it is not taught in the original to undergraduates, it does not often feature in introductory courses in Greek or Roman civilization ("civ"), it is not on graduate reading lists, it is not in graduate survey courses. "Women in Antiquity" is very rarely taught as a graduate seminar—the only regularly offered course, to my knowledge, is team-taught by Sharon James (Classics, UNC-Chapel Hill) and Sheila Dillon (Art History, Duke). The teaching of this course at any level, in any department, depends on the presence of a person in the department with the desire to teach it, because it is not perceived as a course that must be taught—it is not a required course. This means that most people who teach the course are starting from scratch; plentiful (although now outdated) materials are available on the website *Diotima*, but training is in short supply. Similarly, the big introductory civ courses, which usually serve as requirements for the major and which, in addition, are offered to large numbers of students who will never take another course in Classics, deal with women only if the instructor wants that to happen.[11] For the big civ courses, women and gender are still generally seen as special topics that have to take their chances with the array of possible topics to be dealt with in the ten to fifteen weeks of a college term; a thematically-organized course might devote a week or a day to the topic, or not, while the old-school chronological/ political approach could find very few women to include: Aspasia, Lucretia, Cleopatra, Livia . . .

This segregation and optional status are replayed at the most serious level of the field: scholarship itself. It is undeniable that the study of women came in with the arrival of women in the field, and that those writing and teaching about women have mostly been women (cf. Dixon 2001: 14); a department looking to add "Women in Antiquity" to its curriculum is usually looking for a woman to teach it—women's work. The usual implications of "women's work" thus apply, and this is the case even though since the 1970s there have been men who not only sympathized but wrote in the field themselves, as is evident from some of the lists above. Jack Peradotto and John Sullivan organized the first conference on the subject, and *Roman Sexualities* is dedicated to Sullivan (Hallett and Skinner 1997); Gordon Williams, Jack Winkler, and Jeffrey Henderson at Yale, William Anderson at Berkeley, John Henderson at Cambridge, Jerzy Linderski at North Carolina, all helped women do graduate work on gender-related subjects; Susan Treggiari thanks Peter Brunt, among her other teachers. Yes, Elaine Fantham served as reader for *The Garden of Priapus* and gave me a great deal of help; so did Alan Cameron. Scholars like Roger Bagnall, Thomas McGinn, Holt Parker, John Starks, Heinrich von Staden, and Terry Wilfong have made major contributions to the field. To the degree that all scholarship is specialized, the predominance of women writing on women does not currently look like a problem, especially now that it is easy for a press or a journal or a tenure committee to find readers to whom the study of women looks like scholarship (not true early on); the field was fortunate that the journals *Arethusa* and *Helios* existed in the 1970s, both radical and fearless—both also sited at the margins, one published at SUNY Buffalo (a byproduct of Sullivan's departure from Texas in the 1960s in the diaspora), the other at Texas A&M.

But not all scholarship *is* specialized, and we have a big problem in books that present overviews: handbooks, introductory texts. Marilyn Skinner commented long ago (1987b: 1) that the typical scholarly presentation of ancient women is in a collection of essays, and essay collections continue to come forth (e.g., Churchill, Brown, and Jeffrey 2002, McHardy and Marshall 2004, Faraone and McClure 2006, MacLachlan and Fletcher 2007, Parca and Tzanetou 2007, Suter 2008, Glazebrook and Henry 2011). This is a good thing in that it produces a wide scope, but a problem in that these essay collections are essentially producing compensatory history, documenting *women* in religion, *women* in public life, *women* lamenting; in addition, in a collection with any chronological scope, Rome tends to get short shrift (so also Dixon 2001: 8), and late antiquity is often missing altogether, despite its abundance of evidence (the new Blackwell *Companion to Women in the Ancient World*, edited by Sharon James and Sheila Dillon [2012], is a welcome exception in this regard). Moreover, these collections have a decreasing presence outside the field of Classics itself: at the enormous book display at the 2008 Berkshire Conference, they were not to be seen. Meanwhile, the typical handbook in the great proliferation of handbooks now being produced by Cambridge, Oxford, Routledge, and Wiley-Blackwell will have one chapter, amongst dozens of chapters, on women and/or sexuality—I've written several; this usually entails writing on all classes of women over a span of centuries. And the typical general overview does not even have an entry for "women" in the index; we might, since many authors do not write their own indexes, see this as a problem only with index-writing, but I use "no women in the index" as shorthand for a basic cognitive issue. Suzanne Dixon (2001: 4) notes the invisibility of women in general histories as a problem in the past, but it is remarkable to what a degree the problem persists. It is also odd that scholars accustomed to a strong male bias in ancient texts should so often wind up making women even *more* invisible than they were in those texts (see Dixon 2001, Holland 2012, Richlin 1997a on the adoption of textual bias by scholars). As with the problem of civ courses, this issue is part of what feminists in the 1970s called "mainstreaming": how to transform our perception of the cultures we study into a holistic one.[12] A gender-inclusive history, for example, is likely to be social history rather than political history.

No women in the index: how could that be? The conservative identity of Classics as a discipline led in the 1970s to a peculiar attitude toward "theory," by which was meant the proliferation of critical theories growing out of continental philosophy in the mid-twentieth century; feminism, and the study of women along with it, occupied a prominent place in the gallery of bogeymen. At the 1987 APA, the WCC took on the infamous case of the essay "*AJP* Today," in which the then-incoming editor of *American Journal of Philology* announced that the journal would not accept articles using theory—an amazing indicator of the distance between Classics and other disciplines in the 1980s (Luck 1987). Rereading Georg Luck's essay today, you can see his point; he wants to preserve his journal for work that is "philological" in the technical sense, asking plaintively, "But what could be more important than to define the exact meaning of a word in a given context?" He seems to mean that there were other journals to take theoretical work; the problem was, first, that younger scholars were beginning to hold that there was no such thing as a non-theoretical reading, next, that the enthusiasm for strictly philological work was waning, and, on the practical side, that *AJP* was a leading journal in the field, and younger scholars desperately needed to place their work well in order to get tenure. The author of the essay is actually listed as "Editorial Board"; at the time, Mary Lefkowitz was the only woman on a board of ten. After the APA session, the situation was expeditiously transformed, and Barbara Gold soon became the first woman editor of *AJP*, so you would think this issue was settled, but Luck's remarks were still being echoed in 1995 in David West's presidential address for the Classical Association, titled "Cast Out Theory" and ending, "My advice to the young would be to cast out theory, and get down to real work on the texts, the monuments, the surviving objects, the evidence." As if the two were mutually exclusive; it all depends what you mean by "real work."

Although nowadays, even in Classics, the use of theory is widespread, at the same time the status of "feminism" has become somewhat troubled in the wide world (can a revolution be passé?). Even at FC6, where all the papers were about gender, if not about women, there was a conspicuous lack of feminist theory on people's handouts; there was talk of putting together a reading list for FC7. Meanwhile, the woman problem continues. The collection *Classics in Progress*, for example, edited by T. P. Wiseman and published in 2002 to mark the centenary of the British Academy, and looking back to the collection *Fifty Years of Classical Scholarship* published in 1954 to mark the Jubilee of the Classical Association, made almost no note of the arrival of the subject of women on the British intellectual scene since 1954 (see Richlin 2004). Among field-specific overviews, I will pick on the study of ancient religion, although other fields could well be adduced. Religion is something, an anthropologist might expect, that everyone in a culture had and did. Clifford Ando (PhD Michigan 1996) is widely recognized as one of the most acute scholars working in the field; in *Roman Religion* (2003), he put together fourteen essays he considered crucial, knitting them together with substantial introductions and ending with recommendations for further reading organized by topic. This lively, intellectually vigorous book has no entry for "women" in the index; "women" does not appear among the topics in the recommendations for further reading; you have to read very closely to find a single statement on the coed nature of Roman religion (58): "Excluded from [Roman writers' accounts] . . . were an enormous range of priests and religious authorities, male and female of all social ranks, not least *patresfamiliae*, whose piety was not so much irrelevant as taken for granted." There follows a long footnote, of which women take up a prepositional phrase—citing, I must admit, chapter 7 below, along with Boëls-Janssen 1993, and that's it. Perhaps it is rude to observe that twelve of the fourteen contributors are male, and that the two female contributors, Mary Beard and Sabine MacCormack, had both published—elsewhere—on women and religion.

Other major writers on Roman religion: John Scheid produced a handbook account of "the religious roles of Roman women" in 1992 that listed a good many women's religious practices and yet labeled each as somehow an exception to the rule that Roman religion was a male thing; women's practices were marginal, foreign, passive, subordinate, secondary, or "bizarre," although still "indispensable" to the state. In his 2003/1998 overview of Roman religion he devotes less than a page to women, and even that mostly states what women could *not* do, although he concludes that "it is incorrect simply to declare that Roman women were excluded from religion." It would in fact be nonsensical to declare that Roman women were excluded from religion, unless religion is defined as "what men do."

Jörg Rüpke's fascinating and sophisticated 2001 account of Roman religion, translated by Richard Gordon (Rüpke 2007a), presents an accessible narrative backed by a lengthy technical bibliography, notes, and indices, lavishly illustrated with all sorts of material not generally seen, and has over twenty entries for "women" in its index (in fact underreporting), but still falls short. Women appear occasionally in inclusive lists: 11, religious experts were perhaps "only the old women, only the heads of families"; 15, *exempla* teach you to do "as Regulus did, as Claudia did"; 23, on the Ara Pacis, "magistrates, women and children together"; 148, "the donor, male or female"; 161, "couples and women with children"; 172, "by an acknowledged wise-man or -woman." Less comfortably, as add-ons: 15, in family cult, "and the women too (cf. Schultz 2006)"; 48, in the archeological record, "Of course women's graves were also found." Religious veiling is several times pointed out for women alongside men: 23, on the Ara Pacis; 95, "or in the case of women, the stola"; 147, "(or, in the case of women, the stola)." The list of religious offices (223–28) includes many of those held by women, but there is no indication of the kind of frequency demonstrated in the epigraphic record for Italy (see chapter 7 below). Women appear, just like men, in examples: dancing in the cult of Isis (100, with plate 10); dedicating a model uterus (159); Pompeia Agrippinilla, a priestess of Dionysus (214). Women flash past without comment in the copiously quoted texts: Isiac initiates, side by side with men, in Apuleius's *Metamorphoses* 11.8–17 (90–93); a half-dozen women at a pontifical banquet (219). There are occasional comments inspired by a feminist critique, although the supporting bibliography falls off here: the *senatusconsultum de Bacanalibus* is described as "a bit of misogyny that wonderfully reveals the character of dominant Roman values" (32); women's use of love magic may be "a response to the actual asymmetry of power in the relationship" (172).

But although practices like the offering of votives or family worship are duly treated as involving everyone, most festivals involving women do not appear as such (or at all). Caninia Fortunata, a (possible) priestess, appears because she paid for the restoration of a monument commemorating a dedication by a male public slave (158); that the dedication was to Bona Dea passes without comment about her worship as gendered, nor does Bona Dea appear elsewhere. The three women's festivals discussed look odd (190–91):

> The *Matronalia* on 1 March was a day of "misrule" . . . in theory at any rate female slaves were waited on by their mistresses, though in fact all it probably amounted to was some better food and extra time off. . . . In June, women were allowed to participate in bare-foot processions to the temple of Vesta . . . and to visit the temple of Mater Matuta. But there is no evidence that either of these festivals, any more than the Liberalia, enjoyed a wide appeal.

The idea that women needed permission to engage in ritual I do not think can be supported by Roman texts, and I miss here a description of what the Matronalia and the cults of Vesta and Mater Matuta were basically about (cf. Dolansky 2011c); I do not suppose a student would notice the lack. As for evidence of wide appeal, I appreciate the argument that Roman antiquarians dredged up many practices practiced by nobody for a long time, yet I do not like to see women erased from the little we do have; both at Satricum and Rome, Mater Matuta received a lot of offerings, certainly including women's gear (Smith 2000). Similarly, Rüpke discusses Juno Lucina in Horace's *carmen saeculare* (helpfully quoted in full, 120–21) and, almost incidentally, in discussions of the grove of Lucina (120, 231–32), the second time elbowed aside by the extremely helpful quotation in full of the *lex Libitina* from Puteoli, with all sorts of details about burials, slave burial workers, and the business of punishing slaves, "male or female" (232–33). Juno Lucina gets lost in the shuffle.

The evidence is arguably less lopsided than the analysis. Rüpke prints a nice grave monument (224) for a married couple, Licinia Flavilla and Sex. Adgennius Macrinus, who appear, as not uncommonly, side by side, equal in size, with side-by-side labels; the caption comments, "whereas in the case of the wife . . . the personal priesthood of the *divae*. . . represented the sole form of public responsibility available to her, the pontificate . . . of her husband . . . takes its appropriate place in the . . . enumeration of his civic and military career." This is a gesture toward Rüpke's biographical dictionary of Roman priests (2007b); he is thinking of the relation of religious to other public office for men, but I think the monument was perhaps intended to display an equivalency (message: "We were a power couple"). And, to return to indexing, of 148 named individuals in the "Persons" index, 5 are women—and one of these is Cleopatra. Pompeia Agrippinilla is another, but Caninia Fortunata does not appear there, nor does Licinia Flavilla (or her husband).

Using only these books, it would be difficult to teach an undergraduate course on Roman religion that would leave students with the impression that women were much involved, except of course for the ever-popular Vestal Virgins (typically, in Rüpke they appear smack in the center of his argument about "material theology" [115], the assumption being that the reader already knows all about them). The Vestals were *not alone*. Even Valerie Warrior's handbook, published in a series explicitly addressed to undergraduates (2006), although it appropriately works men and women alike into illustrative examples, nonetheless remarks that a procession, at first neutrally described (25), included women "in subordinate roles" (30). A caption for the Amiternum relief notes the presence of "the women of the family," but not of the *praefica* (34). There is, after all, a limited amount of space. Except, of course, in Ross Kraemer's sourcebook on *women's* religions (1988 [2004]), now close to 500 pages long; how much of that material is familiar to classicists? A student, here or there, might be given the *option* of writing a paper on the part women played in religion, and assigned to read Celia Schultz's book (2006), although neither Kraemer nor Schultz appears in Rüpke's suggestions for further reading, and Kraemer's work is not in his bibliography; nor is either of Beard's essays on the Vestals. Polity Press, on the back jacket, touts Rüpke's book as "the perfect introduction to Roman religion for students of Ancient Rome and Classical Civilization." Not yet.

This is a problem anthropologists dealt with some time ago; Jane Goodale's book *Tiwi Wives* was produced in 1971 as a corrective to the then-current habit of writing books on "the Tiwi" that ignored women (see chapter 10). Some fields in Classics have perforce never had a big issue with paying attention to gender, notably family history; you cannot write about a family without women. Jonathan Edmondson and Alison Keith coedited a collection on Roman dress (2008) that had no trouble incorporating male and female writers on male and female dress; everybody wears clothing. I repeat the often-repeated idea that we cannot get an accurate idea of what ancient cultures were like from the extant sources, and need to push them a lot harder in order to arrive at a description of, for example, Roman religion that a Roman woman would have recognized. John Scheid did see that women were "indispensable"; to understand strongly sex-differentiated traditional cultures, we need to think further about the participants' self-perception.[13] Women's processions, indeed mixed processions, are everywhere in descriptions of Roman ritual; if a triumph paraded empire, maybe processions (like the Memorial Day parade) paraded community, and neither the women on parade nor anyone else present thought of women as "subordinated." It is true that Sherry Ortner, in her classic description of "the universal fact of culturally-attributed second-class status of women in every society," listed rituals exclusive to males as an indicator (1974: 68, 70); it is true that in this very collection I myself argue that many Roman cultural practices subordinated women, to put it mildly. Identifying the subject position of the oppressed is hard (Gates 1988; Scott 1990); optimism and pessimism arrive at different evaluations of women's culture (see chapter 10). The slave woman who was driven out of the precinct of Mater Matuta by *matronae* was indispensable; did that make her feel proud? Yet I am sure a true account of Roman religion would look quite different from the current picture.

The question is, who will write that account? If the pipeline producing scholars trained in women's history is narrowing rather than expanding, as most of those who developed the study of women in antiquity retire without a legacy of graduate students, will changes in the field's basic paradigms continue? Juliet Mitchell described the liberation of women as "the longest revolution" in 1966; as the generation of the Second Wave was joined by the next generation, we faced the problem of whether the revolution as envisaged by Second Wave feminism would continue as such, or at all. In 1996, at FC2, I asked, "If revolution is a *res nova*, what happens to revolutions when they become middle-aged? What happens to the shock of the new when it's not new?" Indeed, as Genevieve Liveley points out in her account of the transition from Second Wave to Third Wave receptions of women's history, "postfeminism" was heralded already in 1985 by Alice Jardine (Liveley 2006). Liveley's essay focuses on Marilyn Skinner's project of "Rescuing Creusa" (1987b) and on Phyllis Culham's position at the 1985 WCC panel, and she argues that "Culham's quest to rescue Creusa, to recover the truth about 'women's lived reality' in ancient Greece and Rome misses the point then—that such 'truth' is constituted always and only at the point of its reception." But possibly Liveley is here missing Culham's point, which is that male authors' ideas of women tell less than some other kinds of material do—the catalogues of priestesses and donations at the end of chapter 7 here, for example; general histories have tended to lack assemblages of such material.[14] Whether or not you believe there is such a thing as a fact, it does really make a difference to your understanding of Roman religion if you have or have not read the pertinent epigraphic material.

It might be posited as an axiom in intellectual history that each generation needs to reject the ideas of the previous one in order to make a case for the necessity of its own ideas, what I like to think of as the "Year King phenomenon." What happens, perhaps, from generation to generation is as much a shift in disciplinary predominance as one in mindset; the disappearance of ancient history from history departments may be pushing a swing in Classics toward literary theory, always disposed toward skepticism (not that history-writers aren't—but less so). In fact my critique of the state of the question in Roman religion was concisely preempted by Lora Holland (PhD UNC-Chapel Hill 2002) in a recent overview (2012: 204–6, 213), and Rebecca Flemming (PhD UCL 1997) tackled Scheid squarely as representative of an approach that forced out the copious counterevidence in order to argue for a subordination presumed to be there (2007a). Fanny Dolansky and others are working toward a gender-integrated model of Roman religion, and I hope someday something similar will be achieved for ancient sex trafficking, in the wake of Kathy Gaca's monumental new work (2008, 2010, 2010–11, 2011, and ongoing; cf. Marshall 2013). Among younger scholars, a search for women's experience appears, for example, in the work of Elizabeth Pollard, trained at Penn by Ross Kraemer and Brent Shaw, or of Karen Hersch, trained at Rutgers by Corey Brennan; Hersch's book on Roman weddings leads, tellingly, from Victor Turner on Ndembu ritual and the difficulty of reaching "an adequate understanding of what the words and movements mean to *them*" (2010: 1). The concern with a real, reachable *them* is what fueled the essays in this book, and still does.

I remain worried that all that recovery work could disappear again, as it did after the First Wave, and before then; as Judith Bennett remarks, "Until the eighteenth century, each subsequent generation had painstakingly to recreate feminism" (2006: 46). Perhaps it is an illusion to believe that the goal of scholarship is a permanent remembering. I haven't done much work specifically on Roman women myself since 2001, and all of us have had, along with administrative work and family obligations, other preoccupations, other things we wanted to study; a long-term project on the circulation of knowledge about the ancient sex/gender system in modern Europe has led me into archives where I can see for myself how writers turn to dust. The interdisciplinary women's groups and women's journals have lost interest in the premodern, and, with it, a tolerance for the kind of technical apparatus that accompanies a collection like this one; I may feel that the new World History or an understanding of Orientalism badly need to know about gender in the ancient Mediterranean, but I very much doubt that anyone outside Classics is paying attention.[15] But perhaps it is only naive to see scholarship as working toward a permanent anything; in "The Ethnographer's Dilemma," critiquing teleological models, I instanced Mr. Ramsay in *To the Lighthouse*, ever striving to get beyond Q to R, if not to Z. Perhaps it is the action itself that matters, and we should think of "remembering" as an iterative verb, an ongoing process, a continuing conversation; maybe that is what Genevieve Liveley meant about the constitution of truth. With no prompting from me, the UCLA graduate students ran their conference in November of 2010 on the topic "That's What She Said: The Construction and Expression of Women's Voices in Antiquity," bringing together young scholars doing exciting new work, including, for example, Elizabeth Greene on women's friendship networks in the frontier camps of the Roman army and Meghan DiLuzio on the self-attested religious life of Fabia Aconia Paulina in fourth-century CE Rome. This is where the conversation was that fall: new. Certainly the experience of amassing even a sample of recent work on Roman women has convinced me that the thing keeps going.

Agripina's Bridal Shop

Living in Los Angeles takes you down some strange streets; the day I came across Agripina's Bridal Shop on Washington Boulevard, I took a picture, and I keep it in my "Women in Antiquity" teaching notebook. The world, as always, is changing, getting bigger, and, if Rome and Greece are no longer at the center, people still like to hear about them. As critical attention and activism turn to the transnational, global present, classicists can contribute a much-needed sense of the past. Who better to talk about empire, the ideas of "East" and "West," human trafficking, the common cultural roots of Christianity and Islam, and the world before either? Our history now fits into the big paradigms of World History; if the individual lives of Aspasia, Clodia Metelli, even Cleopatra, are too small to register, the systems of sex work, circulation of knowledge, and Orientalism in which these women participated remain on the table (see Pollard 2008, 2010). Elizabeth Pollard's essay on teaching World History begins with the heading "You Expect Me to Teach *What*?" (2008: 49); we may all expect increasingly to be asked to paint with a broad brush.[16] The more publicly we do it, the better. At the Berkshire Conference, the lives of premodern women have been swamped by the vast flood of knowledge being produced about women in the much better-documented modern period; Judith Bennett presents pages of grim statistics on the disappearance of the premodern from the Berks and of history itself from the feminist journals (2006: 30–53). At the 2008 Berks, there were four papers presented on women in antiquity (two on a panel, two singletons) out of a total of over 800 papers; the call for papers for the 2011 Berks did note that "special consideration" would be given to papers on premodern topics, and there were indeed seven panels on medieval and/or premodern women—but only two papers on women in antiquity. We need to work to keep premodern history in our history departments, keep ancient women on the radar of Women's Studies departments and programs, and team up with scholars working on the ancient Near East, with Byzantinists, with Egyptologists, with Arabists, and, if we are lucky, with those who work on the other big antiquities—China, Southeast Asia, "Indomediterranea" (see Pollard 2009, 2013). Antiquity returns to the 2014 Berks with sessions on family, the body, and human trafficking from Bronze Age Greece to the early Islamic period.

I called this book *Arguments with Silence* not just to commemorate my own truculence but because I believe that history-writing both presupposes the existence of the past and calls it back to speak to the present: keeping a firm grip on Eurydice's hand. This is how I ended what I said in 1996, standing in the Princeton classroom where I had sat as a student in 1973:

> Looking to the future I see us breaking open the definitions that have held us in, and writing the history of a gendered world before the modern era, exploring the history of race, of otherness, of empire and margins. But I can't see that future clearly, and I call on the new ones here, you who are just beginning, to take the lead, and go on. And I think of the ancient women and men whose lives we have called back from the shadows, whose ghosts we have made to drink from the pool of blood; I call you to testify! I call on your ghosts to bear witness that we have not forgotten you!

CHAPTER 1

Approaches to the Sources on Adultery in Rome

Introduction

"Approaches to the Sources on Adultery in Rome" was written in the summer of 1980 thanks to the encouragement of Helene Foley, who was visiting Hanover, NH, where I then held a visiting position at Dartmouth. I was just beginning to turn my dissertation, a lexicon and motif index of Roman sexual humor, into the book that was to become *The Garden of Priapus* (first published in 1983), and I had collected a great many Roman texts about adultery. My first article (1981b) had focused on lurid punishments for adulterers in satire, specifically on the use of *irrumare* in Catullus and Martial, and readers as I was working on it repeatedly expressed doubt that Romans had really practiced oral rape as a punishment for adultery—even that such an act is possible (we live now in less innocent times). At that time I was, therefore, looking for texts that would tell me what really happened to those caught in adultery; the elusiveness of the answer taught me a lesson about history-writing that influenced all my later work. At the same time, the experience of writing for Foley's collection brought me into a scholarly network that had been growing since the early 1970s; the referee was Susan Treggiari. When Helene Foley joined Natalie Kampen and Sarah Pomeroy to organize the 1983 NEH Summer Institute on Women in Antiquity, I was ready to sign on.

I had kept the original manuscript all these years, always intending to put back all the cruelly pruned-out material; when I took a look at it in the summer of 2009, it turned out to be little more than a list, though a long one. Rereading the published version now, I am struck by how, as a young scholar, I had imitated the unquestioning adoption of the Roman sources' point of view then current, using phrases like "compliant husband" and words like "adulteress" and "cuckold." Shackleton Bailey, for example, commenting in 1965 on one of Cicero's letters to Atticus, writes, "L. Lucullus's wife Servilia . . . was eventually divorced by her long-suffering husband for loose conduct" (332). The fact that Servilia's voice was absent barely registered; some revisions to this chapter try to correct this. In 1981, taking "what happened to a man and woman caught in adultery" as the object of study, I focused on the fascinating fact that different kinds of writing tell very different stories, without thinking too much about the oddity of the object of study itself. The very word "adulteress" now sounds almost biblical, certainly finger-pointing. The Roman definition of the act as extramarital sex between a wife and a man not her husband, and the almost total lack, after Plautus, of a sense that a wife is wronged by a husband who has sex with others; the way in which such a wife's feelings repeatedly show up in texts in the form of the wife's jealousy; Augustus's conversion of the act into a crime; the class-related differences in the way the law was defined, so that, for example, a waitress could not be prosecuted for adultery, as if such women had no honor (here buried at the end of a footnote)—in 1981 I saw the historiographical problem as one concerning kinds of sources more than as one concerning the history of women.

Also because I was new to writing, and intended my writing to be read by other classicists, I assumed that the sources needed no description or analysis; although the essay first appeared in *Women's Studies*, my goal was to speak to the elder initiates of classical philology as if I, too, were familiar with what was familiar to them. I did not reflect that experts on Roman law would not read *Women's Studies*, nor would feminists generally be familiar with the *Digest*. But, even for a classicist, *Digest* 48.5, one of the major texts discussed here, needs not just a gloss but some reflection, as does the *Digest* itself as an amalgamation of layers and layers of legal opinions by jurists, all of them male. The sheer weight of this male-authored law on Roman women whose responses are now lost is a fact that should not be taken for granted, as is the weight of the two thousand years of interpretation that have buried women like Lucullus's wife Servilia. In writing the essay printed here as chapter 2, on invective against women, I first came to grips with the relation between male writers and Roman women. In chapter 1, the main idea I wanted to convey was that, by reading a wide range of kinds of sources against each other, a reader could begin to make out the shape of a social phenomenon and understand a cultural obsession. I assumed then, and still do, that there was a real social phenomenon to observe, and that it was accessible through texts, though not from any single text. One lamppost problem leaves you in the dark; multiple lamppost problems can be treated as a simultaneous equation. It was writing this essay that first put me in mind of the scene in *Forbidden Planet* when the invisible monster was outlined by a circle of questing beams of light. Accordingly, what I did in this essay as a matter of course I still, and urgently, believe to be important: I used jokes and gossip alongside law and serious history—low alongside high. This I take to be a fundamental need for any historian, for high and low make culture together.

ৰ ৰ ৰ

Since the rise of Christianity, indeed even earlier, observers of Roman culture have had a lot to say about the sex lives of the Romans. These comments vary from tirades against license to speculation on the amount of sexual freedom enjoyed by free Roman men and women (sexual unfreedom being a mark of the slave). This freedom certainly involved many types of liaison—same-sex as well as male-female; from casual use of prostitutes to established concubinage—as well as the use of the slave's unfreedom. In a society where marriage was common, many of these relationships entailed adultery, and the surprising thing is that a society with so many sexual outlets, where divorce was legal and acceptable, was so obsessed with adultery—or rather with one particular sort of adultery, a wife's infidelity. The purpose of this study is to present different sorts of evidence on extramarital sex between men and women, especially evidence which reflects social attitudes toward such relationships, and to draw attention to problems in the evaluation of this evidence. The answer to the question "What happened to Roman adulterers?" turns out to be a classic case of "depends who you ask." But no matter what texts you consult, some answers are constant: the Roman concept of adultery constituted a major part of the Roman construction of male and female sexuality and particularly of what made a woman good; all Roman sexual categories depend on civil status (slave or free) and on relative social status.

To Romans, the concept of marriage was full of heavy moral and social significance; it follows that their reactions to adultery were not simple. This study lays out five categories of evidence on Roman attitudes toward adultery—law, history, moral anecdote and exempla, gossip, and satire. Can the contradictions among these kinds of evidence be resolved? Or are we left instead with a demonstration of how a social problem projects multiple images in the written record?[1]

A few facts can be relied on as landmarks. The most important are that before the time of Augustus there was no criminal law about adultery, which previously had been strictly family business, and that Roman law generally from its earliest times was the custom of a public community. The family had a great degree of jurisdiction over its members, with the *paterfamilias* at the head, his descendants in direct line under him, along with women married *in manu* (a class which by the late republic was not so numerous), and the freed slaves and slaves under all. Execution of the law depended at all times on self-help, since there was not much of a police force; therefore, the concerned parties had to decide among themselves whether to go to court, settle within the family, use force, or do nothing, and the Twelve Tables are full of the most physical instructions—for dragging your adversary off to court, for keeping debtors imprisoned in chains at your house or cutting them into bits, for the surrender of children into slavery to repay damages. A thief caught in the act could be killed.

It is also important to keep track of changes in manners—to historicize. The late republic and early empire seem to have been characterized, in the city of Rome, by a certain flamboyance of behavior among the upper classes; the end of the Julio-Claudians and the beginning of the Flavians seem to have marked a general return to a love of respectability, and it looks as if, by the time of Trajan, after the reign of Domitian, the Senate was no longer so interested in drawing attention to itself. Not that we can be at all sure that such generalizations are anything more than an artifact of accidents of textual survival; moreover, the overwhelmingly elite authorship of the extant texts from these periods leaves us in the dark about most Romans, even most free Romans. If we go back to the earliest extant texts, the comedies of Plautus from the middle republic, the adulterous wife and her lover, ubiquitous sources of humor later on, hardly make an appearance, maybe because adultery was not so interesting to the slaves and lower-class men who produced comedy.[2] Yet adultery by wives seems to have been a stock theme of mime (see Reynolds 1946)—but we have no trace of the unscripted mime of Plautus's day.

All the literary sources here surveyed were written for the city of Rome, usually for and sometimes by senators and equestrians, while the legal sources were compiled in Constantinople in the sixth century for the benefit of the entire empire.[3] Furthermore, almost all the material was written by men, so that whatever picture of Roman sexual mores can be established can only be one-sided, without much direct evidence from women themselves (but see chapters 3 and 4).

Legal Sources

The legal sources are largely limited to those of the late empire, especially *Digest* 48.5 and *Codex* 9.9. Yet this includes two earlier bodies of writing: the comments of the jurisconsults who wrote under the Severan emperors and earlier, and in turn their citations from a particular law enacted by Augustus, the *lex Julia de adulteriis coercendis*. Here and there in the legal sources are rescripts by emperors of the first and second centuries. The late collection known as Paulus's *Sententiae* also devotes space to the *lex Julia* (2.26) and offers, if dubiously, some information mentioned nowhere else in the legal sources.[4]

The comments of the jurists are unfortunately ambiguous. Rarely do they give a direct quotation from the Julian law; on the other hand, they often use the phrase "the law says. . . ." Whether this refers directly to the *lex Julia* or to the body of commentary surrounding it is not possible to say; it seems likely that what the jurisconsults say can be accepted as at least consistent with the tenor of the law for the period between the passage of the *lex Julia* and the reign of Severus Alexander.

The *lex Julia de adulteriis coercendis* was passed by Augustus as part of his campaign for the moral reform and eugenics of the Senate and *equites* in 18 BCE,[5] and was complemented in 9 CE by the *lex Papia Poppaea*, which, among other things, forbade a senator to marry a convicted adulteress. The law on adultery seems to have included a great deal of regulation of procedure. Most important was its establishment of a *quaestio perpetua* for the hearing of accusations of adultery, similar to those already in existence for the hearing of other *iudicia publica* (parricide, acts of violence, murder, treason). This alignment of what is essentially a civil affair with crimes of violence should be noted as a significant aspect of Augustus's political program, and indeed it was to prove a fertile source of the *delatio* (politically motivated informing) that made the first century CE such a miserable time to be a member of the senatorial class. It certainly shook the generation that followed the one decimated by the proscriptions Augustus sanctioned when he was still just Octavian: a distracting turn from mass murder to a moral purity campaign.[6]

The law delineated the steps to be taken prior to the *quaestio*. The husband was to divorce his wife as soon as he found out she was adulterous, or he would himself be liable for prosecution for *lenocinium*, pimping.[7] He had sixty days in which he or his now ex-wife's father had the exclusive right to accuse her of adultery.[8] However, the adulterer had to be accused first, and his trial would be first. If he were found guilty, the woman would then be tried. If he were found innocent, and the woman had remarried, she could not be tried.[9]

The law further delineated the circumstances in which the husband or father could kill the wife and/or the adulterer. Any killing had to be done *in flagrante delicto*[10] and only in the husband's or father's house. The father had unlimited rights, but had to kill both parties. The husband could only kill the adulterer if the adulterer was *infamis*—a person stigmatized by the censor, or a member of an infamous profession (an actor, a gladiator, a pimp, a prostitute; see Edwards 1997).[11]

When two months had passed after the act of divorce, any third person could bring the accusation of adultery, within the next four months—evidently an open door to spies and informers. There was a five-year statute of limitations on the accusation.[12]

Neither the *Digest* nor the *Codex* makes any mention of the penalties to be imposed by the court on those found guilty of adultery. To sum up, the *Digest* does cite the following penalties: the father's right to kill the wife and adulterer caught *in flagrante delicto*; the husband's right to kill the adulterer, within limits; limits on the punishment of a husband who killed his wife *in flagrante delicto*; the husband's right to inflict injury (*contumelia*) on the adulterer, since he has the right to kill him; the husband's risk of being accused of *lenocinium* if he does not divorce his wife; and the culpability of any accessories to the adultery as adulterers themselves, which seems to be an amendment to the original law (*Digest* 48.5.9[8], 9[8].1, 10[9], 10[9].1, 10[9].2, 13[12], 33[32].1).[13]

Paulus's *Sententiae* give the statutory punishment for adultery (2.26.14): the wife and the adulterer were subjected to *relegatio* (exile), to separate islands; the woman lost half her property and a third of her estates, and the adulterer lost half his property.[14] According to the Julian marriage laws, women found in adultery, as well as other women of low moral standing, were prohibited from remarriage to freeborn Romans.[15]

It will be noticed that the only situation legally defined as adultery was sexual intercourse between a *matrona* and a man not her husband. A married man could legitimately have intercourse with any male who was not freeborn, or with any woman who did not have the status of *matrona* and was not engaged, married, or in concubinage, and he could keep concubine(s) of either sex in his household.[16] If he did have sex with a married woman, his own wife did not acquire the explicit right to prosecute him for this until the late empire; of course there is no reason why she or her representative should not have been eligible to prosecute the adulterous pair as third parties after the husband and father.[17]

That the *lex Julia* was revived by Domitian, though this is mentioned in only extralegal sources, suggests that its implementation, after Augustus, was not wholly successful. There is no legal description of what was entailed by Domitian's reenactment of the law.

The jurisconsults themselves represent a stage in the history of the law on adultery. Each of the excerpts in the *Digest* and *Codex* is taken from a book or section of a book by that jurist on adultery or on the *lex Julia* itself. The chief concern of each jurist seems to have been to define the rules as to the time allowed for bringing accusations, and occasionally to define the circumstances under which the husband or father could kill the adulterer and/or the wife. It might, then, be postulated that the chief area of confusion and concern for those wishing to accuse under the law was when they might do so; perhaps this is more naturally a question for a third party wishing to accuse. Certainly it is hard to find historical examples of husbands or fathers bringing a criminal prosecution, much less killing anybody; there are some exemplary tales of fathers killing daughters or their lovers for premarital sex, even for a kiss (Valerius Maximus 6.1.3, 4, 6), or of a husband clubbing his wife to death for drinking wine (Valerius Maximus 6.3.9, an example of justifiable *severitas*). The law nonetheless manifests a preoccupation with controlling women's sexuality that is easy to match in Greek culture (see Lysias *On the Murder of Eratosthenes*), and in most other kinds of Roman sources, where adultery is a popular topic. The law's quest to get people to redefine themselves—husband as pimp, wife and adulterer as criminal—seems to have succeeded mainly in providing new terms for use in jokes.

Historical Sources

The historical sources extend back to the early republic, although from no earlier than the standpoint of Augustan Rome; that their evidence is thus skewed is certain but not consistent. The earliest statement is from Cato's speech *On the Dowry* (recorded by Aulus Gellius, 10.23, in a section on old-fashioned Roman severity toward women), asserting that a wife would not be able to lay a finger on her husband if she caught him in adultery, while the husband could have killed her with impunity if he had found her so. Cato is expounding on the husband's general *imperium* over a wife he is divorcing; his rhetorical goal here is not recoverable. The adultery law cited by Dionysius of Halicarnassus as instituted by Romulus (2.25; cf. Plutarch *Romulus* 22.3) resembles Cato's description of current custom.

Livy shows no concern for factual cases of adultery in the extant books. Instead, in the stories of Verginia and especially of Lucretia (1.58), he depicts an idealized version of the embodiment of chastity—outraged *matrona*, staunch husband, slain seducer—which has little to do with history and much in common with the moral tales of a writer like Plutarch. The tales of Lucretia and Verginia are so much more exempla than historical episodes that they cannot be compared with the narratives of adultery found in other historical sources.[18]

Still, it is possible to find what look like real-life accounts in sources of all kinds. Cicero and his correspondents mention many scandalous divorces, some of which found their way into later biographies.[19] One of the great sensational divorce cases of the late republic was Caesar's divorce of his wife Pompeia on suspicion of adultery with Clodius, involving his intrusion at the rites of Bona Dea;[20] this cause célèbre contributed to Clodius's hatred of Cicero, who was the witness who destroyed Clodius's alibi during his trial for this religious offence.

The double standard that prevailed in Roman society is suggested by two cases, one famous. Antony flaunted his affair with the actress Volumnia Cytheris, freedwoman of Volumnius Eutrapelus; it was one of the things which galled Cicero most bitterly about Antony (*Att.* 10.10.5, 10.16.5, 15.22). Yet it was only the parade of it that was so bad; Cicero could tolerate Cytheris, although he disapproved, when Eutrapelus gave a dinner party and had her seated next to himself (*Fam.* 9.26.2; cf. 14.16.1). It seems that Cytheris and her function were acceptable, as long as she stayed in her place.[21] On the other hand, a married woman could have no such concubine; when

Caecilius Epirota, Atticus's freedman, was suspected of having sex with his patron's married daughter Caecilia Attica, the liaison was, as a matter of course, not tolerated. Epirota, dismissed from his job as the young woman's teacher, landed on his feet under the patronage of Cornelius Gallus—a patronage which later influenced Augustus against Gallus (Suetonius *Gramm.* 16). As will be seen, some *liberti* who had sex with the wife or daughter of a *patronus* experienced much more serious reprisals.

After the passage of the *lex Julia*, the limited evidence suggests only that the law's application was irregular, although the possibility must be kept in mind that only irregular cases were recorded by contemporary writers. Of the three main stages prescribed by the law—divorce, trial, and exile—there is very little evidence that is not in some way aberrant. Divorces for adultery in the family of the *princeps* included those of Julia and Tiberius (Suetonius *Tib.* 10.1, 11.4), Nero and Octavia (Suetonius *Ner.* 35.1–3), and Domitian and Domitia Longina (Suetonius *Dom.* 3.1, 13.1; especially hypocritical, cf. *Dom.* 8.3). As for the trial stage, most recorded by Tacitus were held before the Senate, most in Suetonius before the *princeps*; the emperors had a special interest in the *equites*,[22] and (perhaps following Caesar's example as dictator, Suetonius *Jul.* 43.1) set themselves up as censors (*Aug.* 37, 39; *Tib.* 35.1; *Calig.* 16.2; *Claud.* 15.4, 16.1; *Dom.* 8.3). The *quaestio perpetua* established by Augustus could have disappeared completely, for all that the sources have to say about it (see Garnsey 1967); the format of the procedure was not what writers other than lawyers cared about. We must assume that it existed, and that normal cases (those not involving senators or high-profile *equites*) were heard, but that it was also gradually dying, and was (unfortunately) being replaced by the process of *cognitio*, administered by the urban prefect. In this court, the punishment was left to the discretion of the judge, giving him a great deal of freedom to impose irregular sentences.[23] A further factor in this confusion is that Tiberius reaffirmed the jurisdiction of the family council over "unchaste" married women (Suetonius *Tib.* 35.1).

Most of the exiles on record are involved with offenses to the reigning dynasty. Those of the two Julias[24] were implemented by Augustus himself as *paterfamilias*, without recourse to the *lex Julia*; the poet Ovid (whose poetry was itself too favorable to sexual activity to jibe with the Julian laws) was perhaps exiled as an accessory under the law, if he was officially charged at all. The younger Seneca was likewise implicated in a dynastic adultery (said to have been trumped up, Dio 60.4–6). The most notoriously unfair example of such an exile was that of Octavia by Nero (Suetonius *Ner.* 35.1–2).

Adulterous relations between freedmen or slaves and upperclass women were severely punished by Augustus, as they had been by Caesar before the Julian laws (*Jul.* 48; *Aug.* 67.2, cf. 45.4; *Vesp.* 11).[25] As such cases and particularly the case of the Julias indicate, the *lex Julia* did not abrogate the rights of the *paterfamilias* to act for himself; Augustus was a strong proponent of the *mos maiorum*, and, in addition, seems to have considered himself *paterfamilias patriae* as well as *pater patriae*. Freedmen were supposed to behave in a dutiful manner; slaves were, legally, things (Joshel 1992b: 50, cf. 28–32; 2011: 215–16); both were legally subject to punishment by owners or former owners (Joshel 1992b: 33–34; Treggiari 1969: 68–81). In general, however, any Roman who offended against a class above his own was in an especially bad position; compare the case of the centurion who had sex with a tribune's wife (Pliny *Ep.* 6.31.4–6). This principle affected upper-class men as well; Plutarch, giving the back story of the T. Vinius who corrupted the future emperor Galba, tells of his flagrant episode with his commanding officer's wife and recounts that the emperor Gaius had Vinius imprisoned (*edêsen auton*, *Galba* 12)—if true, an anomalous punishment, though, as will be seen, also attested under Tiberius.

On the other hand, this very Vinius exemplifies one great recourse from legal sanctions: amnesty. He was set free (*apeluthê*) when Gaius died; if, then, an exile could survive, he or she might come home when the new emperor took over, just as Gaius called home all who had been exiled under Tiberius (Suetonius *Calig.* 15.4).

Tacitus's accounts of adultery must be read carefully, since they are closely related to some of his most personal interpretations of the history of the early principate; thus they are here considered separately. Where you would expect to find scattered accounts of cases of adultery and of the normal procedure, Tacitus records only stories which depict the immorality of upper-class women, the cruelty of the *princeps*, or the savage greed of *delatores*—all three, if possible. The cases he reports are irregular and inconsistent, probably because most of the people involved were senators and/or relatives of the ruling house.[26] In the case of Appuleia Varilla, granddaughter of Augustus's sister, Tiberius intervened to lessen the penalty (*Ann.* 2.50); he also brought D. Silanus, exiled for adultery with the younger Julia, back from his *relegatio* (*Ann.* 3.24). Yet he later intervened to make penalties more rigorous, as in the case of Aquilia (*Ann.* 4.42).

Irregularities for the senators and *equites* were fostered by the boom in *delatio* under the Julio-Claudians. *Delatores* were attracted by the bounty set by the *lex Papia Poppaea* (*Ann.* 3.25):

Nor, therefore, were marriage and the bringing up of children made popular, childlessness prevailing: meanwhile the great number of those endangered was increasing, when every home was undermined by the legalistic machinations of informers, and, as previously trouble came from immoral behavior, so now it came from the laws.[27]

This law was used by Tacitus as the premier example of the invasion of private life by the principate through the agency of *delatio* (*Ann.* 3.28). *Delatores* received a substantial cut of escheated property; the ability of a third party to prosecute under the *lex Julia de adulteriis coercendis* provided a perfect opportunity. A husband who wished to allow his wife sexual freedom, or just not to prosecute her for a crime, risked a great deal.

That some husbands resisted the law is seemingly evidenced by the case of Vistilia in 19 CE (*Ann.* 2.85; cf. Suetonius *Tib.* 35.2):

> In the same year the wantonness of the women was put under control by severe decrees of the Senate, and provision was made that no one whose grandfather, father, or husband had been a Roman knight should prostitute herself. For Vistilia, born of a praetorian family, had publicly registered with the aediles her availability for sexual intercourse, in the traditional manner, which held that there was enough punishment of unchaste women in the very profession of their flagrant crime. Moreover, it was demanded of Titidius Labeo, Vistilia's husband, why he had neglected the revenge furnished by law in the case of a wife openly guilty. And when he gave as his excuse that the sixty days allowed for consultation had not yet gone by, it seemed enough to make a decision about Vistilia; and she was put away in the island of Seriphos.

Did Vistilia really become a prostitute? As readers, we might speculate that such a registration (if any) was a manipulation of a system which could define female behavior as "wanton" and in need of control. As a tactic, such an action would have exempted Vistilia not only from prosecution for adultery, since she was now *infamis*, but from the provisions of the *lex Papia Poppaea* penalizing the failure to marry and have children.[28] It is striking how cynically (or defiantly) the husband in this story hides behind the letter of the law; clearly the whole business is as irksome to him as it is to his wife.

Tacitus perceives an ominous connection between the use of charges of *maiestas* (treason against the *princeps*) and charges of adultery for political ends. The very first example he gives of the abuse of *maiestas* is the case of Appuleia Varilla, cited above; the charge is linked with adultery in a most sinister way (*Ann.* 2.50):

> Meanwhile, the treason law was coming of age. An informer summoned even Appuleia Varilla, the granddaughter of Augustus's sister, on a charge of *maiestas*, since she had made fun of the deified Augustus and Tiberius and his mother in indecent speeches and, a relative of Caesar, was held for adultery. . . .

Other cases where Tacitus suggests a link between *maiestas* and adultery, or hints that evidence of adultery was manufactured, include those of Antistius Vetus (*Ann.* 3.38), where Tiberius intervened drastically; Aquilia, who appears in a list of those charged with *maiestas* (*Ann.* 4.42); Claudia Pulchra, Agrippina's friend and cousin (*Ann.* 4.52); and Faenius Rufus, in the time of Nero (*Ann.* 15.50).[29]

The case of Albucilla (*Ann.* 6.47–48), late in the reign of Tiberius, demonstrates how freely a *delator* could use the law as a political lever, implicating as many eminent culprits as suited him:

> Then Albucilla, notorious for love affairs with many men, and who had been married to Satrius Secundus who informed on [Sejanus's] conspiracy, was denounced for disloyalty to the emperor; Cnaeus Domitius, Vibius Marsus, and Lucius Arruntius were linked with her as her accessories and adulterers. . . . But accounts sent to the Senate indicated that Macro had presided at the interrogation of witnesses and the torture of slaves, and the fact that no letter of the *princeps* was attached led to the suspicion that most of it was made up, the *princeps* being ill and perhaps unaware of the whole thing because of Macro's well-known grudge against Arruntius.

Domitius and Vibius survived, Arruntius killed himself, and Albucilla tried to kill herself and ended up, as T. Vinius was to do, in prison (*carcerem*, 6.48.6); in the end, three more men were exiled or degraded on her account. The lurid case of Nero's wife Octavia (*Ann.* 14.60) is an extreme example of what the law meant to Tacitus: a perversion of moral law by a vile *princeps* and his unscrupulous henchmen, for the persecution of a hunted nobility.

Tacitus expresses his feelings about moral ideals and, indirectly, his conviction of the inappropriateness of the *lex Julia* in Chapters 18–19 of the

Germania.[30] He is in the midst of praising the Germans, whose military prowess he has earlier touted in a manner reminiscent of Livy writing of early Rome:

> Marriage, however, is very strict there, nor would you give more praise to any part of their *mores*. For, almost unique among barbarians, they are content with a single wife, except for only a few, who undertake many marriages, not for the sake of lust but because of their nobility. . . . By these means the women live their lives with their chastity firmly girded, corrupted by no alluring extravaganzas, no excitingly unsettling dinner parties. Men as well as women know nothing of secrets in letters. Adulteries are very rare in such a numerous people, for which the penalty is to hand, given over to the husbands: the husband drives the wife naked from home, her hair cut off, in the presence of her relatives, and drives her through the whole village with a whip; for there is no mercy for a virtue that has become public property; she will find a husband not by looks, youth, or money. For no one there laughs at vices, nor are corruption and being corrupted called "the times." Indeed, still better are those states in which only virgins ever marry, and put an end to matrimonial speculation and utter their wife's pledge once and for all. . . . And good *mores* have more force there than good laws elsewhere.

Here Tacitus combines the castigation of common Roman vices, a stock piece in contemporary rhetoric, with an unusual and oddly wistful description of a sort of physical punishment which at Rome was reserved for slaves, complete to the shaved head. What can his wife's life have been like? (He had one—the *Agricola* is a biography of her father.) What about his mother? (She supervised his education in philosophy.) What do we know once we've read *Germania* 18–19?

Moral Anecdotes and Rhetorical Exempla

Tacitus's parable in the *Germania* makes a good introduction to another kind of writing that often concerned itself with adultery: moral anecdotes and rhetorical exempla and exercises.[31] We now leave sources that try to make it happen (law) or which tell what happened as they see it (history) and turn to sources that tell of ideal cases, what they would like to have happen. Note that, as with Livy, there is often an overlap between these two forms of discourse; the anecdote collections, however, explicitly announce their usefulness, whether for character-building in general or for building a court case in particular. The rhetorical exercises constituted practice for young men hoping to argue in court one day—in the elder Seneca's collection, we find his memories of things people actually said. Bearing the Julian marriage laws in mind, we should think, as we read these collections, of what a woman might expect to experience in court.

Valerius Maximus's rhetorical handbook does include several cases which are realistic rather than idealistic. The account of the trial of Fannia before Marius (8.2.3; cf. Plutarch *Marius* 38), although suspect in several details, seems to be an account of a common republican procedure—the *actio de moribus* (suit for immoral conduct) brought by a husband in an effort to retain part of his wife's dowry after a divorce. The case of Calidius Bononiensis (8.1.*Absol.*12), on the other hand, shows an adulterer (presumably after 18 BCE) making an ingenious, if disreputable, excuse in court for his presence in a married woman's bedroom (he said he was there to meet a slave boy). Finally, Valerius Maximus 6.1, *De pudicitia*, includes an account of cases of adultery in which the husband resorted to "self-help" punishments (6.1.13):

> But if I might quickly also run through a list of those men who resorted to their own feelings instead of the public law in vindicating their honor: Sempronius Musca caught Gaius Gellius in adultery and flogged him; Gaius Memmius caught Lucius Octavius in a similar situation and beat him with [illegible];[32] Carbo Attienus (caught by Vibienus) and Pontius (caught by Publius Cerennius) were castrated. And the man who caught Gnaeus Furius Brocchus handed him over to his slaves to be raped. That these men had given in to their anger was not grounds for a lawsuit.

As will be seen, this is a rare instance in which literary—and mostly comic—accounts of what happens to adulterers are borne out by a real-life account. The killing of a wife and her lover caught together, or just of the lover, a central concern of the new Augustan laws, forms the worst-case scenario in a range of scenarios commonly played out in fiction; usually the punishments are savage but not fatal; the list in Valerius Maximus 6.1.13 is incomplete but representative. Although there is no way of identifying or dating the men involved, their very obscurity lends them an air of reality.

Exempla generally, however, are unrealistic and apocryphal; their characters are often famous men and women or people proverbial for especially virtuous actions. Valerius Maximus 6.1 begins with Lucretia and Verginia, and ends with three non-Roman exempla. These relate marvelous tales of the extremes to which chaste women have gone in the defense of their honor. This is the pattern of a sort of moral tale of which not only Livy but preeminently Plutarch was very fond; in *The Bravery of Women* (*Moralia* 257–61) he tells several stories in which the slain seducer plays a leading role. Camma poisons an unwanted admirer (258b-c); Chiomara's unwelcome seducer is beheaded (258e-f—the same story as Valerius Maximus 6.1.*Ext.* 2, in which the woman is not named); Timocleia of Thebes pushed hers down the well (259d-260d, = *Alex.* 12); Eryxo's brothers stabbed her would-be lover (260e-261b). At the end of this series, the stock villain appears, the tyrant who preys on free women and boys (261f). Apuleius's story of Charite (*Metamorphoses* 8.13) repeats the pattern, with gruesome embroideries of blinding and suicide. This moral comic book seemingly so appealing to Greek and Roman audiences of the first two centuries CE bears a family resemblance to the ideal of the *univira* and the death of Dido; a set of cultural norms takes shape.[33]

Such situations were also popular in the exercises of the rhetorical *scholae* that flourished from the death of Cicero onward, where young men learned how to argue a case. The *controversiae* of the elder Seneca and the *declamationes* of pseudo-Quintilian and Calpurnius Flaccus favored gruesome crimes as subject matter for their mock trials, as being most challenging—and, presumably, most enjoyable.[34] Of these crimes, adultery was a favorite, especially the situation in which a husband found his wife *in flagrante delicto* and killed her, or tried to. Of seventy-four *controversiae* in Seneca's collection, fourteen deal with adultery and other sexual crimes. The case of the foreign merchant (*Controv.* 2.7), which preserves the only complete speech in the collection, incorporates a wide range of normalizing accusations that could be made against an apparently blameless woman—a useful companion to the specifics of Cicero's speech *Pro Caelio*. Here, for example, the speaker sets rules for behavior in public (2.7.3–4):

> A married woman who wants to be safe against the lust of a seducer should go out bedecked (*ornata*) only enough so that she doesn't seem unkempt/dirty (*immunda*); let her have companions of such an age that she may move any unchaste man (*inpudicus*) to respect for their years, if nothing else; let her fix her eyes upon the ground; to anyone who greets her too attentively let her be rude rather than unchaste; even when she is forced to return a greeting, let her do it in confusion and with many

blushes. She should pledge herself to modesty in such a way that she denies her unchastity with her expression long before any words are spoken. No lust will break into these bastions that preserve her purity. (4) Women, go ahead: go out with a look on your face all set to pimp yourself, only slightly less naked than if you had taken your clothes off, with your voice tuned up for all kinds of flirting, only so far short of asking for it that anyone who sees you won't fear to approach you; then be surprised if, when you've put out so many signals of your unchastity, by your dress, your walk, your voice, your face, a man is found who doesn't avoid this adulteress in his path.

This pedagogical preoccupation with adultery seems to have continued strongly through the years; of the fifty-three *declamationes* of Calpurnius Flaccus preserved by his editor, eight (2, 11, 17, 23, 31, 40, 48, 49) are concerned with adultery. Pseudo-Quintilian has at least fourteen cases of adultery out of 145 cases (*Decl. min.* 244, 249, 273, 275, 277, 279, 284, 286, 291, 310, 335, 347, 357, 379). These are substantial percentages of collections which assemble a wide range of bizarre circumstances.

Yet the same writer who paints his moral comic book in primary colors can introduce shading into a somewhat more realistic context. In the *Coniugalia praecepta*, addressed to a young couple he knows, Plutarch advises the prospective bride that it is better for her to shut her eyes to a little philandering than to wreck her marriage, recommending a sweetly indulgent attitude (*Mor.* 140b); he does exhort the husband not to provoke his wife unduly by flaunting his relationships with other women (144d), and urges both to consider the holiness of procreation (144b). The jealousy between wives and female household slaves is briefly mentioned (144c). The bride's sexual fidelity is taken for granted, but Plutarch is one of the very few writers to discuss sex between husband and wife in a serious way (138f, 139c, 139e, 140c, 143d-e, 144f), presuming the existence of a positive female sexuality.[35] He also, however, tells the bride not to give her husband aphrodisiacs, a mistake he says Circe made with Odysseus (139b); and he seems to approve of confinement to the home, silence, and veiling, even recommending the husband to take his wife's shoes away to encourage her to stay home (142c-d). In the world of these *exempla*, even in Rome where women wore veils only on occasion and routinely moved around in public, writers like the men of the *scholae*, Valerius Maximus, and Plutarch could express approval of gross cruelty and see the harsh punishment of wives as belonging to the good old days (see esp. Valerius Maximus 6.3.9–12).

Gossip and Slander

The fourth category to be considered here merits special consideration, first because it constitutes a sort of history of events too minor to make the history books, and especially because it represents one practical form of the *infamia* which resulted from behavior classed as immoral. As rhetorical *exempla* constitute a conscious presentation of idealized behavior, so gossip shows what Romans said when they were being malicious. Of all the ephemera of antiquity, conversation is the most thoroughly lost to us; still it remains, in fossil form, in the shape of insults, scandal, and rumors recorded in all genres.

Cicero's letters, dating from before the Augustan marriage laws, are surprisingly rich in gossip about sexual misconduct; in fact, he was renowned as a wit in his own time and long afterwards, and many of the jokes attributed to him are sexual. One such joke he preserves himself: in a letter to Atticus (2.1.5), he boasts of a retort he claims he made to Clodius, a joke not only insulting but obscene. Clodius had complained that his influential sister would not even give him one foot of room at the games; Cicero says that he replied, "Don't complain about one of your sister's feet—you can always raise the other" (= "you can always get her to spread her legs"). Even if this is only what Cicero wishes he had said, it gives some idea of the way in which Roman gossip could slander a married woman. These letters, and later biographies, talked about events that were verifiable, like divorces and attendant circumstances, but they did not stop there. As Cicero said in a letter to Atticus, "We are both awfully nosy" (*sumus ambo belle curiosi*, Att. 6.1.25), and it was true.[36]

Caelius, missing Cicero, sends him the latest gossip (*Fam.* 8.7.2): Paula Valeria has sent her husband notice of divorce on the day he was to return from his province, and she plans to marry Decimus Brutus; "Servius Ocella would never have convinced anyone he was an adulterer if he hadn't been caught twice in three days." Caelius teases Cicero by not telling where Ocella got caught, and says it tickles him to think of Cicero, the great general, asking people "what woman some guy got caught with." In these brief stories, it is notable how women's agency figures on a par with men's, and how little blame there is—just glee.

Smutty stories clung to the great, as they always have; not only the dissolute Antony (Plutarch *Ant.* 6) but Pompey (Plutarch *Pomp.* 2, Suetonius *Gramm.* 14) and even the elder Cato (Plutarch *Cat. Mai.* 24) had their names bandied about in connection with women. There were stories in circulation about the profligacy of every emperor. The pages of Suetonius, and later of Dio and the *Historia Augusta*, are full of shocking anecdotes, but the similarities between stories about different emperors (e.g., Suetonius *Aug.* 69.1 and *Calig.* 36.2) ought to warn the reader.

It has likewise always been popular to make up jokes about those in power. Among others, there is a series of jokes about Augustus's daughter Julia, in which she plays the part of the clever protagonist (see chapter 3); her clothing, her companions, her method of birth control, and her sexual attitudes all provided matter for amusement (Macrobius *Saturnalia* 2.5, esp. 2.5.2–3, 5, 6, 9, 10). The implications in these jokes that she was committing adultery would have, in her case, an unfunny outcome. A particularly Roman kind of joke was the jingle set in an elegiac couplet, which might have been painted on a wall as graffiti or passed around in oral circulation; Suetonius preserves one about Otho and Nero (*Otho* 3.2):

> You ask why Otho's in exile, though it's called a promotion?
>   He'd begun to be somebody's wife's lover—his own.

Suetonius explains that Otho had married Poppaea so that Nero could enjoy her, but then kept her to himself; Nero sent him off to Lusitania on government business.

That so many of these stories concern the most eminent Romans of their time is sometimes the result of deliberate propaganda, such as, perhaps, Antony's smearing of Octavian. These stories do not tell us anything directly about their subjects. They do attest to some culture-wide attitudes about what constituted bad behavior. People otherwise unknown appear in graffiti as the perpetrators of nasty sex acts; the relation of these acts to their marital status depended on recognition by an audience to whom they were not unknown. But we can see that celebrity gossip did reach the general population, at least in Italy, from speech acts such as the obscene messages about Antony's wife Fulvia on the sling-bullets from the siege of Perusia, or the soldiers' songs at Caesar's triumph (Suetonius *Jul.* 49.4), or the popular reaction against Octavia's suffering (Suetonius *Ner.* 35.1–2).[37] The existence and preservation of these stories show that at least some parts of their contemporary audience found them not disgusting, but titillating, as indeed audiences would continue to do right through the Middle Ages to modernity; these same stories now enliven television and film versions of Rome. The reader will notice that gossip never mentions anyone being killed when caught in adultery; nobody is raped or castrated in retaliation, as they are in the comic sources below. In gossip, what happens if you get caught is just that you become the topic of conversation.

Satire and Related Literary Genres

Satire, on the other hand, paints a lurid picture of adultery and those involved in it; it is important to note the formal relation of this picture to what we have seen in rhetoric and history, but also to remember that here the picture is intended to amuse. Indeed, the moralist's frown powers the comedian's laugh, as Roman comic writers repeatedly remarked. Moreover, it seems obvious that no humorous genre could have amused its audience without being recognizable, if exaggerated. Satire, that quintessentially Roman genre, included among its close relatives epigram (Juvenal and Martial were friends), comedy of all kinds, and satiric novels like the *Satyrica* and Apuleius's *Metamorphoses*. On the other hand, satire might best be conceived of as akin to stand-up comedy, with the comedian addressing primarily an audience of citizen men like himself, with some rhetorical training; stage comedy, addressing a mixed audience and staged by slaves and lower-class men, has some themes of its own. In any case, it should be kept in mind that, in the multilingual world of the Roman Empire and probably before, the same jokes were made in Greek as in Latin (see Richlin 1992: 47–52, 130–31).

The two largest areas of obscene humor in Latin literature are those related to male-female and male-male intercourse. Of the male-female jokes, one very large subgroup deals with adultery, with a division of the comic roles among wife, lover, and cuckolded husband; the reverse situation (husband, mistress, and jealous wife) is much more rarely used, except in comedy. The rest of male-female humor is generally concerned with the excessive sexuality and other faults of unmarried women (prostitutes, widows, divorced women, old women, ugly women), on which see chapter 2. Women bear the brunt: although adultery takes two, and the word *moechus* ("adulterer," from the Greek *moikhos*) was a common pejorative term in satire and epigram, the adulterous wife attracts more blame.

The depiction of adultery in satire bears a family resemblance to a sort of bedroom farce which was a common skit in mime, as attested by several direct references in satire and by various Greek and Latin mime fragments (see Reynolds 1946). The episode involved a stupid husband, a buxom wife, and a dashing lover. The adulterer, although he proverbially hid in a chest, afraid for his life (Juvenal 6.44), at some point turned around and buffeted the hapless husband, Panniculus ("Little Rags"; Martial 2.72.3–4, 3.86.3, 5.61.11–12). The husband was always jealous of the wife (Juvenal 8.197). These scattered references convey the impression that, in mime, the husband was despised, the adulterer was a successful villain, and the wife, though appealing, was upstaged by both.

This situation is the focus of Horace *S.* 1.2, in which the poet exhorts his audience not to bother with coy, troublesome married women, but to stick to willing slaves (male and female) and freedwomen. Horace uses this idea repeatedly in his satires (1.4.27, 111–15; 2.7.45–57, 72), along with the cynical generalization that adultery came into being with the dawn of civilization (*S.* 1.3.105–110). This idea, in turn, is the takeoff point for Juvenal's sixth satire, which is all one enormous argument against marriage, addressed to a putative prospective bridegroom; Juvenal paints pictures of many special types of disagreeable wife, but again and again returns to the way wives cuckold their husbands.

A special satirical persuasion against adultery was the list of horrific punishments visited on the adulterer by the cuckold. Humorously speaking, the adulterer ran the risk of castration, being beaten, or paying a fine,[38] mutilation,[39] death,[40] anal rape[41] or the simulation of it,[42] or irrumation, in which the husband forced the adulterer to fellate him.[43] The only punishment of adulterous wives mentioned in satire is that they had to abandon the dress of a respectable woman, the *stola*, for the toga that was, according to these texts, worn by prostitutes.[44]

One legalistic vignette in satire shows a husband who pimps his wife, as in Juvenal 1.55–57:

when the pimp accepts the adulterer's bequest,
if the wife has no right to inherit—he's well trained
to look at the ceiling, trained to snore in his cups
with wakeful nose. . . .

This goes back to a proverbial passage in Lucilius (1223 Marx): Cicero twice (*Fam.* 7.24, *Att.* 5.39.2) uses the tag from it, "*non omnibus dormio*" ("I don't close my eyes for every man").[45] Such an action is sometimes linked in satire with *captatio* (legacy-hunting), as at Horace *S.* 2.3.231, 237–38, or at *S.* 2.5.75, where Teiresias advises Ulysses to hand over Penelope on demand; or with an effort to cover up the fact that the husband is a *cinaedus* (Juvenal 9.40–86).[46]

The hapless cuckold appears, if rarely, as the butt of jokes in epigram (Martial 3.70, 6.31, 10.69, 12.93); Claudius is the most eminent model cuckold (Juvenal 6.115–32, 10.329–45), asleep while his wife prostitutes herself and commits bigamy. The paradigmatic cuckold is the innocent interlocutor of Juvenal 6, addressed as *tu*, who walks unknowing through the traces of his wife's debaucheries (312–13)—in this case, atypically, sex with another woman; the two women first urinate on the cult statue of the goddess of chastity.[47] The bulk of the examples in Juvenal 6 clearly highlight the fear underlying this cultural preoccupation: your wife's adultery makes a fool of you and palms off other men's children on you.

The favorite picture is simply that of the adulteress. She entraps even effeminate men (Martial 2.47), divorces her husband for her lover (Martial 3.70, 4.9, Juvenal 6.100) or just cheats on her husband, in many ingenious ways (Lucilius 680 Marx, 781 Marx; Martial 1.73, 2.56, 3.26, 4.58, 6.90, 11.7, 11.71; Juvenal 6.140–41, 277–79, O.31–34, 464–66, 487–89, 548, 567). Most of Ovid's *Ars amatoria* displays a woman who is and is not an adulteress; his contemporary, the elegist Sulpicia, remarks in her first poem that it's boring to be chaste. Was it glamorous, then, to be bad? In the upside-down satirical world of the *Satyrica*, the paragon of marital fidelity, the Widow of Ephesus, proves the moral that even the chastest of women is a whore at heart (110.6–112.8); her story, when told by Eumolpus on board the ship of Lichas, provokes a blush even from Tryphaena and a laugh from the (textual) audience. Similarly, Petronius's upper-class women enjoy low lovers; Circe's maid (*Sat.* 126.5–11) gives a cynical account of her owner's preference for base men (slaves, messengers, gladiators, teamsters, actors), while she, the slave, turns up her nose at any but men of rank. Both Habinnas and Trimalchio boast of how, when they were slaves, they used to perform sexual services for their owners' wives (69.3, 75.11). Such women appear in Martial (6.6, 12.58) and throughout Juvenal 6. Slaves who do this in rhetoric get killed; in satire, they get away with it—with the exception of Glyco's wife's lover, a slave, who is thrown to the beasts (*Satyrica* 45.7–8). His story provides the (textual) dinner party with a bit of gossip and a joke.

A topic peculiar to the reign of Domitian is the revival of the *lex Julia*. Some of Martial's epigrams on this subject are seriously laudatory (6.2, 6.4, 9.6), but many more attack women (rarely, men) whose behavior undermines the intent of the law.[48] Juvenal mentions the law only to sneer at Domitian's hypocrisy (2.29–33) or that of those who accuse women (2.36–78). Similar jokes resurface in Ausonius two hundred years later (*Epigrams* 99, 101), suggesting the persistence of this taste in humor, or at least of an interest in imitating it. Ausonius, however, also says that his wife trusts his fidelity (19), not a claim found in Martial; and one of his vignettes of the rhetoricians of Bordeaux tells of Dynamius, forced to leave town and change his name due to charges of adultery (*Prof.* 23).

The only satirist to make a stock villain of the adulterer corrupting an innocent wife is Juvenal. At 3.45–46 he wants no part of such goings-on—"let others carry what the adulterer sends to the bride"; at 3.109–13 the obnoxious Greek upstart seduces everyone in the house. The infamous Crispinus was interested only in adultery (4.2–4), and had actually seduced a Vestal Virgin (4.8–10). The repulsive Naevolus in *Satire* 9 is paid by the *cinaedus* Virro to penetrate both himself and his wife, begetting the children that Virro cannot.

The male bias in Latin literature is most obvious in sexual humor. In satire, married women are always unchaste, just as prostitutes are either too promiscuous or too hard to get; they are all always described as they would be seen by the male lover or husband. The places where the poet, as narrator, talks of his own sexual feelings are rare, and limited to laments over impotence; a poem like Martial's exhortation to his "wife" to be more sexy (11.104) is even more unusual. The only area in sexual humor in which the woman does not play the central, specularized role is in the depiction of punishments of adulterers; here, the woman sits and shrieks in the background while the husband and adulterer fight it out—in short, the *Iliad*. The tantalizing scraps of Sulpicia the elegist and, above all, of Sulpicia the satirist remind us of the stories that are not told (see chapter 4); indeed, Sulpicia the elegist castigates her lover for carrying on with a woman she labels a slut (*scortum*, [Tibullus] 3.16.4).

How did the fear expressed in satire affect the married and marriageable women who lived with it? Surely it affected them, not only directly (divorces, beatings, gossip) but in more subtle ways: how they thought of themselves, how they thought of other women, how they felt about their husbands and the slave women who surrounded them. Slave women had more complicated problems: slaves could not marry legally, but their informal marriages were recognized; what did it mean to a slave woman to be used by the owner, or to see her husband, perhaps, or her child so used? What did it mean to a male slave that his wife's body was open to use by others? The elusive Petronius makes the freedman Hermeros say, "I bought my *contubernalis*, so no man could wipe his hands on her [body]" (*Sat.* 57.6).[49] What did it mean to slave men and women to be both part of the system of *pudicitia* and outside it? It is odd that we have to look for answers in texts that predate Lucilius: another lamppost problem. The slave women in Plautus who hope for freedom do so as part of a package involving legitimate marriage to a citizen; Toxilus in *Persa*, still a slave, thanks the gods for this day when he can put his arms around his beloved, now a free woman, for whose freedom he has paid her pimp (773a-74). Although, as far as we know, all the actors and writers of Plautine comedy were male, the plays are full of the problems posed by the sexual availability of the bodies of slaves and freed slaves, male and female.[50]

Husbands in Plautus routinely lust after slave women or prostitutes and are sometimes caught and punished by their wives; in a radical departure from Aristophanic comedy, wives are not shown as adulterous, with the huge exception of Alcumena in *Amphitruo*—she is certainly lust-filled and heavily pregnant, but also believes her sex partner to be her husband (see Christenson 2000: 37–45 on the debate over Alcumena as tragic figure; also Langlands 2006: 211–18). Whereas satire is full of repulsively randy old women (see chapter 2), there is no amorous *anus* to match the randy *senex* of comedy—nothing like the hags scene in Aristophanes' *Ekklesiazousai*—and the old woman in comedy is defined as outside the sexual (e.g., at *Most.* 274–77; turned into an old-wife joke at 280–81). It is almost as if the categories "wife" and "old woman" are merged in comedy; the young wives in *Stichus* are exceptional. Although male slaves in Plautus often express a desire for sex with off-limits women, the owner's wife is never the woman desired—indeed, she is usually an awe-inspiring figure, even repugnant. Husbands, moreover, often explicitly depict their own wives as repulsive, and are never shown coveting someone else's. The one man who tries to have sex with a *matrona*, the soldier in *Miles*, is in fact dealing with a freed slave prostitute and, even so, is still tortured onstage and threatened with castration, which he professes to deserve. The adulterer's risk of castration is an easy joke in Plautus, but it is a joke made by slaves about what happens to free men.

It is, then, all the more remarkable in comedy that the wronged wife is present onstage and voices her wrongs; some wives get the better of their husbands; the slave woman Syra in *Mercator* even makes a speech declaring the unfairness of the double standard for husbands and wives (817–29; see James 2012, Starks 2010). The *lena* in *Cistellaria* (36–37) says that wives hate *meretrices* because they are rivals for their husbands' affections; wives work to keep their husbands from having sex with *ancillae* (*Casina*, Caecilius Statius *Plocium* in Gellius 2.23.10). The *Poenulus* prologue addresses an audience that includes *matronae* (32–35), and it seems that this one form of humor aims to please, to some degree, the various non-hegemonic elements of its mixed audience. Perhaps, to that audience, a wife's infidelity was not funny—Alcumena, then, being doubly transgressive, only possible because mythological. Nor was every male present in the theater legally able to have a wife. There is some bitterness in the often-quoted words spoken by the slave Palinurus in *Curculio* (33–38):

> No one keeps you away from here [the pimp's house], nor forbids you
> to buy what's openly for sale, if you have the cash.
> No one keeps anyone from going down the public road—
> as long as you don't make a path across posted land,
> as long as you hold off from a *nupta*, a *vidua*, a *virgo*,
> the *iuventus* and free boys, love what you want to.

Palinurus here addresses his owner, explaining how not to risk castration. His lines are a joke—all desirable bodies, if free, are off limits—but there is a further qualification: you need money even to have what is "openly for sale." The list serves as a tacit reminder of the availability of slave bodies and of the difficulty of access, for male slaves, even to purchased sex. Palinurus's owner has a slave prostitute; Palinurus has nobody.

Conclusions

There are obvious contradictions in the evidence presented here. If any one of the five categories were used alone to illustrate Roman sexual attitudes, the picture would be a false one. The law, from Augustus onward, lists clear sanctions against all who commit adultery and are accused and found guilty; the reader assumes that such people were often brought to court, found guilty, and punished according to the law. From historians and other sources presenting information as factual, we can surmise that the Julio-Claudian emperors used the law exactly as they wished, that it presented an opportunity for *delatio*, and, overall, that it was imposed on a nobility which had enjoyed great sexual freedom, and that it thereby caused a long and deeply-felt resentment. It is startling to turn to contemporary rhetoric and exempla and find that the law is not mentioned, or appears only in a distorted and hardly recognizable form; on the other hand, the speakers in these set pieces espouse moral ideals which would make the reader think the *lex Julia* could hardly have been necessary. (At the same time, however, the speakers of the *controversiae*, practicing for court, seem to take these ideals less seriously than do writers like Plutarch; they wallow in murder and adultery.) Then again, despite the terror caused by the *delatores* according to Tacitus, we find that people must have been happily spreading scurrilous rumors about each other not only before but after the *lex Julia*. Finally, satire describes a wholly different situation. Here, adultery is common, but the sanctions of the *lex Julia* are unheard of, and the law itself not mentioned until the time of Domitian, when it is often broken. Instead of legal appeal, outraged husbands exact their own vengeance, raping, mutilating, fining, even killing the unlucky adulterers. Wives within these texts are the ones who punish their husbands, by betraying them. The legal, rhetorical, and comic texts, then, like invective, serve as a preemptive punishment of real-life women: they cast all women's fidelity into doubt, they suggest that a good woman would stay at home, they set up the attack plan against any woman who ventured into public. This in a culture where women were omnipresent in public. Were real women ever killed? Such murders, like spousal abuse, do not show up in the texts, but I would hesitate to interpret the meaning of this silence.

How is it possible to reconcile these accounts, and why should they disagree so wildly about a fact of everyday life? The first, obvious, answer is that each obeyed the conventions of a genre, and told the portion of the truth which its audience expected (see Dixon 2001). This, however, leaves us weighing the reliability of genres if we still want to ask how things really were, or just falling back on a postmodernist denial of the knowability of anything outside the text (see chapter 10). In fact we have a great many stories, which, put together, make, not a chaotic answer, but a three-dimensional answer.

The factors which will have allowed the different accounts to evolve were those which allowed irregularities in the administration of the law. Exile was administered in varying degrees, sometimes not at all, sometimes for a term of years, sometimes to a pleasant place and sometimes to a desert island; the powerful will always have been favored, especially against a weak plaintiff. Most of the inhabitants of the empire before Caracalla, not being Roman citizens, will have been subject to harsh and sometimes arbitrary treatment—if any. So it is easy to see how notorious women may have continued to live in Rome, or in the resort towns around Naples; it is also easy to see how famous people might have either evaded the law, or been hurt badly by it; clearly, the degree of sexual freedom and attendant risks depended on who, when, and where you were.

At the same time, the great variety in the sources is a sign that adultery was a major preoccupation of Roman society. The number of books interpreting the law, the amount of gossip, the number of jokes, testify to a practical, everyday concern with sexual goings-on at least from the late republic on, and presumably earlier as well. For free people, the normalcy of husbands' infidelity, the fear of wives' infidelity, even the criminalization of wives' adultery—all these were perhaps not so hard to live with as long as divorce continued to be easy. And then things changed.

CHAPTER 2

Invective against Women
in Roman Satire

ᥫ᭡

Introduction

This essay was a spin-off of *The Garden of Priapus*; there were further questions I wanted to raise about some of the texts discussed in chapter 5 of the
book. The basic conclusion reached here—that texts about women written
by men are in fact texts about men, with the corollary that such texts do have
profound social effects on women—fed directly into a growing discomfort
among feminist classicists about what we were doing with male-authored
texts. This issue was brought to public discussion in the famous 1985 Wom-
en's Classical Caucus panel at which Phyllis Culham asked whether there
was any point in reading Ovid to find out about real women (see volume
introduction). As it turned out, even feminists in Classics, unsurprisingly,
went on reading and teaching canonical Greek and Latin literature anyway—it was our job, what we had trained in; feminist approaches did come
to influence mainstream treatment of amatory genres like elegy. Satire and
invective, however, since around 1900, have been among the less-read literary genres—difficult, offensive, minor; mainstream discussions even of
satire still tend not to deal with gender or sexuality. The expurgated reading
of Catullus has been remedied, at least in the scholarship, but the *Carmina
Priapea* remain pretty much unknown.

Back in the early eighties, this essay was reacting against some common ways in which invective texts were then being read within Classics —again, when they were read at all. Scholars dealing with Roman invective as a genre had dealt mainly with its debt to Greek invective; women were dealt with separately, part of the softer side of social history. But both literary critics and historians writing on Roman women had tended to find texts like Juvenal's sixth satire irresistible and to feel that they could mine such texts for bits of truth. It is hard not to agree that Juvenal 6 might contribute to our ideas about women's literacy or religious practices or freedom of travel. What I wanted to resist was the long-standing reading of invective texts as evidence of women's misbehavior. A few examples will illustrate the state of the question in the late 1970s; first, from Gilbert Highet, in his general book on Juvenal (1954: 102, on Juvenal 6):

> Of course the satire . . . has seemed false in ages when family life and sexual relations were well adjusted. Yet because of the long degeneration of Roman morals it was probably close to the truth in its own time; and so many quotations and imitations have been inspired by it in the last 1,500 years that it must contain a large proportion of permanent truth. . . . Evidently the profound spiritual maladjustment from which Rome suffered in Juvenal's day had sucked away the strength of her men and intensified the passions of her women.

J. P. V. D. Balsdon, the title of whose book (*Roman Women: Their History and Habits*, 1962, rev. ed. 1975) suggests an attitude about to become extinct, swings between gallantry supported by a well-informed consciousness that all the texts are written by men, and a tendency to construct a sympathetic narrative out of unsympathetic materials, for example (1975: 261):

> Make-up and scents, . . . reasonably enough, . . . constituted the centre of interest in the lives of a very great number of women, in particular of Ovid's own clients, the expensive courtesans. In pagan Rome only the Vestal Virgin was forced to suppress a sigh, knowing that such vanity was not for her.

Awareness of bias does not make him critical (213): "the addiction of women to the novel oriental cults . . . did not escape the satirist's contemptuous notice." He plainly states his views on how to read satire (16): "To call Juvenal and Martial—even to call Tacitus—misogynists is stupid." Why? Because satirists also attack men. But satire must be somewhat true: "That there were women in Rome of the types which Juvenal and Martial described is certain enough." Just not *all* women.[1]

R. P. Bond in 1979, influenced by the women's movement, to judge by the title of his essay ("Anti-feminism in Juvenal and Cato"), nevertheless argues (418):

> The contention will be that Cato and Juvenal both belonged to the same misogynistic tradition and were, in a sense, partially responsible, along with the men who shared their views, for much of the female behaviour which they so trenchantly condemned.

Bond traces the trajectory of misogyny in Roman texts from the elder Cato to Juvenal, draws comparisons between these texts and the "reactionary view" critical of women's liberation in the twentieth century, and concludes by deploring the Roman failure to "accept a need for change and educate women and society accordingly" (447), from which we, reading now, should "derive a valuable lesson." Apart from the circularity of Bond's basic contention, the methodological question still arises: to what extent, if at all, can invective be considered an historical document? Does it tell us anything more than, as a fact in itself, what Roman women had to put up with—the stereotypes that policed their behavior?

The reading preoccupied with historicity is sidestepped altogether by the now common preference for reading invective texts, particularly Juvenal's, as not meaning what they say—as exposing the comedian rather than the joke's butt. The chief proponent of this approach, which goes back to William Anderson's work in the 1960s, is Susanna Braund, for example in her essay "Juvenal: Misogynist or Misogamist?". Arguing that Juvenal 6 is based on a long tradition of rhetorical attacks on marriage, she posits that the misogynistic speaker fails in his task and is "a kind of Roman Alf Garnett, created for the audience's amusement. . . . It is characteristic of satire to explore an issue. . . . through an extremist character and to undercut that character without taking sides. In this way the author of satire has it both ways" (1992: 85–86). That is, the comedian gets to *say* all that invective but, more fundamentally, is mocking anyone who would say such things.[2] This ironic pose is easy to instantiate in current work like *South Park*, and for that matter in Sarah Silverman's work; it is hard to believe, however, that most watchers of *Team America: World Police* (Parker and Stone 2004) took the theme song "America! Fuck Yeah!" to mean that the characters created by Trey Parker and Matt Stone are stupid—this song alone had, in 2010, a Google rating of 7,050,000, and was still over a million in the summer of 2012.[3] I would still stick with Freud and maintain that listeners to this song, as with all transgressive humor, enjoy hearing someone else say something that is usually forbidden. The satirist, performing before his audience, is in the position of a stand-up comedian: charismatic, daring, cool.

A particular problem I faced in the early 1980s was that Roman invective texts, like more elevated literature, had been explained mainly as efforts to copy Greek originals; I wanted to read these texts in terms of their specifically Roman qualities and of their possible effects on contemporary people, taking it as axiomatic that people only copy what they find useful. As a result, this essay skates past "the Greek comic stereotype of women"; later, in critiquing Foucault, I had to point out how very negative that stereotype could be, and bring up Greek invective texts that are usually not read (see Richlin 1991: 172 on Antipater of Sidon). Indeed, "Invective against Women" deliberately flattens historical differences in the use and content of invective within Roman culture(s), and I would like to see the passing references here to Ausonius and Fulgentius developed into a consideration of what happens to invective in late ancient Christian contexts, for example starting with Tertullian; Procopius's *Secret History* can certainly be discussed as part of this tradition, yet Byzantium has a set of ideas about women that are special to itself (see chapter 3, and Vinson 1998, Garland 2006). Although there is now substantial work on female characters in Roman comedy (see Dutsch 2009, with bibliography; Feltovich 2011), it would be useful to contrast the performance of the abject female body in second-century BCE Rome with that in Old Comedy, and with verse invective; much remains to be said about the complex use of the female material bodily lower stratum by masked male actors (see Gold 1998b on cross-dressing; chapter 6 below now includes a brief overview).

Finally, I still want to stress this essay's contention that "Jokes, like laws, act prescriptively to police desire and behavior." It seems to me that a great deal also remains to be said about the contribution made by invective to war effort, to imperialism, and indeed to all forms of hierarchical coercion down to daily miseries. Some work is being done, but not enough to do justice to this busy area of ideological activity—so common, indeed so low, that it is hardly visible to cultural critique (but see Harper 2002, Prum et al. 2007, and issues of *Journal of Hate Studies*, starting in 2001). Jalna Hanmer long ago argued, in passing, in her fundamental essay "Violence and the Social Control of Women," that "Joking . . . represents the most subtle form of the threat of force and is at one extreme of the continuum of violence" (1981: 31), and there is now a massive legal and sociological literature on hate speech, including its effect on women and particularly in the work-place, where it is recognized as a form of harassment. It seems, however, that once such speech crosses the threshold into print and becomes litera-ture, its status as art shields it, with the extreme cases, like the *Priapea*, sim-ply being shunted off into obscurity, as if they had no organic connection to high art and no real-life effects—a problem tied to the pornography-related issues dealt with in chapter 5 below.

Sometimes, of course, readers control texts: it is a great historical curios-ity that Anne Lister, in the early nineteenth century, took erotic inspiration not from Sappho, but from the harsh invectives against *tribades* in Martial (Clark 1996; on these texts, see Brooten 1996: 42–57; Hallett 1997). At an institute held at Dartmouth in 2007, "No Laughing Matter: Visual Humor in Ideas of Race, Nationality and Ethnicity," the participants' projects uni-formly focused on humor as a means of subversion, even though most were examining reactions against heinous forms of racial stereotyping (David Bindman, one of the directors, studies the aesthetics of race in the eigh-teenth century and the history of Western images of Africans, e.g., Bind-man 2002). But this stereotyping is often itself coated in comedy, which makes it sell; and Anne Lister was a wealthy heiress who owned her own library. Sex sells, money shops.

And power makes the archives, so I can only guess, but am still certain, that Roman women produced an invective of their own, and incorporated negative stereotypes of men, and each other, into their daily joking speech; I take it as certain that it was there and that we do not know much about it because Roman women's work did not circulate widely—or because what did circulate was not preserved as the centuries rubbed on (but see chapters 3 and 4). Sarah Levin-Richardson (2013) argues that we cannot just assume that men wrote all the graffiti in Pompeii, and that women may have writ-ten some of the sexual insults against men, or even lines like *Murtis felatris*, which she optimistically translates as "Murtis the blow-job babe": a boast-ing re-appropriation by a woman with no social honor, or flouting honor. Indeed women may have written graffiti about each other. I imagine that Roman *matronae* made jokes about slave women (think of Sulpicia the ele-gist's remarks about the "slut weighed down by a wool-basket," [Tibullus] 3.16.4, with discussion in Keith 1997: 304–5), and that slave women made jokes about female owners; I imagine that Claudia Severa, whose precious letter inviting a friend to her birthday party attests to the life of an officer's wife on the British frontier, made jokes about the locals, who made their own jokes about her. Women's ritual joking is well attested in Greek culture (see O'Higgins 2001, 2003, stressing women's agency in producing invective); did it play a part at the Bona Dea celebrations, or at the Matralia (see chapter 7)? If male Roman satirists played the role of a stand-up comic, did women do this? We do have a fragment from the work of one female satirist (see chapter 4), a respectable married woman: could she, could any woman, have given public readings of her work? It is a good question for future comparative study: what, within a given culture, makes it possible for women to perform formal invective in public? Such performance is attested, for example, in the work of the fifteenth-century Welsh poet Gwerful Mechain; indirectly attested for medieval Islamic cultures; relatively plentiful in seventeenth- and eighteenth-century England; and thriving today in Anglophone cultures.[4]

"Invective against Women in Roman Satire" briefly discusses the roles of the comedienne in its conclusion; it is true that, twenty-five years after this essay was written, comediennes look different—Sarah Silverman, not Phyllis Diller. The transgressive potential of the "unruly woman" was mapped, optimistically, by Kathleen Rowe (1995) in the early 1990s. Today you can hear plenty of invective against men and view a whole play dedicated to the vagina; in *Jesus Is Magic* (Silverman 2005), you can watch Sarah Silverman pretend to sing through her vagina and anus, while in *The Aristocrats* (Jillette and Provenza 2005) she substitutes a charge of rape for the punch line of the joke. Indeed, as the (just a joke) raped woman turned the joke inside out, it became readable as an unfunny attack on the man accused; according to Dana Goodyear's account (2005), he considered suing, to which Silverman said in public, "He doesn't have the balls to sue"—an assumption of the pose of Priapus by a woman speaker. Yet as female comics, like male comics, use their own bodies as the substance of humor, this can still drive them back into traditional concepts of the abject feminine, as seen in Rachel Lee's analysis of Margaret Cho's use of her "dirty vagina" and alien body played against a specularizing audience (Lee 2004; cf. Arthurs 1999; Lavin 2004). Female rappers like Lil' Kim ("Suck My Dick") and Queen Latifah ("Latifah's Had It Up to Here," "Cell Block Tango") call men out, but there is no shortage of misogynistic invective among women rappers in general, and even Awkwafina's "My Vag" manifests a certain ambivalence. Sightings continue of the frat party sign "No Fat Chicks" and similar prescriptive texts telling women who belongs where, who is sexy, who is not.

Parallels, I would guess, are easy to find in any historical period. Explanations are harder to find. In 1983, writing this essay and as yet unaware of Julia Kristeva's *Powers of Horror*, I could resort only to Freud on the Medusa's head and to his follower Karen Horney; in 1986, Mary Russo appealed to Bakhtin's optimistic model of the pregnant, laughing hag to understand the female grotesque (Russo 1986; cf. Russo 1994: 53–73). Russo concluded, though, that Bakhtin's model, taking the hag as emblematic of the life-in-death at the heart of the carnivalesque, does not account for the real-life oppressiveness of this stereotype. Kristeva (1982) associates the whole category of the abject with concepts of ambiguity and pollution (as in the work of Mary Douglas) derived from the maternal body. Today, hunting for further theoretical work on invective and misogyny, even on women in stand-up comedy, even just on stand-up, I do not see much; analyses keep coming back to Bakhtin and to writers influenced by Bakhtin—Natalie Zemon Davis, in her essay "Women on Top" (1975b); Russo.[5] Jalna Hanmer commented (1981: 30) on how the consciousness of cultural hostility toward women is repressed, even once remembered, and the fact is that not a lot of people want to think about these texts. But they are everywhere, and they still make their bid to control our lives.

ﷺ   ﷺ   ﷺ

Nescis. . . quantum Satyram matronae formident.
Fulgentius, Mitologiae 1.23

Discussion of the nature of invective against women in Roman satire begins here from two axioms: that Western published literature has largely been written by and for the benefit of men; and that (perhaps, therefore) much of Western literature concerns tensions between levels in social hierarchies. Satire is a genre intrinsically concerned with power; the satirist writes against those who oppress him or those whom he feels he ought to be able to oppress, depicting himself worsted by plutocrat, general, or noble, or sneering at out-groups (foreigners, sexual deviants, women, slaves and freed slaves, and combinations of these groups). By expressing his hostility, the satirist asserts his own power, and makes himself and his like-minded audience feel better. At the same time, the performance of the satire reinforces the desired social norms. For Roman satire, as for the satire of many other cultures, the satirist himself is a male self-defined as normal. There is now a long history, very visible today, of comics who themselves belong to out-groups, but we see this in Rome only behind the masks of comedy or in the animal bodies of fable, not in the first-person voice of satire—or only insofar as Horace plays the son of a freed slave, or Juvenal, a poor *cliens*. Still male, still normalizing.

Satire often attacks by means of a stereotype, and it has too often been assumed that such stereotypes constitute exaggerated, but basically realistic, versions of their prototypes.[6] This assumption directs attention toward the chimerical figures of the victims of satire and away from the one set of people for whom the stereotypes constitute evidence—the normative males themselves. For any stereotype surely must encode a statement about the writer's and audience's feelings about the real people satirized; invective against women can best be understood as the concrete manifestation of a social notion of women. The hugely exaggerated and emphasized features in the stereotype tell us nothing (directly) about Roman women, but plenty about the fears and preoccupations of Roman society (including and affecting women themselves) with regard to women, as enunciated by male satirists.

The body of ancient literature that contains invective against women, or comic stereotypes of women, is enormous; in Latin, a list of only the most notable sources would include the comedies of Plautus and Terence, a substantial portion of Catullus, Horace *Epodes* 5, 8, 12, 17 and *Satires* 1.2, Ovid *Ars amatoria*, *Remedia amoris*, and *Medicamina faciei femineae*, Petronius *Satyrica*, the *Carmina Priapea*, Martial, Juvenal 6, Apuleius *Metamorphoses*, especially Book 9, and Ausonius *Epigrams*. The purpose of the present study is only to bring forward the most striking and idiosyncratic features of Roman invective against women, and so no chronological examination of the sources will be made. It is enough to note here that their picture of women is entirely consistent, and shares many features with the Greek comic stereotype of women. But while a great number of the particulars of the Roman stereotype are traditional[7] and conventional,[8] the prominent and large space allotted to misogynistic invective in Latin literature and the freedom and variety of the use of stock motifs suggest that the material is not just there pro forma. In addition, misogynistic invective is the same at all levels, from graffiti to formal verse satire. If a literary theme can be viewed as anthropological artifact, the nature of Roman invective against women has clear implications for the function of Roman satire within Roman society as a means of controlling women and defining normative sexuality.[9] Jokes, like laws, act prescriptively to police desire and behavior.

To begin with, the Roman satiric stereotype of women can be broken down into three main categories: young women (attractive), young women (repulsive), and old women (repulsive). This definition depends entirely on sexual and physical qualities. Social status—married, unmarried, or divorced; slave, freed, or freeborn; prostitute or not—often plays a part, but the frequent lack of specification of such status is a well-known problem.[10] Status is clearly only an incidental feature. Yet stereotypes would have had a particular effect on slave women in their capacity as commodities, assigning beauty to sex work, and ugliness, sometimes ethnically determined, to hard labor (cf. Plautus *Mercator* 210–11, 395–417; Starks 2010).

Satire depicts some women as attractive, some as repulsive. In all cases the poet, a male narrator, defines what attracts and what repels. Attractive women—young wives and mistresses—are typified as promiscuous[11] and drunken,[12] sometimes as jealous[13] or mercenary.[14] This stereotype reflects the same concerns evinced by the Roman laws on marriage, divorce, and adultery, especially the early law, which, tradition held, placed drunkenness on a level with adultery as cause for divorce.[15] The obsession with adulterous behavior in wives can easily be understood in an ancestor-worshiping society; the reasons for the association between adultery and drunkenness are less obvious.[16] Though drunkenness is occasionally connected with promiscuity (Juvenal 6.300–45), it can stand alone to typify misbehavior by a woman—she makes a spectacle of herself at a dinner party (Juvenal 6.425–33). The stories of the early sources indicate that the husband and agnates wished to prevent (or detect) secret drinking. These stories imagine a structure for the early Roman household in which the husband is often away from the house, and his wife is left in control; ideal behavior is manifested by Lucretia, who spins late into the night with her maids while her misbehaving counterparts spend the evening drinking and carousing (*in convivio luxuque*, Livy 1.57.9), like men. Both sets of women are available for discovery; a wife's behavior, then, is always potentially either helpful or detrimental to her husband's *dignitas*. The attractive wife must be safely incorporated into her husband's persona, and must not take on the manly role of initiating a party. As in Greek symposiastic literature, there is a general belief that women who drink at parties are available for sex.

Repulsive women populate the pages of satire: why? The poet and audience must be taking pleasure in examining them and proclaiming their disgust. One whole class of such women differs from the attractive ones only in physical form; they are would-be wives and mistresses, promiscuous and drunken like the rest, but depicted by the writer as so hideously ugly that he must refuse them when they pursue him.[17] The other class of repulsive women is old: their age and decrepitude are enormously exaggerated; they, too, like to drink; and, though they often offer the narrator money or a large dowry to marry or have sex with them, he usually resists, with loathing.[18] The interest of Roman satire in graphic descriptions of this repulsive stereotype seems much more difficult to understand than the interest in the attractive stereotype; the reasons for it may perhaps be sought in the peculiar features of Roman invective against women.

The fantastic age of the old women attacked in Roman invective is conventionally expressed by a list of hyperbolic comparisons with heroes and heroines of Greek mythology. Some examples:[19]

quae forsan potuisset esse nutrix
Tithoni Priamique Nestorisque,
illis ni pueris anus fuisset

who perhaps could have been the wet-nurse
of Tithonus, of Priam, and of Nestor,
if she hadn't been an old woman when they were boys

(*Priapea* 57.3–5)

Pyrrhae filia, Nestoris noverca,
quam vidit Niobe puella canam,
Laertes aviam senex vocavit,
nutricem Priamus, socrum Thyestes

Daughter of Pyrrha, stepmother of Nestor,
a woman whom Niobe as a girl saw white-haired,
Laertes as an old man called his grandmother,
Priam his wet-nurse, Thyestes his mother-in-law

(Martial 10.67.1–4)

istud . . . belle
non mater facit Hectoris, sed uxor

This thing
not Hector's mother does becomingly, but his wife.

(Martial 10.90.5–6)

The lists share a basic structure: they define the women in terms of family relationships. Not only are these old women coevals of the proverbially elderly, they are part of the family, and they are not wives. They are daughter, stepmother, grandmother (also in Martial 3.93.22, contrasted with wife), mother-in-law, sister (*Priapea* 12.2), wet-nurse, even mother (*Priapea* 12.1; specifically contrasted with wife, Martial 10.90.5–6, 11.23.14). At *Priapea* 57.7–8 and Martial 10.90.3 (cf. 8.79), the old woman is also specifically denied the appellation of "girl," *puella*. The point of this definition of the old woman is that in each case she remains extremely eager for sexual intercourse, often directly rejected as a partner by the narrator in the crudest terms: *ne desim sibi, me rogat, fututor,* "she begs me that I not desert her as her fucker" (*Priapea* 57.6, cf. 12.5–7); *vis futui gratis cum sis deformis anusque,* "you want to be fucked for free, when you're ugly and an old woman!" (Martial 7.75.1). The unbecoming behavior of the woman in Martial 10.90 is the depilation of her crotch; she is told that this activity is proper to wives, not mothers. Thus in each case old women are marked off from sexual union with men (or wifehood) by a demonstration of disgust at sexual desire in old women, and the statement is clearly made that sexual desire is attractive and appropriate only in young women (prostitutes or wives). This both tallies with and, interestingly, differs from the stereotype in Plautine comedy, in which wives are old and sexually repulsive, age transforms sex workers into body servants or madams, and only young women are sexually desirable.

As the fantastic age and nonmarital family status of old women bars them from intercourse, so the bestial ugliness of all repulsive women in satire stigmatizes intercourse with them as disgusting—though not inconceivable. Animal invective is unusual in Latin;[20] by far the most extreme examples apply to women.[21] At its mildest such invective compares old women to crows, proverbially long-lived (but also carrion-eaters);[22] the woman who persists in depilating her crotch is told not "to pluck the beard of a dead lion" (Martial 10.90.10).

The invective becomes more specific when it deals with a woman's physical flaws, either part by part or focusing on a single part. The most notable examples of the part-by-part technique[23] are Horace's *Epodes* 8 and 12: in 8, the woman is described as old (1–2), black-toothed and wrinkle-browed (3–4), with flabby stomach and misshapen, swollen legs (9–10), with an anus like that of a cow with diarrhea (5–6) and breasts like a mare's teats (7–8); in 12, she is "fit for black elephants" (1), and smells like an octopus or a goat (5), bedaubed with cosmetics made from crocodile dung (11). Martial (3.93) compares a woman with cicadas, ants, spiderwebs, crocodiles, frogs, gnats, owls, goats, and ducks. When a poet focuses on a single part, it is generally the woman's genitalia: often depicted as filthy and loose (compared with the buttocks of the statue of a horse, the gullet of a pelican, and a salt fishpond, Martial 11.21.1, 10, 11, with other, non-bestial comparisons; described as crawling with worms, *Priapea* 46.10); sometimes too bony (Martial 3.93.13, 11.100.4); sometimes white-haired (Martial 2.34.3, 9.37.7); too noisy (Martial 7.18; *"Quid hoc novi est?"* 37, below).

Some generalizations can be made about the referents chosen. Many of the animal referents are exotic, and have unusual shapes and sizes as well (elephant, octopus, crocodile, pelican); insects are even further removed from humanity. The descriptions often allude to diseases, smell, and/or fecal matter, and relate the woman to one of an animal's orifices, especially mouth or anus (cf. Catullus 97.7–8, where the mouth of a male victim is compared with the vagina of a urinating she-mule). At the same time the idea of decay is also often present (*putidam, putres*, Horace *Epodes* 8.1, 7; *putida, Priapea* 57.2; *putidula*, Martial 4.20.4), so that the worms of *Priapea* 46.10 are surely those of decomposition, despite the fact that the woman is addressed as *puella* in the first line of this poem. Old women themselves are repeatedly addressed as corpses, from the imagined funeral of Horace *Epodes* 8 to direct equation (*caries vetusque bustum,* "decay and old tomb," *Priapea* 57.1; *mortua, non vetula,* "a dead woman, not an old one," Martial 3.32.2); one woman is imagined as lusting in her grave (Martial 10.67). What is more startling, the genitals themselves are treated as the women's relics or tombs (*inter avos . . . tuos,* "among your ancestors," Martial 9.37.8; *busti cineres,* "the ashes of your funeral pyre," Martial 10.90.2), and Martial concocts an elaborately grotesque funeral/wedding, ending with the line *intrare in istum sola fax potest cunnum,* "only a funeral torch can get into that cunt of yours" (3.93.27; compare Bodel 2000 on Roman ideas of death-pollution). Perhaps the disgust attributed specifically to the female genitalia, as an outlandish, foul-smelling, possibly diseased or decayed, and bestial orifice, is generalized in satire to the woman as a whole, and especially when the narrator wishes to reject women as desiring subjects.

In fact, old women evoke the most intense expressions of fear and disgust, along with a sense that they constitute a sort of uncanny Other. The role of old women in ancient literature includes a range separate from the role of mother—old wet-nurse and adviser, madam, witch; and the sphere of activity of the witches/nurses/advisers in Latin literature is primarily sexual and perverse (see chapters 7, 8, 9). Like the aged nurses of tragedy and epic who lead Phaedra and Myrrha astray, Dipsas in Ovid's *Amores* (1.8), the *lena* of Tibullus 1.5, and Acanthis in Propertius 4.5 serve as the companion of the poet's mistress and advise her to be promiscuous. Their function is to remove the attractive young woman from the poet's exclusive control and to pervert the sexual behavior of the mistress; the old woman's role easily combines that of witch and madam (cf. Martial 9.29.9–10). Witches also have the ability to charm a beloved (Vergil *Aeneid* 4.478–521; Horace *Epodes* 5.81–82). But their charms include abortifacients (Juvenal 6.595–97; cf. Ovid *Amores* 2.14.27–28) and poisons (Juvenal 6.610–17), so that they pervert the traditional female functions of procreation and feeding and make them deadly.

Moreover, witches can directly threaten male characters. Horace's awful Canidia tortures a little boy (*Epodes* 5) and shuts up the *Epodes* poet himself (17). The witches in Horace *Satires* 1.8 perform fearsome magic rites near the statue of Priapus, making wax dolls with which to control desire; he frightens them away by farting, and undercuts their importance by revealing them as old women with false teeth and hair (46–50). The crone at the start of what remains of the *Satyrica* (7–8) puts Encolpius in his place—a brothel—while the crones at the end of the novel (134–38) try to restore his sexual potency with an eye to their own satisfaction, finally inserting in his rectum a leather phallus anointed with a mixture of oil, pepper, and nettle seed. The witches in Trimalchio's tale steal a baby and beat a strong man to death (*Sat.* 63); the vampire grannies of Ovid's *Fasti* suck the blood of a royal baby (6.131–50). The witches of Apuleius's *Metamorphoses* embody wrongful knowledge: Meroe, who urinates on the narrator and causes the horrible death of the man who tries to desert her, the narrator's friend Socrates (*Metamorphoses* 1.11–19); the anonymous witches who cut off Thelyphron's nose (2.30);[24] and, paramount, Lucius's dangerous hostess, whose arts provide the means whereby his mistress turns him into an ass (3.24–26). Old women in these cases represent a side of female behavior that maliciously threatens males with cuckoldry, sterility, usurpation, rape, or death, all of which activities any male would presumably wish to discourage, and all of which undermine male control over women.

The same sort of threat appears to emanate from female genitalia.[25] Witches turn into animals (*striges*, screech owls) and turn their enemies into animals; invective turns women into animals and likens their bodies to animal parts. Witches deal in death and speak with the dead; invective perceives women's genitals as decayed or dead. It should be noted that nowhere in Latin is there a favorable direct portrayal of female genitalia;[26] they are depicted only as part of repulsive women.

The outstanding example of such a description forms part of the Priapic poem from the *Virgilian Appendix*, listed in the Oxford text (pp. 151–53) as *Priapeum "Quid hoc novi est?"* (83 Bücheler). The poet threatens his recalcitrant penis: instead of lovely boys (21–23) and girls (24–25), the penis will be forced to enter the horrible vagina of a very old woman (26–37):

> *bidens amica Romuli senis memor*
> *paratur, inter atra cuius inguina*
> *latet iacente pantice abditus specus*
> *vagaque pelle tectus annuo gelu*
> *araneosus obsidet forem situs.*   30
> *tibi haec paratur, ut tuum ter aut quater*
> *voret profunda fossa lubricum caput.*
> *licebit aeger, angue lentior, cubes,*
> *tereris usque donec, a, miser, miser,*
> *triplexque quadruplexque compleas specum.*   35
> *superbia ista proderit nihil, simul*
> *vagum sonante merseris luto caput.*

> A two-toothed mistress who remembers old Romulus
> is ready, amidst whose dark loins
> lies a cave hidden by a flaccid paunch,
> and, covered by skin wandering in year-long cold,
> cobwebbed filth obstructs the door.   30
> She's ready for you, so that three or four times
> this deep ditch can devour your slimy head.
> Although you'll lie there weak, slower than a snake,
> you'll be ground repeatedly until—o wretch, wretch,
> you fill that cave three times and four times over.   35
> This pride of yours will get you nowhere, as soon as
> your errant head is plunged in her noisy muck.

In this poem the threat embodied by the vagina is abundantly clear. It is to be feared by the personified phallus; it is foisted off onto a repulsive person, the aged woman, while the attractive boy and girl in lines 21–25 tempt the reader with only external parts of their bodies. The old woman, punningly, is both "two-toothed" and a sheep to be used for sacrifice (*bidens*). The vagina is sinister (*latet, abditus*, 28) and physically dangerous; a cave or deep ditch (*specus*, 28, 35; *profunda fossa*, 32), it will devour and grind the phallus (*voret*, 32; *tereris*, 34), for which the author expresses pity (34). It is filthy; hidden by the belly (*iacente pantice*, 28) and covered by folds of skin (*vagaque pelle tectus*, 29), it collects dirt over the years (*araneosus . . . situs*, 30). It is also intrinsically foul—cold (*annuo gelu*, 29) and mucky (*sonante . . . luto*, 37).

Latin, as compared to Greek, is weak in metaphorical obscenities,[27] and the presence of any consistent sexual analogy is worthy of notice. Female genitalia in Latin are compared with foul, wet, enclosed spaces and with the enclosure of the tomb: the *fossa* of line 32 appears also in the *Priapea* (46.9, 78.6), and is used for the abject anus of the *cinaedus* in Juvenal's second satire (2.10); compare *barathrum*, "abyss" (Martial 3.81.1); *recessus*, "inner parts" (Martial 7.35.7). This negative view places the writers of invective in an ambivalent position. They can discover the genitalia, exposing what really lies inside the shell of a woman, as does this Pompeian graffitist, who wrote on a doorway (*CIL* 4.1516):

> *hic ego nu<nc> <f>utui formosa fo<r>ma puella*
> > *laudata a multis set lutus intus eerat*

> Here I now fucked a gril beatiful to see,
> > prased by many, but there wuz muck inside.

But this implies personal experience; the narrator has touched the foul substance. Alternatively, he can define female genitalia out of the realm of the sexual, as does Martial (10.90.7–8):

> *erras si tibi cunnus hic videtur,*
> *ad quem mentula pertinere desit.*

> You're wrong if this seems to you to be a cunt,
> when a prick has nothing to do with it.

Cunnus then = *id ad quod mentula pertinet*, dependent for its existence as such on the phallus; no more specific positive description exists in Latin. The satirist looking at women must then experience what he despises in order to expose it, or reject it without explaining what he would prefer.

Roman humorists thus use two stances when writing invective against repulsive women: rejection, in which the male narrator refuses to have anything to do with the woman beyond describing her; and revelation, in which the male narrator describes the loathsome features of a woman with whom he has had sex. The first stance seems logical, separating the narrator from the foul qualities he enumerates. The premise is that the woman begs the narrator to have sex with her, and he tells her to go away; for example, *Priapea* 12, in which the god spends the first six lines on the great age of the woman, 7–9 describing her prayer that the god's *mentula* not desert her, and the last six lines speaking his command to her. He tells her to remove her genitalia from his presence: *tolle . . . procul ac iube latere*, "take it far away and order it to hide" (12.10).[28] But the disgust and desire for separation evinced by such a stance are somewhat undercut by the narrator's attention to detail, for the reader is obviously meant to be fascinated as well as repelled; the moralistic speaker of Martial 10.90 uses some of the crudest obscenities in Latin.

And so in Horace *Epodes* 12, as in other poems,[29] the narrator specifically describes himself in bed with the woman he loathes. This imagined coupling has great force, repeatedly and graphically exposing the reader to smell, sound, and feeling, as well as to sight. The writer commonly rejects the woman not only verbally but physically, boasting that she cannot arouse him; usually cause for shame and chagrin (e.g., Ovid *Amores* 3.7), impotence here signifies the woman's failure. Appropriately, it is the writer's genitalia which reject such women on his behalf.[30] Yet the writer is somehow sexually involved with the woman; in "*Quid hoc novi est*," the act of being ground up paradoxically (and, in the poem, regrettably) causes the penis to grow (33–35).

Like the women whom the writer does not touch, these women beg, offer gifts (Horace *Epodes* 12.2), and even promise large amounts of money. The ludicrous monster in Horace *Epodes* 12 reverses the norms of elegy, comparing herself with the beast of prey and her lover with the fleeing lamb or kid (12.25–26). She has the alarming strength of a wild animal; so, too, the writers attribute strength to the offers of money, which can be persuasive.[31] Thus this theme is tied with that of *captatio* of wealthy old women by impecunious suitors (e.g., Juvenal 1.37–44).

The revelatory descriptions aim, then, at exposing and vitiating imagined female attempts to control a sexual situation in a male way. Where the woman offers money (as male lovers in epigram often do), the narrator wants to make it clear that the money itself is the only attraction—

the woman is worthless in herself, and the narrator is doing her a favor by even touching her. Where the woman offers only herself, the narrator again wants to make it clear that the initiative rests with him: he decides whether the woman should be rated as human or bestial, and without his arousal there is no sex. The underlying message is not one of fear but of assertion. In negotiating sex, the male retains control by his right to choose how he will perceive the female.

Conclusions

The nature of Roman invective against women leads to three generalizations. First, at the most elemental level, invective against women flows from the wellspring of satire, fear of the Other: in this case, female genitalia and old women other than wives and mothers. (Note the implication that extant Roman satire itself is male; we have little trace of what Roman women may have said about women or men, though see chapters 3 and 4.) Fear produces mockery, which disguises the fear as contempt (fear plus power), adds the further disguise of humor, stratifies the situation (the satirist has the better of his victim), and establishes an otherwise unattainable control over the feared object. The practice of genital depilation by Roman women demonstrates their cooperation with the male anxiety expressed in invective—though the practice itself is attested largely in satiric texts.[32] The female genitalia, which apparently swallow up the phallus, and the anomalous old woman (too old to be a wife, yet not a mother), once stereotyped and castigated no longer have as much power over the male. They are recreated to conform with the satirist's fantasies: thus he controls them. For the issue is not primarily one of sex, but of power—or it is sexual only insofar as sex can be used to implement and signify power. The reduction of women, first separated into "attractive" and "repulsive," to stereotypes viewed part by part, enables the satirist to view women as intrinsically vile, both morally and physically. (And surely, when the elegists invert this relationship between normative male and flawed woman, the change is only superficial; the relationship remains preoccupied with power, the woman viewed part by part is controlled by the viewer, dominance pairs off with submission, and the inversion serves mainly to titillate poet and reader.)[33]

The more specific significance of the female genitalia can be seen by comparison with invective against *cinaedi*. The beautiful boy is the male equivalent of the attractive woman, and the penis, anus, and thighs of such boys are often described and praised, unlike the genital area of attractive women.[34] Adult males said to desire to be penetrated are the male equivalent of old and/or repulsive women, and the anal orifice of such men is often depicted, as seen above, in terms similar to those used of repulsive female genitalia.[35] Only very rarely are male genitalia described as disgusting (an old man's penis, Catullus 25.3; Martial 11.46). It is clear that an orifice which is penetrated by the penis, or which submits to the penis, is intrinsically disgusting, and becomes more so when the one who submits is normally barred by age from such submission. Being penetrated always signifies submission; but where it is proper, in Roman culture, for young women and boys to submit to adult males, it is not proper for old women and adult males to do so. Hence their orifices are perceived as improbably overused and stained; hence it is the word *puella*, "young girl," "girl child," which is very commonly used to mean "mistress" or "prostitute," just as *puer*, "young boy," "[boy] child," "slave" commonly means "boy sex object." But why is there no praise for the genitalia of the young woman? The answer seems to be that, in fact, there is only a *cunnus* when the *mentula* does *not* pertain to it (when the woman is old); the *cunnus* of the mistress, wife, and mother simply does not exist. *Cunnus* in relation to a sexually attractive woman signifies an undescribed but inferior orifice (Martial 11.43.11–12); the contaminator of the cunnilinctor (common in graffiti, cf. Martial 12.59); or, by pejorative synecdoche, the woman herself (Martial 6.45.1; cf. Horace *Satires* 1.2.69–71, *Priapea* 68.9–10). In short, the negative perception of the female genitalia precludes their specific association with attractive women—just as breasts are seldom explicitly mentioned except in derogatory contexts.[36] Conversely, the anal and genital orifices conveniently represent people deemed inappropriate as sexual partners—old women and adult males.

Finally, the fear of female genitalia per se, along with their function as a pejorative sign, falls into alignment with the social function of Roman invective against women.[37] As invective demonstrates the intrinsic vileness of the female, as it bars certain women from sexual acceptability, so it publicly indicates the correct place of women. The rare attacks on lesbians predictably focus on a woman's preemption of a male role in sex.[38] The stereotypes, both attractive and unattractive, present women in the real world with a finite and predetermined set of options: the attractive stereotypes, along with those in moralistic literature, give women a set of aspirations (though satire makes it clear that men expect even attractive women to be seriously flawed—frivolous and oversexed—and so these flaws are incorporated into the stereotype "attractive"); the repulsive stereotypes give women a set of boundaries, warning them that certain types of women can expect only mockery and revulsion for manifestations of sexuality, even for existence. Hence the use of bizarre animals in invective against women: inappropriate behavior removes women from humanity.[39] Free women exposed to invective must acknowledge that the acceptable married woman produces legitimate children and limits her sexual activity to her young married life; slave women have a grim reminder of their marketability; public performance of invective, from graffiti to formal verse satire, serves as a societal endorsement by the whole audience—including any women present—of the norms outlined therein. The accounts of performances of verse satire place them in a public space, like stand-up comedy; Martial claims women as an enthusiastic part of his textual audience (3.68, 11.16). Such extreme sanctions would seem to be needed by a society that married off most free women, at an extremely young age, and demanded marital fidelity of them, while free men married later and usually had access to prostitutes and to slaves of either sex, and both married women and slaves had to live with that.[40] At the same time, however, this was a society that offered easy divorce and set few limits on free women's ability to own and inherit property, so that a young woman could marry her way through a series of much older husbands, accruing wealth and power as she went: scary. Sarah Levin-Richardson (2013) argues that women themselves wrote and read graffiti, and that we can there see women "trying on" dominant sexuality, even embracing sexual agency through their own abjection. Julia's jokes (chapter 3) and perhaps even Sulpicia's satire (chapter 4) might be doing the same kind of thing.

Invective against women demonstrates the place of women with respect to literature: the female is subject matter, the narrative voice is male. A woman who wishes to write satire must somehow malign herself and her kind, since satire by nature and tradition consists partly in the maligning of women; and so today we have the comedienne—the dumb blonde, the strident shrew, the fat woman, and the hag. If the women's movement abandoned this sense of humor, no wonder.

CHAPTER 3

Julia's Jokes, Galla Placidia, and the Roman Use of Women as Political Icons

ᕲᕲ

Introduction

This essay is yet another spin-off of the research for *The Garden of Priapus*; Julia's jokes make a brief appearance in chapter 1 above. When I first read these jokes in Macrobius's *Saturnalia*, I gave no thought to Macrobius or the time when he put these jokes into his book, but just lumped them in with all the other instances of reported speech and gossip. In the spring of 1982, burrowing into Dartmouth's Baker Library, I began to explore the life of Galla Placidia and Macrobius's Rome.

That fall, I left the idyllic setting of Dartmouth for the satanic mills of Bethlehem, Pennsylvania, and a job at Lehigh University, where I found myself surrounded, as was common in those days, by a large and active community of feminist scholars, all interested in studying women. In those days before the Internet and e-mail, we communicated with other such groups by letter, and in November, 1983, Marilyn Skinner forwarded to me a letter from an Australian feminist and Roman historian, who by November of 1984 was signing her letters: "In sisterhood, Suzanne." It turned out that she was about to organize a conference on women and power at the University of Queensland, and in August, 1986, I flew halfway around the world, feeling as if propelled by a giant slingshot, to take part. The conference drew together scholars from many disciplines and pushed me to think about my material as an example of a cross-cultural, transhistorical phenomenon, affecting real women. Suzanne Dixon and her research partners had previously put together a short book, based on an earlier conference, called *Pre-Industrial Women: Interdisciplinary Perspectives* (Dixon and Munford 1984); through their work I began, belatedly, to continue the theoretical thinking on gender politics that I had begun in the third chapter of *The Garden of Priapus.*

For, while feminists in other fields started out with political theory in the 1970s, most classicists did not; it was not until I took up a joint appointment in Classics and Gender Studies at the University of Southern California in the fall of 1989 that, by teaching "Introduction to Feminist Theory," I came to understand the theoretical foundations of the work we were all doing. The collected papers from the 1986 Queensland conference (Garlick, Dixon, and Allen 1992) put together examples from a wide range of ancient and modern cultures, analyzed in the volume introduction by political philosopher Arlene Saxonhouse and in the conclusion by Suzanne Dixon in terms of then-current debates about the public/private dichotomy within individual states and in the context of women's real intersections with political action. It would be interesting to see the material from the collection rethought in terms of the work on transnationality and gender discussed in the introduction to this volume: the real-life worship of the wife of the *princeps*, for example, is widely attested throughout a Roman Empire that included women of very different cultural backgrounds (see chapter 7); women commonly moved around the empire, with the army (Greene 2011, Phang 2001), and, wretchedly, with the slave trade (Gaca 2010, 2010–11); Stephen D. Moore's ongoing work suggests how the goddess Roma was read as monstrous among early Christians (2006: 97–121). The making of empire certainly depended on gendered concepts in antiquity, many of which have continued into modernity.

The basic theoretical argument in "Julia's Jokes" comes from "The Virgin and the State" by the anthropologist Sherry Ortner, famous in the 1980s for her essay "Is Female to Male as Nature Is to Culture?" And "Julia's Jokes" does contribute to a discussion of the symbolic use of the female body in relation to the state, a discussion still ongoing, as seen, for example, in current work on antiquity by Kate Cooper (2007), Kristina Milnor (2005), and

Holt Parker (2004 [2007]). Meanwhile, as the 1980s turned into the 1990s and the essay was rewritten for publication, I arrived at a surprised, almost resigned, realization that, once again, it had proved next to impossible to get at the real woman; the conclusion, written without reference to the New Historicism, nonetheless makes the thoroughly New Historicist observation that "When we look at texts and objects to discover reality, it is as if we looked at a scene through a screen on a window; as we become interested in the screen and its properties, we suddenly notice that the scene is in fact painted on the screen itself. What lies beyond is unknown."

Yet this uncharacteristic lapse into epistemological pessimism (see chapter 10) constituted the endpoint of a project in history-writing that had begun with the sense that I was, at last, working with a text that came directly from a woman. These jokes circulated in the lifetime of a woman who really existed, and who, along with the otherwise unknown Populia, is one of very few Roman women whose witticisms—and witticisms about her own body—were recorded. "Julia's Jokes" deals with the unavoidable uncertainties related to the attribution of material in oral circulation by constructing two analyses. In one, these were her own jokes; in the other, they were made up by others and ascribed to her, either to support her or (bearing "Invective against Women" in mind) to attack her. The jokes, if not something she said, were something she had to put up with. The essay works with the historical sources on Julia's life, although (with "Approaches to the Sources on Adultery" in mind) these sources are not themselves taken as veridical—an attitude toward the use of dynastic women by Roman historians that was in dialogue with ongoing work by Sandra Joshel, as in her 1997 essay on Messalina.

Moreover, in this essay I tried for the first time to come to grips with a text's double context: in Macrobius's own time as well as in the time of Julia and her father Augustus. Many Roman texts have two sets of meanings, and often are really about the time of writing and not about the time they profess to be writing about; this way of using the past to write about the present is a characteristically Roman way of telling truths too dangerous to express explicitly. As noted in the volume introduction, the project of writing about "women worthies" early fell into disfavor among feminist historians (see Bennett 2006: 23–24), but, in writing about Julia's jokes, a historian has the opportunity to see how Macrobius recycles her in the age of Galla Placidia, of Western and Eastern empresses, women with Attila the Hun looking over one shoulder and the Virgin Mary over the other. It is instructive to see what stays the same in these very different contexts. Kate

Cooper has argued that Mary was a model who appealed to women of all ranks (2007: 112–13), a kind of modeling aspired to by the Roman dynasts from Augustus and Livia onward; in that context, we have to wonder about a writer who cites as witty Julia's line, "I never take on a passenger unless the ship is full." What women read Macrobius?

ⁱ⸾   ⁱ⸾   ⁱ⸾

Preserved in Macrobius's *Saturnalia* lies a group of jokes attributed to Julia, daughter of Augustus (39 BCE–c. 14 CE). They constitute only the last of many accounts of a remarkably well-attested Roman woman: her lurid story appears in the most nearly contemporary extant Roman historian, Velleius Paterculus, and is retailed in turn by the younger Seneca, the elder Pliny, Tacitus, Suetonius, and Dio. We hear of her again from the antiquarian Macrobius in the fifth century. Historians today use these sources to determine what really happened to Julia, but this chapter instead considers how Romans and others use prominent women as political icons. Texts by Roman women are so rare that the jokes compel attention; their double context—in Augustus's court in 2 BCE and in the Christian Rome of the fifth century CE—lets us align a double set of implications. Overall, this text supports several levels of inquiry: into the lives of Julia and her peers, into Roman political ideology, into the re-use of oral material, and, finally, into patriarchal ideology in general.

Stereotypes of Women in Power

Stereotypes of Western royal women are clearly linked to sexuality. At the center lies the normative model of the ruling woman as perfect wife and mother, the "first lady." Modern examples include Queen Victoria and Michelle Obama; ancient ones may begin with the Hellenistic queens, sometimes worshiped along with their consorts, prominent for their public works, and touted as patterns of wifeliness.[1] Augustus's second wife, Livia, cast herself in this mold, in the Roman tradition of female decorum (see esp. Flory 1984); we see few imitations among her immediate successors, but the model returns in the women around the adoptive emperors and in the much-memorialized Julia Domna, wife of Septimius Severus.[2] Macrobius's contemporary Eudocia, wife of the fifth-century Byzantine emperor

Theodosius II, represents a tendency toward this model in the Christian empresses. The typical text that makes a first lady is the eulogy, citing her children, her dutifulness as a wife, and her modest comportment; the result resembles the standard ancient praise of good wives but sets the normal virtues in light of their value to the dynasty. These women produce legitimate heirs, or at least provide living proof of the high moral tone of the regime.

The advent of Christian asceticism made a new model possible: the celibate. Pulcheria, Eudocia's sister-in-law and rival, at an early age forswore marriage to live a life of exemplary Christian piety—a clear example of a ruling woman using this model to avoid the lessened status entailed by marriage (we may compare Elizabeth I of England). But Pulcheria derived much of her authority from the model of the Virgin Mary as Theotokos, mother of God, and from the doctrine that Mary had redeemed the inherent sinfulness of women by her double status as virgin and mother.[3] The model of the celibate here represents a transformation of the model of wife and mother; thus eulogies preserve this stereotype, too.

At the other extreme, some royal women are labeled promiscuous. This model exceeds the normal stereotype of the adulteress just as the model of first lady exceeds that of wife, by emphasizing the stakes: power and dynastic succession. The stereotype of the *meretrix Augusta* seems also to be compelled by the oxymoron, and to be reacting against the first lady model. The typical text for such women is the racy anecdote: their children are of dubious paternity, or they use birth control; they are adulterous or too often married; their dress and comportment are questionable. Julia's jokes provide a rare example of this stereotype supposedly professed by its objective correlative; more often, the stories are hostile, as is the case for the exile of Julia and her daughter Julia the younger, or for the fifth-century pair Galla Placidia, half sister of the emperor Honorius, and her daughter, Justa Grata Honoria. The stories grow with the power involved, culminating in a Cleopatra or a Catherine the Great.[4] Both positive and negative models were at work in public discourse on the life of Princess Diana.

Thus images of ruling women range from the sexless celibate (has no mate) modeled on Mary who attained motherhood without sexuality, to the wife and mother (has one mate) who produces children but maintains perfect fidelity, to the promiscuous one (has many mates) whose maternity is only a by-product of her sexuality.[5] Only occasionally can we tell how much of an image stems from real behavior, how differently the women involved perceived themselves, and whether the image was deliberately sought by them or was created by their families—or enemies. In several cases, including those of Julia, Galla Placidia, and Justa Grata Honoria, conflicting stereotypes are applied to the same woman; in the case of Julia, the relation between the two is particularly clear.

Like ruling men, but unlike other women, women who rule appear in a wide range of especially formal media. Whereas an elite woman such as Clodia or Sempronia appears in anecdotes, history, letters, law court speeches, and even poetry (suitably disguised), while the odd benefactress or female relative takes her place in inscription or *laudatio*, and the lowliest slave woman haunts the epigrams that deny her any individuality, ruling women duly appear in the same histories, eulogistic poems, speeches, coins, and (sometimes) monumental sculpture as do their male kin. Female virtues thus have a more specifically political use for ruling women than for their female coevals, for the sexuality of these women is being consciously used by their male kin—and sometimes by themselves—to represent something else. So the icon covers over the woman inside it; the fascination of commentators with such women at the time, and since, is only the worship the icons elicit.

But why should ruling women's sexuality bear such significance? Why does the icon take this shape, and what is its use? Sherry Ortner links the high valuation of female purity with "states, or at least systems with fairly highly developed stratification." Rejecting functionalist explanations, she argues that female purity is valued where there is hypergamy, or "vertical alliance"—intermarriage between classes (1978: 32):

> The assumption of hypergamy would also account for one of the major puzzles of the female purity phenomenon, namely, that the women of a given group are expected to be purer than the men, that upon their higher purity hinges the honor of the group. . . . the women are *not*, contrary to native ideology, representing and maintaining the group's . . . *actual* status, but are oriented upwards and represent the ideal higher status of the group. . . . female purity . . . in fact . . . is oriented toward an ideal and generally unattainable status. The unattainability may in turn account for some of the sadism and anger toward women expressed in these purity patterns, for the women are representing the over-classes themselves.

For Roman women, we do not have to deal with Ortner's examples of sadism—branding the genitals or confinement to the seraglio. Nevertheless, we do have in Rome an actively hypergamous system in which contamination of women's purity leads to punishment, sometimes capital. Applying Ortner's theory to Julia's jokes, we will have to ask what "over-classes," or what "unattainable status," may be represented by the purity of Roman imperial women.

Julia's History

The sources cited at the start of this chapter make up a patchwork narrative of Julia's life. Suetonius gives the greatest detail (*Aug.* 65). She was born, in 39 BCE, of Augustus's first marriage, to Scribonia (*Aug.* 63.1), which ended in divorce on the day Julia was born (*Aug.* 62.2; Dio 48.34.3). Augustus's second marriage, to Livia, soon followed, and Julia was raised in her father's house, where she was taught to spin and weave and was strictly chaperoned (then and afterward) in quasi-republican austerity (*Aug.* 64.2). She would have been eight years old in the year of Actium (the beginning of Augustus's rule) and marriageable in 27, a year after her father first attempted to reform Roman marriage law. Suetonius reports Antony's claim that Augustus intended to betroth Julia to Cotiso, king of the Getae, in exchange for Cotiso's daughter (*Aug.* 63.2); this claim must be seen in the context of the civil war and Antony's own extra-Roman alliance with Cleopatra. Her first marriage, to the adored heir apparent Marcellus (*Aug.* 63.1), took place when she was fourteen, in 25 BCE, and lasted until Marcellus's death in 23. In 21, she was married to Agrippa (who was made to divorce his second wife, Marcellus's sister, *Aug.* 63.1); thus Agrippa and Julia had previously been brother- and sister-in-law. This marriage lasted until Agrippa's death in 12 BCE. In the course of these nine years, Augustus's marriage laws were passed, with their strictures against adultery and rewards for production of children. Julia, traveling with Agrippa, bore him five children—three boys, Gaius, Lucius, and Agrippa (born after Agrippa's death), and two girls, Julia and Agrippina (*Aug.* 64.1). She was married off a year after Agrippa's death to her stepbrother Tiberius (*Aug.* 63.2), to whom she bore one child, who died in infancy (*Tib.* 7.3). Tacitus says that she "scorned him as beneath her" (*Ann.* 1.53); Suetonius says that Tiberius married her with regret, because he was forced to divorce his own beloved wife for a woman whom he considered unchaste (*Tib.* 7.2).[6] This beloved wife was Vipsania, Agrippa's daughter by his first wife Caecilia Attica, so that Tiberius had also previously been Julia's stepdaughter's husband: another problem.

Nine years later (2 BCE), with Tiberius living abroad, amid great scan-

dal Julia was exiled, charged with multiple adulteries (Velleius Paterculus
2.100.3; Pliny *HN* 7.149; Suetonius *Aug.* 65.1, 2–4). Velleius comments that
the scandal broke in a glorious year that featured Augustus's dedication of
a temple to Mars (2.100.2); this year also saw Augustus named *pater patriae*. Later writers add torrid details of Julia's nocturnal debaucheries in
the Forum, even on the rostra (Seneca *Ben.* 6.32.1–2; Dio 55.10.12–13), and
especially near the statue of the satyr Marsyas (Dio), which Pliny says she
garlanded (*HN* 21.9): significant, since Marsyas's statue represented political freedom. Seneca quotes Augustus's denunciation of her defilement of
the very rostra from which he had put forth the adultery laws—an echo of
the favorite rhetorical topos about Cicero's head being nailed to the rostra
from which he had spoken, and ironic, since Cicero died in the proscriptions of the Second Triumvirate. Augustus chose an apparently remarkable
manner of accusation of behavior now criminal (see chapter 1): he made
his accusation public (*in publicum emisit, publicaverat,* Seneca *Ben.* 6.32.1,
2; cf. Pliny *HN* 21.9 *litterae gemunt*), although, as Seneca adds, he later re-
gretted this decision. Suetonius says more specifically that Augustus "made
it known to the Senate in his absence, a communiqué being read off by a
quaestor" (*Aug.* 65.2), which Dio echoes (55.10.14); Tacitus's statement that
Augustus exceeded the law "by labeling her crime with the weighty name
of wounded piety and violated majesty" (*Ann.* 3.24) perhaps alludes to this
communiqué. Augustus also caricatured normal procedure by sending Julia
a divorce decree in Tiberius's name, prompting Tiberius to write from exile
in his wife's defense (Suetonius *Tib.* 11.4).

Velleius gives a list of five adulterers, all bearing noble republican names:
Iullus Antonius (2.100.4); Quintius Crispinus, Appius Claudius, Sempro-
nius Gracchus, and Scipio (2.100.5). He says there were many others, less
illustrious, as well. The sources differ as to these adulterers' fates (Seneca
Clem. 1.10.3; Tacitus *Ann.* 1.53, 3.24). Dio (55.10.15) says that Iullus Antonius
was executed, along with some other suspect aristocrats, and that the rest
were exiled to islands. This execution, Dio says, was on the grounds that Iullus was plotting a coup; Pliny hints this of Julia herself (*HN* 7.149), as does
Seneca (*Brev. vit.* 4.6): "once again a woman to be feared with an Antony."
The explicit analogy between Julia and Cleopatra recalls the feverishness
of the propaganda against Augustus's old enemy, whose defeat at Actium
alongside Antony (Iullus's father) enabled Augustus to reign: Cleopatra was
not only foreign but also Egyptian and Eastern; she worshiped strange gods,
and was drunken and profligate. Augustus declared war only on her, and
not on Antony, and there were rumors that she wanted to take Rome itself
(cf. Horace *Odes* 1.37). This is what Seneca is talking about.[7]

Suetonius mentions only a later plot involving an attempt to restore Julia (*Aug.* 19.2). Hers was a harsh exile, to the island of Pandateria (Tacitus *Ann.* 1.53; Dio 55.10.14), where Augustus prohibited her from drinking wine and limited her contacts to people whose exact physical description was given to him (Suetonius *Aug.* 65.3). Her mother, Scribonia (*gravis femina*, "a serious woman," Seneca *Ep. mor.* 70.10), chose to accompany her (Velleius 2.100.5; Dio 55.10.14), and there was a public outcry for Julia's return, rejected in an assembly (Suetonius *Aug.* 65.3; Dio 55.13.1). Augustus eventually moved her from Pandateria, after five years, according to Suetonius (*Aug.* 65.3); to Rhegium, according to Tacitus (*Ann.* 1.53). But there were stories of his anger: Julia's freedwoman Phoebe hanged herself when the scandal broke, and Augustus said he would rather be Phoebe's father (Suetonius *Aug.* 65.2; Dio 55.10.16); and he called Julia, her daughter Julia, and her son Agrippa Postumus his "three boils and three cancers" (Suetonius *Aug.* 65.4). Yet Julia seems to have communicated with her father from exile; once, if Dio is to be believed, to bargain over Tiberius (55.13.1a). Her father died leaving her out of his will and excluding both Julias from the family tomb (Suetonius *Aug.* 101); as for Tiberius, Tacitus hints that, on his accession, he so straitened the terms of her exile as to bring on her death (*Ann.* 1.53; cf. Suetonius *Tib.* 50.1).

Julia's daughter Julia was herself exiled for adultery at Augustus's behest. She was suspected of an affair with the aristocrat D. Silanus (Tacitus *Ann.* 3.24.5) and exiled to the bleak island of Trimerus in 8 CE; she died there twenty years later (Tacitus *Ann.* 4.71.6–7). Others besides Augustus lump the younger Julia's exile for adultery in with her mother's (Pliny *HN* 7.149; Tacitus *Ann.* 3.24.2), and Suetonius adds that the younger Julia's baby, born in exile, was "forbidden to be recognized or fed"—that is, was left to die (*Aug.* 65.4; see Barnes 1981).

These post-Augustan narratives all appear to be strongly colored by hindsight and propaganda; when they mention Julia they are conscious of her spectacular exit from Rome and her miserable end. They provide, nevertheless, some basic assertions of fact: her strict upbringing, her immediate experience as a child and adolescent of the realities of dynastic marriage, her exemplary fecundity as Agrippa's wife and mother of the new heirs apparent Gaius and Lucius, the parallels between Augustus's political progress and Julia's marriages, and the protest against her exile by the people of Rome along with Augustus's remarkably public breast-beating. The special position of daughters within the elite Roman family (Hallett 1984: 35–149) may explain the preoccupations of our sources. Still, as J. P. V. D. Balsdon points out, they shy away from any description of Julia herself. Macrobius's version, Balsdon thinks, may come from the possible lost source for *Satur-*

nalia 2: a collection of witticisms by the Augustan poet Domitius Marsus, perhaps augmented by a slightly later collection. Whatever his date, this collector is also the only one to attribute to Julia words of her own.[8]

Modern scholars, following the mainstream of the Roman sources, have debated what really happened in 2 BCE: Was Julia an adulteress or a conspirator? (For a survey of arguments, see Ferrill 1980.) Thus, like their sources, they write from the end of a story that lacks her voice, only incidentally seeking Julia.[9] I would suggest that in looking at Julia's jokes in Macrobius's *Saturnalia* we are at once closer to her life, in a period before 2 BCE, and closer to the strategies by which this set of political events reached its conclusion.

Julia's Jokes

The *Saturnalia* is a fictional dinner party, in the tradition of symposiastic literature; its guests mostly discuss Vergil. In Book 2, however, they tell jokes, among which we find Julia's. The speaker, Avienus, leads into them with an *apologia* (2.5.1):

> "Do you all want me to recount some sayings of his daughter Julia as well? But if I will not be thought garrulous, I want to preface this with a few remarks on the woman's morals, unless one of you has serious and edifying remarks to add here." When everyone urged him to continue with his undertaking, he began to tell about Julia with these words: "She was in her thirty-eighth year, a time of life, if her mind were still sound, verging on old age; but she was abusing the kindness of fortune as much as of her father, although otherwise a love of literature and much learning, which was easy in that household, along with a gentle humanity and a spirit in no way cruel, earned the woman great indulgence and favor, while those who were familiar with her vices marveled as well at such a contradictory personality."

The section on Julia follows a group of stories about Augustus, and Avienus presents her as a sidetrack. He contrasts her sayings with "serious and edifying remarks," of the sort needed to critique her morals, before proceeding. The anomaly of Julia's behavior apparently centers on her age; at thirty-seven (in the year of her exile), she does not conform to the rules for a mature woman. The supervisor of her behavior is her father; her audience is a double one—those whom she charms and those few who know what she really does. But this is a fiction, since those who hear the jokes are about to know all. Indeed, the whole situation of vice, secrecy, and knowledge is a fiction whose purpose is to bring the intratextual audience into the circle of those who know about Julia. They all want to know, and Macrobius assumes his readers want to know, too.

So far Julia is established as a woman who acts too young, a woman who imposes on her father, a woman of education, and a woman who deceives people. Avienus continues his character sketch with an illustration (2.5.3):

> Her father had warned her more than once, with his speech still tempered between indulgence and seriousness, that she should moderate her extravagant dress and her conspicuous entourage. Then when he had reflected on his crowd of grandsons and their likeness to Agrippa, he blushed to doubt his daughter's chastity.

The text now projects Julia through the figure of her father; the conflict read into the signs of Julia's character reveals both what is feared and how those fears are translated. Her chastity is in question, but her father chides her only for external attributes—dress and companions—when he really means to tell her not to have sexual relations with any man but her husband. Julia's children and their resemblance to Agrippa become signs to balance against the others. Her anomalies—age, filial behavior, education, and deceit—thus combine with her dubious appearance to mark her as unchaste, while her childbearing and her father's blush mark her as chaste.

The jokes themselves, the first of which follows directly on this introduction, use the same criteria. They cover three main areas: Julia's personal appearance, including dress and hair; her relations with men, including her behavior as a daughter, marital status, affiliation with younger men, adultery, childbearing, and birth control; and her use of money and power. The series includes six stories about Julia (2.5.4–9) and one about an otherwise unknown woman named Populia (2.5.10).

Text

(2.5.4) So Augustus cozened himself into believing that his daughter had high spirits leading to an appearance of shamelessness, but was free from guilt, and he dared to believe that, among our ancestors, Claudia had been such. And so he said among his friends, "he had two spoiled daughters, whom he had to put up with—the republic and Julia."

(2.5.5) She had come to him with a rather daring outfit and had offended the eyes of her father, who said nothing. She changed the manner of her dress the next day, and embraced her father with an affectation of primness. But he, who had contained his pain the day before, could not contain his joy and said, "How much more proper this dress is for the daughter of Augustus!" But Julia was not at a loss to defend herself, with these words: "Why, today I decked myself out for my father's eyes, yesterday for my husband's."

(2.5.6) Another famous one. Livia [Julia's stepmother] and Julia had diverted the attention of the populace to themselves at the show of gladiators because of the contrast between their entourages; while serious and important men surrounded Livia, Julia was flanked by a flock of young men, and profligate young men at that. Her father warned her in a note that "she should notice how great a difference there was between the two first ladies." She replied elegantly, "These men with me will also become old men."

(2.5.7) This same Julia had begun to have grey hairs prematurely, which she used to pluck out in secret. Once a sudden arrival of her father surprised her slave beauticians (*ornatrices*). Augustus dissembled, though seeing that there were grey hairs on their clothing, and, drawing out the time with other topics of conversation, he introduced a mention of her age and asked his daughter "whether, after some years, she would rather be grey-haired or bald?" And when she had replied, "I would rather be grey-haired, father," he cast her mendacity up to her in this way: "Then why are those women making you bald so rapidly?"

(2.5.8) Likewise, when Julia had heard a serious friend arguing that she would do better if she had modeled herself after the exemplar of her father's frugality, she said, "He forgets that he is Caesar, but I remember I am Caesar's daughter."

(2.5.9) And when those who knew of her sins used to marvel at how she gave birth to sons resembling Agrippa when she made such public property of her body, she said, "Why, I never take on a passenger until the ship is full."

(2.5.10) A similar quip by Populia, daughter of Marcus: To someone wondering why it is that other beasts never desire a male unless when they want to become pregnant, she replied, "Because they're beasts."

Analysis

The question of the appropriateness of Julia's appearance figures in three of the jokes—dress (2.5.5), choice of companions (2.5.6), and removal of grey hairs (2.5.7). The last is resolved to Julia's disadvantage; although this sign of old age is false, visited upon her too early, her father confronts her with a sentence to senility: She must either be grey-haired or bald. That old women's ugliness included baldness was a commonplace in Roman jokes against women (see chapter 2 above).

The jokes at 2.5.5 and 2.5.6 are resolved to Julia's advantage. In 2.5.5, improper dress is compared with proper. Augustus tells Julia that the second dress is more becoming to "the daughter of Augustus," *filia Augusti*; he emphasizes her position in his state. Her reply—the first dress was for her husband, the second for her father—redirects the emphasis onto her family ties to men of different generations. She also implies that dress for the husband must naturally be too sexual for the father, pretending to speak in the conventional language of Roman kinship (cf. Hallett 1984: 102–9). But what the joke skirts (and thus stresses) must be the appeal of Julia's first dress to men besides her husband; the joke, like the dress, plays peek-a-boo with her sexual body. Augustus's euphemism allows Julia's manipulation, underscoring the hypocrisy of both participants (note her "affectation of primness"). She makes a fool of him.

In 2.5.6, Julia's entourage poses a similar problem. While her stepmother surrounds herself with elder statesmen (*graves viri*), Julia chooses profligate young men (*iuventus luxuriosa*). She resolves this, with insolent absurdity, by saying that her followers will also turn into old men (*senes*), here changing, again, the grounds from chastity to generational differences. Augustus's phrase *principes feminas*, "first ladies," like his *filia Augusti* in 2.5.5, only raises the stakes—a woman should be chaste, a woman of the ruling family all the more so. By sidestepping this issue Julia belittles it; her answer belittles her elders as well.

Each joke asks: What behavior is appropriate for a grown daughter of an emperor? Dress, hair, and even companions serve as signs, and Julia's father attempts to make her abandon the signs of sexuality (the open body) for those of asexuality (the closed body). As at 2.5.3, promiscuity and illegitimate children form the unspoken signified. Julia hangs on to her sexuality by translating "sexual" as "younger" and "asexual" as "older," associating her father with asexuality. He only wins by associating her with age (2.5.7).

Julia's evasions here succeed because she (ab)uses the male generational categories in which Augustus thinks (resemblance of sons to father comforts grandfather); she subverts Augustus's discourse. The joke at 2.5.9 opens up his discourse along with Julia's body: on the one hand, she bears children who look like Agrippa; on the other, "she made such public property of her body." Her own answer affirms this objectification. She calls her womb, pregnant with (Admiral) Agrippa's child, a full ship; her lovers, apparently numerous and random, are anonymous "passengers"; she reduces the child to an implied cargo, merely a prerequisite for taking on new passengers. Her metaphor not only adopts and transforms the common erotic image of woman as ship; more radically, it shows that the signs on which her father most relies are unreliable (cf. 2.5.3).[10]

Julia's attitude toward her children here parallels Populia's in 2.5.10, where Populia defines the limiting of sex to procreation as bestial. In Augustus's terms, legitimate children betoken a wife's chastity, and the point of chastity is the production of legitimate children. Julia's joke undercuts Augustus's system, making chastity unnecessary and legitimate children no proof of anything, not only a possible disguise for adultery but also a positive means of indulging in adultery without fear. The shock of 2.5.9 and 2.5.10 comes (on the surface) from two noblewomen's rejection of the roles of daughter, wife, and mother, against the wishes of a father; at a deeper level, surely the shock emanates from the claim of these female figures to control their bodies and their bloodline for their own sexual pleasure. Pregnancy normally signifies one of two things in histories of Roman women: either fulfillment of the role of wife, or evidence of unchastity, as was possibly the case with Julia's daughter, and was certainly the case with Galla Placidia's daughter.[11] Julia and Populia assign unorthodox meanings to pregnancy—a serious iconoclasm in a society of ancestor worshipers. The joke's identification of Populia by her patronymic ("daughter of Marcus") reminds us that she, like Julia, throws doubt on the very assumptions underlying patronymics.

At the same time, the text denies the sexuality of women in previous generations. Augustus himself compares Julia with her ancestor Claudia (2.5.4), whose chastity had been doubted but vindicated (see chapter 7 below), and contrasts her with her stepmother Livia (2.5.6). The text suppresses the scandal that surrounded the marriage of Augustus to the divorced and pregnant Livia (Suetonius *Aug.* 62.2; *Claud.* 1.1), who here takes on the asexuality attributed to the older generation by Julia.[12] She does not even have any wifely sexual relations with Augustus, nor are her two children or Julia's mother Scribonia mentioned. Like Augustus's marriage laws, the jokes concern themselves with the regulation of women's sexuality only up to a certain age, after which it is not expected to exist.

In this text, Julia accepts the status of *filia Augusti* only when it signifies an increase in power, rather than a limit. The joke at 2.5.8, which reproves Julia for her lack of frugality, is resolved by her statement that her father forgets that he is Caesar, while she remembers she is Caesar's daughter. She here literally entitles herself to money and power. The phrase *Caesaris filiam* recalls the loaded words of 2.5.5, *filia Augusti*, and of 2.5.6, *principes feminas*. But in the earlier jokes, where her father emphasized *Augusti*, Julia emphasized *filia*. Here, where his rank gives her privilege, she accepts it, though rejecting him as a model and reducing their relationship to a dynastic one. Once again the joke works by Julia's play with emphasis, and again she belittles Augustus and his values.

Thus we have a series of *dicta* attributed to Augustus's daughter in which she embodies and arrogantly espouses behavior Augustus was seeking to thwart, both in the state and in his family. Whose icon is this Julia?

Double Context: First Century BCE

Assuming these jokes go back to an Augustan source, we can set Macrobius aside for the moment and examine them first in an Augustan context. We can begin with the question of their origin and audience and ask whether the jokes may be anti-Augustan, and whether they may be women's humor. Then, considering the events of Julia's life and the rhetoric of Augustus's political career, and adducing some nonverbal evidence, we can look for an idealized picture of Julia against which to set these jokes. Finally, we can apply Ortner's hypothesis and consider what "unattainable status" may have been represented by the purity of this emperor's daughter.

The first joke (2.5.4) suggests the level of signification present here. Augustus is said to have drawn an analogy between Julia and the state as his two "spoiled" (*delicatas*) daughters; the language comes from the warm affect of Roman father-daughter relations (Hallett 1984). But Augustus's head-shaking indulgence toward Julia in this joke actually signifies his control over her and his desire that she conform without coercion; the same applies to the state as a whole, hence his moral legislation (for a summary, see Brunt 1971: 558–66; chapter 1 above; cf. esp. Dixon 1988: 71–103). Augustus was, in the year of these jokes and Julia's exile, proclaimed *pater patriae*, "father of the fatherland"; the daughter becomes a living metaphor for the state. A Roman audience would find such a metaphor the more ominous in that Roman private law gave the *paterfamilias* power of life and death over all members of his household, a power that would be used especially to punish any breach of moral codes. The mapping of the morals of the body politic onto a woman's body was a common feature in literature of the Augustan regime, and the early books of Livy's history are littered with corpses of women whose living bodies had threatened to let corruption into the state (see Joshel 1992a). This perhaps begins to suggest who listened to the jokes when they were new, and why they survived Julia's outlawry: to people who did not wish to be controlled, her obstinacy may have represented freedom.

We can, of course, not know whether the obstinacy was really hers. The figure of Julia in the jokes counters the figure of Augustus as in political cartoons. However, based on what Suetonius says about her girlhood, and the simple facts of her birth, marriages, and pregnancies, the content of the jokes is consistent with Julia's experience. The ostentatiously strict upbringing results in a taste for display; the chain of broken marriages results in cynicism about the purpose of marriage; Augustus's incentive plan for marriage and childbearing is matched by an alternative plan. If these *dicta* were really spoken by the real Julia, she elicits our sympathy as do few other Roman wits. (And, as a wit, in Macrobius she rubs shoulders with Cicero.) But the force of jokes goes far beyond the figure to whom they are attributed; though here the real Julia seems to stir within the icon, it is the icon that remains for us to examine.

There is some evidence within these jokes indicating who told them, or who is supposed to have told them. The internal audience is restricted to those at Rome, usually to Julia's immediate circle. In 2.5.4, Augustus talks with his friends; while 2.5.6 concerns public behavior and comment by the *populus*, the real dialogue consists of a written message from Augustus to Julia, with her reply; the interlocutor in 2.5.8 is one of Julia's friends; 2.5.9 mentions "those who knew of her sins" (*conscii flagitiorum*). The only participants in 2.5.5 are Julia and her father; in 2.5.7, the only other participants are Julia's slave women.

The evaluative words used in the jokes define an audience that recognizes the norms Julia is breaking. The puritanical, old-fashioned plainness that Augustus wished to revive in Rome is associated with the behavior

Julia usually rejects: her stepmother's companions are *graves viri* (2.5.6), the friend who lectures her in 2.5.8 is *gravis amicus* and recommends *paterna frugalitas*. When Julia plays the role expected of her in 2.5.5, she embraces her father "with an affectation of primness," *affectata severitate*. Her normal behavior is associated with pejorative terms: "spoiled" (*delicatas*, 2.5.4), "rather daring" (*licentiore*, 2.5.5), "profligate" (*luxuriosae*, 2.5.6), "her sins" (*flagitiorum*), "such public property of her body" (*tam vulgo potestatem corporis*), the analogy between her body and a ship (2.5.9).

Yet, with all this, the joke teller and his audience do not make Julia the butt of the joke; in most cases (2.5.4, 5, 6, 8, 9), she gets the better of her father. There is a sense of being in on her secrets, one of the select circle who knew what she really did; with *qui vitia noscebant* ("those who knew of her vices," 2.5.2), compare *secrete* ("secretly," 2.5.7), "those who knew of her sins" (2.5.9). Moreover, those who comment on her anomalous behavior often do so with admiring wonder, never with disgust: *mirantibus* (2.5.2), *mirarentur* (2.5.9), like Populia's interlocutor, *miranti cuidam* (2.5.10). Most telling of all, Avienus characterizes her retort in 2.5.6 with the epithet *eleganter*, an attitude Macrobius may well have picked up from his source.

The jokes that include Augustus manifest the joke teller's desire to control Augustus's behavior while allowing Julia free rein: he is Elmer Fudd to her Bugs Bunny. In 2.5.3, he moderates his reproof of her, and then regrets having said anything at all. In 2.5.4, he fools himself and only speaks of her to his friends, and then indulgently, rather than chiding her. In 2.5.5 he holds himself in at first; in 2.5.6 he chides her only in a mild note, not face to face; in 2.5.7 he reserves his comment for a later time. On the other hand, in 2.5.7 he does have the last word, and the joke depends on the circumstance that he walked in on her while she was dressing.

The original audience for these jokes, then, would have consisted of people who wished Augustus had less power to interfere with *mores* than he did, but were familiar with the wide range of his actual power and desire to interfere. They had internalized the values Augustus wished to enforce, but could tolerate the infringement of these values. They seem to have been decidedly of Julia's generation, or younger, seeing Livia's friends as *senes* and Augustus as past sexuality. They wished to seem to be in the know about goings-on in court circles. And of course the jokes may have originated outside the court, among people who were watching it for signs of their own fate. All these things considered, it seems quite possible that these jokes were told, and spread, by the senatorial and equestrian women of Rome (among others). Perhaps the jokes later entertained women like Appuleia

Varilla, Augustus's great-niece, who "made fun of the deified Augustus and Tiberius and his mother in indecent speeches" (chapter 1).

If the jokes were indeed collected by Domitius Marsus, this would set them in a familiar context: the social and literary circles that surrounded both Julias. A protégé of Maecenas who wrote a lament for Vergil and Tibullus, remembered by Ovid in exile, classed by Martial with Catullus for the lasciviousness of his epigrams (1.intro.), Domitius also wrote an epic on the Amazons that Martial characterizes as both *levis* ("light") and long (4.29.8). This makes it an apt companion piece for his book *De urbanitate*, a careful study of the theory of humor. His poem on the Amazons might well have appealed to those who told the jokes about Julia—and perhaps also listened delightedly to Ovid's *Ars amatoria*.[13] And such a circle might equally have inspired the description of Julia in Avienus's introduction, with its emphasis on her "love of literature and much learning," and on the way her (Julian) virtues ("gentle humanity," "a spirit in no way cruel") "earned the woman great indulgence and favor." Marsus also praised the literary acumen of Caecilius Epirota, whose suspected seduction of Agrippa's first wife Augustus had found seriously unamusing (Suetonius *Gramm.* 16); the publication of a collection that included these jokes may well have been intended to embarrass the *princeps*.

On the other hand, perhaps the *princeps* could not only tolerate the jokes but use them. He did cultivate a reputation for tolerance of such things (Seneca *Clem.* 1.10.3; Macrobius *Sat.* 2.4.19), and this would certainly make their survival easier to understand.[14] After all, the jokes damn Julia's morals thoroughly, and out of her own mouth, while Augustus remains benevolent and indulgent throughout, at worst paternal. Moreover, no matter how the jokes side with Julia, we can assume that such a publication of her vices (and shadow on her sons' paternity) would have pleased her stepmother Livia, especially after 2 BCE—as it would have continued to suit Livia's son Tiberius to have Julia remembered as a wanton betrayer of Augustus.[15] Avienus (2.5.2) begins his narrative by placing Julia in the year of her exile—a more than convenient time for those who want to paint her character black. We recall the public outcry for her return. The date may well have been grafted onto the jokes, either by Macrobius or by an earlier collector. For the situation portrayed in the jokes is not that of Julia's last year in Rome. Three times mention is made of Agrippa, or of a husband present in Rome (2.5.3, 5, 9); 2.5.3 concerns children, 2.5.9 actual pregnancy. Conceivably, the jokes may have been circulated in written form at the time of the exile, but a joke about Julia and Agrippa must come from his lifetime. Whoever collected and published them, pro- or anti-Julia, was using them outside their original context.

If the jokes really favor Julia, does anything, apart from the question of *cui bono*, mark them either as women's humor or as radical humor? The nature of subversive humor has been well theorized by James C. Scott (1990); Julia's jokes provide a Roman test case, rare in its use of an historical woman speaker (see Richlin 2014 on comedy; cf. Levin-Richardson 2013). Scott argues against the commonplace in anthropological theory that jokes opposing social rules in fact reinforce them, since stories of outrageous behavior sharply define what is normal.[16] Such a model eliminates the possibility of genuinely revolutionary humor. What makes a joke about the powers that be different from a joke about the powers about to be ousted? One study differentiates on the basis of the degree of power imbalance within the joke. Whereas common jokes about authority figures (e.g., policemen) are conservative, jokes about inflated authority figures who brutalize the joke's protagonist (e.g., policemen as "pigs" beating demonstrators) are radical (Webb 1981). Scott's paradigmatic case of speaking truth to power involves a tenant woman telling off a landowner (1990: 6–10), and real-life retellings of such a story by tenants would fit comfortably into Scott's "hidden transcript." In a Roman context, retellings of Julia's jokes would offer the favorite strategy of plausible deniability (cf. Ahl 1984), becoming more risky after her exile and death. To the degree that moral legislation can be said to constitute oppression in a society comfortable with slavery, Julia's jokes serve an oppressed group, who, after all, like her, faced possible exile or death.

Julia's jokes certainly differ from the usual Roman jokes about women, which create and deride a consistently negative stereotype (chapters 1, 2; cf. Chapman and Gadfield 1976), or blacken a noted woman's reputation to attack her family (Skinner 1982b, esp. n. 33). Julia's behavior may be bad, but, within the joke, she is admired. She is verbally adroit; the point is not so much her promiscuity as her strength. And she gets the better of her father. The Hellenistic collections of the witticisms of famous Greek prostitutes— preserved in Athenaeus *Deipnosophistae* 13, and evoked in Alciphron and in Lucian's *Dialogues of the Courtesans*—remind us of Julia's jokes. In Latin, only in comedy do we see a woman—usually a prostitute or slave—have the last word in a similar manner. Odd company for the emperor's daughter; the parallels only heighten the contrast. As discussed in chapter 4, a slutty pose is all the riskier for a woman in a traditional society.

So Julia's jokes may have been revolutionary not only in the political sense; they are likely to have been repeated by those who rejected traditional female norms. Joanne Cantor's 1976 studies of gender and joking found that most people surveyed did not like jokes in which a woman wins out over a man; the only exceptions were active feminists. Men and traditional women found jokes in which men bested women much funnier (Cantor 1976; cf. Neitz 1980). The late first century BCE had no women's movement, but it was certainly a time when tradition became politicized (cf. Hamer 1988; Milnor 2005); many have defined this period, including the reign of Augustus, as a time when male gender rebels become visible as well, precisely among the circles in which Julia moved.

Does the content or structure of the jokes mark them as female rather than male? It has been suggested that women's oral humor follows patterns unlike those of male humor (which would not be surprising; cf. chapter 2).[17] And it would be pleasant if we could believe that the hostility and machismo of mainstream humor were counterbalanced by a humor showing "female" traits—a humor without aggression. Marie Maclean (1987) summarizes arguments for the existence of "oppositional practices" by which the weak subvert the power of the strong; she attributes these especially to women's oral narrative (cf. Davis 1975b). Cantor's study suggests, however, that human acculturation is so male-biased that most women adopt a male viewpoint in their humor preferences, incorporating self-hatred into "femininity." Co-optation must always weigh against subversion.[18]

Still, Julia's jokes do without physical aggression, while she remains decidedly assertive and opposed to norms. If the women's humor described by Green 1977 and by Johnson 1973 can be aligned with jokes among other under-classes, which satirize their victimization as a sort of survival training (see also Walker 1988), then Julia's jokes suggest that assertiveness in jokes rises with the amount of perceived power—as, in Cantor's study, feminist women were able to perceive female dominance as funny. That is, the degree of assertiveness in a social group perceived as funny by any member of the society will rise according to the amount of control exercised by that group. So, if Julia's jokes were popular, this means that elite women in Rome must have been feeling their strength, and that elite men in Rome must have recognized it.

Of course, there is no happy ending; Julia died in exile. So much for the oppositional voice. The jokes are a curiosity for Rome: an example of the deliberate use of a traditionally negative stereotype to represent something positive, here self-assertion in the house of a *princeps*. They must have been told first in the period of her marriages, before her exile—coexisting with the many positive images of Julia, perhaps reacting against them—within a group that expected to survive and prosper. The exile of the real Julia shows who really controlled the stereotypes.

Julia's positive images show what was at stake. On July 4, 13 BCE, with Agrippa ensconced in the imperial favor as father of the heirs apparent, Augustus consecrated the site for the Ara Pacis. He still stands there, carved on its side, *en famille*, amid emblems of Julian and Roman fecundity.[19] In that same year, two of the three moneyers give prominent space to Agrippa, while Julia herself is thought to appear on three coins of the moneyer C. Marius. Especially pertinent here are *RIC* 404 and 405 (plate 7), on which Julia's head appears beneath a wreath, flanked by the heads of her sons Gaius and Lucius; the obverse of these coins depicts Augustus (Sutherland and Carson 1984: 72). This constitutes a remarkable honor paid to an achievement of the real Julia by the year 13 BCE: her production of the imperial heirs. Even Livia, who is often claimed to appear on coins of Tiberius in allegorical guise (e.g., Giacosa n.d., 24; cf. Sutherland and Carson 1984: 87, 96), makes no monetary appearance *in propria persona*. A Tiberian coin with the legend *SPQR Iuliae August.* shows only a *carpentum* (*RIC* 51, plate 12), the two-wheeled carriage that was the sign of a respectable *matrona*.[20] Instead we find Livia buttressing the political message of the Ara Pacis with a shrine to Concordia, dedicating this temple of wifely affection on the Roman equivalent of Mother's Day, the Matronalia (Flory 1984; see chapter 7, and cf. Dolansky 2011c).

In this firmament shone Julia's star, her face stamped onto money in her role as *genetrix*. Suetonius tells us how her father's clothes bore witness that she spent time spinning and weaving (*Aug.* 73); courtly poetry inscribed her maiden betrothal to Marcellus (Cameron 1980). Later, the dead and perfect wife Cornelia, in a poem by Propertius, imagines herself mourned by Augustus as worthy to be Julia's sister (4.11.59; Hallett 1984: 53–54). Thus the authorized version in the period before the exile portrays Julia, with enormous publicity, as playing the role expected of her. For Augustus she was an important icon of wifehood and motherhood, in a state in which he had just made adultery a criminal offense. For some Romans, this was a joke.

As summarized by Gordon Williams (1978: 68–69), the rhetoric of 2 BCE conforms with the iconography of Julia before her fall as much as it conflicts with the iconoclasm of Julia's jokes. The "emphasis on home and family" in Messalla's speech bestowing the title of *pater patriae*—a title inscribed on the porch of Augustus's house—tallies with Augustus's insistence on public exposure of his daughter's sins and on listing the public places she desecrated. Rome has become his house, public space has merged with private, a letter to the Senate and an assembly of the people of Rome take the place of the family council. The temple he dedicated in the year of her exile was to Mars the Avenger, and "housed the deities of Mars, Venus Genetrix, and Divus Julius—a symbol of the family . . . that had brought him to power." If, as Williams suggests and as seems likely, Augustus had been planning Julia's exposure for some time, the gods he installed in 2 BCE make a fit trinity to supervise it: Mars the Avenger, father of the Roman people; Mother Venus, mother of Aeneas; and the deified Julius Caesar, who in turn was Aeneas's descendant and Augustus's adoptive father. The temple officially closed (and marked) his debt to the slain Caesar; but in effect this temple was a shrine to Augustus's ancestors—all gods. The image of Mars and Venus caught in Vulcan's net belongs to Ovid and not to Augustan public art.

This context perhaps suggests what "unattainable status" was represented by Julia's purity, and also what "over-class" the emperor's daughter could possibly marry into. As he tried to make her life conform with the *mos maiorum*, the "way of the ancestors," so she is to continue the divine line of Caesars. Reaching childbearing age in effect catapulted Julia into the divine, into the future of the dynasty, and into the past of the *maiores*. The human sexual level was not for her; the jokes, as well as the tales of her enormities, represent the opposite extreme of ideology (cf. Populia's "because they're beasts").

Double Context: Fifth Century CE

To return to our text with a double context: what were these jokes doing in Macrobius's book? It seems safe to assume that Pulcheria, in Byzantium, would have been "not amused" by Julia's jokes; how far were such attitudes prevalent in the West? What is the meaning of a nostalgia that includes this sort of emperor's daughter? And were there any fifth-century equivalents of Julia's jokes and Julia's coins?

In light of the nature of the *Saturnalia* and its participants, the presence of the jokes about Julia in this text is at first surprising. Alan Cameron's discussion (1966) fixes the *Saturnalia* in the tradition of the nostalgic dialogue, set in a revered past at a poignant date just prior to the death of the chief participant—in this case Praetextatus, leader of the last great generation of Roman pagans (for a description of this group and their history, see Bloch 1963, and now, problematizing this picture, Salzman 2002, Cameron 2011).[21] The text thus has a redoubled context, that of the date of publication (probably the early 430s CE) and that of the dramatic date, December, c. 383 CE.

Despite the quiet and apolitical tenor of the conversation, the setting ten years before Flavianus's suicide at the Frigidus bespeaks a political intent. Yet the conquered who rule this Saturnalia stand for no unbridled license; as Robert Kaster has shown (1980), the structure, the protocol, and the content of the *Saturnalia* manifest a rigid hierarchy, an insistence on continuity between past and present, and a high-minded morality, all encapsulated in the virtues of *verecundia* ("modesty/chastity") and *diligentia*. A less likely setting for Julia's jokes can hardly be imagined, unless we bear in mind the object of the *Saturnalia*'s nostalgia: the Augustan past and the heritage of the Roman aristocracy.

Macrobius introduces the whole section of jokes in the *Saturnalia* (2.2–2.7) as a memento of "ancient and noble men" (2.1.8), and indeed, as Kaster points out, it is the first barrage of jokes (2.2) that demonstrates the *ordo* ("protocol") of the dialogue (1980: 228). Their presence would seem to foster hierarchy, then; but what of the subversive content of Julia's jokes? The speaker, Avienus, starts out in the dialogue as a doubter of the value of the past, a brash young man who learns better, unlike others at the table.[22] Avienus tells most of the jokes (2.4–2.7), and, as Cameron notes (1967: 396), wins only praise from the other guests (2.8.1). His jokes both provide a Saturnalia's obligatory *lascivia* and represent a beginner's effort at reverence for the past.

Macrobius clearly feels some unease about Julia's jokes; we recall the apology he puts into Avienus's mouth at 2.5.1–2. He later again marks the series as a departure from the other jokes in Book 2 (all of which, in fact, have male protagonists), sharply demarcating the end and unity of the section with the words of Avienus which open 2.6.1: "But that I might revert from women to men and from lewd (*lascivis*) jokes to respectable (*honestos*) ones." The alignment of women with lewd jokes and men with respectable ones is clear. Symmachus had initiated the whole series at 2.1.8 with the suggestion that the guests make "sprightliness without lewdness" (*alacritatem lascivia carentem*) the subject of their after-dinner conversation (he specifically decries vulgar humor). The jokes continue through 2.7.19. Of all 105 jokes, only seven besides Julia's concern women at all; in five of these (2.2.5, 6, 9; 2.4.12, 20), the point is that the women are adulterous, while a sixth (2.2.11) concerns the high prices of the prostitute Lais. A joke where Cicero says to his daughter Tullia, "walk like your husband" (2.3.16), does make a good comparison with the jokes about Julia's comportment. But none of these jokes has a protagonist like Julia; despite the label *lascivis*, her jokes stand out from the other, more stereotypical jokes.

In fact, Roman anecdotes featuring a single female protagonist are altogether unusual. The other series of jokes in Macrobius *Saturnalia* 2 feature men, most notably Cicero (2.3.1–16) and Augustus (2.4.1–31). Women do appear in moral *exempla* and *ainoi*, but most are one-shots, which describe either paradigmatically good behavior (Cornelia: "These are my jewels," Valerius Maximus 4.4.*pr.*) or paradigmatically bad behavior (Claudia: "I wish my brother were alive to lose another fleet," Valerius Maximus 8.1.4). As we have seen (above, n. 12) the sayings of Livia emphasize virtues that are the reverse of Julia's vices. The jokes about Julia constitute the only extant series of Roman stories with a clever woman as protagonist. Of all the stories Macrobius had to choose from, why preserve these?

It was emphatically not the case that the tradition of praise and blame of women, with its rigid list of virtues and vices, had fallen into abeyance (see Lefkowitz 1981; cf. Atkinson 1985 on the construction of St. Monica). In looking backward, Macrobius could have called on a list of exemplary empresses that stretched from the women of Trajan's house to Dio's encomia of Julia Domna to the much-praised Christian empresses, from Helena to his contemporary, Pulcheria (sources above, n. 2). Even for commoners, the ideal of the *univira* ("woman married only once"), an eminent feature of late republican moral praise, flourished in fifth-century Rome (Williams 1958; Lightman and Zeisel 1977). We can see the ideals of Macrobius's own characters in the famous epitaph of Praetextatus and his wife Fabia Aconia Paulina (*CIL* 6.1779), set up by her, which gives her a list of virtues that would not be out of place during the republic, and certainly include chastity: "putting her husband before herself"; "chaste, faithful, pure in mind and body, kind to all, useful in her home"; "kindling of modesty, chain of chastity"; "with the *pietas* of a mother, the dearness of a spouse, the closeness of a sister, the deference of a daughter"; "helping her husband, cherishing him, ornamenting him, caring for/worshiping (*colens*) him." For Christian women, however, another ideal was becoming important: asceticism.

In fact, in the late fourth and early fifth centuries, we find a split between various ideas of correct female behavior that is even more traumatic than the division induced by Augustus's moral legislation. Peter Brown argued that the aristocratic families of Rome who accepted Christianity did so largely through their female members, who eventually began to adopt asceticism, even, as in the case of the younger Melania, to the detriment of their pregnancies and patrimonies. Melania was active in the 430s, the decade that saw the *Saturnalia* published (Brown 1961, 1988; Corrington 1986; cf. McNamara 1984 on these women's self-empowerment through asceticism, refusal to bear children, and female bonding, especially mother-daughter; and now Cooper 2007). But Michele Salzman has demonstrated that these women were exceptional (2002: 138–77), and Christian moralists found women to frown upon who were unsatisfied to have only one husband or no husband at all. Back around the time of the dramatic date of the Saturnalia, Ambrosiaster was complaining that now, since Julian's edict, women have the power to divorce their husbands, and are doing so "daily."[23] What we see here is that not only have the traditional Roman female virtues survived, they have been exceeded and subverted by the new Christian female virtues. Women's behavior is now scrutinized and prescribed not only by an Augustus (or Theodosius), but also by a Jerome.

To the Roman aristocracy, the ideals of asceticism were fundamentally threatening, undermining as they did the old ideals of fecundity, transmission of patrimony, and coupled unity. Julia as a figure from the venerated Augustan past has characteristics that would appeal to the audience of the *Saturnalia*: the "love of literature and much learning" on which Avienus lays stress; her "humanity" and lack of cruelty, perhaps a contrast with ascetic extremes; her skill in the art of safe dissent; her fulfillment of her dynastic role, even if on her own terms; and her ultimate fate. Like Flavianus, she is a rebel in the old style. Her jokes recall an ancien régime.[24]

The effect of the Christian model for female behavior on the ruling women of the Eastern court has been described at length by Kenneth Holum (1982). Whereas Flaccilla and Eudoxia justified themselves by producing heirs to the dynasty, and Eudocia attempted to do the same, Pulcheria identified herself with and drew her power from the sexless motherhood of Mary. But Macrobius, in the West, had before him a different *exemplum* of imperial womanhood, whose life recalled aristocratic traditions and the example of Julia. Galla Placidia, born to Theodosius I and his second wife in 388 or 389, came to the West and the court of her half brother, Honorius, as a child of six.[25] A dynastic marriage would have been expected for her; by 398 there were courtly hints of her marriage to Stilicho's son Eucherius (Cameron 1970: 47, 154). Instead, she became a hostage of the Visigothic leader Athaulf, whom she married in 414; her husband and their infant son died in 415, and she was returned to Ravenna and married off to Constantius III in 417. Their daughter Justa Grata Honoria was born in 418; a son, Valentinian, in 419. By 423 she had been named Augusta, Constantius had died, and her constant siding with the barbarian elements in Ravenna had forced her to flee with her children to Constantinople. She had returned to Italy by 425 and spent the last decades of her life as a pillar of the church. Meanwhile, her unmarried daughter Honoria was found to be pregnant;

this was seen to pose the threat of her lover's rise to power (cf. both Julias' rumored involvement in coups), and so he was killed and Honoria was exiled to the custody of Pulcheria, or at least sequestered. (She supposedly then wrote a letter proposing marriage to Attila the Hun.[26])

Like Julia's daughter, Honoria found out what it meant to be pregnant at the wrong time; even her mother Galla Placidia, who had produced a legitimate heir, was attacked after Constantius's death by insinuations that she was committing incest with her half brother Honorius (Matthews 1975: 377; cf. Oost 1968: 171). Yet after her restoration we find on coins icons of both women as Augustae, as impressive as any images of their Eastern sisters: Galla Placidia on a solidus, crowned by the hand of God; on a gold multiple, wearing a diadem and chlamys, just like the emperor's regalia—and, on the reverse, enthroned; and Justa Grata Honoria on a solidus, wearing the regalia.[27] Galla Placidia also left public religious monuments behind her; moreover, we have the letters she wrote to Theodosius and to Pulcheria on the Monophysite controversy, and Theodosius's reply to her (Migne *Patrologia Latina* 54.859–62, 863–66, 877–78). They contain little more than formalities, but it is something to see those formalities attested.[28] St. Peter Chrysologus, bishop of Ravenna 432–50, himself addressed her in a sermon with these words (*PL* 52.556–57):

> Indeed, there is present the mother herself of the eternal and faithful Christian empire, who, while she follows and imitates the blessed Church in honor of the Trinity by faith, by works of mercy, by sanctity, has been worthy to give birth to, to embrace, and to possess the august Trinity.

The direct analogy here between Galla Placidia and the Church is less startling in the context of the sermon as a whole, which begins with an invocation of *Ecclesia mater* in bridal garb, and goes on to describe the children of this mother (i.e., Christians), whose conception is (like that of Jesus in Mary) "unknowing of sex, knowing of conception, aware of birth, unaware of corruption, of unbroken chastity, of closed unbrokenness, chaste in its children, diffuse in its fecundity." In the Church, sex and gender have become active metaphors for power relations; alluding to Galla, the bishop turns this around, claiming to see these power relations enacted in the real sexuality of the empress. As mother of the emperor, but also as Augusta, Galla Placidia has become an analog of the Church itself; the bishop can even proclaim in her, Augusta and mother and wife of Augusti, a kind of Trinity (Oost 1968: 266–67). The contrast between this eulogy and the earlier attacks on Galla—both centering on her sexual body—strongly recalls the contrast between the two versions of Julia, and of course foreshadows the double image of Theodora in Procopius's *Secret History* and the Ravenna mosaics (see Allen 1992, Brubaker 2004, Fisher 1984, Herrin 1983).

On the content of the *Saturnalia*, Alan Cameron once remarked, "In a sense . . . this antiquarianism *was* bound up with the traditions of the pagan past. But there is no suspicion of polemic, nothing at all to offend the most narrow-minded Christian" (1966: 35). I would submit that any publicly pious Christian would have found Julia's jokes shocking and the epithet *eleganter* applied to her witticisms distasteful, and that he or she would have been horrified at the suggestion that such words from an emperor's daughter were in any way admirable, even though she came to a bad end. I think we must posit here a connection between the figure of Julia in these jokes and the changing images of Galla Placidia and her daughter. The revival of the jokes in Macrobius's *Saturnalia* constitutes recognition of an empress's power in the early fifth century CE and its source: her self-control in procreative sex. The concurrent ideal of female purity recalls Julia's uncomfortable proximity to the gods; Pulcheria aims at the "unattainable goal" of entry into heaven. Sabine MacCormack comments (1981: 263–64):

> A canon of virtues and deeds for emperors had been laid down during centuries of Roman politics and public life. In late antiquity, it became possible for empresses to be represented in art in the light of this canon, as was Galla Placidia . . . , but this defined their role only very partially. For, while the figure of the emperor remained caught in debates as to the nature of the imperial power which carried over from the pagan into the Christian empire, it was possible to catalogue and expound the virtues of a Christian empress independently of this legacy of the past. In this new context, the virtues and deeds of an empress were directed not merely toward the manifold contingencies of this life, but toward the ultimate goal of the life to come.

Julia's jokes suggest that the virtues of emperors' female kin, and of all women who rule, had been measured by similar criteria long before emperors were Christian.

Conclusions

Julia's jokes work similarly in both of their contexts, the early principate and the fifth century CE. In both cases, the live models have idealized images against which their negative images react. All the images concern sexuality, especially childbearing, and this focus not surprisingly reappears in the recorded events of these women's lives. But both life and icons are manipulated for political ends, with a strong identification between the woman's body and the health of the state.

This study suggests some general rules. Jokes about the sexual impurity of women in power must normally represent a mediation of that power, perhaps a translation of that power in terms of the class fiction Ortner describes.[29] Julia's jokes, if they are an exception to this rule, owe their survival to it; they are seen as "jokes about Julia" rather than as "Julia's jokes" (cf. Walker 1988: 120–22). Moreover, if, as Ortner claims, female purity is the key to class movement upwards, purity disparaged will cancel this out, hampering the claims to superiority of the women's male kin. On reflection, the phenomenon must be, as Ortner suggests, inherent in the patriarchal state: if you invent the sepulchre, someone is bound to point out that whiting it does not disguise its nature; if you have a Caesar, you must suspect Caesar's wife. Such a phrase is inherently loaded, like *Augusti filia*.

Contemplation of the icons of Roman ruling women leaves us with the uncomfortable feeling that we can hardly know the real women inside them at all; we seem to be looking at a long series of constructs, remade whenever women arrived at a certain kind of power. Did Livia really set herself in the first lady mold? And is that icon of her merely the one that survived, while another one of Livia the adulteress disappeared? After all, we have conflicting images not only for Julia, Galla Placidia, and Justa Grata Honoria, but for many other ruling women. What of pre-Hellenistic women? More questions arise. Natalie Kampen (1985) points out how Julia Domna's images rely on Livia's; do icons validate themselves by reference to other icons? Is a sort of inter-referentiality among past, present, and future characteristic of such images (cf. Atkinson 1985; Hamer 1988)? And are icons also invented for the past at the convenience of the present? Livy's story of Lucretia and the Tarquins' wives begins to sound like only a variant of Julia's joke about her followers versus Livia's.

Was Horace looking for the real woman within the icon of Cleopatra when he saw her refusing to be led in the triumph—*non humilis mulier*? Is history a branch of poetry? When we look at texts and objects to discover reality, it is as if we looked at a scene through a screen on a window; as we become interested in the screen and its properties, we suddenly notice that the scene is in fact painted on the screen itself. What lies beyond is unknown. Perhaps there are principles that determine the projection and interpretation of reality onto the screen; if so, the study of ideology serves in the search for them.

CHAPTER 4

Sulpicia the Satirist

ﷺ

Introduction

In 1991, an article appeared in *Classical World* on an obscure Roman writer, a woman named Sulpicia. She is not that semi-familiar figure, the elegist Sulpicia, whose few extant poems have elicited a substantial amount of scholarly writing, but a satirist, a contemporary of Martial, a tantalizing figure known mainly to Romanists who haunt the low dives of Latin literature. Her work survives only in a short quotation by a scholiast of Juvenal, but the *CW* article did not mention that quotation. So it was that Judith Hallett, Holt Parker, and I all read the *CW* article, leaped as if stung by separate but synchronized bees, and began to write responses. We soon discovered that we were all working on the same project and shared what we had written; Parker chased down the Renaissance commentaries, Hallett focused on elegy, and I thought about what it would have meant for a woman to write satire. The results were published together in a later issue of *Classical World* and stand as a pleasant example of collaborative work.

In writing this short essay I was so obsessed with having the words of not only an actual woman writer but a writer of satire that I did not pay enough attention to the content of the two lines that constitute her extant work. Parker did, and commented accordingly on Sulpicia's "astonishing outspokenness." It is a very odd coincidence that, in classical Latin literature, we have two women writers, both named Sulpicia (on which, see the very different theories proposed by Hubbard 2004 and Stevenson 2005: 45); just as oddly, both write about their sexual feelings and experience with male lovers, although, as Parker notes, the second Sulpicia is much more explicit. In antiquity, writing by women about their desire for men is vanishingly rare, and, until the rise of the modern novel and the woman novelist, it is none too common in world literature generally. It is so rare that we have no idea, for instance, of what (if anything) Roman women found attractive in Roman men, for not even the two Sulpicias tell us this. It is then perhaps not so surprising that historians of sexuality, not only of ancient sexuality but of sexuality in general, have tended to consider women's sexual desire for men only where it makes a splash in the historical record, although it must belong to the everyday. Moreover, feminist theorists, at least in this wave, have often been governed by an inhibition that prevents any serious consideration of the pleasure in what used to be called "sleeping with the enemy." The branch of theory known as "sex-positive" is much less well known (see Johnson 2002), but necessary to account for not only the two Sulpicias but the jokes attributed to Julia and Populia (chapter 3).

In the study of antiquity, unpaid sex between women and men is most thoroughly considered by Susan Treggiari in her authoritative study of Roman marriage (1991). Treggiari was able to document in detail the language of love between husbands and wives, along with the extensive remarks of moralizing writers and occasional thoughts of poets on the place of sex in marriage, and she marshals a huge array of anecdotal evidence about the erotic behavior of Roman men and women. But what did women want? Treggiari discusses the first Sulpicia's poems as the romantic preliminaries to a marriage (1991: 122), while Sulpicia the satirist appears attached to a discussion of Sulpicia the elegist in a footnote which only recaps Martial's account of her (1991: 303 n. 28)—a sort of text burial that epitomizes the proportion of male to female testimony within the history of sexuality. Giulia Sissa's *Eros Tiranno* (2003 [2008]), which aims to redress the imbalance in the representation of ancient thought on male and female desire, still has to focus on male writers; the two Sulpicias do not appear. Lesley Dean-Jones (1992) discusses Greek medical theories about women's sexual desire, charting change over time. Suzanne Dixon's brief but trenchant overview (2001: 36–44) focuses on male-authored texts. For all historians, even if so inclined, the lack of evidence, due to the overwhelming control of textual production by men in most cultures until around 1800, of course bears some responsibility for the silence. We still might look again at letters and graffiti (see Stevenson 2005: 50–52 for some examples, and Levin-Richardson 2013 for a substantial study of graffiti, with further bibliography). No one, of course, doubts that at least some women have, historically, felt sexual desire for men, because texts by men talk about this all the time, but a reader has the strong feeling that on this point in particular we would want to hear women speak for themselves. They do, when they get the chance (Lady Murasaki, Marie de France, countless novelists, blues singers, ballad singers, girls jumping rope). It seems that Sulpicia the satirist did, too, and it is maddening but telling that we have so little of her work.

An easy-to-miss aspect of "Sulpicia the Satirist" is the use it makes of the testimonia to Sulpicia the satirist by three writers from late antiquity: Ausonius, Sidonius Apollinaris, and Fulgentius. Writing as Christianity began to clamp down on literature with explicit sexual content, these authors manifest a fond attachment to classical Roman texts that is symptomatic of their age; it is responsible for what Macrobius does in the *Saturnalia* as well (chapter 3). For them, satire and invective were part of that world; to them, Sulpicia was still available, and they speak of her as a writer they know, or at least know of. As with the material surveyed in chapter 2, an understanding of Roman satire and invective still awaits a full and close reading of these writers, dancing with the devil one last time. An understanding of Sulpicia must break off in mid-sentence

&a.   &a.   &a.

It is one of the mysteries of Latin literature that a culture in which women were literate and literary should have so totally failed to preserve those women's writing. Jane Snyder's survey of women writers in classical Greece and Rome (1989) devotes a total of 29 of 156 pages to writing by Roman women, and, of those, 15 pages deal with Christian women. The fact is, of pre-Christian Roman women, almost no writing remains. Six or eight poems by Sulpicia the elegist, two spurious letters of Cornelia, a Greek version of a speech by Hortensia, some mutilated letters from a frontier fort in northern Britain; we hardly know what was lost, though the fact that it includes the memoirs of Agrippina gives an indication of its caliber. Certainly we have clear Roman indications that women's abilities with language were respected, if marginal; Quintilian echoes and adds onto a little historical survey from Cicero (Snyder 1989: 123), while Cicero attributes to upper-class women an old-fashioned sociolect (*De orat.* 3.45). Perhaps Juvenal's opinion (6.434–56) of literary women was widely shared, and their work was never widely circulated, though his anger seems to have been provoked by actual female literati. Or perhaps it was just the triage of the ages, that has generally had so unkind an effect on women's work.[1]

The remains of the extensive poetry by Greek women are far more numerous and have aroused a correspondingly populous bibliography, despite, even inspired by, the largely fragmentary state of the corpus. As Jack Winkler noted (1981: 63), Monique Wittig and Sande Zeig began their history of women writers with a blank page dedicated to Sappho. While Sappho in particular has stimulated the imaginations of critics outside Classics as much as within the field, other Greek women writers remain to us; Marilyn Skinner has drawn attention to Sappho's literary granddaughters, Corinna and Nossis. For all these writers, their words are amplified by the accompanying silence, the loss of most of what they wrote.[2]

If silence can be eloquent, one Roman writer, to whom Snyder allots a sentence and a footnote, seems worthy of closer inspection. She is another Sulpicia, a satirist, or erotic poet, or both, who evidently lived at the time of Domitian. Her extant oeuvre consists of a two-line fragment preserved in the scholia on Juvenal, and a seventy-line hexameter satire under her name that is now generally thought to have been written in late antiquity.[3] Contemporary testimonia to her appear in two epigrams by Martial (10.35, 38); later writers include her in lists of poets who represent the satiric tradition—Ausonius in the fourth century CE (*Cento nuptialis* ad fin.), Sidonius Apollinaris in the mid-fifth century CE (*C.* 9.261–62), and Fulgentius, obliquely, in the late fifth century CE (*Mitologiae* 1.4, 23). Before 1992, the only recent treatment of Sulpicia the satirist was Merriam 1991, which omitted any mention of the one extant fragment of Sulpicia's work; the fragment was definitively treated by Parker 1992b, while Hallett 1992b treated Sulpicia as a poet in the tradition of Propertius.

I want to pause here to mark, like a memorial plaque, the grief and anger appropriate to a scholar beginning an assessment of a woman writer of whose work only two lines remain. In the much-vaunted Western tradition, the handing down involved a lot of throwing overboard; at some point, the rest of Sulpicia's work went over the side. It would be nice to have more of it to work with, and I want to emphasize that we can be certain that there originally *was* more of it. Sulpicia is not a two-line poet. She is a lost Roman satirist, the only woman writer associated with any comic genre in antiquity as far as I know. (I use "satire" here in a broad sense; it seems likely that Sulpicia did not write hexameter satire. Testimonia to her, however, place her in the company of writers who produced satiric/erotic texts: Martial, Juvenal, Catullus, Apuleius. Compare the range of writers in Richlin 1992 and chapter 2 above). Only one line and a papyrus fragment of Gallus survive, yet his life and status as founder of Latin love elegy are widely discussed. It should be possible to say something about Sulpicia.

Martial's Lady Poet

The late antique scholia of Probus on Juvenal, preserved by the Renaissance humanist Giorgio Valla, quote two satiric lines, written in iambic trimeter, which Probus attributes to a Sulpicia (actually, in Valla's account, to a Sulpicius, on which see Parker 1992a and b); the lines mention a man named Calenus who seems to be the writer's sexual partner. This ties the satirist in question securely to the Sulpicia about whom Martial writes in two epigrams (10.35 and 10.38):

10.35:
    Let all girls read Sulpicia
    who desire to please one man alone;
    let all husbands read Sulpicia
    who desire to please one wife alone.
    Not she to assert the madness of the woman of Colchis,   5
    nor to tell of the meals of dire Thyestes;
    nor does she believe Scylla or Byblis even existed;
    but she teaches chaste and proper loves,
    tricks, delights, frivolities.
    One who judges her songs rightly,   10
    will say no woman is naughtier (*nequiorem*),
    will say no woman is holier (*sanctiorem*).
    I would believe the sallies (*iocos*) of Egeria
    were such, in the dripping cave with Numa.
    With her as fellow student, or with her as teacher,   15
    you would have been more learned, even chaste, Sappho;
    but as much as he loved you, as soon as he had seen her,
    hard Phaon would have loved Sulpicia.
    In vain; for she neither as the wife of the Thunderer
    nor as the girl of Bacchus or Apollo   20
    would live, if Calenus were taken from her.

10.38:

> O sweet fifteen to you, Calenus,
> those years which, conjugal, with your Sulpicia,
> the god has vouchsafed you, and achieved!
> O each night and hour, marked
> by the dear pebbles of the Indic shore!   5
> O what battles, what fights on both sides
> the happy little bed and lantern saw,
> drunk with clouds of Nicerotian incense!
> You [have] lived, Calenus, thrice five years;
> that is the sum total of your life   10
> and you count only your days as a husband.
> Of those should Atropos return to you
> even one long-begged-for day,
> you would prefer it to four times the age of Nestor.

These poems carry with them a large amount of literary luggage, which we can at least try to unpack.[4] First of all, we can gather that Martial is making for Sulpicia's poetry the highly conventional claim that, though it deals with sexual love, this is chaste love—a claim that goes back to Catullus 16 via Ovid's *Ars amatoria*, both in quite different contexts. Martial imitated Catullus's disclaimer for himself, as many later poets were to do (Richlin 1992: 2–13). In 10.35, rather than a male poet claiming that writing love poetry does not mean he himself is *mollis*, "effeminate" (Catullus), or a male poet claiming that he is not teaching readers how to commit adultery (Ovid), we have a male poet claiming that a female poet is writing of an erotic love such as might exist between happy husband and wife—that is, she herself is not promiscuous: the adjective *castus* means something different for men and women. (Note how this preeminent claim to subjectivity is here preempted, by a male on behalf of a female.) The impression given of Sulpicia's poetry is of a sort of candy-box verse ("none naughtier, none nicer"—that is, this is erotic verse proper to the bonds of matrimony), an effect enhanced by the jingling repetitions of 1–4, 11–12. The penultimate awful comparison to Sappho—but a chaste and heterosexual Sappho who could stand to learn a thing or two about poetry and beauty from Sulpicia (a topos, see Hallett 1992b: 103)—is capped by a *recusatio* on Sulpicia's behalf of the roles of Juno (?) or of any of the generic *puellae* chased by Bacchus and Apollo through the pages of Ovid, for example. Indeed Martial's poem adumbrates a Sulpician mythology: not the bad women who populate neoteric poetry, elegy, and Ovid's *Metamorphoses* and *Heroides*, but the learned nymph and her Roman king. The emphatic placement of Sulpicia's name at the beginning and the name of Calenus, her husband, as the last word, emphasizes their conjugal bond; and, by playing with the word order, Martial leaves the reader with the final thought that Sulpicia would not live were Calenus to be taken from her.

The second poem seems to give us even more firm information about the married life of a real Sulpicia and her Calenus. This poem, clearly framed as a companion piece, is addressed directly to Calenus by the poet, who felicitates him on his love. The first three lines tell us that Calenus and Sulpicia were married or have been married for fifteen years. Given the norms of age at marriage for Roman men and Roman women (Scheidel 2007), this would make Calenus at least thirty-five, probably forty, and Sulpicia at least thirty. This information is recast in lines 9–11; but lines 12–14 leave the reader with the uncomfortable feeling that perhaps Sulpicia and Calenus are no longer one, with their (possibly) gloomy talk of "if you could only have even one of those days back again, *diu rogatam*" and preferring this to the longest of old ages. Sulpicia seems to be dead (thus Kroll 1931, followed by Parker 1992b). The mortuary effect is enhanced by the fact that tombstones commonly noted the number of years husband and wife had lived together (Shaw 2002), and that another common use of the epigram form, besides for love poetry, was for literary/fictive epitaphs.

We would then have a sad, but also odd, pairing of poems, in one of which Sulpicia certainly seems to be alive and joined indissolubly with Calenus, in the second of which she seems to be gone from his life. Yet, if she is dead, why the erotic interlude in 10.38.4–8, lines that belong to the world of amatory epigram, not to that of the epitaph? *Proelia* and *pugnae*, used of lovemaking, are a commonplace of elegy.[5] Perhaps all of 10.38 is no more than a working out for Calenus of the sentiment sketched more briefly for Sulpicia at the end of 10.35: as she would not wish to live, even as the wife of a god, were Calenus to be taken from her, so Calenus would not wish even for the long life of Nestor, if he could have back only one day of his life with Sulpicia—the implication being, *if* she were taken from him. Perhaps this is not sad at all, but an anniversary poem, also evoking the poetic tropes of Calenus's wife.

The biographical reading of these poems that I have just concocted is unfortunately and drastically undercut by the poems' literary predecessors, which hover intrusively around them. Martial's fondness for imitating Catullus is well known; he routinely uses Catullan meters, as here the hendecasyllabic, along with Catullan vocabulary and content; he names Catullus as one of his chosen models (1.intro., 4.14; see Richlin 1992: 6–7).[6] Although the vocabulary here is pervasively Catullan, one poem in particular seems to me to determine the structure of these two: c. 45, in which Catullus, in uncharacteristically saccharine tones, describes the mutual love of Septimius and Acme. The opening lines of 10.35 are modeled closely on Catullus 45.21–24:

> *unam Septimius misellus Acmen*
> *mavult quam Syrias Britanniasque:*
> *uno in Septimio fidelis Acme*
> *facit delicias libidinesque.*

Compare Martial 10.35.1–4:

> *Omnes Sulpiciam legant puellae*
> *uni quae cupiunt viro placere:*
> *omnes Sulpiciam legant mariti*
> *uni qui cupiunt placere nuptae.*

Catullus's poem consists of two sections, in which each lover in turn swears his/her love (Septimius goes first), followed by a third section in which the poet comments: *mutuis animis amant amantur* (20), "with mutual souls they love and are loved."

This amoibaic structure and sense seem to be what Martial is trying to replicate in his pair of poems; I would not, however, argue that the recognition of this high degree of artifice at once removes us from the world of living people, where names in poems have real referents. Rather, as is common in Martial, we are left with the feeling that he is tinkering with the border between fictive writing and writing about real people.[7] Not that Catullus was not doing this, or indeed not that any writer does not do this; but this was Rome just after the reign of Domitian, where an anonymous Flavian lady had her sculpted head planted onto the shoulders of a goddess's body (see D'Ambra 1996). In much the same way, Martial here takes the presumably real Sulpicia and Calenus and sticks them into two Catullan poems (one of which is about writing Catullan poetry); perhaps he is also dressed up in Sulpicia's own wording; the effect is like those scenic flats with holes cut out for faces, behind which you can stand and have your photograph taken.

Sulpicia the Satirist

Carol Merriam (1991) argues that Martial in 10.35 is seriously defending Sulpicia's poetic and moral reputation: "her poems, if not precisely 'chaste,' were at the very least faithful expressions of joy in a legal marriage" (305). This argument depends on an inference from the later testimonia that a reputation for lasciviousness adhered to Sulpicia in her own day. Such a hypothesis is made much more likely by the extant fragment of Sulpicia's work. We owe the fragment to its use of the rare word *cadurcum*, picked up by Juvenal after Sulpicia (6.537);[8] the commentator writes (see Parker and Braund 2012 for full exegesis):

> *cadurci:. . . est instita qua lectus intenditur. unde ait Sulpicia:*
> *si me cadurci restitutis fasciis*
> *nudam Caleno concubantem proferat*

> *cadurci*: It is the band on/with which the bed is spread/stretched.
> Whence Sulpicia says:
> If, the straps of my *cadurcum* having been restored,
> [someone? something?] should show me lying naked with
> Calenus

The word comes from the name of a Gallic tribe, the Cadurci, and the *cadurcum* seems to be a kind of linen bedding, textiles being a popular Gallic export and linen a specialty of this tribe (Strabo 4.2.2). The elder Pliny, discussing the uses of linen, says that "the Cadurci take the prize for mattresses (*culcita*)" (19.13). Juvenal, picking up *cadurcum*, uses it twice: synecdochically at 6.537 for "bed," here the bed "violated" against religious rules; contemptuously at 7.221, as something sold, along with *hibernae tegetis*, "a [beggar's] mat suitable for [or, as cold as] winter," by an *institor*, a peddler or traveling salesman (also a term of contempt, cf. Horace *C.* 3.6.30, where *institor* has the sexual connotations of "traveling salesman"). The peddler's *cadurcum* is "snowy" (that is, white). Varro says that *tegetes* are made of *linum* (flax), as well as of hemp and various kinds of reeds (*R.* 1.22.1), and the flax fibers that made linen also made string and nets for hunting and fishing. Martial uses Gallic-made clothing to denote what is barbaric, rugged, even greasy (1.53.5, 1.92.8, 4.19). So the register of the word *cadurcum* is low by its association with a crude culture, cheap trade, and rough materials; it is a loan word from a colonized language; not only is it part of that homely piece of furniture, a bed, but it constitutes a (literally) low part of the bed, and, here, of the bed as used for sex. If the *lectus* is the bed frame, the *cadurcum* must be a sort of coarse mattress, tied onto the frame, over which the covers were spread. As the platform against which the force of sex pushed, perhaps it had the same crude tone as the word *culcitulam* used in a comic setting (Plautus *Most.* 894–5, one slave to another: "The owner knows me." "Sure, he ought to know his little mattress"). The register of the expression might be conveyed by translating, "if my bedspring got its screws put back" or "if my sofa-bed frame got fixed." It is a low description of a broken bed.

There is much here to startle the reader expecting a lady writer, naughty but nice. These are iambic trimeters, not hendecasyllables or elegiac distich; the vocabulary is abrupt and strange, reminiscent of both Juvenal and Persius. The word *cadurcum* thus evokes the domestic exoticism proper to satire and invective, the exoticism of a textile, an everyday item, manufactured far away by uncouth people. It is also (possibly) being used with an energetic synecdoche again proper to satire: the *cadurcum* made to stand for the couple's marriage. Specifically, it stands for the sexual side of marriage; that is how *cadurcum* is used in Juvenal 6, where a married woman is seeking absolution from an Egyptian priest for not abstaining from sex on a holy day: *magnaque debetur violato poena cadurco*, "and a great penalty is owed for the violated *cadurcum*" (537). This Juvenalian bed is literally violated, as the thought continues from the word *concubitu*, "sexual lying together," in the previous line. The low word is typically chosen by Juvenal to contrast with the dubiously holy setting, as, in reverse, he puts the emperor's *pulvinar* in the same verse with the "foul smell" of the *lupanar* (6.132)—a scene in which, we note, the *meretrix Augusta* sets out wearing a Gallic cloak (6.118). In satire, synecdoche is usually pejorative rather than euphemistic.

Indeed, what *is* Sulpicia talking about here? Here she is in her own poem exposing herself naked with her husband, called by his own name; contrast the effect of Ovid's description of Venus and Mars in the net, or the effect of Horace or Ovid talking about his own sexual performance and the nameless woman in bed with him. It is part of the job of a male satirist, as well as of the elegist, to expose the female body to the public gaze (Richlin 1992: 67–70, 109–16, 131; chapter 2 above, chapters 5 and 6 below). There would have been no rules for a female satirist to follow; Sulpicia here seems to be taking the bull by the horns, and exposing her own self—a daring form of reappropriation (see Ostriker 1985; and now Levin-Richardson 2013). For the wording, we might compare Catullus's exposure of a friend's bed in c. 6 (where the friend's bedmate is a *febriculosum scortum*, "disease-ridden whore"), or of himself in c. 32, both vivid expressions of what is normally in Latin a male subject position and a male prerogative.

A lot depends on what the lost context of these two lines was. *Si . . . pro-ferat* begins a conditional sentence; how did it end? Who or what was the subject of *proferat*? Several conflicting reconstructions suggest themselves. Morel explained the lines thus: "*optat, ut sibi lectus genialis nescio qua de causa turbatus restituatur*"—"she prays that the marriage bed, broken up by some unknown cause, be restored to her" (1927: 166). The sense of the fragment then hinges on *restitutis*, "restored." In this scenario, the subject of *proferat* would have been something like *dies optata* "some hoped-for day," and the conclusion of the condition would be, "how happy I would be!" The *proelia* and *pugnas* of Martial's second poem (10.38.6), along with the *felix lectulus* at 10.38.7, might be a reminiscence of Sulpicia's own description of her *lectus* here (so Kroll 1931). Not, perhaps, in the best of taste, but a possible reaction to something written by Sulpicia herself.

Other possible subjects for *proferat*, other endings to the conditional, however, suggest different scenarios. *Profero* is commonly used of displays on the theatrical stage, and the two lines might suggest the spectacle of the display of bodies on the *ekkyklema* at the height of a Greek tragedy. Is the subject of *proferat* another poet, who has written about Sulpicia's sex life in his poetry? Perhaps a rival satirist who has, in traditional manner, impugned her mores? Or perhaps the offender is Martial himself, and it is Sulpicia who picks up *lectulus* with her *cadurci*, rather than the other way around; perhaps she did not like having her *felix lectulus* praised. Holt Parker rightly points out that sometimes a *cadurcum* is just a *cadurcum*—the graphic description of the bed here may indeed be recalling the scented, rumpled, creaking bed of Catullus 6—so that "the text itself . . . gives a re-markably vivid picture of the bed and its underpinnings rucked up by the intensity of her and her husband's lovemaking" (1992b: 93). If she is reacting to Martial's poem, this would indicate that she was not in fact dead when 10.38 was written. If the poem from which the fragment comes is typical of her work, Martial's first poem constitutes some serious whitewashing.

For the tone of the fragment is arguably angry, too strong and sexually explicit to be *nequam*, and hardly *sanctus* at all, despite Martial's encomium. A possible end to the condition in this case would be, "I would not give a damn." Or, if the subject of *proferat* were "some ill-starred day," a possible apodosis would be "I would be making a big mistake," or "This time I would just use him and walk away" (think of the end of Catullus 8, or c. 76, where he rejects his beloved).

Another possibility: if we take Sulpicia seriously as a satiric writer, the fragment may be part of a poem "On Marriage"—from a woman's point of view. The topic was a favorite of the rhetorical schools (cf. Braund 1992), and it is pleasant to imagine that, at least once, a woman replied. In that case, the subject of *profero* might be "some force," and the end of the condition would be: "Then you'd see what it's really like!" Or, most radical of all, the end of the condition might be, "Then you'd see how pleasurable that is for me"—for, as Parker points out, this text is one of the only places in all of ancient literature where a woman talks about being in bed with a man.

We are left with the impression of a strong writer, a stylistic link between Persius and Juvenal. It even seems likely, despite his avowed distaste for female literati, that Juvenal had these lines in mind when he picked up *cadurcum* to use in his sixth satire. The word appears in Latin this once in Sulpicia, twice in Juvenal, and not elsewhere. As noted, the word *concubitu* appears at Juvenal 6.536, a line above his *cadurco*; compare the innovative form *concubantem* in the second line of Sulpicia's fragment. The phenomenon whereby women writers are disparaged by those who imitate them is also historically familiar (see Richlin 1991).

The Reception of Sulpicia

If Juvenal did emulate Sulpicia this far, we cannot know how much further, due to the loss of the rest of her work. A study of the influence of Sulpicia on later satire is one of the tasks not possible for us; it would be easy to hypothesize that her influence must have been negligible, precisely because no one bothered to save her work. But this might not be a good hypothesis. Her work seems to have been known to writers in the fourth and fifth centuries, at least by reputation: Ausonius and Sidonius lump her with Plato, Cicero, Martial, and Juvenal; Ausonius refers to her *opusculum*, which must mean at least a substantial poem or group of poems. The scholiast on Juvenal is familiar enough with her work to remember the parallel use of a rare word in it. And—or so scholars have come to believe—in the fourth or fifth century, someone went to the trouble of writing a satire under her name.

Why would someone have done such a thing? There was a vogue for literary nostalgia among writers of the late empire; this poem pretends to be situated in Domitian's Rome.[9] As for why a late ancient writer would pick a woman's voice, this was a time when Christian women were attaining a new prominence both in public affairs and in writing. We might compare the way in which the highly nostalgic Macrobius chose Julia's jokes to include in a section of his book otherwise devoted almost exclusively to men's witticisms—jokes in which Julia's subjectivity is expressed in no uncertain terms (see chapter 3 above). Indeed, Sidonius Apollinaris says that a writer named Julius Titianus, a contemporary of Juvenal's, wrote a collection of letters in the name of "eminent women" (*inlustrium feminarum, Ep.* 1.2), although he therein tried to imitate, not the women's style, but Cicero's. But even where male writers have made up texts for women, this does not mean the women never wrote.[10] The satire we have under Sulpicia's name seems to have been written by someone anxious to include recognizable details, to strengthen the impersonation; the result provides us with some clues.

The poem is set up as a speech addressed to the poet's Muse—the first word in the poem is *Musa*, and the speaker invokes their habit of "intimate consultation" (*penetrale . . . consilium,* 3–4); this speech concludes at line 63. The Muse then replies, and finishes out the poem (65–70). The whole—an echo of Sappho LP 1? of Sulpicia the elegist? Did all women poets do this?—is thus framed as a dialogue between women, a conceit reinforced by the Muse's epithet for the poet: *cultrix mea,* "my worshiper [fem.]" (65). Not that there has been much to identify the speaker as female before this point, although the poem begins with an eleven-line proem in the first person; the name of Calenus is dragged in, without explanation or much context, at 62. A chummy allusion to Egeria in the Muse's speech echoes Martial 10.35.13–14, suggesting that perhaps Egeria, Numa, and the cave showed up in the poems of the real Sulpicia (67–68; so also Parker 1992b: 92 n. 24):[11]

> *Nam laureta Numae fontisque habitamus eosdem*
> *et comite Egeria ridemus inania coepta.*

> For we frequent the laurel-thicket of Numa and the same fountain,
> and, with Egeria as our companion, we laugh at [the emperor's] vain
>   undertakings.

The Muse says this in order to reassure the poem's speaker that the wicked emperor Domitian will meet with the fate he deserves. Most of the poem is devoted to a variation on the *locus de saeculo;* the speaker laments the decline of Roman arts in these times of peace and luxury, and in particular the expulsion of Greek philosophers from Rome by the man "who rules among the Romans as king" (35–44). The Muse's comforting prediction of the tyrant's end in itself separates this poem from literature either of the reign of Domitian or the period that followed. Nobody at the time of Domitian criticized his policies directly, or directly called him *rex* or *tyrannus*, while the post-Domitianic literature is marked by the bitterness of its professions of loss (see Boyle 1990); if Sulpicia outlived Domitian to write this poem, it would have sounded feeble next to Juvenal's savagery or Tacitus's dirges. The Muse's prediction reads not only like hindsight but like hindsight long after the fact, and the poem arguably reads like an exercise, festooned with period details.

Certainly the poem lacks any of the linguistic audacity that characterizes our two-line fragment. Contrast the two lines above on Numa's grotto with the description of it at Juvenal 3.12–20: the place where Numa met up with his "nighttime girlfriend," the grove of the sacred fountain rented out to Jews, "the woods begging, the Camenae kicked out," the old rustic spring covered by a fancy new marble rim. Even Martial's "sallies" in a "dripping cave" (10.35.14) are more vivid than the wording of this satire, which barely uses an uncommon noun in seventy lines.

The proem does include one other hint about the possible nature of the poetry of the real Sulpicia. The opening four lines consist of an appeal to the Muse to permit the poet to write in hexameters; she goes on to reject hendecasyllables, iambic trimeter, and scazons (4–6). We might guess that the writings of the real Sulpicia included all these meters; even, more hesitantly, that she never did write in hexameter, the meter, as the proem emphasizes, of *heroas et arma* as well as of satire. As Parker points out (1992b: 91–92), the presence of trimeter in the list tends to support the authenticity of our trimeter fragment.

The proem also includes the line *primaque Romanos docui contendere Graiis*, "I was the first woman to teach the Romans to vie with Greeks [in writing in these meters]," 8; a Renaissance editor emended *Romanos* to *Romanas*, causing this writer to attribute to Sulpicia a claim to have led the way for other Roman women writers. Note how the word depends on the editor, the claim depends on the later imitator, the original poetry of Sulpicia is gone, the writings of "Roman women" lie in the dream of a shadow.

So the hexameter satire attributed to Sulpicia tells us some things about her; more than nothing. Apparently references to Calenus, and to Egeria, were enough to serve as trademarks of her work. In addition, it seems possible that she wrote consciously as a woman to a female audience, and that this helped to determine the presence of the sisterly Muse and the hypothetical Roman women in the satire.[12] The list of rejected meters suggests quite strongly that these were meters in which the real Sulpicia wrote; the use of her persona to speak a satire suggests that her tone, if not her form, was compatible with satire. And, most of all, the fact that hers was an adoptable persona meant that some centuries after her death people still knew who she was. The writer of the satire could expect an audience to tie together an anti-philosophic emperor, Calenus, Egeria, a woman writer, and come up with the name not mentioned in the text itself: Sulpicia.

The cluster of references to Sulpicia herself in the fourth and fifth centuries CE confirms her reputation at that time. Not only does the commentator Probus think of her when reading the newly popular Juvenal; Ausonius, writing in the mid-fourth century, includes her in one of his own *apologiae*, along with a significant collection of male authors.[13] Ausonius's *Cento nuptialis* is an *epithalamion*, a wedding poem, in the form of a *cento*, a poem made up out of fragments of well-known hexameter verse—in this case, as commonly, Vergil's. However, in keeping with the conventionally ribald tone of the poem and the patchwork nature of the verse, Ausonius stitches onto his poem a prose introduction and conclusion, somewhat in the style of Menippean satire, which shifts back and forth from prose to verse. The conclusion is a tour-de-force combination of two apologetic themes from earlier satire: the claim that "my page is wanton, my life is chaste" and the list of eminent predecessors. Along with Sulpicia, Ausonius cites and/or describes Juvenal, Martial, Pliny, Apuleius, Cicero, Plato, Annianus (2nd c. CE), Laevius, Evenus, Menander, the comic poets, and finally Vergil, whose verse has after all provided all Ausonius's lines (he displays no knowledge of the obscene poetry attributed to Vergil). He quotes Martial's *lasciva est nobis pagina, vita proba* ("my page is sexy, my life respectable," 1.4.8), a line in which Martial himself is paraphrasing Catullus (16.5–6; Richlin 1992: 2). To parallel this, Ausonius says of Sulpicia, "Sulpicia's little book itches with lust, her brow does a goat"(*prurire opusculum Sulpiciae, frontem caperare*); this last odd phrase evidently refers to the frown conventionally said to be directed against such verse by the prudish (Richlin 1992: 10–11). We might compare Martial 10.64, in which he asks Lucan's widow Polla not to read his "sallies" (*iocos*) with "frowning brow" (*tetrica . . . fronte*, 2). This puts Sulpicia into the odd position of combined erotic writer/ straitlaced *matrona*, providing a hint perhaps of the divided mind a Roman would expect from a respectable woman who wrote erotic verse—again recalling Martial's *apologia* on her behalf at 10.35.

In the fifth century, Sidonius Apollinaris similarly inserts Sulpicia into a list, this time of poets he will *not* try to imitate—perhaps the longest *recusatio* in Latin, a poem of 346 hendecasyllabic lines. The first part of the poem

(*C.* 9.1–210) amounts to a catalogue of poetic topics which the poet will (not) describe. The second part (211–317) is a catalogue of 46 poets, mostly Roman, of whom only two are women—Sappho and Sulpicia. The immediate context in which Sulpicia appears marks her verse as erotic (9.259–73):

> Not Gaetulicus will here be read by you,
> not Marsus, Pedo, Silius, Tibullus,   260
> nor any sally (*iocus*) Sulpicia's Thalia
> wrote, sweet-talking stuff, to her Calenus,
> not the stiffness of Persius or the charm of Propertius,
> nor hundred-meter Terentianus.
> Lucilius is not here, nor Lucretius,   265
> not Turnus, Memor, Ennius, Catullus,
> Stella, nor Septimius, nor Petronius,
> nor Martial, endlessly biting,
> nor the one who, at the time of the second Caesar,
> lived at Tomis, forever unacquitted,   270
> nor the one who, in the end, in similar fall,
> at the light breeze of common talk
> became an exile over an angry actor.

The first two lines of this section are a direct borrowing from the introduction to Martial's first book of epigrams, in which he defends the explicit treatment of sexuality in poetry: *lascivam verborum veritatem . . . excusarem, si meum esset exemplum: sic scribit Catullus, sic Marsus, sic Pedo, sic Gaetulicus, sic quicumque perlegitur,* "I would make excuses for the sexy explicitness of my words, if I were setting the mode: but so writes Catullus, so Marsus, so Pedo, so Gaetulicus, so whoever is read all the way through" (discussed in Richlin 1992: 6–7). This section in Sidonius is clearly divided generically from the one that precedes it, which deals with epic and tragic poets; Sulpicia is surrounded, with few exceptions, by writers of epigram, elegy, and satire, in whom Sidonius sees something in common. Probably this is explicit erotic content; Lucretius must be there because of the section on sex at *DRN* 4.1030–1287 (on which see Gordon 2002). Moreover, although he focuses on the pleasantly amorous side of Sulpicia (*non quod Sulpiciae iocus Thaliae/ scripsit blandiloquum suo Caleno*), and associates her with the comic Muse, it is thought-provoking to find her in a list that also includes the decidedly raunchy Persius, Lucilius, Catullus, Petronius, Martial, Ovid, and Juvenal. And in this company Sidonius gives her two lines to herself, an honor he accords elsewhere in this section only to Ovid, Juvenal, and some later writers.

Finally, Fulgentius, writing later in the fifth century, mentions Sulpicia twice in the extraordinary introduction to Book 1 of the *Mitologiae*. The narrator, who calls himself Fulgentius, describes his flirtatious conversations with the Muse Calliope and her promises to him of further fun with her attendant, Satyra. The Muse in the end manifests herself like a vengeful Propertian Cynthia (1.23), and the whole prologue is marked by a blurring of lines between history and literature, source and text (among which are marked borrowings from the prologue to Apuleius's *Metamorphoses*). This is the context in which we read Fulgentius's references to Sulpicia. First, he claims for his work (1.4):

> *Neque enim illas Eroidarum arbitreris lucernas meis praesules libris, quibus aut Sulpicillae procacitas aut Psices curiositas declarata est. . . .*

Nor should you imagine that those lamps of the *Heroides* will lead the procession in my books—those lamps by which the wantonness of little Sulpicia or the curiosity of Psyche was shown forth. . . .

Here Sulpicia appears sandwiched between Ovid's *Heroides* and Apuleius's Psyche, probably reflecting her status as a figure written about as well as writing. Psyche's lamp shows up again later (1.20) as something to be rejected; what is interesting here is that Fulgentius equally associates Sulpicia with a *lucerna*. We might speculate that Fulgentius found this in Martial 10.38, and that Martial in turn found it in Sulpicia; even, possibly, since we have only one fragment on which to hang all our thoughts about Sulpicia, that the missing subject of *proferat* was *lucerna*. What is most important, this mention of Sulpicia's *lucerna*, with the epithet *Ausoniana* for her later in the prologue, assures us that both Fulgentius and Ausonius were talking about Sulpicia the satirist and not about Sulpicia the elegist.

Fulgentius's second mention of her continues the blurry association of Sulpicia with fictional characters. In a remarkable statement on satire, he writes (*Mitologiae* 1.23):

"You don't know," said [the Muse], "Fulgentius, crude neighbor of the Muses, how much respectable women (*matronae*) fear satire/Satyra. Granted that, before the verbal waves of women, lawyers (*causidici*) yield (*cedant*), schoolteachers (*grammatici*) can't make a peep, the pro-

fessor (*rhetor*) is silent and the auctioneer (*praeco*) shuts up his shout-
ing; [satire] is the only thing that puts a limit to their raving, even when
Petronius's Albucia is in heat.[14] Indeed when satire is mocking, the own-
ership of Plautine Saurea goes to sleep, and the gabbiness of Ausonian
little Sulpicia dies (*Sulpicillae Ausonianae loquacitas deperit*), and the
songful singing of Sallustian Sempronia grows hoarse, though Catiline
himself be present."

Here we find Sulpicia embedded in another literary-historical set piece. Fulgentius's attack on speaking women is modeled closely on Juvenal's dismissal
of female literati in the sixth satire (***cedunt grammatici***, *vincuntur* **rhetores**,
omnis/ *turba tacet, nec* **causidicus** *nec* **praeco** *loquetur*, 6.438–39)—Sulpicia
seems doomed to sneak through history arm in arm with her evil twin. Satire (here voiced through a double ventriloquism, Fulgentius's Muse speaking of her female proxy, Satyra) is said to silence women, even women who
silence men. The examples given are themselves embedded in texts: Albucia
in Petronius (this is her only testimonium); Artemona (angry wife, owner
of the slave Saurea) in Plautus's *Asinaria*; Sempronia, a real woman of the
late republic, in Sallust's history of the Catilinarian conspiracy—Sallust describes her as Catiline's co-conspirator, notorious for her cultural skills; and
Sulpicia in Ausonius. Though at least Sempronia and Sulpicia are described
in their texts as verbally gifted, and Artemona threatens her husband with
a beating at the end of her play, Fulgentius cuts them down to size in several ways. He combines fictional with real women; he describes them with
adjectives based on the names of male authors (*Petroniana, Plautinae, Ausonianae, Sallustianae*); and he chooses verbs that reduce their substance:
obdormit, deperit, raucescit, "goes to sleep, dies, grows hoarse." He speaks of
Sulpicia, here and above, using the familiar diminutive form, "Sulpicilla."

   Thus, although we might deduce from the string of mentions of Sulpicia
in late antiquity that her work was taken seriously at this time, the nature of
our last word of her prepares us for the subsequent silence.

An Unsuitable Job for a Woman

Overall, the outstanding fact about Sulpicia is the exceeding oddness of a
woman writing satire, or erotic iambics, in this culture. The whole structure
of Roman satire aims at the social subordination of women, among others
(chapter 2)—as Fulgentius explicitly says. It is striking that Ausonius and

Sidonius incorporate Sulpicia in lists that include Juvenal, Martial, Cicero, Plato, Apuleius; other such lists in Latin, the younger Pliny's for example, restrict themselves to male poets. Sulpicia here is distinctly a woman in the boys' club. We can see why a satiric text by a female author would have made readers uneasy; when Catullus and Petronius barely made it through the monasteries, we need not be surprised that a woman's text resembling the fragment we have would not have found space in the copying schedule.

Where would Sulpicia have gotten the idea that a woman *could* write like this? Virginia Woolf says, "We think back through our mothers if we are women." Perhaps it is not a coincidence that, of the few women writers in Latin whose names are even known to us, two have the same name. We might, then, expect to find in the work of Sulpicia the satirist a tribute to her famous predecessor. And perhaps, then, the voice of Sulpicia the satirist was something like the voice of Sulpicia the elegist at her most feisty: as, for example, when she is telling off her lover Cerinthus for preferring a "slut" to her ([Tibullus] 3.16.3–4); or when she flies in the face of all the rules of matronly decorum by claiming she prefers a good lover to a good reputation (3.13). This strongly asserted subjectivity tells us a lot. It tells us that, despite conditions of production that we have every reason to believe were highly daunting for a woman, female subjectivity and the desire and ability to present it were present in Roman culture. It tells us that the objectification of women in Roman elegy (cf. Wyke 2002; Fredrick 1997), the literary ventriloquism by which Roman male poets spoke instead of women, were noticed and countered by Roman women writers. Holt Parker (1994) has argued that two poems long attributed to a ventriloquist of the elegist Sulpicia were really by her, and that she there achieves the "revision and subversion" of "the masculine tradition of elegiac poetry."

Thus, following the first Sulpicia, Sulpicia the satirist is committing a double breach of barrier. Whereas the first Sulpicia both broke into a male job (writing) and a male genre (elegy), turning the lover's gaze back on a male object, the second Sulpicia broke into writing and into the position of Priapus. The savage and angry voice, the insolent spleen, that characterized her fellow satirists, seem also to have characterized her work.

For a woman to write at all is no longer a curiosity, though it has proved difficult for female humorists to break out of a pattern in which they themselves are the butt of the joke (see chapters 2 and 3). It is likewise possible that there were Roman women writers who stuck to safer paths and whose work was simply not considered important enough either to mention or to preserve. But a woman writing satire is different. To capture the transgressive force of Sulpicia's satires, we might compare in our own time the shock value of paintings by women artists that reclaim female subjectivity (Kent and Morreau 1985). For a woman to write of herself naked with her lover is, in Roman terms, a claiming of the male gaze. If both Sulpicias, along with Julia and the obscure Populia, talked about their sex lives, they testify to a certain amount of leeway in Roman culture. On the one hand, it conforms with ancient ideas of women's tendency toward lust that all these women writers take a stance that would now be identified within feminism as "sex-positive"; on the other hand, Sulpicia the satirist and Julia, along with the lost epigrammatist Cornificia and the Sempronia attacked by Sallust, were admired by male writers for their wit (see Stevenson 2005: 33–35, 44–48). Like Sappho, the poet most commonly invoked to connote "literary woman," they were not only writers but erotic writers. Considering the nature of Roman invective, it must have taken a lot of nerve to write like this—as Michelle Cliff put it, "claiming an identity they taught me to despise." As we turn to chapter 5, I wish we had Sulpicia's comments on Ovid's rapes.

If all this is true, what are we to make of the reading of Sulpicia offered us by Martial, her contemporary? We might believe his poem 10.35 to be special pleading. Judging by the only two lines of Sulpicia we have, it is also a spectacular case of misreading. The dainty language of girls and games, delights and naughtiness, does not well describe a woman who wrote of herself displayed "lying naked with Calenus."

But otherwise, there is very little we can say, because two lines are all we have. And so I would like to dedicate to Sulpicia a blank space of her own.

CHAPTER 5

Reading Ovid's Rapes

ॐ

Introduction

Marilyn Skinner became my co-conspirator and inspiration in the early 1980s, when she was teaching at Northern Illinois University. In 1985 I experienced the hospitality of DeKalb, Illinois, at first hand, and Marilyn, ever keen to clue me in, took me to see a screening of a new documentary, "Not a Love Story," which focused on the exploitation of women in the sex industry and on the objectification of the female body in popular culture. This film moved me to tears; it is easy now to shelve the preoccupation of late-1980s feminism with rape and pornography under the label "Sex Wars," easy to diminish it under an historical label—over, a phase—but my tears sprang from the recent death of a friend who had been raped and murdered, and I do not think the abuse of women is over.

In the 1980s, Second Wave feminism in the United States and Britain seized on pornography and rape as major issues to be dealt with by the movement. This action had profound consequences, proving to be highly divisive, as temperance had been for First Wave feminism in the 1800s; eventually feminists just got tired of arguing for and against pornography, and the idea of controlling it fell by the wayside. But in the late 1980s the topic was central; Sandra Joshel and I put together a session on rape and

Roman history at the Berkshire Conference in June 1987, and, egged on by Marilyn, I organized a WCC panel on pornography in ancient texts for the December 1987 APA. The original panel included Madeleine Henry, Molly Levine, Terri Marsh, and Robert Sutton; we went on as a collective to organize a volume of essays, and the call for papers netted (or extorted) proposals from a bemused archaeologist (Shelby Brown), an art historian turning to the then-still-little-explored topic of pederastic vase painting (Alan Shapiro), an historian of slavery turning here to historiography (Sandra Joshel), a rogue rhetorician dragged into the seamy depths of the ancient romance (Holly Montague), a specialist in Apuleius and staunch feminist (Helen Elsom), a brand-new PhD (Holt Parker), and a longtime veteran of the WCC (Bella Vivante, then writing as Bella Zweig)—also my future comrade in editing, Nancy Rabinowitz. As, in that time before e-mail, we read each other's papers and argued over the phone and at conferences, we developed an interpretation of ancient literature much darker than anything anticipated back at the 1985 WCC panel (see volume introduction), which, after all, had focused on the reappropriation of Ovid's poetry by feminist readers.

As "Reading Ovid's Rapes" was being written, a letter from Alan Shapiro appeared in the *New York Times* (November 8, 1987), pointing out that Ovid had recently been represented simultaneously on both the nonfiction bestseller list, for the *Ars amatoria*, and on the fiction list, for the *Metamorphoses* ("25 Years of University Press Best Sellers," October 11). Our work raised serious questions about what happens when texts like these are presented to students as canonical—questions still being asked (see James 2008; Kahn 2005); this issue was the subject of a panel led by Sharon James at the conference "Feminism and Classics 5" (2008), a round table led by Nancy Rabinowitz and me at the APA (2009), and a workshop led by Kathy Gaca and Lillian Doherty at the APA (2010). The introduction to *Pornography and Representation* lays out the arguments of the feminist critique of pornography; in a decade that has seen the explosion of pornography on the Internet, the proliferation of human trafficking, and the continued political use of the female body, the issue continues to be urgent (for recent bibliography, see Bumiller 2008).

The original idea for the essay was sparked by an invitation to speak on Ovid at Carleton University in 1986; I remain grateful to Leslie Cahoon, Mary-Kay Gamel, and Molly Myerowitz Levine for their great intellectual generosity in including me in their ongoing discussions of Ovid and putting up with my attacks on their beloved writer. "Reading Ovid's Rapes" entered into a conversation on Ovid and Roman elegy that already included many scholars and continues to draw new participants (see particularly the essays collected in Ancona and Greene 2005; Fear 2000; Fredrick 2002). The issues raised by Susanne Kappeler and the other theorists considered in the essay should remind the reader of the power grid written into Roman texts, especially now, when the principle prevails in Latin studies that the separation of textual persona from historical author governs the text's meaning, even in deeply misogynistic texts (see introduction to chapter 2).

Moreover, as demonstrated by the range of the essays in *Pornography and Representation in Greece and Rome*, the reader needs to get well off the beaten path in considering how a gaze conditioned by gender and the slave system operated within Roman culture. "Reading Ovid's Rapes" should be read while thinking about the conditions of production of drama and dance, along with the use of consumer goods decorated with images of women, in built environments decorated with images of women; Ovid's poetry should be compared not only with drama but with the novel and with texts like Athenaeus *Deipnosophistae*, a textual dinner littered with fragments of women (Henry 1992; McClure 2003). We need to read further, and more widely, and think about the part played by women themselves in a culture like this, at different times and places in an ancient Mediterranean that included many more than two cultures. We need to think more about how slavery conditioned sexuality.

It seems possible that Julia, granddaughter of Augustus, was associated with Ovid—both were exiled in 8 CE (see Fantham 2006: 111ff., and chapter 3 above): is his poetry about her? Did she hear it read? Is there a relation between the content of her mother's jokes and the content of his poetry? If, as I argue here, figures like Marsyas and Philomela recall Ovid's own exile, his own removal from speech, we might recall from chapter 3 that the elder Julia was said to have had sex near the statue of Marsyas. Did she and her daughter know Ovid's fellow poet, Sulpicia the elegist, who was the niece of Ovid's patron Messalla, the man who named Augustus *pater patriae*?

And were there slaves in the room to overhear all this poetry about rape, or to read it aloud, or to write it down from dictation? Was it about them, or might they have thought so? Jane Stevenson has revived the idea that the verse epitaph of a (freed) slave named Petale, or Sulpicia Petale, was written by Sulpicia the elegist; Petale was the dedicator's *lectrix*, her "reader-aloud" (2005: 42–44). The epitaph also notes that Petale, who died at the age of thirty-four, had a son; no father is named. The writer and enslaved war captive Parthenius wrote for the poet Gallus a little book of plots much like those in the *Metamorphoses*, suitable for making poetry out of—the *Erôtika pathêmata*—and we might take these plot lines to have some connection with his own broken life. Kathy Gaca's work re-marks the ancient landscape with the brutality of enslavement in war (2008, 2010, 2011, 2010–11).

"Reading Ovid's Rapes" is, in a way, another spin-off of *The Garden of Priapus*; although Ovid's rapes make no appearance in the book—not even those committed by Priapus in the *Fasti*— feminist theory on the pornographic does. Perhaps the most adequate theoretical models for Roman humor in *The Garden of Priapus* are those I found in a 1980 collection edited by Laura Lederer, *Take Back the Night*. This book was an early fusillade in the Sex Wars; at the time I took it to be about violent fantasy, which is basically what *The Garden of Priapus* is about. Reading all that invective as a first project made me aware of how sexual aggression pervades the structures of Roman society, and, as further reading has suggested, of many other societies. In the late 1970s and early 1980s, I had a subscription to the *National Lampoon*; it was not possible to read its pages alongside the *Carmina Priapea* without thinking that an explanation of the similarities required grand theory (see chapter 10). As I went on talking about pornography and rape in the early 1990s—with Gender Studies students and colleagues at USC, with students in the Law School at the time of the Anita Hill hearings, with feminists in Classics—it became clear that opinions both on the texts and on grand theory were divided, and today it is hardly even possible in the academy to espouse the concept of long-term historical continuities. I still think that if more people read invective, they would not be so averse to grand theory.

❧   ❧   ❧

You are the inspiration for a poet, he seemed to say. If you think you are being spied on, tell your parents. They will think you are silly and hysterical. They will tell you how great art is made.

Laurie Colwin, "A Girl Skating" (1982)

He gives kisses to the wood; still the wood shrinks from his kisses.
To it Apollo said, "But since you cannot be my wife,
you will surely be my tree."

Ovid, Metamorphoses 1.556–58 (Apollo and Daphne)

I don't particularly want to chop up women but it seems to work.

Brian De Palma (quoted in Pally 1984)

A woman reading Ovid faces difficulties. In the tradition of Western literature his influence has been great, yet even in his lifetime critics found his poetry disturbing because of the way he applied his wit to unfunny circumstances. Is his style a virtue or a flaw? Like an audience watching a magician saw a lady in half, they have stared to see how it was done. I would like to draw attention to the lady.

Consider Ovid's *Metamorphoses*, cast as a mythic history of the world: more than fifty tales of rape in its fifteen books (nineteen told at some length). Compare his *Fasti*, a verse treatment of the Roman religious calendar: eleven tales of rape in six books. These vary in their treatment; some are comic. In general, critics have ignored them, or traced their literary origins, or said they stood for something else or evidenced the poet's sympathy with women.

But we must ask how we are to read texts, like those of Ovid, that take pleasure in violence—a question that challenges not only the canon of Western literature but all representations. If the pornographic is that which converts living beings into objects, such texts are certainly pornographic. Why is it a lady in the magician's box? Why do we watch a pretended evisceration?

Critical Orientation

Before beginning to analyze the text, I offer some cautions and a theoretical framework.

Problems in writing: (1) The text I am writing is metapornography and partakes of the same subject-object relationship, the same "gaze," that structures its object. (2) Similarly, criticism and theory have been tools of patriarchy, and may not bolster the effort to subvert it—can perhaps not change anything (see Jehlen 1981; Kaplan 1983: 313; Lorde 1984). (3) To write about Ovid keeps the focus on the male writers of the canon. But this does not exclude ancient women: the nature of Ovid's rapes surely bears on the lives of the women who heard his poems and live(d) in the sign system that produced the canon (see chapter 2). One option is to do the best we can with the tools and materials at hand.

My goals are to hold up the content of some canonical texts to a political scrutiny and to suggest a theoretical model that enables escape from the trap of representation within hierarchy.

Axioms: Content is never arbitrary or trivial; content is not an accident of a text but an essential part of it. A text about rape may also be about something else, but it is still a text about rape. A seductive treatment is standard equipment for any fantasy; stylistic analysis does not replace content analysis and, in fact, leaves us to explain what the style is doing on that content, like a bow on a slaughterhouse.

Moreover, there is a reciprocal relationship between the content of the text and the lives of the text's consumers. Stylistic beauties serve to expedite the absorption of content by the audience, though the narrative structure directs audiences even without the stylistic adornment of high-culture texts—tragedy is to weep at, comedy is to laugh at, and so on. To resist the direction of narrative because of content is to break the rules; but such a breakdown in the perpetual motion of text and life is possible, even here, in the thick of metapornography.

My theoretical framework is fourfold:

Rereading in the Classics

As its name suggests, the discipline of Classics is not wide open to the idea of a re-formation of the canon. This has been true even for feminists in the field (see analysis in Skinner 1986, 1987a, 1987b). So even studies of Ovid by feminists (Myerowitz 1985; Verducci 1985) have kept their eyes focused on the magician rather than on the lady; others have set out to absolve the poet of his apparent sexism, concentrating on the distinction between poet and persona, and on the effect this has on the message of the text (Cahoon 1985; Hemker 1985).[1]

But such readings join the magician's act as he saws away. Erased from the field of vision: the price of admission, the place of male and female onstage, the experience of the magician's assistant, the voyeurism and gaze of the audience, the motivation of the magician himself, the blood that is not really dripping from the box. In order to confront the canon and explain what is going on in Ovid's act, we need other ways of reading.

Feminism for and against Pornography

The feminist controversy over the nature and danger (or use) of pornography contributes a basis for a political critique of texts like Ovid's. The argument against pornography holds that the common images of women contribute to the oppression of women (e.g., Echols 1983; Griffin 1981; Lederer 1980); the argument in favor of pornography has highlighted sadomasochism, both in fantasy and in reality, as a valid sexual mode, and/or claimed that violent images are cathartic and/or not harmful. The nonjudgmental stance coincides with the anthropologist's and the classicist's yearning for objectivity (see chapter 10). But these arguments again elide some questions. Why should sexuality and violence be so commonly connected? Represented? Can a person have a right to be physically abused? Is violence inevitable and uncontrollable? Do cultural or historical differences excuse anything?

Fantasy and Representation

Theories of representation, starting with the formulation of the gaze as male, trace the link between gender and violence (esp. Berger 1972; de Lauretis 1984; Kaplan 1983; Mulvey 1975). This position defines the pornographic as the source of both danger and pleasure, and as a model for all representation. Studies sometimes claim that the explicit content of a fantasy is not its meaning. Here, as E. Ann Kaplan has noted (1983: 320), there is a danger of losing sight of content altogether: "If certain feminist groups (i.e., Women Against Pornography) err on the side of eliding reality with fantasy . . . , feminist [literary] critics err on the side of seeing a world constructed only of signifiers, of losing contact with the 'referred' world of the social formulation."

Thus, analysis of Ovid's rapes as figures of the artist's predicament dodges some questions: Why is rape the figure of choice? What effects might this choice have on the audience?

Questions of complicity and origin arise in any discussion of culture-wide fantasy. What of the women in the audience? Is there a female gaze? Is gaze itself gendered, in a way separate from social gender? Whose idea is it to saw a lady in half? Any volunteers? Can specifically female fantasies be isolated? (This critique dates back to Mary Wollstonecraft.) It is possible to trace historical change (see, e.g., Thurston 1987); still, within the closed system of the patriarchy (what Audre Lorde called the "master's house"), women, as a muted group (Ardener 1975), can speak audibly only in the master's language, whether or not their speaking transmutes the language (as claimed, e.g., by Maclean 1987). This paradox was clearly outlined by

Xavière Gauthier in 1974: women can write either in men's language or in a language defined as womanish by men.[2]

Yet if, with the most radical critiques, we say "Art will have to go" (Kappeler 1986), where do we go? The problem here is the gap between our ability to analyze the problem and our ability to realize a solution.

Gender and Reading

Feminist literary criticism endeavors, in part, to come to grips with problems of gender and reading (so also Gubar 1987). Two of its strategies—canon re-formation and appropriation—are particularly pertinent to reading Ovid.

As Teresa de Lauretis says (1984: 107), "any radical critique [entails] a rereading of the sacred texts against the passionate urging of a different question, a different practice, and a different desire." Feminist critics advise readers to resist the text (Fetterley 1978), to read against the text, to misread or reread the text (Kolodny 1985), to reject the canon of Western literature and make a new one, or end canons altogether (Fetterley 1986; Kolodny 1985; Showalter 1985: 19–122). Three things to do with a lot of male-based texts: throw them out, take them apart, find female-based ones instead. (This critique goes back to *A Room of One's Own*.)

Another approach is of special interest; our prefeminist sisters had it as their only option other than silence or co-optation. This is the appropriation of male-based texts—becoming, in Claudine Herrmann's phrase, *voleuses de langue*, "women thieves of language" (or "of the tongue"), taking myths and looking at them in a different way (Ostriker 1985; see chapter 4). As it happens, a myth of Ovid's has seemed important to steal: Philomela, raped, her tongue cut out, weaving her story to her sister who had thought her dead; Philomela, who may have become the nightingale. Her story has been claimed by a male critic as the voice of poetry (Hartman 1970) and reclaimed by a feminist as a paradigm of woman writer and reader (Joplin 1985); claimed by Virginia Woolf in *Between the Acts* and reclaimed by her feminist reader (Marcus 1983, 1984). The misreading of texts here is deliberate, heroic; as Patricia Joplin says (1985), "We have a rescue to perform. Those who gave us the sad news that we had no sister lied to us." But we realize just how heroic an act the rescue of myths must be when we look at how Philomela and her sisters are known to us.

Gazing at the Text

Texts are inseparable from their cultures, and so, before looking at Ovid's rapes, we need a context. We know that Ovid was a popular writer; law students emulated his rhetorical tricks, schoolboys read his stories (Bonner 1949; 1977: 217). How might Ovid's rapes have fit in with the cultural experience of his audience?

We know that great numbers of people attended theatrical shows and wild beast "games" that exhibit some of the same traits as Ovid's writing: portrayal of sexual scenes from Greek myth, especially in the polymorphous theater of the pantomime (Lada-Richards 2007, 2013); savage and gruesome deaths (Barton 1993; Coleman 1990). Wealthy people adorned their houses with representations of such scenes (Brown 1992; Fredrick 1995; Myerowitz 1992). The practice cases of the rhetorical schools where Ovid was trained often dealt with rape and violence (Bonner 1949; see chapter 1). Roman humor is full of rape; a series of first-century comic poems focuses on the god Priapus, who graphically threatens male and female thieves with rape (Richlin 1992; see chapter 2). And in Pompeii archaeologists have found phallic wind chimes, birdbaths, statues of Priapus, phallic paving stones (Grant 1975; Johns 1982). Roman law on rape was ill-defined, real cases rarely attested, and the victim was blamed (Dixon 1982; Fantham 1991; Gardner 1986: 117–36; Joshel 1992a). All slaves were, more or less, the sexual property of their owners; on the other hand, in Ovid's Rome the new emperor Augustus was criminalizing extramarital sex with married women (see chapters 1 and 3).

Ovid's rapes play a significant role in his work. He was the last great Augustan poet, having outlived his more conventional coevals, and he wrote prolifically; here I will look at sections of only three of his works, though my analysis could well be extended (see chapter 6). In the *Metamorphoses*, rape keeps company with twisted loves, macabre and bloody deaths, cruel gods, cataclysms of nature (the Flood, Phaethon's fire), wars, and, of course, grotesque transformations. Rapes (some Ovid's) fill Arachne's tapestry in Book 6, and, like threads in a tapestry, the themes in the poem run in and out of sight; sometimes a horror in a half-line, sometimes half a book, sometimes gone. The rapes in the *Fasti* adorn the etiologies of Roman religious festivals, while the two in the *Ars amatoria* contrast with the normal suavity of the narrator's advice. But the poems overall share a certain point of view, and the rapes capture its essence.

The Metamorphoses: *Rapes and Transformations*

Daphne's Fearful Beauty

The attempted rape of Daphne by Apollo, one of Ovid's best-known passages, is almost the first event in the poem after the Flood. At once the narrative directs the reader's gaze. Daphne begins the episode as a nymph and ends as a laurel tree; in between, she flees from the god, who appears ridiculous and fails to rape Daphne as a nymph, although in the end he has his way with her when she is a tree. But look at Daphne in her flight (1.525–30):

> As he was about to say more, the daughter of Peneus, in a frightened
> rush,   525
> fled from him, and left his uncompleted speech, along with him.
> Even then she looked [literally *visa (est)*, "was seen"] pretty; the winds
> laid bare (*nudabant*) her body,
> and the gusts that met her fluttered her clothing as it tried to resist
> (*adversas*),
> and the light breeze made her locks go out behind her as it hit them
> (*impulsos*),
> and her beauty (*forma*) was increased by her flight.[3]   530

Evidently your looking at her is the point. Does the fact that the narrator's voice is not identical with the voice of the historical Ovid undercut this? Is this just the viewpoint of the buffoonish god? Hardly; glazed thinly, if at all, by its literary mechanisms, there is Daphne's body. The display itself is subtly violent, as the very air that surrounds the running woman anticipates the violence she fears: *nudabant, adversas, impulsos.* Ovid liked this trick; he says of Leucothoë during her rape, "fear itself became her" (*M.* 4.230); of Europa, "and fear itself was a cause of new beauty" (*Fasti* 5.608); of the Sabines, "and fear itself was able to adorn many of them" (*Ars amatoria* 1.126); of Lucretia, spied on by her future rapist, "this itself was becoming; her chaste tears became her" (*Fasti* 2.757). The display of the woman's body and fear to her rapist-to-be (and reader) often precedes her rape; Arethusa, who flees her rapist naked, is made to testify: "because I was naked, I looked readier for him" (5.603). Leo Curran (1978) argued that the narrator's consciousness of the victims' fear shows his empathy for them; but the narrator stresses how visually attractive the disarray of flight, and fear itself, made the victim (see Joshel 1992a).

Philomela's Tongue

Ovid's rapes are not sexually explicit, shifting the focus to the buildup and aftermath. No such limits hamper the poem's use of violence, which thus sometimes stands in for the sexual, as most vividly in the story of Philomela (*M.* 6.424–674; see Liveley 2011: 73–76).

Ovid begins the tale when Procne, daughter of the king of Athens, marries the barbarian Tereus. They go off to Thrace, and Procne duly bears a baby boy, Itys. Five years pass; then Procne wants to see her sister, Philomela. Tereus goes down to Athens to fetch her, gazes at her, and lusts after her; he wishes he were Philomela's father, so he could fondle her (475–82); and he fantasizes about the body that lies beneath her clothes (490–93). On the ship back to Thrace, he cannot take his eyes off her (516–18), and this is emphasized by an animal simile in which Philomela is a rabbit, Tereus an eagle (518): "there is no flight for the one captured, the captor (*raptor*) watches (*spectat*) his prize." In Thrace, he takes her, not to her sister, but to a hut in the woods, where he rapes her; throughout this scene, he is the subject of all the verbs, she is the object, except where the verbs signify fear (*tremit, horret, timet,* 527, 530). Indeed, the poet here uses a technique that will later (555–56, 639–40) describe other significant objects, as he turns Philomela into an object with a cluster of modifiers: *pallentem,* "growing pale"; *trepidam,* "trembling"; *cuncta timentem,* "fearing all things"; *cum lacrimis ubi sit germana rogantem,* "asking with tears where her sister was" (522–23). At this point she can still speak. The rape itself takes only two lines, the action being expressed in two words, *vi superat* ("he overcomes by force," 525); it is not sexually explicit, but when Philomela is next compared to an animal, she is a lamb wounded by the wolf's mouth, a dove with feathers bloodied by greedy talons. The reader is reminded that she had been a virgin.

After the rape, Philomela makes a long and rhetorically polished speech; as we will see, the ability to speak under torture recurs in the poem, but here it provokes reprisals. Tereus's fear and anger at her threats are so strong that he cuts out her tongue (549–60):

> After the wrath of the wild tyrant was stirred up by such words,
> no less his fear, spurred on by either cause,   550
> he frees from its sheath the sword that was belted on him,
> and he forces her, having been grasped by the hair, with her arms bent
>   behind her back,
> to suffer bonds; Philomela was readying her throat

and had conceived a hope of her own death once she had seen the
   sword;
he, as [ ] was reproaching and calling out on the name of "father"   555
and struggling to speak while grasped by the forceps, her tongue—
he cut it out with his savage sword; the stump of the tongue flickers,
[ ]self [ ] lies and, trembling, mutters into the dark earth,
and as the tail of a mutilated snake will jump,
[ ] quivers, and, dying, seeks the trail of [ ] mistress.   560

Tereus's first action after the rape (551) is to remove the sword from its
sheath; an action parallel to the rape is about to take place. But here we get
details not given for the rape, with a list of further actions—by, as we gradually discover, three actors: Tereus, Philomela (who only bares her neck and
hopes for death), and Philomela's tongue. Tereus's next action as subject
(555) is "he ripped out" (557), and he acts on a single object heralded by
a remarkable cluster of modifiers: "reproaching" (555), "calling out" (555),
"struggling to speak" (556), "grasped by the forceps" (556). The surprise for
the reader is that the postponed object (indicated by [ ] in the text) is not
Philomela, as the feminine modifiers lead the reader to expect, but *linguam*,
"tongue" (556)—a feminine noun that here stands in for the feminine victim both grammatically and literally.

The action now belongs to the tongue itself: 557, *radix micat* (the flicker-
ing stump of the tongue, like a clitoris, makes Philomela's ruined mouth a
simulacrum of her ruined genitals); 558, *ipsa iacet*, "herself, she lies there"
(like a person, a victim of violence); 558, *terraeque tremens inmurmurat
atrae* (the tongue itself makes its own speech; note the effect of the repeated
t's and *r*'s—when you read the line aloud, you have to move your tongue);
560, *palpitat*, "she quivers" (recalling, with "trembling" [558] the verbs of
earlier clusters associated with Philomela [522–23, 527–30]). Finally, dying
as Philomela cannot, the tongue like the snake's tail seeks the body of which
it once had been a part.

What are we to make of "muttering into the dark earth" and the comparison to a snake? This image complex is more familiar from the *Eumen-
ides*—a woman, the earth, darkness, the snake (often opposed as a sign to
the eagle, here associated with Tereus). Earlier, Procne's marriage had been
attended by the Furies; later, the two sisters turn into Fury-like creatures
(esp. 595, 662). The "dark earth" tallies with the dark night within human
beings (472–74, 652), and with the locus of the crimes committed in this
tale—against Philomela in the hut in the deep forest, and soon against Itys

in the depths of the house (638; cf. 646, "the innards of the house [*penetra-lia*] drip with gore"). The stump flickers like a snake's tongue; the severed tongue, like a loyal slave woman, mutters (*inmurmurat*, 558) to the gods below on behalf of her mistress (*dominae*, 560).[4] The simile, so close to her mutilation, surprises the reader with a new view of Philomela—a snake rather than a lamb or dove. Is the text shifting its sympathies?

The end of the tale bears out this suggestion. Tereus keeps Philomela shut up in the hut, and rapes her occasionally, for a year. The narrator ex-presses surprise (*vix ausim credere*, 561). Philomela cleverly weaves an ac-count of her experience and sends the weaving to her sister by giving it to Procne's unknowing slave woman (578-80); her mouth "lacks an *index*" (574)—a telltale—so she must substitute the weaving, an *indicium* (578). Procne, reading Philomela's web as a "pitiable poem" about "her own" lot (582; see Gamel n.d.), is at first herself silenced (583–85); then she rushes out to rescue Philomela. First threatening to burn down the house with Tereus in it, or to cut out Tereus's tongue, eyes, and genitals, or to kill him, she chances on her revenge: Itys wanders in, and she stares at him, then says, "Oh, how you resemble your father" (620-22). The two sisters will butcher Itys, cook him, and serve him to Tereus for dinner. Marking the shift in the narrative's sympathy, when the sisters seize the boy, the poet describes him with an object cluster (639–40) like the ones used of Philomela and of her tongue earlier: *tendentem manus*, "holding out his hands"; *iam sua fata vi-dentem*, "now seeing his approaching end"; "*mater, mater*" *clamantem*, "cry-ing out 'mother, mother'"; *colla petentem*, "trying to put his arms around her neck." Philomela cuts his throat, and the two sisters serve him up for dinner. When Tereus calls for his son (*Ityn . . . accersite*, 652), Procne actu-ally makes a pun (655): *intus habes, quem quaeris*, she says—"You have the one you're looking for inside/Itys." Tereus calls on the *vipereas sorores*, the "snaky sisters" (that is, the Furies, 662) and jumps at the two sisters before him with his sword; they turn into birds with marks of blood on their feath-ers, while he turns into a bird with a spearlike bill.

So the sympathy the reader builds up for Philomela by the midpoint of the story is undercut, to a degree, by its ending.

Ovid's story of Philomela has been construed as a sympathetic and ac-curate picture of a rape and its aftermath, and of a reading of one wom-an's plight by a sister woman (Bergren 1983; Curran 1978; cf. Gamel n.d.; Joplin 1985; Marcus 1983, 1984). But something else is going on here. Ovid has shifted the focus of dramatic attention in this tale forward off the rape and backward off the metamorphosis, onto the scene of the cutting out of

Philomela's tongue. Is it decorum that makes the poet omit the details of the rape? If so, it is a decorum that allows him to show us what the inside of her mouth looks like with the tongue cut out of it. This is a conflation of violence with sex.

The cutting out of Philomela's tongue is the sort of set piece that was increasingly to characterize Latin literature in the first century CE (Williams 1978: 184–92). Her unexpectedly eloquent speech immediately after her rape, which seems to make the mutilation such a comment on speech and gender, is also the kind of anomaly Ovid plays with elsewhere; for example, Latona's speech to the farmers when she is too thirsty to speak (*M.* 6.349–59), or the clever speech that the satyr Marsyas makes as he is being flayed (*M.* 6.385–86). I second the critics who quote Dryden's comment on Ovid's Narcissus: "If this were Wit, was this a Time to be witty, when the poor Wretch was in the Agony of Death? . . . On these Occasions the Poet shou'd endeavour to raise Pity: But instead of this, *Ovid* is tickling you to laugh."[5] In fact the very source of this wit is the delighted incongruity of clever style with gruesome subject matter (cf. Verducci 1985).

The bodies of Philomela, Marsyas, and many others feed the magician's box. This poetry depends for its elegant existence on the display of violence: the flaying of Marsyas, the opening of Philomela's mouth.

Myrrha's Body

The cutting out of Philomela's tongue is a transformative point in the tale, turning her from object of violence to perpetrator; her literal metamorphosis at the end is abrupt and relatively unstressed. But Philomela's mutilation has much in common with the metamorphoses suffered by many victims in the poem, mostly female; for example, Daphne into laurel, Io into a cow, Callisto into a bear, Actaeon into a stag, Arachne into a spider, and many into trees (Phaethon's sisters, Dryope, Myrrha), pools (Cyane, Arethusa, Byblis), and statues (Phineus's men, Niobe). All lose the ability to speak with a human voice; if they have been turned into animals, their efforts to speak, resulting in grunts, and their horror at this, are recounted. A favorite tactic is to trace the metamorphosis step by slow step, particularly horrible in the case of Myrrha, whose metamorphosis into a tree encases her pregnant belly in wood (10.489–513): roots burst through her toenails, her skin "hardens with bark" (494), she voluntarily sinks her face into the uprush of wood (497–98), but her pregnancy advances and the birth splits her open, nor has she a voice with which to cry out (503–13). In the similar transformations of Phaethon's sisters and Dryope, one mother tries to pull the tree off her daughters and can only mutilate them (2.345–63); another, having herself unwittingly enacted a like mutilation (9.344–45), feels her breasts harden to her nursing child, and tells what that feels like, until the transformation closes her lips (9.349–93).

So the metamorphosis of women can be something special. In some cases, their previous beauty is grotesquely disfigured, and just those details are given that drive this home in Roman terms (Callisto's hairy arms, Io's comic bovine grin). In many cases, illicit sexuality is the catalyst for metamorphosis, and whereas a rape is normally not explicitly described, the text makes up for its reticence in the metamorphosis. It is as if there were an analogic or developmental relationship between rape and mutilation. Several women are transformed as a *punishment* for their rape (Io, Callisto, Medusa), and two are killed outright by their angry fathers (Leucothoë, Perimele).

The place of rape in Ovid's texts is thus one where pleasure and violence intersect. Fear is beautiful; violence against the body stands in for rape.

Salmacis's Desire

The only rape scene in the *Metamorphoses* that involves explicit physical contact also involves a major role reversal: the rape of Hermaphroditus, a beautiful boy of fifteen, by the naiad Salmacis (4.285–388). Her proposition to him makes him blush, "and to have blushed became him" (330)—fear again beautiful, here at some length (331–33). Salmacis then spies on the boy as he first dips his toes in her pool, then strips; her voyeurism here (340–55) rivals that of Tereus.

Bathing scenes recur as incitements to lust in the poem (see esp. Arethusa); they combine the innocence and tempting solitude of other favorite settings (picking flowers, sitting on the riverbank, wandering on the beach) with an opportunity to show the body naked. In this instance, both the rape victim and the (female) rapist strip down. Indeed, the passage overdetermines Salmacis's desire and marks its abnormality: not only does she burn, but her *eyes* burn, and they burn like the sun (Phoebus, a familiar rapist in the poem) reflected in a mirror, *opposita ... imagine* ("with opposed image," 349). She is a looking-glass rapist. The boy is compared (354–55) to an ivory statue or white lilies; her likenesses are not so nice. In a switch on the usual comparison of rapist to eagle or wolf, Salmacis is compared to a snake *attacking* an eagle, and (unique in the poem) to an octopus (361–64, 366–67).

The result of this rape is twofold: Salmacis and Hermaphroditus, in response to a prayer of hers, become joined into one creature, a hermaphrodite, who speaks with the boy's (dismayed) consciousness; and he prays that the pool will henceforth turn any man who swims in it into a *semivir*, a "half-man" or eunuch (386), and gets his wish.[6] Salmacis's body remains only as the female part of the new body, while her consciousness is gone; as so often in ancient tales, not what she prayed for.

Other women in the *Metamorphoses* pursue men out of excessive desire (the maenads, Byblis, Myrrha, Circe), never with good results. But here the poet experiments with a female who has all the trappings of the most forceful rapist, and the interchange of roles results in a permanent and threatening confusion of gender. We will see male rapists who dress as women, even a male raped because he is dressed as a woman, and these events turn out well; when a female acts male, the result is the unmanning of all men, and the narrative makes it clear that this is a bad thing (e.g., 4.285–86). A character in Book 12 shows what is at stake: Caenis, raped by Neptune and given a wish in return, replies (12.201–03):

> This injury produces a great wish
> now to be able to undergo (*pati*) no such thing; give that I not be a
>   woman—
> you will have given everything. . . .

In the world of the *Metamorphoses*, a sensible request. As we will see, to *try on* a female role is important for Ovid; but that role, like the trying on, has its limits.

Rapes in the Ars amatoria

It has been argued that the two scenes of rape in the light, witty *Ars* reflect Ovid's knowing use of an unreliable narrator, the *praeceptor amoris* ("teacher of love"), and that these scenes represent love that the *praeceptor* deplores (Myerowitz 1985: 66), or that the poet rejects (Hemker 1985). If so, how is it that he has used the same voice in the *Metamorphoses* and the *Fasti* as well? At least it is safe to say that the poet found this sensibility congenial.

The poem's attitude toward women has well been described as seeking control (Myerowitz 1985, 1992; compare Parker 1992a). In this setting, we find the rape of the Sabines and the tale of Achilles and Deidamia, texts that share with the rapes of the *Metamorphoses* the content that lies between the brackets of narratorial persona.

The Rape of the Sabines (*AA* 1.99–134)

At 1.99, the *praeceptor* sets up his account of the incident, so hallowed a part of Roman history, in terms of his own present and of the gaze. Women, he claims, now come to the theater to watch and be watched. The tale of the Sabines is adduced as an *aition* (origin story) for this putative phenomenon; the setting of the rape in the theater is Ovid's innovation and suggests he is not just telling a story but staging a scene. At 109, the *praeceptor* begins his description of the mass kidnapping:

> [Romulus's men] look around, and each marks for himself with his
>   eyes the girl
>   whom he wants, and with silent heart they plan many things.   110
> [And while the performance was going on onstage, as the audience
>   began to applaud,]
>   the king gave the looked-for signal for loot to his people.
> At once they jump up, showing their hand with a shout,   115
>   and lay their greedy hands on the young girls.
> The way doves, the shyest flock, fly away from eagles,
>   the way the little new lamb sees the wolves and runs for it,
> so the girls feared the men, now rushing without restraint;
>   each turned color, none looked the way she had.   120
> For there was one fear, but not one face of fear:
>   some tear their hair, some sit there, out of their minds;
> one, sad, is silent, in vain another calls her mother;
>   this one complains, that one's struck dumb; one stays, another
>   runs;
> the captured (*raptae*) girls are led, marital loot,   125
>   and fear itself looked good on many of them.
> If one fought back too much and said no to her partner,
>   the man picked her up himself in his greedy arms,
> and said: "Why wreck those tender little eyes with tears?
>   What your father is to your mother, I'll be to you."   130
> Romulus, only you knew how to give your soldiers benefits;
>   if you give benefits like that to me, I'll be a soldier.

As in the Philomela episode, the men are here the subjects of action verbs, especially of the gaze (109); the women begin as objects of action. This situation is reversed in lines 117–26, but, like Philomela, the women act only to show fear. The simile of doves and lambs is similarly familiar, and was in fact a commonplace; so for Lucretia in the *Fasti* (below), and in Horace *Epodes* 12.25–26 (a cross-sex travesty, see chapter 2 above) and *Odes* 1.23 (to "Chloe"). In the climax of the scene (121–26), the narrator sketches the crowd of girls in a series of short subject-verb clauses. But the summary subject—"girls"—is in apposition with a concrete noun—"marital loot" (125)—and the actions these women perform again only mark their vulnerability.

These clauses are remarkable in Latin for the neatness of their construction, one figure balanced against the next by parison, chiasmus, and asyndeton, in the smallest possible space—Ovidian prestidigitation. By their brevity they achieve the effect of a miniature, with little figures mouthing inaudible cries and stamping inaudible feet. But we do not have to rely on aesthetics for a reading of the passage; the narrator tells us: "And fear itself looked good on many of them" (126)—the voice of the *praeceptor*, but also, as we have seen, that of the *Metamorphoses* and the *Fasti*.

At 127, the possibility of fighting back is conceded, but we know the women must be captured; the man's action and speech are indulgent, amatory, and paternalistic (128–30). He marks only her tears, annulling her resistance; carrying her off like a child, he talks of her "tender little eyes," as the poet Catullus does in a poem to his beloved as she weeps over a dead sparrow (c. 3).

Once again the narrator tells us how to read this, declaring that he would volunteer as a soldier himself if he could get such a reward (131–32)—recalling Ovid's beloved metaphor, *militat omnis amans*, "every lover is a soldier" (see Cahoon 1988). But metaphors often convey a literal perception, and a poet who sees love as comparable to battle might well see violence as part of love.

Remarkably, this passage has been read as a strong anti-rape statement by Ovid (Hemker 1985). The premise of the argument is that the *praeceptor* is so obviously wrongheaded that the reader sees the falsity of all he says, as if the whole poem were in quotation marks and the quotation marks nullified the content. Yet it is simultaneously argued that Ovid's description "sympathetically conveys the horror of the situation"; the climactic vignette of the women in flight shows "the women's perspective" (45).

Such a reading ignores the tone of the passage: the women's fear is displayed only to make them more attractive. We have this myth, too, in comedies and action romances (squeaky voice: "Put me down!"); it is part of the plot. Indeed, in the 1954 movie musical *Seven Brides for Seven Brothers*, based on Stephen Vincent Benét's story "The Sobbin' Women," the brothers sing a song about the Sabines. Reception here does not alter the meaning of the original: for Ovid's Sabine women, there is really nothing to be worried about, because they are getting married ("What your father is to your mother, I'll be to you"—compulsory heterosexuality in action). Their fears are cute (see Modleski 1982: 46), and the whole thing is a joke. Again the text uses women's fear as its substance (see Myerowitz 1985 on the female as *materia* in the *Ars*). There are indeed quotation marks around the text, the marks that tell the reader "this is amusing"; they act, however, not to attack the content, but to palm it off.

Achilles and Deidamia (*AA* 1.663–705)

Toward the end of Book 1 of the *Ars amatoria*, the *praeceptor* illustrates his contention that no means yes (663–80) by telling the story of Achilles and Deidamia. He has been arguing that the lover should mix kisses with his wheedling words (663), whether or not the woman wishes to kiss him (664). If she fights and calls the lover "naughty" (665), nevertheless "she wants herself to be conquered in fighting" (666). A man who has taken kisses and not "other things" (669) was not worthy even to get the kisses (670). Once he got the kisses, how close he was to his "full desire" (671); such hesitance was not *pudor* ("modesty/chastity") but *rusticitas* ("acting like a hick"), the *praeceptor*'s bane (672). Then he generalizes (673–78):

> You may call it *vis* [rape/force]; that *vis* is welcome to girls;
> "unwilling," they often wish to have given what's pleasing.
> Every woman violated by the sudden seizing of sex   675
> rejoices, and "naughtiness" does them a favor.
> But a woman who has departed untouched, when she could have been forced,
> though she simulates gladness with her face, will be sad.

Women's emotions are consistently unreal throughout this passage—"unwilling" (674) must describe a feigned emotion; "naughtiness" (676) must represent a feigned scolding as in 665; even their facial expressions are artificial (678). The pupil is to believe that women do have emotions with which to enjoy the experience, but there is apparently no way to tell for sure. What *does* a woman want? The deletion of women's voice here is even more thorough than in the tale of Philomela.

At this point, reaching for mythic justification, the *praeceptor* briefly instances the rape of the daughters of Leucippus, who are said to have enjoyed it (679–80; see Sutton 1992), and then launches into his illustrative set piece. Having sketched the beginning of the Trojan War in six lines, he takes the same time to show us the young Achilles in drag, disguised as a girl on the island of Skyros. Still in drag, the boy becomes a rapist. He is put in to room with the royal princess, "by chance" (697), and—*voilà!*—*haec illum stupro comperit esse virum*, "she knew him to be a man by means of rape" (698), *stuprum* apparently the acid test. The *praeceptor* goes on to hint that it was no rape at all (699), saying that she desired it (700) and begged Achilles, now in armor and hurrying off to war, to stay (701–4). *Vis ubi nunc illa est?* he asks, smirking—"Where's that 'rape' now, eh?" (703). He concludes, "You see, as it's a matter of *pudor* for her to begin certain things first, thus it's pleasing to her to undergo them (*pati*) when another begins" (705–6). His point is that *pati*—"to suffer," "to be passive," "to be penetrated sexually"—is pleasing to women, and this is the mark of the woman, as *vis*, "force," is the mark of the man (see Parker 1992a). When we want to know the gender of the adolescent hero dressed in women's clothing, the signifier of his maleness is his ability to commit rape. Ovid was to repeat the idea of transvestite rape several times in the *Metamorphoses* (4.217–33, 11.310, 14.654–771), most notably when Jupiter, disguised as Diana, embraces Callisto and *nec se sine crimine prodit*—"does not thrust out/reveal himself without crime" (2.433); gender revelation equals penetration.

These two passages from the *Ars amatoria* deploy both the eroticization of women's fear and the objectification of women. Whereas *pati* is repugnant to men, here *pati* is women's nature, and they enjoy it (but contrast Caenis). As in New Comedy, the outcome of rape is happy.[7] Happy endings do occasionally appear in the *Metamorphoses*, for example, for Orithyia and Boreas, immediately after Philomela; they marry, and Orithyia has twins (see Modleski 1982: 35). Happy endings sometimes appear in the *Fasti* as well. But note again the intersection of pleasure with violence, now with fun in place of pain (Richlin 1992: 156–58). The erasure of female subjectivity is complete; the poem presents the female reader with no exit (see chapter 2 above).

Rape in the Fasti: *Comic Relief*

The rapes in the *Fasti* are a mixed bag. Three (1.391–440, Priapus and Lo-tis; 2.303–58, Faunus and Omphale/Hercules; 6.319–48, Priapus and Vesta) are comic: a rustic and ithyphallic god attempts to rape a nymph/Amazon/goddess in her sleep, and is interrupted in comic fashion before he succeeds. Three rapes (5.193–206, Chloris and Zephyr; 5.603–20, Europa and Jupiter; 6.101–28, Crane and Janus) have fortunate outcomes: Chloris mar-ries Zephyr and becomes the goddess Flora, Europa names a continent, and Janus gives Crane a goddess's power over all house boundaries. The rape of Callisto, a repeat from the *Metamorphoses*, is passed over in a phrase or two, as the narrative dwells on her punitive transformation (2.153–92; see John-son 1996). Another rape (2.583–616, Mercury and Lara) is also punitive, but ends well, since Lara gives birth to twins, the Lares Compitales who guard Rome's boundaries. Finally, three rapes are connected with Rome's mythic history: the stories of Lucretia (2.723–852), Rhea Silvia (3.11–48), and the Sabine women, part II (3.187–234). Rhea Silvia and Lucretia, like the comic victims, are asleep as their rapists approach (cf. in the *Metamor-phoses* only Thetis—who, however, also has to be tied down—and Chione); Lara has had her tongue ripped out, and Lucretia is repeatedly said to be dumbstruck. Through rape, Crane and Lara assume the guardianship of boundaries; Chloris/Flora gives Juno the power to bear a child without a father. Common elements, then, are the powerlessness of the women and the potential for unlocking that results from their penetration; hence the catalytic function of the historical women (see Joshel 1992a). Like the Vir-gin Mary, they are lowly creatures whose very humility and penetration foster the creation of power.

As in the *Metamorphoses*, these rapes have Hellenistic models; the model, however, is the poet's choice, and footnotes do not cancel content any more than narrative structures do. These rapes echo the rapes of the *Metamorphoses* and *Ars amatoria* and provide us with a new element: a paradigmatic structure.

Rape as a Joke

The three comic rapes are peculiar in that they are almost identical and seem to be Ovid's invention (see Fantham 1983); Priapus's attempted rapes of Lotis in Book 1 and of Vesta in Book 6 are the same in all but name. The shared elements are summed up in Table 1.

Table 1. Comic Rapes in Ovid's *Fasti*

Common features	Lotis (1.391–440)	Omphale (2.303–58)	Vesta (6.319–48)
Marked as comic tale		*Antiqui fabula plena ioci* (304)	*Multi fabula parva ioci* (320)
Women provide visual stimuli.	Scantily clad naiads reveal bits of their bodies (405–10).	Omphale goes walking with Hercules, alluringly clad (*aurato conspicienda sinu*, 310).	
Rustic gods look and are excited.	Satyrs, Pan, and Silenus are aroused by the nymphs (411–14); Priapus wants Lotis.	Faunus sees Omphale and Hercules and falls for her at once.	Priapus, who has been chasing nymphs and goddesses, sees Vesta (335).
An idyllic party is in progress.	A Bacchic rout in a forest glade	Hercules and Omphale go into a cave, switch clothes, feast, and go to sleep.	Party hosted by Cybele, including drinking, dancing, and wandering the valleys of Ida.
The woman targeted goes to sleep	Lotis, at the edge of the group	Omphale, in her bed in the cave	Vesta, in the grass
The rustic god approaches stealthily	Long description of silent approach on tiptoe	Long description of Faunus searching through the cave	Priapus approaches with careful steps (337–38).
Details of the rape attempt	Priapus balances himself (429) and pulls off Lotis' covers from the feet up (431); his erection is described later.	Faunus climbs onto Hercules' bed, misled by cross-dressing; his erection described (346); pulls up Hercules' dress from the feet up; surprised; tries "other things" (345–50).	*ibat, ut inciperet* ("he was going up to her to begin")
Sudden alarm	Silenus's ass brays.	Hercules wakes up and dumps Faunus.	Silenus's ass brays.
Discovery	Lotis runs away; Priapus exposed.	Faunus exposed in light	Vesta gets up; all gather. Priapus runs away.
Everybody laughs.	All laugh at Priapus and his erection (437–38).	All laugh at Faunus (355–56).	

The poet clearly marks these stories as jokes, with labels or narrative elements ("everyone laughed") or both. Note the element of visual stimulus in the two longer tales: the nymphs show their breasts, legs, and naked feet through openings in their clothing (1.405–10); Omphale's fancy clothes leave her "well worth looking at for her gilded bosom" (2.310). All three tales remark the gaze of the potential rapist. But more, the voice of these women is one that is "asking for it." The circumstances allow license; most curious is the intimate dinner in the cave (a location marked as both ritual and bucolic), with its cross-dressing (both traditional and ritual) which turns the rape of Omphale into the rape of Hercules.[8] The poet gives a detailed description of Hercules in Omphale's clothing, bursting the seams with his huge body (2.318–24); the scene reverses Achilles' transvestite rape of Deidamia. The targeted woman falls asleep, but attention is focused on the god's stealthy approach. Slowly he comes, step by step . . . he pulls the covering up from the bottom . . . we hold our breath; this is the technique of the striptease (or of the horror story, or of the Hellenistic love charm, see Winkler 1990b), highly erotic, and the reader is seduced into the scenario. As Elaine Fantham points out, such scenes were common in Roman wall painting (1983: 198–99). The explicit descriptions of the god's erection embody the source of the narrative's desire—Faunus is assimilated to Priapus (2.346). Alarm, discovery, everyone laughs; the sight of the tumescent god in mid-rape is the primal scene of comedy.

The Comic Structure Dressed Up

This comic structure recurs, surprisingly, in punitive and historic rapes in the *Fasti*, notably those of Lucretia, Rhea Silvia, and Lara.

Ovid's version of the Lucretia story follows the account in Livy's history of Rome (1.57–59; see Joshel 1992a), but changes the focus significantly. Livy puts Lucretia *in medio aedium*, "in the middle of the hall" (1.57.9); Ovid puts her, with her wool baskets, *ante torum*, "next to the bed" (2.742)—elliptically, the *lectus genialis* that stood in the *atrium* as a symbol of marriage, and then again, a bed. Along with the men, the reader spies on her there and overhears her worrying about her husband (2.741–58). The narrator likes to see her cry: "this itself was becoming: her chaste tears became her" (757)—like Daphne's fear, like the Sabines' fear. The narrator describes her beauty (763–66), and then, like Tereus, Tarquin gloats in his memory on the details (769–74)—again an expansion by Ovid of Livy's two-line account (1.57.10). Her crowning attraction is *quod corrumpere non est*, "that it is not possible to seduce her" (2.765).

The staging of the rape enacts its meaning. Tarquin enters—*hostis ut hospes init penetralia Collatini*, "enemy as guest, he goes into the house/ innards of Collatinus" (787); en route to Lucretia's room (793), he "frees his sword from its sheath"—like Tereus after the rape (*M.* 6.551), like Cinyras after his daughter seduces him (*M.* 10.475).

The rape itself includes physical details unusual for Ovid except in the comic rapes (794–804). Tarquin presses Lucretia down on the bed (795); she feels his hands on her breast, "then for the first time touched by a stranger's hand" (804). Lucretia is compared to a lamb *lying under* a wolf (799–800). The narrative presents her mute thoughts, and her difficulties with speech continue in the scene that follows the rape (823–28); the narrator tells us that the need to retell her experience feels to her like a further assault by Tarquin. The physical details of her suicide are strikingly emphasized: she falls *sanguinulenta*, "bloody" (832), rather than simply *moribunda*, as in Livy; Brutus pulls the dagger from her "half-living" body (838); her corpse shows her approval by moving its eyes and hair; and, the last we see of her, her wound (not just her body) is being exhibited to arouse the populace—*volnus inane patet*, "her gaping wound lies open" (849). She ends as she began, as object of the gaze. As in the comic rapes, the viewer/voyeur sees, burns, and acts; in the tragic version, we get to see the woman die as well. We even get to see inside her wound, as inside Philomela's mouth. (Indeed, the poet moves from this episode to a brief allusion to Procne and Tereus, 853–56.) This version is not a send-up, like the rape of the Sabines in the *Ars amatoria*, and yet the historic *exemplum* has been sensualized.

Familiar elements recur in the rape of the Vestal Virgin, Rhea Silvia, by the god Mars (3.11–48), which resulted in the birth of Romulus, founder of Rome. We see her tripping down the path to fetch water; she sits on the riverbank; she opens the front of her dress (15–16) and pats her hair. Then she falls asleep in her idyllic surroundings. Mars sees her, desires her, and has her (21), and she wakes up pregnant (23)—"for, to be sure, the founder of the Roman city was within her guts" (*intra viscera*). Why does she have to open the front of her dress?

Like Philomela's, Lara's story involves not only rape but also the punishment of sisterhood through silencing and mutilation. The story is given to explain who the *dea Muta* ("mute goddess") is (2.583), so presumably Lara is to be elevated to divine status; this is not narrated. What is told is that the naiad Lara, known for her loquacity, has warned the nymph Juturna that Jupiter intends to rape her (603–4) and has also told Juno (605–6). To punish Lara, Jupiter rips out her tongue and gives her to Mercury, conductor of souls, to be taken down to live "with the ghosts in Hades, as the proper place for those who are silent" (609). En route they pass through a grove, where the mutilated Lara excites Mercury's lust: "she is said then to have pleased the god, her guide" (612). He "gets ready" for rape (613, *vim parat*, a recurrent phrase in the *Metamorphoses*). She tries to plead with him but cannot: *voltu pro verbis illa precatur, / et frustra muto nititur ore loqui*, "she begs with her face in place of words, / and in vain she struggles to speak with mute mouth" (613–14); speaking line 613 makes your mouth work, while the mimetic effect of 614 can be compared with that of *M.* 6.558, Philomela's tongue muttering into the ground. The instant result is that she becomes pregnant with twins who turn out to be the Lares Compitales (615–16)—the happy ending.

Familiar here are the incitement to lust inherent in the woman, the bucolic setting that serves as license, and the postponement of rape with compressed reference to male arousal (*vim parat*, both elliptical and insistent). In this case the postponement comes not from the tease of the rapist's stealthy approach but from the efforts of a woman who is both speaking and silent, like someone attempting to speak in a dream: terror made voluptuous. What is the reader to make of this? No stage directions are given, but the story is ostensibly in the poem to explain the Roman calendar—to show why, on the day of the Feralia, the day of the dead, an old woman sits among girls and performs an elaborate ritual for *Tacita*, "the silent one" (2.571–82, see chapter 7); also to illustrate the calendar—Lara is Miss February 21, setting up for Lucretia, who is Miss February 24. As with calendar pictures, as in the Callimachean *aitia*, the calendar is in fact there as an excuse for the illustration. And when the author has substituted Lara's terrified gasping for the striptease of the comic rapes, can we not recognize that both are presented for the reader's pleasure? The muting and mutilation of Lara, like Philomela's, propel a story not her own.

Rape: The Insertion of Theory into the Text

To deal with these texts, I now present three theoretical models, in search of one that might offer a way out of the trap of representation.

The Pornographic Model: Rape Is Rape

Content analysis allows us to see past the legerdemain of style. As Laurie Colwin's poet points out in the first epigraph to this chapter, "great art" shares its mechanisms with pornography. The episodic structure, the elision of the act of rape, and the physical cruelty of the *Metamorphoses* recall Angela Carter's analysis of Sade, especially of the scenarios of *Justine* (Carter 1978: 39); Ovid's endless supply of innocent nymphs prefigures Justine's picaresque resilience (44), as the dissolution of bodies in metamorphosis prefigures the fantasies of the Freikorps men discussed by Klaus Theweleit (1987: 171–204). When Susan Griffin says of the pornographer, "He gives woman a voice only to silence her" (Griffin 1981: 40), can we not apply this to Philomela? Lara? Lucretia?

We must be conscious of these poems not only as texts that are read but as texts that are taught. The scholarly custom of referring to scenes of rape as "the loves of the gods" has been well dealt with by Eva Keuls (1993: 43–55); Zola Packman (1993) titled her essay on translations of Roman comedy "Call It Rape." A class of students, among whom in all likelihood there is at least one person who has been raped, cannot be expected to regard these texts as unproblematic. When this happens it is a reinscription of rape, an endorsement of it.[9]

The pornographic model, then, allows us to take Ovid's rapes literally; to realize that they are, if not the whole text, an important part of it, not to be ignored; and to consider what we want to do with a canon that includes many such texts, finally weighing their hurtfulness in with their beauty. We want a way out. But then we must keep faith with history. Maybe the Marquis de Sade should not get so much credit for initiating modern sensibility; maybe history provides no way out. The average inhabitant of Rome enjoyed watching spectacles in real life that Sade could only enjoy in his imagination. We must recall that to a Roman of the literary class, a story about a raped woman with a Greek name would have a peculiar resonance, suggesting not only the abstract figures of Greek erudition but the looted marble figures in his garden, the enslaved (= sexually accessible) and living figure serving him dinner. Or serving her dinner.

The Cross-Sex Fantasy Model: To Rape Is to Be Raped

Et qui spectavit vulnera vulnus habet.
[And a man who has seen wounds has a wound.]

Ovid AA 1.166

The question of the experience of Ovid's audience raises the possibility that the pornographic model is incomplete. If, as theorists of fantasy argue, subjectivity oscillates, could Ovid have provided, even enjoyed, a female subjectivity? Before I consider what good this would do the (female) reader, I need to establish how it might have been possible in Ovid's world.

The construction of Roman sexuality and textuality included two pertinent features. First, Roman men of the literary class often professed a complex sexual orientation (Richlin 1992, esp. 220–26). Normative adult male sexuality, as expressed in love poetry, gossip, and political invective, took the form of attraction to both women and adolescent males. Freeborn adolescents, though in principle off limits, were at least conscious of their attractiveness to older men, and there was no lack of slave boys; all males, then, went through a phase in which they were the object of the gaze and knew it. Attraction of adult males to other adult males, however, was, in these texts, considered loathsome; adult males were not supposed to be the object of anyone's gaze. Being penetrated (*pati*) was seen as a defilement of the body, which illuminates the claim, discussed above, that women enjoyed it; the younger Seneca describes women as *pati natae*, "born to be on the receiving end" (*Ep. mor.* 95.21). We recall Caenis; the *Fasti* narrator says of Callisto's rape, "she underwent Jupiter against her will" (*invito est pectore passa Iovem*, 2.178).

Our sources on the construction of Roman women's sexuality are too indirect and fragmentary to tell us much; women were expected to marry, often in their teens, and might well divorce and remarry (see chapters 1, 3, 4, 7, 8).

Second, the theater at Rome in Ovid's time (Lucian *On Dancing* 34) included an extremely popular form, pantomime, in which a male dancer was the central figure, often playing a woman. A line of musicians and singers sang the story in Greek, and a second actor played any necessary minor characters; the first dancer was the star and danced all the main roles (hence *panto-mimus*) of the play.

Pantomime sets Ovid's rapes in 3-D. That it was so popular testifies to a special ambivalence in Roman culture, which commonly stigmatized dancing as effeminate (Richlin 1992: 92–93, 98; Corbeill 1997; cf. Pliny *Panegyric* 54.1). Meanwhile, the satirist Juvenal indicates that pantomimes in his day sometimes depicted the sexual misadventures of mythic heroines: Leda (6.63), Pelopea (who bore Aegisthus to her father Thyestes), and Philomela (7.92).

Gossip records that dancers were desired by the rich and famous (so of Sulla and Metrobius, Plutarch *Sulla* 36; Bathyllus and Maecenas, Tacitus *Annals* 1.54.3). Satire avers that women found the dance of rape sexually exciting (Juvenal 6.63–66):

When effeminate Bathyllus dances the pantomime Leda,
Tuccia can't control her bladder, Apula squeals,

as if in an embrace, suddenly, a wretched sostenuto.
Thymele pays attention; then rustic Thymele learns.

"Leda" would be the rape of Leda by Zeus in the form of a swan. Is the
male actor called effeminate because he is? Because he is dancing? Because
he is playing a woman? Because he is dancing a rape? Because he is dancing
a man/bird/god raping a woman? Does the women's purported reaction
have an objective correlative? We think of Visual Kei, of David Bowie, of
Mick Jagger in lipstick. That such a spectacle would have been considered
dangerous for a respectable young man to see is attested by a letter of Pliny
(7.24), in which he describes the situation in the house of Ummidia Qua-
dratilla: a racy old aristocrat, she considered her troupe of pantomime actors a good relaxation for herself, but she always sent her grandson away to
study when they were about to perform.

Was this any more to Ovid than part of his social milieu? It seems so.
The elder Seneca's rhetorical memoirs include a sketch of Ovid, the star
student, in his college days; Seneca ends by observing that "Ovid rarely de-
claimed *controversiae* [arguments], and only *ethicas* [ones involving character portrayal]; he much preferred *suasoriae*" (*Controversiae* 2.2.12). *Suasoriae* were speeches given in character, usually of a famous historical person;
this penchant for dramatics pervades Ovid's poetry. Other writers wrote
for the *pantomimi*, especially when they needed money: the son of one
of Ovid's fellow students, who, as Seneca complains, "polluted his talent"
(*Suasoriae* 2.19); the first-century poets Statius, who, according to Juvenal,
sold an *Agave* to the *pantomimus* Paris to make ends meet (7.82–92), and
Lucan, who wrote fourteen *salticae fabulae*, "scripts for the dance" (*Lucani
vita*). Ovid explicitly denies having done any such thing—even though his
poems are appearing on the stage, "danced to a full house," during his exile
(*Tristia* 5.7.25–28). On the other hand, in a more elaborate literary-historical
defense of his oeuvre, addressed to Augustus, he says (*Tristia* 2.519–20):
"And my poems have often been danced for the people,/ often they have
detained even your eyes." This follows the argument "If slapstick comedy
about adultery is all right, why not my poems?"; it precedes the argument
that paintings of sexual and violent scenes are commonly to be found in
Roman houses (see Myerowitz 1992). Ovid himself, in short, argues for an
equivalence between his earlier poetry and other art forms: the adultery
mime, pantomime dance versions of his poetry, and paintings of erotic and
violent scenes.

The seriocomic dialogue *On Dancing*, by the Syrian Greek writer Lucian, composed at some time in the mid-second century CE, testifies to the conservative view of pantomime as effeminate (1, 2, 3, 5), both in itself and in its effect on the audience; to the frenzy of the audience (2, 3, 5); and to the prominence in the performance of the man dancing the woman's role, especially that of a raped woman (2, 28).[10] The crusty interlocutor describes being in the audience of the pantomime (2), "watching an effeminate person mincing daintily about with delicate clothing and unbridled songs and impersonating sexy women, the lewdest of those in antiquity, Phaedras and Parthenopes and Rhodopes." (Parthenope was a Siren who yearned for Odysseus; Rhodope married her own brother.) Lucian describes the dancer's flowing silk garb (29–30, 63, 66) and his masks—five for one performance would not be unusual. The mask was beautiful (unlike those of comedy and tragedy), and had a closed mouth.

But what most suggests a tie with Ovid is Lucian's list of the topics that a good *pantomimus* must know by heart (37–61), which tallies closely in order, arrangement, and content with the *Metamorphoses* as a whole (cf. Galinsky 1975: 68–69, 132, 139). It includes the tale of Procne and Philomela (40): "and the [daughters] of Pandion, both what they suffered in Thrace and what they did." Also the tale of Pelopea (43), which Juvenal mentioned as well—a father seduces a daughter. The *pantomimus* is to learn, in particular, transformations (57) and, most of all, the loves of the gods (59)—that is, their rapes of goddesses and women. This list mentions fifty-six women's roles, including two historical figures (Stratonice and Cleopatra) plus one for a man in drag: Achilles on Skyros. This recalls not only the tale of Achilles and Deidamia in the *Ars*, inset into the text like a dramatic interlude, but also the *Fasti* and the attempted rape of Hercules (which Elaine Fantham suggests came from pantomime, 1983: 200–1); the freeze-frame tableaux of the Sabines running (set in the archaic theater and forerunner of the experience of women at the theater of the *Ars*); and the rapes by gods in drag in the *Metamorphoses*.

Describing a great dancer at the court of Nero, Lucian stresses the way he could tell a whole story in gesture. This might explain one curiosity of Ovid's style; look again at *M.* 6.551–57 (Philomela's mutilation). With one hand, Tereus unsheathes his sword; with the other, he grabs Philomela by the hair; with the other, he bends her arms behind her back; with the other, he chains her wrists; with the other, he grabs her tongue with a pair of forceps; and finally he uses the sword to cut out her tongue. And compare 6.338–68, in the comic tale of the goddess Latona and the Lycian farmers: throughout, Latona carries her newborn twins in her arms (338); they even play a part in the drama (359); at 368, the angry goddess dramatically raises her palms to the sky to curse the oafish farmers. What has happened to the babies? Perhaps this is not baroque illogic but cubist logic; perhaps this transformative poem derives its poetry from motion, the motion of the dance.

Lucian also draws a direct comparison between dancing and rhetoric (65), basing it explicitly on the shared art of impersonation, especially as found in rhetorical exercises, Ovid's old specialty. Rhetoricians' anxiety over the occasionally necessary impersonation of women is widely attested.[11]

The connection between Ovid's poetry and the pantomime accords well with the model of fantasy derived from psychoanalytic theory, in which the subject is said to oscillate between the terms of the fantasy (Fletcher 1986; Kaplan 1986, based on the work of Laplanche and Pontalis). Thus, in one of the basic schemas, "a father seduces a daughter," the subject can be in the place of "father," "daughter," or even of the verb "seduces." The interrelations between this concept, Ovid's poetry, and the pantomime are most striking. The model exactly describes the performance of the dancer—first one character, then another, with the essential need to enact the interaction between the characters; and not just any characters but, often, the father who seduces a daughter (Pelopea) or an equivalent (Leda). Or vicariously: Tereus imagining himself in Pandion's place *so that* he could fondle Philomela. The poet's fascination with the reversal, whereby a [daughter] (Medea, Scylla, Byblis, Myrrha) seduces a [father], is delimited by the extreme anxiety of the Salmacis episode, where the female has become subject rather than object, and the male is forced not only to become but to remain female.

Roman poets generally published their works by giving readings, usually to circles of friends; and we recall the male Roman's experience of being the object of the male gaze, as an adolescent.[12] So can it be said that Ovid empathizes with his rape victims? Certainly—as a great *pantomimus* might; but not with any but a delicious pity for them, a very temporary taking on of their experience, their bodies. How beautiful she looks in flight; one woman feels the hot breath of the rapist on her neck, another is caught bathing naked, a third taken by surprise on her way to visit her sister. For a few, the rapist even first dresses as a woman, so that the phallus can be a surprise, and teach its lesson about gender again. I imagine the poet himself (or the narrator, or both) "dancing" his characters one by one: a father, seduces, a daughter.

Ovid's special circumstances lend themselves to this imagination. The *Metamorphoses* was completed when Ovid was in exile, for offenses connected with his poetry (Goold 1983), to the cold wilderness of Tomis. The silenced victims, the artists horribly punished by legalistic gods for bold expression—Marsyas, and especially Arachne, even the co-opted Daphne—read like allegories of Ovid's experience, and at a time when his fellow declaimers remembered the death of Cicero, his head and hand nailed to the rostra (Richlin 1999). Philomela weaves a message to her sister; the unvoiced Cyane with her "inconsolable wound" (5.426) gives Proserpina's belt to Demeter as a sign; Arachne weaves her own tapestry of rapes. At this level it might be possible to argue for Ovid as metapornographer. But if the *Metamorphoses* lays bare a cruel cosmos, it does so voluptuously.[13] Even the declaimers, who loved him, thought he overdid it; Cestius Pius remarks, criticizing Ovid's witty wrap-up of Erysichthon's self-ingestion, that this is the poet "who filled this era not only with *Erotic Arts* but erotic wordplay" (*amatoriis non artibus tantum sed sententiis*, Seneca *Controv.* 3.7). It was catching; and that was Cestius's point.

The pleasure of the style and the pleasure in the content are congruent. Moreover, the universe described horrifies and attracts us precisely because it is out of kilter, as is the style with the content. Perhaps this is why rape is such a suitable scenario for the *Metamorphoses*, which comes to involve dissolution of the boundaries of body, genus, gender, and genre. (And not rape alone; the poem is full of incest, the mating of human with statue, cross-sex transformations.) A similar phenomenon appears in Greek literature (Bergren 1983; Zeitlin 1985), long before Latin. But perhaps Roman culture, so obsessed with boundaries, so permeable, as permeable slave morphed into impermeable citizen, is precisely the place for it. Rape as a passport to death, or to dissolution of the body, may have made sense to Ovid and his audience.

Compare a story in Tacitus about the daughter of Sejanus, Tiberius's ex-henchman (*Annals* 5.9):

> It was then decided that punishment should be visited upon the remaining children of Sejanus, though the rage of the mob was lifting, and many were placated by the executions that had already taken place. So they were carried into the prison, the boy understanding what was about to take place, the girl so much still unaware that she kept asking over and over what she had done wrong and where she was being taken, and saying that she would not do it again, and that she could be let off with the beating usual for children. The authors of that time say that because it was considered unheard-of for a virgin to be subjected to a

capital execution, she was raped by the executioner with the noose lying next to her; then they were throttled and their bodies, so young, were thrown out on the Gemonian steps.

The execution was, except for the rape, comparable to those of other political prisoners in those abnormal times (see Williams 1978: 184; Richlin 1999: 195–96). The story appears again in Suetonius (*Tiberius* 61.4–5), generalized to many victims of the atrocities late in the reign of Augustus's successor: "and among them women and boys. Young girls, since in the custom handed down to us it was a *nefas* for virgins to be strangled, were first spoiled (*vitiatae*) by the executioner, then strangled." Editors compare a case during the triumviral proscriptions (the years into which Ovid was born), reported by the much later writer Dio (47.6), in which a young boy was put forward into the class of men—made to assume the *toga virilis*—so that he could easily be executed. The sixteenth-century classicist Justus Lipsius comments that the same reasoning underlies the case of Sejanus's daughter—that once having been raped and deflowered, *mulier videretur*, "she would seem a woman."

The case of Sejanus's daughter comes from 31 CE, fourteen years after Ovid's death, the accounts of it from the early second century CE; but the logic of it, rape as a *rite de passage*, atrocity as it is to Tacitus and Suetonius, informs their texts as it does Ovid's. Tacitus's account of the young girl crying out in the prison echoes Ovid's description of Philomela in the hands of Tereus.

We begin to look for ways out; the model begins to feel like a trap.

First, what about the female members of Ovid's audience? Is it possible that this poetry includes a female subjectivity? In chapter 3 I suggested that the jokes about Julia, daughter of Augustus, might have formed part of a resistant discourse among elite men and women; chapter 4 brings in Sulpicia the elegist and her rebellion against expectations. Ovid would have known those exiled and driven to suicide, as would those listening to his poems—slave and free. Yet the Laplanche-Pontalis model works both ways, and I think of Angela Carter's description of the women listening eagerly to a male speaker in Sade's *Philosophy in the Boudoir* (1978: 143): "Since he is good enough to class them with the masters, they, too, will be permitted to tyrannise as much as they please. Libido . . . is genderless." If women are invited to identify across gender boundaries, the process is not necessarily revolutionary (Kaplan 1986).

Isn't this just the pornographic again? In Sade, and often in literature, the assumption of a female voice is a central technique (Kappeler 1986: 30; and see Henry 1992; Joshel 1992a; Parker 1992a): ventriloquism. Even dominance by women, when written into the scenario, is just another thrill (Carter 1978: 20–21). Fantasy of movement within the system is not escape from the system.

But some argue that fantasies mean something completely different from what they say—for example, that fantasized violence provides an excuse for cuddling (Russ 1985), or that the mutilation of the love object, so common in romances (the blinding and maiming of Mr. Rochester) is a covert expression of anger at the object's power (Modleski 1982: 24–25). The implication that the degree of the "covert" anger correlates directly with a real power is very disturbing when applied to fantasized violence against women; anger against women's supposed power resounds in man-in-the-street narratives about rape (Beneke 1982). Nina Auerbach took as the epigraph for her book about Victorian misogynist fictions of women, *Woman and the Demon* (1982), a line out of context from Maxine Hong Kingston (1976: 19): "Perhaps women were once so dangerous that they had to have their feet bound." Rather than congratulate ourselves, we must bear in mind the disparity between the reality of women's historical power and the size of the shackles historically placed upon it.[14]

Like the pornographic model, the cross-sex fantasy model offers no exit from gender hierarchy. The female is still the site of violence, no matter what the location of the subject. Even if the magician and the lady change places, *he* is still taking *her* place.

A Political Model: Rape Is Rape, Resistance Is Possible

Proprium humani ingenii est odisse quem laeseris.
[It is proper to human nature to hate one whom you have hurt.]

Tacitus Agricola 42.3

We need a political model that will both describe the magician's act and suggest a way to end it. The problem is not gender but hierarchy: within hierarchy, violence is a right, and the control of violence diminishes liberty. An anarchic system is thus a precondition for the deletion of the pornographic. Though escape from hierarchy has seemed impossible, perhaps there are some discourses that permit it, are open: theory, mathematics, nonrepresentational art, some forms of music. Other systems—humor, fantasy, narratives, representational art, all interrelated—form the bars around hierarchy.

The structure of these closed discourses is political, and they have four main characteristics:

(1) They contain a cue that says any item is untrue ("It's just a joke!"). Ovid actually asserted this in his poems from exile (e.g., *Tristia* 2.491–96). High art has developed a whole array of distancing devices, barricades against the explicit meaning of content (Modleski 1982: 31), including the art form itself. But the continuum between high art and low art is very strong (Kappeler 1986), and a tragic and a comic cue may very well introduce the same material (cf. Donaldson 1982: 100 on the "mutually reinforcing" nature of the tragic and comic views of the rape of Lucretia). We must keep our wits about us, and not close off high art from the rest of the experiential universe, like the art historian writing on the rape of the Sabines and of Lucretia who comments that rape has nowadays "disappeared . . . from coherent and transmissible iconographies" (Bryson 1986: 173). No; as Barbara Kruger's piece puts it, "Your gaze hits the side of my face" (in Vance 1984: 212).

(2) Content follows function and is not arbitrary. Content is the commodity, it is what you pay for. It is a wish, more or less disguised.

(3) The relation between each item and reality depends on the status of the users; these discourses maintain the status quo. This is the model implied in Susanne Kappeler's parable of the white Namibian farmer who had himself photographed while torturing one of his black workmen (1986: 5–10). This is the model implied by the photographs from Abu Ghraib. This is the model exemplified by Seneca's *controversia* about Parrhasius torturing a captured slave as a model for a painting of Prometheus, in which the declaimers attack Parrhasius by describing the torture. Seneca comments that no one wanted to defend Parrhasius, and proceeds to lay out a substantial defense of artistic freedom, but the *controversia* itself enjoys that freedom (see Morales 1996). The structure of the subject's sentences is always subject-verb-object (Kappeler 1986: 104); hence the passive periphrastic construction that comes about when an individual normally the object is reconstructed as a subject: "she has to be punished." As Angela Carter remarks of the story of the pornographic object, "to exist in the passive case is to die in the passive case—that is, to be killed" (1978: 75–77), an apt conflation of the accusative case with the passive voice. Or, as Laura Mulvey famously put it, "Sadism demands a story" (1975: 14).

(4) Historically, though perhaps not necessarily, hierarchy has been gen-

dered. The object of study is written about; Kaja Silverman says that, in *The Story of O*, O's body is made readable by her whipping (1984: 337). Brian De Palma says, to explain his film *Body Double* (in Pally 1984), "[It's just a] genre convention . . . like . . . using women in situations where they are killed or sexually attacked. . . . I don't particularly want to chop up women but it seems to work." As Angela Carter says, "Art with work to do."

Work on what? The position at the bottom, so often a woman's, has never been pleasant; something in it "exposes the meatiness of human flesh" (Carter 1978: 140; see Brown 1992; Kappeler 1986: 63–81; Parker 1992a; Rabinowitz 1992). Catharine MacKinnon says of the history of sexuality (1992: 122–23): "The sexualization of aggression or the eroticization of power and the fusion of that with gender such that the one who is the target or object of sexuality is the subordinate, is a female, effeminized if a man, is relatively constant. . . . Hierarchy is always done through gender in some way."

Where does this leave us? On the one hand, history weighs heavy, and closed discourse is more comfortable than open. Revolutionary discourse is intrinsically unamusing. How ephemeral, how negligible, how little, how dull this essay is compared with the lovely monument of Ovid's poetry! And insofar as it amuses, it fails. On the other hand, when we see problems of discourse as systemic, we can gauge our task. The female can no longer be by definition the site of violence—nothing can. What does happen if we say, as Susanne Kappeler does (221), "Art will have to go?" Maybe there is something else. Meanwhile we must use what exists to show what is wrong.

Conclusion

How *can* women read? And why should we read Ovid? How badly do we need this history? I'll borrow an answer from Toni Morrison. We're stuck with Philomela; she's like Beloved, the dearly beloved ghost of grief, and to be blind to her is not to exorcise her. We need to know her and keep faith with history.

The battle for consciousness must go on (see de Lauretis 1984: 185) and focus on concrete political improvements in women's lives. As classicists, as scholars, as teachers, as women and men who speak to other people, we can fight in this battle. What can we do?

(1) We can speak and write about antiquity for other feminists and people outside the academy. We can remake our disciplines (Hallett 1985). We can move outside of Classics, and we can open up the boundaries of Clas-

sics itself, as this essay and the rest in *Pornography and Representation in Greece and Rome* were trying to do.

(2) We can blow up the canon. Canons are part of social systems. We recognize the one we have as dysfunctional. It must and will change; we can surely critique the pleasure of the text without fear of breaking anything irreplaceable.

(3) We can claim our lack. We can ask, where am I in this text? What can it do for me? What did it do to its audience?

(4) We can appropriate; we can resist. The old stories await our retelling; they haunt our language anyway. Ovid's *Heroides* inspired women writers for a thousand years.[15] And if the only names we have to speak in are names of blood, maybe we can speak the blood off them. History is what groups write as they gain a voice.

CHAPTER 6

Making Up a Woman

The Face of Roman Gender

&

Introduction

It was a lucky benefit of an unlucky situation that, in the 1980s, I found my-self spending a lot of time talking to scholars in the history of religion. Few large Classics departments in the 1980s were interested in hiring feminist scholars; some departments still had no women at all, or felt that one was plenty. Most feminist scholarship was being produced by scholars working in programs or small departments, and I was no exception, teaching in a three-person department at Lehigh University, best known as an engineering school. But it had a very good liberal arts college, and the faculty were necessarily thrown together; the Religion Department was just upstairs from Classics. Thanks to the generosity of those colleagues, particularly Norman Girardot, Lydia Speller, and Chava Weissler, my eyes were opened to the ancient Mediterranean as a place where Jews and Christians *were* Greeks and Romans, and where "Greek" and "Roman" are really inadequate maps to describe the terrain; the discipline of Classics was still, at that time, largely immured in the separation from biblical studies in effect since the mid-nineteenth century (see Marchand 1996), and, due to my training, it came as news to me that, for example, Jewish history and Greco-Roman history are contemporaneous.

In addition, thanks to Lehigh's "Validity in Interpretation?" reading group, and to the Lehigh Valley Feminist Research Group, which draws on scholars at five local colleges, I began to learn to make my work intelligible to a nonspecialist audience—not, at that time, a major concern of classical scholars, then still clinging to a sort of Olympian aloofness.

So, in 1989, when I left the Lehigh Valley for Los Angeles, I was used to working with groups across disciplines; by another stroke of luck, one of the first colleagues to greet me here was Karen King, then teaching at Occidental College. Thanks to her openhanded friendship and her work on gnostic Christianity, I got to meet a whole group of Southern California scholars studying ancient religion and women's religion. In turn, thanks to Chava Weissler, I had the chance to participate in a colloquium on "Women in Religion and Society" in 1991 at the Annenberg Research Institute in Philadelphia, where I met a galaxy of scholars who would influence my work, including Marilyn Booth, Daniel Boyarin, and Howard Eilberg-Schwartz. This chapter was born at that meeting when I was asked if I would be interested in contributing to a collection, to be edited by Eilberg-Schwartz and the great comparativist Wendy Doniger, on the unusual topic of the female head; I immediately thought of Ovid's *Medicamina faciei femineae*.

The finished essay shows traces of many other early-90s influences. The collection, as might be expected from the editors' body of work, concerns the symbolic use of the female body across time and space—a topic I had begun thinking about in the mid-1980s, growing out of the work on Roman invective seen in chapter 2, which was turning into a projected book, *Roman Witches*, sections of which constitute chapters 7 and 8 in this volume. I had therefore been reading in comparative anthropology for some time, and, thanks to a 1987–88 NEH Fellowship, had read all the way through Pliny's *Natural History*, an experience that greatly contributes to this essay, as well as to chapter 8. Meanwhile, Judith Butler's *Gender Trouble* had appeared in 1990, and I had been reading and teaching similar theoretical work by Wendy Chapkis and Monique Wittig on the construction of gender since 1989: this approach was indispensable to any discussion of cosmetics. The allusion in the second paragraph of this essay to Jennie Livingston's film *Paris Is Burning* takes me back to a New York sidewalk in 1990, where Sandra Joshel, Terri Marsh, and I were standing, deep in argument about what we had just seen. The experience of working on *Pornography and Representation in Greece and Rome* is all over this essay and its bibliography; Molly Myerowitz Levine wrote an essay for *Off with Her Head!* and we continued, long-distance, our long-standing dialogue about the experience of femininity in the ancient world. Colleagues and students at USC, particularly Lois Banner and David Fredrick, gave me more to think about; meanwhile, ongoing work on women in ancient medicine had led to a special issue of *Helios* in 1992 that included Heinrich von Staden's compelling "Women and Dirt." In those years, the air was full of questions about the ways in which gender is constructed through body modification; Maria Wyke's essay on Roman women's cosmetics appeared in 1994, and in 1997 she edited a special issue of *Gender & History* on "Gender and the Body in Mediterranean Antiquity."

"Making Up a Woman" also incorporates the beginnings of two new lines of inquiry in my work, both of which have old roots. The section "Making Up Gender, Making Up Empire" goes back to an undergraduate interest in ethnographic stereotyping in Latin literature, begun as a paper on the Gauls in Livy and continuing through a senior thesis on Roman Britain and graduate work on Roman provinces; the section "Slippage in the Courtroom" goes back to an interest in Roman rhetoric first developed by Bernard Fenik in a Princeton reading group on the elder Seneca and continuing into a USC graduate seminar on rhetoric and a projected book on gender and manhood in Roman oratory, bits of which have been published elsewhere. Both these interests feature in my current work—on slaves in Plautus, on the orator Cornelius Fronto—and the whole package serves to show how what we know depends on who we are, how writing distills the endless mash of experience.

The essay's cheerful tone, especially considering the loathing for the female body expressed by many of the writers considered, marks a change from chapters 2–5 and deserves some comment. It was hard, in those days, not to be wooed by the exuberance of the pro-pornography feminists, the anything-goes, in-your-face attitude of queer theory. Those were the days when the "lipstick lesbian" had begun to supplant the flannel-shirted separatist, but postmodernism had not finally clobbered political theory. It was easy to lighten up, and I was just happy to be in California. But the observations in this essay on the construction of masculinity, and on women's own attested use of makeup, should not detract from the mass of textual evidence here presented that adds to the material in chapters 2 and 3, or from the realization that gender and ethnic stereotypes are connected.

&a.   &a.   &a.

It is noticeable in many societies, of which ancient Rome is certainly one, that women wear makeup and men do not.[1] Sometimes, where this is so, it seems as if wearing makeup is almost constitutive of femaleness, or of femme-ness. Why should this be so?

One explanatory model might suggest a functional reason: women wear makeup to look beautiful and so attract lovers. But this amounts to saying that women wear makeup to show that they are female and looking for a sexual partner, since "beautiful" generally means "conforming to (an arbitrary set of) gender ideals (usually female), hence sexually attractive." This is an instance of what Judith Butler describes as the performative aspect of gender; it is as if, in the Rodgers and Hammerstein tune "I Enjoy Being a Girl," the verb "being" were transitive. As the character Linda Low says shortly before launching into the song, "I want to be a success as a girl. . . . The main thing is for a woman to be successful in her gender."[2] Thus the terms "look beautiful," "wear makeup," and "attract lovers" become interchangeable, synonymous; and beauty seems to lie, not only in the eye of the beholder, but in the labor of the beheld: the pure act of applying makeup becomes a token of the lengths to which the beheld is willing to go for the beholder. And thus, in the transsexual beauty contest known as "voguing," the assumption of women's clothing and makeup pushes biological males over the line into femaleness. Makeup then becomes the mark of gender—or *a* mark of gender.[3]

Of course, the usual mark of gender is elsewhere, lower down; perhaps this suggests a better model to explain why women wear makeup and men do not. Perhaps the reason women paint their *faces* is to hide something: by painting the outside, they contain what is inside; by painting the top, they conceal (but mark) the bottom. Nancy Vickers writes, apropos of the face of Medusa as a sign of her rape, "The obsessively spoken part—the face—[becomes] the other side of the obsessively unspoken . . . part—the genitalia . . . and fear of the female body is mastered through polarized figurations that can only denigrate or idealize" (Vickers 1985: 220). And the reason *women* paint their faces is to hide something men do not have. After all, the faces of women are like the faces of (clean-shaven) men, with eyes, nose, mouth; to look at them, you would not know that there was something completely different down there. Or perhaps women use makeup to mark something they are missing, something that men do have; hence the erotic allure of the bearded lady.[4] And hence the transsexual's makeup lays claim to a lack. A man wearing makeup and long hair, or a woman wearing no makeup and short hair, can in this culture provoke the fascinated question "Is that a boy or is it a girl?" Once the signs on top are blurred, the real question comes out: what is the bottom line?

Likewise, the application of makeup—cosm-etics—has implications for the universe—the cosm-os. The Greek root *kosm-* means "order," and the same double use of the root had symbolic meaning in Greek culture. In Rome, the word for makeup, *medicamina*, had a different set of associations: with medicine, poison, and witchcraft. Both sets of meanings resonate with the concealment and marking of gender; the female body becomes the site of gender's dirty work: "The female body is revealed as a task, an object in need of transformation."[5] Medicine, poison, witchcraft, and makeup are all crafts or skills aiming at a certain kind of control over the body and its surroundings; keeping the female body in order is an important aspect of keeping the universe in order.[6] Both Greeks and Romans saw the universe itself as gendered, so that the marks their culture imposed on people as determinants of gender formed part of a larger system. The ordering of people into males and females tallied with categorizations of classes into free and slave, of nations into civilized and barbarous, and of the world into heaven, earth, and underworld, center and edge.

In this system, women's own subjectivity is hard to find. Indeed, as has been remarked by feminists studying women's relation to their own bodies, women's choice to beautify themselves is particularly problematic, peculiarly self-deconstructing, since this focus on the surface calls into question the existence of any underlying self. As Howard Eilberg-Schwartz argues (1995: 2), in cultures where woman is aligned with the body anyway, painting over the face and mouth obscures the one part of the body from which a female self might speak. Roman sources consistently link women's use of makeup with deception, covering a body often described by men as inherently repugnant (see chapter 2); moreover, free women who use makeup are said to align their bodies with the open bodies of slaves and prostitutes. As will be seen, the exceptional cases where men use cosmetics point to areas of danger, disorderly zones in the order of Roman culture.

Vanishing Cream: (Un)making Women

Consider Ovid's fragmentary poem *Medicamina faciei femineae*— "Medicines/Cosmetics for the Female Face." Like some of his other works— the three books of the *Ars amatoria* ("The Art of Love," 1 BCE), and the briefer *Remedia amoris* ("Remedy for Love")—the *Medicamina* is a mock-didactic poem. Roman writers were fond of didactic, and Ovid often takes this impulse and runs with it; the *Ars amatoria* is an instruction manual on how to pick up a lover (two books addressed to men, one to women), the *Remedia* tells the reader how to get rid of a lover no longer wanted. As has been amply demonstrated by Molly Myerowitz (1985: 104–28), the instructor/narrator of the *Ars amatoria* treats the woman and her body as the *materia* of his *ars*, and esteems women more highly than men precisely because women's relationship to their own bodies is more (literally) artificial.

Thus the opening of the *Medicamina* (written by Ovid at a time between the writing of books two and three of the *Ars*) sets the reader on familiar ground (1–10):

> Learn what care (*cura*) will recommend your face, girls,
>> and by what means your beauty should be watched/guarded.
> Cultivation (*cultus*) has ordered sterile soil to pay out the bounty
>> of Ceres, and the toothed brambles have died;
> *Cultus* also remedies the bitter juices in fruits,   5
>> and the split tree takes in adopted aid.
> *Culta* things are pleasing: lofty roofs are smeared (*linuntur*) with gold,
>> the black earth hides under its superimposed marble.
> Fleeces are dyed (*medicantur*) over and over in the purpling cauldron;
>> India offers ivory to be carved for our delectation.   10

Throughout his writing, Ovid plays with the conventional elegiac preference for urban over rural, toilette over dishabille; in the lines that follow these, he contrasts the women of today favorably with the rustic matrons of the mythical Italian countryside. On one level, this is a send-up of the traditional Roman preference for country over city, agriculture over any other way of life. But on another level, the poet is setting up a symbolic opposition between control and cultivation—*cultus*, culture—and the physical nature that is its *materia*, its raw material. City then is to country as *cultus* is to chaos.

Thus when the analogy is extended to the female body, as in this proem, that body is likened to nature in the raw, and in some unpleasant forms. The woman's unadorned, undepilated body is here compared with "sterile soil" (3) and its "toothed brambles" (4), and to "bitter juices" in fruit (5), which can be amended by grafting onto the tree—here described as "split" in the process (6). High things are made pleasing by being "smeared" with gold (7; the same verb is used elsewhere of putting on makeup); the "black earth" below is hidden by means of a marble covering (8). Wool, like hair, is dyed; ivory, like flesh, is to be shaped. These half-similes summon up a half-vague map of a woman's body, aided by the commonness of the ancient use of plowing (*cultus*) as a metaphor for sexual intercourse (see Carson 1990; duBois 1988: 65–85). The sterile soil, with its brambles and bitter juices, is to be cured or amended by *cultus*; this is the black earth that needs to be dressed, covered over, in marble (hard and bright, not muddy and dark), as the higher parts are smeared with the golden mark of value.

These themes announce programs which Ovid develops at much greater length in Book 3 of the *Ars amatoria*. Ovid himself cues his reader back to the *Medicamina* at *AA* 3.205–8:

> I have, in which I told the *medicamina* for your *forma*,
>> a little booklet, but a great work in its *cura*:
> In it, too, you should seek aid for your damaged form;
>> my art is not artless/impotent (*iners*) on your behalf.

This third book of the *Ars* was, so the poem claims, added on at women's popular request (2.745–46); women, too, says the narrator in his new proem, deserve and need instruction. After a gloomy reminder of the imminence of old age and wrinkles (3.59–82), concluding with the remark that having babies shortens youth and "the field grows old with continual harvest" (82), and after further reflection to the effect that, though iron and flint wear out with use, a woman's "part" need fear no such loss (91–92), the poet launches into his new book with the words *ordior a cultu*, "I commence from *cultus*" (101). This gives him the occasion for his most famous rejection of Roman ancestral simplicity and embrace of the sophistication of present-day Rome (113–28); here again, the polish of the well-kept body is aligned with the gilded architecture of the modern city, as opposed to wattle huts and cow pastures.[7]

After remarks on the best style of dress and coiffure for different kinds of figure (3.135–92, including a tip on where to buy a wig), the narrator goes on to give detailed instructions on makeup and personal hygiene. The armpits should not smell (literally, "no fierce goat should go into your armpits," 193); no rough hair on your legs (194); brush your teeth (197), wash your face (198); make yourself fair with powder (199), make yourself blush by *ars* (200), and by *ars* fill out your eyebrows (201), and mask your cheek with a little patch (202). And "there's no shame" in marking your eyes with a thin line of ash (203) or saffron (204). (Here follows the author's plug for the *Medicamina*, quoted above [205–8].) Then the narrator explains how vital it is to conceal the whole cosmetic process from the lover (209–34):

But don't let your lover catch, exposed on the table,
    your *pyxides* [makeup jars]; a feigned art helps the face.   210
Who would not be offended by scum smeared all over your face,
    when it runs into warm folds, slipping with its weight?
Oesypa—what do they smell like, though sent from Athens,
    the juice taken from the unkempt fleece of a sheep?
Nor would I approve if you put on your deer-marrow mixture   215
    in his presence, or brushed your teeth, either.
These things give you beauty (*forma*), but they are ugly (*deformia*) to
look at,
    and many things foul to do please once they are done.
[examples from the work of smith and sculptor]
You also, while you are being cultivated, let us think you are
sleeping;   225
    you will be seen to better advantage after the finishing touch.
Why should I know the cause of the fairness of your complexion?
    Close the door of your bedroom; why do you give away the
unfinished work?
There are many things it's proper for men not to know; most things
    would give offense, if you did not conceal the things inside
    (*interiora*).   230

In their developed form, then, Ovid's instructions include a strong recommendation to hide the process itself from its intended audience—for two reasons. First, the lover should believe no effort has been involved; this is a familiar idea in Ovid, for whom *ars est celare artem* (art is the hiding of art) is a motto, though a somewhat paradoxical one for such a consciously artificial poet. More important for us, and more taken for granted by the poet: the actual ingredients used in the effort are repellent. The "inside," the bedroom, conceals *pyxides* full of scum (*faex*), in fact runny scum; *oesypa* (grease from wool); deer-marrow paste; as well as ash, saffron, and chalk powder.

Ovid repeats the same themes, more strongly, in the *Remedia amoris*, which teaches lovers how to fall out of love. Recommending that the lover go to his girlfriend's house early in the day, before she has performed her toilette, he explains (351–56):

Then also, when she is smearing her face with her poison (*venenis*)
  concoctions,

go to your mistress's face, and don't let shame stand in your way;
You will find *pyxides* and a thousand colors of things
    and slopped *oesypa* running into tepid folds.
Phineus, *medicamina* like that stink of your tables;   355
    nausea has come to my stomach from this more than once.

The identification of makeup as *venena*, literally "poisons," aligns this description with the placement of makeup in the Roman materia medica (below); *venena* and *veneficia* are, with *medicamina*, among the words encompassing the range of meanings poison/potion/medicine. The makeup box, the *pyxis*, reappears here in close association with its repulsive contents. And the whole picture is linked to the monstrous via an image from Greek mythology: the tables of Phineus, the blind king plagued by the Harpies, who steal food from his tables and befoul them with their excrement. Vergil describes these creatures as birds with women's faces (*Aeneid* 3.216–18): "Maiden-like the faces of these birds, but most foul/ the off-pouring of their bellies, and their hooked hands, and their countenance/ always pallid with hunger." The contrast between the maiden-like face and the foul belly structures Ovid's picture of the mistress's dressing table that causes his nausea.[8]

Such themes are hardly unique to Ovid in Roman culture. The mysteries of the boudoir were produced onstage two hundred years earlier in Plautus's play *Poenulus*, in a lavish musical number featuring two slave prostitutes and their attendants (210–52). "From sunup this morning," sings Adelphasium, "the two of us never stopped/ washing or rubbing or scrubbing or dressing,/ buffing, re-buffing, painting, primping" (217–21). Her sister Anterastilis comments in turn (240–47),

Think, sister, please, how people say that we're
just like they say pickled fish are—
without any taste, without sweetness:
if they're not soaked a lot and a long time
        in lots of water,
they stink, they're salty, so you wouldn't want to touch them.
That's what we're like,
women are of that ilk,
        not too pretty and not too lovely
        without a makeup job and lots of cash.

In the context, the comparison of unbathed women to fish is a shock—a laugh line—and elicits a joke from the listening male slave. Onstage, the female character [her]self confesses how bad women naturally smell; but the speaker is a male actor.

A similarly elaborate dressing scene occurs early in Plautus's *Mostellaria* (157–312). In this play, the freed slave prostitute Philematium preens herself in front of her old slave woman Scapha, while her lover spies on them. Like the prostitutes in *Poenulus*, Philematium has just had a bath; she enters with the comment that it is a long time since a bath has made her so *deficatam*, "free from scum (*faex*)" (157–58)—like the *faex* Ovid observed in the dressing table *pyxides*. As requested, Scapha holds a mirror and jewel box for her (248), helps her with her hair (254), and hands her the white lead (258); she refuses, however, to give Philematium the rouge (261), protesting that her owner is too young to need makeup, and she also advises against wearing perfume—"because, by Castor, a woman smells good when she doesn't smell at all" (273). Herself an old woman (takes one to know one), she declares that it is old women who have to conceal the faults of their body with makeup and their sweaty smell with perfume (274–78). "That's right," says the eavesdropping lover, "and you guys out in the audience with old wives at home know it" (280–81). Compare the wife's *palla* in *Menaechmi* (167–68): "It's best to smell the top part of women's clothes," says the *parasitus* Peniculus, "because that other part" (holds it up and sniffs) "stinks up your nose with a smell that won't wash out."

These comic set pieces are clearly not novelties, but share familiar jokes with a mixed audience that included both prostitutes and their customers, along with *matronae*, or so the *Poenulus* prologue tells us. Thinking of gender as performative, we might reflect that, onstage, each primping whore—and Scapha, too—is a woman with a man inside, played by a man with a woman inside, for behind her mask is the actor's face, and inside his mouth are her words. Each masked male actor plays "Scarlett" or "Mammy" or "Rhett," depending on and reinforcing stereotypes already held in common by their varied audience—here, that women stink. Moreover, as Philematium literally specularizes herself—at one point, she kisses the mirror—so her lover specularizes her within the diegesis, encouraging the audience to do the same: her pretty-girl makeup covers a mask that covers an actor, always potentially himself an object of lust (cf. Juvenal 6.63–75). Hence the disdainful observer of a Greek actor remarks (Juvenal 3.96–97): "you'd say everything was empty and smooth/ below his belly (*ventriculum*), and split by a slender crack." Comedy performs the performance of gender and teaches the audience how it's done while it teaches what to laugh at: "then country-girl Thymele learns" (*Thymele tunc rustica discit*, Juvenal 6.66; see chapter 5 above on the *pantomimus*).[9]

Fifty years before Ovid, a serious didactic poet, Lucretius, produced a picture of a woman's boudoir that was to proceed down the ages, via Ovid to Swift and beyond (*De rerum natura* 4.1174–91).[10] *Inside* the house, the woman "fumigates her wretched self with foul smells" (*miseram taetris se suffit odoribus*, 1175), as her maids run to get away from her, giggling; *outside*, the stock character of the *exclusus amator* ("shut-out lover") hangs flowers and garlands on the doorway, anointing the doorpost with perfume, kissing the doors. Lucretius sums up: women know that if men realized what it was like inside, they would run away; "so all the more/ they conceal from [their lovers] all the backstage (*poscaenia*) of life" (1185–86). The woman's body, as often, is mapped onto the parts of the house; this jibes especially well with Robert Brown's comments on *suffit*, which, as he argues, does not mean "reeks" (the usual interpretation) in this context, but literally "fumigates," in the medical sense. Fumigation as a medical process "involved the application of strong-smelling fumes to the nostrils or, commonly in the case of gynecological complaints, to the womb by means of a tube introduced into the vagina."[11] Thus the lover kisses, perfumes, and garlands the door, the face of the house, while in an inner room the mistress pipes smells up her vagina. Brown notes that favorite fumigations included sulfur, burnt hair, urine, and dung.

Procreation itself is depicted as marring women's bodies; both Ovid and Martial describe women taking action to avoid or conceal stretch marks on their bellies. Ovid posits this motive briefly at the start of the second of his two poems reproaching Corinna for an abortion (*Amores* 2.14.7); Martial describes a woman using bean meal (*lomentum*) to conceal the "wrinkles of her uterus" (3.42.1), and attacks a woman who "wants to be fucked" by him but will not bathe with him, by listing what he suspects lies beneath her clothing (3.72): wrinkled, sagging breasts, wrinkled belly, gaping labia, "something sticking out of the mouth of your cunt." Lose-lose: giving birth produces ugliness; refusing to give birth betrays vanity (cf. Juvenal 6.592–99). The *venter* occupies a sort of bodily limbo: a smooth (*planus*) *venter* is on the list of beautiful features in Corinna's body (Ovid *Amores* 1.5.21), but it is perilously close to the unbeautiful parts below, and so a *venter mollis* features in a list of ugly body parts (Horace *Epodes* 8.9).

Latin invective insists that makeup is itself horrible and must be covering something horrible, cataloguing the flaws of the female body (see Richlin 1992: 109–16). Here we might review the invective poetry surveyed in chapter 2 above, and see how it emphasizes the contrast between painted surface and repulsive interior. The august Augustan poet Horace, in one of two *Epodes* describing a repellently ugly woman who is in bed with the narrator, lists among her unpleasant physical features (goat in armpits, sweat, bad smell) her "wet powder" slipping off and her complexion "colored with crocodile dung" (12.10–11). Old age in Roman invective makes women both sexually repellent and greedy for sex, and so they resort to cosmetics as camouflage. An old woman in Martial wears a coating of chalk on her face (8.33.17). A woman rejected by the poet's penis (9.37) "lies stored away in a hundred *pyxides*": her hair, her teeth, her dresses, her face, her eyebrows, all are removed at night, and her "white-haired cunt" can be numbered among her ancestors. An old woman is told (10.90) not to bother using depilatories on her crotch anymore, since it has ceased to be of interest. The anonymous poet of the *Priapea* (46) addresses a girl "no whiter than a Moor, shorter than a pygmy, rougher and hairier than bears, looser than the pants that Medes or Indians wear"; "looser" here refers to her vagina, and he goes on to say he would need a powerful aphrodisiac to "bang the swarming worms of your cunt." Note the use of animal/exotic referents for her body parts, coupled with her internal decay. That such perceptions were shared by elite and popular culture alike is attested by the Pompeian graffito discussed in chapter 2 (*CIL* 4.1516), in which the *puella* is beautiful on the outside but (the writer reports) had "muck" (*lutus*, cognate with *pollutus*) on the inside.

Cosmetics themselves could be directly connected with the vagina. Depilation of the female genitalia is said to make for attractiveness (Mart. 3.74); Martial says that such *munditiae* are for *puellae*, not for an old woman (10.90), though one Pompeian graffitist prefers a "hairey cunt" to a smooth one because it "holds in the steam" (*CIL* 4.1830; see chapter 2, n. 21). Depilation was carried out by plucking (Mart. 10.90), ointments (Mart. 3.74), or resin (Mart. 12.32.21–22, where the resin is "foul" and the property of the "wives" of the red-light district, i.e., prostitutes). In this context it is helpful to remember that the depiction of the female genitalia in Roman texts is overwhelmingly negative, while poetic praise of the female body omits the genitalia altogether: "it is as if there were a blank space in the middle of the woman" (Richlin 1992: 47, and in general 46–47, 67–69). Like the leaky Greek women described by Anne Carson (1990), the vagina in Latin is smelly, dirty, wet, loose.

By extension, the box that contained the makeup becomes sexualized, abjected. A famous and obscure dirty joke in the court case between Clodia and Caelius depended on what was contained in a *pyxis* sent by the young aristocrat to his equally aristocratic ex-mistress—possibly a depilatory, as Marilyn Skinner suggests.[12] Or possibly *unguentum*, "ointment" or "perfume"; Catullus (c. 13) praises Clodia's *unguentum* and says it would make the addressee wish to become "all nose"—a facial/genital transformation much remarked by modern commentators (e.g., Dettmer 1989). Certainly, as seen in Ovid's prohibitions above, *pyxides* were strongly associated with women and with makeup. Moreover, makeup boxes often were decorated with scenes of women applying makeup (Wyke 1994: 143–44), so that, pretty on the outside, they would often have contained substances arousing the uneasy horror evoked by pollutants (much as the old tampon boxes used to be a plain demure blue, without any label, decorated by darker blue sprigs). They might contain spare body parts, as in the *Satyrica*, where Tryphaena's slave restores Giton and Encolpius to their former good looks by producing her mistress's wigs, along with "eyebrows from a *pyxis*" (110.1–5; cf. Mart. 9.37). A female practitioner packages fertility drugs in a *pyxis* (Juvenal 2.141). One of the Augustan declaimers remembered by the elder Seneca, and cited by him as particularly gauche, used *pyxides* and *medicamina* as emblems of the female (*Suasoriae* 2.21):

> This is the Corvus who, while he was running a *schola* at Rome, . . . declaimed the *controversia* about the woman who was preaching to the *matronae* that children should be abandoned at birth, and so was on trial. . . . In this *controversia* this line of his raised a laugh: "Among the *pyxides* and *medicamina* for fragrant breath there stood the assembly in their Oriental headgear (*mitrata contio*)."

What is notable here is the representation of a convocation of women of the respectable class as an "assembly wearing the *mitra*," that is, with headgear also Asiatic and foreign, and surrounded even in public with their pots of makeup. As seen in chapter 1, the *scholae* taught young men how to portray women in court, and a lesson is taught here: cosmetics make women ludicrous; women in groups are ludicrous; motherhood is always in jeopardy; cosmetics hide something bad.

Pyxides, as part of the personal possessions to which women were legally entitled (Paulus *Sententiae* 3.6.83), belonged to the *mundus muliebris*, the "woman's equipment." *Mundus*, as a legal term, could be used without the qualifying adjective *muliebris* with this meaning; the word *mundus* = "sky, universe, world" may have developed from the legal *mundus* in the same way the Greek *kosmos* developed. Another *mundus*, possibly the same word, was a ritual pit, the "gateway to hell" (*ostium Orci*), associated with the goddess Ceres; when it was opened, it let out the spirits of the dead, and public activities were curtailed (Spaeth 1996: 63–65). Indeed, the Roman grammarian Varro himself derives the legal *mundus* from *munditia* (*De lingua latina* 5.129)—the noun form of an adjective *mundus* "free from dirt or impurities, clean; cleared of superfluous growth; elegant" (*Oxford Latin Dictionary* s.v.).[13]

Although my focus here is primarily on Rome, a few important Greek precursors should be noted. Paramount among these is the scene of the dressing of Pandora in Hesiod's *Theogony* and *Works and Days* (eighth century BCE). Hesiod leaves his audience in no doubt that the first woman was a bad thing. In fact what he really stresses is that she was paradoxical in this regard, a "beautiful bad thing" (*Th.* 585). She is beautiful on the outside, especially when Athena has dressed her (*kosmêse*, WD 72, *Th.* 573), but bad on the inside (*WD* 60–82): a "trick" (*dolon*, WD 83, *Th.* 589), delighting in her *kosmôi* (*Th.* 587). The form of Pandora—beautiful and beautified on the outside, bad on the inside—serves as a paradigm for the general shape of things in Hesiod. Not only does she carry a jar with evils inside it; she herself is a miniature of tricky Gaia, the deified Earth who contains a hollow space from which Kronos reaches out to castrate his father (*Th.* 158, 174, 178). Her crown, moreover, is carved with images of monsters (*Th.* 582, *knôdal'*), so that she also recapitulates the horizontal shape of Hesiod's universe: the map with monsters at its margins, for example Medusa (*Th.* 276), or Echidna, pretty nymph on top and slithering snake on the bottom, who lives in a cave and eats raw meat (*Th.* 295–305). Women, at least in Hesiod's version of the Greek origin myth, are a snare and a delusion, and their nature is expressed in their bodies; their *cultus* both constitutes them as pitfalls and is necessitated by their bad insides. Anne Carson suggests that this idea of the duplicitous nature of women may be connected with the Greek perception of women as wet, prone to rotting via sexuality, and hence unbounded, polluted. This would certainly tally with the Roman perception of makeup as something icky put over something icky.[14]

Working from the same premises on women's nature, the model husband Ischomachus in Xenophon's *Oeconomicus* (Athens, ca. 362/1 BCE) instructs his wife that she should avoid wearing makeup, which will not make her as attractive to him as a rosy complexion derived from vigorous housework (10.2–13). His wife, as he tells it in the dialogue, provokes his lecture by wearing white lead on her face, alkanet juice on her cheeks, and boots with platform soles; these he condemns as deceitful, like falsified material goods, and liable to be found out. According to the dialogue, she obeys his recommendations with alacrity; indeed, his final remarks indicate the presence of certain class/gender motivations (10.12–13):

> But [a wife's] looks, when she tries to outdo her servant, being more pure/clean and clothed in a more seemly fashion—it's [sexually] exciting (*kinêtikon*), especially when the fact that one woman willingly gratifies/ pleasures (*kharizesthai*) [you] is compared with the fact that the [other] woman is forced to serve/obey [you]. But women who are always sitting grandly around offer themselves to be judged by the standard of bedizened (*kekosmêmenas*) and seductive/cheating women. And now, Socrates, he said, you may well believe that my wife lives her life behaving herself just as I taught her and just as I now tell you.

This writer portrays the husband as the focus of efforts to arouse his sexual interest on the part of three classes of women: wives, slaves, prostitutes.[15] The text shows a marginal consciousness of the bitterness that may well have existed between women in the same household sharing—on very different terms—the same man (see chapter 7). Roman texts suggest that such ill feeling may have been acted out precisely in the arena of the toilette. In the uppermost reaches of Roman society, the very application of makeup was a servile occupation; Ovid, in the *Ars amatoria*, suggests that it is not nice for a woman to scratch the face of her *ornatrix* ("hairdresser," "beautician") with her fingernails or stick hairpins in her arms, causing the servant to curse the head she works on (3.239–42). Juvenal picks up the same motif (6.487–507), in the context of the flogging of slaves by their bored female owners. The comedies of Plautus—acted by slaves—repeatedly portray the wife as the angrily unsuccessful rival in the competition with prostitutes, yet Plautine wives fear not only prostitutes, normally kept outside the home, but the rivals within. *Casina* centers on a wife's need to control the sexual use of *ancillae*; *ancillae* are not to be too pretty, unattractive Syrians or Egyptians being the most suitable for hard work (*Mercator* 210–11, 395–417; see chapter 2 on stereotyping and slaves as commodities). In a fragment of Caecilius Statius's comedy *Plocium* (in Gellius 2.23.10), a husband complains that his wife has made him sell an *ancilla* she suspects of being her *paelex*—that is, of having sex with her husband—one who, in the common comic epithet, "looked good enough to be free" (*facie haut inliberali*, in Gellius's paraphrase, 2.23.8). A group of *ornatrices* represented with their owner on a Gallic funerary monument shows baldly how class, gender, and ornament were interwoven in this society: four (slave) women stand, one holding a mirror, around a woman seated in an elaborate wicker chair. The younger Seneca (*Ep. mor.* 95.48) suggests that the truly pious worshiper not "hold a *speculum* for Juno," for "a god does not need servants"; he picks this action, like toting Jupiter's gym bag, as a gendered synecdoche for servile praxis.[16]

The wife's misguided use of cosmetics in Xenophon at the same time shifts her over into the category of prostitutes—women whom he labels both deceitful and sexual. The distinction between the undisguised looks of respectable women and the deceptively dressed-up appearance of prostitutes became a topos in moral literature and satire.[17] The declaimer Latro, in one of the elder Seneca's *Controversiae*, delivers a set of rules for the behavior a *matrona* should adopt outdoors to mark herself off from a recognizable *adultera*; she should be bedecked (*ornata*) only enough so as not to be *immunda* (*Controv.* 2.7.3; cf. chapter 1 above on this speech). In the second century CE, Plutarch is still saying that an extremely virtuous wife might shun even a hint of pomade and makeup, avoiding what is "sluttish," *hetairikon* (*Coniugalia praecepta* 142a; discussed in Carson 1990: 150); he also, as seen in chapter 1, advises wives not to be jealous of the female household slaves (144c). The use of makeup did occasionally form part of the list of attributes of a prostitute in a Roman brothel. This can be seen, for example, in another *Controversia* (1.2), the point of which is to differentiate what makes a priestess from what makes a prostitute: "You stood ornamented (*ornata*) so as to please the people, in clothing a pimp gave you" (1.2.7); compare Juvenal 6.131, Messalina going home from work at the brothel "foul with her darkened (*obscuris*) cheeks," or the "painted whore" (*picta lupa*) set to stand outside the Circus wearing her *mitra* (Juvenal 3.66).

Thus the subsequent appearance of the same theme in Christian tirades constitutes, not a new attitude (despite the Christian claims against the wicked pagan Other), but a reworking of an old one. Tertullian's short two-book work *De cultu feminarum* ("On Women's Dress," late 2nd c. CE) is the locus classicus (cf. also Cyprian *De habitu virginum* ["On Maidens' Dress"], and see D'Angelo 1995, esp. on Tertullian's connection between covering the head and covering the genitals). Blaming the female sex, in a famous exordium, for all the ills of humankind starting from Eve (1.1.1–2), Tertullian asserts that the inventors of women's adornment were the fallen angels who mated with the daughters of men (Genesis 6:1–2, *Book of Enoch* 8.1–3). They are the ones who invented the worldly arts, including metallurgy, herb lore, charms, science, and astrology; likewise, they are the ones who gave women

jewelry, dyed wool, and eye makeup (also at 2.10.3). To dress, Tertullian attributes the vice of ambition; to makeup, that of prostitution. Having dealt
with dress in Book 1, he proceeds to makeup in Book 2. His point is that
the purpose of makeup is to entice men to desire women; women should
be responsible for avoiding both the lust and the temptation (2.2.1), and
should not lead others astray. He lists "anointing the face with cream, staining the cheeks with rouge, and lengthening the eyebrows with antimony" as
sins against God (2.5.2), and equates "having a painted face," "lying in your
appearance," and "committing adultery in your appearance" (2.5.5). He concludes with a section on the association between makeup and whores (2.12):
"The alluring display of beauty is invariably joined with and appropriate to
bodily prostitution" (2.12.2). Likewise, the outer appearance should betoken
what is inside (2.13): "Let whiteness come from simplicity, modesty produce
your rosy complexion; paint your eyes with demureness, your mouth with
silence, hang on your ears the words of God, bind on your neck the yoke
of Christ, bow your heads to your husband—that's ornament enough. . . .
Dress in . . . the purple of chastity . . . and you'll have God himself for a
lover" (2.13.7).[18] As in other cultures, and as previously and contemporane-
ously in Greco-Roman culture, the painted face here serves as an index to
the woman's freedom with her genitalia.

Similarly, the Christian poet Prudentius, writing in the late fourth century CE, includes the wearing of makeup by women in his catalogue of sins,
the *Hamartigenia* (258–76). The poem moves from the *mundana machina*
("earthly machine") wobbling under the burden of sins, to women's deceitful devotion to bodily artifice, to the effeminacy of men who reject their
position as *caput muliebris corporis et rex* ("head and king of the woman's
body," 279). Again, the emphasis is on deceit and falsity: the woman "falsi-
fies her outer [or: another] form" (*externam mentitur . . . formam*, 265);
women "dye (*inficiunt*)/ their forms with stain, so that their skin, smeared
with pigment,/ loses what it had been, not to be recognized under its false
color" (274–76).

Cosmetology and Beauty Culture

So far, we have seen ample evidence that the female body in Roman culture
was considered intrinsically disgusting; that makeup itself and the circumstances of its use were considered disgusting; and that women were often
enjoined not to use makeup, or at least not to let themselves be caught put-

ting it on. As the female genitals are at the bottom of all this disgust, so (male-authored) moralizing texts repeatedly claim that makeup is used by women to increase their opportunities for sexual activity—a bad thing, of course. Ovid's advice to women on how to use makeup and maximize their sex life is in keeping with his general (tongue-in-cheek?) flouting of cultural norms, his mocking of Augustan moral edicts. Meanwhile, the displacement of the disgust from the genitals, concealed both by clothing and by physiology, to the face, which in Rome was normally not even veiled, parallels the repeated claims that makeup is deceitful, that it hides what is really there. Makeup is part of a female trickiness that is fundamentally determined by the structure of the female genitals: hence the jokes about what's in the *pyxis*, the makeup box.

Lo and behold, despite all the disgust, a second and large group of texts consists of recipes and recommendations for making makeup, locating makeup within the body of scientific and didactic works that merged what we would call chemistry, botany, pharmacology, medicine, and magic. Of these works, moreover, all those extant have male authors. We see here how the moralizing texts coexisted in tension with a contemporary technology, a science in cahoots with industry—literally, to use Teresa de Lauretis's term, a technology of gender (de Lauretis 1987). Yet these texts, along with the material remains of the Roman cosmetics industry—sometimes decorated, as noted above, with painted depictions of painted women— provide us with a fossilized indication of the real women who were the real market for Roman cosmetics, with scattered traces of women's own beauty practices (compare the medical practices seen in chapter 8). There are even fragments of texts by female experts in *medicamina* for women, though, as with most ancient women writers, most of their writing is lost.[19] The casual wreckage of Pompeii has yielded plentiful remnants of cosmetic apparatus (Allison 2004: 125–58), while grave goods supply, as Rita Berg says, "true sets of objects that physically surrounded women" (2002: 23; see also Swift 2009); the motifs decorate goods that, Berg suggests, women shopped for (66). For Vedia Izzet, the mirrors found in Etruscan tombs form part of "the creation of social personae" for the dead (2012: 72). Charming remains of girls' dolls have been found, complete with little cosmetic kits, so that, as has been noted, girls could learn how to be women (D'Ambra 2007b: 61, 63; Dolansky 2012; Shumka 2008: 174). Moreover, as Leslie Shumka argues, for the *ornatrix* herself, beautification was a skill to be proud of, so that her tools might be displayed on her gravestone (2008: 185). Thus, in Roman culture as today, real women can be said both to implicate themselves in a system by which they adapt their bodies to suit a standard (beauty) at least partly designed by themselves, and to be implicated in a system that conceals, disguises, derides, and silences them. Such processes of co-optation seem indispensable to patriarchal societies, Rome among them. The term "beauty culture" incorporates the paradox whereby a cultural practice simultaneously constructs and erases its practitioners.

Ovid again provides a starting point. After his cosmogonical introduction, the instructor of the *Medicamina faciei femineae* goes on to give some specific tips for how to achieve the desired *forma* (35–100, where this fragmentary poem breaks off). Significantly, he begins with a warning that women should not rely on magic arts to achieve the desired end (35–42):

> Thus rather [should] love [arise] than by powerful herbs,   35
>   which the magical hand cuts with awesome art;
> don't you believe in plants nor in mixed juices
>   and don't you try the hazardous poison of the loving mare.
> (Nor are the middles of snakes split with Marsic chants
>   nor does the wave run backward to its sources;   40
> and even if someone has moved the Temesean bronze,
>   the moon will never be shaken off her horses.)

This standard list of magical acts—cutting special plants, making potions, using the *hippomanes* (a membrane from the forehead of a newborn foal), the Marsic snake charm, forcing streams to flow backwards, drawing down the moon—calls to the reader's mind a whole field of methods for attracting a lover by forcing his emotions (as do the evil witches in Horace *Satires* 1.8 and *Epodes* 5).[20] The instructor continues with a pious recommendation that "girls" (*puellae*) should please men instead by their good morals, which will last even after age has devastated their *forma* and they are ashamed to look in the mirror because of their wrinkles (43–50). But the initial rejection of magic (in the literal sense: *maga . . . manus*, "the magical hand," 36) anticipates the whole next section of the poem, in which the instructor, after his nod to good conduct, proceeds to concoct potions of his own. He clearly wishes his recipes to suggest a field other than magic: medicine. That the border between these two fields was a contested one can clearly be seen in the texts, and is underscored by the range of the term *medicamina* itself: what cures, what amends, something concocted.

In its present incomplete form, the *Medicamina* gives only four recipes and the beginning of a fifth, and even these are not sharply divided one from the other, so that the effect is of a long grocery list. The first (51–68) recipe is for a night cream for the complexion, and calls for African grain, vetch, ten raw eggs, stag's horn, pounded narcissus bulbs, gum with spelt, and honey: "whatever woman will apply this *medicamen* to her face,/ will shine more smoothly than her mirror" (67–68). The second (69–76), another skin cream, calls for lupines, beans, white lead, fine red soda, and Illyrian iris. A *medicamen* derived from birds' nests, called *alcyonea*, will "rout spots from the face" (78); this should be mixed with honey for better smearability. A fourth recipe (83–98) finds a new use for old incense, along with soda, gum, myrrh, honey, fennel, dried roses (a handful), Libyan salts, frankincense drops, and barley water: "just let this be smeared on your soft face for a little while,/ there will be no color on your whole face" (97–98). The poem breaks off with a recommendation of poppy paste for the cheeks. The ingredients, largely vegetable-based and pleasant-smelling, contrast with the invective picture of makeup as disgusting. They range from the common to the expensive and exotic, and the labor entailed ranges from the girl's own pounding of poppies (99–100) to the hired labor of mills (58) and men (75). The effect is highly technical, combining the didactic with the catalogue, and represents a poetic version of the encyclopedias for which the Hellenistic world had such an affinity. Its application to makeup here might seem like an Ovidian send-up, except for the equally serious and much lengthier treatment in the work of the elder Pliny.[21]

The effort to distinguish between magic and medicine is one of Pliny's primary concerns in his *Historia naturalis* (*Natural History*).[22] This amazing compendium (77 CE) describes the physical world from iron ore to human beings. Along the way, Pliny includes tantalizing throwaway lines (for example, on the efficacy of wearing a woman's brassiere on your head to cure a headache [28.76]—see chapter 8), but, most of all, he lists various elements and their medicinal use, lecturing on the difference between such use and the practices of the Magi (26.19–20, 27.57, 28.4–9, 30.1–16, 30.95, 37.54), whom he sees as unscrupulous eastern charlatans, "barbarians and outsiders" (*barbari externique*, 28.6).

In the course of his exegesis, he tells us some things about women's beauty aids which tally with the list of ingredients in the *Medicamina faciei femineae*. Some of his information is unique, and purports to tell about real women's real practices—beauty culture. He notes that some women have their eyelashes dyed every day (11.154), a practice he feels is excessive (*tanta est decoris adfectatio*, "so great is their yen for beauty"); he concludes by remarking that it is said that too much sex makes the eyelashes fall out,

and deservedly so (*haut inmerito*). Antimony is used by women to make
their eyes look larger (33.102). Pliny lists some hair dyes: red, 28.191 (used in
Germany; cf. Martial 8.33, Ovid *AA* 3.163 *Germanis . . . herbis*),15.87; blonde,
26.164; black, 32.67–68 (by means of leeches, but you have to keep oil in
your mouth or your teeth will turn black, too), 26.164; unspecified, 16.180,
35.194 (also used as mascara). He does not, however, associate this practice
strongly with either gender. On the other hand, he says that he considers
depilatories to be "women's *medicamenta*," adding that they are now used
by men (26.164, also 36.154), a situation he deplores (14.123). As will be
seen below, depilation was on the list of bad behaviors attributed to *cinaedi*
(adult men who allowed themselves to be penetrated by other men).

By far the majority of Pliny's recipes have to do with women's skin. Most
familiar might be the use of asses' milk, made notorious by Nero's wife Poppaea, who, Pliny says, used to travel with five hundred she-asses so that she
could keep up her regimen of bathing in a tub of their milk (*HN* 11.238);
the idea was that it "smoothed her skin." Elsewhere Pliny notes that some
women bathe their faces in asses' milk seven times daily, emulating Poppaea (*HN* 28.183). Wrinkles, we recall, were singled out by Ovid to represent
what ends beauty; as we have seen, male writers portray women as worrying not only about the wrinkles on their faces, but also about stretchmarks
from childbirth, and Pliny has a remedy for stretchmarks: a lotion made
from salt and melanthium (31.84). White earth of Chios is good for women's
skin, and can also be used to touch up whitewash (35.194). For skin care,
women use fat from a sow that has not littered (28.139). Pliny apologizes
for giving a recipe for face cream made from the jelly of a bull calf's bone:
frivolum videatur, non tamen omittendum propter desideria mulierum, "it
might seem frivolous, but it should not be left out, because of what women
want" (28.184). He appends to this a recipe employing bull's dung to make
the cheeks red, though *crocodilea* (crocodile intestine salve) is better (recall Horace's invective description of women's cosmetics, which includes
crocodile dung; see von Staden 1992 on the association of dung therapies
with women in ancient medicine). Women also "nourish their skin" with
the foam of the various kinds of beer made out of cereals from across the
empire—*zythum* from Egypt, *caelia* and *cerea* from Spain, *cervesia* and others from Gaul (22.164)—and also use the red seed of osyris (27.111). Pliny
repeatedly appeals to women's own practices, even attributing *desideria*—
desires, tastes, a market—to women.

Curiously, most of Pliny's skin-cream recipes are designed to conceal or
remove freckles.[23] The ash of murex shell with a mixture of honey for seven

days, followed by an eggwhite fomentation on the eighth day, clears spots on a woman's face, removes wrinkles, and fills out the skin (32.84); also recommended for spot removal (as well as a shampoo) is lead sulfide (33.110), while another lead derivative (34.176) gives women a bright complexion, the only drawback being that it is "deadly" (*letalis*). Similar trade-offs faced nineteenth-century women, as discussed in Banner 183: 40–42, and indeed white lead is attested as a cosmetic frequently from antiquity through the modern period, probably due to the fact that Pliny's *Natural History* continued to be widely available. Specifically for the removal of freckles, Pliny lists the following plant products: elaterium (cucumber juice) smeared on the face in sunshine (20.9); red bulbs in the sun with wine or vinegar (20.103); rocket and vinegar (20.125); wild cumin and vinegar (20.162); gith and vinegar (also good against leprosy, 20.183); corchorus (2.183); alkanet and vinegar (22.49) and bugloss root ointment (22.52), both also good against leprosy; *sium*, also used as a night cream for "flaws on women's faces"; barley meal, vinegar, and honey (22.124); a decoction of wild lupines (22.156), also good for the skin generally; white grape juice (23.23, also good for "faults of the skin on the face" in general, and for bruises, scars, and warts); oil of ben nut (23.89); wild fig juice (23.126); decoction of white myrtle leaves (23.163); plane tree seed balls in vinegar and honey (24.44, also good for cancerous sores and pustules); agnus castus seed, saltpeter, and vinegar (24.63, also good for lichens); rosemary seed (24.100); paste of arum and honey (24.145); fenugreek meal and sulfur (24.186, also good for leprous sores); *telephion* ointment (27.137). Inorganic ingredients include soda (31.122, also good for leprosy) and the marshy *adarca*, which "removes freckles from women's faces" (32.140). At 32.85 Pliny lists ways to remove freckles and "other flaws" with cuttlefish bones (other fishy remedies at 32.87, 97, 98). Orache is said to *cause* freckles and pimples (20.219). Lest there be any puzzlement as to why anyone would want to go out and get some orache, another observation suggests an answer: Pliny notes that a *stelio* (spotted lizard) drowned in urine makes a *malum medicamentum* that causes freckles on the face of one who drinks this potion, and so "those plotting against the beauty of their husbands' girlfriends (*paelicum*)" kill such a lizard in her face cream (29.73). The remedy is egg yolk, honey, and soda. Real women, real rivals, real heartbreak, real home remedies? The figure of the *paelex* haunts even the makeup counter.

That women themselves were indeed particularly concerned about freckles and other marks on their faces is claimed by Celsus, another medical authority of the first century CE: *Paene ineptiae sunt curare varos et len-*

ticulas et ephelidas, sed eripi tamen feminis cura cultus sui non potest, "It is almost silly to treat (*curare*) pimples and freckles and moles, but the concern (*cura*) for their *cultus* cannot be torn away from women" (6.5.1). Again, this gives us a rare insight (if we believe it) into women as consumers with desires of their own. Two surprising asides from Pliny suggest that more than vanity was at stake: he says that divinities (*numina*) do not obey those with freckles, and cannot be seen by them (30.16); and after a list of freckle cures, he comments: *Invenio apud auctores his qui lentigines habeant negari magice sacrificiorum usum,* "I find in my sources that to those who have freckles is denied, in Magic custom, the practice of ritual offerings" (28.188). The latter comment brings us around from the *materia* of Pliny's *ars*—the women whose faces need to be cured—to his rival and rejected *ars,* that of the Magi. Not only are freckles an outward bad sign, a *vitium,* to be worked on by Pliny's science; they suffice in themselves to disqualify the freckled from practices of which Pliny disapproves anyway.

It is as if freckles were like the bad spots on a piece of fruit: repellent in themselves, also perhaps indicative of interior decay. Compare Kathy Peiss on a similar idea in the early twentieth century (1990: 147):

> For beauty culturists, as for many nineteenth-century Americans, the face was a window into the soul, and complexion problems were indicative of a life that was disordered, out of balance. Thus Susanna Cocroft asked women: "Is your complexion *clear*? Does it express the clearness of your life? Are there discolorations or blemishes in the skin—which symbolize imperfections within?"

A parallel may be found in Pliny's recommendation for getting back at your rival. What must Roman face cream have been like, we wonder, if your rival would not notice that a lizard had been killed in it? As seen above, Latin invective portrays the very makeup on a woman's face as repellent, crumbling, decaying. Makeup itself is to be concealed, hidden, kept inside, made up, as it is, of repellent ingredients: crocodile dung, scum, smelly wool grease, lizards.

Juvenal touches on this aspect of makeup in his immense satire on women (6.457–73). A woman in a facial mask made of bread is described as *foeda aspectu,* "foul to see," and *ridenda,* "laughable" (461); her face cream smears the lips of her "wretched husband" (463; elsewhere he is befouled by her urine [313], or nauseated by her vomit [432–33]), while her lover sees the clean end result (464–66), the product of exotic cosmetics. Like Poppaea, she bathes in asses' milk (468–70). Juvenal poses the rhetorical question (471–73), "But something that is covered and bathed in so many varied *medicamina*, and receives the lumps of cooked and soaked cream of wheat—should it be called a face or a wound?" What links the two senses of *medicamina* as "medicine" and "cosmetic," then, is the notion that the woman's face, like a wound, is something that is being cured—or that needs to be cured. Yet implied in these cosmetological texts are real women, briefly visible to us—women who literally bought into a system that could see a woman's face as a wound.

Making Up Gender, Making Up Empire

If makeup is a sign of the female—of the difference between outside and inside, top and bottom—and the makeup itself is a paradoxical substance—repellent in content but producing beauty—it makes sense that the (imputed) wearing of makeup should have been used in Roman culture by extension to mark other kinds of difference as well: among males, to mark off those who, as adults, wanted to be penetrated sexually by other males (loosely lumped together here as *cinaedi*); among nations, to mark off barbarians from their conquerors.

Roman ethnographers like to describe how tribes on their borders painted themselves, in order to confirm the Greco-Roman definition of barbarians as Other, just as women are Other in relation to men.[24] Those at the center (Rome) are normal and do not paint themselves; those at the margins are abnormal, and do. This is only one example of the more general Roman use of accounts of barbarians to talk about what it meant to be Roman, most notably in Tacitus's *Germania* (early second century CE), as seen in chapter 1. The tone of these accounts is well represented by the locus classicus on the Britanni painting themselves with woad. Caesar writes, in his *Gallic Wars* (5.14.3):

> Indeed, all the Britanni dye themselves (*se . . . inficiunt*) with woad, which produces a blue (*caeruleus*) color, and by this means they are a more horrible sight when they go into battle; their hair is long and flowing, and every part of the body is shaven, except the head and the upper lip.

This blue color, the color of the ocean at the margin of the world, recurs in other accounts of distant peoples: Pliny describes the Agathyrsi as having "blue hair" (*HN* 4.88); Silius Italicus writes of the "blue inhabitant of Thule" (17.416). Painting the face or body is attributed indifferently to both male and female barbarians; thus Pliny (22.2):

> Likewise I notice that, for the sake of beauty (*forma*) and of traditional rituals, some of the foreign (*exterarum*) races use certain herbs on their bodies. Indeed, the women among the barbarian peoples smear their faces, some with one [herb], some with another, and among the Dacians and Sarmatians even the males inscribe their bodies. There is in Gaul [a plant] like the plantain, called "woad," and the wives and daughters-in-law of the Britanni, smeared over their whole bodies, walk naked in certain rites, reproducing the color of the Ethiopians.

The Ethiopians here connote the extreme of exoticism, and their color is often treated as unattractive in satiric contexts.[25] Vergil cites the *picti Agathyrsi* in one list of exotic peoples (*Aeneid* 4.146) and the *picti Geloni* in another (*Georgics* 2.115). The word *picti* can mean "painted"; it can also, however, mean "embroidered," and there is a chance that these exotic skin decorations, as with Pliny's "inscribed" Dacians and Sarmatians, were achieved by tattooing rather than by paint. The third-century CE historian Herodian thinks the Britanni tattoo themselves with designs and pictures of animals (3.14.7); the fourth-century CE poet Claudian, in his *Getic Wars* (416–18), speaks of Roman soldiers who have read the "figures marked with iron" on the body of a dying Pict. In classical Greek culture, decorative tattooing is reported and depicted as a practice of the paradigmatically barbaric Thracians. Like the long, unkempt locks and checkered trousers of barbarians and Amazons, marking of the skin provides an easy means of differentiating marked from unmarked groups of people.[26]

The content of Caesar's description of the painted Britanni presents them as antithetical to the female, extremely warlike. Similarly, Tacitus says that the savage and half-known Harii paint themselves (black?) and carry black shields when they make their sneak attacks in the dead of night (*Germania* 43.5). For Sidonius Apollinaris, writing in Gaul in the fifth century CE, the frontier has moved; he sees himself as Roman, humorously beset by seven-foot-tall Burgundian neighbors who grease their long hair with butter (*C.* 12.3, 7, 11). Yet these outsiders paradoxically combine an ultravirile proficiency in war with qualities and external attributes considered female by the Romans. The long, loose locks of barbarian men are described with phrases usually used in Latin to describe the hair of a distraught or grieving woman (e.g., *crinibus effusis*, Lucan 1.443; see chapter 9 below). Such warriors associate themselves with women in battle; the tribesmen defending the island of Anglesey against the Romans are, according to Tacitus, accompanied by Druids and by women looking like Furies, with their hair hanging down (*crinibus deiectis*, *Annals* 14.30.1).[27] At the extremes of the known world, some even sink so low as to be ruled by women (Tacitus *Germania* 45.9—"to such a degree do they degenerate not only from freedom but even from slavery"). Thus Tacitus, describing the elaborate chignons of the Suebi, feels compelled to defend them from suspicions that they may be more interested in romance than is consistent with virility (*Germania* 38.4): "This is their beauty regimen (*cura formae*), but it is not harmful; for they are adorned not in order to make love or be loved, but to create terror as they go into war, their hair arranged for the eyes of the enemy."[28]

Conversely, barbaric *cultus* is contrasted in Roman texts with the proper beauty of Roman women. Martial writes of the good wife and mother Claudia Rufina (11.53.1-3):

> Though Claudia Rufina is descended from the blue (*caeruleis*) Britanni,
>> how she displays the breast of the Latin race!
> What beauty of form (*decus formae*) she has!

He goes on to praise her for her conformity to Roman ideals of behavior for married women. On the other hand, the elegist Propertius (first century BCE) scolds his mistress (2.18.23–32):

> Now, crazy woman, you even imitate the dyed (*infectos*) Britanni,
>> and you fool around, staining your head with foreign colors?
> As nature made it, that's the right look for everyone: 25
>> a Belgic color is foul on a Roman face.
> May many bad things happen under the earth to that girl
>> who foolishly changes and falsifies her hair!
> Take it away; to me you will certainly seem pretty,
>> to me you are pretty enough, if only you visit me often.   30
> But if some girl has stained her temples with blue dye
>> then is a blue beauty (*forma*) good?

It is hard to be sure even what the poet is accusing his mistress of: painting her face with woad? Dyeing her hair? Using blue shadow to contour her face? What is clear here is that her makeup aligns her with the barbarian Other, and that the practice of using makeup itself is aligned with barbarian "staining." In the poet's eyes, what the *puella* has done to make herself beautiful is wrong; he can tell her what is right, what will give her the correct *forma*.[29]

Whereas barbarians paint themselves because they are barbarians, men who are said to like to play the part of women sexually—*cinaedi*, who let themselves be penetrated by other men—are said to mark this by wearing makeup like women, along with women's clothing (Edwards 1993: 63–97; Richlin 1993: 541–54). Petronius vividly describes the decaying makeup of a *cinaedus* who is sexually molesting the narrator: "Streams of hair gel ran down his forehead as he was sweating, and there was so much chalk in the wrinkles of his cheeks that you'd have thought a wall with the plaster worn away by rain was collapsing" (*Satyrica* 23.5). Elsewhere, a slave woman takes the narrator, Encolpius, for a prostitute because of his styled hair, makeup (*facies medicamine attrita*), use of his eyes, and gait (126.2). Juvenal, in an extended vignette of *cinaedi* at home (2.83–114), imagines them wearing women's clothing; one applies eye makeup (93–95), his eyebrow "painted with wet soot" (*madida fuligine tinctum*), another wears a hairnet. Similarly, in a description of *cinaedi* who insinuate themselves into your (i.e., a man's) home and corrupt your wife, the poet claims that "this adulterer in a hairnet feeds his eyes with soot" (*oculos fuligine pascit . . . reticulatus adulter*, 6.O.21–22—*adulter* ends the line with a surprise). The effeminate emperor Otho bequeaths to the group in *Satire* 2 a mirror (typically a woman's accoutrement) in place of armor, and the poet pictures him using it to apply a facial mask (2.99–109).

Over two hundred years earlier, the statesman Scipio Aemilianus, probably in a speech made as censor in 142–41 BCE (quoted by Aulus Gellius, 6.12.5; see Astin 1967: 255), had defined a *cinaedus* by his appearance:

> For a man who daily is adorned before his mirror (*adversum speculum ornetur*), covered with perfumes, whose eyebrows are shaven, who walks around with his beard plucked out and his thighs depilated . . . does anyone doubt about him that he has done the same thing that *cinaedi* do?

Gender here is again performative; but note how affect is equated with sexual behavior. Compare another of the elder Seneca's cases (*Controv.* 5.6), which debates whether a young man who has been gang-raped after dressing up as a woman on a bet should suffer the restrictions on civil rights of an *impudicus*, literally an "unchaste man." One orator, arguing against the young man, declaims: "He put on womanish clothing, he arranged his hair in a woman's style, he circled his eyes in girlish pimping, he colored his cheeks." Another: "Give him girl's clothing, give him night: he'll be raped." The speakers assume both the inevitability of the rape of women, and the permeability of a man who could pass as a woman. In this stereotype, the feminization of the *cinaedus* and the foreigner become conflated in the image of the effeminate (Greek) easterner, as for example in a poem of Martial which contrasts the addressee, a Greek with oiled hair and depilated skin, with the poet, a shaggy Spaniard (10.65; see Richlin 1992: 44, 136–37). We might compare this with Seneca's description, discussed earlier, of a gathering of women as a *mitrata contio* (*Suasoriae* 2.21).

Thus, in Book 1 of the *Ars amatoria*, when still addressing men, Ovid makes it clear what they are *not* to do: curl their hair (1.505), depilate their legs with pumice (506)—this is for the eunuch priests of Cybele (507–8). *Forma viros neglecta decet*, "neglected beauty is becoming to men" (509); *munditie placeant, fuscentur corpora Campo*, "let them be pleasing by their neatness, let their bodies be painted/tanned from the playing fields" (513). Men's togas should fit well and be clean (514), their teeth should be clean (515), their shoes should fit well (516), their hair should not be cut too short so that it is bristly (517), but hair and beard should be nicely cut (518). Fingernails should be cut short and clean (519), no hairs should stick out of the nose (520); no bad breath (521), no goat in the armpits (522). The poet concludes: "Let wanton girls do the rest,/ and whatever not-really-a-man (*male vir*) seeks to have a man" (523–24). For the younger Seneca, one of the sons to whom the elder Seneca dedicated his rhetorical work, *virtus* = manly = "dusty and tanned (*coloratam*), with calloused hands"; *voluptas* = "soft and emasculated" = "painted and embalmed like a corpse for a funeral" (*fucatam et medicamentis pollinctam*, *Vit. beat.* 7.3; so Gordon 2002: 91). Makeup makes the woman, and unmakes the man.

Slippage in the Courtroom

It is, then, quite startling to read among the letters of the younger Pliny, a cheerful, kindly millionaire and civil servant under the emperor Trajan, the following reminiscence of the accomplished orator and informer, Marcus Regulus (*Letters* 6.2):

The very fact that he used to outline either his right eye or his left (the right if he was about to act for the claimant, the other if he was about to act for the defendant); that he used to move a white plaster to one or the other eyebrow; the fact that he always used to consult soothsayers on the outcome of the case; [all this] used to come from an excess of superstition, to be sure, but also from the great seriousness with which he took these endeavors.

This extraordinary (and, to my knowledge, unparalleled) example of an orator in makeup points to an interesting area of slippage in Roman gender construction.[30] For there is something of an overlap in Roman culture between the behavior of an orator in the courtroom—that quintessential proving ground of Roman manhood—and the sexually suspect movements of a dancer. The orator's movements, known as *actio*, were influenced by the practice of actors, though the great first-century CE professor of rhetoric Quintilian repeatedly distances the proper behavior of the orator from that of the stage performer (11.3.89, 103, 123, 184). *Mollis* (effeminate) *actio* is "to be put as far away from you as possible" (11.3.128); the orator is to exhibit "firmness of the body, lest our voice be attenuated to the weakness of eunuchs, women, and sick people" (11.3.19). Again, such behavioral marking connects the sexual and the ethnic; the flamboyant style in Roman oratory was known as "Asian" (connoting the effeminate East), the minimalist as "Attic" (here connoting severe style rather than Greekness). Thus one of the great practitioners of the forensic art, Quintus Hortensius, was attacked for his effeminacy (Aulus Gellius 1.5); his rival in a court case called him "Dionysia," after a famous female dancer.[31] Ironically, the definitively manly Roman art of oratory, enacted in the Forum at the center of the city of Rome, itself incorporated certain marginal elements.

Conclusions

In Roman thought, the use of makeup seems primarily to be connected with the idea that the female body is something that needs to be fixed. This idea appears to underlie both the real use of makeup by real women, as far as we can know about it, and the references to makeup in the works of male authors. Cosmetics are assimilated to the medical-magical substances catalogued by the elder Pliny and others, which were assembled and marketed by both male and female practitioners. Disgust with the lower parts of the female body—what Bakhtin calls the "material bodily lower stratum" (1984: 303–436)—is generalized to the whole body, dealt with palpably on the face, and generalized further to the cosmetics applied to the face and body, even to the pot they come in. Makeup is not to be used by men; painted men become Other, categorizing themselves with women and/or barbarians. The adjective *externus/a/um* appears sometimes applied to the surface of the body and sometimes applied to the marginal areas of the world; the *interiora* are paradoxically troublesome in the same way.

What are we to make of the variety of personal categories associated by Roman male writers with the use of cosmetics—women, but also barbarians, *cinaedi*, and the odd orator? Here it may help to move from the symbolic to law, and think about the relationship between the head and the citizen. Appropriately for our purposes, citizenship at Rome was sometimes called, in law, *caput*—"head." Change in a person's social status was termed *capitis deminutio*, literally "lessening of head." This could happen, for instance, with the loss of freedom through sale into slavery, or the loss of citizenship through exile; *caput*, as "civil honor," was stained by the censor's black mark which denoted official *infamia*—incurred, for example, by adult males who "suffered womanish things in their body." A slave's *caput* had no rights.[32] Free Roman women, who were citizens of a sort—owning property, moving about in public, acting as parties to contracts, literate—nonetheless could not vote or hold office, and their right to public speech was highly problematical; when women did make forensic speeches, they were written about as if they had opened their bodies to penetration.[33] (Indeed, within the Roman sexual system, the face and mouth—often denoted by the same word, *os*—are seen as peculiarly vulnerable to sexual violation and staining; Latin has a word for oral rape, *irrumare*, and there are many Roman jokes about the mouth tainted by oral intercourse.)[34] The extremes of invective against Roman women astonish us, considering their degree of social power; Roman invective against women must have constituted a form of extralegal social control (see chapters 2, 3, and 5 above). Roman cosmetic culture, then, forms an elaborate part of that control. Like barbarians, who have no *caput*, and *cinaedi*, whose *caput* is dishonored, Roman women lived in a state of partial decapitation. Even the hinted presence of orators in this group thus seems odd, unless we realize the extent to which Roman oratory played with the boundaries of manhood. Yet for male orators it was always a game; they, by definition, spoke—women did not.

A commentator on the cross-cultural construction of masculinity writes (Gilmore 1990: 11):

Although women, too, in any society are judged by sometimes stringent sexual standards, it is rare that their very status as woman forms part of the evaluation. . . . Rarely is [women's] right to a gender identity questioned in the same public, dramatic way that it is for men. . . . It usually involves questions of body ornament or sexual allure, or other essentially cosmetic behaviors that enhance, rather than create, an inherent quality.

But this misses the point. To return to Butler's notion of the performative aspect of gender: it is clear that in Roman culture, and arguably in others, femaleness is not only problematic but precarious. The invective poems against old women make it clear that it is possible to cease being a woman, to be even more repulsive; I think of Martial's poem in which he tells an old woman to stop believing that what she has is a *cunnus*, since a phallus no longer will have anything to do with it. In this sense, the *medicamina* for the female face are cures that can never succeed, able neither to make nor to mend.

CHAPTER 7

Carrying Water in a Sieve

Class and the Body in
Roman Women's Religion

༄

Introduction

This essay, written in 1994, sprang from two sources. The project on Roman witches that first emerged in chapter 2 was pushing me to look for explanations for Roman beliefs in general Roman culture. If women, particularly old women, were thought to use magic and *venena* to meddle in sex and procreation, and if they posed such a threat to babies, I needed to find out what these beliefs might have to do with Roman women's religious practices and with Roman ideas about the female body. "Carrying Water in a Sieve" summed up some of the material I put together to deal with religion, while "Pliny's Brassiere" (chapter 8) did the same for the body; together, they show that Roman religious practice has an ideological basis similar to that seen in medical practice, and closely related to the themes examined in chapters 2 and 6 above.

In addition, as a result of my new acquaintance with the world of scholarship in religion (see chapter 6 introduction), I began talking about this material to a range of audiences that included students and scholars in the history of religion; this was what I brought to the Annenberg Conference, and finally to a 1992 conference on "Women and Goddess Traditions" at the School of Religion at Claremont Graduate University, organized by the New Testament scholar Karen Jo Torjesen. That conference brought together scholars working on goddess worship across a broad range of cultures ancient and modern, and included feminist scholars for whom goddess worship marked a particularly positive aspect of the female—a position going strong in 1992 within the academy, and still today, although mostly outside the academy (see chapter 10). Classicists still must address the issue of whether prehistoric goddess worship attests to matriarchy (most recently, Talalay 2012). The collection in which this essay originally appeared was made up of the papers from the Claremont conference; the essay as published is thus shaped by the need to address that audience, bringing the unwelcome news that Roman women's religion, even when involved with the worship of goddesses, incorporated a large element of class differentiation, nor did it celebrate the female as separate from and superior to the male. Free Roman women used religious practice to reinforce their identity as superior to that of slave women, the sexual exclusivity of the body being central to various cult practices. Women's cult practice, as far as we can tell from the textual evidence, revolved around wifely fidelity, childbirth, and motherhood.

At the same time, however, it seemed to me that there was good news as well. Conventional histories of Roman religion up until the 1990s barely mentioned women at all, especially not as priests, yet the epigraphic evidence told a different story. During my NEH Fellowship year in 1987–88 I read, along with Pliny's *Natural History*, the *Corpus Inscriptionum Latinarum* (*CIL*) for most of Italy outside Rome, and it turned out that the whole countryside was studded with women with official titles in cult practice. These titles do show traces of the status division seen in textual accounts of women's cult, yet they also show women with different status histories acting together; slave women show up occasionally as dedicators of offerings or as participants in cult, and so we do have concrete evidence of slave women's agency in religious life. The difference between the picture presented by textual evidence and the picture presented by epigraphy and archaeology provides another instance of the methodological model evolved in chapter 1: depends who you ask.

Furthermore, putting together a calendar of women's festivals shows how rich the year was in events in which women held center stage in the city or on the farm, and also how important women's presence was in some festivals in which men were the chief actors. Without Ilia, no Romulus and Remus, we might say—and the consciousness of women's value in fact pervades Roman cult. A list of women's activities also suggests how central religion was in their lives, not only, or even mostly, in organized cult, but in daily household ritual, in small practices that bespeak an underlying worldview (for example, in the use of apotropaic charms, which shade right over into medicine). This is not to say that religion was more important for women than for men, but, rather, that we can know quite a lot about the ways in which religion was important for women, just as we can for men.

This is an area of study in which much new work has been done in the past decade; books by Celia Schultz (2006) and Sarolta Takács (2007) have treated Roman women's religion in detail, historicizing the textual sources that "Carrying Water in a Sieve" treated without much attention to source criticism, indeed without reference to specialists in Roman religion and historiography who focus on individual sources. Barbette Spaeth's study of the goddess Ceres (1996) appeared when this essay was in press, and I am sorry not to have had the chance to benefit from her insights. Any study of ancient women's religion must profit from the massive work done by Ross Kraemer; the experience of teaching courses on "Women in Antiquity" using her sourcebook has done a great deal to shape my thinking.

Major work remains to be done toward understanding Roman religion as an organic system that involved men and women together. The volume introduction and the new note 2 in this chapter give a brief survey of the scholarly landscape since the 1990s; until very recently, a field that had generally omitted women altogether was still divided into "Roman religion" (no women) and "Roman women's religion." Judith Hallett's early work (1984) on the importance of Roman women within the family—well attested—should have prompted more holistic studies of Roman culture; see the volume introduction for gender as a force operating within scholarly practice itself. A new generation now argues for the treatment of religion in the context of households, and against any idea of women as marginal (see Dolansky 2011a, 2011b, 2011c; Flemming 2007a; Holland 2012; Mueller 2011). Cults long designated "women's" in fact included men, and vice versa (Holland 2012: 210–11, with bibliography; Smith 2000); material evidence helps us see worship in the house (Clarke 2003: 73–94). I still think the category "women's religion" is a useful one, since it is clear that many cults were based on gendered concepts, and that religious praxis was one of the main means by which women constructed their gender in antiquity. For enslaved women, the inability to follow in a mother's footsteps would have been a major element in their natal alienation.

The study of women and religion in the ancient Mediterranean today also needs to join in the urgent conversation within Women's Studies on postcolonial and transnational issues involving women and religion. Roman religion was local—indeed, it could be broken down, if we had the data, into an infinity of local practices across Italy and then across an enormous empire—but it also deeded its belief structure to form part of the inheritance of the new religions that were to subsume that empire, eventually to encircle the globe (see Richlin 2010). The study of women's religious practices throughout the Mediterranean at the time of the Roman Empire will help scholars understand Christian practices today, just as the study of veiling in that disparate, intermingled, and deeply rooted set of cultures (see Hughes 2007; Llewellyn-Jones 2003) will help scholars understand veiling in Islam—and vice versa. Global history begins in antiquity.

❧   ❧   ❧

. . . and as she sat there weeping a most curious image, born perhaps from that other image of the spilt milk, arose in her mind. She saw herself as a cup of clear water, which she herself was somehow bearing through a crowd, and which she should have carried carefully, steadily, losing not a drop, so that when *he* asked for it the cup was still full and unpolluted. But instead of that she had let anyone drink who wished. . . . And the strange image grew, till Julia saw all the race of women bearing their vessels of water and passing to and fro among the thirst-tormented race of men: and in the forefront she saw her daughter, carrying a cup of crystal, and holding it high over her head.

Margery Sharp, The Nutmeg Tree, 248–49

When people talk about "goddess worship" today, they often have in mind a cultural formation in which femaleness enjoys a high cultural value and women benefit thereby. The goddesses of the ancient Mediterranean world are still familiar names in the West, and some might expect that Greek and Roman women's religion would have been focused on these goddesses, and that the presence of goddess worship would have influenced, and for the better, not only women's lives but their whole culture. To test this idea, it is important to take a close look at the cultures of the ancient Mediterranean—distinct, various, and many. Of these, Rome is too often lumped in with Greece; it had, in fact, a fascinating and peculiar set of religions all its own, as well as many borrowings. In Roman religion can sometimes be seen practices that would be transformed into Christian festivals and cults of saints. Yet while the beginning of the Roman Empire is roughly contemporary with the beginning of Christianity, Rome had, by that time, existed as a republic for five hundred years and more. Our fragmentary sources thus allow us to see something of Roman women's religion over a long span of time. What we see is a decidedly phallocentric culture, in which femaleness is officially valued only insofar as it is connected with fertility and governed by chastity; compare the kind of social policing seen in chapters 1, 2, 5, and 6. As in the vision of Margery Sharp's modern Julia, Roman women must have viewed their bodies as vessels borne through life, not only precariously but competitively.[1] For, as in her vision, women were divided according to the openness of their bodies: slave bodies were open, but slavery was a civil status, not a social class, and slaves could be freed, thus becoming citizens, if stained; freedwomen certainly married, but their position as *matronae* was marred by prior slave status; as seen in chapter 1, free prostitutes, even waitresses, had less social honor than other free women; even honorable free women were divided into upper-class and lower-class. Each woman would have known her place in what might be called a sex/class system. The good news is that we can see women managing that system, and can thus observe Roman religion as a gendered whole; moreover, considering the attitude displayed by that other Julia, daughter of Augustus (chapter 3), and the two Sulpicias (chapter 4), we can be sure that some Roman women talked back to the police.

The study of Roman women's religion was in its early days when this essay was in the making, and in it I juxtaposed two kinds of material not previously considered together: the historical evidence for women's leadership in public religion throughout Italy, and the symbolic meaning of women's cult in the larger culture.[2] The tension between the resulting stories has turned out to be a main issue for new work in the field. Studies of women's religion that would treat the category "Roman" as non-homogeneous are still much to be desired; I am afraid this essay does not do much in that direction, although the listing of epigraphic evidence by location might still, I hope, prove useful. I would like, someday, to establish for Rome the relation of women and the sacred to women and the monstrous. In particular, I want to understand some negative stereotypes that pervade Roman culture (and many others)—stereotypes in which female monsters, or witches, do things like eat babies, poison people, and transform people into animals. One of my hypotheses is that this kind of thing can be understood as a symbolic inversion of what was normative behavior for real Roman women, and of the female, with respect to religion and ritual. Apart from culture-wide festivals (e.g., the Saturnalia) and foreign imports (e.g., Magna Mater, the Bacchanalia), Roman women's cults show a preoccupation with the female body—with chastity, lactation, childbirth, the nurturing of children, marriage—and with the sex/class divisions relevant to the female body: *matrona*, slave, prostitute. The same concerns are shown in household cult and ritual, in medical beliefs associated with the female body (e.g., beliefs in the curative or harmful uses of menstrual blood and women's milk; see chapter 8), and in state rituals like the Fordicidia that enacted beliefs about birth and fertility using animals' bodies. Whereas the monstrous/female kills (and sometimes eats) children, feeds people poison, and breaks boundaries, the sacred/female values the bearing and nurturing of children and reinforces boundaries.

Such questions about symbolic meaning can only be asked after inquiry into the varieties of Roman women's religious experience. What was it? How was it structured? Did the worship of goddesses in a pantheon correspond with an elevation of the female in Roman symbolic systems? Any examination of Roman women's rituals raises issues about the way in which these women may have accepted, and defined themselves by, rituals that identified them with their bodies—limit or celebration, depends on your point of view; and about how these rituals may have been used by one class of women to express their power over other classes of women, in a culture in which most kinds of public power were vested in men. This in turn raises overall issues of women's complicity in patriarchy. On the other hand, the extant sources also raise the definite possibility of female solidarity and group identification in Roman culture; it is probably of a sort not uncommon in societies with strong gender differentiation, and it can simply reinforce the oppression of women, but it can also be a source of women's strength and female consciousness (see, for comparison, Buckley and Gottlieb 1988: 13 on the enjoyability of menstrual seclusion; du Boulay 1986; Giovannini 1981). Jack Winkler, in "The Laughter of the Oppressed" (1990c), analyzed Athenian women's rituals in such a positive light, and compared them with similar rituals of modern Arab women (see now O'Higgins 2001, 2003); in chapter 8, I consider how women may have used beliefs about the special powers of the female body for their own purposes. This whole problem ties in with current concerns about ethnography and epistemology: how can we, as outside observers, evaluate the experience of Roman women?[3]

In framing answers to these questions, I am following in the footsteps of feminist historians of religion, whose projects have made scholars aware of whole new ways of looking at religion in culture: Bernadette Brooten's recovery of women leaders in the ancient synagogue; Karen Torjesen's recovery of women in the early Church; Ross Kraemer's treatment of the ancient Mediterranean as a world full of women visibly active in religion, a world that Greeks, Romans, Jews, and Christians inhabit together. Whereas Kraemer (1992: 80–92) asks what it meant for Roman women to be priests, Mary Beard (1990: 41–47) asks what it meant for any Roman to be a priest. Chava Weissler, in her study of Jewish women in the early modern period, points out (1987: 86–87) that

> making gender a category of analysis enables us to understand Ashkenazic Judaism as a *total* social system in which both men *and* women participated . . . it leads . . . to the investigation of the distribution of domains of the religious life between women and men.

Their work made this essay thinkable, and informs my efforts to imagine real Roman women as active participants in an intelligible cultural system.

In what follows, the reader may feel, with dismay, that I am here leaving out the most familiar faces in the world of Roman religious culture: Christian, Jewish, and imperial cults receive no attention here, and I give short shrift to weddings and funerals, which of course played important roles in Roman women's lives (see chapter 9 on funerals, and now Caldwell 2007, Hersch 2010 on weddings). The day-to-day or "folk" aspect of women's religious practice could also be much more fully documented than the scope of this essay allows; I have dealt elsewhere with women's use of magico/medical rituals and amulets (chapter 8), and there is more to be said about women's involvement in "magic" generally (see now Brooten 1996: 73–114; Faraone 2001), as well as about daily observance associated with the home and with women's duties (see now Dolansky 2011a, 2011b, 2011c, 2012). The Vestals show up here only intermittently, as do the more familiar goddesses in the Roman pantheon and the notorious gods and goddesses of imported cults: Bacchus, Isis, Magna Mater, all popular with women. Here I want to focus mainly on those aspects of Roman women's religious life that were most peculiarly Roman, and in the context of Roman Italy.

Sources

The religion of Roman women, and Roman women in Roman religion—which are two different things—have been very imperfectly known, dependent as they are on scattered data that have yet to be assembled in full (some in Kraemer 1988 [2004]). The extant Roman sources for women and religion are like tattered lacework: the original Roman treatises on the subject, such as they were, are lost, and even the testimonia of them are fragmentary. We must depend on Roman anecdote collectors, encyclopedists, and cultural historians, sometimes fleshed out by Ovid's *Fasti*.[4] What we have from them is tantalizing—for example, the source usually known as Paulus ex Festo.

One of the obscure characters on the edges of a classical education, Paulus is even blocked from the general reader by his peculiar name: "ex Festo" is clearly not a cognomen. He turns out to be three people: Verrius Flaccus, who put together a marvelous dictionary of Roman lore in the early first century CE; Pompeius Festus, who epitomized this dictionary in the late second century CE; and Paulus Diaconus, who excerpted from Festus in the eighth century CE (hence the name Paulus ex Festo). Lindsay's Teubner text obligingly prints the fragments of Festus interspersed with the excerpts from Paulus: so in some places we have both Festus's original and Paulus's excerpt; then there are places where there are shreds of Festus, partly reconstructed from Paulus's excerpt; and, unfortunately, there are long runs where we have only Paulus. And here before our eyes we see the process by which women get erased from history.

First, it is clear that Verrius Flaccus drew on several books about rituals involving substantial participation by women. Festus will give long runs of entries about women and mourning, or wedding customs, or women in ritual generally (e.g., 282–84L). And it is clear that, just as Paulus excerpted from Festus, and Festus from Verrius, so Verrius was copying out of something like *The Big Book of Roman Weddings*. Such sources are all lost.[5] Second, although Paulus does keep a lot of items about women, we can see, when we have both the passage from Festus and the excerpt from Paulus, that sometimes he did not. For example, Festus records (152L) a taboo on wearing footgear made from the skin of a dead cow, for the *flaminicae*, high priestesses at Rome; in Paulus (153L), Festus's *flaminicis* has become *flaminibus*, so that the priestesses are replaced by priests. So when we have long runs of Paulus and Festus is lost, we know that a lot about women is lost, too.[6] I dwell on the case of Paulus ex Festo here to emphasize that the state of our knowledge of Roman women's participation in cult may well mislead us as to the original attitude toward this phenomenon in pre-Christian Roman culture. When it has been pieced together, the evidence suggests that Roman women participated actively in cult at all levels.

A different sort of lacy data, more directly attached to real women, is available from Latin inscriptions from all over Italy; it shows, roughly, that there were priestesses, and precincts of dedication special to women, in numerous places. But, though it is useful to have the map of Italy dotted with these points of light, each individual case brings with it only the sketchiest context. Moreover, the way in which the *CIL* was assembled means that we have a sample that looks larger than it is. In the late nineteenth century, a team of energetic German classicists began scouring Italy and the former Roman Empire for inscriptions, most of them religious dedications and tombstones. They not only examined stones themselves—Theodor Mommsen climbing up a ladder to look through a spyglass at an inscription incorporated into a church tower—but collected reports of stones, some long vanished, that had been turned up by eighteenth-century plows. The resulting enormous collection, assembled in huge volumes with meticulous reproductions, organized geographically, town by town, province by province, gives the impression of comprehensiveness. In fact, what we often get is ten stones from one village, a hundred or so from a big town, all spread over a period of five hundred years. The resulting picture could be called "suggestive," no more. Thus, although my preferred goal would be a picture of religious life throughout the Italian peninsula, I am forced, as usual, to depend for my main narrative on textual sources based in the city of Rome. At least sometimes these sources indicate that they describe life in the countryside, or in other towns.[7]

Priestess Terminology

H. S. Versnel begins his essay on Roman women's worship of Bona Dea with an apposite quotation from the elder Cato (second century BCE), describing the duties of the *vilica*, the slave housekeeper on a plantation (*De agri cultura* 143.1; in Versnel 1992: 31):

> She must visit the neighbouring and other women very seldom, and not have them either in the house or in her part of it. She must not go out to meals or be a gad-about. She must not engage in religious worship

herself or get others to engage in it for her without the orders of the master or the mistress; let her remember that the master attends to the devotions for the whole household.[8]

Versnel goes on to base his otherwise convincing and lively argument on a putatively strict division of the Roman religious sphere by gender as seen here in Cato: ritual is a male thing, not for women. This is also the impression you would get from most handbooks on Roman religion: the Vestals are the exception that proves the rule. But perhaps the real situation was not so clear-cut, just as (we might assume) Cato's housekeeper was doing something that prompted him to say no. Indeed, Cato himself goes on to suggest that the *vilica* should garland the hearth on holidays and pray to the *Lar familiaris* (143.2)—a suggestion we find made onstage in a comedy by Cato's coeval Plautus, this time directed to the free mistress of the house (*Rudens* 1206–8). Moreover, Cato suggests that the *vilica* do this *pro copia*—"according to her means"—pointing to the ability of slaves to use their discretionary funds, here for religious purposes. There is also textual evidence that women were involved in public rituals as well as in household cult, sometimes as priestesses or sacrificers. At the Liberalia, old women sat selling cakes, each one with a little grill (*foculum*) on which she sacrificed for each buyer (Varro *De lingua latina* 6.14, cf. Ovid *Fasti* 3.763–67). Old women were also important during the rites of the Feralia, when the ghosts of the dead were placated (Ovid *F.* 2.571–82). A woman called the "Petreia" used to lead processions in the provincial towns, imitating a drunken old woman (Paulus 278, 280L). More vaguely, we hear that there were some rites that had to be performed by women, so the wives of the priests were assigned these (Dionysius of Halicarnassus 2.22).

Sources like Paulus give us the words for types of women involved in ritual: an *armita* was a maiden sacrificing with the fold of her toga thrown back over her shoulder (4L); a *simpulum* was a little cup used for libations, so women dedicated to religion were called *simpulatrices* (455L). Festus says that a public chorus of maidens sang a special hymn during the Second Punic War (446L), and that there were Salic maidens, like the Salic priests (439L), who made sacrifices.

Women who were expert in religion, or who carried out sacrifices, were called *sagae*, *piatrices*, *expiatrices*, or *simulatrices* (Festus 232L, 426L; Paulus 303L). Women priests were usually just called *sacerdotes*, the same word used for men, but sometimes were called *sacerdotulae* (diminutive ending), or *antistitae* (feminine ending).[9] They wore a special head shawl called a *rica* when sacrificing (Varro *LL* 5.130; see now Fantham 2008). The wife of the *flamen Dialis* (the priest of Jupiter at Rome) had the title of *flaminica*, and respected all the same bizarre taboos he did, plus a few more. She had her own bizarre outfit, including the *rica*, which Festus describes as "square, fringed, and purple" (152L, 342L, 368L). She also had a special tall headdress called a *tutulus*, tied onto her hair by a purple ribbon (Festus 484L). She had to wear a dyed (*venenato*) dress, and a twig from a fruitful tree (*de arbore felici*, literally "from a lucky tree") in her *rica*; she could not climb higher than three rungs up a ladder, except for a certain kind called a "Greek ladder"; and she could neither smile, bathe, comb her hair, nor arrange her hair when she went to the festival of the Argei (Aulus Gellius 10.15.26–30; Plutarch *QR* 285a). The *flamen* had to resign if she died, perhaps because of the fact that some rites could not be performed without her (Plutarch *QR* 276d-e). There was a *regina* who made sacrifices, as well as a *rex*; she wore a twig of pomegranate on her head (Paulus 101L). Priestesses used the same sacrificial knife as priests, and *virgines* did as well (Paulus 472L). Some goddesses had their own priestesses: Bona Dea's was called the *damiatrix* (60L), and Ceres had special ones (Valerius Maximus 1.1.1; see now Spaeth 1996).[10]

Priestesses from Roman Italy

The *CIL* leaves us in no doubt that women were active in public cult throughout Italy. This took several forms: (1) priestesshoods in imperial cult, almost always the cult of a female relative of the emperor, (2) priestesshoods in the cult of various goddesses, (3) participation as worshipers, involving large or small dedications (gifts to god or goddess).[11]

Several titles recur in inscriptions to indicate that a given woman holds a priestesshood (see appendix A). Most commonly found is *sacerdos*; evidence is extant of at least eighty-four women from all over Italy who held this title, of whom twenty-four —only about 29 percent—were involved in imperial cult. In contrast, the title *magistra* is found thirty-six times, and is never, or perhaps once, associated with imperial cult. *Ministrae* are sometimes found accompanying *magistrae*, occasionally alone; there are ten of these, none of them associated with imperial cult. Both of these terms have male equivalents, *magister* and *minister*, titles used in a range of contexts from politics to the army to education; both masculine and feminine forms might be translated "superior officer" and "inferior officer." In a religious context, they are normally used of officers in a religious association.[12] The last commonly found title is *flaminica*, a term best known as applied to the wife of the *flamen Dialis* at Rome (above); but the names of at least twenty-five *flaminicae* from all over Italy are extant, of whom ten (40 percent) served in the imperial cult. A couple of rare titles exist that describe groups of female worshipers: a group of *cultrices* from the *collegium* of the small town of Fulginiae (*CIL* 11.5223); and a group of *consuplicatrices*, "fellow women suppliants," of Mater Matuta from Cora in Latium just south of Rome (*CIL* 10.6518).

Outside of imperial cult, the terms *sacerdos*, *magistra*, *ministra*, and *flaminica* are associated with a wide range of particular goddesses. Of the fifty non-imperial *sacerdotes*, thirty were involved with the worship of Ceres and/or Venus; the public priesthood of Ceres and Venus was a major municipal honor in the area around the Bay of Naples. Numerous examples survive from Pompeii, including the benefactress Eumachia, whose statue is a familiar figure to students of women in antiquity.[13] Other *sacerdotes* were in charge of the rites of Magna Mater (eleven examples), Juno Populonia (three), Minerva (two), Isis (two), Fortuna Redux (one), and Jovia Veneria of the people of Abellae (one). The goddess most commonly served by *magistrae* was Bona Dea (nine), followed by Mater Matuta (three); *magistrae* of some other goddesses are attested only singly: Dea Obsequens ("Goddess Obedient"), the spirit of Diana Augusta, Ceres Augusta, Minerva, Fortuna Melior ("Better Luck"), and Juno. A pair of *magistrae* served Proserpina at Vibo in the toe of Italy (*CIL* 10.39), and Venus seems to have been served by teams of *magistrae* at Furfo in the Aternus valley and at Cupra Maritima, a small town on the Adriatic coast (9.3518, 5295). *Ministrae*, who occur more rarely, naturally show a narrower range: three for Bona Dea, one for Magna Mater, one for Salus, one for Juno Populonia, and four unspecified. *Flaminicae* outside imperial cult are often unspecified (twelve of fifteen), and there is a chance that some of these are really in imperial cult, the connection being implicit. Of the remaining three, one represents Feronia, while the other two are described only by place name, the *flaminica pagi Arusnatium* up in Cisalpine Gaul (Italy north of the Po; 5.3928) and the *flaminica* of Pisaurum and Ariminum, neighboring towns on the Adriatic coast (11.6354). One woman is described as both *sacerdos* and *flaminica* of Julia Pia Augusta, of Mater Deum ("Mother of the Gods," i.e., Magna Mater), and of Isis Regina (9.1153), showing how the worship of the empress could blend with the worship of goddesses.

Tombstones quite often give age at death and other biographical information about the person commemorated, and we might hope to find out from inscriptions something about the age at which a woman might become a priestess, or how long she might serve; the Vestals, for example, had well-known rules about this (Plutarch *Life of Numa* 10.1–2; Aulus Gellius 1.12). However, the available information is disappointingly sparse, although still better than nothing. A tombstone from the thinly-settled coast between Barium and the mouth of the river Aufidus (*CIL* 9.307), set up by an unhappy mother to her daughter, tells us that Petilia Secundina, daughter of Quintus [Petilius], was priestess of Minerva and lived for nine years, seven months, and eighteen days; her mother commemorates her *infatigabilem pietat(em)*, her "tireless sense of duty." So from this backwater we get a glimpse of something almost unattested elsewhere: a child priestess, and one evidently engaged in religious activity. Another woman, *ministra* of Salus in the hilly countryside near Amiternum, died at the age of thirty, having served as priestess for thirteen years (9.4460); here we have something that looks more familiar, a woman becoming active in religion around the age at which she would be taking on the role of *matrona*. At the other end of the life cycle, a woman who held the high-ranking job of *sacerdos publica* of Ceres at Puteoli on the bay of Naples died at the age of ninety-three, according to her tombstone (10.1829).

We have much better luck with the question of civil status. For present purposes, I will begin with a crude division of these women into freeborn (certain and uncertain), freed (certain and uncertain), and slave. Roman nomenclature makes this fairly easy to do: freeborn men and women were entitled to give their "filiation," their father's name, while slaves and freed slaves (who legally had no parents) were not; instead, freed slaves gave their former owner's name in the "libertination" formula "freedwoman of So-and-so," and slaves their owner's name in the genitive case. Slave women have only a single name, while freedwomen tack their slave name as a cognomen onto their former owner's *nomen*. Guesswork comes in when there is no filiation or libertination and you have to go by the name itself, hence the category "uncertain." So Flavia Coelia Annia Argiva (*CIL*10.4789) is probably not only freeborn but elite, judging only on the basis of her quadruple name; Tillia Eutychia (10.4889) is probably a freed slave, with her Greek cognomen meaning "Good Luck."[14] Of the 148 priestesses in appendix A whose names are susceptible of interpretation, 80 are certainly freeborn women, and 39 are uncertain freeborn. Of this group of 119, which constitutes over 80 percent of the whole, 45 (38 percent) have some definite marker of elite status, in the form of money, other rank markers, or rank markers of their kin.

Freedwomen are obviously much rarer, but they do make themselves known. Twelve priestesses identify themselves clearly as freed slaves, and another fourteen are likely to have been so. There are even three priestesses definitely identified as slaves (*CIL* 9.3518, 10.202, 11.4635). So we might assume that becoming a priestess was something that a freeborn woman might expect and a freed slave might aspire to.[15]

However, the freeborn/freed division here may be quite misleading. Even for the elite women, it is not always clear that they come from an aristocratic family or even from a family that has always been free. Most of the members of one honor-laden family have the Greek cognomina characteristic of freed slaves (*CIL* 10.4790); we can occasionally see the move from freed slave to town bigwig in a series of inscriptions. One set of probably linked inscriptions from Ovid's home town of Sulmo outlines the following family tree (9.3087, 3091, 3092):

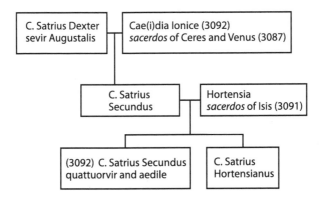

Dexter's office of *sevir* marks him as (probably) a successful freedman, while his wife's Greek cognomen makes her a probable freedwoman; their son marries a woman with a very high-class name; their grandson holds a respectable magistracy, probably the highest in the town.[16] The tombstone of one freeborn priestess, Ninnia Primilla, daughter of Quintus [Ninnius], bears a touching poem explaining that she sprang from humble origins (*CIL* 9.3358): "I was born of freed parents, both of them, poor people in terms of their income, but of freeborn character." She became priestess of Ceres in the small town of Pinna Vestina. On the other hand, of the twenty-five certain or uncertain freedwomen priestesses, eleven (44 percent) have some definite tie to money or public prestige. Ninnia Primilla's tombstone reminds us, if we needed a reminder, that slavery put a stigma on the person; still it was not an insuperable barrier to social success.

The inscriptions also give us fascinating insights into women acting together, sometimes across status boundaries. A stone from Aquileia, in the far eastern reaches of Cisalpine Gaul, commemorates a gift or gifts from four women (*CIL* 5.762):

To Bona Dea Pagana ["of the village"?]
Rufria Festa daughter of Gaius [Rufrius]
Caesilia Scylace freedwoman of Quintus [Caesilius]
magistrae
with their own money;
Decidia Paulla daughter of Lucius [Decidius]
and Pupia Peregrin(a) freedwoman of Lucius [Pupius]
ministrae
of Bona Dea
built this temple
with their own money.

"With their own money" is a formula in this sort of inscription, not at all unique here (for the same phrase in Greek inscriptions, see MacMullen 1980: 216); it underscores that aspect of Roman religion that has more to do with conspicuous consumption than with spirituality. But this inscription also hints at a priestessly hierarchy about which I yearn to know more. Why does each rank include one freeborn woman and one freedwoman—was this a necessity or an accident? Clearly here being a freed slave is not what separates the *magistrae* from the *ministrae*, and all the women have "their own money," as this durable witness has been telling all viewers for two thousand years.[17]

A similar group from Furfo, northeast of Rome, lists two freeborn women, two freedwomen, and a slave woman, all *magis(trae)* of Venus; they seem to be listed in descending status order (*CIL* 9.3518; cf. 5.757, from Aquileia, one freeborn and two uncertain freed *magistrae* of Bona Dea). A group from Tridentum, back in the ultimate far north of Italy, suggests another possible criterion for division in rank (5.5026):

Mag(istrae)
Cassia Marcella
Iuentia Maxsuma
Firmidia Modesta
Numonia Secunda

Min(istrae)
Iuentia Secunda
Manneia Pupa
Loreia Prima
Vettia Secunda

Two of these women are possibly sisters—Iuentia Maxsuma and Secunda—and, by the convention of old-fashioned Roman naming in which all sisters in a family have the same name with some numerical marker, they would be an older and a younger sister. Three of the *ministrae* in fact have such markers: Iuentia and Vettia are "Number Two," and Manneia is "Doll" (that is, "Baby"). One of the *magistrae* is also a "Number Two," but it seems at least possible that women moved up in rank with age. What cult these women served is unspecified here; more than anything, they present a marked display of Roman naming in a part of Italy where a lot of the inscriptions are bilingual in Latin and the local Celtic language. Indeed, "Manneia" may well be a hybrid name—a Roman name-form grafted onto a Gaulish root.[18]

Most priestess groups, like this one, are made up of women of the same status.[19] Likewise, women make dedications within status boundaries: the *matronae* at Interamnia put up a statue together to honor a woman (*CIL* 9.5071), and so did the *matronae* of Surrentum (10.688); three probably freeborn women made a dedication to Bona Dea together at Tuder (11.4636). Sometimes priestesses are buried together (10.4789–91, possibly part of a larger burial ground). Very occasionally, we find female kin engaged on a religious project together: a freeborn woman and her mother who set up and ornamented a statue to Venus Augusta (5.835); a pair of freeborn sisters who contributed generously to the temple of Demeter at Cumae around 7 CE (10.3685, 3688). Some mother-daughter pairs hold the same priestesshood (9.1153 and 1154; probably 10.1074), while a mother and her daughter-in-law hold different ones (9.3087, 3092, seen above). At Veii, her "most pious sisters" set up a major inscription in honor of Caesia Sabina, *sacerdos* of Fortuna Redux (11.3811): "she alone of all women gave a banquet to the mothers of the magistrates and to [their] sisters and daughters and her fellow townswomen of every rank, and during the days of the games and banquet of her husband she gave a bath [i.e., admission to the baths] with free oil."[20]

But women also act with men. There are several priest/priestess pairs (*CIL* 5.3922, 3923, both at pagus Arusnatium; 9.3146; 11.3196); several kin groups (husband and wife, 5.6514, 10.1549; the two sisters noted above, acting with their male kin, 10.3685); and some women acting with men presiding or helping (5.6412). Where extended families are visible in inscriptions, we can sometimes see how priesthoods and similar offices run in families (5.3926–3928, 3962, 7788). Women who were priestesses would have been very likely to have male kin who held priesthoods, and probably perceived religious activity as something men and women had in common, not something that separated them.[21]

It has become almost a commonplace to say that the municipal aristocracy defined itself through office-holding.[22] The main function of cult often seems to have been as a prestige marker in small towns and cities; the upper ranks of the local bourgeoisie would be honored by rank in a cult, and would in turn express their gratitude by substantial grants to the town, in the form of buildings, public banquets, gladiatorial games, or simple bundles of cash (*CIL* 9.1153, 14.2804). Or vice versa: giving the cash might result in a priesthood. (We must bear in mind that we have records only of people who could afford to have an inscription made.) As seen above, the correlation between holding a priesthood and other elite markers is very high.

There also was a well-established connection between freed slaves' upward mobility and priesthoods. A freedman who made enough money could aspire to be a *sevir Augustalis*, a member of the board of six men annually appointed to oversee the cult of the emperor; freedmen are conspicuous in the inscriptions as public-spirited members of the community. In many honorific decrees we see the sevirs and the priestesses bowing and curtseying to each other (*CIL* 10.51, 10.54, 11.5752, 11.6172), and indeed the female kin of *seviri* might well be priestesses (5.3438, 10.3087, 3092). As seen in the case of the *magistrae* and *ministrae* of Aquileia above, this might give a freedwoman the chance to hobnob with the freeborn ladies, to be invited, as it were, to join the Junior League. Being a priestess was above all a way in which women became visible in public: thanked by groups of men, their names put up in large letters (sometimes carefully larger than other names, 5.4458, 9.5841, 10.1074), giving multiple gifts "with their own money."

It would be a mistake, however, to think that this nexus of public service, class, prestige, and piety necessarily implies hypocrisy or lack of religious feeling. The separation of church and state is not a new idea, but when Jesus said to render unto Caesar what is Caesar's and unto God what is God's, it was in direct contravention of the Roman idea of being a good citizen. A good citizen was, among other things, active in the temples—as indeed is the case in many modern communities. How can we document spiritual feeling, so long gone? The inscriptions are a sort of fossil, the stony remainder of an impulse strong enough to make someone spend money on a commemorative plaque to mark an action now lost to us. Another study might consider women's votive offerings, replicas of body parts and babies, which seem somehow more affect-laden.[23] But the question of priestesses' actual involvement in religious cult is perhaps addressed by a small group of inscriptions that foreground sacrifice. A *magister* and *magistra* of Ceres set up an inscription on the "day of the sacrifice," April 19, 18 CE (*CIL* 11.3196). The *ordo* of Capena, outside Rome, set up a stone to a *sacerdos* of Ceres "to honor the ceremonies most respectably provided" (11.3933). A tombstone commemorating a *sacerdos* of Ceres and Venus at Sulmo, commissioned by her, has reliefs of a torch, an altar, a woman sacrificing, and a child holding an animal (9.3089). On the tombstone of a *sacerdos* of Ceres at Atina in southern Italy is carved a *culter*, the sacrificial knife, and a sow (10.5073; cf. similar carvings, 10.129, 10.1812, both also priestesses of Ceres). As Versnel notes, women did carry out blood sacrifices in the rites of Bona Dea (1992: 32, 43, 48); as seen in Festus, priest and priestess used the same knife. In an impassioned dedication to Venus Proba, one male worshiper gave her the epithet of *sacrificatrix* (10.3692). These examples should make us rethink the generalizations set out by John Scheid in 1992 (see volume introduction).

Women's devotion to goddesses (and some gods) can also be seen in dedicatory inscriptions (see appendix B). The inscriptions surveyed include twenty-seven major donations, from Forum Vibii in the Ligurian Alps to Campania (but not further south), many of them statues and altars but also including temples, porticos, whole temple complexes, a fishpond, and a silver dish weighing 1 lb. 7 oz. More humble (but not cheap) dedications seem to consist largely of the inscription itself, probably with an ephemeral offering attached or made during an accompanying ritual. The dedications to Magna Mater provide a good illustration of this tie between writing and ritual, since they are often made *ob taurobolium*, "on the occasion of a *taurobolium*," and we know what this was: a ritual in which the initiate stood in a pit, under a grating, and bathed in the blood of a bull slaughtered above the grate. It seems safe to say that some religious feeling accompanied this experience (see Ferguson 1970: 104–6, for a full description).[24] Counting the forty-one ordinary donations with the major donations in appendix B, Bona Dea receives the largest number, five major and ten ordinary; Magna Mater is second, with ten offerings, and Juno (in various manifestations) and Mater Matuta are tied for third, with six each. Other well represented recipients include Venus and Ceres with four each, and the Matronae with three. A long list of other deities with one or two dedications from women completes the roster—mostly, but not exclusively, goddesses: Fonio (evidently an adjunct of Bona Dea, *CIL* 5.757, 758), the Parcae, Minerva, Fortuna, Demeter, Dea Obsequens, Diana Loch(ia?), Isis—and also Saturn, Silvanus, and Jupiter Optimus Maximus.

Some geographical patterns are discernible. The Matronae and Junones, singly or together, are popular in Cisalpine Gaul, probably due to the influence of nearby Celtic peoples (cf. Ferguson 1970: 16–17 and fig. 8 for brief description and illustration). Dedications to Mater Matuta come only from Campania, with one notable exception, while the dedications to Bona Dea come from every part of Italy. Two dedications to the Matronae are made by a woman for the sake of another woman (*CIL* 5.4134, 4137); similarly, a freedwoman makes a dedication to Bona Dea "for the wellbeing of our (A)tel(li)a," evidently her former owner (9.5421). A mother makes a dedication to Venus Aug(usta) in memory of her daughter (5.836); a freedman, with his wife (a *flaminica*) and four children sets up an elaborate dedication to Juno to honor his *patrona* (5.7811).

Most intriguing of all are what appear to be two sites of cult in which women played an important role: a shrine of Minerva Memor ("Remembering") near Travi in Etruria (*CIL* 11.1292–1309); a women's shrine at Pisaurum with dedications to at least ten different goddesses (11.6294–6302), possibly dating to the second century BCE. The dedications at the shrine of Minerva Memor in fact include more by men (eleven) than by women (seven), though two of the men are there on behalf of female relatives. Several dedications indicate what was special about this manifestation of the goddess:

11.1297: To Minerva Memor, Coelia Iuliana, freed from a serious illness by the grace of her medicines, placed this gift.

11.1305: To Minerva Memor, Tullia Superiana, on the restoration of her hair, made good on her vow willingly and deservedly.

11.1306: To Minerva Medica Cabardiacensis, Valeria Sammonia from Vercellae made good on her vow willingly and deservedly.

This Minerva is a doctor, to whom women and men came to be cured; the alternate cult title in 11.1306 makes Minerva's function here explicit. Valeria Sammonia, like others who visited the shrine, has come a long way to see the goddess; Vercellae is in Cisalpine Gaul.[25]

The shrine at Pisaurum is attested by a group of thirteen plain stones in the shape of truncated pyramids, found in a field about a mile from Pisaurum in 1738, with "a quantity of votives of metal and terra cotta, large statues of terra cotta, mountains of offerings . . . and more than four thousand coins," as the *CIL* editor relays to us from the original report. Most of the stones hold only the name of a deity, usually a goddess: Fides, Juno, Juno Loucina, Mater Matuta (twice), Salus, Diana, Feronia, Juno Regina. Three women's names are given as dedicators—Cesula Atilia (*CIL* 11.6298), and Mania Curia and Pola Livia (11.6301)—and one stone seems to indicate that the dedicators are the *matronae* of Pisaurum as a group (11.6300). The attestation of cult centers like this, however sketchy, fills out the picture suggested by better-known cults like that of Diana at Aricia or of Mater Matuta at Satricum—and here she is in Pisaurum on the Adriatic coast. Women might, then, have both a special local place, perhaps a grove or rural shrine, at which to worship, and a reason for travel to well-known cult centers, where they might meet and mix with women from all over Italy.

But the gender balance at the shrine of Minerva Memor reminds us that many cults mixed men and women. The worship of Magna Mater involved an elaborate and mixed-gender hierarchy, as seen best in a series of inscriptions from Beneventum (*CIL* 9.1538–42). The officers include a *cymbal(istria) loco secundo*, a male augur and *sacerdos*, and two female *sacerdotes xv vir(ales)*, one of whom shows up in two other inscriptions, where she has become *sac(erdos) prima* (9.1538; cf. 1541, 1542); a female *sacerdos* (1539); a male *sacerdos* and his female *consacerdos* (1540); a male *primarius* and a female *sacerdos secundo loco xv vir(alis)* (9.1541); and a *tympanistria* (9.1542). A priest and a *ministra* of Magna Mater made a joint dedication at Corfinium, 9.3146; the "inferior officer" paid for a new statue of Bellona and one of the goddess and had the goddess gilded, along with the hair on the statue of Attis. Two women (one probably freed, one a slave) who celebrated their taurobolia at Puteoli were supervised by the same priest, Tiberius Claudius Felix, one in 134 CE, one in 144 CE (10.1596, 1597). Furthermore, many men set up dedications to goddesses, especially to the Junones and Matronae in the north; in so doing, they were, in turn, sometimes supervised by priestesses (10.39, 10.6640).

Men also served as priests of goddesses: there is a group of *magistri* of Venus Jovia at Capua in 107 BCE (*CIL* 10.3776), and a *magister* of the shrine of Juno at nearby Cubulteria (10.4620). Such a mix of genders is familiar from many aspects of religion in the city of Rome: the pontifex maximus and the Vestals, the *flamen* and the *flaminica*, the *flamines* of various goddesses (see chart in Beard 1990: 20–21). What is startling is the evidence of men's involvement in the cult of Bona Dea, the one goddess whose cult at Rome was strictly off-limits to men (so also Kraemer 1992: 53, following Brouwer 1989: 258; also in Warde Fowler 1916). There was a male priest of Bona Dea at Puteoli in 62 CE, a freedman, Claudius Philadespotus freedman of the emperor (10.1549); and a "*collegium* of male worshipers of the heavenly Bona Dea" at Venafrum (10.4849). One man set up a dedication to Bona Dea in Cubulteria (10.4615), ornamented with carvings of a man and a woman carrying baskets of fruit. All these sites are in Campania or on the road north of it; perhaps the importance of Ceres and Venus on the Bay of Naples and of Mater Matuta at Satricum (Bettini 1991: 77–78) and Cales (where she and Juno had temples, 10.4650, 4660) somehow attracted some men to women's cults.[26] But well to the north, at Spoletium, a grove of Bona Dea was "dedicated so that it might be permitted to be cleaned up again by men," though the names given in the inscription are those of the presiding priestess and of a woman, a centurion's wife, who dedicated an altar there (11.4767).

This fragmentary survey of some remnants of women's cult practice serves as a useful reality check. It reminds us that women held the title of "priestess" all over Italy. It suggests a relationship between status and religious office, with freeborn women predominant but freedwomen forming an important minority, and sometimes participating alongside freeborn women. It confirms that public, high-prestige priestesshoods were indeed one way in which women were active in public; but it also shows that not all priestesshoods were like that, and that priestesses can be found in some very small towns. As objects of devotion, Bona Dea and Mater Matuta are as well represented as Juno and Minerva. Women gave large sums of money to support cults; they also traveled to the country, or to far-off towns, in order to carry out their worship. And they worshiped often with other women, but not infrequently alongside men.

There is one major absence. In all this testimony of women's worship, there is almost no trace of slave women (see Holland 2008). One *ministra* of Bona Dea at Tuder, Quieta slave of Atia Pieris (*CIL* 11.4635); one *magistra* of Venus at Furfo, Sperata slave of Aulus Munatidius, among a group of free *magistrae* (9.3518); one *magistra* at Grumentum who gave a chest and candelabrum to Juno, and (because of Juno's relation to marriage?) identifies herself as "Pietas, slave-wife of Secundus" (10.202). A worshiper of

Magna Mater, Thalame slave of Hosidia Afra (10.1597), commemorates her *taurobolium*. Apart from the household cult of the house that owned them, what religions did slave women practice? Some, especially the field slaves who had no hope of being freed, would have been captives who brought their religion with them; many others would have been born in Italy, or bought from Greece or Asia for the household, positioned as outsiders who might someday move inside—but as slaves, outsiders literally inside the house. To understand their part in Roman women's religion, we must return to texts.

Roman Women's Groups

Texts can give us more of a story about women's religious practice, and we have nowhere else to turn if we want to ask further questions: how we can interpret the inscriptions; what Roman women thought they were doing; what other people thought they were doing; what was the meaning of women's cults. Unfortunately, these texts bring with them problems of their own. Not only do they provide meager information, but they are uniformly written by Roman and Greek men, who may well have their own axes to grind in the account they give of women's cults.[27] For instance, Ross Kraemer usefully suggests that the recurring focus on chastity cults in some accounts may have more to do with the current political agenda at the time they were written than with women's actual preferences and practices (1992: 55, 58–60). But these texts can at least attest to the attitudes of elite male writers to women's cult, and sometimes they seem to provide us with plain statements of fact: what a priestess wore, where a temple was.

In order to talk about "Roman women's religion" meaningfully, we need to look for further evidence that Roman women thought of themselves as a group. It seems that some did, but the word "some" here is important. It is a common pitfall of scholarship on ancient women that we find ourselves saying "Roman women" or "Greek women" when what is meant is "freeborn women," or even "elite women." As if slaves and freedwomen, of course, did not count, or were not "women." Moreover, there is a larger problem with the word "Roman": Is "Rome" just a city? Or is "Rome" everyplace ruled by Romans? Here, when I mean "wives of Roman citizens," I will use the word *matronae*, and will say "Roman women" only when I mean "female persons living in Roman Italy." Much could be said about women who identified as Roman and lived outside Italy, but, since this essay adduces epigraphic evidence only from Italy, and Italy outside the city of Rome at that, I can claim to present here only an incomplete set of jigsaw puzzle pieces from part of the puzzle. As shown above, inscriptions conventionally indicate the status of persons relative to slavery; we have to keep slaves in mind.

Matronae first of all were clearly marked, like all inhabitants of the Roman world, by their dress. Paulus defines them as "those who had the right of wearing *stolae*" (112L), and we read elsewhere what this *stola* was like: a long dress that covered the woman up very thoroughly, even to her feet—it had a sort of flounce at the bottom, the *instita*. The satirist Horace remarks on what a bad idea it is to chase after *matronae*, since you can never see what you're getting—much better to go for a freedwoman or a slave or a prostitute, who (he claims) wore clothes you could see through. He is clear that it is senatorial *matronae* who are most to be avoided; married freedwomen evidently do not count as *matronae* to him here, and he sees them as safe targets.[28] *Matronae* also had folkways of their own—a preferred drink, for example; Paulus, in talking about the wine called *murrina*, says "women (*mulieres*) call this *muriola*," which is a diminutive form, like a nickname (131L). We read elsewhere that older women drank *passum*, raisin wine, and other sweet drinks (Varro in Non. 551M); Pliny tells us (*HN* 22.45) that women (*mulieres*) chewed gum. Aristocratic *matronae* of the early first century BCE apparently kept an old-fashioned way of speaking (Cic. *De or.* 3.45). *Matronae* rode around the city of Rome in special kinds of carriages, called *pilenta* or *carpenta* (Paulus 225L, Festus 282L), a right which we hear was given them because they gave gold as a group to ransom the city from the Gauls (cf. Festus 138L).[29] In the theater, at the time of Nero, all women seem to have sat together—and in the back, among the poorer spectators (Calpurnius Siculus *Ecl.* 7.26), following an innovation introduced by Augustus as part of his moral reforms (Suetonius *Aug.* 44.2–3, *feminis, muliebre secus*)—although Ovid in the *Ars amatoria* is still explaining how a man can flirt with the woman next to him, a theme for which his version of the rape of the Sabines serves as an illustration (see chapters 1, 5).

Matronae had other special rights that had to do with their bodies. The reconstructed text of Festus tells us: "*Matronae* were not moved aside by magistrates, lest they should seem to be pushed or handled, or pregnant women be jostled" (142L). Similarly, Valerius Maximus, who is something of an extremist on female chastity, says (2.1.5): "They did not permit one carrying out a summons to touch a *matrona* with his body, so that the *stola* should be left unviolated by the touch of an alien hand."

The specialness of the body of the *matrona* again comes into play when the title itself is being defined. Aulus Gellius, arguing against Aelius Melissus, quotes him as saying (18.6.4), "A *matrona* is a woman who has given birth once; one who has done this more often is called a *materfamilias*; just as a sow which has given birth once is called a *porcetra*, and one who has done it more often, a *scrofa*." Gellius heaps scorn upon this, suggesting that Aelius has made it all up, at least the part about women; but he goes on to say that it is more likely, as most authors he has consulted say (18.6.8), "that a *matrona* is a married woman, even if she has no children; and she is so called from the name *mater*, not yet achieved, but with the hope and omen of soon achieving it, whence *matrimonium* itself is named."

So we see that, on the one hand, *matronae* have some group definition, and, on the other, that it is biologically determined—it relates to their reproductive function.

We do have some specific instances of the *matronae* acting as a group, as the *ordo matronarum*—not always in a reproductive context.[30] One of the most interesting is one of the latest instances, in which Hortensia, daughter of the famous orator Hortensius (first century BCE), pleaded the case of the *ordo* before the triumvirs when these women were being heavily taxed (Val. Max. 8.3.3). Entering the historic record so close to the date of performance, this event must really have taken place; still, Hortensia's action has mythic justification going back to Rome's origin stories: the Sabine women, Rome's first women, acted as a group to intercede between their fathers and their new husbands. Traditionally they were led by a woman called Hersilia (Gellius 13.23 records the supposed wording of her prayer); and there is a further tradition that, in gratitude, Romulus named the thirty neighborhoods of Rome after the thirty women on the embassy (Dionysius of Halicarnassus 2.45, 47.3). A story also told by Valerius Maximus takes the *ordo* back to the earliest republic (5.2.1), in the context of the story of Coriolanus's wife Volumnia and his mother Veturia, and how the Senate rewarded them for turning him back and protecting the city from invasion. The Senate at this time supposedly gave the *ordo* distinctive signs: men should yield to them on the sidewalk; they could wear *vittae* as well as gold jewelry, purple clothing, and gilded flounces; and they also set up the temple and altar to Fortuna Muliebris. The *matronae* most famously acted jointly to lobby for the repeal of the Oppian law, which limited female practice of conspicuous consumption. Phyllis Culham (1982) interestingly ties in this sumptuary regulation of women with "increased religious activity and displays of wealth by women," possibly linked, during the Hannibalic wars. She also suggests that women were able to organize to resist the law through "contacts and skills" acquired through cult participation (1982: 791). Again, for "women" here read "rich elite women"; among their new possessions would have been slave women. The same caveat applies to the story of Hortensia, for the later historian Appian (*Civil Wars* 4.32–34) specifies that the tax was levied upon the 1400 wealthiest women in Rome. Moreover, we should ponder not only the story of the Oppian law but what our sources make of it; Valerius Maximus comments as follows (9.1.3): "But why do I speak further of women? Whom both the weakness of their intellect, and their exclusion from the more serious sort of work, encourage to bestow every effort on the more painstaking cultivation of themselves." This, once again, in a sourcebook for speakers (see chapter 1; Langlands 2006: 123–91).

Valerius's obsession, however, also leads him to comment on how the *matronae* voted for Sulpicia as the most chaste *matrona* (8.15.12):

> Deservedly is Sulpicia, daughter of Servius Paterculus, wife of Q. Fulvius Flaccus, brought to the commemoration of men. The Senate had decreed, after the Sibylline books had been inspected by the decemviri, that a statue of Venus Verticordia ("Who Turns the Heart") should be consecrated, so that the will of maidens and women might be turned more easily from lust to chastity. From all the *matronae* one hundred were selected by lot; from the one hundred, again ten were selected, and they passed judgment about the most holy woman (*sanctissima*). She was then chosen out of all [women] for her chastity.

This supposedly happened in 112 BCE, fairly late in the republic—a time when free women were supposedly leaving behind their traditional restrictions.

Once again it is hard to know how optimistic to feel about this story, in the terms laid out in chapter 10 (cf. Kraemer 1992: 57; Stehle 1989: 153). On the one hand, you get women, together, apparently in large numbers, voting, and about something with which they are credited with expertise. They are being consulted about the state religion, by the men's legislative body, about goddess worship. So far, so good. But then we get the casual equation of *castitas* with *sanctitas*. These women are co-opted into memorializing their own unreliability; look who approves (Valerius Maximus); look what kind of goddess this is. It seems to me that stories like this should be enough to make people think twice about the significance to women of goddess worship. Not all goddesses imply women's autonomy. On the other hand, autonomy is not always what women want.[31]

222 · ARGUMENTS WITH SILENCE

So what can be said about this evidence for (some) Roman women's self-perception as a group? First, our evidence, as testimony to women's groups, is extremely weak. Scholars who work in more modern periods have the benefit of first-person testimonia from women; it is overwhelming to realize that such evidence is almost entirely lacking for pre-Christian Rome, with the exception of inscriptions—necessarily limited in scope. Moreover, it is almost impossible to trace changes in Roman women's groups over time; the evidence is so fragmentary that we have to pick up a piece here and a piece there. Second, what we seem to be seeing is that *matronae* at Rome did have the sort of network, extending over at least several centuries, that did enable them to act in groups on occasion; but that such groups were heavily enmeshed in an ideological system that was always ready to belittle them, and that approved of them only insofar as they ratified the social assessment of themselves as the property of individual men for the production of children, and that saw them as always prone to lapses into unchastity.[32] Third, at the same time, we must now be on the lookout for the practical implications of the classism built into this system, whereby the honor of the *matrona* is constructed in opposition to the dishonor of slaves and prostitutes—overlapping groups, in any case (Harper 2011: 291; Joshel and Murnaghan 1998a: 4; Saller 1998: 87–89). As seen in chapter 6, slavery is structurally implicated in the process of women's beautification, which then means, as always, something different to the practitioner and her owner. What about all the Roman women who did not count as *matronae*? Did they have any group unity? Did they feel solidarity with *matronae*? How did they fit into the ideological system in which the *matronae* were enmeshed?[33]

One answer to these questions may be summed up in a brief story of a pair of women, both from Capua, who helped the Romans out during the Second Punic War (Val. Max. 5.2.1). One was a *materfamilias*, and one was a *meretrix*, a prostitute; one "sacrificed daily for the safety of our army," the other gave food to the captured Roman soldiers. The Senate, after the Romans won, rewarded these women. Valerius Maximus, typically, comments: "How marvelous that the fathers [i.e. the senators] took the time during such rejoicing to thank two humble women." But we note the way their labor is divided: the sacrifice belongs to the *matrona*.

Along these lines, Roman comedy from around 200 BCE—performed at the ostensible date of Valerius Maximus's story—provides another enormous but cryptic source on the relations between *matronae*, prostitutes, and women slaves (see Feltovich 2011; chapters 1 and 6). The twenty extant plays of Plautus are full of *ancillae* and their owners—some *matro-*

nae, some prostitutes—and there are several speeches by freed and slave women that deal with women's lot and sex/class divisions among women. The speech of the unnamed *lena* in *Cistellaria* (19–37) claims that *matronae* set a good example by the loyalty of their friendships to each other, but that they despise *meretrices,* whom they see as rivals for their husbands' affections (*paelices*). The *lena* states that her freed slave status is the direct cause of her work as a prostitute (38–39). In contrast, the old slave woman Syra in *Mercator,* as seen in chapter 1, delivers a monologue on the injustice of the double sexual standard for wives and husbands (817–29); this character is made to speak on behalf of "women" (*mulieres,* 817) and mean *matronae.* The plays include a female *sacerdos* of Venus (*Rudens*) who takes in two shipwrecked prostitutes, and numerous forms of worship by women, including *meretrices.* For comedy to work, the social forms it presents must be recognizable to the audience; the audience for Plautus included slaves and prostitutes both male and female, alongside *matronae* and their families, while the actors included slaves and freed slaves. These actors, however, along with the playwrights, were exclusively male, as far as we know; they acted to please the various members of the audience, who would react in various ways when Syra gave her speech (see James 2012). But at least we can be certain that her lines were spoken to a mixed group, which is more than can be said for the rest of the textual evidence considered here.

The complexity of Roman cultural co-optation of women through religion, and the difficulty of recovering it, may further be illustrated by a deceptive passage from Petronius's *Satyrica.* During a dinner party held at the home of the vulgar nouveau riche freedman Trimalchio, one of the guests complains that things are not what they used to be (44.17–18):

> Why, nobody thinks that heaven is heaven, nobody fasts, nobody gives a rap for Jupiter, but everybody is counting up their goods when their eyes are covered [in prayer]. In the old days women used to go in their *stolae,* barefoot, to the hill, with their hair hanging down and their minds pure, and pray to Jupiter for water. And so just like that it rained buckets, then or never, and they all went home like drowned rats.

This picture of married women's good behavior in the good old days comes not from some Cato-like Roman aristocrat but from a freed slave with a Greek name, Ganymedes—perhaps a hint at his employment by a former master as cupbearer and sex toy. By his own account, he arrived in Italy as a boy from Asia Minor (*Satyrica* 44.4, 6), an origin widely associated in Roman elite texts with effeminacy and cultural degeneracy. Moreover, he is not a real freed slave but one imagined by Petronius, who was, perhaps, a Roman noble at Nero's court. Can we believe that his speech represents a real social attitude among freed slaves in Roman Italy? Surprisingly, it does not seem impossible. The epigraphic evidence surveyed above suggests that some freedwomen were indeed involved alongside *matronae* in public cult; so, alongside the sex/class *divisions* to be examined below, we might also keep in mind an ongoing system of sex/class and status *transition*, in which women formerly slaves moved up in the religious world, while their husbands, perhaps, urged them on.[34]

Women's Individual Cult Practice at Rome

As we move now into looking at evidence for Roman women's religion, we are on our guard. We have already seen that goddess worship is hardly a guarantee of feminist consciousness. As we look at the circumstances of ritual in which Roman women would have gotten to know each other, we need to consider ways in which the centrality of the body in women's religion ties in with problems of class and civil status. On the one hand, the evidence is abundant that we have in Rome a society with extended networks of kin, stretching not only all over the city, but across the Italian countryside, reinforced by all sorts of political and economic obligations (Bradley 1991; Dixon 1988; Hallett 1984). On the other, this coexisted with and depended on another society, made up of slaves and freed slaves, characterized by broken kinship, cultural, and ethnic bonds. Religious rites would have meant very different things to women in the two groups. Sandra Joshel (1986) shows how slave child-nurses might have experienced lopsided and painful affective ties to an owner/child, with comparisons to the situation in and after American slavery. Certainly slave women might have had good reason to fear or distrust free women as well as men in their households, and, in a system in which their bodies were the sexual property of the owner, would have experienced their own bodies very differently from the way free women did.[35]

I look first here at evidence on individual women's participation in ritual.

A story in Valerius Maximus testifies to a rite de passage for freeborn Roman girls that also suggests a special intergenerational bond (1.5.4):

> But Caecilia, wife of Metellus [this probably dates the story to 212 BCE], while she sought wedding omens for her sister's daughter, a grown

maiden, in the traditional manner (*more prisco*), by an all-night vigil, made the omen herself. For when she had been sitting in a certain shrine for this reason for some time, and no utterance relevant to the purpose had been heard, the girl, tired out by the long delay of standing, asked her aunt (*matertera*, mother's sister) that she give her a place to sit down for a bit; the aunt replied to her: "Truly, I willingly leave my seat for you." Which statement, made out of kindness, turned out to be a sure sign: since Metellus, not much after this, when Caecilia had died, married the maiden of whom I am speaking.

As the epigraphic evidence seen above occasionally shows us sisters or mother-daughter pairs engaged in cult activity together, this story hints further that there was a tradition at Rome that bound together each (freeborn) woman with her sister's daughter, at least in that the two of them participated together in an important rite de passage for the young woman; the importance of the *matertera* shows up elsewhere, as will be seen. Freeborn Roman women were expected to marry, and their first marriage would normally take place at or soon after puberty (Hopkins 1964–65, but see now Scheidel 2007); thus this ritual would help to mark the girl's transition into adulthood.[36]

The concern with marriage is reflected in the stories about deities worshiped especially by women. The temple of Fortuna Muliebris, at the fourth milestone outside of Rome on the via Latina, supposedly marked the occasion when Coriolanus was talked out of attacking Rome by his mother and his wife (Val. Max. 1.8.4). Festus says that it was a *nefas* (sin) for the cult statue there to be touched except by a *univira*—a woman who had only had one husband (282L; cf. Williams 1958). Likewise, in the temple of patrician Pudicitia in the Forum Boarium, along with the temple of plebeian Pudicitia in the Vicus Longus, it was a *nefas* for any woman to sacrifice who had either never been married, or had been married more than once (Festus 282L, Val. Max. 2.1.3). The shrine of Dea Viriplaca specialized in a sort of couples counseling (Val. Max. 2.1.6)—one-sided, judging by her name, "Goddess Husband-Pleaser."

Livy tells the tale of the founding of the cult of plebeian Pudicitia (10.23.3–10; see Kraemer 1992: 58) as the story of a patrician woman who marries down, is barred from the cult by the other *matronae*, and goes off and starts her own shrine at home. He also says that the cult has lapsed due to being "made common by polluted (*pollutis*) women, not only *matronae* but women of every order." Writing under Augustus, Livy is looking back three hundred years, to a time when "patrician" and "plebeian" were still meaningful class divisions; to him, the divided cult means the marking of a division between levels of women. Wider access to the shrine results in the breakdown and disappearance of the cult itself, which must exclude in order to have meaning; exclusion in turn is defined in terms of access to the woman's body, for "polluted" means "insufficiently chaste."[37]

"Polluted," however, can certainly also mean "dirty." Julius Obsequens preserves in his collection of omens a story from 90 BCE, in which a woman called Caecilia Metella—like Caecilia wife of Metellus, a noble name—was responsible for the cleansing of the temple of Juno Sospita after it had been soiled by women's bodies:

> Caecilia Metella said that she had seen Juno Sospita in a dream, running away from her temple because it was being befouled (*foedarentur*) in an unclean manner (*immunde*), and had called Juno back with difficulty by her prayers. She restored the temple to its former sparkle by cleaning out the shrine, which had been stained by the dirtiness of the *matronae* and their obscene bodily services (*ministeriis*)—a bitch even had her nest of puppies under the statue of the goddess there.

No further details are given: what is imagined to have gone on in this famous shrine to Juno at Lanuvium? Here a woman goes on public record with a dream of women's bodies as intrinsically dirty, even animal-like, and leaving behind them the stain—of what? Body fluids? Gynecological instruments? Cult practices? The *ministerium* here is a you-word, not the power claimed by *ministrae* in their dedications.

But women are also said to have sacrificed especially to goddesses of childbirth. At one point, when Aulus Gellius is talking about breech births at some length, he quotes the first-century BCE writer Varro (Gell. 16.16.4):

> Since . . . women then labor with more difficulty, for the sake of praying to avert this danger, altars have been set up at Rome to the two Carmentae, of whom one is called "Postverta," the other "Prorsa," from the power and name of straight and backward birth.

Paulus says that pregnant women sacrificed to the nymph Egeria—Numa's friend; according to him, because of her name: *e-gerere* means "push out" in Latin (67L). Three statues in front of the shrine of Minerva on the Capitol were called the *nixi di*, the "straining gods," as they were thought to preside over the labor of pregnant women, though Festus notes those who say their odd posture may have derived from their former location in Greece, where they had been seated at a table—here Romans superimpose onto borrowed gods a meaning to do with childbirth (182L).

Of course Juno was the chief goddess of all these things. Here we pick up another bit of information about sex/class distinction in religious practice (Paulus 248L, cf. Gellius 4.3.3):

> *"Paelices"* is a name indeed now given to those who lie under those not belonging to them, not only women, but even males. The ancients properly called a woman a *p(a)elex*, who married a man who (already) had a wife. For this class of women indeed a penalty was established by Numa Pompilius in this law: "Let a *paelex* not touch the altar of Juno; if she does, let her sacrifice a female lamb to Juno with her hair let down."

A *paelex,* as in the complaint of the *lena* in *Cistellaria,* was a concubine, usually a mistress, a kept woman. Juno in the *Fasti* transforms Callisto into a bear to make this *paelex* ugly (2.179), like a wife tampering with her rival's face cream (chapter 6). The word is often construed in Latin with the name of the wife depending on it in the genitive; for example, Ovid's Philomela is ashamed to be *paelex sororis,* "my sister's *paelex*" (*M.* 6.537, 606; see chapter 5). It has connotations of rivalry, of "the other woman." But normally the *paelex* is a slave, or a freedwoman, not a threat to the wife. Why can she not touch Juno's altar? Two forces are operating here: (1) focusing on the words "not belonging to them": the *paelex* takes the blame for the lack of symmetry in the couple's monogamy—in literature, Juno was always depicted as resentful of Jupiter for his affairs; (2) the *paelex* is contaminated by her status, by the very "lying under someone." In Roman sexuality, it is a commonplace that slaves are thought less of, de-grad-ed, not only for their lower social status, but because they have been sexual common property. The one penetrated ("not only women, but even males") is thereby stained.[38] As seen above, one of the few first-person women's voices we have from Rome, that of Sulpicia the elegist, includes a protest against her lover's betrayal of her, an elite woman, with a female slave, a "slut with a wool-basket" ([Tibullus] 3.16.3–4). To complicate things further, the slave Syra in *Mercator,* discovering a *meretrix* established in their house, says to her female owner (689–90), "Come with me, so you can see/ your *paelex* Alcumena, my Juno." In this joke, the slave woman herself identifies the *matrona* who owns her with Juno, and the *meretrix* with Juno's *paelex*—Alcumena, herself the center of Plautus's *Amphitruo* (see chapter 1).

Juno was worshiped at Rome as *Juno Iuga*, because she joined (*iug-*) marriages (Paulus 92L)—a street was named for her altar; *matronae* also worshiped her as *Opigena*, because she gave help (*Ops*) to women in labor (Paulus 221L). She was frequently invoked as Juno Lucina, the main goddess of childbirth. Paulus says that *matronae* celebrate the first of March, the Matronalia, because it is the anniversary of the opening of the shrine of Juno Lucina (131L). The explanations of her name, Lucina, produce some oddities. Varro says (*LL* 5.68, partly paraphrased):

> The moon is called "Noctiluca" on the Palatine, because from there her temple shines at night. . . . (5.69) But she is also called, by the Latins, Juno Lucina; either because she is also the earth, and shines (*lucet*); or because from her light in which conception occurs to the one in which she has brought forth into the light (*produxit in lucem*), the moon helps (*luna iuvat*) until she has brought [the child] into the light (*lucem*), and the name "Juno Lucina" is thus made up from *iuvando* and *luce*. From this fact women in childbirth invoke her; for the moon is the guide of those being born, because hers are the months. It is clear that the women of old times saw this, because women gave credit for their eyebrows most of all to this goddess.

Festus (396L) also has this; the strangeness of it lies beyond our asking.

Women's Festivals

We move now from women's individual worship to festivals that were special to women. The Roman year was defined by the procession of days marked by religion (see Salzman 1990; Takács 2007: 25–59), and women played a part in many of the general festival days. Indeed, Roman women should be imagined like women in Orthodox Judaism, their lives patterned by carefully observed ritual—though the pattern was capable of variation. Outside of Rome, each town might have celebrated some of these festivals, and would presumably also have had some of its own. A list of only those festivals with a special significance for women would include (based on general descriptions in Scullard 1981):

> January 11, 15, Carmentalia. Carmenta or Carmentis, a goddess of childbirth, had a temple at the foot of the Capitol, near the Porta Car-

mentalis, and her own *flamen*. Her altars and her powers over breech births have been noted above, though for Varro she is a double goddess.

February 1, Juno Sospita. Girls' ritual at Lanuvium: blindfolded girls feed cakes to the snake in the sacred grove; their proven virginity ensures a good crop.

February 15, Lupercalia. Young aristocratic men run naked through the streets of Rome, flogging the bystanders, especially women (Varro *LL* 6.13; Paulus 49L), with thongs of bloody goatskin from the goat they have just sacrificed.

February 21, Feralia. Old women and girls propitiate the Silent Goddess, the mother of the Lares (Ovid *F.* 2.571–80; see chapter 5 on Lara). This was part of a three-festival period of placating the dead that took up most of February (see Dolansky 2011b, Mueller 2011).

March 1, Matronalia. Sacred to Juno Lucina; this is the date on which her temple on the Esquiline was dedicated by the *matronae*. Husbands prayed for the health of their wives and gave them presents; the wives got dressed up, paid visits, probably went to the temple, and entertained their slaves and served them food (see Dolansky 2011c).

March 17, Liberalia. This is the festival of the god Liber, sometimes associated with the Greek Dionysus; in the town of Caere, his female counterpart Libera was worshiped as well. At Rome, old women sat selling sweet cakes and sacrificing on small altars; at Lavinium, according to Augustine, a *matrona* had to garland the large phallus that represented Liber. This was also the festival at which freeborn boys, after an inspection of their genitals, changed the boy's toga for the man's toga.

April 1, Veneralia. Upper-class and lower-class women worship the goddess Fortuna Virilis in separate groups, some in the men's baths; they may also bathe the cult statue of the goddess. This is also the festival of Venus Verticordia.

April 23, Vinalia. During this wine festival, prostitutes sacrifice to Venus Erycina.

April 27, Floralia. Games are held, including theatrical shows at which actresses danced naked.

May 1, Bona Dea. This temple festival includes the offering of a sow; rituals involving wine; and wreathing the goddess's head with vine leaves.

June 9–15, Vestalia. Barefooted *matronae* bring offerings to the temple of Vesta.

June 11, Matralia. Rites are held at the temple of Mater Matuta in the

Forum Boarium, where only *univirae* can decorate her statue. *Matronae* bake special cakes (Varro *LL* 5.106). *Matronae* gather in the temple, a slave woman is let in, and the *matronae* drive her out by slapping her; they then pick up and cuddle the child of a sister.

July 6, Fortuna Muliebris. *Univirae* decorate the cult statue (?).

July 7, Nonae Caprotinae ("Fig-tree Nones"). Slave women hold a feast and mock battle outside the city, commemorating a time when Roman slave women saved the *matronae* from being raped by an invading enemy force by standing in for them. *Matronae* and slave women worship Juno Caprotina.[39]

August 13, Diana on the Aventine. At Aricia, processions of women march to Diana's cult center, holding burning torches, to thank the goddess for answering prayers. Votive offerings at Aricia include "models of reproductive organs and women with infants."[40] Slaves have the day off. Women wash their hair.

November 13, Feronia. Freedwomen make an expiatory gift to the goddess Feronia, a patron of slaves, at her temple in the Campus Martius; *matronae* make a gift to Juno Regina on the Aventine.

December 3, Bona Dea. A ritual is held in the home of the wife of one of the consuls or praetors, attended by Vestals, *matronae*, and female musicians (probably slaves). Men were strictly barred from the ceremonies, which involved drinking unwatered wine. The location in a private house must have limited the number of attendees.

This calendar emphasizes the degree to which Roman women, like Roman men, must have measured their lives from festival to festival. The rhythms of women's year synchronize with those of the culture as a whole, with a preponderance of activity in the late winter through early summer. Combined with household cult and personal religion, this program must have kept women busy, ever conscious of religion as a factor in their lives.

Living through the calendar would also have greatly contributed to Roman women's sense of who belonged where. As Richard Gordon says of municipal cult, "divisions of the local society are repeatedly rehearsed" (1990b: 228). Juvenal in his sixth satire (6.314–51) describes the Bona Dea rites as bestial orgies in which women get drunk, dance lewdly, and finally cry out for men to be brought in to service them sexually. There is the same prurient curiosity as in Aristophanes' *Women at the Thesmophoria*, a need to know what it is that women do when they are alone together. But Juvenal gives one suggestive detail: he describes a competition in dancing between the aristocratic women and prostitutes (6.320–23, cf. 350–51). Slave "women" form part of the transvestite imitation of the Bona Dea cult in his second satire as well (2.83–116, esp. 90, 98). Such a two-class distinction shows up in several other women's rituals—most notably, the Matralia (*matronae* slap slave woman), but also at the Matronalia (*matronae* serve slaves), at the cult of Fortuna Virilis at the Veneralia (upper-class and lower-class women worship in different places), at the Nonae Caprotinae (legend of the substitution of slaves for *matronae*), and in the freedwomen's offering to Feronia (*matronae* offer to Juno instead). That is, six of seventeen festivals involving special women's rituals include a marked element in which women are divided into classes (seven, counting Bona Dea twice). Moreover, several more festivals depend on sex/class identity: the Vinalia is just for prostitutes, Diana's day off is just for slaves, and the cult of Fortuna Muliebris is just for *univirae*. No prostitutes walk to the temple on the Vestalia (they could not go near the Vestals anyway); no *matronae* dance at the Floralia. The only festivals that seem to cross these boundaries are the Carmentalia (for all women who give birth) and the Lupercalia (the goatskin thong treatment seems to be for everyone); and it seems that any woman could march in the procession to Diana at Aricia.

Putting the calendar together with textual accounts, however biased, begins to give a body to the scattered bones of the inscriptions. The remarkable description of the cult of Mater Matuta—surely connected with the ritual whereby aunts and nieces wait together for an omen of marriage—suggests what events may have accompanied the dedications to her. Archaeological work on her temple in Satricum has recovered terra-cotta votive offerings like those for Diana at Aricia, along with mother-child statuettes; there are over ninety of them in the museum at Capua, and many of these show a seated woman with multiple babies—as many as a dozen (Bettini 1991: 77–78; French 1987; see now Smith 2000). In the Roman material on witches and in negative stereotypes of women, there is great anxiety over fostering of children by women other than their mothers; surely this women's ritual is aimed at affirming kin ties, while emphasizing status barriers. Where there is no mother, aunts are good, wet-nurses are bad.[41] The need of *matronae* to mark their superiority to slave women determines the shape of Roman women's religion.

In large part these festivals remind us of the way women were marked off into classes according to the degree of access to their bodies they allowed. Roman women's rituals insist on the danger of the permeability of women's bodies and on the high price to be paid for wrongful openness.

Perhaps the best instance of this idea comes in a story about one of the Vestal Virgins, who for ordinary women must have served as a constant reminder of the possibility of a completely closed body and the very high price to be paid for its breach.[42]

The worst crime for a Vestal Virgin was to be unchaste; they were punished for this by being buried alive. So, naturally, if a Vestal was accused of unchastity, she took it seriously. Valerius Maximus tells the story of one who did, the Vestal Tuccia (8.1.absol.5):

> By the same sort of aid the chastity of Tuccia, the Vestal Virgin, accused of the crime of unchastity, emerged when obscured by the cloud of slander. She, with the consciousness of her certain purity, dared to seek hope of her safety by a dangerous proof. For she took up a sieve [a ritual implement in Vesta's cult, Paulus 94L], and said, "Vesta, if I have always moved chaste hands to your rites, let it be that I may take up water from the Tiber in this and carry it to your temple." Boldly and rashly the vow of the priestess was cast; the very nature of things gave way.

It seems to me that this story of a holy woman sets up the model for all Roman women; they are permeable yet must be impermeable, they must carry water in a sieve. That *matronae* accepted this symbolic logic, enacted it in their rituals, and enforced it on girls and on non-*matronae*, is amply attested. This suggests further that the negative images of the monstrous female may well have been fostered by women; the two systems are complementary not only in terms of their symbolism, but also in terms of their social function.

What, then, is the bottom line for Roman women's religion? The focus on chastity always reminds me of values within some modern Italian cultures, as seen for example among the Sicilian townspeople in Maureen Giovannini's study (1981). It is hard to doubt that the townspeople have internalized the values their code imposes on women. We need not doubt that Roman women—probably from household slaves on up—shared ideals, though we might see the Roman state as using their bodies to think with (Joplin 1990, Joshel 1992a). Thus, when we see women proudly connecting religious leadership with affluence and upward mobility, we must also realize that the religion itself was ambivalent about femaleness. Still, when women put their cult titles on a tombstone or dedication along with their names, they were claiming that title as part of their identity, as Sandra

Joshel has shown for freed slaves' identification with their labor. The name of priestess is, as we say, written on their grave.

APPENDICES

Appendix A: Priestesses from the *CIL* for Italy

The following list divides priestesses according to title and follows the numerical order of the *CIL*. The volumes of the *CIL* cover various geographical regions: volume 5 covers Cisalpine Gaul, volume 9 covers the east coast of Italy, volume 10 covers the west side of southern Italy, Sicily, and Sardinia, volume 11 covers Italy north of Rome and south of the Po, volume 14 covers Latium. Each "s" on this list means "one *sacerdos*," each "m" means "one *magistra*," and so on.

sacerdos

5.520, Usia L. fil. Tertullina, s. divarum

5.2829, Asconia C. f. Augurini, s. divae Domitillae

5.3438, Veronia Trofime, s. Matris deum

5.4387, Aemilia C. f. Aequa, s. divae Plotinae

5.4400, Caecilia Procula, s. xv viralis

5.4458, (P)ostumia P. f. Paulla, Avidia Procula, Rutilia Proba, s(ss?). div(a)i August

5.4485, Clodia Q. fil. Procilla, s. divae Plotinae

5.5647, Caesia P. f. Maxima, s. divae Matidiae

5.5862, Gei(inia . . .) C. Var(i) Elpidephori, s. Matr Magn deum Ideae

5.6412, Petilia Q. f. Sabina, s. Minervae

5.7617, [no name extant], s. (di)vae Plotinae (P)ollentiae divae Faustinae Taurinis divae Faustinae Maioris Concordiae

9.307, Petilia Q. f. Secundina, s. Minervae

9.1100, Eggia Sabina Bast . . . , s. M.D. Mag

9.1153, Cantria P. f. Longina, s. and flam divae Iuliae Piae Aug et Matr deum . . . et Isidis Regin

9.1154, Cantria P. fil. Paulla, s. Augustae Aeclano

9.1538, Servilia Varia and Terentia Elisuiana, ss xv vir; . . . Ianuaria, cymbalistria

9.1539, Mummeia C. f. Atticilla, s

9.1540, Cosinia Celsina, consacerdos Matri deum

9.1541, Terentia Flaviana and Servilia Varia, s. secundo loco xv vir; [s prima (same woman in 1538)]

[9.1542, Servilia Varia, s. prima (same woman in 1538)]

9.2569, Helvia Mesi f., s. Vener

9.2670, Suellia C. f. Consanica, s. Cerialis deia libera

9.3087, Caeidia . . . , s. Cereris et Veneris

9.3089, Helvia G. l. Quarta, s. Cere(ris et Veneris)

9.3090, Mamia V. f., s. Cereris et Veneri(s)

9.3091, Hortensia, s. Isidis

9.3166, Acca Q. f., s. Veneris

9.3167, Accia and Modia, ss. Veneris

9.3170, Attia Mirallis, s. Cereris

9.3358, Ninnia Q. f. Primilla, s. Cereria

9.3429, Nummia Varia C. f., s. Veneris Felicis

9.4200, Tamudia M. f. Severa, s. public Cerer

9.5068, Attia P. fil. Maxima, s. Augustar

9.5428, Antonia Cn. fil. Picentina, s. divae Fau(sti)nae

10.51, Latia P. f. (and?) Auleia Aurina, s(s?). Aug

10.54, . . . Quinta . . . a, s. per(petua) (divi Fausti)nae

10.129, Bovia Maxima, s. xv viral, to Ceres

10.343, Lucia M. l. Suettia, s.

10.680, . . . a L. f. Magna, s. public (Vene)ris et Cereris

10.688, [no name extant], (s) public Vener (et Cereris?)

10.810, Eumachia L. f., s. publ [also 811, 812, 813]

[10.811, same as 810]

10.812, Eumachia L. f., s. publ; Aquuia M. f. Quarta, s. Cereris publ; Heia M. f. and (Ru)fula L. f., ss. Cereris publ

[10.813, Eumachia, s. publ]

10.816, Mamia P. f., s. public [also 10.998]

[10.998, Mamia P. f., s. publicae]

10.999, Istacidia N. f. Rufilla, s. publica

10.1036, Alleia M. f. Decimilla, s. publica Cereris

10.1074, Clodia A. f. and Lassia M. f., ss. publica Cereris

10.1207, Avillia Aeliana, s. Ioviae Veneriae Abellanorum

10.1798, Faltonia Procula, s.

10.1812, Sabina, s. Cereris public

10.1829, . . . na Mun . . . , (s. public)ae Cereris

10.3911, Herennia M . . . , s., to Ceres

10.3926, Icuria M. f., s. Cerialis mundalis

10.4673, Aria C. f., s.

10.4789–91, Flavia Coelia Annia Argiva, s. Iunonis Populonae; Nonia
Prisca, s. Iunon Populon; Vitellia Virgilia Felsia, ministra sacrorum
publ (p)raesidis Iu(n)onis Populo(n)

10.4794, Staia M. f. Pietas, s. Cerer(is) publ prima

10.4889, Tillia Eutychia, s.

10.5073, Munnia C. f., s. Cer

10.5144, . . . asennia, (s) (Vene)ria

10.5191, Agria Sueia N. f., s. Cerer et Veneris

10.5201, Pompeia Cn. f. Phoebe, s. divarum

10.5413, Dentria L. f. Polla, s. divae Augustae

10.5414, Floria C. f. Posilla, s. publica

10.5656, Saenia Cn. f. Balbilla, s. divae Faustinae

10.6018, Pompeia Q. f. Catulla, s. August

10.6074, Decimia C. f. Candida, s. M. D.

10.6075, Helvia Stephanis, s. M. M. I., a *taurobolium*

10.6103, Caesia No(vi) f., s. Cereri(s)

10.6109, Sallustia Saturnina, s. deae Cereris

10.6640, Iulia Procula, s. [Cereris] (presides over ded.)

10.7352, Antia M. f. Cleopatra, s.

10.7501, Lutatia C. f., s. Augustae imp perp, wife of flamen of Livia's cult;
dedication to Ceres Iulia Augusta

11.407, Cantia L. f. Saturnina, s. divae Plotin

11.3810, (Caesia) Sabina, s. Fortunae Reducis

11.3933, Flavia Ammia, s. Cereris

11.6172, Curtilia C. f. Priscilla, s. divae Augustae

11.6520, Cetrania P. f. Severina, s. divae Marcian

14.2804, Agusia T. f. Priscilla, s. Spei et Salutis Aug

magistra

5.757, Aninia M. f. Magna, Seia Ionis, and Cornelia Ephyre, mmm. B.D.

[5.758, Seia Ionis, m. (B.D.? to Fonio)]

5.759, Petrusia Proba . . . Galgesti Hermerot(is), m. to B.D.

5.762, Rufria C. f. Festa and Caesilia Q. l. Scylace, mm. to B.D. Pagana
(with ministrae)

5.814, Leuce Anspaniae l. (and?) Occusia Venusta, mm? to dea Obsequens

5.5026, Cassia Marcella, Iuentia Maxsuma, Firmidia Modesta, Numonia
Secunda, mmmm (with min)

5.7633, Valeria Epithusa, m., to numen Dianae Aug

9.805, Vergilia Prisca, m. Bonae (Deae?)

9.3518, Salvidia T. f. Secunda, Quinctia Sex. f. Secunda, Casnasia Q. l. Rufa,
Casnasia G. l. Sperat(a), Sperata Munatidi A(uli) ser, mmmmm(?)
Vene

9.5295, Veidia T. l. Auge and Iulia C. l. Urbana, mm. Veneri (?)

10.39, Helvia Q. f. and Orbia M. f., mm of Proserpina

10.202, Pietas Sec(un)di contuber(nalis), m. to Juno

10.5192, Fabia Philema(tium?), Baionia Philema(tium?), and Graecina
Myrinna, [mmm?]

10.6511, Cervaria Sp. f. Fortunata, m. Matri Matutae

11.3196, Bennia Primigenia, m., with mag(ister) pagi, to Ceres August

11.3246, Servilia L. l. Felix, m., to Minerva

11.4391, Iulia M. f. Felicitas, m. Fortunae Melioris

11.4767, Pom(p . . .), com(magi)str(a), in dedication to B.D. by wife with
husband

11.6185, Rufellia L. l. Tych(e), m

14.2997, Publicia L. f. Similis, m. Matris Metut

14.3006, Sulpicia Sergi filia, m. Matris Matutae

14.3437, Iulia Athenais, m. Bonae Deae Sevinae

ministra

5.762, Decidia L. f. Paulla and Pupia L. l. Peregrin(a), mm. to B.D.

5.5026, Iuentia Secunda, Manneia Pupa, Loreia Prima, Vettia Secunda,
mmmm

9.3146, Acca L. f. Prima, m. Matris Magnae, on altar with priest

9.4460, Plaetoria Secunda, ministra salutis

[10.4791, m. sacrorum publ . . . (see above under s.)]

11.4635, Quieta Aties Pieridis, m. Bone Die, (and?) proma[gistra?]

flaminica

5.3916, Cusonia Maxima, f., to Saturn, with a man (her husband?)

5.3922, Pomponisia Ponti fil. Severa, f., with a man

5.3923, Cassia P. f. Iustina, f., with a man

5.3928, Octavia M. f. Magna, f. (pa)gi Arusnati(um)

5.3930, Tullia Tul. f. Cardelia, f.

5.6365, Catia M. f. Procula, f.

5.6514, Albucia M. f. Candida, f. (di)vae Iuliae No(var) and f. (d)ivae
Sabinae Ticini, with her husband

5.6840, Octavia Elpidia, f.

5.6954, Tullia C. f. Vitrasi(?), flaminicia [sic] Iulia August

5.7345, . . . a M. f. Secunda Aspri, (flam)inica divae Drusillae

5.7629, Tullia C. (f.), f. Iulia Augusta

5.7788, . . . nia M. f. Mar . . . and . . . a A. f. Sabina, ff. divae Aug

5.7811, Metilia Tertullina, f., with husband and four children, to Juno
regina, for *patrona*

[9.1153, see under *sacerdotes*]

[9.1155, f. divae Aug—same woman as in 9.1154 under *sacerdotes*]

9.1163, Neratia Betitia Procilla, f. Faustinae Aug

9.4881, Egnatia A. f. Aul(ina), f. in colonia provinciae Narbon

9.5534, Vitellia C. f. Rufilla, flamini(cae) salutis Aug

9.5841, Vibia L. f. Marcella, flamina [sic] Aug

10.5924, Flavia Kara Gentia, f.

10.6978, Messia Prisci fil. Crispina, f. divae Aug

10.7602, Iulia Vateria Vateri fil., flamen [sic]

10.7604, Titia Flavia Blandina, f. perpetua

11.5711, Camurena C. fil. Celerina, f. Feron

11.5752, Avidia C. f. Tertullia, f.

11.6354, Abienia C. f. Balbina, f. Pisauri et Arimini

cultrix

11.5223, cc collegii Fulginiae

consuplicatrices

10.6518, Paul(a) Toutia M. f., with c.

hymnetria

10.7426, Nicarin Munatiae L. l. Zosimae filia, h. a s(acris?)

Appendix B: Dedications by Women

The following dedications by women are cited or discussed in the text above. This does not by any means constitute an exhaustive list of such dedications; see for example Brouwer 1989 for a complete list for Bona Dea.

Major Donations

5.412, temple, statue, and portico to Juno Feronia
5.757, temple, to Fonio
5.761, temple to Augusta Bona Dea Cereria
5.762, temple, by *magistrae* of Bona Dea
5.781, temple, statues, porticos with markets and kitchen, to Iunones
5.835, statue and ornaments to Venus Augusta
5.7345, fishpond, by *flaminica* of Drusilla
5.8242, altar to Parcae, silver dish to Bona Dea
9.3146, altar commemorating restoration and gilding of statues of Magna
    Mater, Attis, and Bellona
9.5428, statues for theater, by *sacerdos* of Faustina
9.5071, statue to Feronia [? or to a woman named Feronia]
10.810, buildings attached to the temple of Concordia Augusta
10.3685, 3686, 3688, 3689, temple and portico, etc., to Demeter; and
    dedications by the same people
10.3817, statue to Mater Matuta
10.3818, statue to Mater Matuta
10.3819, statue to Mater Matuta
10.4635, temple to Magna Mater
10.5192, steps and *epimedia*, by three *magistrae*

10.6074, (statue of?) Attis, by a *sacerdos* of Mater deum

10.6640, statues in shrine of Ceres

10.8416, statue of Jupiter to Mater Matuta

11.574, site for temple of Isis

11.4767, altar in grove of Bona Dea

11.1291–1306, shrine of Minerva Memor

11.6290–6302, shrine at Pisaurum

14.3437, temple pavement and roof repair, by *magistra* of Bona Dea

Ordinary Donations

5.758, to Fonio, by *magistra* of Bona Dea

5.759, earrings (?) for the statue of Bona Dea, by a *magistra*

5.814, to Dea Obsequens, by a freedwoman (or women?)

5.836, to Venus Augusta

5.3240, to the Junones, by a *sacerdos* and a man

5.3264, to the Matronae

5.3916, to Saturn, by a *flaminica* and a man

5.4134, to the Matronae

5.4137, to the Matronae

5.5647, to Jupiter Optimus Maximus, by a *sacerdos* of Matidia

5.6829, two vessels and a mirror to Jupiter, Juno, and Minerva

5.7811, to Juno, from a family, to honor *patrona*

9.684, to Bona Dea

9.1538, *criobolium*, by a *cymbalistria*

9.1539, *taurobolium*

9.1541, *taurobolium*

9.1542, *taurobolium*

9.1552, to Silvanus Staianus, on behalf of a son

9.3518, to Venus, group of five *magistrae*

9.5295, to Venus, two *magistrae*

9.5421, to Bona Dea

10.129, to Ceres

10.202, chest and candelabrum, to Juno, by *magistra*

10.467, to Ceres

10.816, to the Genius of Augustus, by *sacerdos*

10.1549, to Bona Dea

10.1555, to Diana Loch(ia?)

10.1596, *taurobolium*

10.1597, *taurobolium*, by a slave

10.3911, to Ceres, by a *sacerdos*

10.5383, to Bona Dea

10.5384, by the same woman, to Fortuna Sancta

10.6075, *taurobolium*, by *sacerdos* of Magna Mater Idaea

10.6511, to Mater Matuta, by a *magistra*

10.6518, to Mater Matuta, woman with *consuplic(atrices)*

10.6595, to Bona Dea

11.3246, to Minerva, by *magistra*

11.4636, to Bona Dea

11.6185, to Bona Dea, by *magistra*

11.6304, to Bona Dea

11.6305, to Bona Dea

CHAPTER 8

Pliny's Brassiere

ॐ

Introduction

The collection *Before Sexuality* came out in 1990, reflecting the enthusiastic reception by classicists, especially Hellenists, of Foucault's *History of Sexuality*; it is subtitled *The Construction of Erotic Experience in the Ancient Greek World* (Halperin, Winkler, and Zeitlin 1990). The collection was remarkable for its conflation of "antiquity" with "Greece," and Romanists who had been working on Roman sexuality since the 1970s felt that some balance was called for. So, around 1992, Judith Hallett, Marilyn Skinner, and I began work on a collection that would pull together some of the main areas in Roman culture then under discussion and deal with Roman sexuality in its own right; Skinner's introductory essay is titled *"Quod multo fit aliter in Graecia . . ."* ("It's done much differently in Greece"). After I had to drop out, they soldiered on, and *Roman Sexualities* came out in 1997.

"Pliny's Brassiere," like "Carrying Water in a Sieve," comes from the project on Roman witches, and presents some of the medical evidence, concentrating on the copious but widely scattered remarks on women's bodies in Pliny's *Natural History*. It began as a talk titled "Blood, Milk, and Poison" first given at the 1986 Brown conference on "Roman Women: Critical Approaches," and continued through numerous permutations in the early 1990s. The published essay draws on the approach first developed in chapter

241

3 above and continuing in chapters 4, 6, and 7, looking for women's agency in the same texts that treat women as objects, as the same glass is both half empty and half full. Pliny, who is not a doctor—who, in fact, distrusts doctors and other scientists—includes among his gigantic collage of snippets of information a considerable number of statements about what we might call women's folk practice. As the religious calendar in chapter 7 shows women incorporating rituals into their daily lives, so Pliny shows women festooning their bodies (and those of their loved ones) with amulets, necklaces, anklets, bracelets, and plasters, tending to each other, taking advice from midwives and prostitutes, and taking deliberate action to attain health. The religious interest in reproductive achievement laid out in chapter 7 not only is reiterated in Pliny, but is shown to be balanced by women's interest in curtailing reproduction—a dichotomy that also directly addresses the fears expressed in witch beliefs, where one of the main activities attributed to witches is the killing of babies.[1] As *venenum* means not only "poison" but "potion," and a witch is a *venefica* ("poison-maker"), so Pliny's medicines overlap with *venena*, and he lists all kinds of amulets aimed at safeguarding the user against *veneficium* and the evil eye. He may be a hostile witness, but he's a talkative one.

My desire to find Roman women was fostered by Linda Gordon's 1986 essay "What's New in Women's History," which discussed the structure versus agency debate (see chapter 10); at the same time, my need was exacerbated by the lack of female subjectivity in Foucault's version of ancient sexuality. I did not see how a history of sexuality could exclude women. Yes, from early on it had seemed to me that Roman texts about women were primarily about men, and I had felt it essential to be conscious that this was so when reading any Roman text; now I wanted to try to see women anyway. "Pliny's Brassiere" appears in *Roman Sexualities* in a section on "Male Constructions of 'Woman'" that includes Sandra Joshel on Tacitus's Messalina, Judith Hallett on the othering of love between women in Latin literature, and Pamela Gordon on the Sappho constructed by Ovid, but I don't see Pliny's text as doing entirely the same thing those texts are doing; I think that's a real brassiere on his head, not a fictitious garment, and that he literally incorporates some real women's practices while going about his own business. Since "Pliny's Brassiere" first appeared, what that business was has been the subject of considerable discussion, and critics now treat Pliny's text as artful (see especially Doody 2010); perhaps an historian might conceive of the *Natural History* as a collage incorporating photographs, with all that implies.

Certainly the photographs are often unflattering. The juxtaposition of "Pliny's Brassiere" with chapter 2 above (on invective against women) and chapter 6 above (on makeup) adds to the current of disgust that runs alongside the female beauties sung, or stripped, in poetry, and adorning markets, houses, dishes. The female genitalia in invective texts are repeatedly compared with foul substances and bizarre animals, and then makeup is portrayed as itself, often, compounded of foul substances—"something icky put over something icky." The same could well be said of Pliny's pharmacopoeia, nor is this idea restricted to Pliny, as demonstrated by Heinrich von Staden in tracing the connection between women and dung therapy (1992). The extent to which Roman women internalized the idea of their bodies as dangerous and powerful, through the special properties of their body fluids—saliva, breast milk, and menstrual blood—is hard to tell; some folk practices attested here suggest that they may have done so.

The agency of women in medicine is thrown further into shadow by Rebecca Flemming's argument about the female practitioners cited by Pliny (2007b: 271–76). Pointing out that Pliny's lumping together of *obstetrices* with prostitutes categorizes them all as "experts in a type of innate female knowledge that is essentially about being a woman, rather than being based on any kind of training" (274; cf. Parker 1992a: 106), she places Pliny's Lais and Elephantis, Salpe, Olympias and Sotira with the exotic male names evoked in pseudepigraphical medical literature (Zoroaster, Petosiris). The *obstetrix* in this context "stands for the foreignness within"; Pliny's female sources "are all made to speak directly from their bodies, their femininity," and "are all there to legitimate and sell certain types of information" (275–76). It is no accident that they appear mainly in the "disgusting" Book 28, on medical uses of the human body; Flemming argues that Pliny probably did not read their recommendations at first hand, but lifted them from references in a book on this subject (271–73). They resemble, then, the glamorous brand names in Kathy Peiss's study of early twentieth-century cosmetics (see chapter 6 above), paralleled more recently by Helena Rubinstein, Prince Matchabelli, and Coco Chanel—these all, however, are "real names," as we happen to know. The relation between ordinary women and Pliny's female authorities might be compared with the relation between women in the audience and the women acted out onstage, for example the two prostitutes in *Poenulus* who sing a song about women needing to scrub themselves so they don't smell like fish, discussed in chapter 6. Complicated; yet even the skeptical Flemming also documents an unglamorous, everyday world where women practiced medicine alongside men (see esp. Flemming

2000: 383–91, a list of female practitioners in inscriptions). Most *obstetrices*, as she points out, were freedwomen and slave women (2000: 52; cf. Kampen 1982). We might doubt that midwives looked as unimportant to women generally as they did to medical writers generally (so also Flemming 2000: 38–39, 360).

Indeed, Flemming's questions suggest the fascinating possibility that, amongst the pseudepigraphical subliterary texts on useful knowledge, magical and otherwise, that circulated in antiquity, were texts addressed particularly to women, as *Aristotle's Masterpiece* circulated in early modern England and Ireland (see Fissell 2003): not actually by Aristotle. Flemming well argues that "the rhetorical purposes these names serve, from those of Elephantis and Lais to Olympias and Sotira, are all too clear," and argues less convincingly that behind these adopted names must be a man (2007b: 275).[2] We might, as in "Pliny's Brassiere," push beyond this point to ask what these names might have meant to a female readership, and who might have bought their books. A job for the papyrologists.

ⁱ⁝⁝   ⁱ⁝⁝   ⁱ⁝⁝

As we try to write the history of Roman sexualities, the sexual experience of women is most difficult to recover, almost unknown at first hand, heavily screened in male-authored erotic and literary texts. The journey you are about to undertake travels through little-known wildernesses of Roman texts in search of the sexual experience of Roman women. These texts are far from erotic, a jumble of encyclopedias and agricultural handbooks. In treating their content as pertinent to women's sexual lives, I have to point out that *Our Bodies, Ourselves* has occasionally been targeted as pornographic and is seen even by its creators as an important step forward in women's sexual freedom.[3] Similarly, the material to be examined here brings us into the everyday world of women's sexual experience, including mundane topics like menstruation, fertility, contraception, abortion, aphrodisiacs, pregnancy, childbirth, and well-baby care. The texts treat having babies as part of having sex, and I will, too; though babies are few and far between in love elegy or invective, in the wholly marriage-centered world of the encyclopedias, babies are everywhere.

The question of women's place in ancient medicine was the subject of much study in the 1980s and 1990s. Despite this, and somewhat surprisingly, the reader in 1997 would have found most of the Roman material here new. Even so eminent a scholar as Ann Hanson, writing about ancient medical writers, treated Soranus as a Greek along with the Hippocratic writers, and moved to the Middle Ages when she wanted to talk about *Gynaikeia* in Latin (1990: 311). The majority of the then-new feminist work on ancient medicine was Hellenocentric, and many studies were not primarily concerned with placing the systems they analyzed in a broader cultural context.[4] Heinrich von Staden's analysis of Celsus on the female body (1991) was exceptional in its attention to the Roman ideologies behind Celsus's ambivalence. Here I will be relying mainly on the *Natural History* of the elder Pliny (24–79 CE), along with the lexicographer Pompeius Festus (familiar from chapters 6 and 7), the agricultural writer Columella (60s CE), and other technical writers. Although they often leave us in a murky ancient Mediterranean soup of sources, they also on occasion tie in their dicta with observed practice in the Italian countryside, or let us know that they are turning to female practitioners or popular belief as their source. These writers are not, properly speaking, medical writers; they have no medical training; but they hold up for our perusal a collage of beliefs from many strata of their society, and they richly repay study.

How were these writers different from medical writers as such? What can they tell us about Roman women that medical writers might not? Pliny himself makes a good starting point. As G. E. R. Lloyd suggests in his brief but pointed overview (1983: 135–49), Pliny has the virtues of his faults. His vast encyclopedia is built along contradictory lines: much of it derives from his enormous reading, yet he generally recognizes the value of experience, and sometimes turns to his own observations; he often inveighs against magic and superstition, then in the next breath records lists of magical cures, with or without negative comment; sometimes he follows Greek scientific sources almost word-for-word, elsewhere he reports what he has seen in the Italian countryside. Cures using bugs are dubbed almost too disgusting to relate (29.61), while earthworms are acclaimed as so versatile that they are kept in honey for general use (29.91–92). He could never be called a critical reader in any consistent sense; as his nephew innocently remarks of him (*Letters* 3.5.10), "He read nothing without making excerpts from it; indeed, he used to say that there was no book so bad that some part of it wasn't useful." Although he writes a crabbed and difficult prose, often sounds cantankerous, and was certainly a terrible bigot, the *Natural History* exudes a sort of sweetness, like the monologues of the old codger in *The Wrong Box*. That he was extremely curious is well attested by the manner of his death; the *Natural History* itself shows that he carried this curiosity to the point of gullibility, as for example in his account of the herb doctor he met who told him he could get him a thirty-foot moly root (25.26–27).

He had the deepest contempt for doctors.[5] In a long tirade (29.1–28) he makes it clear that this contempt is ethnic and class-based. Pliny was a wealthy man, a Roman equestrian, a naval commander, author of a book on cavalry tactics, a book of military history, and a book on rhetoric, as well as a slave owner, landowner, scientist, encyclopedist, and friend of emperors.[6] For him, doctors and their medicine are Greek and worse than useless to Romans; when he proclaims (29.1) that "the nature of remedies . . . has been treated by no one in the Latin language before this," he ignores Celsus and Scribonius Largus—perhaps because they counted as "no one" to him (Scribonius was not only a doctor but probably a freed slave; Celsus, though not a doctor, still does not register with Pliny). Again and again he reviles doctors for making huge profits; this is the contempt of a Roman equestrian for a tradesman. He compares doctors to actors (29.9), persons whose civil status was diminished due to the dishonor felt to adhere to their occupation (see Edwards 1997). He associates medicine with the luxury and moral corruption which it was a cliché, in Roman oratory, to associate with the Greek East (29.20, 26–27). He repeats in all seriousness what was a standing joke, for example in the epigrams of Martial: that doctors murder their patients (29.11, 13, 18). The Roman people, he says, did "without doctors but not without medicine" for six hundred years (29.11), and he quotes in its entirety a letter of the elder Cato to his son Marcus dismissing Athens, Greek literature, and Greek medicine, with loathing (29.14): "A most worthless and intractable race . . . They have sworn to kill all of us, whom they call 'barbarians,' by their medicine . . . I prohibit you from all doctors." Cato's authority here is guaranteed, in very Roman terms, by reference to his triumph, censorship, age, public service, and experience (29.13, 15). Pliny goes on to claim that he himself is making use of Cato's own book of home remedies (29.15), and insists that *Romana gravitas* must separate Romans from the practice of medicine, even from the writing of medical books in Latin.

Yet he compiled the *Natural History*. There is thus in his text always a tension between the matter at hand and Pliny's attitude toward it; he writes, not (shudder) as a medical professional, but as a Roman equestrian eager to make useful knowledge of the natural world available to Romans. (In this he succeeded. Despite its chaotic organization, the *Natural History* proved popular; it was to have a long afterlife, enjoying honor and respect down through the Middle Ages and Renaissance [Chibnall 1975; Doody 2010], and it is still in print today after two thousand years.) Pliny's book, despite overlaps, is thus essentially different from the texts produced by Roman medical writers: for example, not only Celsus and Scribonius Largus, but also the second-century doctors Galen and Soranus, and the sixth-century writer Metrodora.[7]

For one thing, the last three of these writers were Greeks, though Galen and Soranus practiced in Rome; and they wrote in Greek. Soranus looks down on his adopted city: "the women in this city do not possess sufficient devotion to look after everything as the purely Grecian women do" (2.44, trans. Temkin). For another, they are concerned, in their writing, to present a system of health care; a section of Metrodora's work is even arranged by headings in alphabetical order, for ease in consultation. Though Soranus's book is largely concerned with advice to women and midwives, he brings up folk medicine in order to discredit it (1.63, contraceptive amulets; 2.6, why women loosen their clothing and hair during childbirth), or patronizes women's beliefs: "Even if the amulet has no direct effect, still through hope it will possibly make the patient more cheerful" (3.42, trans. Temkin; but cf. Lloyd 1983: 168–82, who credits Soranus for his willingness to humor his patients). To Pliny, doctors, the Magi, peasants, and his own observations are all grist to the mill; just as Cato wrote a *commentarium* for the use of his wife, son, slaves, and *familiares* (*HN* 29.15), so Pliny is writing one for a larger circle. The medical writers write as outsiders, or from above, as professionals; Pliny writes from inside.

This essay takes its name from a brief remark in the *Natural History* (28.76): "I find that headaches are relieved by tying a woman's brassiere on [my/the] head." The strangeness of this image, outstanding even in Pliny's weird parade, has haunted me since first I read it. Of course it made me laugh; I always think of a man in a toga sitting and working late into the night by lamplight, with something on his head that looks like something Lady Gaga would wear.[8] In fact Roman brassieres probably looked more like Ace bandages; yet the image is still strange, because Pliny does not just mean that a headache is cured by wrapping a stretchy thing around your head. He is talking about the medicinal uses of the female human body, and he seems to believe that something is exuded from women's bodies that would make a brassiere cure a headache. Strange as his belief system may be to us, it seems possible to ask what it could have meant to Pliny's female contemporaries.[9] Pliny and his bra may be useful as a symbol embodying the yin-yang of Roman medicine: we can focus on Pliny, and consider what his gynecology, his use of the brassiere, has in common with his status in Roman culture; or we can focus on the woman whose brassiere it was.

Linda Gordon, in an important article (1986), delineated two opposing approaches to the writing of women's history. In one approach, the historian paints women as the victims of an oppressive structure, showing how patriarchy and patriarchs keep women downtrodden. In the other approach, the historian paints women as agents, working out their own strategies to deal with whatever system they find themselves in. This second approach often tries to locate and analyze "women's culture": sets of strategies that women at particular times and places have adopted.[10] I will here argue that the episode of Pliny's brassiere can be used as a starting point for both these approaches, and I will begin with Pliny.

Pliny and the Brassiere

> I thought of that old gentleman, who is dead now, but was a bishop, I think, who declared that it was impossible for any woman, past, present, or to come, to have the genius of Shakespeare. He wrote to the papers about it. He also told a lady who applied to him for information that cats do not as a matter of fact go to heaven, though they have, he added, souls of a sort. How much thinking those old gentlemen used to save one! How the borders of ignorance shrank back at their approach! Cats do not go to heaven. Women cannot write the plays of Shakespeare.
>
> *Virginia Woolf, A Room of One's Own (1957 [1929]: 48)*

What does it mean when Pliny puts a brassiere on his head? Why do we laugh? Partly, at least, because of who he is. He's a man in a toga; the brassiere doesn't suit his dignity. What's a man like that doing with a bra on his head?

The relation between Pliny the scientist and the brassiere on his head might be taken as a symbol of the way Roman medicine colonizes the female body. Pliny's *Natural History* includes a major section in Book 28 on the medical uses of the female human body; this section has a lot to say about menstrual blood, about which there is also another section in Book 7, and it should be emphasized how extremely strange it is to find so much discussion here of a substance rarely so much as named in Latin.[11] In addition, there are a great many other bits about the female body dotted throughout the text; and other writers, as well, talk about the issue—not medical writers, but agricultural writers like Columella, and lexicographers like Pompeius Festus.

The point is not only that these writers view the female human body as raw material for medicines. The point is the reason why they think this would work. Evidently the female body itself is intrinsically powerful— both harmful and helpful; almost uncanny, evidently due to its special processes, not only menstruation but also childbirth and lactation. Anne Carson (1990) has talked about the symbolic properties attributed to Greek women's bodies in literary texts; in Roman technical writing we see similar attitudes given practical form. Indeed, the Roman texts provide a perfect example of the kind of ambivalence suggested by Thomas Buckley and Alma Gottlieb as the paradigm for menstrual "taboos."[12] So, as we look at the Roman texts, it is useful to contrast them with studies of attitudes toward the female body in other Mediterranean cultures, especially those influenced by Christianity, Judaism, or Islam. Rome has nothing to compare with the theological basis for menstrual disgust in the Turkish village culture studied by Carol Delaney (1988), nor is there any mention of prohibitions concerned with religious ritual.[13] The beliefs attested by the technical writers are secular and practical in their area of concern; while they use evaluative language, like *tantum malum* ("so great an evil") or *monstrificum* ("monstrous"), there is apparently no theological or cosmological reason for it (but see chapter 6 on the *mundus muliebris*).[14]

Sometimes just the female body itself, even the sight of it, can be dangerous. Describing the frankincense trade in Arabia, Pliny notes that those who trade in this precious commodity cannot let themselves "be polluted (*pollui*) by any meeting with women or with funeral processions" (12.54).[15] The appearance of a woman as a bad omen or pollutant is not uncommon; Pliny describes what he calls "the rustic law on many Italian farms," whereby care is taken to keep women from walking down the road using a spindle, or even carrying one in the open, since such a sight would "blight all expectations," especially for the crops (28.28). While the ostensible source of the problem here is the spindle, the virtual identity between women and spinning/weaving is surely in play.

Often the power of the female body is associated directly with menstruation. Its powers to help are awesome, almost frightening, and are noted with a certain ambivalence; as Pliny says, "many say there are remedies, too, in such an evil." Hailstorms and tornados are driven away "by the sight of a naked, menstruating woman" (if this is what *mense nudato* means); likewise storms at sea are turned aside by the sight of a naked woman (?), even without menstruation (*etiam sine menstruis*, 28.77). Menstrual blood has general powers to cure diseases, especially epilepsy (28.44), rabies, fevers

(28.82–86)—all illnesses involving loss of bodily control.[16] And it is particularly useful to the farmer. Columella lists a whole series of spells to rid the garden of pests, things like caterpillars (*Rust.* 10.337–68). But the best, he says, is to send a menstruating virgin to walk around the fields (10.357–66):

> But if no medicine (*medicina*) has the power to repel the pests,
> bring on the Dardanian arts, and let a woman with bare feet,
> who, first occupied with the regular laws of a girl,
> drips chastely with her obscene blood, 360
> with her dress and hair unbound, and serious face,
> be led three times around the fields and garden hedge.
> And when she has purged them by walking, amazing to see!
> . . .
> The caterpillars roll to the ground with twisted bodies.

Columella repeats this advice elsewhere (11.3.64), without specifying that the woman needs to be a virgin, and citing a Greek text, Democritus's *On Antipathies*. Pliny repeats the same advice for getting rid of caterpillars, worms, and beetles, along with other pests (28.78); the woman should be naked. He also there cites a recommendation of Metrodorus of Scepsis, derived from Cappadocia, for getting rid of cantharides in the fields: he says the woman should go through the middle of the fields with her dress pulled up above her buttocks. (Presumably Columella, with his "Dardanian arts," is also thinking of Metrodorus; Scepsis is in the Troad.) Other possibilities are for her to go barefoot, with her hair hanging down and her dress unfastened; but care should be taken lest she do this at sunrise, for this will dry up the crops. Moreover, if she touches them, young vines will be permanently damaged, and rue and ivy, those "most medicinal things" (*res medicatissimas*) will die on the spot. In a discussion of ridding trees of pests (17.266–67), Pliny repeats that many people say caterpillars (*urucae*) can be killed if a woman just beginning her period walks around each of the trees, barefoot and with her tunic ungirt (*recincta*). Since both writers cite Greek or Asian sources, we cannot tell to what extent such rituals may have been practiced in the Italian countryside, but we gain the added idea that such rituals may have been practiced throughout the Mediterranean. Dangerous rituals: we note that even in Columella's discussion of the useful powers of a menstruating woman, the blood itself is referred to as "obscene blood," *obsceno cruore* (10.360). The semantic range of *obscenus/a/um* in Latin leaves us in no doubt that Columella associates the blood with things both sexual and repulsive, things that should not be seen or spoken about (Richlin 1992: 9; cf. von Staden 1991: 284–86). The mixed emotions attested here are echoed by Pliny's warning about the danger to crops.

Thus it is no surprise to find that, in Pliny's *materia medica*, menstrual blood can do harm. Pliny introduces both of his discussions of menstrual blood with warnings: "Nothing may easily be found more monstrous than the flux of women" (7.64); and "Indeed, from the menses themselves, elsewhere monstrous, . . . they rant dire and unspeakable things" (28.77). Intercourse with menstruating women can be "deadly" for men (28.77–78). Speaking of the *violentia* of menstrual blood, Pliny gives a list of its effects (28.79–80): it can put bees to flight, stain linens black, dull barbers' razors, tarnish bronze and give it a bad smell, cause pregnant mares to abort (even when the women are only seen at a distance, if this is the first menstruation), and, even when burnt to ashes, ruin dyes (cf. 28.78, where purple is said to be "polluted" by menstruating women during the times of especially deadly menstruation). Even women themselves, usually "immune among themselves to their own evil" (*malo suo inter se inmunibus*) can be forced to abort by a smear of menstrual blood, especially if a pregnant woman walks over some (28.80). Pliny cites Bithus of Dyrrhachium as the authority for one remedy: mirrors that have been dulled by the glance of a menstruating woman can recover their shine by having the woman look at the back of the mirror; and this whole problem can be averted by having menstruating women carry a particular sort of fish around with them, a mullet (28.82).

In another list of the harmful properties of menstrual blood (7.64), Pliny says: contact with it sours new wine; crops become barren when touched by it; grafts die; the seeds are burned up in the gardens; fruit falls off the trees; mirrors are dimmed by menstruating women looking into them; the edge of iron tools is dulled; the shine on ivory is dulled; beehives die; bronze and iron corrode, and bronze smells bad; and it gives rabies to dogs who taste it and infects their bites with incurable poison (*venenum*). Even ants, people say, can sense it, and will spit out fruit tainted by it, nor will they go back to it afterwards (7.65). Likewise, bees, who appreciate cleanliness, hate both scurf and women's menstrual blood (11.44). All kitchen plants grow yellow at the approach of a menstruating woman (19.176).

Many of these beliefs have an agricultural context, and indeed Columella includes a few remarks on menstrual blood among his most humdrum comments on gardening. Like Pliny, he says that plants will dry up if touched by a menstruating woman (*Rust.* 11.3.38); this passage, like most of Columella, is down-to-earth in its tone, and explicitly takes its authority from peasants (*ut rustici dicunt*, 11.3.43, 12.10.1) and from Columella's own experience (11.3.61). He also advises that no women at all should be allowed near cucumbers and gourds, for "the growth of green things droops at contact with them": sympathetic magic? This is even worse if the women are menstruating, at which time they will kill the new growth just by looking at it (11.3.50).

These beliefs are in keeping with attitudes expressed toward menstruation in other kinds of Roman texts. Menstruation and menstrual blood are mentioned only a few times in Roman satirical and moralizing literature, uniformly negatively. Attitudes toward the female genitalia generally in Roman texts are highly negative; descriptions appear only in invective, and invective of a most savage sort (see chapter 2 above).[17] Thus Festus lists the word *ancunulentae*, which he says is used to refer to "women . . . at the time of menstruation"; he suggests that the Latin word *inquinamentum*, which means "stain," comes from this word (10L). *Inquinamentum* is not a neutral word, and its cognates appear with some frequency in sexual contexts (Richlin 1992: 27).

It is not just menstrual blood, though, that comes into these medical texts. Another peculiarly female body fluid, breast milk, plays a large part in Pliny's account of the female body. Unlike menstrual blood, however, breast milk is uniformly helpful. Pliny rates women's milk as one of the most useful remedies (28.123):

> Foremost we will expound the common and particular remedies from animals, for example the uses of milk. Mother's milk is the most useful thing for anybody. . . . Moreover, human milk is the most nourishing for any purpose, next goat's milk; the sweetest after human [milk] is camel's, the most effective [after human milk] comes from donkeys.

Again, we might be startled to find women listed here among animals, and take this as similar to the attitudes that link menstruating women with animals, crops, and the monstrous. Still, Pliny has many good things to say about women's milk. Tellingly, as opposed to the *venenum*-like qualities of menstrual blood, it is an antidote to poisons, and cures many illnesses, especially illnesses of the eye. A man anointed with the milk of a mother and daughter at the same time, Pliny says, is freed from all fear for his eyes throughout his life (28.73).[18] Other effluvia from women's bodies are also powerful and can be beneficial, including urine, hair, and saliva. Pliny says, for example, that the saliva of a fasting woman is good for bloodshot eyes and fluxes; the corners of the eye are to be moistened with the saliva occasionally. This works better if the woman has fasted on the previous day as well (28.76).

With all these recommendations, we find ourselves wondering how often people actually used cures like this. We have a useful attestation in a story about the father of the emperor Vitellius. Suetonius is not sure he approves of him, and describes the senior Vitellius as "a man harmless and industrious, but thoroughly notorious for his love of a freedwoman. He used to bathe his windpipe and throat as a remedy with a mixture of her saliva with honey, and not secretly or occasionally but daily and right out in the open" (*Vitell.* 2.4). Presumably what is disgraceful here is the openness and the breach of status boundaries; Suetonius does not really seem to question the belief that her saliva would have curative powers. As will be seen, there are several accounts of the use of women's saliva to protect babies from harm.

It seems, overall, that Roman medical uses of the female body tie in with a set of beliefs about the female body that is characterized by a deep ambivalence, which might usefully be compared with the ideology of women's religion in chapter 7. The body is powerful, but in a frightening way. There is a familiar division between the lower-body fluids and the upper-body fluids—the fluids from the lower body having the power both to help and to harm, while the fluids from the upper body are just helpful. Menstrual blood protects, or harms, a long list of products of culture—crops, metal tools, domesticated animals, dye. So when Pliny puts on that brassiere, he is using the female body to think with in more ways than one.[19]

But who gave him the brassiere? Several of the cures from the female body involve a large degree of cooperation and participation on the part of women themselves: for example, the caterpillar-removal procedure, in which a woman has to walk through the fields barefoot. This certainly implies a scenario with a woman and her powers as the center of attention, and this is not the only such case. One female practitioner whom Pliny quotes, the *obstetrix* Sotira, recommends a cure in which the soles of the patient's feet are smeared with menstrual blood; she notes that this works especially well if the smearing is done by the woman herself (*HN* 28.83). The saliva to be obtained from a fasting woman implies not only her cooperation in providing the saliva but in fasting as well. We might guess that the elder Vitellius got the saliva from his mistress with her knowledge; likewise for the other cures and harms. We might extrapolate that this body of medical knowledge implies a great deal about women's experience of themselves in the world. We might further expect that women's beliefs about their bodies might vary according to status and sex/class, or urban/rural divisions; in any case, we might well turn our attention from the man wearing the brassiere to the woman he got it from.

The Woman behind the Brassiere

> I did not spend the next two weeks worrying about my period. If it did
> not show up, there was no question in my mind that I would force it to do
> so. I knew how to do this. Without telling me exactly how I might miss a
> menstrual cycle, my mother had shown me which herbs to pick and boil, and
> what time of day to drink the potion they produced, to bring on a reluctant
> period. She had presented the whole idea to me as a way to strengthen the
> womb, but underneath we both knew that a weak womb was not the cause of
> a missed period. She knew that I knew, but we presented to each other a face
> of innocence and politeness and even went so far as to curtsy to each other at
> the end.
>
> *Jamaica Kincaid, Lucy (1990: 69–70)*

Feminist historians of medicine have made us familiar with the idea that women played an important part in folk medicine in Western Europe.[20] In the Roman period, the divisions among different kinds of medicine were much blurrier than they are today. There evidently were such divisions; Pliny spends a lot of time complaining about the kinds of medicine he disapproves of, especially "magical" cures—that is, the cures of the Magi, practitioners from Asia Minor (see Lloyd 1979: 13 n. 20; 1983: 140–41). But for us, it is very hard to tell the difference between the Roman forms of what we would call folk medicine, scientific medicine, and magic. This section looks at how women themselves might have taken an active role in their cures. These cures definitely sound folksy; the reader should be aware, however, that they do not generally sound more folksy than the general run of cures in Pliny's *Natural History*.

Pliny certainly does not cite many female medical authorities as sources. His sources are most often male, when he cites them, and it is always a question how much descriptive validity we can ascribe to his recommendations. Still, what I will try to do is to recover from Pliny's *Natural History* some idea of women's own health practices in first-century CE Rome.[21]

How might we imagine women involving themselves in medical practice? The epigraph to this section comes from the Antiguan writer Jamaica Kincaid; her youthful protagonist has just come to New York City from her island home to work as an *au pair*. In her own memories, this young woman and her mother are both active and knowledgeable, and the sort of medicine they practice is immediately recognizable in the pages of Pliny's *Natural History*.

If we look long enough, we find that some of Pliny's recipes do involve action by the woman herself. For pains in the *muliebria loca*, women are to wear "constantly" a bracelet containing the first tooth of their child to fall out, which should never have fallen on the ground (28.41). So we can imagine women saving, in their medicine boxes, their children's first baby teeth. To stop menstruation, Pliny recommends catching a spider spinning a thread as it ascends again, crushing it, and applying it (30.129). For a variety of ills, Pliny recommends calf's gall sprinkled on the genitals during menstruation, just before intercourse (28.253); so we have to imagine a woman saying, "Excuse me while I just sprinkle on some of this calf's gall." Taking a purge could apparently be a complex and drawn-out process: women are to take a decoction of linozostis in food, starting on the second day of menstruation (*purgatio*), and then for two further days; on the fourth day, after a bath, they are to have sex (25.40). In a rare ethnographic description of actual female practice, Pliny says that the *agrestes feminae*, "peasant women," in Transpadane Gaul wear amber necklaces, mostly as ornaments, but also as *medicina*, to ward off throat problems (37.44).

Another branch of ancient *medicina* that demands active involvement of its consumers is love medicine. Despite disclaimers, Pliny describes more than sixty different aphrodisiacs and more than twenty-nine different antaphrodisiacs. He even has several lists of such materials (26.94–99; 32.139), including one from the Magi (30.141–43), and credits a range of sources, all male.[22] These are mostly given without comment, though Pliny chides Theophrastus for his description of a plant that provokes the desire to have sex seventy times (26.99). Considering the common Roman idea that women specialize in potions (see below), the all-male cast is surprising; Metrodora does include a number of aphrodisiacs in her book (1.26, 1.38, 1.39, 4.20–23).[23]

The market for these products seems to be mixed. Some are listed specifically as "for men" (a total of twelve), "for women" (a total of seven); scandix is for those "exhausted by sex or shriveled from old age" (22.80).[24] Rarely are circumstances specified; Pliny does not tell us of limits on use for oneself, as opposed to use on others. Hyena genitals in honey are said to stimu-

late desire "even when men hate intercourse with women"; and so (what's a
wife to do?) "the harmony of the whole house is preserved by keeping these
genitals, along with a vertebra with some of the skin attached" (28.99).[25]
For antaphrodisiacs, several motives seem to be in play. Repeatedly these
drugs are said to stop wet dreams (*libidinum imaginationes in somno*, literally "imaginings of lusts in sleep") or sex dreams (*somnia veneris*) (20.68,
20.142–43, 20.146, 26.94, 34.166). Some aphrodisiacs are clearly aimed at in-
fluencing an object's desires without his/her knowledge—sprinkling seeds
on a woman to augment her eagerness (20.227); placing a southernwood
sprig under the pillow (21.162). Others would be harder to miss: putting
hyena muzzle hairs on a woman's lips (aphrodisiac, 28.101) or rubbing her
groin with blood from a tick or giving her he-goat's urine to drink (antaph-
rodisiac, 28.256). Erynge root (22.20) is said to make a man who gets hold
of it *amabilis*; this, Pliny says, is how Phaon of Lesbos made himself beloved
by Sappho. The Magi, among many other powers they attribute to the hyena (including a cure for *probrosa mollitia*, "disgraceful effeminacy"), claim
that a hyena's anus worn on a man's left arm will make any woman follow
him the minute he looks at her (28.106). By way of comparison, Metrodora
seems equally to be writing for a mixed audience; five of her eight aphrodisiacs are "for erection" (4.20–23), while one is headed "so that she will howl
and make all kinds of sounds" (1.39, Parker trans.). A remedy entitled "for
a woman, so she will not be promiscuous" (1.36) requires the man to rub
medicine on his penis; another charm promises "to make her confess her
lovers" (1.37).[26]

Nowadays we expect women to be concerned with abortion.[27] Roman
culture, though, highly valued women's fecundity, and Pliny's text reflects
that attitude. His expressed attitude toward abortion is negative, and he
mostly gives recommendations for ways to increase fertility and to promote
successful delivery of a child. However, he does in fact give formulae for
abortifacients, as well as for emmenagogues. (These remedies are referred
to by Pliny as "calling forth the menses," much like the cures described by
Jamaica Kincaid's narrator; the distinction between such a medicine and an
abortifacient appears, then, to be a fine one, although in fact, due to beliefs
about the optimal time for conception, perhaps not fine at all.[28]) In this
context, it seems significant that Pliny attributes the invention of abortion
to women; he exclaims (10.172), "Males have figured out all the back alley-
ways of sex, crimes against nature; but women figured out abortions." This
despite evident ideological disincentives.[29]

Pliny himself connects abortion not only with "unnatural" sex, as here, but also with magical potions that cause insanity and/or love and lust (25.25):

> But what excuse could there be for showing how minds could be un-hinged, fetuses squeezed out, and many similar things? I do not discuss abortifacients (*abortiva*), nor even love potions . . . nor other magic por-tents, unless when they are to be warned against or refuted, especially when confidence in them has been undermined.

One such refutation concerns two female practitioners, Lais and Elephan-tis. Pseudonymous or not, they receive the same basic treatment from Pliny *eques* as the rest of his Greek authorities: a curt nod. They do here rate par-ticular disapproval; in his summary of their accounts of the abortifacient powers of menstrual blood, he faults them for contradicting each other, and concludes (28.81): "When the latter says that fertility is brought about by the same methods by which the former pronounces barrenness [is], it is better not to believe [them]." This tells us a good deal. On the one hand, Pliny's attitude is quite negative: he sums up their accounts as *monstrifica*, in keeping with the general tone of his remarks on menstrual blood, nor is he deferential to them as female authorities on abortion. On the other hand, we know through him that these female authorities were cited on both abortion and fertility. He reproduces the lists of *abortiva* attributed to them—among them, a warning that barley tainted by menstrual blood will block conception in she-asses (or not).[30]

Furthermore, Pliny himself tells us some things about women's prac-tice. A section headed "Wine, too, has its amazing qualities" moves from fertility to poisons, taking in abortion along the way. Wine flavored with hellebore, cucumber, or scammony, he notes (14.110), is called *phthorium* ("destructive") because it produces abortions (*pthorios pessos* is the term for "abortifacient" in the Hippocratic Oath).[31] One wine from Arcadia pro-duces *fecunditas* in women and madness (*rabies*) in men (14.116); in Achaia, there is a wine reported to expel the fetus (*abigi partum*), "even if pregnant women eat one of the grapes." An Egyptian wine has the nickname *ecbolada* (Greek for "throw-out"), because it brings on an abortion (14.118). Similarly, ground pine has the Latin name *abiga* ("push-out"), "because of abortions" (*propter abortus*, 24.29). Perhaps these descriptive names are folk terms. Similarly, in a discussion of the properties of the willow tree, Pliny notes (16.110) that Homer calls the willow *frugiperda*, "destroys-fruit" (*olesikar-pon, Od.* 10.510), and comments, "Later ages have interpreted this conceit according to their own wickedness, since it is known that the seed of the willow is a *medicamentum* of barrenness for a woman." The prescriptions attributed to Lais and Elephantis may have been part of a how-to guide; similarly, in a discussion of the gynecological properties of mallow, Pliny notes that another female practitioner, Olympias of Thebes, says that mallows with goose grease bring on abortion (20.226). Rebecca Flemming's objections to the facticity of these women as practitioners raises the interesting possibility that books of cures circulated under these names as cookbooks circulate now under the name of Betty Crocker, aimed at a female market; the history of such subliterary texts is a long one (see, e.g., Weissler 1998, with remarks on authorship at 9–10). That a woman might not wish to conceive is recognized by another recipe, directed at a male market: a woman unwilling to conceive is forced to, by means of hairs taken from the tail of a she-mule, pulled out while the animals are mating, and woven together when the man and woman are (30.142)—this time, a remedy making considerable demands on the male sexual partner.

Pliny's connection of female practitioners with abortifacients and love potions is common in literary and legal texts. Apart from whatever doctors may have done, Roman writers portray a market of female consumers whose needs are met by women who concoct potions. Thus the satirist Juvenal, writing against women fifty years after Pliny (6.594–98):

> Nary a woman gives birth in a gilded bed—
> so great is the power of the arts and drugs of that woman   595
> who makes women sterile, and kills human beings in the womb
> for a fee. Rejoice, unfortunate man, and you yourself give her
> whatever it is she must drink.

The point is that wealthy women, who can afford the cost, would rather pay for an abortion than bear a child; (cuckolded) husbands are Juvenal's intended audience. Similarly, at least one legal text envisions the makers of potions as female; the jurist Marcian, writing in the early third century CE on murder and poison, notes (*Digest* 48.8.3): "By law that woman is ordered to be relegated who, even if not with malice aforethought, but setting a bad example, has given any medicine to promote conception by which the woman who took it died." The law is concerned to regulate all hazardous potions, including those related to sex. Pliny disapproves of abortion, but still provides a list that seems to reflect folk practice as much as "medicine"; by the early third century CE, abortion was considered a serious crime in need of legal attention, whether self-inflicted (Ulpian, *Digest* 48.8.8) or performed by others by means of "potions" (Paulus, *Digest* 48.19.38.5, also against aphrodisiacs). Yet it does not seem that abortion was illegal before the Severan period, or that this female market was ever rigorously controlled.[32]

Pliny devotes much more attention to the methods by which women may cure barrenness and promote conception. He recommends a wide variety of substances, from cow's milk to partridge eggs, and he strongly implies an active female market for these medicines.[33] He even cites from one of his sources a text unfortunately lost—a poem by a woman crediting a gemstone with helping her to conceive (37.178): "What paneros is like is not told us by Metrodorus, but he quotes a not inelegant poem by Queen Timaris on it, dedicated to Venus, in which it is understood that the stone aided her fertility."

A picture begins to emerge of activities undertaken, mostly by women, in order to ensure the fertility that was so essential to them. The waters of Sinuessa are said to cure barrenness in women (31.8); a spring at Thespiae and the river Elatum in Arcadia help women conceive, while the spring Linus in Arcadia prevents miscarriage. We might imagine women making pilgrimages to these rivers in order to attain their goal, much like the well-attested fourth-century BCE pilgrimages to the temple of Asclepius at Epidaurus, where women sought help toward conception, among other cures, via incubation (Lefkowitz and Fant 2005: 285–87); we might compare women's travels to religious centers as seen in chapter 7. "Some people," says Pliny, "out of superstition, believe that mistletoe works more effectively if it is gathered from an oak at the new moon without iron or touching the ground, and that it cures epilepsy and helps women to conceive if they just keep it with them" (24.12). Women are also advised to keep cucumber seeds fastened to the body, without letting them touch the ground (20.6); thus we imagine the hopeful mother bedecked with seeds and plants. Another recommendation (*tradunt*, "they say") is to smell the plant ami during sex (20.164); so we might imagine rituals of the bedroom, as with the calf's gall cure above. (Compare Serenus Sammonicus's recommendation that a woman and her husband pluck the "herb of Mercury" together when they are hurrying to bed at night, *Liber medicinalis* 32.613–14). Various medicines are said to foster conception, and some of them are not so appealing: the Magi promise that a barren woman will conceive in three days if she takes a hyena eye in her food with licorice and dill (*HN* 28.97); small worms taken in drink promote conception (30.125), as do snails applied with saffron (30.126); likewise hawk's dung in honey wine (30.130).

We might pause here to notice how awful some of the medicines sound. A lot of Pliny's recipes suggest how different the experience of medicine would have been for a Roman from what a modern patient experiences. For the breasts, Pliny recommends crabs applied locally (*inliti*, 32.129); this sounds impossible, but elsewhere he recommends tying frogs backwards onto a baby's head for siriasis (literally "dog-star-itis," a name for infant sunstroke, 32.138); the skull has to be moistened, he notes soberly. Other recommendations for women include the use of beaver testicles, scrapings from the gymnasium, chewed-up anise, earthworms taken in sweet wine, beetles, and a wide variety of kinds of animal dung. There are recommendations for tying on fish, and recommendations for fumigation with a dead snake, or with lobsters. The example of the frogs on the baby shows that it is not just women who get stuck with this kind of medicine; however, there does seem to have been an association between disgusting ingredients and women patients. Heinrich von Staden (1992) has pointed out how overwhelmingly such cures are reserved for women, especially the use of dung.

So far we have seen women actively engaged in medical treatments affecting menstruation, abortion, and conception. Once conception was achieved, expectant mothers ran tests to determine the child's sex. For example, Pliny (10.154) says that, as a young woman, Livia, wife of Augustus, was eager to have a boy, and, when she was pregnant with Tiberius, used a special way, "common among girls" (*hoc usa est puellari augurio*), to tell the sex of her baby. Suetonius (*Tib.* 14.2) gives a more detailed description:

> Livia, when pregnant with [Tiberius], wanted to know whether she would give birth to a male [child], and tried to find out by various omens; she took an egg stolen from a setting hen and cherished it continually, sometimes in her own hand, sometimes in her maidservants', taking turns (*nunc sua nunc ministrarum manu per vices ... fovit*), until a chick was hatched, with a marked crest.

Here this procedure is made into a joint effort by owner and slaves, all participating together, although, as in cosmetics and religion, the practice is focused on the body of the dominant woman; at least, as far as Suetonius noticed.

Pliny also lists recommendations for materials that will affect the sex of the baby, not just tell the mother what it is. Many of these aim at helping to conceive a male child. Some involve activities by father and mother together (for example, taking crataegonos in wine before supper for forty days before conception, 27.63); often the recommendations are for special additions to the mother's diet.[34] Once in a while, the properties of substances to produce either a girl or a boy are listed; so maybe some people were trying for girls (compare the short list of such medicines in Metrodora, "for the birth of a boy or the birth of a girl," 1.33). On the other hand, there are hints here and there that boy babies are better, and a complete absence of recommendations aimed solely at conceiving a girl baby. So though there is nothing here to indicate any widespread practice of gender-based abortion, there does seem to be an assumption that women will be trying to have male children.[35]

By far the bulk of Pliny's material on fertility has to do with pregnancy, and especially with childbirth. It is ironic that one of the very few reported sayings we have from Roman women has to do with a subversion of what seems to be the norm expected by Pliny. One of the jokes attributed to Julia, daughter of Augustus, has her claiming to use her pregnancies to enable her to have sex with men other than her husband (Macrobius *Saturnalia* 2.5.9): "And when those who knew of her sins used to marvel at how she gave birth to sons resembling Agrippa when she made such public property of her body, she said, 'Why, I never take on a passenger until the ship is full.'" As seen in chapter 3, Julia, in contemporary histories, has the character of a renegade, a woman who goes against what is expected of women. Certainly, if the list of remedies in Pliny is anything to go by, we would expect that many Roman women were deeply concerned about carrying a baby to term.

Pliny's encyclopedia contains more than 140 remedies concerned with pregnancy and childbirth. A significant category contains substances that help hold off miscarriage or are to be avoided because they will cause miscarriage. Pliny includes miscarriage among the hazards of sexuality, saying that "a yawn indeed is fatal [to a woman] in labor, just as sneezing during sex causes miscarriage" (7.42). Some substances are to be avoided by pregnant women as dangerous, even by proximity; sometimes miscarriage is a risk or side effect. Thus the cases in which activity by the woman is demanded include many aimed at staving off miscarriage. Most interesting is a group that involves things women should not step over: these include menstrual blood (28.80); a viper or a dead amphisbaena (30.128); a

262 · ARGUMENTS WITH SILENCE

raven's egg, which will cause her to miscarry through the mouth (30.130); and beaver oil, or a beaver (32.133). These are among the most hallucinatory episodes in the *Natural History*: how is it imagined that a woman might accidentally step over a beaver? Did anyone really believe in oral miscarriage? Additional information only raises further questions. Pliny (30.128) offers two remedies for stepping over a dead amphisbaena—a snake with a head at each end of its body. One involved carrying a live amphisbaena on your person in a box; the other was to step immediately over a preserved amphisbaena. So we have to imagine the household in an uproar, and somebody yelling, "Marcus! Quick, run down to the drugstore and get a preserved amphisbaena!" The dangers of raven's eggs are clarified by Pliny's notes on the raven (10.32); he says it is a popular belief (*vulgus arbitratur*) that ravens lay eggs or mate through their beaks, and hence a pregnant woman, if she eats a raven's egg, will bear her child through her mouth, and will have a difficult labor if a raven's egg is brought into the house. Although Aristotle is cited for a counter-opinion, it seems at least possible that Pliny is preserving a folk belief here—though one that can hardly have had much in women's experience to support it.

Most of the miscarriage insurance is less exotic, and involves amulets, like this one (36.151):

> Eagle stones, wrapped in skins of sacrifical animals, are worn as amulets by women or quadrupeds (*mulieribus vel quadripedibus*) while pregnant, to hold back the birth (*continent partus*); these are not to be removed until they give birth, otherwise the vulva will prolapse. But if the amulet is not taken away while they are in labor, they cannot give birth at all.

This kind of recommendation is found for other amulets as well, so when we think of amulets, we also should imagine that each one carries with it its proper procedure.

Indeed, the recommendations here imply women's activities and involvement with the medical care of their own bodies. A woman might experiment with a range of pessaries, ointments, and potions. Pliny recommends tying thirty grains of git to the body with linen to aid in removing the afterbirth (20.183). A woman might also use a hare-rennet ointment, unless she had bathed the day before (28.248); if she takes sow-thistle potion, she must then go for a walk (22.89). Substances or objects she might keep with her or carry include not only the preserved amphisbaena but a stick with which a frog has been shaken from a snake (30.129); a vulture's feather under the feet (30.130); a torpedo fish, brought into the room (32.133); and a "round ball of blackish tufa" taken from the second stomach of a heifer and not allowed to touch the ground (11.203). Amulets to aid labor include those made from plants sprouting inside a sieve thrown away on a cross-path (24.171); a stone eaten by a pregnant doe, found in her excrement or womb (28.246); and chameleon tongue (28.114). Some amulets or substances have to be placed on certain parts of the woman's body: the afterbirth of a bitch (30.123) and the snakeskin (30.129) have to be put on the woman's groin; the stingray-sting amulet is to be worn on the navel (32.133); the stone voided by a bladder victim is to be tied over the groin (28.42). Some procedures are very elaborate indeed, involving the central participation of other people. To hasten birth, the father of the baby is to untie his belt and put it around the woman's waist, and then untie it, saying the *precatio* "I bound you, and I will set you free"; he then leaves the room (28.42). Another remedy involves someone throwing over the house where the woman is in labor one of two things: a missile that has killed with one stroke each a human being, a boar, and a bear; or a light cavalry spear pulled from a human body without touching the ground (28.33–34). Or someone might just bring the spear into the house.

Pliny also lists some medicines that counteract the effects of witchcraft against conception, pregnancy, and childbirth. Some of these indicate women's concern to protect themselves against witchcraft, a sense of the vulnerability of a pregnant woman. The stone called aetites, found in eagle's nests, is also said to protect the fetus "against all plots to cause abortion," *contra omnes abortuum insidias* (30.130). Eating wolf meat is recommended for women about to give birth, or else having someone who has eaten wolf meat sit next to them as they go into labor; this prevails even against *inlatas noxias*, "harmful things carried in" (28.247). The idea here that it is harmful specifically to bring certain things into the house where a woman is in labor recurs in several cases, and the implication is that ill-wishers might do this on purpose. The same may be true of the objects not to be stepped over; perhaps these should be thought of as placed in the woman's path—the beaver, for example. These all seem to be actions it would be hard to do unintentionally, and so are to be understood as malicious; likewise, Pliny notes that hanging the left foot of a hyena above a woman in labor is fatal (28.103). So we should imagine pregnant women as on their guard, having to be vigilant to make sure nobody is surrounding them with beavers and hyena feet. The secretion of harmful substances or objects near an intended victim played a part in general Roman *veneficium*, as in the case of Germanicus (Tacitus *Annales* 2.69.5); we might compare the use of goofer dust in African-American hoodoo.

Similarly, women are vigilant in protecting the babies once they are born. A fascinating set of texts talks about the use of amulets and other medicines by mothers or *nutrices* to protect young babies.[36] Baby amulets cited by Pliny include branches of coral (32.24); amber (37.50); gold ("so that *venefica* that might be carried in may do less harm," *ut minus noceant quae inferantur venefica*, 33.84); malachite (37.114); galactitis (37.162); beetles (11.97); a dolphin's tooth, for children's "sudden terrors" (*pavores repentinos*, 32.137); similarly a wolf's tooth or wolf's skin (28.257); a horse's baby teeth (28.258); and bones from dogs' dung, for siriasis (30.135). One cure especially for girl babies is an amulet of goat's dung in cloth (28.259), recalling von Staden's association of dung therapy with women. The use of protective medicine could continue past babyhood; Suetonius says that Nero continued to wear on his right arm the cast-off skin of a snake, enclosed in a gold bracelet, "at his mother's wish" (*ex voluntate matris*, *Nero* 6.4). This suggests to us (1) that the amulets do not just appear in some Greek medical sources collected by Pliny, but reflect actual Roman practice, (2) that they were used and controlled by concerned mothers, and (3) that they were worn by children as a sign of their mothers' protection.[37] Moreover, David Soren's excavation of an infant cemetery from the late ancient period in the Italian countryside suggests that animals like those recommended in Pliny were indeed fastened onto ailing children.[38]

The classic baby amulet is the *fascinum*, a phallic amulet of which many exemplars survive today. The paramount example of a *male* body part with beneficial properties, the phallus has powers to counteract witchcraft and the evil eye, as has been widely discussed.[39] But Pliny introduces his account of the *fascinum*—protector, he remarks, of babies and generals alike—in the context of women's pediatric practice. Dismissing some practitioners' claims about the use of saliva, he remarks, scornfully, "If we believe those things are done aright, we must think likewise of these, too: that the wet-nurse (*nutrix*), at the approach of a stranger (*extraneus*), or if the infant is looked at while sleeping, spits [*adspui*, on the baby? at the onlooker?] three times" (28.39). Here, as elsewhere, the *nutrix* is the protector of the baby, and her saliva has a protective force against the evil eye.[40]

The satirist Persius, Pliny's contemporary, describes the same practice. He is talking about what is best to pray for, and he uses as a negative illustration a picture of a baby and the women who are taking care of him (*Satire* 2.31–40):

Behold, a grandmother or gods-fearing mother's-sister (*matertera*)
has taken the boy from his cradle and averts evil (*expiat*) from his
    forehead and wet lips
with her obscene middle finger (*infami digito*) and her purifying
    (*lustralibus*) saliva,
skilled at holding back burning (*urentis*) eyes;
then she brandishes the baby and, with suppliant prayer, she points
    him,   35
her skinny hope, now toward the fields of Licinus, now toward the
    house of Crassus:
"May king and queen choose this boy for son-in-law, may girls
fight over this boy; whatever this boy steps on, let it turn into a rose."
But I don't trust my prayers to a wet-nurse (*nutrici*). Deny,
Jupiter, these things to her, though she ask you clad in white
    (*albata*).   40

Persius, perhaps the least interested in women of all Roman satirists, here affords the reader a sidewise glance at women's folk practice.[41] He lists as possible baby-minders not only the *nutrix*, but two important kinds of female kin: the grandmother, and the mother's sister, the *matertera*—a family member who shows up elsewhere as important in a child's life (Hallett 1984: 151, 183–86; chapter 7 above). He despises them, with their use of the obscene, low body, and their vision of the rich man and his wife as *rex* and *regina*—a usage that belongs, in Latin, to the view from below. To them, the wealthy freedman Licinus is the same as the wealthy aristocrat (Licinius) Crassus. But Persius still depicts these women as actively concerned to protect the baby, and using their saliva as an important means of protection against the evil eye. These women pray for riches for the baby, for a good marriage, and for love; and they get dressed up to pray. They have health care down to a system.

Beyond Lingerie

And so we leave Pliny, sitting up late at night, laboring away at the *Natural History*, with a bra on his head. This is surely a case where the cup, so to speak, is both half-empty and half-full. What Pliny tells us certainly gives us information about Roman women's lives that is both new and disturbing. If we want to view Rome as an oppressive patriarchy, we can carry with us the image of Pliny's recommendation that a menstruating woman should carry a mullet with her so she will not dull the shine on mirrors (28.82). Yet, while Pliny and the other technical writers are indeed a rich source on fears about the female body, they also display beliefs about its powers. We might compare this ambivalence with Judith Hallett's model (1989) of "woman as same and other" in day-to-day relationships in the Roman elite; or with the perilously permeable boundaries so characteristic of Roman culture, where slave could be freed, Greek could come to Rome, and Pliny could write the *Natural History* and loathe doctors at the same time. The picture of the female body in Pliny also sheds further light on what Roman men feared when they accused each other of effeminacy, as they so frequently did (Richlin 1992; chapter 6 above). On the other hand, thanks to Pliny, we are able to fill in a picture of women's lives otherwise only known from material remains and from the somewhat more one-sided view of professional medical writers. Archaeology can give us votive offerings, dedications, and burials; Pliny and his friends can give us more of a context for them—can help us connect the dots. Pliny and his bra bring us just a little closer to Roman women themselves.

CHAPTER 9

Emotional Work

Lamenting the Roman Dead

ﾰﾟ

Introduction

This book is dedicated to Judith Hallett and Marilyn Skinner, companions along the way, but "Emotional Work" was dedicated to Gordon Williams, without whom, it is fair to say, I would not have set out at all. In the now hard-to-imagine world into which my generation of women emerged— emphatically a men's world—there would have been no women's voice at all if some men had not been happy to listen. Judy and Marilyn dedicated *Roman Sexualities* to the memory of J. P. Sullivan. The great thing about Gordon as a dissertation director was that it never crossed his mind to hang back; he was interested in all things Roman, anyway, and urged me endlessly onward. In 2010 I spoke at his memorial and cleaned up his study for his dear wife Jay, who soon followed after him. *Tibi cano et Musis.*

As well as being a dedicated object, *Arguments with Silence* is also commemorative, an epitaph, a remembrance of the lost world of Roman women, but this essay deals with mourning for the dead not only because of an interest in Roman women's public speech. I dropped my part of editing *Roman Sexualities* because, in 1993, my father died, and my mother was diagnosed with dementia, and the 1990s for me were a time when death became familiar and I saw up close what it means to lose speech. Taking care of my mother and my family while trying to keep working taught me the truth of Virginia Woolf's message in *A Room of One's Own*; writing became, for me, a longed-for luxury, at the same time that my mother descended into an endless regret for what she had lost by leaving school at sixteen to go to work, and both of us mourned for my father.

The writing of this essay, then, comes not only from the scholarly impulse that made me read through Paulus ex Festo and make a collection of Roman *neniae*—trivial things—or the theoretical impulse to treat trivial things as telling, derived from *Sittengeschichte* by way of the *Annales* school. It comes from the experience of teaching for ten years in USC's Gender Studies program, from which I derived the firm belief that women's everyday experience is knowable, that it can be shared and compared across cultural and temporal divides, and that it is a big part of history. I feel no hesitation in positing that "women" is a transhistorical category—which hardly means that all women have had the same experience or nature. The action of mourning, as attested in Roman culture, was certainly defined by Roman writers in gendered terms, and we can instructively watch them both following and breaking their own rules. We can also see them, as in chapter 7, assigning roles according to class; for me, the most surprising and enlightening thing in this essay is the realization that, for these Romans, to dress in black was to dress like a poor person—that they felt themselves to be expressing loss in a concrete way. Death impoverished them, took from them. The poor, of course, were already dressed in black.

Once again, the job of the *praefica* can be seen either as the abuse or the empowerment of the low. She is the final woman in this book, and I see her standing, as on the Amiternum relief, with her arms raised in the air, leading the chant for the dead. At the center of the relief is a dead man; other men are carrying him, or blowing horns, or playing the *tibia*; carved in stone, the women are speaking, and the *praefica* leads them. You have to listen if you want to hear.

*a.   *a.   *a.

In 1958 Gordon Williams published "Some Aspects of Roman Marriage Ceremonies and Ideals" in the *Journal of Roman Studies*, dedicating it to his friend and colleague, Eduard Fraenkel, "in the year of his seventieth birthday." That essay was framed as a contribution to Fraenkel's signature study of what was Roman about Plautus's comedies, and, as such, it rummages around in the Roman lumber room in satisfying and productive ways, searching lexica and literature for souvenirs of Roman wedding ceremonies: the role of the *pronuba*, the possible meaning of the term *morigerari* and its relatives, the ritual of the threshold, the importance to Roman women of being *univira* and the adaptation of this ideal by Christian writers. Epitaphs of faithful wives are made to yield up the ghost of societal expectations. In the end, all this erudition is brought to bear on two vexed passages, one in Propertius and one in Plautus's *Mostellaria*, but the essay's conclusion has sweeping things to say about what is Roman about Roman weddings and married women. In 1958 Gordon Williams could hardly have suspected that, twenty years later, the study of women in antiquity would have sprung up as a contender for the attention of classicists, and that his own early essay would figure as an important contribution to the understanding of the status of married women in Latin literature and Roman life. But that is in fact what happened.

Maybe because the study of women in antiquity grew, if decorously, out of the sexual revolution and the crucible of Second Wave feminism, it fastened with fascination on the figure of the *univira* and the ideal of wifely obedience. Citations of Williams for these notions have a pedigree reaching back to the founding mothers of the field, starting from Judith Hallett's "The Role of Women in Roman Elegy: Counter-Cultural Feminism," which appeared in the first *Arethusa* issue on women in antiquity (see chapter 10). Hallett uses Williams's essay "to substantiate our initial assertion that Roman society relegated women to a subservient, confined role" (1973: 104). Sarah Pomeroy's *Goddesses, Whores, Wives, and Slaves* boils down Williams in her discussion of Roman marriage customs (1975: 161): "The ideal of the *univira* and the eternal marriage was strictly Roman, and without counterpart in Greece." Helene Foley's 1981 collection *Reflections of Women in Antiquity* included a citation of Williams to support a reference to "the ideal of the *univira* and the death of Dido" (Richlin 1981a: 390; see chapter 1 above). Jane Gardner's basic reference work *Women in Roman Law and Society* cites Williams to underpin a description of Roman wedding ceremonies (1986: 44). This cavalcade of acknowledgments culminates in Susan Treggiari's magisterial work on Roman marriage; her chapter on "*Coniugalis Amor*" begins with the words, "In a seminal article in 1958, Gordon Williams traced specifically Roman ideas of marriage," and devotes the subsequent page to a summary (1991: 229–30). Williams's tribute to Fraenkel, it turns out, was widely appreciated by an audience of women, most of whom were still in grade school when "Some Aspects" was published, and all of whom took Williams to have been writing about women.[1] Indeed, amidst the scant and dismal bibliography on ancient women that existed before 1970, Williams' essay shone like the lights of home. He took women seriously, and without the coy fidgeting then common, simply because questions involving women were important to his understanding of Roman culture as a whole. His approach here served as a model for uncountable later studies of how ideas about women worked in Roman culture; in what follows, I can only provide a small descendant, with thanks for the *exemplum*.

Emotional Work

The term "emotional labor" was made famous by the sociologist Arlie Hochschild in 1983, in reference to "work that is done for wages and that is meant to achieve a desired emotional effect in others" (Andersen 1997: 108); she was focusing on airline flight attendants. In addition, the term "emotion(al) work" is used in feminist theory to refer to the work that is done by women within families in tending to the emotional needs of family members: celebrating birthdays, keeping in touch with an extended family, marking big events like graduations, listening to people's troubles. The two main ideas in both of these related terms are (a) that tending to emotions is work, and (b) that women tend to carry the can. Here I will use "emotional work" to take in both terms and will transfer this term to Rome to talk about lamenting the dead: who did it and what it was.

The topic of women and mourning has been dealt with from early on in the study of women in antiquity, mostly in relation to Greece—for example, Margaret Alexiou's study of the ritual lament in 1974, or Christine Havelock's study of women mourners on Greek vases in 1982—and more recently by Nicole Loraux (1998; published in French in 1990) and Karen Stears (1998).[2] Relatively little has been done on women and mourning in Roman culture (for a general overview, see Treggiari 1991: 483–98; and now esp. Corbeill 2004: 67–106, Šterbenc Erker 2011).[3] In general, most work on women and mourning falls into the "structure versus agency" debate (see chapters 8 and 10): is women's relation to lamenting the dead a sign of women's oppression or of women's power? Is it part and parcel of the idea that women are polluted, wild? Or is it one part of a vital, and culturally crucial, women's culture— what Anna Caraveli concisely calls "a universe of female activity outside the realm of men" (1986: 169)? I want to complicate this debate here, while thinking more about Roman women: how mourning worked for them, and what it meant. And I will deal in order with the two parts of the term: emotional; work.

Emotional

Is this work associated in Roman culture with the emotions, and, if so, what does that have to do with its gender associations—with what might be called a gendered division of labor?

I will take the first part of this question as a given; all available evidence associates mourning with the representation of emotion. However, although there is a consistent association between such showing of emotion and women in Roman thought, nevertheless it was not, in fact, restricted to women. This is no huge surprise; in any culture, there is always a gap between normative statements and behavior.

That this behavior was associated with women is widely attested, for example by Cicero in the *Tusculan Disputations*: "Those various and detestable kinds of mourning: dirt (*pedores*), and womanish lacerations of the cheeks, and beating the chest and thighs and head" (*Tusc.* 3.62). The younger Seneca in the *Consolatio ad Helviam* is similarly dismissive: "lamentations, indeed, and wailings (*heiulatus*) and other things, through which as a general rule womanish grief (*muliebris dolor*) makes a commotion" (*Helv.* 3.2). Note that, where this generalization is made, it is made in a pejorative sense; displays of grief are something women do, and they are bad. They are woman*ish*, not woman*ly*.

Legal and historical texts continue the association, along with the sense that women's mourning is something to be controlled. The XII Tables concerns itself in Table Ten with limiting the display at funerals, and includes the specification that "women must not tear cheeks or hold wailing on account of a funeral."[4] Lawmakers set up expected time frames for mourning, none longer than a year (Treggiari 1991: 493–95). Historians report cases in which women's mourning was limited, ad hoc, for example after the battle of Cannae, when the Senate "decreed 'that *matronae* should not extend their mourning beyond the thirtieth day,' so that the rites of Ceres could be performed by them. . . . And so the mothers and daughters, the wives and sisters of the newly slain, wiping away their tears and putting away the marks of grief, were forced to put on white clothing and set incense on the altars" (Valerius Maximus 1.1.15). Note that, at least in Valerius's golden hindsight, it matters to the Senate that women should perform these rites (see volume introduction and chapter 7 on the dispute over women's importance to public worship). The younger Seneca, commenting on the standards set by law, writes (*Ep. mor.* 63.13):

> The *maiores* set a year [as the limit] for women's mourning; not so that they would mourn for so long, but so that they would mourn no longer; but for men there is no set time, since there is no time at which it is honorable for men to mourn. Yet what woman will you give to me of those little ladies (*mulierculis*) scarcely pulled away from the pyre, scarcely dragged off the corpse, whose tears have lasted for a whole month?

Here he manages to suggest not only that women in particular display emotion at funerals, and that it is wrong to do so, but that these women's grief is ephemeral. Unlike his.

For Seneca's complaint points to the gap between Roman men's normative associations between women and mourning, on the one hand, and actual practice, on the other. The point of Seneca's essay is that he himself grieved very much for his friend and kinsman Annaeus Serenus. It is not hard to think of Roman men who made a display of their grief, at least in textual form: Catullus's famous poem for his brother; Cicero's lengthy correspondence about his beloved daughter, in which are recorded his efforts to acquire property on which to make a temple for her. His letters document a grief so marked that others went out of their way to get him to return to more appropriate behavior; he claims his way is the right way (Skinner 1983a; Treggiari 1998: 14–22). Moreover, there was a common situation in which men conventionally made a display of mourning: when they wanted to enlist public sympathy for their own plight. The *sordidus*, the man dressed in mourning, is a familiar figure in Roman culture. For a full catalogue of such behavior, the reader can consult one of the *controversiae* of the elder Seneca (*Controv.* 10.1): "The Son of a Poor Man, Dressed in Mourning, Follows a Rich Man." This *controversia* lists the following elements in such display: letting your beard grow, groaning, wearing dark clothes, and *squalor*—letting your body and clothes become stiff and dark with dirt. Seneca quotes Porcius Latro as defending the young man's practice: "How many people do it!" (*Controv.* 10.1.9).

Finally, moralizing stories about men who do not grieve suggest that this represented unusual self-control. Livy provides an early example in the tale of the consul Horatius (2.8.7–8). One day he is dedicating a temple, and his enemies, the jealous relatives of Valerius, cannot bear that he should so occupy the public stage. So they send a messenger to tell him that his son has died, and that he cannot dedicate a temple while his household is in mourning, *funesta familia*. Livy speculates that he either did not believe them, or just had great strength of spirit, *robor animi*; he simply gave orders for the body to be buried, and went on dedicating the temple.

This Horatius is a sort of mythistorical archetype for others who show similar fortitude. The elder Seneca, in the preface to Book 4 of the *Controversiae*, tells how Asinius Pollio noticeably held back from a display of grief at the death of his son Herius. Seneca first tells a story in which Augustus complains to Pollio that a friend of his had had a dinner party when Augustus was grieving for his grandson Gaius; Pollio replies that he himself had hosted a dinner on the very day his own son had died. Seneca then continues (*Controv.* 4.pr.6):

> You great men, who don't know how to give in to fortune, and make your troubles the test of your virtue! Asinius Pollio declaimed three days after he had lost his son: it was the declaration of a great spirit vaulting over its trials. But on the other hand I know that Q. Haterius bore the death of his son Sextus with such a weak (*inbecillo*) spirit that he not only yielded to his grief when it was fresh, but could not bear the memory of it even when it was old and worn away. I remember, when he was speaking on the *controversia* about the man who was dragged away from the graves of his three sons and so is bringing suit for *iniuria*, his speech, right in the middle, was broken up by his own tears; then he spoke with so much greater force, so much more wretchedly, that it was clear how great a contribution grief can sometimes make to talent.

Despite the disapproving adjective *inbecillo*—a quality often associated in Roman moralizing texts with women—Seneca returns to Haterius's tears at the end of this preface, and makes this very *controversia* the first one in Book 4. The *controversia* now exists only in excerpted form and none of it is particularly attributed to Haterius. But some speaker or speakers, according to Seneca, made the old man say (*Controv.* 4.1):

> An old man, childless, wretched, I take only this solace amidst my misery, that I cannot be more miserable. I see the ashes of my sons in the tomb. It is a great solace to call again and again the names of children who will not respond. Here is where I must live, so that I will not meet

anyone thinking about marriage or children, and make a bad omen for him.

His age, his cries, populate the spaces surrounding the epitaphs we still read.

Putting all these texts together, we can gather that, on the one hand, displays of mourning are often considered a bad thing. It is women's duty to mourn, it is their job; conversely, there is something woman*ish* about it. When they do it right, all is as it should be, and yet what they do is not a good thing even for them, and the state has to be careful that they should not do it too much. When a man grieves, it is bad because he is breaking gender norms, acting like a woman; also the acts themselves are the kind of thing men are not supposed to do if they want to perform their masculinity correctly, or show they are made of the right stuff. Moreover, the circumstance of being in mourning would normally stop a man from performing a positive holy act like dedicating a temple: mourning taints certain actions, including actions of state business, which is usually manly business. The sight of a mourning person is an ill omen.[5]

At the same time, these writers show or say that men feel grief strongly, and that not displaying it is a great feat of self-control. Self-control then also figures when they display grief intentionally, as a deliberate strategy to elicit sympathy; this is culturally approved. The case of Haterius suggests that, in the courtroom or the practice hall, displaying grief was expected, if you were acting out someone else's grief. The declamatory texts themselves are melodramatic, for strong emotion is their stock in trade, chosen as a way to train the speaker to pull at the heartstrings of a courtroom; the old man at the grave sounds like one of the female lament poets Anna Caraveli recorded in modern rural Greece, whose job it is to inspire others to grieve with them. So a sad theme might remind a speaker of his own real grief— might test his self control. If his own grief intervened, that was out of place, but could nonetheless be effective. As I have argued elsewhere (1997b), Roman experts on rhetoric consistently show unease when performances implicate speakers in impersonations of unmanly behavior. But they always wanted to win.

So, in dealing with the first part of the term "emotional work," we wind up with a basic ambivalence.

Such an ambivalence indeed also characterizes Greek cultures, ancient and modern, where mourning practices have been studied. Nicole Loraux finds in both Greek and Roman cultures "the topos of a feminine nature prone to tears" (= bad) (1998: 29); Anna Caraveli says that the laments she is studying are generally held, in modern Greek village culture, to be "worthless songs" (1986: 170). Yet, as Karen Stears argues (1998), women's funeral rituals in ancient Greece play an important role in their families, and constitute a duty, a privilege, honor to the family, womanly decorum, and a key element in holding onto family property: a proper funeral plays a major role in claiming an estate. She suggests that the women's lament may have constituted a sort of family history, and that periodic visits to the tomb would have provided a chance for women's sharing of information (or what might otherwise be called "gossip") and acquiring more data (a chance to watch the passing scene). Similarly, Caraveli outlines the ways in which women's laments today are regarded as art by other folk performers, forming part of a vigorous system of folk aesthetics and religion that provides women with a means of social/political critique and a way to bond among themselves. She also cites instances in which men lament—usually when alone.

Loraux's main concern in the third chapter of *Mothers in Mourning* is to define what is special about ancient Greek laments by contrasting them with Roman practices. As a distinguishing feature, she singles out the Roman practice of assigning to *matronae* the job of public mourning for outstanding men. She argues that, although Romans as well as Greeks looked down on mourning as "womanish," they made an exception for what she calls "the put-on tearless mourning of the matron" (1998: 31). Whereas in Athens a public funeral means the removal of a person from his family and his accrual to the state, in Rome public funerals represent display by great families, in which female kin played a featured role. This distinction recalls Gordon Williams's conclusion to "Some Aspects of Roman Marriage Ceremonies" (1958: 28):

These . . . ideals are Roman and in no way Greek . . . a peculiar creation of the Roman genius. . . . They reflect the far greater importance and dignity which Romans attached to the institution of marriage, one-sided though their conception of its obligations often was, and the dignified and important position in society which they accorded to married women. Aristocratic in origin, by a familiar shift (visible, for instance, in the relation between the Theognidean code of aristocratic behaviour and Aristotle's bourgeois ethics), they became the conventional ideals of middle-class and lower-class citizens whose remains are commemorated in the majority of our preserved epitaphs.

Loraux's treatment of this issue is quite brief, and I think her focus leads her to miss an important point, of which Williams here takes note: *matronae* are not the only Roman women, nor are elite *matronae* the only *matronae*, and mourning concerned women outside the ranks of married women of whatever class. Here, as elsewhere in the gendering of Roman religion, the class division among women is being inscribed at the state level (see chapter 7 above for an overview). This brings us to the second element in the term "emotional work."

Work

Karen Stears, in arguing that women's funeral rituals are an instance of women's power, rejects the idea that "mediation of pollution is indicative of lower social status, and of marginality" (1998: 118). But, as I will argue, that idea gives a fair description of what Romans thought mourning actually was. And in a much more literal sense than I think Stears means: not that all women are second-class citizens, hence mourning is for them; but that mourning is a low-class job.

The list of mourning behaviors is learned by students alongside the principal parts of verbs, and becomes so familiar that these odd actions seem natural. I will try to defamiliarize them. The list includes: letting your hair hang down; wailing; the lament itself, the *nenia*; beating your body; lacerating your cheeks with your nails; tearing your clothes; wearing dark clothes.

(1) Letting your hair hang down. Most people who learn Latin go through a kind of rite de passage during the first few years, as they learn idioms; *crinibus passis* must be one of the first ones. *Passis*, from *pando*: the hair of women with *crinibus passis* is open like a flower, or like the horns of cattle, splayed out, displaying what is usually unseen. I learned what the phrase means so long ago that I came to associate this *passis* with *patior*, as if the hair itself were suffering.

This idiom becomes boringly familiar, so that its strangeness becomes hard to see; you get used to women with their hair hanging down. An obvious literary example, from Lucan's *De bello civili*: Marcia, ex-wife of the younger Cato, married off by him to his childless friend Hortensius, comes bursting in from Hortensius's funeral to beg Cato to take her back (2.333–37):

> . . . but, after she'd stored in the urn
> his last ashes, with pitiful face, shaken—
> her hair flowing down, she'd torn it, she'd beaten her breast   235

with dense blows, and heaped on herself the ashes of the tomb
(otherwise she wouldn't look good to her husband)—thus she sadly
addressed him.[6]

Lucan's point here demands that Marcia be *comme il faut*, if not more
so; her hair is duly down. Livy (26.9.7) even has the *matronae* sweeping
the altars with their *crinibus passis*. (They in fact are not mourning, but are
participating in a familiar parallel activity: praying to the gods at a time
of public crisis.) The stock nature of this theme results in a parody at the
cena Trimalchionis, where one of the freedmen, Ganymedes, talks about
the good old days, as seen in chapter 7 (*Sat.* 44.18): "In the old days women
used to go in their *stolae*, barefoot, to the hill, with their hair hanging down
and their minds pure, and pray to Jupiter for water. And so just like that it
rained buckets." The ideal scene: troops of respectable matrons, intentionally disheveled, on public display, and on display to the gods.

What did this mean, anyway? Why let your hair down to indicate grief?
Plutarch asked the same question in his *Roman Questions*; unfortunately, he
makes things more confusing rather than less (*Mor.* 267a-b): "Why do sons,
on the one hand, escort [the bodies of] the parents with their heads covered,
while daughters [do so] with their heads bare and their hair unbound?"
Among the answers he suggests is this one: "Or is it that, in mourning, what
is customary is what is not usual, and that it is more usual for women to be
veiled, but for men to go out in public uncovered? And indeed among the
Greeks whenever some misfortune occurs, the women cut their hair while
the men grow theirs, because it is usual for the men to cut their hair while
the women grow theirs." Elsewhere, as we will see, Plutarch says that Roman women who mourn wear white veils.

So we are left with a whole list of binary oppositions to puzzle over:
women/men; young women/*matronae*; veiled/unveiled; hair up/hair down;
cut hair/uncut hair. Molly Levine, in her overview of ancient hair symbolism, adds to this the rule that unmarried girls' hair is usually worn down,
while wives cover their hair (1995: 95–96). In fact, Roman women of all
classes in visual representations cover their hair only occasionally, and often in the context of religious ritual, when everybody covered their hair;
Lisa Hughes, dispelling the widespread notion that associates veiling with
freedwomen or lower-class women, interestingly suggests that some veiling
by women in Italy might have marked their foreign ethnic status (2007:
235).[7] For women in the western Mediterranean, then, the veil might feel
slightly exotic, as well as holy.

Plutarch's idea that the unbound hair of women at Roman funerals was (only?) for "daughters," and that it was a marked alternative to veiling, may well be a mistake; this same passage includes a clear misinterpretation of a story in Valerius Maximus. But, as Levine reminds us, unbound hair does suggest youth or premarital status for women. In addition, as many of her examples show, unbound hair characterizes the monstrous female: Medusa, the Furies with snaky hair, bacchantes running wild through the town and out into the woods. Meditating on the meaning of hair in its connection with mourning, Levine notes that hair itself is both alive and not alive, that it mediates between life and death (1995: 86).

The overtones of unbound hair to a Roman viewer are perhaps suggested by a deliberate misreading of this sign in Ovid's *Ars amatoria* (3.431–32). In a passage clearly meant to be naughty, the *praeceptor* suggests that unbound hair is sexy, and that a woman can attract a new lover at her own husband's funeral. This brings us back to the time before Ovid's exile, when Julia, Agrippa's unruly widow, had just been exiled, and a joke circulated about Julia's slave women plucking out her grey hair; to Daphne's locks floating out as she runs from Apollo; to the scenes of hairdressing in satire and the decorative arts; and to the hairy girls and bald old women of invective (see chapters 2, 3, 5, 6): women's hair is intimately connected with beauty, the erotic, cruelty, luxury, disgust. Perhaps this in turn should remind us of who it was in the Roman sex/gender system who was conventionally thought of as *capillatus*: not a woman at all, but the adolescent male, whose long hair is invariably thought of as a big part of his allure (Richlin 1992: 44). Going back to Lucan's Marcia, we might meditate on his odd phrase, *non aliter placitura viro* (2.337). Overtly, this means that Marcia pleases her old husband, Cato, by observing all the forms of mourning for her dead husband, his dead friend; but putting together the elements of mourning, unbound hair, Ovid, and Lucan's black humor—and Lucan's Cato being who he is—this phrase must also mean "this is the style of beauty to captivate the kind of husband Cato is." It is no surprise that this love scene is immediately followed by a funereal wedding, in which every pleasurable event of a normal wedding is listed but undercut by the occasional *non* (itself a riff on the dire wedding of Procne and Tereus at Ovid *Metamorphoses* 6.428–32). Cato himself appears in shaggy mourning (372–91), and much emphasis is placed on the total absence of sex from this new union. Cato has Rome instead of sex (388–91); Marcia's appearance then embodies this counter-sex. Captive women in Roman relief sculpture have their hair undone; dishevelment shows devastation, abandon(ment), the eroticized prelude to rape and enslavement (see Dillon 2006, Uzzi forthcoming).

No simple meaning attaches to the female mourner's flowing, spreading, suffering hair. It is safe to say, though, that the hair, like the other parts of the mourning act, served to make a spectacle of the woman. Indeed, this is characteristic of mourning behavior generally; this is surely part of the reason why it is governed by sumptuary legislation. Roman feelings about the repercussions of being a spectacle have been much studied since the early 1990s, notably by Catharine Edwards (1997); they might be summed up, "Making a spectacle of yourself is not very nice." There is something erotic about being looked at, always; what Laura Mulvey called "to-be-looked-at-ness" (1975: 12). And usually there is something female about it as well.[8]

(2) Wailing. In Dublin in 1987, I heard a tape of old women keening. I had always thought that "keening" was something Celtic, romantic; I was surprised to hear that it sounded exactly like my own grandmother moaning to herself: "Oy, oy, oy." Unfortunately no tapes are available of Roman women wailing; we can only conjecture. Roman writers conventionally call a certain sound "womanish" or "female" or "not manly": Horace has a "not manly *eiulatio*" (*non virilis eiulatio*, Epod. 10.17); Tacitus a "womanish *eiulatus*" (*muliebri eiulatu*, Ann. 16.10.5); and Vergil, in the case of Euryalus's mother, has a "female *ululatus*" (*femineo ululatu*, A. 9.477; see Sharrock 2011). None of these words are restricted to women, by any means; men make *eiulationes* (or *heiulationes*) and, very commonly, barbarian men ululate, usually in battle. (In fact they also wear their hair down; femaleness and foreignness often map onto each other in Roman thought—see chapter 6 above.) Both *eiulatio* and *ululatio* are onomatopoeic, and *(h)eiulatio* is simply saying *(h)ei*, as in the common phrase *ei mihi*; compare *oimoi* in Greek. Ululation presumably was what it sounds like. Similarly, people speaking English said "Ay, me," until fairly recently, or "Alas," and people speaking French said "Hélas." In English today we conventionally represent a sob as "boo-hoo"; these words render a sob as "ei" or "hei" or "ulu," with the important difference that this is, or can be, a stylized sobbing, not given way to spontaneously, but performed on certain occasions.

The point seems to be that words or sounds like this are conventional signs for an emotion, and are speech acts, in that they are not about grief, but perform grief. In the context of the lament for the dead in Rome, when women say *ei* or ululate, this is part of an expected performance, associated with grief and especially with sobbing. Anna Caraveli, in describing the lament poets of contemporary rural Greece, emphasizes that they are considered particularly skillful when they can call forth grief from others by using a set of conventions, particularly melodic cues (1986: 175). These are learned responses. As a parallel in Anglo-American culture, I would suggest the opening words of Kaddish at a Jewish funeral, "Yisgadal v'yisgadash shemay rabbo"; or the opening words of the Episcopal Rite of Burial of the Dead, "I am the resurrection and the life." The first time you hear these words, they may have no effect on you; like me, you may not even understand the meaning of the words in Kaddish; after you have stood at enough funerals and heard them roll inexorably out, they may cause you to collapse, as if the words were the death. The power to bring this about is what is being associated with women in Caraveli's account.

(3) The *nenia* (sometimes *naenia*). The word *nenia* in Latin has an odd range of meanings. It means the dirge that is sung at a Roman funeral; or a song; or a magical incantation; or a jingle; or silly rubbish, trifles; or, possibly, the end of the intestines. What kind of dirge, we ask, and what does this range of meanings mean? And is the *nenia* also associated with women?

Quintilian says (8.2.8) that *nenia* is the proper name for a *carmen funebre*; Suetonius says that at the very elaborate funeral held for Augustus, the *nenia* was sung, by decree of the Senate, "by the children of eminent men, of both sexes" (*principum liberis utriusque sexus, Aug.* 100.2). The word is defined by Pompeius Festus, as reconstructed (154–56L): "*Naenia* is the song which at a funeral is sung to the *tibia* to praise [the dead person] . . . [thus] Afranius in [his play] *The Maternal Aunts*. . . and Plautus, 'For this loving man my mistress has said the *naenia* among us at home'; because the complaint of people weeping is quite similar to this word. Some say that the word *naenia* is taken from the word for the end of the intestine."[9] He then refers (156L) to a "goddess Naenia," whose shrine is outside the Viminal gate (see Bodel 2000: 138).

Some points in Festus's definition recall other things presented so far. That the *nenia* was sung to the tibia reminds us that there is another dimension of Roman funeral performance we cannot recover: the music. Caraveli's notion of melodic cues presumably applies even more to the *nenia* than to the wailing. The idea that the *nenia* praised the dead person recalls Stears' suggestion and Caraveli's claim that laments constitute a family history; of course many elements in a Roman funeral aimed at contributing to such a history (Bodel 1999; Flower 1996; Johanson 2011), and, as Nicholas Horsfall has demonstrated (2003 [1996]), the Roman *plebs* customarily transmitted cultural information through traditional song forms. Elizabeth Tylawsky (2001) shows just how detailed such a history could be, and points out that this was a history that included women as its subject matter as well as its performers. (Indeed, we might well ask whether dirges were sung for dead women as well as for dead men, since all the examples deal with women mourning for men; on women as ancestors, see now Flower 2002.) Then there is the hint that Afranius's *Materterae* included something about the *nenia*—tantalizing, since, as seen in chapters 7 and 8, the *matertera*, the mother's sister, is an important figure in the Roman kin system, and at the Matralia served as a sort of surrogate mother in opposition to the slave wet-nurse. The fragments of Afranius's *togata* suggest a dying mother giving her daughter to her sisters, weeping, sex, a funeral—the perfect setting for a song of family history. The claim that *nenia* is onomatopoeic suggests the sounds of wailing discussed above.

For an explicit association between the *nenia* and women, however, we have to look at one of its other senses: *nenia* as magic spell. In every instance, it is used of a witch: Canidia (Horace *Epod.* 17.29), Medea (Ovid *AA* 2.102), and, most thought-provokingly, the *striges* who suck the blood of babies in Ovid's *Fasti* (6.141–42): "whether these birds then are born (so), or whether they become (so) by a charm (*carmine*), / and the Marsian *nenia* shapes old women into birds." Thus the old women who sing the *nenia* turn into shrieking *striges* who eat babies; this strongly suggests the witch story in Petronius, where Trimalchio tells the story of something that happened when he was still a slave (*Sat.* 63.3–4): "Our owner's sweetie (*delicatus*) died. . . . So when the poor little mother was lamenting him and most of us were in miserosity, suddenly the *strigae* started up; you'd think a dog was chasing a rabbit." The mother (here a slave accompanied by slaves) laments the son; the witches start to howl.

Finally, Emily Gowers (1993: 59, 107–8), in looking at the range of meanings for *nenia*, associates it with the Bakhtinian world of reversal, where the worthless is valued: the *nenia* is a trifle, something low, and associated with festivals celebrating Roman popular culture. So if the *nenia* is gendered, it is gendered through women's magic, a magic that was either erotic or deadly or both (see chapters 6, 8); it may have been sung for Augustus by the children of *principes*, but it is commonly associated with the low-class and trifling.

(4) Beating your body, cutting your cheeks: Of the mother in Petronius's story, it is said *plangeret illum*, and I translated *plangeret* "she was lamenting." Literally, *plango* means "I beat," and this verb is used, with synonyms, to describe another behavior that is part of the lament; again oddly, "beat" [your own body] comes to mean "mourn" [somebody else]. The mourner might beat her (or his) upper arms, head, thighs, and particularly the chest and breasts, and women are said to tear their cheeks with their finger-

nails; Stears discusses Greek vases with little ornamental figures of mourning women on the handles, with bars of red paint on their cheeks (1998: 115).[10] In line with the discussion above of the counter-eroticism of women's loosened hair, it seems that at least sometimes a mourning woman would expose her breasts as she beat upon them; Petronius, in the story of the Widow of Ephesus, points out that her mourning exceeded the "common custom" (*vulgari more*) of letting her hair hang down and beating her bared breast for everyone to see (*Sat.* 111, *nudatum pectus in conspectu frequentiae plangere*).[11] This is clearly not erotic in intent—think of Hecuba holding out her aged breast to Hector—and yet, like Ovid's sexy widow, the Widow of Ephesus is certainly eroticized. Similarly, mourning behavior includes tearing your clothes; again, sometimes, this is specifically aimed at baring the breast—it is the top of the clothing that is torn (Ovid *M.* 5.398, *summa vestem laniarat ab ora*, of Proserpina lamenting her rape by Dis, see chapter 5; Juvenal 13.132, *vestem diducere summam*, treating the gesture as unisex and token).

So what do we have so far? Unbinding your hair, wailing, singing the *nenia*, beating your breasts, slashing your cheeks: all could be interpreted simply as expressions of grief, of the desire to hurt yourself, to look as much unlike yourself as possible, to express how bad things are by making yourself look bad and feel physical pain. It is a kind of reversal of makeup. Perhaps, as Marilyn Skinner suggested to me, an element of self-punishment is involved, as if the woman is expected to blame herself for the death; this is a common reaction to the death of someone you define yourself as taking care of, even in this culture—how much more so in a culture of *pietas*? But the moves are not arbitrary, left up to each person to invent for herself; and they are associated with women, even if not exclusively so.

They are also associated with class, which brings us back to Stears's denial that the "mediation of pollution is indicative of lower social status." On the contrary, it seems that, when Romans put on dark clothing, they were dressing not like a sad person but like a poor person.

Some sources stipulate that dark clothes are worn at funerals especially by female kin: Varro says (*Vit. pop. R.* 3 apud Non. p. 549, 550) that the women "should mourn at the funeral dressed in dark (*pullis*) *pallae*," and that "the young women kin should follow their grief in coal-black (*anthracinis*) [clothing], the closest female kin should wear a blackish (*nigello*) cloak, and have their hair let down." The suggestion of some kind of age differentiation here recalls the possible range of meanings for hair. Does wearing black read differently on an *adulescentula* and a *matrona*? Plutarch confuses things again here; he asks, in the *Roman Questions* (*Mor.* 270d-e), "Why do women wear white *himatia* when in mourning, and white veils?" And he answers: "[Is it that], just as they wrap the body of the dead person in white, they require this of the relatives?"

Elsewhere, dark clothes are just stated flatly to be requisite dress for either women or men in mourning. Juvenal describes a man growing old in black (*nigra*) clothing (10.244–45); when the rich man's house burns down (3.212–13), the *matrona* goes shaggy-haired, the leading citizens are dressed in dark clothing (*pullati*).

Elsewhere again, this dress is explicitly stated to be a sign of class. Lucan describes the public mourning in the city as the Civil War begins (2.18–19): "every honor hid, covered with plebeian (*plebeio*) clothing; the purple accompanied no fasces." Mayor (1979 [1877] on Juvenal 3.213) glosses this baldly: "In public mourning the nobles dressed as the vulgar." This takes us back to Seneca's *controversia* where the poor young man follows the rich man clad in mourning; declamations repeatedly interpret *sordes* as marking poor opposed to rich, poor man vs. the white-clad *candidatus*, defendant vs. plaintiff. Whereas in a Western the man in black is the villain, in any hierarchical situation in Rome the one in black is the underdog.[12]

Quintilian says that one kind of *actio*—one which in the context of this essay surely recalls the behavior of mourners—is particularly appealing to the cheap seats, the poor people, the people dressed in black (2.12.10): "To strike your hands together, to stamp your foot on the ground, to strike your leg, your chest, your forehead, works wonders with the *pullatus circulus*."[13] Elsewhere he associates untrained oratory with the *pullata turba* (6.4.6); he makes it clear (11.3.123) that the kind of *actio* described here is regarded as stagy. As Catharine Edwards has amply shown, anything tied to the stage is, in Roman terms, socially suspect; in this context, as I have also argued about Roman rhetoric, part of the problem is that acting stagy is acting woman*ish* (Richlin 1997b, chapter 6).

At the theater itself, the crowd in dark clothing was made to sit separately by Augustus, as were women, as seen in chapter 7 (Suet. *Aug.* 44.2–3); the categories there manifest a notable double bias along lines of sex and class, with concern shown both for separating lower-class from upper-class and distinguishing among degrees within classes, and for achieving a sort of moral segregation such that sex objects (women and boys) were separated from (upper-class) men. The interesting result of this seating arrangement is described by the humble shepherd narrator of one of the *Eclogues* of the Neronian poet Calpurnius Siculus: "We came to the seats where the dirty crowd in dark clothing/ was watching, among the women's chairs" (*venimus ad sedes, ubi pulla sordida veste/ inter femineas spectabat turba cathedras*, 7.26).

So we are here rummaging through a sort of drawer, in which are jumbled up together a set of cultural modes and practices and groups: mourning, acting, a style of rhetorical *actio*, dark clothes, women, and lower class people, especially a lower-class audience.

This audience is variously valued, when it is noticed. The younger Pliny says (*Ep. 7.17.9*) that even an audience made of laborers—people who are dirty and wearing black—can be intimidating: "we also stand in awe of those *sordidi* and *pullati*." We might juxtapose another well-known story in Suetonius about Augustus (*Aug.* 40.5); here he is indignant at the sight of a crowd of *pullati* at a *contio*, and he decides to make the aediles keep any man not in a toga out of the Forum. He is supposed to have cited Vergil on the lordly toga-wearing Romans to explain himself, and Suetonius brings up the story to illustrate the statement that Augustus wanted to bring back traditional dress and manners; but the explicit meaning of the story is that Augustus wanted to see men in togas at *contiones*, and not men dressed as laborers (slaves evidently here invisible).[14]

If dressing in black made you *look* low-class, conversely, the people who took care of funerals *were* low-class. The *libitinarii*, the undertakers who operated out of the grove of Libitina on the Esquiline, were male, but they had female co-workers, whose job description takes us back to the lament.[15] These women take their place among all the other working women seen here: the makeup artists in chapter 6, the wet-nurses of chapter 7, the health care workers of chapter 8. Indeed, several analyses have treated mourning women symbolically as "midwives to the dead" (see overview in Šterbenc Erker 2011: 46–47); as Rebecca Flemming's survey reminds us, real midwives occupied a similarly low-class position.

Laments, it seems, need a leader, as in one of the earliest and best-known laments in antiquity, the lament for Hector at the end of the *Iliad*. It is a triple lament, and for each woman—first Hector's wife, Andromache; next his mother, Hecuba; and last his sister-in-law, Helen—Homer begins her speech with the phrase *êrkhe gooio* (*Iliad* 24.723, 747, 761). (Note again here the connection between the lament and witchcraft, as in *nenia*: *goaô* = "wail," *goos* = "wailing," but *goês* = "magician," *goêteia* = "witchcraft.") Juvenal, in retelling this story, sets it (10.260–62) "among the tears of the Trojan women, as Cassandra began to give the first laments, and Polyxena, with torn *palla*."[16] The position of leader of the laments turns out to be a well-defined one.

And you could hire one. Lucilius, the earliest source, describes *praeficae* as "women who, hired for a price, weep at a stranger's funeral" (*mercede quae conductae flent alieno in funere*, 955M). Paulus Diaconus defines *praeficae*: "*Praeficae* are women hired to lament a dead person, who give the others the cadence for lamenting, as if set in charge of this. Naevius says: 'God, she must be a *praefica*, I think, since she praises the dead man so'" (250L).[17] Varro also has something to say about this character; commenting on a line in Plautus, he explains (*LL* 7.70),

> The *praefica*, as Aurelius writes, is a woman who is hired from the grove [presumably of Libitina] to sing the praises of the dead man in front of his house. Aristotle writes that this used to be done, in the book which is titled *Barbarian Customs*, to which this is a confirmation, which is in Naevius's play *Fretum*: "God, she must be a *praefica*, I think, for she praises the dead man." And Claudius writes: "A woman who is put in charge of the female slaves, [to show them] how they should lament, is called a *praefica*." Both show that the *praefica* is so called from being put in charge.[18]

Returning again to Williams's "Some Aspects of Roman Marriage Ceremonies," I cannot help being reminded of the *pronuba*, who played a central role in Roman weddings. She would have been responsible for the *dextrarum iunctio*, the joining of the hands of bride and groom, which Williams describes as "a general form of ceremony in which a woman of some dignity . . . hands the bride to her new husband"; she may have uttered a ritual phrase as she did so (Williams 1958: 21). In the example Williams cites, the *pronuba* is the bride's mother, and we might then expect the *pronuba* to be a close kinswoman (Dido, so far from home, has Juno); a late encyclopedist specifies that she must be a *univira* with a living husband (Treggiari 1991: 164). The *praefica*, then, is a kind of photographic negative of the *pronuba*: leading the ceremony, but not a member of the household; a leader, but not a woman of dignity. She is, perhaps, a stand-in for the closest kinswoman, who is not expected to lead anything at this moment.

Gellius, finally, sews up the connection between *praeficae*, lamenting, women, and worthless work, by recording the following insult (*NA* 18.7.3): A silly *grammaticus* remarks to Favorinus, "You philosophers are nothing but what M. Cato calls 'shrouds'; for you collect bits and pieces of lexical nuggets, things repulsive and weightless and trashy, like the words of the women [called] *praeficae*."[19]

The *praefica* can be seen at work in the context of an entire funeral in a bas relief from Amiternum (fig. 4).[20] The relief shows the body of a man carried on a bier. The artist has been very careful to mark the social status of the participants in the funeral. Although this relief is taken to be the cultural product of freedmen, the dead person is marked as an important man; he is wearing a toga, and has a tapestry over his head embroidered with the crescent moon and stars (suggesting the *toga picta* of the *triumphator*?), and other marks of office. He is surrounded by ranks of mourners; his bier is carried on a litter borne by eight men, with their tunics girt high, like workmen; and the whole procession is led by a seven-man brass band, similarly dressed. Karen Stears argues that, in representations of Greek funerals, the chief mourner would be found at the head of the corpse. But that is not the case here. The bier, with its corpse, divides the professionals from the family, low/workers from high/unpaid; and the workers lead the way. The wife of the dead man follows the bier; she is marked as a *matrona* by her long flounced skirt, and her hair hangs down on her shoulders. The two shorter figures next to her, with the same dress and hair, are presumably her daughters; behind and above her are other *matronae,* one with her hair down, the other two with it still up; below them are two possible slave women, their legs displayed. Preceding the bier stand two women who are not wearing the *stola*; their shins are clearly visible. The one closer to the bier is pulling at her unbound hair. But the one to the right, in profile, raises her hand in a version of the speaker's gesture; here is the *praefica* leading the lament, directing the women mourners, and singing the praises of the dead man "before his house" to the tune of the *tibia.*

Conclusions

As a confirmed collector of lexical nuggets, I must side with the *praefica*. Her emotional work suggests how what is ostensibly abject at times takes center stage in Roman culture. Loraux's distinction between women's mourning practices in Athenian culture and in Rome shows up here in Rome's relative complexity. The kind of class division and interaction that so characterizes Roman culture adds dimensions to Roman mourning practices that either are not present or are not traceable in Athens. No one familiar with Roman

Fig. 4. Relief with funeral procession, first century BCE. Amiternum, Italy. (Image © and courtesy of the Regents of the University of California, Christopher Johanson, and the Experiential Technologies Center (ETC), UCLA. This work is licensed under the Creative Commons Attribution 3.0 Unported License. To view a copy of this license, visit http://creativecommons.org/licenses/by/3.o/ or send a letter to Creative Commons, 444 Castro Street, Suite 900, Mountain View, California, 94041, USA.)

women's history would be surprised by the forms of the Roman lament, or by its connection with women. Considering how the rituals seen in chapter 7 emphasize distinctions between *matronae* and slaves, it is not that surprising to see that the Roman lament involved a division of labor not only by gender but (optionally) by class. What is surprising to find is that, even on the symbolic level, mourning is marked by social class. After all, you mourn for something you have lost; bereavement is a kind of poverty, and Roman property law in general is inextricably tied up with the problem of death, of making possessions adhere to people, who are so transitory. As Roman mourning is marked by class, so "mediation of pollution" is indeed "indicative of lower social status." One way to look at it: unless they could palm it off on somebody else, all Roman women were stuck with this. So the ones who had the money hired *praeficae* and *ancillae* just as they hired (or bought) wet-nurses. Another way to look at it: because they wanted to have the most beautiful funeral possible, all Romans who could find the money hired a professional. In Caraveli's terms, the *praefica* is an artist, a lament poet, though she works not (only) out of her personal pain but for hire.

I have had too many occasions recently to consider what a *praefica* does. Why is it that students learn the phrase *crinibus passis* so early on? To us it seems that the Romans were obsessed with death, but they were surrounded by death, funerals were common for them as they were everywhere until the late twentieth century, as they still are in most of the world, as they are now for my parents' friends. After every funeral I go to now, back at the house there is a team of ladies who have put an apron on over their good dresses and rolled up their sleeves and started cleaning the kitchen. I have come to be one of them. Now that I've been in the main supporting role, I know what needs to be done. Things have to be cleaned up, so the people who live in the house know that someone is taking care of them, that they are still alive whether they want to be or not. This is emotional work.

CHAPTER 10

The Ethnographer's Dilemma
and the Dream of a
Lost Golden Age

ᘓ

Introduction

This chapter belongs to a time when not only feminists but many scholars in the humanities believed that what we wrote was directly connected with political action in the world we inhabit. That belief has been sorely tested in the past twenty years, especially for those of us who work on the far past; still, maybe not wrong. Specifically, "The Ethnographer's Dilemma" was inspired by the concentrated reading and thinking I had been doing on feminism and Foucault after moving to the University of Southern California in 1989. My appointment was half in Classics, half in Gender Studies, and for the first time I was teaching feminist political theory with colleagues in anthropology (Walter Williams), history (Lois Banner), psychology (Carol Jacklin), and sociology (Michael Messner, Barrie Thorne). USC's program was an unusual one, founded early on as the Program for the Study of Women and Men in Society, and always involving a large component of Men's Studies; I fit right in, and taught in the General Education courses on women's studies and feminist theory. There I saw at first hand that teaching really can change people's lives—true in gender studies in a way it rarely is in Classics, as students gain political insight and learn to see the workings of gender systems in history and in their own lives. It was a great experience, and I owe a lot to the wonderful range of students USC had in the early 1990s: inner-city kids, single mothers, returning students, the stand-up comedian Emily Levine who sat in on my senior seminar on ancient sexuality, and always the film school group.

It was team-teaching with the ever-cheerful Walter Williams that taught me to think about the glass-half-empty, glass-half-full perspectives, and how they vary according to the personality of the researcher. Ironically, the material surveyed in chapter 10 brings us back to the insight of chapter 1: depends who you ask—a depressingly relativistic conclusion for someone who believes in the existence of historical fact. The early 1990s was a time of great intellectual fervor, in Classics particularly centered on Michel Foucault's late work on the history of sexuality, since he chose to start from antiquity. I wrote a series of rejoinders (1991, 1992: xiii–xxxiii, 1993, 1997a, 1997c), impelled partly by the short shrift Foucault gave to women in his history. Foucault found plenty of defenders (see Larmour et al. 1997, Skinner 1996), and now the whole debate is itself fading into history (Richlin 2013b), although Foucault's dicta have become a solid part of general knowledge about antiquity, impossible to dislodge. But this fade also suggests how chapter 10 might be viewed as an exercise in reception theory, while itself constituting part of the very long history of the reception of classical antiquity. Feminists are hardly the first to invoke antiquity in the service of politics, nor were we in the Second Wave even the first feminists to do so (see Henderson and McManus 1985, Stevenson 2005). The study of reception has been booming in Classics for the past fifteen years, and classicists are now going through something of what anthropologists went through in the 1980s, as described in chapter 10: becoming conscious of the history of what we do (Kallendorf 2007; Martindale and Thomas 2006). "The Ethnographer's Dilemma" fits perfectly well with the remarks of Genevieve Lively addressed in the Introduction: yes, meaning is made at the point of reception. The real point of chapter 10, however, is that scholars' choices have consequences. Without feminists there would be no women's history, and writing that history is important for all women, past and present.

In practical terms this essay began with an APA panel in 1990, organized by Nancy Rabinowitz and me and titled "Feminist Theory and the Classics" (only a cousinly relation to the Feminism and Classics conferences which began in 1992). In the panel proposal, I wrote: "We have consciously organized a panel for the general meeting, rather than one for the Women's

Classical Caucus, to emphasize our conviction that feminist theory is of interest and use to the membership as a whole. These matters need no longer be restricted to the gynaeceum." The panelists were Marylin Arthur Katz, Marilyn Skinner, Tina Passman, Judith Hallett, and Barbara Gold; most of us went on to put together the collection in which chapter 10 appears. A major element in this chapter derives from a letter Marilyn Skinner wrote to her fellow panelists dated October 12, 1990:

> I'm really looking forward to this session. The "essentialists" and the "constructionists" (or, better, the pessimists and the optimists) are forming battle lines, and from the wealth of brainpower and erudition on either side, it'll be one hell of a fight. What *fun*!!

And it really has been a lot of fun. With serious implications.

     ᶩ. ᶩ. ᶩ.

> Every oppressed group needs to imagine through the help of history and mythology a world where our oppression did not seem the pre-ordained order. Aztlan for Chicanos is another example. The mistake lies in believing in this ideal past or imagined future so thoroughly and single-mindedly that finding solutions to present-day inequities loses priority, or we attempt to create too-easy solutions for the pain we feel today.
>   *Cherríe Moraga, "From a Long Line of Vendidas" (1986: 188–89)*

Optimists and Pessimists

Why does anyone study the past? That is, what are people's motives for doing this, and what are the possible results? Looking forward to the panel from which *Feminist Theory and the Classics* began, Marilyn Skinner wrote to me that she expected to see some wonderful battles between "the pessimists and the optimists." I have been thinking about this accurate but odd division ever since. How mysterious: what is there to be hoped for, or despaired of, in the past? Do these hopes relate to our own progress in knowledge? Scholars often talk in terms of "getting somewhere," as if all learning were a quest with a grail at the end of it, or a series of metamorphoses, with a last glorious transformation at the end. Reflecting on the history of a field of scholarship, people tend to divide it into developmental stages, implying, "They were dumb then, but we're smart now." "Beyond X" is a common title: after structuralism comes poststructuralism; after modernism, postmodernism. Like Mr. Ramsay in *To the Lighthouse*, thinkers are obsessed with getting past Q to the next letter of the alphabet, and so finally to some ultimate Z. Or does our optimism or pessimism relate to our actions in the present and our goals for the future? The problem is that the focus on hope or despair, the focus on getting to Z, has obscured political goals and divided writers more and more from any audience outside the academy. As Cherríe Moraga suggests, it is not good to get distracted from what needs to be done.

I myself am a gloomy writer, included among the pessimists in Marilyn Skinner's assessment. My research began in the late 1970s with Roman satire and invective, texts now rarely read outside the field of Classics (see chapter 2). Here is the full text of a poem discussed briefly in chapters 2 and 6 (*Priapea* 46):

> O girl no whiter than a Moor,
> but sicker than all the fags,
> shorter than the pygmy who fears the crane,
> rougher and hairier than bears,
> looser than the pants that Medes or Indians wear,
> [why don't you go away?]
> For though I might seem ready enough,
> I'd need ten handfuls of [Spanish fly]
> to be able to grind the trenches of your groin
> and bang the swarming worms of your cunt.

The *Songs of Priapus*, a group of lyric poems in which the ithyphallic god who watched over Roman gardens threatens to rape intruders, might be dismissed as obscure, second-rate, anonymous. But there is a great deal of material like this in Latin, and indeed in Greek, in later European cultures, and in non-European cultures. The more I looked, the more I found; I soon began to hypothesize that such texts work along with basic social formations, and not only in Rome. This coincided with my growing awareness of violence against women in my own culture, on my own campus, on my own street. Three months after my book *The Garden of Priapus* first came out, the woman who had been my co-captain on the Princeton crew was raped and murdered; she was thirty-two years old.

So I write in anger, and I write so that oppression is not forgotten or passed over in silence. Yet I know this is not the only way to write. I once team-taught a course with Walter Williams, the historian of gender, whose work has emphasized the freedom of sexual identity within Native American and other non-European cultures. He used to tell me that the glass is half full, and that my gloomy views derive from the cultures I have chosen to study. I know that other feminists in Classics do find positive things in those cultures. I also know that it is not part of the traditional practice of Classics to care so much about the social implications of texts. As we read Latin and Greek, we distance ourselves, muffling the meaning with layers of grammar, commentary, previous scholarship. We skip things. I think that is not a responsible or honest way to read, and that reading should be socially responsible; this is one reason classicists need feminist theory—our old way of reading keeps us cut off. As a woman, a feminist, and a scholar, I want to know what relation scholarship can have to social change. This question seems to me to necessitate serious thought about the attitudes we bring to our work—our optimism or pessimism—and their relation to action.

Thinking about optimists and pessimists and their arguments with each other within the academy, I evolved a taxonomy in order to describe them. Sandra Joshel, whose work on Roman slavery figures below, objects that my oppositional categories obscure overlaps and exclude other possibilities: life is not either-or. You can imagine her saying "But . . ." at the end of each paragraph. The making of such a taxonomy is itself characteristic of one of its own main categories, and her objection is characteristic of the other. I believe that my neat categories describe something that really exists, and needs to be addressed in this sort of orderly way; but I concede the overlaps, which indeed give the system its paradoxical energies, and make it possible for us to talk to each other. The chart below groups theorists at two levels: according to their assumptions about knowledge, and according to their feelings about what they study. For feminist theorists, these divisions are already familiar; the consideration of feeling as a motive for theory may be new. For classicists—a group that has come to define itself as apolitical—the struggle in the new millennium to define our public worth in a marketplace of ideas now urges constant self-examination.[1]

The first split lies at the level of epistemology: the question of what is knowable, of how we know what we know. Some people believe in what is called "grand theory," a kind of theory which claims validity across history and cultures.[2] I would call this an optimistic epistemology, since it takes a sanguine attitude toward the ability of a human subject to view a huge mass

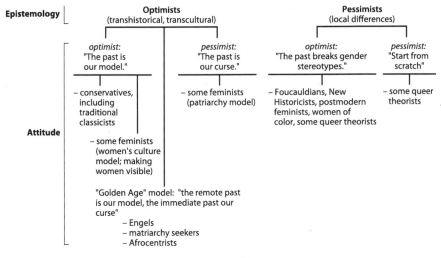

Fig. 5. Optimists and Pessimists

of information and express it in a meaningful order. Other people pooh-pooh grand theory, and, instead, trace local-historical differences. I would call this a pessimistic epistemology, since it takes a negative attitude: huge masses of information are chaotic, and human efforts to reduce them to "order" are futile and self-deluding, because necessarily solipsistic—not only the order but the information itself being invented by the researcher. Thus this group describes the efforts of the first group as "reductionist," and condemns its theories as "totalizing theories."[3] The optimists stress similarities and continuities, the pessimists stress difference and watersheds. Though some optimist groups (for example, Marxists) include historical change in their model, the pessimist groups tend to accuse the optimist groups of being ahistorical and stress their own "historicizing" of phenomena. Often models that posit very slow change—in terms of millennia—seem to register with their opponents as no-change models.

The second split lies at the level of attitude. Optimists see in the past, or in other cultures, good things to be emulated; pessimists see bad things that determine or elucidate our own ills. This split depends on personality as much as on politics. Writers accentuate either the positive or the negative, usually to make a larger point; then the larger point is forgotten or obscured by the dueling details of the positive/negative picture (a major example would be the ongoing debate over ancient sexual identities). Optimists and pessimists tend to annoy each other and quarrel: those who celebrate "women's culture" are attacked as romantic; the cheerful, upbeat, and inventive Foucauldians are critiqued as politically naïve; the glum chroniclers of patriarchy are in turn dismissed for their use of grand theory. What is important is what is getting lost, the larger point at stake, the "so what." "See? Women can be powerful" vies with "See? Women have always been oppressed." The implied "Then . . ." that connects to action usually remains implicit; whole social programs hover—unexpressed—behind articles on Belgian mine workers or ancient Greek pederasty. Sometimes it is hard to tell the players apart; as the chart shows, an optimistic epistemology often goes with a pessimistic tone, and vice versa. To avoid confusion in what follows, I will use "Optimist" and "Pessimist" to refer to epistemologies, "optimist" and "pessimist" to refer to attitudes.

Feminists in the academy in the 1990s were engaged in a running argument about grand theory (see de Lauretis 1990 for overview; Rose 1993). In this case, the issue is cast as "essentialism"—the belief that something (women, patriarchy, sexuality) exists as an abstract entity that would be recognizably the same across time and cultures. Feminist theorists in the 1970s built their political analysis on the idea of patriarchy (gender asymmetry in which power tends to reside in males over females), which they saw as universal, or nearly so. Moreover, whereas a long tradition in Western thought held that women were essentially different from men and inferior to them (Aristotle, Aquinas, Nietzsche), and some feminists countered this by arguing for the equality/sameness of women and men, other feminists countered by arguing that women are essentially different from men and superior to them (Mary Daly, Adrienne Rich). These feminist essentialists stress qualities like nurturance, warmth, kindness as inherently female. But the 1980s saw the rise of postmodernist theory, (still) generally hostile to grand theory, alongside the rising consciousness of differences among women themselves across class, race, sexual, and geopolitical lines. "Difference" for women of color meant the assertion of identity; in contrast, postmodernist theory, despite its emphasis on the particular and on local-historical differences, rejects the idea of the "subject"—the independent individual. Instead, each person represents an intersection of fluctuating currents of power, so that the whole culture makes up a sort of network. Anti-essentialist arguments assert that the female (for example) would have a different meaning in any given culture, even that the category "women" is meaningless (see volume introduction, on Afsaneh Najmabadi); and indeed that some constructs in culture A would not exist as such in culture B (for example, Michel Foucault's claim that "homosexuality" is a nineteenth-century idea [1978: 43]). The strength of the anti-essentialist reaction seems to come partly from a feeling of revulsion against an idea that was for so long used against women; partly from a feeling that totalizing theories involve the theorist in speaking for other people, preempting them (a feeling that can result in aphasia, see Alcoff 1991; hooks 1990: 26); and sometimes also from the paradoxical belief that all totalizing theory is invalid. Thus some feminists have claimed both that the essentialist concept of gender is a trap for women, and that it is not in fact valid. It is important to note that these are separate claims; too often the first ("trap for women") is asserted as if it were the second ("not valid"). I will refer to this assertion as the "wrong because depressing" argument. Long duration does not preclude change, and we have ample evidence that nature itself is an historical entity.

Postmodern ideas have been met by some feminist theorists with interest, by others with indignation.[4] Without the category "women," some wonder, how can we have feminism? The disappearance of the subject, they point out, also neatly deletes the material existence of oppression, of agency and responsibility; this critique often takes the form of what I have called (1991: 161) the "just-when" argument: "Just when women (people of color, colonial people) finally begin to claim subjecthood, Western elite theorists claim there is no such thing." Still, "essentialist" is now a bad word, something no one wants to be, while feminism, having shattered into "feminisms" in the 1990s, is now itself in trouble as a label. Each side in the grand theory debate claimed confidently that its methodology pointed the way to women's future, and would usher in profound social change. Fine: how?

The title of the volume *Feminist Theory and the Classics* invited the question of what contribution feminists in Classics could make to feminist theory in other fields. How you answer this question depends very much on where you stand in relation to grand theory. If you are interested in a construct like "patriarchy" and want to test how long it has gone on, it is helpful to have as much information as you can get about cultures two thousand years in the past. If you are not—and "patriarchy" itself now sounds very dated as a concept (see Bennett 2006)—the value of Classics changes. If we abandon a model that charts a pattern over long periods of time, if each culture is distinct, then time collapses into space and Classics becomes a branch of anthropology, investigating its cultures. Nor can Classics offer a special method; whereas anthropology, for example, not only finds out as much as it can about individual cultures but also posits rules explaining how cultures work, Classics stops at finding out as much as it can about two cultures within a set period (c. 1500 BCE to c. 500 CE), or even just at appreciating them. The rules we have generated have to do with how to find things out more accurately, how to reconstruct our long chain of evidence. Our only special claim was that Greece and Rome themselves were somehow important, either because of their intrinsic worth or because of their putative status as the origin of Western culture. When such claims are abandoned or rejected, what does Classics have to offer? One answer is that, to those who stress difference within our culture, it has been important to stress difference in the Western past. Those who want to prove that the modern period is fundamentally different from earlier periods need to know something about them. The glamour of antiquity is slow to evaporate. Arguments both optimistic and pessimistic often depend on having (or not having) an understanding of what happened in the ancient Mediterranean.

The Ethnographer's Dilemma and the
Dream of a Lost Golden Age

The division into Optimist and Pessimist has taken two special forms within the disciplines of anthropology and history. (1) Feminist and postmodernist anthropologists have, for some years now, been increasingly involved with what I call the ethnographer's dilemma. For example: radical feminists early on decried crimes against women, and gave genital mutilation (clitoridectomy) as a prime instance (Barry 1979: 189–92; Daly 1978: 153–77).[5] They Optimistically assumed their values applied to all cultures. But feminist anthropologists began to wonder whether it is really incumbent upon Western scholars to view other cultures in light of our own values, among which they placed feminism. Suppose that Other women derive pride and satisfaction from practices we find abhorrent ("oppressive")? This principle also applies to less extreme examples, like division of labor (women take pride in weaving, pot-making, tuber-gathering) or religious segregation (the menstrual hut as a source of solidarity, even primacy). Whereas an old-fashioned Marxist analysis would have called pride in clitoridectomy "false consciousness," feminists in the 1990s became uneasy about labeling other people's values false, preferring that each should speak for herself. On the other hand, anthropologists generally have become conscious that the observer cannot escape her own values; we see through the eyes socially constructed for us. For a feminist, the combination of these realizations produces an epistemological double bind (we should try to see things through the Other's eyes, but we can't) and brings into question the whole purpose of the anthropological project. Maybe the West should stop being so nosy. Maybe we should just stay home. But what about home? Does this mean it's all right for women to have cosmetic surgery? And what about false consciousness—should we learn to respect clitoridectomy? Are values ever transferable? The problem of reconciling different gender systems has only grown more pressing since September 11, 2001.

The bogging down of the ethnographer coincided with the rise of the field of postcolonial theory and subaltern studies. During the 1980s, theorists' attention turned to the aftermath of the invasion and occupation of many parts of the world by Europeans in the modern period. Now that these occupations have (at least officially) been over for some time, the people who live in those parts of the world, or who returned to the "mother country," have been writing about what it means to them to have two languages and two cultures, or a mixed culture. The title of Gayatri Spivak's classic article, "Can the Subaltern Speak?" (1988), refers to the problem of finding a voice for those who are outside the structures of power and language in colonial systems (for example, the title character in Mahasweta Devi's short story "Draupadi"). In what language should s/he speak? What gives people the power to speak? These issues, long recognized in feminist theory (see Gal 1991 for a review), take on a new dimension when race, gender, and class combine with a colonial history. The voices speaking out of the colonies have turned the ethnographer's monologue into a conversation, and remind us whose dilemma it is. For the ancient world, the problem is that we do have many "native" voices, but we must scramble to find the voices of women, of slaves, and of those who were literally colonized within that world.[6] Since our conversation has to be one-sided, our dilemma rarely troubles us.

One way out of the ethnographer's dilemma has been suggested by anthropologist Lila Abu-Lughod. In "Can There Be a Feminist Ethnography?" (Abu-Lughod 1990: 26–27), she talks of the practice of anthropology by indigenous anthropologists and "halfies," people of mixed cultural background: "Their agony is not how to communicate across a divide but how to theorize the experience that moving back and forth between the many worlds they inhabit is a movement within one complex and historically and politically determined world." Women studying women, she says, do break down the self/other divide, to a degree. But, unless just being a woman in our field is enough, feminists in Classics can never be "halfies." We cannot even be participant observers. We suffer all the drawbacks of being "colonizers" of the past—thousands of years of skewed sources, invasion into cultures that did not ask us to come—without the advantage of actually being able to go there. On the other hand, we do speak the language, to some degree; and there is no one left to resent us, nor is Messalina here to tell her own story. (Then there is the enormous question of who owns classical antiquity among the modern nations; see Stephens and Vasunia 2010, and ongoing discussion of the phrase "Oriental seclusion" as applied by modern classicists to Athenian women.)

(2) At the same time that anthropologists have been getting nervous about what we do when we look else*where*, historians have been redefining what they think we are doing when we look else*when*. Postmodernist historians, at least, have produced a mode of history-writing that is closely aligned with anthropology and exhibits the same paradoxes (see Veeser 1989 on the New Historicists; Partner and Foot 2013 for this and other varieties). Michel Foucault inspired a school of critics who look for local differences in stretches of the past, mapping a terrain of ideas and social mores.[7] The epistemological problem on which they focus was formulated by Louis Montrose (1989: 20) as "the textuality of history, the historicity of the text" (see chapter 3). That is, as past events are only actually knowable to us through a screen of texts—rather, the screen of texts is all that is knowable to us of the past—so each text must be located in its historical context, and can only be understood within that context. This leaves the historian in much the same position as the anthropologist in her dilemma, able at best to appreciate and understand; value judgments are not part of this method (see Newton 1988 for a feminist critique).

However, ironically, and maybe because appreciation is still part of the method, this school of history-writing falls into what I would call the dream of a lost golden age. Societies in the past, especially precapitalist societies, are privileged; the strangeness of their customs is admired, their emotions seen as free of the dread hand of Freud. This optimistic attitude shows up, to give a classical example, in the work of the Foucauldian John J. Winkler, who often sets up what he calls "ancient Mediterranean" cultures in favorable contrast to what he calls "NATO cultures" (Winkler 1990a: 13, 27, 73, 93). We see here how the elsewhere and elsewhen can be combined.

But it is not only the postmodernist historians who look to the past for something to admire. Other kinds of historians want to use past cultures as a means to redeem the present, or claim the distant past as a charter for future social change. This desire can be seen as a form of what is called in religion studies "chronological dualism"—a belief that there was once a time when everything was wonderful; then there was a Fall, so that we have the long expanse (including now) when everything is terrible; but someday there will come a time when everything will be wonderful again. Models like this combine optimism with pessimism, in stages. The theorists who have chosen this model make odd companions: (1) Some feminist historians and archaeologists have looked to the past for instances of matriarchy, high valuation of women, or goddess worship; the implication is that if such a state of things existed once, it can exist again. (This can be seen to be similar to the feminist anthropologist project of finding models else*where*: if there is gender equality among the !Kung San, we can have it, too. As anthropologist Micaela di Leonardo points out, this move was partly justified by first claiming that cultures elsewhere represented "primitive" societies, living remnants of the elsewhen [di Leonardo 1991a: 15].) Most of the scholars looking for matriarchy in the past focus on pre- or non-Indo-European cultures and the traces of their survival; some, however, have even looked to the Greco-Roman world (see Zweig 1993).

(2) Another group, among those historians increasingly seeking to put the rest of the Mediterranean world back into our picture of antiquity, has integrated Greece and Rome with neighboring African and Semitic cultures (see Haley 1993). For Afrocentrists, this forms part of a political program of reclaiming a great past. (3) An early and influential chronological-dualism model was produced by Engels, who was a contemporary of the early anthropological writers on matriarchy; in *Origin of the Family, Private Property, and the State*, he posited what he called the "world historical defeat of women," a time in the distant past when egalitarian societies gave way to male-dominated ones. This time began with the rise of states and would come to an end with revolution in the means of production. Engels's influence on feminist theory in the 1970s was considerable.[8] (4) Finally, and oddly enough, the romantic view of the golden past also seems to be responsible for the politically conservative discipline of Classics itself: hence the name. You would not think that the august male philologists Wilamowitz and Gildersleeve had much in common with Merlin Stone or Molefi Kete Asante or Engels, but all of their projects are determined by a belief that certain pasts are especially worthy of study and that such study empowers the student. This leaves us with a sad argument for the arbitrary nature of the historical endeavor, since all these romantics have sallied forth into the past and returned with completely different trophies. Even if we agree that all the trophies were there to be found, along with others, there

is still wide disagreement about which ones are worth looking for, and how to establish criteria.

It is my goal here to review the 1990s debates in anthropology, history, and Classics, both (O)ptimist and (P)essimist, ending with some illustrations from the history of ancient women. I have picked these disciplines and these illustrations in order to stress materialities as much as possible, to maintain a focus on women's lives. The last defenders of grand theory fight on (Bennett 2006). My own preference is for an Optimistic epistemology that maps a real reality and then does something about it; difference is a part of reality, not a sign of its demise.

Anthropology, History, Women in Antiquity

Anthropology

The ethnographer's dilemma and the dream of a lost golden age were being discussed in feminist anthropology by the early 1980s. In an excellent overview, Judith Shapiro (1981: 119) divided feminist anthropological work into two types, one seeking "to affirm the universality of male dominance and to seek ways of accounting for it without falling into biological determinism. Another [denies] the generality of the pattern by producing cases to serve as counterexamples . . . showing how sexual differentiation may imply complementarity as well as inequality." The chapters above on sexual invective and rape would fall into the first category (cf. Keuls 1993), the chapters on religion and medicine veer toward the second, the chapters on makeup and mourning combine the two. The perception of the division Shapiro outlined as a choice between grand theory and local-historical differences has driven postmodernist feminist anthropologists into quandaries, for example, Henrietta Moore in *Feminism and Anthropology*, who begins from the premise that "the concept 'woman' cannot stand" (Moore 1988: 7). Moore is then defensive about doing "feminist" anthropology, and states outright that "the basis for the feminist critique is not the study of women, but the analysis of gender relations," dismissing earlier work (1988: vii, 6). In this, she anticipated a trend in which women per se went out of fashion; a collection of essays in feminist anthropology, intended (di Leonardo 1991b: vii) as an update on the classic *Woman, Culture, and Society* (Rosaldo and Lamphere 1974), was titled *Gender at the Crossroads of Knowledge*, underscoring the retreat of feminist scholarship from "women" to "gender" outlined in Tania Modleski's *Feminism without Women* (1991: 3–22).

The ethnographer's dilemma is a specialized form of this grand-theory issue. Judith Shapiro sums up the problem (1981: 117):

> Marxist idealizations of sex-role differentiation in small-scale societies bring us back to the Noble Savage; what we are seeing is an attempt to seek a charter for social change in the myth of a Golden Age. This approach is also a way of avoiding one of the thornier problems that recent sex-role studies have raised for the field of anthropology, which is the question of how we can go about adopting a critical perspective on societies very different from our own. . . . If we engage in a critique of other cultures . . . do we risk engaging in what we have generally seen as the opposite of anthropology—missionization? . . . Do we operate with a theoretical double standard: a critique of society for us and functionalism for the natives?

Again, the problem throws Moore into self-reproach: feminist anthropology, by trying to be inclusive, practiced exclusion; anthropologists were preempting third world women, and thereby being not just ethnocentric but racist (1988: 191). Micaela di Leonardo devotes a whole section of her overview to the dilemma, which she calls "ethnographic liberalism and the feminist conundrum," and which she rightly sets in the context of anthropology's general political relation to its object of study (1991a: 10): "how could we analyze critically instances of male domination and oppression in precisely those societies whose customs anthropology was traditionally pledged to advocate?" Her formulation points to a way in which this issue is relevant for Classics: classicists are trained to feel a strong love for the ancient world, a duty to cherish its memory. Thus her words bear a significant resemblance to the way in which Judith Hallett posed the problem in a 1992 conference paper: "How are we to foster a debate about ancient Greek and Roman constructions of sexuality which acknowledges the shortcomings of Greek and Roman societies?" (1992a: 7). The cultural separation of anthropologists from the cultures they study, and the cultural continuities between antiquity and the present that are part of the self-definition of Classics, both leave the feminist in a position that makes it hard to justify her own critique. Indeed, to many classicists, such critiques are not what the field of Classics is about.

Golden age models and origins theories attempt to escape the ethnographer's dilemma via the past. Both anthropology and archaeology have devoted attention to the question of who is responsible for human civilization, man-the-hunter or the new contender woman-the-gatherer; some want to find woman-centered cultures in the remote past, others at least to make Neolithic women visible (Gero and Conkey 1991). Michelle Rosaldo's classic essay "The Use and Abuse of Anthropology" duly includes a section on the search for origins and universals (1980: 390–96; cf. O'Brien and Roseberry 1991). Best known herself as a formulator of grand theory (so di Leonardo 1991a: 13), she nonetheless directs a frown at origins theories, on the grounds that they depict gender systems as "essentially unchanging" (1980: 392–93). This is a version of the "wrong because depressing" argument; note also here the way "long-lasting" or "slow to change" is read as "unchanging." On the other hand, Rosaldo more or less concedes that "sexual asymmetry" is a universal, and calls ignoring it "romantic" (1980: 396). A good word to choose; surely these arguments about the most distant human past exhibit clearly the mythopoeic impulse driving scholarly endeavors—the rewriting of Genesis.

The discipline emerges as a battleground for Optimist and Pessimist epistemologies, incorporating optimist and pessimist attitudes. Di Leonardo lists solutions theorists have proposed to solve the "feminist conundrum": various types of grand theory, including Engels's Marxist model; various optimistic models, in which women are either said to enjoy high status in a given culture, or the power of their separate sphere is stressed. Her favorites are the *Verstehen* method associated with Max Weber, in which the investigator tries to get into the mindset of the ones investigated, and a sort of feminist Marxist theory that stresses the study of political economy. She rejects postmodernist theory (1991a: 17–27) as nihilistic, incapable of political commitment, and points out that it is possible to see problems in language without throwing the material world overboard. Even Moore (1988: 10–11) posits a kind of feminist postmodernism that will hang on to real women's real experiences, rather than just listing their varieties.

These issues matter to classicists because we, too, have to worry about dealing with cultures not our own. We need a theory that can define our relation to the people we are studying: what is a writer supposed to do who studies cultures buried in the past, who reads "dead" languages? If the goal of feminist anthropology is to replace monologue with conversation, we have no possible equivalent. We, too, have to examine our reasons for writing (about) the past; we need a theory that spells out the relation between "antiquity" and ourselves. Moreover, as we pore over our fragmentary evidence, it is useful to us to make comparisons with other cultures. Work in Mediterranean anthropology (Brandes 1981; Dubisch 1986; Herzfeld 1985) has seemed particularly pertinent (as in Winkler 1990a, and the sources in chapter 9 above); attention is now turning towards Asia, for example through Walter Scheidel's Stanford Ancient Chinese and Mediterranean Empires project. Studies of oral forms like fables or jokes often require a comparative lens. So we need a theory that can justify such comparisons.[9]

But, as feminists, we all need to remind ourselves of why we are doing this in the first place. If the idea originally was to find a charter for social change someplace else, we should not let arguments about how to find the charter keep us from working on the social change. We should not wind up talking about women extremely remote from us in time and space, in language extremely remote from everyday speech, so that we never have time to talk in everyday words with women close to us. We should hold on to the reality of what we are doing.[10]

History

Feminist theory in history has come to focus on problems in dealing with the elsewhen much like those anthropologists have found in dealing with the elsewhere.[11] Historians with differing approaches agree on some surprising points, particularly that the goal of writing women's history is social change. Gerda Lerner begins *The Creation of Patriarchy* (1986: 3) with the words, "Women's history is indispensable and essential to the emancipation of women." Judith Newton emphasizes the point in her materialist critique of postmodern theory (1988: 94); yet the eminent postmodernist Joan Scott also talks of "feminist commitments to analyses that will lead to change" in her classic essay "Gender: A Useful Category of Historical Analysis" (1989: 83). These same critics are willing to begin from the premise that history is mythmaking (Lerner 1986: 35–36; Newton 1988: 92). Lerner both acknowledges the human need for myth and calls on feminists to abandon "the search for an empowering past . . . compensatory myths . . . will not emancipate women in the present and the future" (1986: 36).[12]

Historians, however, are left in an uncomfortable position with regard to grand theory other than golden age models. Accepting the hortatory function of writing history entails a steady reluctance to hear bad news, and more versions of the "wrong because depressing" argument. Thus a model that posits the transhistorical existence of patriarchy is defined by its opponents as ahistorical (that is, wrong), because it involves something that does not change over time (or has not changed yet; or has not changed for as long as we have records). To Joan Scott, patriarchy watchers are pessimists: "History becomes, in a sense, epiphenomenal"; against varieties of grand theory, she sets "my hopeless utopianism" (Scott 1989: 86–87, 91), an interesting oxymoron. More resourcefully, Gerda Lerner suggests that totalizing theory can comprehend change: "anatomy *once was* destiny" (1986: 52–53, her emphasis). Such a position seems to me to be both more productive and more sensible than the wholesale rejection of grand theory. Here Classics has something to contribute: a long view. We are used to noting trends over the two-thousand-year period which is our own domain, along with the fifteen hundred years that came after. In this perspective, capitalism is a flash in the pan. On such a large scale, local-historical differences do not seem so significant, or so different. Rather than serving as an end in themselves, surely their best use is to modify grand theory, not vitiate it.

To solve their problem, some historians fashion a combined model that will let them describe both women's oppression and their agency—the fact that women were not always just victims (Lerner 1986: 4; Newton 1988: 99; Schüssler Fiorenza 1989: xv, 25, 85–86). These two concepts, "oppression" and "agency," correspond with "pessimistic" and "optimistic" expectations on the part of scholars. Linda Gordon (1986: 23–24)—inspiring "Pliny's Brassiere"—sketched three similar pessimist/optimist oppositions: between "domination" and "resistance" models; among Marxists, between structure and agency; and, among feminists, between political history and social history. The social historians who recover women's culture are accused by the gloomy political historians of "romanticization of oppression." Here we have a historical version of the ethnographer's dilemma: is women's separate culture, women's special world, a thing of beauty or part of the problem? This is where the category "women" begins to vanish down the rabbit hole. To reconstruct Greek or Roman women's separate culture requires years of painstaking research, putting together tiny fragments; we long to know more; and yet almost everything we get is filtered through male texts and a culture that favored the male in many ways. A combined model would take into account the male nature of the sources while keeping a firm grip on the women hidden behind them.

An approach like this would be able to test the model of the "world historical defeat of women" tied, by Engels, to the rise of the state as an institution, a model which should be of interest to classicists (see Harper 2011 on law, the state, and sexuality). Rome in particular developed from a small-scale pastoral culture to a large-scale empire, turning other small-scale cultures into colonies as it went along. We might look at Irene Silverblatt's work on the Inca (Silverblatt 1991), in which she takes a strongly optimistic view of women's position; Judith Hallett's work on Roman elite women leads in a similar direction (Hallett 1984, 1989), as does the new work on Roman religion that posits a gender-integrated model (e.g., Dolansky 2011a, b, c; see chapter 7). The challenge, for all periods of history, is to avoid restricting our gaze to the elite, or adopting a strong identification with the studied culture as elite sources portray it. In many cases *Verstehen* all has been to forgive all.

The ethnographer's dilemma is also noted by historians of women as a problem they themselves face; there is the same Self/Other difference, the same imbalance of power between observer and observed. Here, where elsewhere and elsewhen merge, so do the ethnographer's dilemma and the dream of a lost golden age. As Judith Shapiro remarks of the use of the noble savage in anthropology, the distance between now and an imperfectly known then allows for all sorts of wishful projections. The search for validation in the past haunts even those writers who are critical of such searches. Nazife Bashar, arguing against the usefulness of the concept of "the status of women" cross-culturally, surveys a group of English historians of women, all of whom structure their history as a progression—or regression: the bad old days or the golden age. Yet Bashar concludes that, for feminists, without a golden age, "we cannot have our myth of the past as . . . an inspiration for the future" (1984: 46). Those who seek matriarchy in the past have come under attack by historians (Lerner 1986: 16, 26–35, 146–48), archaeologists (see Brown 1993; Talalay 2012; Zweig 1993), and historians of religion (Eller 2000; Schüssler Fiorenza 1989: 18, 21–31). Yet many of these in turn are themselves seeking validation in the past. Lerner's history is a search for a charter: if patriarchy has a historical beginning, it can have a historical ending. Some archaeologists just substitute woman-the-gatherer for the Goddess. Church historians are looking for some Church Mothers. The mythmaking function of history seems inescapable.

But possibly there are other functions. For a classicist, an exciting, and surprising, extra set of motivations comes from Elisabeth Schüssler Fiorenza's *In Memory of Her*, a feminist history of the early Church that devotes three lengthy chapters to theory. There is no doubt in Schüssler Fiorenza's mind about the historical relevance of the first century; to her, the Bible is a living document. Most classicists pay no attention to Christians, a minor cult before the late Roman Empire, or to Jews; yet, all the time, flourishing beside us, large numbers of feminist historians of religion are writing about the periods we regard as our own, and by necessity, many of them, writing about nonelite culture. Feminist biblical scholars often think in terms of salvage, of finding women in the sacred text, but Schüssler Fiorenza recognizes the operation as dangerous: "the source of our power is also the source of our oppression" (1989: xviii, 35). Feminists in Classics should compare our problematic relation to our own canonical texts, and the controversies over "reappropriating" beloved male authors (*Helios* 17.2 [1990]; see volume introduction, chapter 5). Yet Schüssler Fiorenza makes a claim for writing history as activism: remembering the sufferings of women in the past is a way of reclaiming them, for it "keeps alive the suffering and hopes of Christian women in the past but also allows for a universal solidarity of sisterhood with all women of the past, present, and future" (1989: 31, cf. xix–xx, and hooks 1990: 43, 215). In this optimistic model, we are helping, not hurting, when we speak for these dead others. We are actually doing something for them.

Women in Antiquity

If anthropology and history are perhaps overly embroiled in epistemological questions, the study of women in antiquity has been preoccupied with empirical ones. What can we find out from our material? Feminists in Classics are only too familiar with the textuality of history, and have made a business out of reading gaps and silences. We can attest that studying gender doesn't mean not studying women. The nature of our sources has forced us to think in terms of gender systems from the outset; feminists in Classics began working on gender, the body, and sexuality in the late 1970s (Richlin 1991). Most ancient women are outside literary texts; is history, we have asked, a more feminist project than literary criticism? But, in our work, we have rarely paused to worry about the ethnographer's dilemma, and, from the 1970s into the 1990s, we took grand theory for granted. That certainty is pretty much gone.

A 1991 interdisciplinary collection presented the reader with the unusual sight of a feminist epistemologist commenting on a survey of feminist work in Classics (Harding 1991, on Gutzwiller and Michelini 1991). Sandra Harding asked (1991: 103) what are the feminist assumptions that permit contemporary women to identify with other women across two millennia, across the vast cultural differences between Antigone's culture and ours, across the class, race, and sexual identity differences between contemporary female feminist readers and the imagined female audiences for these literatures.[13]

Harding used our praxis—Optimistically—to suggest that the ethnographer's dilemma can be overcome, that all kinds of differences can be bridged. But it's a good question: what *are* our assumptions, anyway? And why do we study the past?

A look at major surveys on women in antiquity in the 1980s shows a narrow range of motives and assumptions, among which it is hard to find Harding's question. The field may be dated to a special issue of the classical journal *Arethusa* in 1973 (carried forward into Peradotto and Sullivan 1984; see Sullivan 1973 for an account of the making of the issue, which shortly preceded a conference held at SUNY Buffalo, April 25–27, 1973). Surveys and collections followed: Sarah Pomeroy's *Goddesses, Whores, Wives, and Slaves* (1975) is still the best known outside the field and, after almost forty years, still in wide use as a textbook, but during the 1980s waves of brave pioneers pushed the frontiers onward (see list in Rabinowitz and Richlin 1993: 306–7; overview in McManus 1997). In accord with the empiricist bent of Classics, some of these justify themselves by the modest claim to be presenting new research results to the reader. Most also refer to the basically optimistic women's studies goal of making women visible in history; Mary Lefkowitz and Maureen Fant (1982), in the most stripped-down version, stop with these two assertions. However, from the beginning a tacitly pessimistic grand theory justification from origins is present; thus Pomeroy (1975: xii):

> The story of the women of antiquity should be told now, not only because it is a legitimate aspect of social history, but because the past illuminates contemporary problems in relationships between men and women. Even though scientific technology and religious outlook clearly distinguish ancient culture from modern, it is most significant to note the consistency with which some attitudes toward women and the roles women play in Western society have endured through the centuries.

Similarly Helene Foley (1981: xii): "In studying these literary texts carefully we examine, in effect, the origins of the Western attitude towards women." John Peradotto and J. P. Sullivan open with an explicitly gloomy version (Peradotto and Sullivan 1984: 1):

> Prejudice against women . . . goes back to the very beginning of western culture . . . we are prone to idealize [Greek and Roman] cultures. . . . Without belittling their achievements and their contributions, however, we ought not to blind ourselves to the seamier legacies they left us.

They go on to say in so many words that they are writing a history of gender oppression, likening the history of women to "the history of slavery and the origins of racial prejudice" (1984: 4; compare Sullivan's similar remarks in the original journal issue, 1973: 5). This is ironic in a collection that barely mentions slave women; the connection stems from the rise of Second Wave feminism out of the Civil Rights movement of the 1960s (Echols 1989), where the analogy took a while to come to grips with realities. The strong consciousness of oppression in Second Wave feminist history-writing comes from the experience of the writers on campuses and in activist groups in the era of Martin Luther King and Vietnam.

The field was looking for patterns rather than differences. A striking instance is the statement by Averil Cameron and Amélie Kuhrt (1983: ix) that "although the societies under discussion vary greatly . . . the questions which suggest themselves are remarkably constant." This seems odd in a collection that includes articles on Greek, Persian, Assyrian, Egyptian, Hittite, Celtic, Hurrian, Hebrew, and Syrian women, from cuneiform tablets and hieroglyphics, papyrus and codex; many of these cultures are not Indo-European, and the time span covered within antiquity is greater than that between late antiquity and the present. The table of contents is broken down into the following sections: Perceiving Women, Women and Power, Women at Home, the Biology of Women, Discovering Women, The Economic Role of Women, Women in Religion and Cult. A postmodernist might argue that the remarkable constancy of the questions that "suggested themselves" belonged to the Ancient History Seminar of the University of London rather than to the cultures studied. A fan of grand theory would counter that the constancy inhered in the cultures themselves, and was discovered, not invented.

A similar faith in unified theory was manifested by Ross Kraemer in the first edition of her sourcebook on women in ancient religion (1988: 4):

> I approach the sources primarily as a feminist historian of religion: I seek to recover and understand the religious beliefs of women and to

integrate that knowledge into a revised, enriched appreciation of human religion. . . . The texts here . . . are where we must begin to reconstruct women's religion in antiquity, to inquire about the differences between women's religion and men's as well as about the similarities, and to revise our models and theories accordingly.

In other words, while she assembles an immense amount of particular knowledge about particular cultures, Kraemer's project involves the categories "women's religion," "men's religion," and "human religion," and the ancient religions studied form part of these possibly transhistorical entities.

In the teeth of these disciplinary, epistemological, and political appeals to grand theory, and of her own oath of fealty to "the basic postulates of feminist theory" including a belief in patriarchy, Marilyn Skinner (1987b: 4) suggested there had been a "far-reaching intellectual shift within our own discipline," which she called "postclassicism":

> most readily characterized . . . by its denial of the *classicality* of the ancient cultural product, its refusal to champion Greco-Roman ideas, institutions and artistic work as elite terrain, universally authoritative and culturally transcendent, and therefore capable of only one privileged meaning. Instead, it subscribes to the idea of all cultural artifacts and systems as broadly accessible "texts" open to multiple and even conflicting readings.

Skinner's move here conceals a step which undercuts grand theory much as in the critiques of essentialism outlined above: some grand theory is repugnant, therefore grand theory itself is bad. Skinner was talking about refusing the privilege accorded to Greco-Roman ideas by conservatives, those on the political right (in the 1980s–90s, Allan Bloom, Camille Paglia). Because of the history of right wing, anti-woman use of Greece and Rome in grand theory, Skinner, and many others, wanted to strip Greece and Rome of their privileged status. There is more than one way to do this: the feminist grand theory approaches listed above make antiquity the oldest trace of something bad rather than the origin of all things good. Skinner describes an alternate way, which pulls the rug out from under the right by doing away with grand theory altogether. "Denial of classicality" is the key element.

In the event, this move proved surprisingly successful, as the 2000-year grip of classical education lost hold of the curriculum; the resulting conservative backlash, in which feminists were blamed for "killing Homer," was countered perhaps most eloquently by Page duBois (2001, 2010), who loves to explore what lies across what Virginia Woolf, in "On Not Knowing Greek," called "a tremendous breach of tradition" between the Greeks and us.[14] Meanwhile, like Skinner, David Konstan and Martha Nussbaum, in a collection influenced by Foucault, and focusing on sexuality rather than on women, criticized the tendency of grand theory to see (or construct) patterns, in quite Woolfian terms (1990: iii): "The appropriation of classical Greece and Rome as origins and models of a so-called 'Western' tradition has helped to obscure some of the deep differences between ancient and modern societies." In order, then, to reject a right wing claim on Greece and Rome as full of things the right wing likes, this group chooses to say not "those things were there but they're bad" but "values are arbitrary" and "different things were also there." Things, as it turns out, that *we* like: different sexualities, different attitudes towards knowledge, women writers. Greece and Rome remain models, sources of inspiration, for "postclassicists" just as they were for conservatives. The difference is that postclassicists look to the past for liberatory models rather than for those that preserve the status quo.

The collections in which chapters 3 and 5 first appeared returned to grand theory assumptions. *Stereotypes of Women in Power* (Garlick, Dixon, and Allen 1992) asked why the same kinds of negative images are used against politically powerful women across cultures and time (see Dixon's "Conclusion," *ibid.*, 209–25). The collection traces what it names as a single phenomenon through Egyptian, Roman, Byzantine, medieval Scandinavian, Ming Dynasty, Renaissance Italian, Victorian, and modern Australian cultures. A related premise initiated *Pornography and Representation in Greece and Rome*, which takes the pornographic to be a transhistorical category. Both collections share a focus on images that are arguably harmful to women, some extremely harsh. In contrast, a recent collection on ancient prostitution, although it explicitly rejects any rosy fantasies (Glazebrook and Henry 2011: 8–9), and includes a lexicon of derogatory terms for prostitutes, begins with a refusal to engage in grand theory. Allison Glazebrook and Madeleine Henry write in their introduction (2011: 4):

> We do not claim to present a unified or unitary point of view. Some contributors definitely see prostitution as an unalloyed form of social oppression; others consider the theoretical aspects more than the experiential. The span of time and space and the nature of the evidence do not permit a grand synthesis.

Prostitution in antiquity is and is not a women's issue: female prostitutes are very visible in our evidence, but male prostitutes frequently show up alongside them, and in the same brothels. Like other big structures—the family, labor, war, all of which shape prostitution—this one would seem to call out for a grand synthesis, but in 2011 that was less possible than in 1991, and much less so than in 1979, when Kathleen Barry published *Female Sexual Slavery*. This state of affairs seems to be a byproduct of the political slow-down within feminism itself, as it has grown less and less possible to speak out against gender bias as systemic. Yet it is hard to see an upside to sex trafficking, and hard not to recognize that it is everywhere and everywhen.

Between the pessimistic grand-theorists and their more optimistic opponents, Harding's question—what are our assumptions?—got left a little in shadow in the 1990s, and might well be revisited now. The final discussion at "Feminism and Classics 6" in 2012 asked what makes research feminist; do we need some common framework? Is women's history necessarily a feminist history, and vice versa? And what kind of feminism?

It would certainly be a feminism that unsettles the nebulous, class-free world in which scholars could say "women" and mean "free citizen women." David Schaps's useful *Economic Rights of Women in Ancient Greece* simply wrote off slaves and prostitutes in the introduction (1979: 2), despite his title. Such a prefatory disclaimer was much disparaged, around 1990, by theorists of difference.[15] Just as critiques by women of color and postcolonial women changed the face of feminist theory, we might have expected work on women in antiquity in the late 1990s through the 2000s to incorporate the subjectivity of slave women and colonized women. Sandra Joshel's work on Roman slave child-nurses (1986) might serve as a model; she went on to co-edit a collection, with Sheila Murnaghan (1998), which traced the overlapping sets {women} and {slaves}. Thomas McGinn's work on the built environment of prostitution (2004) integrates these marginal people into the unzoned streets of the Roman city. The latest, and largest, overview of women in antiquity (James and Dillon 2012) incorporates a wide array of cultures outside Athens and Rome (with maps), meshes textual with material evidence (including skeletons), and spans the millennia from the third BCE (Mesopotamian time-bytes, remarking on the impossibility of the task) well into the first CE (Byzantium); the contributors rigorously interrogate their own methodology, the question of matriarchy and goddess worship is conscientiously reexamined, and, despite a disclaimer ("our decision to focus on genres of evidence means that we have had, for the most part, to overlook the great majority of women in antiquity," 2012:

3), the social purview is pretty wide.[16] When you compare the collections from the 1980s to this one, you see the result of twenty years of legwork between then and now, and the difference that makes to our understanding of women's lived reality. Nobody is ever going to get to Z, if that means shutting down any further arguments. But, even if we cannot arrive at exact knowledge of any woman's life, we can get closer, as a hyperbola approaches its asymptotes.[17]

Pliny's Brassiere: Still Life with Absent Objects

How (O)ptimism and (P)essimism play out in the study of ancient history depends on temperament. The examples that follow might be used to show the longevity of patriarchy, or the ability of women to resist by means of their own culture. They might be used to show the horrors of the Roman colonial system, or to recover the voices of the colonized. The tone of the picture depends on the attitude of the painter, but painting at all is a good trick when the model is just out of sight. That we now have a whole gallery is cause for celebration.

To stress difference, an anthropologist or historian will often stress the strangeness of the studied culture; New Historicists like bizarre anecdotes (Darnton 1984: 3–7). Hence the subtitle of this section, which looks back to the story in chapter 8 in which Pliny says, "I find that headaches are relieved by tying a woman's brassiere (*fascia*) on [my/the] head" (*HN* 28.76). This example exemplifies also the problems of transhistorical interpretation and translation. The word *fascia* is conventionally translated "breast-band" (*Oxford Latin Dictionary* s.v. 2.a), a word with no connotations in English. The oddity of Pliny's behavior is lessened or intensified depending on whether we translate "breast-band" or "brassiere." To understand how various Romans would have seen this action, we would have to know more about Roman attitudes towards women's breasts, and investigate the usage of the word *fascia* (does it appear in Roman dirty jokes? No). The picture of the dignified polymath laboring away late into the night at the *Natural History* with a brassiere on his head can serve the modern reader in different ways. For a New Historicist, it is a reminder of the uniqueness of Roman culture, and a corrective for homogenized pictures of the Romans: not just like us, not just like white marble statues. For a feminist, it raises many questions about the significance of the female body in Roman ideology. Are you an optimist? Pliny valorizes the female body by using it to cure himself: there is no limit to it, he says (*HN* 28.77). Are you a pessimist? This is part of an ideology in which the female body is colonized for male use (look at what Ischomachus said about his wife, chapter 6); or described as filthy (look at the poems in chapter 2, or the makeup in chapter 6, or the story of the pollution of Juno's temple in chapter 7); or feared as monstrous, as in Pliny's discussions of the fearful powers of menstrual blood.

As seen in chapter 7, Pliny also tells us that Roman women chewed gum. The historian, rummaging happily through the volumes of Pliny and other encyclopedists, picks up, here and there, more indicators that Roman women had what ethnographers call "foodways." Women (*mulieres*) are said to have preferred certain sweet drinks; again, we can translate this into Diet Coke and white wine spritzers, or we can refuse to be so misled, and *Verstehen* further, constructing a map of Roman women's tastes. Optimistically celebrating women's culture, we can connect this map with other indicators that *matronae* had a subculture of their own. The texts—not only elite literary texts but laws, anecdotes, and inscriptions—tell us plenty about Roman women's active lives in public and private. Maybe Roman women had a group identity.

Pessimistically, we might ask, *which* women? Is this identity or the face of oppression? Roman lesbians are lost behind a screen of invective (Hallett 1997), and, as Bernadette Brooten has shown, women suspected of same-sex inclinations are viewed in some medical texts as mentally ill and might have been subjected to clitoridectomy (1996: 143–73). Roman women's sexuality in general is very hard to recover (see chapters 3, 4, and 8). Nor, as seen in chapters 6 and 7, do most sources tell us about *all* women, and, when we find material about slave women and their female owners, sisterhood is not what we find. (The rites of Mater Matuta: women's culture?) Yes, there are many stories of slave women who helped their owners, stood up for them, even died for them; whose stories are these? Not many stories go the other way; but then there are all those tombstones "for myself, my husband, and our freed slave men and women," and others set up by freed slaves for themselves and their former owner (see Carroll 2011: 135–41). What did Sulpicia Petale think of Sulpicia?

Similar distinctions between classes of women according to their sexual accessibility seem to have existed in Greek cultures as well; the whole point of the prosecution of Neaira, for example, which tells us so much about the miseries of a prostitute's life in classical Greece, is that she had tried to pass her daughter off as fit to carry out certain ritual roles.[18] In Theocritus's *Idyll* 15, from Hellenistic Egypt, two happy, bourgeois housewives go off to the queen's festival, abusing their maids and leaving the baby home with the nanny. This poem used often to be read in courses on women in antiquity to show how the power of the Hellenistic queens raised the status of women in Hellenistic culture; we might, however, compare Audre Lorde's criticism of white bourgeois feminists whose attendance at feminist conferences depends on household work by women of color.[19] The ancient tchatchke industry, which produced huge masses of terracotta figurines, seems to have included old nurses along with pretty girls (and old men, dwarves, actors) as suitable decorative objects; shades of the Aunt Jemima salt shaker. The pessimist will find further examples of inter-class oppression in art, like the *ancillae* holding mirrors for their owners discussed in chapter 6. This is a good test case for Engels's theory of the world historical defeat of women with the rise of the state; clearly, the institutions of imperialism and slavery are better for some women than for others.

Undaunted, the optimist can turn around and start constructing a subjectivity for the women of the under-classes, about whom the literary texts give us such a small and biased view. Maybe the terracotta figures are theater souvenirs, marketed to the same old women who led the ritual at the Feralia. We know there were slave women in the audience at Roman comedies, who might have found much to inspire them onstage (see chapter 1). The essay by Natalie Kampen from which I abstracted the Gallic toilette scene begins with a full-page photograph of a relief sculpture from Ostia, showing a woman selling vegetables, facing the viewer, her hand extended in what is known as the "speaker's gesture" (Kampen 1982: 62). Whether she is saying, "Buy some asparagus," or "I'm the best vegetable-seller in the Forum Holitorium," this woman made her mark, and had the money to do it. The two workers who stamped their feet on the still-wet roof-tile (see volume introduction) made their mark for free; the hairdressers in chapter 6, the midwives of chapter 8, had their skill carved in stone; the Amiternum grave relief (chapter 9) shows the *praefica* in her position of leadership. Sandra Joshel in a large-scale study (1992b) reconstructed a voice for the slaves and freed slaves of Rome from the inscriptions they placed, usually on their tombs, that talk about their occupations; here we see men, women, kin networks, the interrelationships between owner and owned. We find slave women and freedwomen among the religious inscriptions in chapter 7, and these are just the ones who could afford to commemorate their devotion.[20]

Outside of Italy, there are papyrus letters from Hellenistic and Roman Egypt that often speak to and for women—some even penned by the women themselves; these have much to tell us about women's lives. For example, a soldier's letter home to his wife calmly advises her to keep the baby if it is a boy, and to cast it out if it is a girl. Another letter gives an account of how a peasant woman arrested a bath attendant who had scalded her with hot water. One gives what seems to be a woman's shopping list.[21] Wooden *tabellae* preserved at the Roman fort of Vindolanda on Hadrian's Wall indicate a network of relationships among army wives (Greene 2011, 2013).

The records of ancient empires constitute in themselves an argument for the transhistorical nature of the colonial mindset—indeed, they formed a sort of bible for European colonialism. For that matter, they establish the pedigree of the involvement of ethnography with empire. Page duBois established the intersection of this version of Self/Other with that of gender in *Centaurs and Amazons* (1982a). As we turn to the next decade, we might contribute to the public consciousness of how Orientalism predates Islam; how women wore veils before Islam (see Hughes 2007, Llewellyn-Jones 2003); and how Christendom and Islam grew out of the same Mediterranean matrix. We can show what this meant for women.

Beyond Optimism and Pessimism

In the end, I come back to my original question, Why study the past? If feminists—optimists and pessimists alike—are all really hoping for better days ahead, how can we best use our study of the past to make that dream come true?

The one thing of which I am sure is that we cannot contribute to a revolution if we speak only to each other, and only in scholarly language. Nor is it likely that such writing will change any laws, or feed anyone. Meanwhile, many people outside the academy do want to know about the past; we can write for them. As classicists step up to remind the marketplace what we do, we can see to it that women are at the table—not just *in* it, as in the parable that opened this book.

What are we trying to do? Describe truth? Contribute to a revolution? Achieve immortality through the brilliance of our work? Get tenure? Prove that we're right and the other people are wrong? Sometimes I think that scholarship is just an art form, a weird esoteric art form that often plays to an audience of one or two people; but then I think that this is the ultimate pessimistic epistemology.[22] Sometimes I think that scholarship is just a job, like plumbing or typing; something we do all day, in our radical or conservative way. Revolutionary activity mostly happens outside our working hours, assuming we leave time for it, and most revolutionary activity is carried on by people who are not scholars. But sometimes I do think that there is something revolutionary about knowing the past; that when we recover long-gone women from oblivion we are really shifting some balance; that what is taught in the classroom, what is written in the history books, makes a difference. This cheers me up. Feminists in Classics, however, are going to have to take action to connect the scholarly journals and the streets, at a time when the field of Classics itself is practicing outreach. The Committee on Ancient and Modern Performance publicizes productions of ancient plays almost daily; Nancy Rabinowitz spent a recent year sitting in with Rhodessa Jones on the Medea Project: Theater for Incarcerated Women. Twenty years ago, bell hooks wrote: "We must actively work to call attention to the importance of creating a theory that can advance renewed feminist movements, particularly highlighting that theory that seeks to further feminist opposition to sexist oppression" (1992: 81). Our future depends on keeping faith with our past.

Notes

❧

INTRODUCTION

1. For discussion of the inscription's meaning, see Adams 2003: 124–25; the servile status of the two writers is not disputed, and either one or both of them are women.

2. For a large-scale project by women historians telling their stories, see Boris and Chaudhuri 1999, which includes a piece by my old classmate Nancy Hewitt, who got me to put a revised version of "Hijacking the Palladion" into *Gender & History* when she was editor (see chapter 10). Having spent the past ten years chasing down the connections among nineteenth-century classicists, I think that any effort toward the autobiographical is to the good: a message in a bottle.

3. See Page duBois' evocation of the power of objects to inspire a "passion for the dead" in *Slaves and Other Objects* (2003: 35–58, esp. 35–37).

4. The Berkshire Conference of Women Historians began in 1930 as a group of women professors of history who met in the Berkshires, spurred by the exclusion of women from various American Historical Association events; gaining momentum in the 1970s, it began in 1973 to hold a triennial conference that focuses on the history of women, called (a bit confusingly) the Berkshire Conference on the History of Women (often referred to as "the Berks"). The first conference outside the northeast was held in 1996 at the University of North Carolina at Chapel Hill; the group is now national, the meeting is now international and huge. The Berkshire Conference works closely with the Coordinating Council on Women in the Historical Profession (CCWH), the AHA equivalent of the WCC.

5. This issue contains essays by Sarah Pomeroy and Judith Hallett, Marilyn Skinner, Jennifer Roberts, and Janet Martin; Ann Michelini was the guest editor. *Cloelia*, originally the *WCC Newsletter*, now exists online at www.wccaucus.org.

319

6. On activism and the WCC, see the special issue of *Cloelia* for fall 2005, with essays by Jerise Fogel, Mark Golden, Barbara Gold and Nancy Rabinowitz, and Judith Hallett, among others.

7. For EuGeStA, see www.eugesta.recherche.univ-lille3.fr; for the Feminist Sexual Ethics Project, see www.brandeis.edu/projects/fse/.

8. See, for example, Robin 2007, Ross 2009; ongoing work not only covers the usual territory (Italy, France, England) but has moved into the Iberian peninsula, central Europe (Hungary provides a notable example), and the New World, represented, for example, in Jane Stevenson's massive survey (2005). For an encyclopedia, see Larsen, Robin, and Levin 2007.

9. Courses and scholarly work on sex and gender seem to be less restricted than courses on women—perhaps perceived as somehow less specialized? Similar conditions obtain in England, although the field of Gender Studies is well established at Cambridge and London; see Blundell 2004, who reports a substantially greater percentage of departments than in the United States offering courses on women or gender but the same problems with mainstreaming. The European universities have offered a remarkably mixed reception to the study of women; see Henriette Harich-Schwarzbauer in the fall 2009 issue of *Cloelia* (pp. 17–18) on the situation in Austria and Switzerland.

10. The now-familiar reader first appeared in 1977 as *Women in Greece and Rome*, published by the firm Samuel-Stevens, and, at 225 pages, a little over half the size of the current edition; the editors, in a brief introduction, thanked various scholars for the use of their classroom materials—this book was created by new teaching needs. The re-titled reader was first published by Johns Hopkins University Press in 1982. The 1983 NEH Institute organizers, with the addition of Elaine Fantham and Alan Shapiro, eventually produced a similarly comprehensive textbook (Fantham et al. 1994). On the teaching of undergraduate courses on women in antiquity, see the survey by Geraldine Thomas reported in *Cloelia* 2011, with a supplement giving the raw data.

11. On textbooks and curriculum design in the field of history generally, see Bennett 2006: 128–52, with her remark at 131: "despite concerted feminist critique over the last three decades, textbooks—and the master narratives they convey—remain remarkably unchanged." Without a full survey of current textbooks, I have a general impression that most still deal with women in Roman history by sandwiching brief snapshots of "women" into the old war-to-war narrative (an extreme example is Boatwright et al. 2011, endorsed by Walter Scheidel as "the best textbook on Roman history available in English"; cf. Kamm 2008, 11 of 206 pages). Dillon and Garland 2005, covering just the republic, has a substantial chapter on "Women and the Family" with good bibliography; Ward, Heichelheim and Yeo 2009 at least incorporates snapshots at regular intervals over its huge span. Presumably most courses that use these narrative textbooks also use sourcebooks. It is odd that, for example, Appian's account of the atrocities during the proscriptions includes plenty of women, but the persons named in the standard textbook narrative of these events will all be male.

12. See Bennett 2006: 128–52 for a detailed overview of the problem within the discipline of history. For a striking example in scholarship, see Julia Clancy-Smith's review (2006) of Philippa Levine's edited volume *Gender and Empire* (Oxford 2004), written as a compensatory addition to the *Oxford History of the British Empire*, which, in *five volumes* published in 1998–99, managed to leave out women and gender; compare the

working group fielded by the International Medieval Congress that spent five years in the 1990s studying "The Transformation of the Roman World" but left out gender issues. Both are discussed in Richlin 2010.

13. For previous suggestions along the same lines for Greek culture, see Zweig 1993, and the extensive arguments made in O'Higgins 2001, 2003.

14. To understand the difference it has made to have these collections of material, a reader need only consult the bibliography put together by Sarah Pomeroy and others in Peradotto and Sullivan 1984: 343–72, and, in turn, the bibliographies there cited that were put together in the 1970s, and look at what has been done since. Without this work, there would be silence; see nn. 11 and 12 above.

15. Accordingly, and pugnaciously, I titled a review essay in *Journal of Women's History* "What We Need to Know Right Now" (2010). Because the essays in *Arguments with Silence* originally addressed different audiences, they assume differing degrees of specialist knowledge in the reader, so that, for example, the argument of chapter 7 addresses a question not raised by most classicists, while the argument of chapter 10 assumes some familiarity with Foucault. Meanwhile, the book is full of references to ancient writers festooned with the conventional identifiers; this basic trade code is not intelligible to a wider audience. But, as Judith Bennett notes, it has been very hard for histories of premodern women to be at all audible (2006: 43): "among modernists, these myths [about premodern sexual minorities] still prosper, even decades after they have been demolished by credible scholarly research."

16. For an excellent discussion of curricular issues involved in teaching about gender and colonialism transhistorically and transnationally, see Ballantyne and Burton 2005.

CHAPTER 1

Republished with permission of Taylor & Francis Informa UK Ltd, from *Women's Studies* 8 (1981): 225–50; this issue was published, also in 1981, as *Reflections of Women in Antiquity* (Gordon and Breach), edited by Helene P. Foley, in which this chapter appeared on pp. 379–404. Permission conveyed through Copyright Clearance Center, Inc.

I want to give special thanks to Professor Gordon Williams for many criticisms and suggestions.

1. In this study I have not included specimens of the attitude of serious poetry toward sexual behavior. On the whole, they can be aligned with the fantasies and idealizations of rhetoric described below, and in any case I think it is hard to generalize about social attitudes from Roman epic, elegy, and lyric. The period under consideration here runs from the second century BCE to the early second century CE. Useful sources on adultery at Rome include the following: Rein 1844: 835–56, a clear list of the ancient evidence; Mommsen 1899: 688–99, a technical discussion of points of the law; Corbett 1930: 127–46; Mayor 1989 [1877] on Juvenal 10.314–17, an extensive list of literary sources on the punishment of adulterers; and now Gardner 1986: 127–36; McGinn 1998b: 216–47, authoritative on the Augustan laws; Evans Grubbs 2002; Treggiari 1991: 262–319, with a wealth of Roman material plus comparative discussion of issues including honor and the double standard. Special studies include Garnsey 1967 and 1970, esp. 21–24, 103f., on the administration of the *lex Julia*; Daube 1972, on the culpability of accessories; and

now Bradley 2012: 229–56, Evans Grubbs 1993, Fantham 1991, McGinn 1991, 1998a, 2002, Walters 1993. Bonner 1949 is informative and imaginative on the relation between the legal situations described by the *controversiae* and those of real life. Brockdorff 1977 (in Danish) lists sources of various kinds on adultery and the *lex Julia*, with translations, brief notes, and commentary on the reasons for the lack of success of the Augustan marriage legislation. Langlands 2006, like this essay, approaches the question of Roman *pudicitia* by analyzing a range of sources; similarly, on the case of Julia and Iullus Antonius, Hallett 2006a. See Harper 2011: 289–91, 424–62, on adultery laws as a way for the state to control honor/shame, with the "dishonored" bearing the brunt: "the law was a major prop of systemic sexual exploitation" (290).

2. The original essay made no use of Roman comedy; brief comments now appear at the end of this chapter. See Richlin 2014 on Plautus and slavery.

3. The problem is well defined by Garnsey 1970: 8–10.

4. *Coll.* 4 consists of selected points, especially from Paulus's commentary on the *lex Julia*. Harper calls Paul. *Sent.* an "amorphous body of post-classical law" (2011: 446). For parallels in modern law, cf. Scott 1932, vol. 1: 281.

5. *Dig.* 48.5.1; for arguments regarding the date of this legislation, and a general account of its content, see H. Last in *Cambridge Ancient History* 10.443–47. The law sometimes used the terms *adulterium* and *stuprum* interchangeably; *stuprum* was illicit sex, here between a man and virgin or unmarried woman (*Dig.* 48.5.6.1), but the concern of the *lex Julia* is to police marriage, so here to police marriageability. The law does not seem ever to have been intended to outlaw all sexual relations outside marriage, nor can the procedure under the law very easily have been applicable to unmarried women. See Gardner 1986: 123–25 for discussion; Fantham 1991 for a thorough survey of all pre-Augustan evidence.

6. Last (above) notes that one aim of the law is to avoid harshness by transferring the punishment of the wife from the control of the family to the control of the court, limiting the family's power to kill the woman. This may have been in Augustus's mind, but in all the evidence surveyed there is not a single mention of any real woman ever having been killed by her relatives, and it may be assumed to have been a rare occurrence. It seems to me rather to be the case that Augustus was trying to legislate feelings of shame and punitive severity into the upper orders—an endeavor evidently doomed to failure—and that this is borne out by the treatment of a forgiving husband legally as a pimp, as if, by making this moral judgment true in law, Augustus could instill it in the conscience of the nobility.

7. *Dig.* 48.5.2.2, 2.5, 2.6, 2.7, 12(11).13 (specifically under the *lex Julia*), 15(14).pr., 30(29); Paul. *Sent.* 2.26.8. If the husband took no action against a wife he knew to be adulterous, there was no case against his wife (*Dig.* 48.5.2.3); the *adulter* could try to bring action for *lenocinium* to ensure this, but not once he himself was accused (48.5.2.4). The law was particularly concerned with husbands who took money for their compliance, connivance, or mercy (48.5.15[14], 48.5.30[29].3), and was lenient toward those who concealed their knowledge gratis (48.5.30[29].2) or who were simply ignorant (30[29].4). Women came to be covered under this law (48.5.11[10].1), and Marcianus opines that a woman who receives money for her husband's adultery can be accused as an *adultera* (48.5.34[33].2). A soldier who acted in this manner was released from his oath and deported (48.5.12[11].pr.); see Phang 2001 on soldiers' marriages.

8. *Dig.* 48.5.4.12(11).6, 15(14).2. The sixty days were computed from the date of divorce, in the case of a woman who remarried, or from the date of the act, if she remained single (48.5.30[29].5). The husband had priority over the father, and could bring an accusation even after a third party had begun proceedings, if he had not delayed through negligence (48.5.2.8, 3, 4.2).

9. *Dig.* 48.5.2, 12(11).11, 20(19).3. At 48.5.5 it is stated that the *lex Julia* itself made the following provision: that if the woman were unmarried, the prosecutor could begin with either her or the *adulter*; if she were married, he had to start with the *adulter*. Hence the jurist opines that a divorced woman can certainly be prosecuted (also for a widow, at 48.5.16[15].8). It is pointed out that even if the *adulter* is convicted, a married woman accused of adultery with him might still win her case, if he had been falsely convicted (48.5.18[17].6).

10. The term is modern, not classical.

11. The father's right to kill his daughter and her lover was held to be superior to the husband's, the idea being that the father would be the more likely to show mercy (48.5.23[22].4). This right, over adulterers of all ranks, was stated in the second chapter of the *lex Julia* (Paul. *Sent.* 2.26.1). The law originally specified the right as belonging to the father of a daughter who was in his *patria potestas* (48.5.21[20]), although Paulus's opinion is that a *filius familias* should have the right to kill his daughter (*Sent.* 2.26.2). Killing had to be done *in flagrante delicto* (48.5.24[23]) and only in the father's or husband's house (48.5.23[22].2). The father had to kill the *adulter* and his daughter as simultaneously as possible (48.5.24[23].4). If the father did not kill both, he could be prosecuted for murder under the Cornelian law (48.5.33[32].pr.).

The husband could not kill his wife, and could only kill certain kinds of adulterers (48.5.25[24].pr., Paul. *Sent.* 2.26.4) and only in his own house, not his father-in-law's (also Paul. *Sent.* 2.26.7). The husband, under the law, could kill anyone who was a pimp, a singer or a dancer, one convicted of a criminal offence and not restored to full civil rights, or a freedman of his immediate family. Once he had killed such an *adulter*, he had to dismiss his wife immediately (*Dig.* 48.5.25[24].1) and announce the circumstances publicly (Paul. *Sent.* 2.26.6) within three days.

The right of a man to kill an *adulter* who outranked him was a sticky point; cf. *Dig.* 48.5.25(24).3, 48.5.39(38).9.

A husband who did not wish to kill the *adulter* found *in flagrante delicto* could detain him for up to twenty hours in order to bring in witnesses (*Dig.* 48.5.26[25].pr., 48.5.26[25].5; Paul. *Sent.* 2.26.3 places this rule in chapter five of the *lex Julia*).

The husband who did kill his wife was recommended to the court's mercy in a rescript of Antoninus Pius (*Dig.* 48.5.39[38].8); he was not to suffer the death penalty, but, if of inferior rank, was to be sentenced to hard labor for life; if of superior rank, to *relegatio* to an island. Paulus also recommends leniency (*Sent.* 2.26.5).

Finally, Papinian notes that anyone who may kill an *adulter* has *a fortiori* the right to "treat him with contumely" (48.5.23[22].3)—a noteworthy rule, considering what the nonlegal sources have to say about what happened to adulterers. In conjunction with the rules about the husband's right to kill, this would seem to indicate a modified liability if the husband assaulted the adulterer, should the adulterer choose to bring a suit; in Gaius's *Institutes* (4.4, concerning the delict of *iniuria*) it is noted that the customary penalties in lawsuits for *iniuria* are "honorary"—that is, that "the estimate of the injury is increased or diminished in proportion to the dignity and honorable position in life of the person injured." This principle is a late one; still, if the adulterer were *infamis* to begin with, his "dignity" would not be very high. Of course, the question remains as to how the husband was to ascertain the rank of a naked stranger in bed with his wife. An explicitly stated distinction as to rank is likely to be later than Hadrian, but the principle may well have been implicit earlier; see Garnsey 1970: 103–4, and esp. 156–57.

12. *Dig.* 48.5.2.9, 48.5.4.1 (four-month period), 48.5.14(13).4, 48.5.16(15).5. Anyone could be prosecuted within five years of the committing of the act, even if the woman had died (48.5.12[11].4). It is not clear why the four-month period for third parties was indicated at all, if the statute of limitations was five years; perhaps the five-year period was important if the husband did not divorce, and the evidence of adultery came to light much later than the act (I am indebted to Susan Treggiari for this suggestion). It was also not clear how much freedom to accuse a third party had if the husband chose not to prosecute. Ulpian (*Dig.* 48.5.27[26].pr., 48.5.27[26].1) states that a third party may not accuse at all unless the husband accuses first, or unless he first accuses the husband of *lenocinium*; Papinian (48.5.40[39].1) gives as his opinion that the third party can accuse even if the husband has not been accused of *lenocinium*.

Although a man could not accuse his concubine of adultery as a husband, since he was not her husband, he could accuse her of adultery as a third party, as long as she was of good standing (e.g. a freedwoman who was the concubine of her patron; *Dig.* 48.5.14[13].pr., 48.5.14[13].1).

Other limitations, or lack thereof: the woman could be prosecuted even after the death of her husband (*Dig.* 48.5.12[11].8); the adulterer could be prosecuted even after the death of the woman (*Dig.* 48.5.40[39].2). A woman who had been raped could not be accused of adultery (48.5.14[13].7); a married woman under the age of twelve had to be accused as a fiancée rather than as a wife (48.5.14[13].8). By marrying a woman, a man cancelled her previous wrongdoings and lost his ability to accuse her of adulteries previous to their marriage (48.5.14[13].9–10). The *lex Julia* specifically prohibited the accusation of anyone away on legitimate Senate business during his absence (48.5.16[15].1), as well as action by certain persons, e.g. those under age 25 (48.5.16[15].6).

13. On the fine points of the culpability of accessories, cf. Daube 1972.

14. It seems probable that, by the second century CE, this punishment applied only to culprits of the senatorial and equestrian orders, and that people below those orders found guilty of adultery were punished corporally; cf. the rescript of Pius cited above. Garnsey discusses this question at length (1970: 103–4; cf. esp. 103 n. 2, 111 n. 3, 136, 152, 167, 222). It is important to realize that it would have been normal for the "servile" or harsh physical punishments to have been inflicted upon any non-citizen below the rank of decurion—i.e., on most people. For the different sorts of exile, see Garnsey 1970: 55, 111–22. Confiscated property presumably went to the state, with a percentage going to an informer, if any. The penalty implied by the *lex Papia Poppaea*, that a convicted adulteress cannot take under a will (as *caelebs* and *infamis*), is no small one. Though denial of the *ius capiendi* was used as a club by this legislation in an age of *captatio*, nevertheless it would have been a real deprivation for someone in exile, whose comforts and possibly hopes of return depended upon money.

15. See Greenidge 1894: 171–76 for discussion.

16. According to Papinian, the *lex Julia* applied only to free persons who were involved in adultery or *stuprum*; slaves were covered by the *lex Aquilia*, laws covering the

delict of *iniuria*, or the praetor's action for corruption of a slave (*Dig.* 48.5.6.pr.). If the slave was not harmed, there was no *iniuria* (Paulus *Sent.* 2.26.16). See Gardner's comments on Ulpian's category of those "against whom sex crime is not [held to be] committed" (*in quas stuprum non committitur*; 1986: 124), and esp. Harper 2011: 290, 445–46 for later developments on this point.

17. Despite *Codex* 9.9.1; cf. *Codex* 9.9.34(35). However, a woman or her family did have the right to start proceedings for divorce, at the risk of losing the dowry—cf. Bonner 1949: 95 n. 1 (on the *actio malae tractationis* and the *actio rei uxoriae*), 124 (on the *actio de moribus*). Women could testify in court; there are numerous examples in the speeches of Cicero. A woman could even plead in court, but this was enough of an oddity that Valerius Maximus has several anecdotes on such women; see Bonner 1949: 52.

18. There are, however, some points worth noting in the story of Lucretia, as retold by writers from Livy onwards. The means by which Tarquin forced her into compliance was a threat to rape her, then kill her, placing the body of a male slave beside her, so that it would look as if she had been caught in adultery and killed with her lover. It might be assumed that adultery with slaves was the thing most feared; hence the republican custom allowed the killing of the wife not only in revenge but so that she would not bear the child of a slave. There are few jokes about illegitimate children in Roman satire, but several of these do elaborate on the shame of a man whose children resemble his slaves (Mart. 6.39; cf. Juv. 6.76–81).

19. Cic. *Fam.* 8.7.2, 2.15.5; Memmius and the wives of the Luculli, *Att.* 1.18.3; Lucullus's other marital problems, Plut. *Luc.* 38, *Cic.* 29; the affair of Milo's wife Fausta with the historian Sallust, Gell. 17.18, cf. Shackleton Bailey 1965: 331–32 (on *Att.* 1.18.3); Pompey's divorce of Mucia for adultery with Caesar, with reports of Caesar's affairs with the wives of Ser. Sulpicius, Gabinius, and Crassus and with Servilia, Suet. *Jul.* 50.1; Dolabella as adulterer, Cic. *Att.* 11.23.3, 12.52.2, 13.7, Plut. *Ant.* 9; Cato's divorce of his wife Atilia, Plut. *Cat. Min.* 24.

20. Cic. *Fam.* 1.9.15; *Att.* 1.12.3, 1.13.3, 1.18.2–3; Suet. *Jul.* 6, 74; Plut. *Cic.* 28–29, *Jul.* 9–10.

21. For other famous republican women like Volumnia Cytheris, see Treggiari 1969: 140, 142; on Cytheris herself, see now Keith 2011.

22. Garnsey 1970: 85, 88–89.

23. Garnsey 1970: 103–4.

24. Suet. *Aug.* 34.1, 65.4, 101.3, *Tib.* 11.5, 50.1, *Calig.* 16.3; cf. Williams 1978: 58–61 for other sources, with discussion, and chapter 3 below. This was certainly a test of the new laws which Augustus would not have wished or contrived.

25. On these cases, see Treggiari 1969: 72–73; and now Evans Grubbs 1993 on later law.

26. The legal and political aspects of these cases are discussed fully in Garnsey 1970: 21–24.

27. Translations throughout are my own.

28. Greenidge 1894: 171–72.

29. On the use of stories about adultery in the household of the *princeps*, see Joshel 1997.

30. On Tacitus *Germania* 18–19, see Langlands 2006: 321–29, in a general discussion of Tacitus on *pudicitia* (320–48).

31. On Valerius Maximus, see Langlands 2006 *passim*, esp. 123–91; on declamation, 2006: 247–80.

32. The text has *pernis*, "hams," which seems unlikely; suggested emendations include *nervis*, "straps"; *pugnis*, "[his] fists"; and *perticis*, "switches."

33. Similar connections appear in the passage cited above from Tacitus *Germania*; see Williams 1958: 23–24.

34. So Bonner 1949: 38–41, 83. On the validity of the "laws" on adultery cited in the *controversiae*, see Bonner 119–21, 131–32; Quintilian *Inst. Orat.* 3.6.17, 27; 5.10.36, 39, 104.

35. See Treggiari 1991: 229–38, 253–61 on romance and love within marriage, which are well attested in Roman sources; it is thought-provoking that sex appears in Treggiari's comprehensive overview mainly in the chapter on illicit sexual relations. Yet a chaste (*casta*) wife was not celibate. For ancient (though mostly Greek) attitudes toward legitimate sex between men and women, see Sissa 2003 [2008]; on the range of Roman social expectations about women's sexuality, Dixon 2001: 32–44. For attitudes within ancient rabbinic Judaism, somewhat resembling those expressed by Plutarch but much more interested in women's desires, see Boyarin 1993.

36. Cf. *Att.* 2.24.3, 5.21.9, 9.22.4; Plut. *Cic.* 26; Clodius and Clodia, *Att.* 2.4.2, 2.9.1, but cf. Plut. *Cic.* 29, for a counter-rumor; Servilia and Caesar, *Att.* 2.24.3, cf. Suet. *Jul.* 50.2, Macrob. *Sat.* 2.25. On Clodia, see now Skinner 2011.

37. For discussion of the sling-bullets, see Hallett 1977, 2006a.

38. Hor. *S.* 1.2.41–46, 132–34; Mart. 2.60, 3.85, 3.92, 6.2. Castration as punishment for adultery is also joked about in comedy (Plautus *Curc.* 30–32, *Poen.* 862–63; Ter. *Eun.* 957) and is the basis of an extended scene at the end of *Miles Gloriosus* (1395–1426).

39. Mart. 2.83, 3.85.

40. Petron. *Sat.* 45.7–9, Juv. 10.316.

41. Catull. 16.1, 14; Hor. *S.* 1.2.44, 133; Mart. 2.49, 2.60, Apuleius *Metamorphoses* 9.27–28, on which see Walters 1993, and Bradley 2012: 229–56 on adultery in Apuleius generally.

42. Catull. 15.18–19; Juv. 10.317.

43. Catull. 16.1, 14; 21.7–13; Mart. 2.47, 2.83; Richlin 1981b. These punishments are similar to the threats against thieves made by the god Priapus in the *Carmina Priapea*, esp. *Pr.* 13, 22, 28, 30, 35, 44, 56.5–6, 59, 70.13, 74; for Roman machismo and interest in Priapus in the first century CE, see Rankin 1971: 52ff., esp. 58–63.

44. Mart. 2.39, 10.52; Juv. 2.65. For a description of the humiliation entailed in such a change of dress, see Pliny *Ep.* 4.11. On the toga of the adulteress, see now Parker 1997: 59; Duncan 2006: 157–59, who reads it as cross-dressing. Olson 2002 points out that there is no evidence that either prostitutes or adulteresses were forced to wear the toga, and indeed very little evidence at all.

45. This idea has a close parallel in serious poetry at Horace *C.* 3.6.25–30.

46. Women, too, are said to corrupt their daughters: Petron. *Sat.* 140.1–11, Juv. 6.232–42, 14.25–30.

47. Sex between women is also treated as adultery—just for practice—in one of the cases discussed by the elder Seneca (*Controv.* 1.2.23); see Hallett 1997 for discussion.

48. Mart. 1.74, 5.75, 6.7, 6.22, 6.45, 6.91. On Domitian's moral legislation, see now McGinn 1998a.

49. Mueller prints Burmann's inserted *capillis*, a reminiscence of *Sat.* 27.6; but surely *sinu* vel sim. is more likely.

50. On the sexual use of slave women in Plautus and Terence, see James 1998, 2010,

2012, and work in progress; Starks 2010; Marshall 2013. On male slaves' access to sex in Plautus, see Richlin 2014, and work in progress. For a general legal/social overview, see Treggiari 1979.

CHAPTER 2

Copyright © 1984 by Department of Classics, State University of N.Y. at Buffalo. "Invective against Women in Roman Satire" first appeared in *Arethusa* 17.1 (1984) 67–80. Revised and reprinted with permission by The Johns Hopkins University Press.

1. Balsdon's book went through numerous reprints and a revised edition from 1962 to 1998, and a cursory search in WorldCat shows translations into Danish, Finnish, German, and Greek. It must be the most widely circulated book on the subject.

2. For a similar interpretation, see Plaza 2006: 127–55; for a critique of persona theory, see Rosen 2007: 220–23. Persona theory was widely applied to Ovid by Anderson's former students in the 1980s; see chapter 5 below for response.

3. The day after I first wrote this, the *Los Angeles Times* reported on the *Rolling Stone* story that led to the departure of General Stanley McChrystal from Afghanistan; Michael Hastings said of McChrystal's staff, "They jokingly refer to themselves as Team America, taking the name from the *South Park*-esque sendup of military cluelessness, and they pride themselves on their can-do attitude and their disdain for authority" (*Rolling Stone* 1108/1109, July 8–22, 2010, http://www.rollingstone.com/politics/news/the-runaway-general-20100622). See Richlin 1992: 73 on *All in the Family*, cuing, and the difficulty of distinguishing between the satire of bigotry and empathy with bigotry. Archie Bunker of *All in the Family* was the US version of Alf Garnett, protagonist of several UK television series; Peter Griffin of *Family Guy* is a direct descendant, Eric Cartman of *South Park* plays a similar role, and compare Sacha Baron Cohen in *Borat*.

4. For Gwerful Mechain, see Johnston 1998: 68–71; for a brief overview of material in Arabic, see Peretti 2003: 210–14; for eighteenth-century England, see Staves 2010: 172ff. The seventeenth-century writers collected in Henderson and McManus 1985 make spirited use of Roman satirical invective in defense of women.

5. Suzanne Dixon includes some further invective material in a chapter on "Representations of Female Sexualities" (2001: 32–44), but does not seek further theories to explain it; she offers thought-provoking introductory remarks on issues of approach and the self-imposed exclusion of certain topics (30–31). See essays in Mittman and Dendle 2012, especially by Sarah Alison Miller, along with her earlier work in *Medieval Monstrosity and the Female Body* (Routledge, 2010).

6. For example, on male passive homosexuals, Highet 1954: 59–64, 117–27; on women, Knoche 1975: 148; Bond 1979. On invective against women in Latin literature, see now Gold 1998a, Henderson 1999: 93–113 (on Horace *Epodes* 8) and 173–201 (on satire); for more on the female body as repellent, see chapters 6 and 8 below. See Miller 1998 for a thought-provoking distinction between Roman invective and the Bakhtinian grotesque.

7. Sources collected by Grassmann 1966: 12–22, 23–34; Buchheit 1962: 88–89.

8. Some parallels collected by Opelt 1965: 26–28; cf. also Richlin 1978: 206–16, 229–32, 233–46, 255–68; Adams 1982: 80–109.

9. This technique is well applied in anthropology, usually for material in oral circulation; most helpful for the study of Rome is the work of Gary Gossen on the Chamulas of southern Mexico, who share many cultural characteristics with the Romans. Especially pertinent here are Gossen 1974: 97–109; 1976. For an examination of the social significance of the denigration of the female body, see Russo 1986, 1994, and, from a psychoanalytic perspective, Kristeva 1982; also Slater 1968: 23–99, 410–39. See also duBois 1988; Spelman 1982. Many of the marital patterns described by Slater for Greece apply to the Romans as well, cf. Hopkins 1964–65 (now updated in Shaw 2002; Scheidel 2007).

10. Compare the discussions of the status of women in erotic poetry: e.g., Lilja 1965: 35–42; Williams 1968: 526–42; James 2003.

11. Lucilius 680 Marx, 781 Marx; Catullus 11, 37, 58, 59, 67, 76, 111; Horace *S.* 1.2.77–108; *Priapea* 26; Petronius *Sat.* 16.2–26.6 (Quartilla), 109.2–3 (Tryphaena), 126.5–7 (Circe); Martial 2.31, 4.12, 6.45, 7.30, 8.53; Juvenal 6.100–14, 115–32, 300–34, O. 31–34, 548, 567; 10.220. This was a serious topic in moralistic poetry (e.g., Horace *C.* 3.6.21–32). On the Widow of Ephesus (Petronius *Sat.* 110.6–112.8), see chapter 1; Langlands 2006: 227–30, and 230–46 on Apuleius. On women in the *Satyrica*, see now Richlin 2009: 89–91; on the promiscuous wife in Plautus, see Langlands 2006: 204–18.

12. Juvenal 6.300–51, 425–33; Martial 12.65.

13. In comedy, jealous wives (e.g., in Plautus *Asinaria, Casina, Menaechmi,* and *Mercator*) are not attractive; cf. Habinnas's wife (Petronius *Sat.* 67) and the hypocritically jealous wife at Juvenal 6.279.

14. Mercenary motives are strongly associated with the mistress in elegy (see James 2003), but see also Catullus 110; Horace *S.* 1.2.47–53, 2.5.70–72; Martial 3.54, 9.2, 9.32, 10.29, 11.50; Juvenal 4.20–21, 7.74–75.

15. Especially the elder Cato at Gellius 10.23.4; also Dionysius of Halicarnassus 2.25.6, Valerius Maximus 6.3.9, Pliny *HN* 14.89–90; some discussion in Pomeroy 1975: 153–54. See now Flemming 2007a: 92–97.

16. See Pomeroy 1976; Gardner 1986: 83; Treggiari 1991: 461–62; Clark 1998: 112–13.

17. *Priapea* 32, 46; Martial 11.97; cf. Martial 11.23 (rejection of would-be wife and description of the indignities she must suffer if the poet should take her).

18. Lucilius 282–83 Marx, 1065–66 Marx, and ?302, 766–67 on drunkenness; Ovid *Am.* 1.8.3–4, 114 (drunkenness); Horace *Epodes* 8, 12; *Priapea* 12, 57; *Virgilian Appendix* "Quid hoc novi est?" 151–53; Martial 1.19, 2.33, 3.32, 3.93, 4.20, 7.75, 8.79, 9.29, 9.37, 10.39, 10.67, 10.90, 11.21, 11.29, and cf. 3.72. This essay did not originally deal with Roman comedy; see now chapter 1 on adultery and chapter 6 for extended discussion of the abject female body in Plautus. As now noted in chapter 1, old women do not appear as sexual aggressors in comedy as they do in satire; jokes about the ugliness and bad smell of old women appear at *Most.* 273–78, and the *senex* voices hatred of his wife or of wives in general in *Asinaria, Aulularia, Casina, Epidicus* (briefly, at 175–80), *Menaechmi, Mercator, Miles Gloriosus, Mostellaria,* and *Trinummus*—almost half the extant plays. In particular, the husband in *Asinaria* voices disgust at the idea of kissing his wife, and says her breath stinks (893–95); cf. Caecilius Statius in Gellius 2.23.13–14. The fondness of the *lena* in *Curculio* for wine motivates an elaborate musical number (76–146); the old *ancilla* Scapha in *Mostellaria* advises her female owner to be unfaithful (182–292); see below on old women in elegy.

19. Cf. also *Priapea* 12; Martial 3.32, 3.93, 9.29, 10.39; "Quid hoc novi est?" 26.

20. For the use of animal invective in rhetoric, cf. Nisbet 1961: 195.

21. A few graphic animal comparisons are used of men in Catullus: 25.1–3, 69.5–10, 97.5–8.

22. Pliny *HN* 7.153; e.g., *Priapea* 57.1, Martial 10.67.5.

23. Cf. *Priapea* 32, 46; Martial 3.53, 3.93, 9.37.

24. Mutilation by cutting off ears and nose is cited as a punishment for adulterers (Martial 2.83, 3.85; Vergil *A.* 6.494–97), and in other circumstances where the shaming of the victim was the goal (Tacitus *Ann.* 12.14). See chapter 1 above.

25. See Kristeva 1982: 56–89; Russo 1986, 1994; and the classic study by Karen Horney (1932). For a social science perspective, see Ember 1978. On the general significance for Greek culture of fear and disgust caused by the female genitalia, see Slater 1968: 12–23; he emphasizes the association of pubic hair with women's overpowering sexuality, although his conclusions are disputed by Kilmer 1982. Cf. Martial's comments on depilation, as well as the Priapic allusion to worms in the vagina (46.10).

26. The closest example is perhaps the Pompeian graffito *CIL* 4.1830: *futuitur cunnus <pil>ossu<s> multo melius <qu>am glaber / . . . con<ti>net va<p>orem . . .* ("a hairey cunt is a much better fuck than a smooth one / . . . it holds in the steam"). See also the highly metaphorical treatment at Apuleius *M.* 2.7.

27. Compare in general the vast store of sexual metaphor in Aristophanes collected in Henderson 1975; those for female genitalia there range from very positive to very negative, and the metaphors from holes and hollows are not particularly negative (nos. 150–58).

28. Cf. Martial 3.32, 3.93, 7.75, 10.67, 10.90, 11.97.

29. Cf. *"Quid hoc novi est?"*; *Priapea* 32; Martial 11.21, 11.29.

30. Horace *Epodes* 8.18–20, 12.14–15 (the poet lets the woman prove his potency by complaining of his prowess with another woman); and esp. Martial 9.37, where the *mentula* "sees" the old woman.

31. *Priapea* 57.8; Martial 11.29 (cf. 7.75, 9.37).

32. Martial 3.74, 10.90, 12.32.21–22; see also chapter 6.

33. *Contra* Hallett 1973, with subsequent discussion in *Arethusa* 6, pp. 267–69, and 7 (1974): 211–19; she sees in elegy a sincere ideological counter to traditional Roman attitudes toward women. Cf. Martial 9.37, where the poet virtually dismembers the woman by enumerating her false parts—hair, teeth, complexion, even eyebrows—then lets his *mentula* reject her. The parts listed are not much different from those praised by an elegist. For the technique of part-by-part praise in the Renaissance, see Vickers 1981. Hallett's position on elegy has been addressed by Barbara Gold (1993), Ellen Greene (1998), Maria Wyke (2002), Sharon James (2003), and several of the contributors to Ancona and Greene 2005, among others.

34. See Richlin 1992: 46–47.

35. Catullus 97; the anus is *laxus* ("loose," *Priapea* 17.3); *tritus* ("worn," Martial 2.51.2); and called *fossa* ("ditch"), Juvenal 2.10. Cf. also Martial 6.37. *Cinaedi* were proverbially afflicted by hemorrhoids; the slang term was *ficus* ("fig") or *marisca* ("cheap/coarse fig") (Martial 1.65, 4.52, 6.49.8–11, 7.71, 12.33; *Priapea* 41.4, 50.2; Juvenal 2.13), and Martial once uses *marisca* to mean a wife's anus as compared with the preferable anus of a boy (12.96). Lucilius draws an analogy between befoulment by women and by boys: *haec inbubinat at contra te inbulbitat <ille>* (1186 Marx), "she rags on you, but then again he be-merdes

you"; cf. *Priapea* 68.8, ?69.4; Martial 9.69.1, 11.88, 13.26; Juvenal 9.43–44. On this imagery, see Miller 1998; for more on this system of sex/gender roles, see Richlin 1993, Parker 1997.

36. Horace *Epodes* 8.7; Martial 2.52, 3.53.3, 3.72.3, 3.93.5, 14.66, 14.149. See Richlin 1992: 47.

37. Cf. Horney 1932: 360.

38. Martial 1.90, ?7.35, 7.67, 7.70. "Bassa" is the name of the woman attacked in 1.90; another Bassa (4.4) is the victim of a long invective list attacking her foul smell, including several animal similes resembling those in 11.21. On Roman invective against lesbians, see Brooten 1996: 42–57 (also covering Greek literature from the Roman period); Hallett 1997; Richlin 1992: 132, 134. For a theoretically-informed overview of the female homoerotic/homosocial in antiquity, see Rabinowitz and Auanger 2002.

39. See Leach 1964, esp. 60–61.

40. See Hopkins 1964–5, and now Shaw 2002, Scheidel 2007.

CHAPTER 3

Republished with permission of ABC-CLIO, from *Stereotypes of Women in Political Power: Historical Perspectives and Revisionist Views*, ed. Barbara Garlick, Suzanne Dixon, and Pauline Allen (New York: Greenwood Press, 1992), pp. 65–91. Permission conveyed through Copyright Clearance Center, Inc.

My thanks to the Women's Classical Caucus of the American Philological Association, who heard an earlier version of this chapter; to Sandra Joshel, Natalie Kampen, Lydia Speller, and Gordon Williams for help and comments; to Suzanne Morrison for assistance in research; and to Suzanne Dixon, Pauline Allen, and Barbara Garlick for their warm hospitality and patience as editors.

1. See Austin 1981, document nos. 151, 156, 158, 185, 217; also Theocritus, *Idyll* 15; Pomeroy 1984: 3–40. On the phenomenon in Victorian England, see Auerbach 1982: 35–62. Of course, this is an extension of the praise of good women for which Greek examples go back to Homer's Penelope.

2. On the Trajanic women, see Temporini 1978; on Julia Domna and her sister and nieces, see Dio, Books 75–80 passim; Cleve 1988; Kampen 1985; and, on women of the imperial household generally, see now Fischler 1994, Ginsburg 2006, and the body of work produced by the contributors to Kolb 2010 (students of Temporini among them). For a brief overview on portraits, with current bibliography, see Meyers 2012. On imperial women from Trajan to Marcus Aurelius, see Keltanen 2002, Richlin 2011b. Beth Severy-Hoven (2003, esp. at 180–84) deals with Julia in the wide context of Augustus's ideological use of the family; see also the special issue of *Arethusa* she guest-edited on "Reshaping Rome: Space, Time, and Memory in the Augustan Transformation" (40.1, winter 2007).

3. On Pulcheria, see Holum 1982: 79–111, 147–216, and esp. 139–45, 153–74, and the idea that through her asceticism she would "'receive the king of the universe in her womb'" (142, quoting Atticus, bishop of Constantinople, 406–25 CE). See also Fisher 1984; Herrin 1983, with sources; and now Vinson 2004, and essays in MacLachlan and Fletcher 2007, on the association between virginity and power, esp. Cooper 2007. For

the significance of virginity in classical Greece, see Sissa 1990. Schade 2009 analyzes the divergence between the ascetic ideal of the late-ancient female body and representations of elite women in art, and shows how contemporary heads were placed on older statues, with traditionally feminine bodies—thought-provoking alongside this chapter's analysis of Macrobius's Julia. Compare D'Ambra 1996 on goddess/portraits of ordinary women.

4. The phrase *meretrix Augusta*, "empress prostitute," comes from Juvenal (*Satire* 6.118), in his tale of Messalina, but the figure is common in historians of the empire (Suetonius, Tacitus, Dio, the *Historia Augusta*; cf. Richlin 1992: 81–104, chapter 1 above, and, on Messalina, esp. Joshel 1997). It continues to Procopius's *Secret History* and the caricature of Theodora in the sixth century CE (see Allen 1992; and now Brubaker 2004, with bibliography, and esp. Vinson 2004 on the female body in Byzantine ideology). For models comparable to the present one, see Wyke 2002: 195–243 on the Augustan construction of Cleopatra; Hamer 1988 on the use of Cleopatra in the fifteenth to seventeenth centuries is unreliable on the ancient evidence. On Dido and Cleopatra, see Carney 1988. See Parker 2004 [2007] on the meaning of the Vestals' virginity to the state.

5. For a (non-Western) example of a positive view of the use to a female ruler of bearing children to several fathers, see Hoffer 1974.

6. This and all subsequent translations are my own.

7. Hallett 2006a: 156–60 argues that Seneca is here also, or instead, talking about Antony's ex-wife Fulvia, who was Iullus's mother.

8. See Balsdon 1962: 68–88 for full discussion of the sources on Julia. Hallett 1984 describes the kinship/gender/political systems of Julia's world; see now Hallett 2006a on the story of her involvement with Iullus Antonius, and, for a book-length study of Julia, Fantham 2006. On Julia in the context of Augustan ideology, see now also Milnor 2005: 80–93, 291. On the sources of Macrobius 2.2–2.7, see Wessner 1928; on Domitius Marsus, see Skutsch 1905, Balsdon 1962: 82; and now Long 2000: 344. The overlaps between Macrobius and Quintilian 6.3.1–112 anchor the jokes in the early first century CE, and at any rate it seems natural to assume they were contemporary with their protagonists. See below on the audience for the jokes about Julia.

9. For discussion of the development of the study of female historical figures, with sources, see NEH 1983: 100–08. Studies that share the concerns of the present chapter include Fisher 1984; Skinner 1983a; and now esp. Dixon 2001, 2007; Skinner 2011. Some of the essays collected in McHardy and Marshall 2004 also deal with ancient women and political ideology. See Walcot 1987 for an example of an old-style dragon-lady history, invoking Freud's "Femininity"; compare Cleve 1988, who champions the Severan women's power under the title "Some Male Relatives of the Severan Women" and winds up explaining how they took their power by "manipulating all of their male relatives," "using the same tools and techniques employed by male politicians of their time—albeit with much more subtlety . . . , because they had to rule 'behind the scenes'" (cf. n. 13); and now also Bauman 1992.

10. For woman as ship in Aristophanes, see Henderson 1975: 164–65 (here men also are ships); and cf. esp. *Palatine Anthology* 5.204. For the image in Latin, see Adams 1982: 89, 167.

11. On the significance of Julia's daughter's pregnancy, see Barnes 1981; on Justa Grata Honoria, see below, and note 26. See Williams 1962 for the importance of procreation in the ideology of Horace's praise of Augustus's marriage legislation, esp. *Odes*

4.5.23, *laudantur simili prole puerperae* ("mothers of newborns are praised for children resembling [their husbands]").

12. Livia apparently had her own stories, which directly counter Julia's. Dio says (58.2.4): "Various well-put sayings (*apophthegmata*) of hers are recorded," and gives two: (58.2.4) how she spared the lives of some men who had crossed her path naked and therefore were to be executed, saying that to chaste women (*sôphronousais*) such men are no different from statues; (58.2.5) that she explained her hold over Augustus by saying that she herself was scrupulously chaste, cheerfully did what seemed best to him, did not meddle in his business, and pretended not to hear of or notice his love affairs.

13. On Julia's known circle, see Williams 1978: 63-70; also Green 1982. For sources on Domitius Marsus, see Skutsch 1905.

14. See Zijderveld 1968, esp. 306-7, on the "manipulatory use of joking" by political leaders.

15. See Levick 1975 for a discussion of the factions angling for the succession; she emphasizes the dynastic importance of Julia's progeny and depicts Julia's history entirely in political terms—the "lovers" are Julia's political clique. "Behind the scenes" lurks the "dark figure" of Julia's mother, Scribonia, who cannot forgive her ousting by Livia and promotes Julia's children against Livia's son Tiberius; Livia is at the center of the opposing faction. See Joshel 1997: 229 for a critique of a similar analysis.

16. For example, Fine 1976; Makarius 1970; Turner 1969: 47 and passim; Zijderveld 1968, esp. 297-98; also Barber 1959. See now Russo 1994, and chapter 2 above, with discussion in the chapter introduction.

17. See Green 1977; Johnson 1973; and now Arthurs 1999, Kothoff 2006, Lavin 2004, Lee 2004, Rowe 2001. Some empirical support is provided by Mitchell 1985. Nancy Walker (1988) argues that American women's humor is marked by its domestic content (she does not consider structure), and that it incorporates a veiled and subversive protest against patriarchy; related arguments on Victorian women's writing in Gagnier 1988. Both follow Apte 1985 and Eco 1984. On women cartoonists, see Mitchell 1981; Robbins and yronwode 1985.

18. For an optimistic overview of Roman women writing and reading graffiti, see Levin-Richardson 2013 (above, chapter 2). On subversive discourse in African-American traditions, with important general implications, see Gates 1988.

19. See Kleiner 1978 for one view of who (including Julia) is where on the Ara Pacis, with special consideration of the place of women and children on the monument (a much-disputed issue); Galinsky 1969: 219 on Venus in the Ara Pacis; and, on the ideological use of representations of women in imperial art, see now D'Ambra 1993, 2007b; Kampen 1991; Kleiner and Matheson 1996, 2000; Wood 1999. Cf. Dixon 1988, esp. 71-103, for in-depth treatment of the ideology of maternity in the early principate and for women of the imperial house thereafter; and now Milnor 2005 on gender in Augustan ideology. For discussion of women as patrons underwriting public art, see Meyers 2012, Woodhull 2004.

20. See discussion of a *sestertius* of Caligula showing Agrippina with a *carpentum* on the reverse, in Breglia 1968: 46 and facing plate.

21. For an overview of revisions of both Bloch's model of the "last pagan generation" and Cameron's model of literary nostalgia, along with discussion of Macrobius's project as grounded in struggles for cultural prestige between Constantinople and Rome, see

Ando 2001; Cameron discusses the pagan/Christian dichotomy as irrelevant to Macrobius at 2011: 231–72. Salzman 2002 provides a detailed quantitative survey of the Roman aristocracy's conversion starting in the century before Macrobius.

22. Kaster 1980: 242–48, 240, n. 64; cf. Cameron 1967 for the identification of Avienus with the fabulist Avianus who dedicated his book to Macrobius around 430 CE.

23. Ps.-Aug. *Quaestiones* 115.12, 16, = *CSEL* 50.322, 323; Brown 1961: 7 n. 50 takes the passage to refer to a relaxation of divorce laws for *clarissimae feminae* (women in the elite social class), but the question is vexed.

24. I owe these insights to the helpful reading of Martha Malamud. For detailed consideration of Julia's jokes in Macrobius's text and moral context, see now Long 2000.

25. For a full, if dramatic, account, see Oost 1968; also Matthews 1975: 224, 248, 316–18, 354–55, 377–80. On Galla Placidia, see now Sivan 2011, with discussion of her relation to Julia's jokes in Macrobius's *Saturnalia* at 101–3, and useful remarks on the arguments in this essay.

26. Holum 1982: 1; Oost 1968: 282–85; but cf. *PLRE* 2 (Jones et al. 1971): 568–69. On Honoria, see now Sivan 2011: 153–58.

27. Galla Placidia, in MacCormack 1981: 228 and plates 59 and 60; Justa Grata Honoria, in Holum 1982, figure 14, and discussion of all the coins, 129–30.

28. Oost 1968: 290 sees the letter to Pulcheria as a "less formal" sharing of religious feeling.

29. Compare Green 1982, who sees the accusations of sexual misconduct against both Julias as camouflage for accusations of political conspiracy in which the women served as tools; Hallett 1984: 141–42, 328, who sees Roman fathers' concern with their daughters' chastity as stemming from "paternity anxiety."

CHAPTER 4

Republished with permission of the Classical Association of the Atlantic States. This article first appeared in *Classical World* 86 (1992): 124–50. Permission conveyed through Copyright Clearance Center, Inc.

Many thanks to my former colleagues at the University of Southern California; I am especially indebted to suggestions by Martha Malamud and Diane Pintabone, who heard my early musings on Sulpicia. Holt Parker (1992b) and Judith Hallett (1992b) most kindly let me see their work before it was published.

1. Besides Snyder 1989, see: on the earlier Sulpicia, Hinds 1987; Lowe 1988; Parker 1994, with extensive discussion of women in the Roman literary tradition; now Keith 1997, Skoie 2002, Hallett 2006b (with numerous other publications on this author); on Cornelia, Dixon 2007, Hallett 2004. Holzberg 1998–99 revives the argument that the poems attributed to the earlier Sulpicia were written by a male author, while Hubbard 2004, calling the biographical reading of these poems "naïve," argues that they were written by author(s) unidentified but unlikely to be her; see comments in Keith 2006 (with Hallett 2006b, in a special issue on this Sulpicia). On educated women in general, see Hallett 1989, and now Hemelrijk 1999, Churchill et al. 2002, and esp. Jane Stevenson's comprehensive history of women writing in Latin (2005). Stevenson argues forcefully that the numerous women poets attested from the first century BCE through late

antiquity were well-respected in their own day and thereafter, and that, after all, the work of most attested classical Latin writers is lost (2005: 31–48). On the best-known Vindolanda letter, see Bowman and Thomas 1987: 137–40, and now Elizabeth Greene 2011, 2013, on the much broader evidence for this letter's social context. On women's letters from Egypt, see now Bagnall and Cribiore 2006, Rowlandson 1998, and further work by Cribiore and Rowlandson on women's education in Egypt. See Richlin 2013a for a reconstruction of the letters of Terentia, wife of Cicero.

2. On Sappho, see Stehle 1990, with bibliography, and duBois 1995; on Nossis, Skinner 1989, 1991; on Corinna, Skinner 1983b.

3. For sources on the textual history of both the fragment and the hexameter poem, see Parker and Braund 2012: 454–56, updating Parker 1992b. James Butrica (2006) argues that the hexameter poem was in fact not late at all, but, along with a fragmentary but racy poem on Penelope that appeared next to it in the manuscript, was written by Martial's Sulpicia.

4. See Hallett 1992b: 105–19 for in-depth discussion of the literary antecedents of these poems, focusing on Catullus and especially on Propertius; see further Parker 1992b: 94 n. 36.

5. Parker 1992b: 94 argues that this is a close paraphrase of one of Sulpicia's poems; Hallett 1992b: 110–14 provides background for the elegiac pedigree of these lines, and explores the implications of Martial's choice of words. See Cahoon 1988, with bibliography.

6. On Catullus and Martial, see Hallett 1992b: 105–9; Richlin 1992: 127–41; Sullivan 1991: 95–97, in an enlightening discussion of the epigram tradition.

7. For the disappearance of Sulpicia herself from Martial, see Parker 1992b: 94–95 and Hallett 1992b: 122–23, arguing against Merriam's claim (1991: 305) that 10.38 is cast as an address by Sulpicia herself to Calenus.

8. Book 10 of Martial, a second edition, dates to the reign of Nerva (see Sullivan 1991: 44–49); Juvenal 6 is pretty securely dated to 116 CE by lines 407–12 (see Courtney 1980 ad loc. and p. 1). It seems at least a strong possibility that our fragment of Sulpicia was part of a poem or poems that either inspired Martial 10.38 or reacted directly to it; see below. In either case, Juvenal would be picking up the outlandish *cadurcum* from Sulpicia, and not vice versa.

9. On literary nostalgia, see Browning 1983: 16, 81–82; Roberts 1989: 57–58 on the period's taste for "mosaics" of bits of earlier writers; and now Cameron 2011.

10. See Parker 1992a: 93 on the repeated tendency in literary history to deny women's authorship; see Holzberg 1998–99 for an example.

11. See below on Numa's cave in Juvenal 3. Perhaps it is also significant that the hexameter poem brings in the stock description of primitive humans as living on acorns (*glandibus*, 20), an item that features vividly in the opening of Juvenal 6 ("[a wife] shaggier than her acorn-belching husband," *uxor . . . / horridior glandem ructante marito*, 6.5, 10); another Juvenalian borrowing?

12. Parker 1992b: 94 rejects this as a fantasy of the Renaissance editor, pointing out that Martial says Sulpicia's poetry is suitable for both male and female audiences; but Martial's reading of Sulpicia may be on the revisionist side.

13. On Juvenal's virtual disappearance between his lifetime and the fourth century CE, and his subsequent revival, see Highet 1954: 19, 181–88.

14. Accepting Bücheler's emendation *subet* for the text's *subit*, which Helm retains.

CHAPTER 5

Republished by permission of Oxford University Press, Inc, from *Pornography and Representation in Greece and Rome*, edited by Amy Richlin (1992); Chapter 8 "Reading Ovid's Rapes" by Amy Richlin.

Thanks to Marilyn Skinner and Susan Kapost for the bibliography that got me started; Terri Marsh for much help along the way; groups at Carleton University, University of California, Santa Cruz (especially, and always, Mary-Kay Gamel), Hamilton College, and Amherst College (especially Holly Montague and Carlin Barton) for critical listening; and the Lehigh Valley Feminist Research Group for jumping in. To the readers of the manuscript—Sandra Joshel, Molly Myerowitz Levine, and Robert Sutton—I am more indebted than I can say.

This essay was written in memory of Carolyn Hamm.

1. There has been a tremendous boom in the study of Ovidian erotics since this chapter was first published; see the bibliography provided by Keith 2009, and, most pertinently, Salzman-Mitchell 2005. On rape and violence in Ovid, see Johnson 1996 on the rapes of Callisto in the *Metamorphoses* and *Fasti*, and Segal 1998, who points to the violence against male characters, even to the landscape, and to what he sees as a lack of pleasure in sex in the *Metamorphoses*. For a collection of essays using gaze theory to analyze Roman culture, see Fredrick 2002. New work on the rapes in Ovid's *Fasti* has concerned itself with issues of genre and intertextuality rather than with content, a somewhat disturbing return to business as usual; see most recently Hejduk 2011, with bibliography. Feminist work on the *Heroides* has focused on the subjectivity of these *scriptae puellae*, to use Maria Wyke's term; see Fulkerson 2005, Spentzou 2003. On persona theory and invective, see introduction to chapter 2. The groundbreaking essay on rape in the *Metamorphoses* was Curran 1978, which dealt with more of the questions raised here than I gave credit for, and did claim to be responding to the "reaction to Ovid's rape stories on the part of contemporary young women" (241 n. 37). On rape in antiquity, see now also Deacy and Pierce 1997, which however focuses largely on Greek culture; more usefully, see Kathy Gaca's ongoing work on rape, war, and enslavement, esp. 2010-11. In light of Gaca's work, I now think that many of the passages in Ovid discussed in this chapter should be rethought in terms of the rape of girls in war; moreover, the ecphrastic quality of episodes like the rape of the Sabines in the *Ars amatoria* suggests a relation with visual portrayals of soldiers dragging women, best attested in art after Ovid (see, for example, Dillon 2006 on the column of Marcus Aurelius), but surely familiar to Roman viewers from the painted tableaus in triumphal processions—of which the *praeceptor* places his interlocutor and his quarry as spectators, *AA* 1.213-28. This chapter is necessarily much less optimistic about female subjectivity than Levin-Richardson 2013, which does not engage with the critique of the pornographic. See Marshall 2013: 194-96 on graffiti in Thai child brothels.

2. This issue raises interesting questions for the model of subversive discourse defined by James C. Scott (1990; see chapter 3). Although I would argue that, in Roman comedy, enslaved people pushed the boundaries of Scott's "hidden transcript" into a public space (Richlin 2014), the language of comedy is hedged about with defenses, and is definitely not the master's language. See Le Guin 1994 for a parable on the limits of tolerance in the language of muted groups. The limits on women's public speech are still readily visible.

3. All translations are my own.

4. On the association between *murmuro* and slaves' semi-audible speech, see Richlin 2014.

5. From the Preface to *Fables Ancient and Modern* (1700); the Bodleian copy available through Early English Books Online shows on the title page the owner's mark, "Anne Sylvius . . . the gift of my nephew: Hennery Cowes Howard," an indication, if one were needed, of female readership. Dryden's line is quoted, in parts, by Galinsky 1975: 77 n. 79, 132–33; also at Gamel n.d.: n. 17.

6. For other sources on this spring, see Vitruvius 2.8.12 and Pompeius Festus 439L; discussed briefly in Richlin 1992: 288. On the episode in Ovid, see also Nugent 1990, and, for an approach through queer and psychoanalytic theory, Zajko 2009. Romano 2009 deals with mythic elements in Ovid's story in the context of the historical sources on the spring.

7. On rape in New Comedy generally, see Fantham 1975, and now also Pierce 1997. Sharon James (1998) argues that the two Terence plays centered on rape, *Eunuchus* and *Hecyra*, are "designed to disturb, not to amuse." See chapter 6 below on the subject position of the female spectator of Roman stage performance, particularly of comedy.

8. See Loraux 1990, Kampen 1996. Hejduk 2011 points to the parallels between Omphale's cave and Dido's in *Aeneid* 4.

9. The repercussions of teaching the *Metamorphoses* are explored in chapter 2 of Madeleine Kahn's *Why Are We Reading Ovid's Handbook On Rape?* (2005), and, alongside other Latin texts, by Sharon James (2008, 2014) and Sanjaya Thakur (2014). This issue is not new; see Marjorie Woods's study (1996) of the prominence of rape texts, including Ovid's, in medieval anthologies used in boys' schooling.

10. On Lucian's *On Dancing*, see now Lada-Richards 2007, esp. 53, 64–78; on dance in Ovid, Lada-Richards 2013. For women dancers in the later *pantomimus*, see Starks 2008.

11. On rhetoricians and actors, see Gleason 1995, Gunderson 2000, Richlin 1997b, and chapter 6 below. On the male/female subject position of the medieval student of rhetoric, see Woods 1996.

12. On the position of the publishing poet as akin to flirtation, see esp. Fitzgerald 1995: 44–58.

13. For a political reading of the *Metamorphoses*, see Johnson 2008, who revives and expands arguments on the parallels between Ovid and his artists.

14. August 19, 2012: US Representative Todd Akin says, "[Pregnancy as a result of rape is] really rare. If it's a legitimate rape, the female body has ways to try to shut the whole thing down." Akin serves on the House Committee on Science, Space, and Technology. By the time this book is in print, we will know who won the election, Akin or his female opponent, Claire McCaskill.

15. See Stevenson 2005, passim, for the *Heroides* as model, from the time of Heloise. Angela Carter's own work is a major example of ambiguous appropriation: explicitly feminist, extremely violent.

CHAPTER 6

First published as Amy Richlin, "Making Up a Woman: The Face of Roman Gender," in *Off with Her Head!: The Denial of Women's Identity in Myth, Religion, and Culture,* edited by Howard Eilberg-Schwartz and Wendy Doniger. © 1995 by the Regents of the University of California. Reprinted by permission of the University of California Press.

Many thanks to Howard Eilberg-Schwartz for stimulating me to think about this topic; to my former USC colleagues Martha Malamud and Donald McGuire for their helpful reading; to T. Corey Brennan, Cindy Weinstein, Marshall Cohen, and audiences at Bryn Mawr College, Caltech, and the University of Southern California for kind reception; and to Molly Myerowitz Levine for ongoing discussion. Translations throughout are my own, unless otherwise noted.

1. Maria Wyke, in an essay contemporary with this one, discussed the "Roman rhetoric of adornment" as a way of using the "surface of the female body to define the social and sexual identity of woman as non-male, non-citizen, and seductive trap" (1994: 148); see esp. her concluding section, on "the adorned body's dangers" (146–48). On Ovid's *Medicamina faciei femineae*, see now Rimell 2005. On dress and adornment as socially endorsed means by which respectable women constructed their own femininity, see now Shumka 2008; Rita Berg's lavishly illustrated and well-theorized survey of jewelry and adornment (2002) has particularly telling remarks on class. On Roman veiling and attitudes toward women's hair, see my fellow contributors to *Off with Her Head!*, Molly Myerowitz Levine (1995) and Mary Rose D'Angelo (1995), and now Fantham 2008, Hughes 2007. For further helpful thoughts on "the *uses* of natural matter [as] a significant source of meanings," see von Staden 1992; on technologies of the female body, von Staden 1991.

2. In *Flower Drum Song*, music by Richard Rodgers, lyrics by Oscar Hammerstein II, book by Oscar Hammerstein II and Joseph Fields (New York: Farrar, Straus and Cudahy, 1959). The full song and setting appear on pp. 33–37 of that libretto.

3. Butler 1990: 25, 128–41. On gender as makeup, see Bartky 1988: 68–86, esp. 68–71; Heath 1986; Rivière 1986. Particularly useful for teaching is Emily Prager's short story "A Visit from the Footbinder" (1982). On voguing, see Livingston 1990. Of the explosion of writing on gender construction since Butler 1990, see, for example, Bordo 1993; Edut 1998. For an extended argument on cross-dressers as a third category that calls into question sexual categories themselves, see Garber 1992; on transgender identity, see Stryker and Whittle 2006.

4. See Gubar 1987 on Magritte's *Le Viol* (The Rape), and comments in Eilberg-Schwartz 1995.

5. Bartky 1991: 40. For feminist theory on the politics of the female body, see also Bartky 1988, Chapkis 1986.

6. For this model in Greek culture, see Winkler 1990b. For an application of this model to women's ritual masks in Sierra Leone, see Lamp 1985.

7. On *Ars amatoria* 3, see Myerowitz 1985: 41–149, and esp. p. 58 on *AA* 3.113–28.

8. On the *Remedia amoris*, see now Brunelle 2005.

9. On gender-bending and male actors playing female roles in Greek tragedy, see Rabinowitz 1995, 1998, with bibliography; on cross-dressing in Plautus, Gold 1998b.

10. See Nussbaum 1989: 41–48; she argues that Lucretius is not misogynistic but an advocate of equality in love between men and women: "Male illusion forces the female too to live a dishonest life, staging herself as in a theatre, and concealing the stage machinery" (43). See now Gordon 2002 for a full argument on Lucretius as critic of normative Roman virility. For a third-century CE version of the dressing scene, see pseudo-Lucian *Amores* 38–42.

11. Brown 1987: 296. For discussion of fumigation and the control of the female

body, see King 1994: 109. On ancient dung therapy for women, see the excellent discussion in von Staden 1992; chapter 8 below.

12. Skinner 1982a. Though not because Cicero depicts Clodia as a prostitute and Martial associates the use of resin with prostitutes at 12.32.21–22, as Skinner argues; there is no other evidence to restrict resin to prostitutes (Pliny, in fact, says it is used primarily by men, 14.123), and other sorts of women depilated themselves, as in the Martial poems discussed above. On the connection between women's use of cosmetics and the social meaning of the implements themselves, see further Wyke 1994: 143–44, with illustrations, and now Berg 2002, Shumka 2008.

13. On the *mundus muliebris* in the mundane sense, see now Berg 2002: 18–25 on the legal definition, etymology, and range of social meanings, and 51–52 on women's legacies to their daughters; Shumka 2008: 177–78.

14. Carson 1990. On *cultus*, deceit, and women in Hesiod, see discussion in Boyarin 1993: 84–88, 97–106. For a consideration of the semiotics of Pandora in film, see Mulvey 1992.

15. Sarah Pomeroy points out that the word here translated "servant" (*diakonôi*) is gender-neutral in Greek, and could well stand for male as well as female household slaves, although it is usually here taken to refer to a female slave (Pomeroy 1994: 308); surely the feminine participle "forced" (*anagkazomenên*) argues for a female slave here.

16. For the image, with discussion, see Kampen 1982, fig. 15 (also Wyke 1994, fig. 1). For epigraphic evidence on *ornatrices*, see Treggiari 1976. Both are discussed in Wyke 1994: 142. For numerous further examples of dressing scenes in art and text and analysis of the power relations involved, see now Berg 2002: 66–68; for a scene in mosaic, which shows the owner's face reflected in the glass held by her slave woman, see Schade 2009: 220, fig. 3, with discussion and parallels; for funerary reliefs, Shumka 2008; for incisive analysis of Etruscan mirrors, particularly the elaboration of the male gaze in a scene of the Judgment of Paris, see Izzet 2012: 71–77. For another opposition of female owner and *ornatrix*, see James 1997 on Ovid *Amores* 2.7 and 2.8.

17. See Henry 1992, Richlin 1992: 176–77, and now Olson 2002, Flemming 1999: 57, who sees in Roman texts a sharper differentiation than I do between *matrona* and *meretrix*. On the historical shift on this point in the late nineteenth century, see Banner 1983: 42, 133; Peiss 1990.

18. Trans. Edwin A. Quain; text and translation from *Tertullian: Disciplinary, Moral, and Ascetical Works*, trans. Rudolph Arbesmann, Emily Joseph Daly, and Edwin A. Quain, in *The Fathers of the Church*, 40: 117–49 (Washington, DC: Catholic University of America Press). On this work of Tertullian, see Clark 1989; Shumka 2008: 174–77, with Clement *Paedagogus*; Upson-Saia 2011. Tertullian's substitution of virtues for makeup has a long history, and appears—surely ironically—in speeches by prostitutes in Plautus (*Poen.* 301–7, cf. *Most.* 168); compare Alcumena's substitution of virtues for a dowry (*Amph.* 839–42).

19. For female practitioners and their recipes in Pliny, see for example 28.38, 66, 262, 32.135 (all from the female practitioner Salpe); 28.67 ("midwives"); 28.70 ("midwives and prostitutes"). Holt Parker (forthcoming) cites also Cleopatra (not *the* Cleopatra), who wrote a *Cosmetics* (Galen 12.403–5K); also Elephantis (Galen 12.416K); and the sixth-century woman medical writer Metrodora (her sections 1.55–63, 4.19 bis A). See chapter 8 for further discussion of these sources and the debate over their actual female author-

ship (Flemming 2007b; Parker 2012); on the attitude toward cosmetics in Pliny and Celsus, Flemming 2000: 172.

20. On Hellenistic love charms, see Faraone 1992, Johnston 1995b, Winkler 1990b; and now Faraone 2001, with comments on gender and class.

21. For a detailed assessment of the ingredients Ovid lists in the *Medicamina* and their effectiveness in the light of "modern chemical and dermatological knowledge," see Green 1979 (with bibliography). Green's attitude is that Ovid gives serious scientific advice, while Pliny is "one of the worst offenders" among ancient sources "riddled with old wives' tales and outré, if not downright disgusting materials"; Pliny "seems quite incapable of distinguishing between the functional and the spurious, between scientifically based prescriptions and those dictated by the analogies of sympathetic magic"; Ovid is no "rehash of stale superstitions," measures up to "modern scientific criteria," and "will have no truck with this kind of hocus-pocus" (381–83, 391). Green's expert advisers were a chemist and a "cosmetologist." It is my premise that the division between science and magic which Green uses as a criterion is anachronistic for the culture in which Ovid and Pliny lived.

22. So Lloyd 1979: 13; cf. 37–49, on the overlap of medicine and magic; further on Pliny, in Lloyd 1983: 135–49, and chapter 8 below.

23. The preoccupation with the removal of freckles shows up in modern fiction for young women in the Anne of Green Gables books (in *Anne of Avonlea*, first published in 1909, Anne dyes her nose red with carpet dye, mistaking it for a freckle lotion she had "compounded" herself from a recipe in a magazine; in *Anne of Green Gables* [1908], she had dyed her hair green with dye bought from a Jewish peddler). In the 1950s, Beany Malone, in the girls' books by Lenore Mattingly Weber, is always trying a new freckle cream. In both series, the heroines demonstrate a preoccupation with an externally given ideal: Anne looks to romance novels, Beany to advertising.

24. For Roman attitudes toward northern tribes, see Sherwin-White 1967, Balsdon 1979; for a more complex picture, Isaac 2004: 411–39. For the barbarian Other in Athenian ideology, see duBois 1982a, 1982b.

25. On color, see Snowden 1970: 178–79, 193–94, addressed by Haley 1993, both arguing that dark skin is not disparaged in Roman culture. But cf. Plautus *Poenulus* 1112–13, ?1289–91, *Rudens* 420–23, where color is at least an issue, and is connected with African ethnic origin (Ethiopia, Cyrene, Carthage). Comic caricatures of Africans exaggerate facial traits (see Snowden's plates 2, 5, 6, 7, 10, 36; cf. Petronius *Satyrica* 102.15); on the other hand, erotic epigrams sometimes make a point of finding dark and light skin equally attractive. See Isaac 2004: 65, and passim; Starks 2011 on race and erotics in Vandal Africa.

26. On Thracian tattooing, see Jones 1987: 145–46. On barbarians and Amazons, see duBois 1982a: 35.

27. Barbarian women in battle: Caesar *Gallic Wars* 1.51.3; Tacitus *Annals* 4.51.2, 12.30.3, 34.4, *Germania* 7–8, *Histories* 4.18; Plutarch *Marius* 19.

28. For representations of the hairstyles of the Germans in contemporary Roman art, see Anderson 1938, plates 21–23. The alignment between conquered status and exotic appearance shows up in many Roman depictions of northern Europeans—for example, in Anderson's plate 8 (Roman cavalryman riding over man naked except for a light cloak), plate 17 (dejected woman wearing checked tunic and trousers), plate 24 (man wearing checked trousers, no shirt, and a chignon, with his hands bound behind

his back). See now in general Ferris 2000, and Uzzi forthcoming on the eroticization of captives in Roman relief sculpture.

29. For more on Propertius 2.18, and on the interrelationship between gender construction, the exotic, and ornament in Latin love poetry generally, see Fredrick 1992, chapter 3, pp. 52–61; 1997.

30. Sherwin-White, in his commentary (1966: 357), concentrates on what Pliny says about Regulus's "superstition."

31. Modern critics sometimes replicate the perceptions they study; one of the foremost commentators on Roman oratory, A. D. Leeman, calls *actio* "certainly the most amusing department, especially to the northern reader who is not accustomed to the opera-like performances of the mediterranean orator" (1963: 27). On the sexual ambiguity of dancers, see Richlin 1992: 92, 98, 101, and now Corbeill 1997; on actors generally, see Dupont 1985: 95–110; Edwards 1993: 98–136. On *actio* and Asianism, see Bonner 1949: 20–22, 63. On gender and oratory, see now Gleason 1995, Gunderson 2000, Richlin 1997b, Richlin 2011a, with further bibliography.

32. Paulus at *Digest* 4.5.3.1, 4.5.11; Gaius *Institutes* 1.160–62; see Edwards 1993: 63–136, Richlin 1993: 556, Richlin 1999: 193–95.

33. On Roman women and public speech, see Hallett 1989, and now Hallett 2004, Hemelrijk 1999.

34. Edwards 1993: 71; Richlin 1992: 26–29, 53, 69, 82–83, 93–94, 99, 108–09, 123, 128, 132, 148–51, 169, 170.

CHAPTER 7

Printed with permission from the Continuum International Publishing Group, © Karen L. King (ed.), 1997. Originally appeared in *Women and Goddess Traditions in Antiquity and Today*, ed. Karen L. King, pp. 330–74.

I thank Karen L. King and Karen Jo Torjesen for their patience in dealing with the original essay; their encouragement was truly goddess-like. This essay depended on research carried out under a grant from the even more patient National Endowment for the Humanities in 1987–88, for which I am still extremely grateful. Audiences at Haverford College, Princeton University, Rollins College, Texas Tech University, the Huntington Library, Occidental College, and the Annenberg Institute in Philadelphia, as well as at the Goddess Conference at Claremont, made helpful comments; special thanks to Daniel Boyarin, Howard Eilberg-Schwartz, Ross Kraemer, Joseph Russo, Chava Weissler, to Sheryl Conkelton for aid nobly rendered, and most of all to Karen King, again and always.

Translations throughout are my own except as noted.

1. See now Rebecca Langlands' argument that "*Pudicitia* was a personal quality that needed to be displayed to and seen by others" (2006: 37ff.).

2. Since this essay was written, considerable new work has appeared; see Holland 2012 for an incisive overview. On Roman women's religion, see Green 2008, 2010; Holland 2008, Parker 2004 [2007], Schultz 2006, 2007, Spaeth 1996, Takács 2007. On cults of *pudicitia*, see Langlands 2006: 37–77. Beard 1995 revisits her landmark 1980 study of the Vestal Virgins (on whom, see further bibliography in Holland 2012). A panel at the

2008 APA brought together scholars looking to push the field forward by focusing on a gender-integrated approach to Roman religion, and some of the papers were published in a special issue of *Classical World*—most pertinent to this chapter, Dolansky 2011c, Mueller 2011. On Greek women and religion, see now Cole 2004, Connelly 2007, Johnston 1999; Parca and Tzanetou 2007 covers women in religion from Homer to the early Church. Ross Kraemer's overviews in *Her Share of the Blessings* (1992, chapters 5 and 7 on Rome) provide an invaluable orientation and cover far more ground than can this more narrowly focused study; see now her further thoughts (2011). Boëls-Janssen 1993, overlooked in the original essay, provides an extensive overview of evidence on early Rome; see also her earlier essays cited in Hersch 2010.

In general studies, the contributors to Ando 2003 do not consider gender as an element in Roman religion (see volume introduction); writing on priesthoods, Beard 1990 and Gordon 1990a and 1990b have little to say on women in religious office. Jörg Rüpke's biographical dictionary of priests (2007b) devotes its 239 pages to men alone, from Acilius to Zosimus, placing their priesthoods among other public offices they are known to have held. Rüpke's general handbook (2007a) presents a more inclusive picture, something like John Crook's *Law and Life of Rome*, but oddly patchy (see volume introduction for remarks on this book along with Scheid 1992, 2003). As Suzanne Dixon notes (2001: ix), sometimes the lopsidedness of the ancient sources is outdone by later writers; see note 6 below for instances of the erasure, in late antiquity, of women from Roman texts about religion, and compare Holland 2012: 205, 213, on the double removal of women from the record, which she follows Josine Blok in tracing back to the late nineteenth century. An integrated treatment of religion in Roman society has yet to be written; see Chava Weissler below on religion as a "total social system."

In 1994, the most recent handbook on Roman religion (Latte 1967) likewise said very little about women. Latte's index includes a total of two entries under "Frauen" (he notes that "women" were excluded from the cult of Silvanus; and of Hercules). On the experience of slave women in the Matralia, his only comment is: "Sklavinnen waren, wie selbstverständlich, von einem Fest ausgeschlossen, das der legitimen Weiterführung der Familie galt" ("As is obvious, slave women were excluded from a celebration that had to do with the legitimate continuation of the family," 1967: 97–98). Compare the discussion of the Matralia below. Warde Fowler 1916, perhaps in sympathy with the attitudes of the Cambridge ritualists, has much more to say and is especially interested in women's cult as related to the Earth-mother and fertility. Gagé's *Matronalia* (1963) was ahead of its time and, at the time this essay was written, constituted one of the most important studies of Roman women's cult, but naturally was not informed by feminist theory. The index of Ferguson's *Religions of the Roman Empire* (1970) contains no entry under "Women," "Mater Matuta," or "Bona Dea." Work on Roman women considered for the original essay included Brouwer 1989; French 1987; Stehle 1989; Versnel 1992.

3. On the postmodernist ethnographer's dilemma, see Rosaldo 1986; for feminist precursors, critiques, and updates, see Abu-Lughod 1990; Mascia-Lees et al. 1989; and Shapiro 1981. For an overview of this issue from the perspective of ancient history and feminism, see chapter 10 below.

4. Sources referred to below include: the remains of the book *On the Latin Language* by M. Terentius Varro, an upper-class Roman of the first century BCE; Dionysius of Halicarnassus, a Greek rhetorician at Rome whose *Roman Antiquities* began to appear

342 · NOTES TO PAGES 204-7

in 7 BCE; Valerius Maximus, whose collection is familiar from chapter 1; the *Roman Questions* of the Greek biographer and moral philosopher Plutarch (before 120 CE); and Aulus Gellius, whose *Attic Nights*, a collection of brief ruminations on topics of interest, dates to around 180 CE. Ovid's *Fasti*, seen in chapter 5, breaks off at the end of June.

5. See Gordon 1990a: 184–91, esp. 189 n. 29, for another perspective on the intellectual climate that produced books like Verrius's, which he sees as part of a process of "institutionalizing unintelligibility" (189), the information purveyed by these books being mostly "obsolescent" (188). Festus and Verrius seem to have felt this themselves; see Festus 242L. References to Paulus ex Festo herein are to pages in the Teubner text edited by W. M. Lindsay (1913), hence "282L" for "Lindsay, page 282." This text has not been translated into English.

6. For other examples, see: *Manare solem*, 150L vs. 151L (reference to Matuta gone); *Nothum*, 182L vs. 183L; *Pietati*, 228L vs. 229L; *Propius sobrino*, 260L vs. 261L (female kin disappear); *Plebeiae pudicitiae*, 270L vs. 271L; *Praebia*, 276L vs. 265L; *Probrum virginis Vestalis*, 277L (gone in Paulus); *Pudicitiae signum*, 282L vs. 283L; *Praefericulum*, 292L vs. 293L (reference to Ops Consiva gone); *Redimiculum*, 336L (gone in Paulus); *Strittavum*, 414L vs. 415L (female kin disappear); *Salias virgines*, 439L (gone in Paulus); *Tutulum*, 484–86L vs. 485L; Tarpeia's statue, 496L (gone in Paulus). For Paulus importing (male-male) homophobia into an "excerpt," see 284L vs. 285L, *puer quem quis amabat* vs. *puer qui obscene ab aliquo amabatur.*

7. The present study is also limited in its epigraphic scope: I have surveyed all inscriptions from Roman Italy (*CIL* volumes 5, 9, 10, 11, 14) but not from the city of Rome itself (*CIL* 6) or Ostia (*CIL* suppl.), or (for reasons of scale) the enormous remains from Pompeii (*CIL* 4). And I have used only the *CIL*, without searching more recent sources of inscriptions. Compare the sample in Forbis 1990, which uses sources beyond the *CIL* but omits *CIL* 5.

8. Versnel is here using the translation of William Davis Hooper and Harrison Boyd Ash in the Loeb Classical Library edition of *De agri cultura* (Cambridge, MA: Harvard University Press, 1960). Note that Cato also sets limits on what the *vilicus* can do (5.2–3). Religion is not discussed in the often-cited two-part study of rural women by Walter Scheidel (1995, 1996), still the main resource on this topic; he rightly observes that "a very substantial part of all the people who ever inhabited the ancient Mediterranean . . . would have been women living on the land" (1995: 204), and he sets up a good framework, but his study depends to a surprising extent on textual sources. Papyrology and epigraphy still have much to say here.

9. On the meaning of *sacerdos*, see Beard 1990: 43–47.

10. See now Flemming 2007a for a similar overview of this material, arguing against Scheid 1992.

11. On epigraphic evidence for women's participation in public life during the empire, see Dixon 1992, 2001: 73–132; Forbis 1990; MacMullen 1980; Van Bremen 1983, 1996; essays by Dixon, Hallett, and Woodhull in McHardy and Marshall 2004, by Koortbojian and Laird in D'Ambra and Métraux 2006, and numerous essays in Hemelrijk and Woolf 2013; Meyers 2012, for a brief overview of women's patronage; and further bibliography in Mueller 2011: 229–30 n. 8. For priestesses, see Forbis 1990: 500, 501–2; MacMullen 1980: 211–12, 213, 215. Particularly important for understanding women's participation in religious activity is the new work presenting material from Greco-Roman Egypt:

women's papyrus letters (Bagnall and Cribiore 2006—specifically at 382–85, but, as they note [14], passim), along with inscriptions and artifacts (Rowlandson 1998: 62–70 and passim); and, for late antiquity, Wilfong 2002.

12. The old standard Latin dictionary, Lewis and Short (most recent edition 1975), gave no indication of the commonness of the female forms of these titles in the context of religion. The now standard *Oxford Latin Dictionary* gives a fair account of *magistra* but relies on textual instances of *ministra*. For *magistrae* and *ministrae* in the *collegia* of Bona Dea, see Kraemer 1992: 88, following Brouwer 1989: 280–81.

13. *CIL* 10.810, 811, 812, 813; see MacMullen 1980: 209, for a quick description of Eumachia's activities. For illustration of her statue see Fantham et al. 1994: 335, fig. 12.4.

14. Whether a Greek cognomen certainly indicates freed status has been the subject of debate; see Mouritsen 2011: 123ff. for discussion.

15. See now Hughes 2007: 230–32, for discussion of funerary representations of a freedwoman associated with sacrifice and a freedwoman priestess of Isis.

16. On the sevirate, see Gordon 1990b: 205 ("freedmen aping their social superiors"), 208. In Petronius's *Satyrica*, both Trimalchio and his friends Hermeros and Habinnas are *seviri* (30.2, 57.6, 65.5, 71.12). But not all *seviri* were freedmen. On the use of public display by upwardly mobile freed slaves as a status claim, see Berg 2002; Petersen 2006; Roller 2003. This interpretation of freedwomen's representation of themselves as veiled has been challenged by Lisa Hughes (2007).

17. On this inscription, see Brouwer 1989: 116–17, 281. The inscription is only figuratively durable, because it is now lost. Brouwer found a preponderance of freed slaves in the worship and priesthood of Bona Dea across the Roman Empire. This is markedly at odds with the proportions in the overview of women's worship presented here.

18. See Evans 1967: 222–23 on the stem *mandu-*, "probably to be related to the form *mannus* 'a pony,'" and remarks on names in *mann-* including *Mannia*.

19. Priestess groups: *CIL* 5.4458 (one certain and two probable freeborn); 9.3167 (both probable freeborn); 9.5295 (both certain freed); 10.39 (both certain freeborn); 10.5192 (all uncertain freed); 10.6511 with 6518 (two certain freeborn).

20. *CIL* 11.3811, reading *matribus c vir* as "mothers of the *centumviri*." The *centumviri* were judicial magistrates at Rome and in some towns, of which Veii was one (*CIL* 11.3801, 3805).

21. On women's public activities with their male kin, see Forbis 1990: 502–4, and in general Hallett 1989; and now Dolansky 2011a, 2011b, 2011c. Cf. comments on Licinia Flavilla and her husband in the volume introduction.

22. See MacMullen 1980: 211–12; Gordon 1990b: 224–31; and now Mouritsen 2005, with bibliography, and Margaret Laird's essay in D'Ambra and Métraux 2006.

23. See now Holland 2008 on the dedication of a spear, by a probable freed wet-nurse, to Diana at Aricia around 300 BCE, with the interesting suggestion that the spear commemorated her manumission; Holland contrasts the mixed finds at Aricia with the "high concentration of reproductive models" at shrines elsewhere, with sources (2008: 97–98).

24. Women's *taurobolia* and *criobolia* (ram sacrifices) are commemorated in *CIL* 9.1538, 1539, 1541, 1542; 10.1596, 1597, 6075. For a Victorian fantasy of the *taurobolium*, see Walter Pater, *Marius the Epicurean*, chapter 18: "Some jaded women of fashion, especially, found in certain oriental devotions, at once relief for their religiously tearful souls

and an opportunity for personal display. . . . And one morning Marius encountered an extraordinary crimson object, borne in a litter through an excited crowd—the famous courtesan Benedicta, still fresh from the bath of blood, to which she had submitted herself, sitting below the scaffold where the victims provided for that purpose were slaughtered by the priests." This fabrication appropriates the name of Benedicta, attested only in Marcus Aurelius *Meditations* 1.17, where Marcus says he "never touched Benedicta or Theodotus" and gives no other background information, though Pater is not alone in assuming she was a prostitute. The story itself is perhaps Pater's transformation of a nasty tale in the *Historia Augusta* about the empress Faustina bathing in a gladiator's blood (*Vit. Marc.* 19.3–4).

25. On the geographical distribution of the cult of Minerva as a healing goddess, see Sauer 1996, who focuses on Romano-Celtic areas of the empire; "Cabardiacensis" seems to be a Ligurian ethnic identifier, in keeping with the dedicator's home town, possibly related to the tribe of the Cavares in southern France.

26. On the mixed-gender worship of Mater Matuta at both Rome and Satricum, see esp. Smith 2000; for the general phenomenon, brief discussion and bibliography in Holland 2012: 205, 210–11.

27. On motivated ideology, see Langlands 2006. For an argument that [Tibullus] 4.2, on Sulpicia at the Matronalia, was written by Sulpicia the elegist, see the essay by Judith Hallett in Churchill et al. 2002.

28. On Roman women's dress, see Olson 2002, Sebesta and Bonfante 1994, and essays by Fantham, Keith, Olson, and Shumka in Edmondson and Keith 2008. For *vittae* (fillets, or hair ribbons) and *insita* as the symbol of a chaste Roman *matrona*, see Ovid *Ars amatoria* 1.31–32. For satirical advice to avoid covered-up *matronae*, see Horace *Satires* 1.2.31–120. See Hughes 2007 for a trenchant argument on the various meanings freed and free women may have expressed by commemorative portraits that show them wearing a veil.

29. On the removal of the right to be conveyed in a litter as a punishment for upper-class women known to be adulteresses, see McGinn 1998a. On the *carpentum* on coins, see chapter 3.

30. On the powers, duties, and privileges of Roman *matronae*, see Gagé 1963; also Dixon 1988, 2001; Hallett 1984, 1989; Treggiari 1991.

31. Since this essay was written, an enormous body of scholarly work has arisen concerning women in traditional belief systems. See, e.g., Narayan 1997, Narayan and Harding 2000, Heath 2008, and, on women in the Islamic world, see the journal *Hawwa*.

32. On the cultural unease surrounding the Roman ideology of chastity, see Langlands 2006.

33. On class divisions among Roman women, see also Clark 1998, for the tense relations between slave and free women in the life of Monnica, mother of St. Augustine.

34. For a discussion of freed slaves' movement into Roman identity through work, see Joshel 1992b; n. 16 above.

35. Labor historians and anthropologists have mapped and documented tensions between modern-day women employers and women domestic workers. See Gill 1990; Hondagneu-Sotelo 2007, with recent bibliography on global and transnational issues. Differences of language and culture would also often have affected relations between female owners and slaves, many of whom were imported from across the Roman Empire.

36. On girls dedicating their dolls and togas before their first marriage, see Flory 1984: 314; Kraemer 1992: 55; Hersch 2010: 65–68, with sources and discussion; Dolansky 2012: 257-58, 274, with parallels to women's cult. Keith Hopkins' conclusions about the early age of marriage have been much disputed; Scheidel 2007 sums up ongoing arguments and suggests the late teens as more likely, stressing the tenuousness of the evidence.

37. For *pollutus* as meaning "tainted by sexual intercourse," see *OLD* s.v. 2, 4; it is interesting that *any* sexual intercourse counted as ritual pollution for men or women (not reflected in *OLD*), while *pollutus* also means "tainted by *illicit* sexual intercourse": all sex verges on the illicit, even before Christianity, even without asceticism (see now Harper 2013). See Flory 1984 for an excellent overview of the rich array of cults celebrating chastity and "family values" connected with Augustus's religious revival, under the leadership of his wife, Livia; and now Langlands 2006: 360–61, for brief remarks on resistance to this inspiring role model.

38. On slaves' sexual degradation, see Joshel 1992b: 28–32; and in general, see Richlin 1992: 26–31, 58–59, 66–70, and 1984. On Roman rules regarding adultery, see chapter 1 above; Gardner 1986: 127–32.

39. See Versnel 1992: 41 for a brief analysis of this festival in comparison with elements in the Athenian Thesmophoria; Stehle 1989 for an analysis of its symbolic meaning; also Saller 1998: 88–89.

40. See D'Ambra 2007a for a summary of current arguments, particularly by Lora Holland (2008) and Carin Green (2008), that the cult at Aricia included men; also that the procession marched from Aricia to the sanctuary and not from Rome to Aricia. The evidence is certainly slight, but Ovid *Fasti* 3.270 does seem to imply that the torchlight procession (or walk), at least, was for women, and women's religious processions are amply attested as marked actions, for example in Julius Obsequens.

41. Dumézil 1980: 175–209 provides Vedic parallels. The connection between the Matralia and the story of Caecilia Metella is also made by Gagé 1963: 225–43; Hallett 1984: 183–89; and most thoroughly by Bettini 1981: 67–99. For connections between the Matralia and other women's cults, see Flory 1984: 313–14; note especially the close physical proximity of the temple to the site of girls' dedication of their togas.

42. For the similarly exemplary story of Claudia Quinta and the arrival of Magna Mater at Rome, see Langlands 2006: 67–70 and passim; Hersch 2010: 94 connects this story with reports that brides wore the crown of Magna Mater. Compare the dynastic ideology seen in chapter 3.

CHAPTER 8

First published in Hallett, Judith and Marilyn Skinner; *ROMAN SEXUALITIES*. © 1997 Princeton University Press. Reprinted by permission of Princeton University Press.

1. See now King 1998: 132–56 on contraception and male fears of women's control of household fertility as part of a general fear of women poisoners.

2. For this argument on texts ascribed to women writers, see Parker 1992a, Russ 1983: 20–24, Weissler 1998: 9–10. Holt Parker's 2012 rebuttal of Flemming 2007b addresses, at length, the female sources cited in Galen, but not those in Pliny.

3. The idea is reiterated in the Preface starting from the first edition in 1971. Still in print in 2014, this basic women's health book devotes twenty of its twenty-seven chapters to issues directly related to sexuality, including sections on birth control and abortion, pregnancy, childbirth, and menopause. On attacks on *Our Bodies, Ourselves*, see Hunter 1986: 28 (entries for 1977, 1981), citing the Boston Women's Health Book Collective's own "file on backlash." The book appears on the list of the fifty worst books of the century printed in *The Intercollegiate Review* in 1999 (fall 1999, p. 5); one of the consultants for this list was Victor Davis Hanson, co-author, with John Heath, of *Who Killed Homer?* (see chapter 10). *OBOS* was put together in the first place to provide information to women, by women (hence the title), to counter a long tradition of which Pliny's book forms part. The circulation of accurate knowledge about female anatomy remains a political issue.

4. This landscape was radically altered by the appearance of Rebecca Flemming's major study of women and Roman medicine in 2000; for material discussed here, cf. 129–84. Her later argument on the fictive nature of Pliny's female sources (2007a, cf. 2000: 39–42, 134–35) should be read in conjunction with this chapter, along with Holt Parker's response (2012), which still leaves Pliny's women writers on dubious ground. For earlier studies that linked medical theories with their cultural context, see Dean-Jones 1992, on the social function of Hippocratic theories of women's sexual pleasure; King 1994, 1995, 1998 on women in Hippocratic medicine generally; and, on Rome, French 1986 (on Pliny and Soranus), Gourevitch 1984 (largely a sourcebook), Hanson 1990: 330–31 (Soranus and Roman culture), Pinault 1992 (Soranus and the rise of asceticism). See now Kapparis 2002 on abortion; King 2011, correcting the record on Galen, midwives, and the putative practice of therapeutic masturbation.

5. For discussion of Pliny on doctors, see Nutton 1986, who argues that Pliny overstates his case.

6. On the remarkable life of the elder Pliny, see the younger Pliny, *Letters* 3.5, 6.16. The extant fragment of Suetonius's *Life* of the elder Pliny may conveniently be found in Rolfe 1997: 2.480. On Pliny's thought generally, see Beagon 1992; French and Greenaway 1986; and now Evans 1999 (Pliny's monstrous ethnography, with consideration of gender), with Murphy 2004 (Pliny's encyclopedia as imperialist knowledge). Vons 2000 asks the very good question of what all these women are doing in Pliny's book in the first place, with particular reference to the topics of gynecology and cosmetics, arguing that Pliny's moral system determines his anatomy of nature, as luxury corrupts both women and the state (cf. earlier treatment of Pliny's moralizing in Citroni Marchetti 1991). Aude Doody (2010), in step with recent trends, treats Pliny's book as a literary creation, thus problematizing the idea that knowledge of Pliny's world can be had from his text; she writes a lively history of "using" versus "reading" Pliny.

7. So also French 1986: 69; Flemming 2000: 59, 129, 183 on Pliny as writing for the use of the elite *paterfamilias* (although I cannot agree that his actual audience was so narrow). The text of Metrodora is in preparation in an edition by Holt Parker; see Flemming 2007b: 257, 276–78, for a skeptical analysis of Metrodora's authorial status, in a considered overview of what "authorial status" means in medical texts generally. Compare Parker 2012, esp. 380: "Feminine names are subject to a level of disbelief that is never visited on male names."

8. G. E. R. Lloyd points out (1983: 137) that, when Pliny says *invenio* ("I find"), he often seems to be reporting on what he has read in the course of his research, rather than

on his personal experience. My imaginings about Pliny, then—the toga as well as the brassiere—must be taken more for their symbolic value than as an idea of Pliny's actual practice.

9. This question has not been the primary focus of work on Greek and Roman gynecology, due to the nature of the extant sources, which are written from the doctor's point of view; Flemming comments only that we cannot know how women would have read these texts or lived with the underlying ideology (2000: 184, 373–74), and she believes that they were "excluded . . . from the ranks of those to whom this knowledge was presented, who were intended to act on it" (181–82; but cf. 168, 171). For discussion, see Hanson 1990: 309–11 (with bibliography); Hanson 1992: 47–48; Dean-Jones 1994: 26–40, 247–48; King 1994: 105, 109–10, 1995; and especially Lloyd 1983: 62–79 (on the Hippocratic corpus), 181–82 (on Soranus). Riddle 1992 treats the history of birth control as a slow erosion of women's rights over their bodies; see esp. 165, and compare Kapparis 2002: 91–132.

10. For women's-culture approaches to antiquity, see Hallett 1989, Skinner 1993, Zweig 1993. Buckley and Gottlieb (1988: 12–15, 31–34) argue vigorously for women's agency within menstrual symbolic systems. See further in chapter 10.

11. The major discussion is at 28.70–86, and note the apology at 28.87. Book 28 begins a long section on remedies from animals, which goes on through Book 30. Remedies from human beings begin at 28.4, and include a discussion of verbal charms and superstition and of the uses of human saliva (28.35–39), human hair (28.41) and other body parts (28.41–44), gymnasium scrapings (28.50–52), and urine (28.65–69). The discussion of the female body follows, and from there Pliny proceeds directly to elephants, apologizing for telling the reader so many disgusting things. The discussion in Book 7 comes in a book-long general discussion of the properties of human beings, and commences with the statement *solum autem animal menstruale mulier est* ("but woman is the only menstrual animal," 7.63). Then Pliny labels the *profluvium* as *monstrificum*, and gives a concise but full list of its properties. On the section in Book 28, see Flemming 2007b: 271–72.

12. Buckley and Gottlieb 1988: 7–8, 35–38; they are among the few writers to discuss Pliny in this context, basing their remarks on a 1916 article in the *Johns Hopkins Hospital Bulletin*. They point to Pliny as an example of a positive attitude toward menstrual blood; as will be seen, this is only half the picture. For brief discussion, see Dean-Jones 1994: 248–49.

13. Thus also Cohen 1991: 287. Susan Guettel Cole discusses various conditions in which women were considered polluting in Greek sanctuaries, among them postchildbirth and miscarriage, and during menstruation (1992, esp. 109–111); cf. Dean-Jones 1994: 223–53 on Greek attitudes toward menstruation. On the application of biblical law on menstruation in ancient and medieval Judaism and in ancient Christianity, see Cohen 1991. On menstruation in rabbinic literature, see Wegner 1991: 77–78, 82. On the increase in misogyny in attitudes toward menstruation from the classical rabbinic period through the Middle Ages, see Boyarin 1993: 90–97. On the meaning of menstruation in the medieval church, see Bynum 1987: 122–23 (holy women's bodies as sources of food), 211, 214, 239. On early Islamic attitudes, see Wegner 1991: 91 n. 28. For a women's-culture approach (early modern Jewish women's own prayers, including those concerning menstrual purity), see Weissler 1991, esp. 165–66.

14. Flemming devotes considerable attention to this cosmological question, in par-

ticular to Pliny's project in the *Natural History* of showing the world as designed for men like himself (2000: 77, 131, 149, 157); in general, she posits a fundamental system of ineluctable gender asymmetry which medical writers helped to maintain (361-66), despite "a climate of flourishing cosmological and rhetorical competition" (368). Even I see more room for women's agency than this, at least in Pliny, and Flemming's own account could well support it.

15. Perhaps this prohibition reflects a pre-Islamic Arab system underlying beliefs like those examined in Delaney 1988.

16. Other powers are listed at *HN* 28.80-86: menses act as a solvent on bitumen (also at 7.65); menses cure gout, and menstruating women can cure by their touch scrofula, parotid tumors, abscesses, erysipelas, boils, and runny eyes. Lais and Salpe, as well as a male source, recommend menstrual blood for the relief of the bites of rabid dogs and of fevers. The *obstetrix* Sotira recommends relief of fevers and epilepsy by smearing the soles of the patient's feet with menstrual blood. Icatidas *medicus* says fevers are ended by intercourse when the menses are just beginning. A menstrual cloth can counteract the effects of rabies, due to the fact that rabies is caused by dogs tasting menstrual blood. The blood is also good for ulcers of draught animals, women's headaches, and protecting the house from the arts of the Magi. Cf. Serenus Sammonicus *Liber medicinalis* 12.163, who recommends the *obscenos rores* ("obscene dew") of a virgin as a cure for pains in the ears.

17. See also Richlin 1992: 67-69, 115-16; on menstrual blood, 169, 281-82. Cf. von Staden 1991: 277-80, on Celsus's analogies between womb and anus, labia and wound.

18. On the meaning of the eye in Roman culture, see Barton 1993: 91-98. On the salvific meaning of breast milk and suckling in ancient Italy, see Corbeill 2004: 100-05.

19. On the female body in symbolic systems, see Buckley and Gottlieb 1988: 26-30, including discussion of Mary Douglas and the concept of pollution; Eilberg-Schwartz 1995. On the meaning of the upper body vs. the lower body, see Bakhtin 1984. For Bakhtinian analysis of the female body in Roman invective, see Gold 1998a; Miller 1998 distinguishes the sterile body of Roman satire from the fecund body of Bakhtinian carnival.

20. This model, which in the 1990s gained great popular currency, judging by students' comments in class, is well exemplified by Ehrenreich and English 1973. The model is somewhat contemptuously dismissed by Monica Green (1989), who produces a set of sophisticated and historically informed questions concerning women practitioners and women patients in the medieval and early modern periods. For a brief but compelling account of the historical vicissitudes of knowledge of herbal contraceptives, see Riddle et al. 1994.

21. Contrast the interpretation in Flemming 2000: 183, who takes Pliny's evaluative comments as his "efforts to prevent women from using the world around them to exert their own control over childbearing," and the treatments as "described not for [women's] benefit, but for the benefit of their men" (181). But meaning is made at the point of reception, and there is no sign that women were precluded from reading Pliny, or his sources, for themselves.

22. Sources are given at 20.19, 20.28, 20.32, 20.34, 20.227, 26.99, 28.256.

23. For some examples of texts featuring women who use aphrodisiacs on their husbands, see Faraone 1992: 98-99; add Juvenal 6.133-35, 610-26.

24. For men: *HN* 8.91, 10.182, 22.20, 26.96, 26.98, 27.65, 28.99, 30.141 (four), 30.143. For women: 20.227, 22.87, 28.101, 28.106, 28.256, 30.143 (two).

25. A cure of the Magi. The text says lust is stimulated *ad sexus suos*, "for their own sex"; this does not make much sense with the following clause, and so Mayhoff conjectured *ab sexu suo*, "away from their own sex," that is, the wife lures the husband away from his desire for other males.

26. The aphrodisiacs in Pliny and Metrodora would then not support the argument made by Christopher Faraone for Greek aphrodisiacs (1992): that they tend to aim at controlling the ardent male but arousing the passive female. For more on the gender politics of Greek love-charms, see Winkler 1990b: 90–91, 95–98, and now Faraone 2001.

27. On abortion and contraception in antiquity, see Riddle 1992; Riddle, Estes, and Russell 1994; and now Kapparis 2002, for a thorough treatment of abortion, with an overview of methods at 7–31. On abortion in Pliny, see Beagon 1992: 216–20; Flemming 2000: 161–69.

28. On emmenagogues, see Riddle 1992: 27 and passim; Flemming 2000: 161–63.

29. The incentives, in light of chapter 1, are of course equally obvious; for discussion of women's motives for abortion in relation to their marital status, see now Kapparis 2002: 91–132.

30. For problems with what is knowable from Pliny's citations of female authorities, see introduction to this chapter, on Flemming 2007b and Parker 2012.

31. On abortion in the Hippocratic Oath, see Riddle 1992: 7–10, and now Kapparis 2002: 53–90.

32. *Digest* 48.8.8 (Ulpian): "If it is proved that a woman has brought force to bear on her own innards in order to avoid giving birth, the provincial governor should send her into exile"; *Digest* 48.19.38.5 (Paulus): "Those who make potions, either to cause abortions or love, even if they do not do this fraudulently, still, because it sets a bad example, those of the lower class are sent to the mines, while those of the upper class are relegated to an island and fined part of their property. But if they have caused a woman or man to die, they must undergo the supreme punishment." Gardner (1986: 158–59) is of the opinion that the drugs, rather than abortion itself, are what is prohibited here. See further, on the availability and legality of abortion, Riddle 1992: 7–10, 109–12; Gamel 1989, on abortion in Ovid's poetry; Hopkins 1965, on Roman contraception generally. Kapparis 2002 now provides a fully historicized discussion of Roman abortion law, which he sees as primarily concerned with married women and places in the context of a change in attitudes that begins in the early empire and first shows up in law under Septimius Severus.

33. For conception aids, see *HN* 20.51; 22.83; 23.53; 27.63; 28.52; 28.249; 28.253; 28.255; 30.131. Serenus Sammonicus devotes section 32 of the *Liber medicinalis* to *conceptio et partus*; he cites Lucretius as his authority on the mysteries of conception, and goes on to offer several cures for barrenness (32.607–14).

34. See *HN* 20.263, 25.97, 28.248, 28.254, 30.123.

35. Gender-selective infanticide in antiquity has been the subject of extensive scholarly debate. See discussion in Golden 1992: 235–30, with bibliography; also Boswell 1990: 54 n. 2 (bibliography), 100–103 (primary sources), and in general 53–137; Dixon 1988; Riddle 1992; and now Kapparis 2002: 154–62. For reports on the practice of female infanticide in India and on women's statements about the practice, see Dahlburg 1994, and

now Bhatnagar et al. 2005, Miller 1997, Patel 2007 (on sex-selective abortion), Perianayagam and Goli 2012.

36. On the care of young children by mothers and/or *nutrices* see Dixon 1988, esp.
120–33; Joshel 1986 deals with the subject position of the slave wet-nurse.

37. The persistence of some of these amulets is remarkable. Christiane Klapisch-
Zuber (1985: 149–50, with plate 7.1) publishes a detail of a sixteenth-century Italian
painting showing a coral branch and a wolf's tooth amulet for teething, and discusses
the wet-nurse's responsibility for the child's health (also at 105 n. 25, on protection from
the *maldocchio*). She notes that "dog teeth or wolf teeth" figure in the lists of possessions
of four fifteenth-century male babies (149 n. 64). An eighteenth-century American representation of the "coral and bells" may be seen in the Henry Huntington Library and
Art Gallery, San Marino, CA, in the "Portrait of Mrs. Elijah Boardman and Her Son William Whiting Boardman," by Ralph Earl (c. 1798), displayed alongside a contemporary
English specimen.

38. See Soren 1999; Soren, Fenton, and Birkby 1999. Soren found puppy bones in
with the baby bones; as well as recommending frogs for siriasis (above), Pliny recommends puppies applied to the painful parts of patients for the transfer of the illness, after
which the puppies are to be buried (30.42, 30.64).

39. On the phallus and the evil eye, see Barton 1993: 95–98, 171, 189 and fig. 2; Dunbabin and Dickie 1983; Johns 1982, color plate 10 (phallic amulets), 68 fig. 51 (phalluses
sawing an eye in half), and in general 62–75. Pliny does not discuss the amulet worn
by girls, the *lunula*, the shape of which might have evoked the moon that governed the
female body; for images and discussion, see D'Ambra 2007b: 124–25, 127. Cf. Plautus
Epidicus 640.

40. For other examples of apotropaic spitting in Roman belief, see *HN* 28.35–39; attested as early as Plautus, *Asinaria* 39–43. The nurse as protector of the baby can be
attested in Greek culture at least as early as the seventh century BCE (*Homeric Hymn to
Demeter* 228–30). Johnston 1995a provides full treatment and excellent analysis of ancient Greek and Near Eastern beliefs about harm to babies from demons and witchcraft,
including discussion of apotropaic spitting. For similar beliefs in Jewish folk culture, see
Trachtenberg 1961 [1939]: 121 ("threefold expectoration"), 159, 162; my own grandmother,
born in Lithuania in the late nineteenth century, practiced the same behavior described
by Pliny, and I must admit that it persists at least into my own generation, in the form of
the words "pooh, pooh" or "tu tu tu."

41. For a reading that connects this passage directly with the Matralia, see Smith
2000: 151–52.

CHAPTER 9

Reprinted, by kind permission of the editors, from *Essays in Honor of Gordon Williams:
Twenty-five Years at Yale*, ed. Elizabeth Tylawsky and Charles Weiss (New Haven, CT:
Henry Schwab, 2001), pp. 229–46.

Many thanks to the editors for asking me to contribute to *Essays in Honor of Gordon Williams*, and for their patience. This paper was first delivered at a conference at
St. Hugh's College, Oxford, at the invitation of Patricia Salzman-Mitchell and the late

and much mourned Don Fowler, in March 1999; and then to friends old and new at the New York Classical Club, in June 1999. I am grateful to John Bodel, Judith Hallett, Peter O'Neill, and John Pollini for help and inspiration, and especially to Marilyn Skinner for putting me up to it. Thanks to Christopher Johanson for the image of the Amiternum relief. I write now in loving memory of Gordon Williams; I like to remember him as he was at the Brown conference on women in 1986, laughing as he raised a glass with me.

1. Evidently this appeal might have surprised Fraenkel more than Williams, who repeated a description of Fraenkel's seminar at Oxford as "a circle of rabbits addressed by a stoat" (quoted in Horsfall 1990: 63). Fraenkel was no feminist, but I like to imagine that he might have found something to interest him in the descent line through Williams' essay to this one. Certainly it fits with his interest in Roman customs and rituals, which, like Fraenkel's seminars, were co-ed. Engagement with Williams 1958 can now be traced forward to Hersch 2010, who argues with him (201–2), and was herself born in 1968.

2. See now also Loraux 2002 and Connelly 2007; the important ancient/modern comparative study by Gail Holst-Warhaft (1992) was not included in the original reading for this essay. Suter 2008 usefully covers ancient lament traditions including the Near East, but, still, of the eleven essays in the collection, seven focus on Greece and two on Rome.

3. On the *praefica* and Roman laments for the dead see also Habinek 2005: 233–56. Nicholas Horsfall's indispensable account of Roman folk culture does not discuss the *praefica* and, despite his wish for more women among the Romans he discusses (2003 [1996]: 28), there is no entry for "Women" in his index and indeed very few women in his text, except for generic groups of plebeians (but see 2003 [1996]: 43 on nurses and lullabies). He makes the crucial point that song, in Rome, constituted a major element in popular education and cultural transmission, an idea in turn central to Habinek's book. Schultz 2006, although covering a broad array of women's rituals, does not deal with mourning or the *praefica*. On women's mourning dress, see now Olson 2004–5 [2007]; on Roman funerals, Johanson 2011; on family participation in the Parentalia, Dolansky 2011b, Šterbenc Erker 2011: 55–56; on women's belief in the *manes*, Mueller 2011 (textual and epigraphic evidence); on mourning in the *Aeneid*, Sharrock 2011.

4. *mulieres genas ne radunto, neve lessum funeris ergo habento*; Warmington weirdly translates *lessum* as "chorus of 'Alas!'" (1961: 499). Cicero preserves this line in *De legibus* (2.59), in the famous section where he reminisces about learning the XII Tables in his boyhood *ut carmen necessarium*. He first says that the law limits funeral dress and music and *tollit lamentationem*, "does away with lamentation"; then he quotes this fragment; then he cites two early authorities who are unclear about what *lessum* means, one suggesting that it is some sort of funeral garment, one that it is *lugubrem eiulationem, ut vox ipsa significat* ("a mournful wailing, as the word itself shows"); hence Warmington's "alas" for *lessum*? But see below on the sound of Roman mourning.)

5. On death pollution, see, e.g., Bodel 2000; Šterbenc Erker 2011: 52–54.

6. *sed, postquam condidit urna / supremos cineres, miserando concita voltu, / effusas laniata comas contusaque pectus / verberibus crebris cineresque ingesta sepulchri, / non aliter placitura viro, sic maesta profatur.* On the lament in Lucan, see now Keith 2008.

7. On the gendered meanings of covering the hair in Roman culture, see also D'Angelo 1995, and now Fantham 2008, bibliography in Hughes 2007; on veiling generally in the ancient Greek world, see Llewellyn-Jones 2003.

8. Compare Mary Russo (1986: 213): "There is a phrase that still resonates from childhood. Who says it? The mother's voice—not my own mother's, perhaps, but the voice of an aunt, an older sister, or the mother of a friend. It is a harsh, matronizing phrase, and it is directed toward the behavior of other women: 'She [the other woman] is making a spectacle of herself.' Making a spectacle out of oneself seemed a specifically feminine danger. The danger was of an exposure." On the downside of spectacle for the specularized, see also chapter 5, and Fredrick 1995, 2002, Duncan 2006: 124–59; on the funeral as display, Bodel 1999.

9. *naenia est <carmen, quod in funere laudandi> gratia can<tatur ad tibiam> . . . <Afra>nius in Materte<ris>. . . <Plautus [Truc. 213]:> "huic hom<ini amanti mea era apud nos naeniam> dixit domi"; quod ei voci sim<ilior querimonia flentium> sit. quidam aiunt nae<niae ductum nomen ab extre>mi intestini voca<bulo>.* On the *nenia*, see now Dutsch 2008, who works toward reconstructing its poetic form; Šterbenc Erker 2011: 51.

10. Upper arms, Ovid *M.* 9.637; head and thighs, Cic. *Aer. al. Mil.* fr. 8; breast and cheeks, Sen. *Cons. ad Marc.* 6.1.2, Juv. 13.127–28; breasts, Apul. *Met.* 5.7.

11. On the exposed breasts, see now esp. Corbeill 2004: 85–105; he explains mourning rituals as making an analogy between death and childbirth.

12. Catherine Conybeare remarked to me on this point that the composite picture of the mourning woman—disheveled and dressed in black—has become the ideal of the Christian woman by the time of Jerome; compare Williams's comments on the adaptation of the ideal of the *univira* by Tertullian: "a most interesting and successful attempt to borrow for Christianity the pagan ideal of the single eternal marriage" (1958: 24).

13. Cf. *Rhet. Her.* 3.26, which advises that orators should look like neither actors (*histriones*) nor construction workers (*operarii*). Peter O'Neill has argued (2003) that the term *circulus* is used by elite Roman writers to refer especially to groups of lower-class Romans of whom they disapprove.

14. Judith Sebesta (1997: 529–31) takes the point of this story to be that the *pullati* are wearing Greek clothing, but surely there is a class issue at stake; as if Ronald Reagan had seen a crowd in jeans, and wished to see instead a crowd in jacket and tie.

15. Smith 1975 on Petronius *Sat.* 38.14 cites Val. Max. 5.2.10: *hunc tam contemptum gregem.* For a collection of sources, see Mayor 1979 [1877] on Juv. 3.32, 12.122; on Libitina and funeral workers, Bodel 2000; and, on the *praefica*, Van Sickle 1987: 45–47; Flower 1996: 116; Šterbenc Erker 2011: 48–49, 51; n. 3 above.

16. *inter/ Iliadum lacrimas, ut primos edere planctus / Cassandra inciperet scissaque Polyxena palla.* On *goêteia*, see Johnston 1999: 82–125; she demonstrates that this word denotes a practice of communication with the dead limited largely to male practitioners, and discusses the relation between *goos* and *goêteia* as stemming from the use of song (112).

17. *praeficae dicuntur mulieres ad lamentandum mortuum conductae, quae dant ceteris modum plangendi, quasi in hoc ipsum praefectae. Naevius [Fr. com. 129]: "haec quidem mehercle, opinor, praefica est, quae sic mortuum conlaudat."*

18. Varro is here commenting on Plautus *Truc.* 495, *sine virtute argutum civem mihi habeam pro praefica.* He explains: *<praefica>, ut Aurelius scribit, mulier ab luco quae conduceretur quae ante domum mortui laudis eius caneret. hoc factitatum Aristoteles scribit in libro qui <in>scribitur Nomima barbarika, quibus testimonium est, quod <in> Freto est Naevii: haec quidem hercle, opinor, praefica est: nam mortuum collaudat. Claudius scribit: quae praeficeretur ancillis, quemadmodum lamentarentur, praefica est dicta. utrumque ostendit a praefectione praeficam dictam.*

19. *vos philosophi mera estis, ut M. Cato ait, "mortualia"; glosaria namque conligitis et lexidia, res taetras et inanes et frivolas, tamquam mulierum voces praeficarum.*

20. This relief is discussed by Jocelyn Toynbee (1971: 46–47; cf. also 44–45 on the tomb of the Haterii); Harriet Flower (1996: 98–99, with further sources in nn. 37–39); John Bodel (1999: 266–67); and Anthony Corbeill (2004: 95–96, with comparable images). Compare the relief of a woman's laying-out from the tomb of the Haterii; both Darja Šterbenc Erker (2011: 45–46) and Maureen Carroll (2011: 130, with fig. 8.2) discuss the three women who sit, hunched forward, at the head of the bier, wearing the *pilleus* that marks the freed slave.

CHAPTER 10

Reprinted with permission of Taylor & Francis Informa UK Ltd, from *Feminist Theory and the Classics*, ed. Nancy Sorkin Rabinowitz and Amy Richlin (New York: Routledge, 1993), pp. 272–303. Permission conveyed through Copyright Clearance Center, Inc.

Many thanks to Nancy Sorkin Rabinowitz and Sandra Joshel for yet more hours on the telephone. Lon Grabowski continues to give me hope for life after patriarchy, always nice for a natural pessimist. In memory of S. V. R., with abiding love.

1. In the early 1990s, the problem at hand was that classicists were still largely distancing themselves from the theory wars over essentialism and social constructionism. Now that those wars are themselves over (Richlin 2013b) and the resistance to theory within the field has retired, we find ourselves fighting for our very survival; the institution of the REF (Research Excellence Framework, previously the Research Assessment Exercise) in the UK has mandated the documentation of "impact outcomes" even in the humanities.

2. For this long-standing issue in historiography, see Jenkins 1997, Partner and Foot 2013, Skinner 1985.

3. See, for example, Butler 1992, where totalizing theory is identified with racism and blamed for the Gulf War; in general, see the overview presented in the introduction to Butler and Scott 1992, where "poststructuralism" itself is seen as a totalizing term. For comments on such claims, see Rose 1993. The division I outline is usually historicized as one between the Western humanistic tradition and postmodernism; for a lucid introduction, see Nicholson 1990: 1–4. The anti-grand-theory ideas of postmodernism can be found in the past, for example in the sophistic tradition of the fifth century BCE. For a model comparing various theories of writing history with big-bang versus steady-state theories, see Golden 1992. On the intersection of nineteenth-century schools of historiography with the study of women in antiquity, see the analysis by Josine Blok (1987), who covers the idealism/positivism opposition of which Optimism/Pessimism is a version. For a helpful overview that includes the middle ground of standpoint epistemology, see Harding 1987. The Optimist/Pessimist debate continues in the wrestling match between historicism and formalism within classical literary studies, the topic of a 2008 Princeton conference organized by the historian of slavery Rose MacLean; see Hinds 2010, with illustrations from Roman women's writing.

4. Collections that take a primarily positive attitude toward Foucault or postmodernism include Diamond and Quinby 1988; Weed 1989. Nicholson 1990 includes two especially critical pieces, by Nancy Hartsock and Susan Bordo, to which add Modleski

1991; Pierce 1991. For a critique of postmodernism in anthropology, see Mascia-Lees et al. 1989. Butler 1992 is framed as a response to such critiques, which she refers to as "the chant of antipostmodernism" (Butler 1992: 17); for the volume in which her essay appears, the editors indeed posed a useful set of questions critical of postmodernism for the contributors to respond to (Butler and Scott 1992: xiv–xvii). Contrast hooks 1990: 23–33. For an introduction to the state of feminist theory around 1990, see Hirsch and Keller 1990. For an update with a good selection bridging early Second Wave to current global feminisms, see McCann and Kim 2010.

5. The case of Aminata Diop of Mali prompted the French Commission for Appeals of Refugees to become "the first judicial body to recognize genital mutilation as a form of persecution under the terms of the Geneva Convention," reported in *Ms.* (January/ February 1992), 17. Since 1992, debate and documentation have burgeoned, as the World Health Organization works to eliminate the practice; note that these efforts are still regarded as imperialist by some feminists within practicing cultures. See esp. work by Martha Nussbaum (1999 and ongoing) on ethics and gender in an international framework.

6. The bibliography in postcolonial studies is (still) enormous and growing, now augmented by work in transnational feminism. A good place to start might still be Michelle Cliff's two essays in Rick Simonson and Scott Walker, eds., *The Graywolf Annual Five: Multi-Cultural Literacy* (St. Paul: Graywolf Press, 1988: 57–81). Cliff's training in the classical tradition makes these pieces especially resonant for a classicist. For a sampling of the field to date, see Ashcroft et al. 2006; Aggleton et al. 2012 has an introduction by Henrietta Moore, whose work is discussed below.

7. On Foucault, see bibliography in Diamond and Quinby 1988; and now, for an overview of the field of the history of sexuality, Richlin 2013b; on Foucault and the history of ancient sexuality, Skinner 1996.

8. See Tong 1989: 47–51, 274–78, for a brief discussion and introductory bibliography.

9. The relation between Classics and anthropology is an old one; see Culham 1986: 9–14, Finley 1975, Humphreys 1978, Redfield 1991. Page duBois (1988: 24–29) gives an eloquent account of the implications of the ethnographer's dilemma for her own work on Greek culture.

10. On the politics of theoretical language, see hooks 1990: 23–33; hooks 1992: 80, "It is evident that one of the uses of theory in academic locations is in the production of an intellectual class hierarchy where the only work deemed theoretical is abstract, jargonistic, difficult to read, and containing obscure references. It is easy to imagine different locations, spaces outside academic exchange, where such theory would not only be seen as useless, but would be seen as politically nonprogressive." For a striking case in point, see Alcoff 1991, which, ironically, is actually *about* the problem of achieving dialogue among all kinds of women.

11. For an overview of the field, see Morgan 2006, esp. 49–202 on issues related to grand theory and postmodernism. This useful collection of excerpts also provides a list of where the full essays may be found.

12. Lerner was the keynote speaker for the first "Feminism and Classics" conference, held in Cincinnati in 1992.

13. Note the use here of "Antigone," a character in a play by Sophocles, apparently

to mean "an ancient woman." Feminist work on antiquity has tried to disentangle such constructs; see Rabinowitz 1993. See discussion in the volume introduction of a similar statement by Afsaneh Najmabadi (2006) which comes to a conclusion opposite to Harding's: that this divide is unbridgeable.

14. "On Not Knowing Greek," *A Common Reader: First Series*, p. 23 (New York: Harcourt Brace Jovanovich, 1984 [1925]).

15. See Spelman 1988: 2, 37–56, on women, slave women, and Aristotle. Sarah Pomeroy made this issue a focus of the introduction to her 1975 social history. Studies from the 1980s that look at women across lines of civil status and age include Dixon 1988, Gardner 1986, Kampen 1982. For a critique of the disclaimer tactic, see Lugones 1991: 38; Alcoff 1981: 25; and, in general, Spelman 1988.

16. Ironically, one contributor (Izzet 2012; see chapter 6) ends a trenchant discussion of Etruscan mirrors by stating that she has debunked the previous golden-age view of feminists working on Etruscan women: "the analysis of the mirror here provides a more nuanced feminist reading, a revisionist rebuttal that does not romanticize the seductive visual materials. To say that Etruscan women were just as subject to the male gaze . . . as other women in antiquity is to stop treating them as exotic 'other.' If it is to get anywhere near understanding the complexity of ancient Etruscan lives, the study of Etruscan women now needs to move beyond the doctrines of second-wave feminism" (2012: 77). As this chapter documents, Second Wave feminism hardly held a uniformly optimistic view of the past. In critical arguments, it is hard to dodge Mr. Ramsay's ghost.

17. This comparison first appeared on p. 74 of an expanded version of "Hijacking the Palladion" (Richlin 1990), published in *Gender & History* (4.1 [1992]: 70–83); see also Richlin 1992: xx, in a discussion closely related to "The Ethnographer's Dilemma," and written at the same time.

18. On *Against Neaira*, see Keuls 1993: 156–58; and now Gilhuly 2009: 29–57, with bibliography.

19. On the Theocritus poem, see Gutzwiller and Michelini 1991: 75, and n. 45; and now Skinner 2001.

20. Unsurprisingly, most new work on nonelite women comes from archaeologists and art historians, who treat women in the context of family, work, and home. See, e.g., Carroll 2011; D'Ambra 2007b; D'Ambra and Métraux 2006; Hemelrijk and Woolf 2013; Levin-Richardson 2013; Petersen 2006: 184–226; Shumka 2008: 185; and materials discussed in Dixon 2001: 89–132, Hughes 2007, Roller 2003.

21. The Loeb series provides a large and convenient collection of nonliterary papyri in translation (*Select Papyri*, vols. 1–2, ed. A. S. Hunt and C. C. Edgar [Cambridge and London: Harvard/Heinemann, 1932, 1934]). On infanticide, vol. 1, no. 105; on the bath attendant, vol. 2, no. 269; the shopping list, vol. 1, no. 186. For work on women in papyri and women's papyri, see Bagnall and Cribiore 2006, Rowlandson 1998, Wilfong 2002, and, for a brief introduction, Parca 2012. Bagnall and Cribiore deal with the question of handwriting and provide images of the letters, as well as translations and notes.

22. For discussion of the co-optive force of the academy on feminists, see Bordo 1990; Schüssler Fiorenza 1989: 6. For the postmodern *reductio ad artem*, see di Leonardo 1991a: 22–23, on Hayden White, and, in anthropology, on what she calls the "ethnography-as-text school," who "focus . . . away from the ethnographic experience, onto an analysis of ethnographic texts themselves."

Bibliography

§▲

OLD = *Oxford Latin Dictionary*

Abu-Lughod, Lila. 1990. "Can There Be a Feminist Ethnography?" *Women and Performance* 5: 7–27.

Adams, J. N. 1982. *The Latin Sexual Vocabulary*. Baltimore: Johns Hopkins University Press.

Adams, J. N. 2003. *Bilingualism and the Latin Language*. Cambridge: Cambridge University Press.

Aggleton, Peter, Paul Boyce, Henrietta L. Moore, and Richard Parker, eds. 2012. *Understanding Global Sexualities: New Frontiers*. Abingdon, UK: Routledge.

Ahl, Frederick. 1984. "The Art of Safe Criticism in Greece and Rome." *American Journal of Philology* 105: 174–208.

Alcoff, Linda. 1991. "The Problem of Speaking for Others." *Cultural Critique* 12: 5–32.

Alexiou, Margaret. 1974. *The Ritual Lament in Greek Tradition*. Cambridge: Cambridge University Press.

Allen, Pauline. 1992. "Contemporary Portrayals of the Byzantine Empress Theodora (A.D. 527–548)." In *Stereotypes of Women in Power: Historical Perspectives and Revisionist Views*, ed. Barbara Garlick, Suzanne Dixon, and Pauline Allen, 93–103. New York: Greenwood Press.

Allison, Penelope. 2004. *Pompeian Households: An Analysis of the Material Culture*. Cotsen Institute of Archaeology, UCLA, Monograph 42. Los Angeles: Cotsen Institute of Archaeology.

Ancona, Ronnie, and Ellen Greene, eds. 2005. *Gendered Dynamics in Latin Love Poetry*. Baltimore: Johns Hopkins University Press.

Andersen, Margaret L. 1997. *Thinking About Women: Sociological Perspectives on Sex and Gender*. 4th ed. Boston: Allyn and Bacon.

Anderson, J. G. C. 1938. *Cornelii Taciti de Origine et Situ Germanorum*. Oxford: Clarendon Press.

Anderson, W. S. 1964. "Roman Satirists and Literary Criticism." *Bucknell Review* 12.3: 106–13. Reprinted in *Latin Verse Satire: An Anthology and Reader*, ed. Paul Allen Miller, London: Routledge, 2005, 363–68.

Ando, Clifford. 2001. "The Palladium and the Pentateuch: Towards a Sacred Topography of the Later Roman Empire." *Phoenix* 55: 369–410.

Ando, Clifford, ed. 2003. *Roman Religion*. Edinburgh: Edinburgh University Press.

Apte, Mahadev L. 1985. *Humor and Laughter: An Anthropological Approach*. Ithaca, NY: Cornell University Press.

Ardener, Edwin. 1975. "Belief and the Problem of Women." In *Perceiving Women*, edited by Shirley Ardener: 1–27. London: J. M. Dent & Sons.

Arthurs, Jane. 1999. "Revolting Women: The Body in Comic Performance." In *Women's Bodies: Discipline and Transgression*, ed. Jane Arthurs and Jean Grimshaw, 137–64. London: Cassell.

Ashcroft, Bill, Gareth Griffiths, and Helen Tiffin, eds. 2006. *The Post-Colonial Studies Reader*. 2nd ed. Abingdon, UK: Routledge.

Astin, A. E. 1967. *Scipio Aemilianus*. Oxford: Clarendon Press.

Atkinson, Clarissa W. 1985. "'Your Servant, My Mother': The Figure of Saint Monica in the Ideology of Christian Motherhood." In *Immaculate and Powerful: The Female Sacred Image and Social Reality*, ed. Clarissa W. Atkinson, Constance H. Buchanan, and Margaret R. Miles, 139–72. Boston: Beacon Press.

Auerbach, Nina. 1982. *Woman and the Demon*. Boston: Harvard University Press.

Austin, M. M. 1981. *The Hellenistic World from Alexander to the Roman Conquest*. Cambridge: Cambridge University Press.

Bagnall, Roger S., and Raffaella Cribiore. 2006. *Women's Letters from Ancient Egypt 300 BC—AD 800*. Ann Arbor: University of Michigan Press.

Bakhtin, Mikhail. 1984. *Rabelais and His World*. Trans. Hélène Iswolsky. Bloomington: Indiana University Press.

Ballantyne, Tony, and Antoinette Burton, eds. 2005. *Bodies in Contact: Rethinking Colonial Encounters in World History*. Durham, NC: Duke University Press.

Balsdon, J. P. V. D. 1962. *Roman Women: Their History and Habits*. London: Bodley Head. Rev. ed. Westport, CT: Greenwood Press, 1975.

Balsdon, J. P. V. D. 1979. *Romans and Aliens*. Chapel Hill: University of North Carolina Press.

Banner, Lois W. 1983. *American Beauty*. Chicago: University of Chicago Press.

Barber, C. L. 1959. *Shakespeare's Festive Comedy*. Princeton: Princeton University Press.

Barnes, T. D. 1981. "Julia's Child." *Phoenix* 35: 362–63.

Barry, Kathleen. 1979. *Female Sexual Slavery*. New York: New York University Press.

Bartky, Sandra Lee. 1988. "Foucault, Femininity, and the Modernization of Patriarchal Power." In *Feminism and Foucault*, ed. Irene Diamond and Lee Quinby, 61–86. Boston: Northeastern University Press.

Bartky, Sandra Lee. 1991. *Femininity and Domination*. New York: Routledge.

Barton, Carlin A. 1993. *Sorrows of the Ancient Romans: The Gladiator and the Monster*. Princeton: Princeton University Press.

Bashar, Nazife. 1984. "Women and the Concept of Change in History." In *Pre-Industrial*

Women: Interdisciplinary Perspectives, ed. Suzanne Dixon and Theresa Munford, 43–50. Canberra: Australian National University Printery.

Bauman, Richard A. 1992. *Women and Politics in Ancient Rome*. London: Routledge.

Beagon, Mary. 1992. *Roman Nature: The Thought of Pliny the Elder*. Oxford: Oxford University Press.

Beard, Mary. 1980. "The Sexual Status of Vestal Virgins." *Journal of Roman Studies* 70: 12–27.

Beard, Mary. 1990. "Priesthood in the Roman Republic." In *Pagan Priests*, ed. Mary Beard and John North, 17–48. Ithaca: Cornell University Press.

Beard, Mary. 1995. "Re-reading (Vestal) Virginity." In *Women in Antiquity: New Assessments*, ed. Richard Hawley and Barbara Levick, 166–77. New York: Routledge.

Beneke, Tim. 1982. *Men on Rape*. New York: St. Martin's.

Benjamin, Walter. 1968. *Illuminations*. Ed. Hannah Arendt. Trans. Harry Zohn. New York: Schocken.

Bennett, Judith M. 2000. "'Lesbian-Like' and the Social History of Lesbianism." *Journal of the History of Sexuality* 9: 1–24.

Bennett, Judith M. 2006. *History Matters: Patriarchy and the Challenge of Feminism*. Philadelphia: University of Pennsylvania Press.

Berg, Rita. 2002. "Wearing Wealth: *Mundus Muliebris* and *Ornatus* as Status Markers for Women in Imperial Rome." In *Women, Wealth and Power in the Roman Empire*, ed. Päivi Setälä, 15–73. Acta Instituti Romani Finlandiae, vol. 25. Rome: Institutum Romanum Finlandiae.

Berger, John. 1972. *Ways of Seeing*. Harmondsworth, UK: Penguin.

Bergren, Ann L. T. 1983. "Language and the Female in Early Greek Thought." *Arethusa* 16: 69–96.

Bettini, Maurizio. 1991. *Anthropology and Roman Culture: Kinship, Time, Images of the Soul*. Trans. John Van Sickle. Baltimore: Johns Hopkins University Press.

Bhatnagar, Rashmi Dube, Renu Dube, and Reena Dube. 2005. *Female Infanticide in India: A Feminist Cultural History*. Albany: State University of New York Press.

Bindman, David. 2002. *Ape to Apollo: Aesthetics and the Idea of Race in the Eighteenth Century*. London: Reaktion.

Bloch, Herbert. 1963. "The Pagan Revival in the West at the End of the Fourth Century." In *The Conflict between Paganism and Christianity in the Fourth Century*, ed. Arnaldo Momigliano, 193–218. Oxford: Clarendon Press.

Blok, Josine. 1987. "Sexual Asymmetry: A Historiographical Essay." In *Sexual Asymmetry: Studies in Ancient Society*, ed. Josine Blok and Peter Mason, 1–57. Amsterdam: J. C. Gieben.

Blundell, Sue. 2004. "Gender: The Virtues and Vices of the Mainstream." http://www.stoa.org/diotima/essays/fc04/Blundell.html.

Boatwright, Mary T., Daniel J. Gargola, Noel Lenski, and Richard A. Talbert. 2011. *The Romans: From Village to Empire: A History of Rome from Earliest Times to the End of the Roman Empire*. Oxford: Oxford University Press.

Bodel, John. 1999. "Death on Display: Looking at Roman Funerals." In *The Art of Ancient Spectacle*, ed. Bettina Bergmann and Christine Kondoleon, 259–82. Washington, DC: National Gallery of Art, Center for the Advanced Studies in Visual Arts, *Studies in the History of Art* 56.

Bodel, John. 2000. "Dealing with the Dead: Undertakers, Executioners, and Potter's Fields in Ancient Rome." In *Death and Disease in the Ancient City*, ed. Eireann Marshall and Valerie M. Hope, 128–51. London: Routledge.

Boëls-Janssen, Nicole. 1993. *La vie religieuse des matrones dans la Rome archaïque*. Rome: École française de Rome.

Bond, R. P. 1979. "Anti-feminism in Juvenal and Cato." In *Studies in Latin Literature and Roman History*, vol. 1, ed. Carl Deroux, 418–47. Brussels: Latomus.

Bonner, S. F. 1949. *Roman Declamation in the Late Republic and Early Empire*. Berkeley: University of California Press.

Bonner, S. F. 1977. *Education in Ancient Rome*. Berkeley: University of California Press.

Bordo, Susan. 1990. "Feminism, Postmodernism, and Gender-Scepticism." In *Feminism/Postmodernism*, ed. Linda J. Nicholson, 133–56. New York: Routledge.

Bordo, Susan. 1993. *Unbearable Weight: Feminism, Western Culture, and the Body*. Berkeley: University of California Press.

Boris, Eileen, and Nupur Chaudhuri, eds. 1999. *Voices of Women Historians*. Bloomington: Indiana University Press.

Boston Women's Health Book Collective. 2012. *Our Bodies, Ourselves*. New York: Simon & Schuster.

Boswell, John. 1990. *The Kindness of Strangers*. New York: Vintage.

Bowman, Alan K., and J. David Thomas. 1987. "New Texts from Vindolanda." *Britannia* 18: 125–42.

Boyarin, Daniel. 1993. *Carnal Israel: Reading Sex in Talmudic Culture*. Berkeley: University of California Press.

Boyle, A. J., ed. 1990. *The Imperial Muse: Ramus Essays on Roman Literature of the Empire: Flavian Epicist to Claudian*. Bendigo, Australia: Aureal Publications.

Bradley, Keith R. 1991. *Discovering the Roman Family*. New York and Oxford: Oxford University Press.

Bradley, Keith R. 2012. *Apuleius and Antonine Rome*. Toronto: University of Toronto Press.

Brandes, Stanley. 1981. "Like Wounded Stags: Male Sexual Ideology in an Andalusian Town." In *Sexual Meanings*, ed. Sherry B. Ortner and Harriet Whitehead, 216–39. Cambridge: Cambridge University Press.

Braund, Susanna H. 1992. "Juvenal—Misogynist or Misogamist?" *JRS* 82: 71–86.

Breglia, Laura. 1968. *Roman Imperial Coins: Their Art and Technique*. Trans. Peter Green. New York: Praeger.

Brockdorff, H. 1977. "*Lex Julia*." In *En kvindes chancer i oldtiden*, ed. H. Salskov Roberts, 118–80. *Opuscula Graecolatina* 13. Copenhagen: Museum Tusculanum.

Brooten, Bernadette J. 1996. *Love Between Women: Early Christian Responses to Female Homoeroticism*. Chicago: University of Chicago Press.

Brooten, Bernadette J., ed. 2010. *Beyond Slavery: Overcoming Its Religious and Sexual Legacies*. New York: Palgrave Macmillan.

Brouwer, H. H. J. 1989. *Bona Dea: The Sources and a Description of the Cult*. Leiden: E. J. Brill.

Brown, Peter. 1988. *The Body and Society: Men, Women and Sexual Renunciation in Early Christianity*. New York: Columbia University Press.

Brown, P[eter] R. L. 1961. "Aspects of the Christianization of the Roman Aristocracy." *Journal of Roman Studies* 51: 1–11.

Brown, Robert D. 1987. *Lucretius on Love and Sex*. Leiden: E. J. Brill.

Brown, Shelby. 1992. "Death as Decoration: Scenes from the Arena on Roman Domestic Mosaics." In *Pornography and Representation in Greece and Rome*, ed. Amy Richlin, 180–211. New York: Oxford University Press.

Brown, Shelby. 1993. "Feminist Research in Archaeology: What Does It Mean? Why Is It Taking So Long?" In *Feminist Theory and the Classics*, ed. Nancy Sorkin Rabinowitz and Amy Richlin, 238–71. New York: Routledge.

Browning, Robert. 1983. In *The Cambridge History of Classical Literature*, vol. 2, part 5: *The Later Principate*, ed. E. J. Kenney. Cambridge: Cambridge University Press.

Brubaker, Leslie. 2004. "Sex, Lies and Textuality: The *Secret History* of Prokopios and the Rhetoric of Gender in Sixth-Century Byzantium." In *Gender in the Early Medieval World*, ed. Leslie Brubaker and Julia M. H. Smith, 83–101. Cambridge: Cambridge University Press.

Brunelle, Christopher. 2005. "Ovid's Satirical Remedies." In *Gendered Dynamics in Latin Love Poetry*, ed. Ronnie Ancona and Ellen Greene, 141–58. Baltimore: Johns Hopkins University Press.

Brunt, P. A. 1971. *Italian Manpower 225 B.C. to A.D. 14*. Oxford: Oxford University Press.

Bryson, Norman. 1986. "Two Narratives of Rape in the Visual Arts: Lucretia and the Sabine Women." In *Rape*, ed. Sylvana Tomaselli and Roy Porter, 152–73. Oxford: Blackwell.

Buchheit, Vinzenz. 1962. *Studien zum* Corpus Priapeorum. Munich: Beck.

Buckley, Thomas, and Alma Gottlieb. 1988. "A Critical Appraisal of Theories of Menstrual Symbolism." In *Blood Magic: The Anthropology of Menstruation*, ed. Thomas Buckley and Alma Gottlieb, 3–50. Berkeley: University of California Press.

Bumiller, Kristin. 2008. *In an Abusive State: How Neoliberalism Appropriated the Feminist Movement against Sexual Violence*. Durham, NC: Duke University Press.

Butler, Judith. 1990. *Gender Trouble: Feminism and the Subversion of Identity*. New York: Routledge.

Butler, Judith. 1992. "Contingent Foundations: Feminism and the Question of 'Postmodernism.'" In *Feminists Theorize the Political*, ed. Judith Butler and Joan Scott, 3–21. New York: Routledge.

Butler, Judith, and Joan Scott, eds. 1992. *Feminists Theorize the Political*. New York: Routledge.

Butrica, James P. L. 2006. "Epigrammata Bobiensia 36." *Rheinisches Museum* 149: 310–49.

Bynum, Caroline Walker. 1987. *Holy Feast and Holy Fast*. Berkeley: University of California Press.

Cahoon, Leslie. 1985. "A Program for Betrayal: Ovidian *Nequitia* in *Amores* 1.1, 2.1 and 3.1." *Helios* 12: 29–39.

Cahoon, Leslie. 1988. "The Bed as Battlefield: Erotic Conquest and Military Metaphor in Ovid's *Amores*." *TAPA* 118: 298–307.

Caldwell, Lauren. 2007. "*Nuptiarum Sollemnia*? Girls' Transition to Marriage in the Roman Jurists." In *Finding Persephone: Women's Rituals in the Ancient Mediterranean*, ed. Maryline Parca and Angeliki Tzanetou, 209–27. Bloomington: Indiana University Press.

Cameron, Alan. 1966. "The Date and Identity of Macrobius." *Journal of Roman Studies* 56: 25–38.

Cameron, Alan. 1967. "Macrobius, Avienus, and Avianus." *Classical Quarterly* n.s. 17: 385–99.

Cameron, Alan. 1970. *Claudian: Poetry and Propaganda at the Court of Honorius.* Oxford: Oxford University Press.

Cameron, Alan. 1980. "Crinagoras and the Elder Julia: *AP* 6.345." *Liverpool Classical Monthly* 5, 6, 129–30.

Cameron, Alan. 2011. *The Last Pagans of Rome.* Oxford: Oxford University Press.

Cameron, Averil, and Amélie Kuhrt, eds., 1983. *Images of Women in Antiquity.* Detroit: Wayne State University Press.

Cantor, Joanne R. 1976. "What Is Funny to Whom? The Role of Gender." *Journal of Communications* 26: 164–72.

Caraveli, Anna. 1986. "The Bitter Wounding: The Lament as Social Protest in Rural Greece." In *Gender and Power in Rural Greece*, ed. Jill Dubisch, 169–94. Princeton: Princeton University Press.

Carney, Elizabeth. 1988. "*Reginae* in the *Aeneid*." *Athenaeum* n.s. 66: 427–45.

Carroll, Maureen. 2011. "'The Mourning Was Very Good': Liberation and Liberality in Roman Funerary Commemoration." In *Memory and Mourning: Studies on Roman Death*, ed. Valerie M. Hope and Janet Huskinson, 126–49. Oxford: Oxbow Books.

Carson, Anne. 1990. "Putting Her in Her Place: Woman, Dirt, and Desire." In *Before Sexuality: The Construction of Erotic Experience in the Ancient Greek World*, ed. David M. Halperin, John J. Winkler, and Froma I. Zeitlin, 135–69. Princeton: Princeton University Press.

Carter, Angela. 1978. *The Sadeian Woman and the Ideology of Pornography.* New York: Harper & Row.

Chapkis, Wendy. 1986. *Beauty Secrets: Women and the Politics of Appearance.* Boston: South End Press.

Chapman, Anthony J., and Nicholas J. Gadfield. 1976. "Is Sexual Humour Sexist?" *Journal of Communications* 26: 141–53.

Chibnall, Marjorie. 1975. "Pliny's *Natural History* and the Middle Ages." In *Empire and Aftermath: Silver Latin II*, ed. T. A. Dorey, 57–78. London: Routledge & Kegan Paul.

Christenson, David, ed. 2000. *Plautus* Amphitruo. Cambridge: Cambridge University Press.

Churchill, Laurie J., Phyllis R. Brown, and Jane E. Jeffrey, eds. 2002. *Women Writing Latin.* Vol. 1: *Women Writing Latin in Roman Antiquity, Late Antiquity, and the Early Christian Era.* New York: Routledge.

Citroni Marchetti, Sandra. 1991. *Plinio il Vecchio e la tradizione del moralismo romano.* Pisa: Giardini.

Clancy-Smith, Julia. 2006. "The Intimate, the Familial, and the Local in Transnational Histories of Gender." *Journal of Women's History* 18: 174–83.

Clark, Anna. 1996. "Anne Lister's Construction of Lesbian Identity." *Journal of the History of Sexuality* 7: 23–50.

Clark, Elizabeth A. 1989. "Devil's Gateway and Bride of Christ: Women in the Early Christian World." In *Women and a New Academy*, ed. Jean F. O'Barr, 81–102. Madison: University of Wisconsin Press.

Clark, Patricia. 1998. "Women, Slaves, and the Hierarchies of Domestic Violence: The Family of St. Augustine." In *Women and Slaves in Greco-Roman Culture: Differential Equations*, ed. Sandra R. Joshel and Sheila Murnaghan, 109–29. London: Routledge.

Clarke, John R. 2003. *Art in the Lives of Ordinary Romans: Visual Representation and Non-elite Viewers in Italy, 100 B.C.—A.D. 315*. Berkeley: University of California Press.

Cleve, Robert L. 1988. "Some Male Relatives of the Severan Women." *Historia* 37: 196–206.

Cohen, Shaye J. D. 1991. "Menstruants and the Sacred in Judaism and Christianity." In *Women's History and Ancient History*, ed. Sarah B. Pomeroy, 273–99. Chapel Hill: University of North Carolina Press.

Cole, Susan Guettel. 1992. *"Gunaiki ou Themis*: Gender Difference in the Greek *Leges Sacrae." Helios* 19.1–2: 104–22.

Cole, Susan Guettel. 2004. *Landscapes, Gender, and Ritual Space: The Ancient Greek Experience*. Berkeley: University of California Press.

Coleman, Kathleen. 1990. "Fatal Charades: Roman Executions Staged as Mythological Enactments." *Journal of Roman Studies* 80: 44–73.

Colwin, Laurie. 1982. "A Girl Skating." In *The Lone Pilgrim*, 55–73. New York: Washington Square Press.

Connelly, Joan Breton. 2007. *Portrait of a Priestess: Women and Ritual in Ancient Greece*. Princeton: Princeton University Press.

Cooper, Kate. 2007. "'Only Virgins Can Give Birth to Christ': The Virgin Mary and the Problem of Female Authority in Late Antiquity." In *Virginity Revisited: Configurations of the Unpossessed Body*, ed. Bonnie MacLachlan and Judith Fletcher, 100–15. Toronto: University of Toronto Press.

Corbeill, Anthony. 1997. "Dining Deviants in Roman Political Invective." In *Roman Sexualities*, ed. Judith P. Hallett and Marilyn B. Skinner, 99–128. Princeton: Princeton University Press.

Corbeill, Anthony. 2004. *Nature Embodied: Gesture in Ancient Rome*. Princeton: Princeton University Press.

Corbett, Percy Ellwood. 1930. *The Roman Law of Marriage*. Oxford: Clarendon Press.

Corrington, Gail P. 1986. "The 'Divine Woman'? Propaganda and the Power of Chastity in the New Testament Apocrypha." *Helios* 13: 151–62.

Courtney, E. 1980. *A Commentary on the Satires of Juvenal*. London: The Athlone Press.

Culham, Phyllis. 1982. "The *Lex Oppia." Latomus* 41: 786–93.

Culham, Phyllis. 1986. "Ten Years after Pomeroy: Studies of the Image and Reality of Women in Antiquity." *Helios* n.s. 13.2: 9–30.

Culham, Phyllis. 1990. "Decentering the Text: The Case of Ovid." *Helios* 17: 161–70.

Curran, Leo C. 1978. "Rape and Rape Victims in the *Metamorphoses." Arethusa* 11: 213–41.

Dahlburg, John-Thor. 1994. "The Fight to Save India's Baby Girls." *Los Angeles Times*, 22 Feb., pp. A1, A14.

Daly, Mary. 1978. *Gyn/Ecology: The Metaethics of Radical Feminism*. Boston: Beacon Press.

D'Ambra, Eve. 1993. *Private Lives, Imperial Virtues: The Frieze of the Forum Transitorium in Rome*. Princeton: Princeton University Press.

D'Ambra, Eve. 1996. "The Calculus of Venus: Nude Portraits of Roman Matrons." In *Sexuality in Ancient Art*, ed. Natalie Boymel Kampen, 219–32. Cambridge: Cambridge University Press.

D'Ambra, Eve. 2007a. "Maidens and Manhood in the Worship of Diana at Nemi." In

Finding Persephone: Women's Rituals in the Ancient Mediterranean, ed. Maryline Parca and Angeliki Tzanetou, 228–51. Bloomington: Indiana University Press.

D'Ambra, Eve. 2007b. *Roman Women*. Cambridge: Cambridge University Press.

D'Ambra, Eve, and Guy P. R. Métraux, eds. 2006. *The Art of Citizens, Soldiers and Freedmen in the Roman World*. Oxford: Archaeopress.

D'Angelo, Mary Rose. 1995. "Veils, Virgins, and the Tongues of Men and Angels: Women's Heads in Early Christianity." In *Off with Her Head! The Denial of Women's Identity in Myth, Religion, and Culture*, ed. Howard Eilberg-Schwartz and Wendy Doniger, 131–64. Berkeley: University of California Press.

Darnton, Robert. 1984. *The Great Cat Massacre*. New York: Basic Books.

Daube, David. 1972. "The *lex Julia* Concerning Adultery." *Irish Jurist* 7: 373–80.

Davis, Natalie Zemon. 1975a. *Society and Culture in Early Modern France*. Stanford: Stanford University Press.

Davis, Natalie Zemon. 1975b. "Women on Top." In *Society and Culture in Early Modern France*, 124–51. Stanford: Stanford University Press.

Deacy, Susan, and Karen F. Pierce, eds. 1997. *Rape in Antiquity: Sexual Violence in the Greek and Roman Worlds*. London: Classical Press of Wales/Duckworth.

Dean-Jones, Lesley. 1992. "The Politics of Pleasure: Female Sexual Appetite in the Hippocratic Corpus." *Helios* 19.1–2: 72–91.

Dean-Jones, Lesley. 1994. *Women's Bodies in Classical Greek Science*. Oxford: Oxford University Press.

Delaney, Carol. 1988. "Mortal Flow: Menstruation in Turkish Village Society." In *Blood Magic*, ed. Thomas Buckley and Alma Gottlieb, 75–93. Berkeley: University of California Press.

De Lauretis, Teresa. 1984. *Alice Doesn't*. Bloomington: Indiana University Press.

De Lauretis, Teresa. 1987. *Technologies of Gender*. Bloomington: Indiana University Press.

De Lauretis, Teresa. 1990. "Upping the Anti (sic) in Feminist Theory." In *Conflicts in Feminism*, ed. Marianne Hirsch and Evelyn Fox Keller, 255–70. New York: Routledge.

Dettmer, Helena. 1989. "Catullus 13: A Nose Is a Nose Is a Nose." *Syllecta Classica* 1: 75–85.

Diamond, Irene, and Lee Quinby, eds. 1988. *Feminism & Foucault*. Boston: Northeastern University Press.

Di Leonardo, Micaela. 1991a. "Introduction: Gender, Culture and Political Economy: Feminist Anthropology in Historical Perspective." In *Gender at the Crossroads of Knowledge*, ed. Micaela di Leonardo, 1–48. Berkeley: University of California Press.

Di Leonardo, Micaela, ed. 1991b. *Gender at the Crossroads of Knowledge*. Berkeley: University of California Press.

Dillon, Matthew, and Lynda Garland. 2005. *Ancient Rome: From the Early Republic to the Assassination of Julius Caesar*. Abingdon: Routledge.

Dillon, Sheila. 2006. "Women on the Columns of Trajan and Marcus Aurelius and the Visual Language of Roman Victory." In *Representations of War in Ancient Rome*, ed. Sheila Dillon and Katherine E. Welch, 244–71. Cambridge, UK: Cambridge University Press.

Dixon, Suzanne. 1982. "Women and Rape in Roman Law." *Kønsroller, parforhold og sam-*

livsformer: arbejdsnotat nr. 3. Center for Samfundsvidenskabelig Kvindeforskning (Women's Research Center in Social Science), Copenhagen. Revised in Dixon 2001, 45–55.

Dixon, Suzanne. 1988. *The Roman Mother*. Norman: Oklahoma University Press.

Dixon, Suzanne. 1992. "A Woman of Substance: Iunia Libertas of Ostia." *Helios* 19: 162–74.

Dixon, Suzanne. 2001. *Reading Roman Women: Sources, Genres, and Real Life*. London: Duckworth.

Dixon, Suzanne. 2007. *Cornelia, Mother of the Gracchi*. London: Routledge.

Dixon, Suzanne, and Theresa Munford, eds. 1984. *Pre-Industrial Women: Interdisciplinary Perspectives*. Canberra: Australian National University.

Dolansky, Fanny. 2011a. "Celebrating the Saturnalia: Religious Ritual and Domestic Life." In *A Companion to Families in the Greek and Roman Worlds*, ed. Beryl Rawson, 488–503. Chichester, UK: Wiley-Blackwell.

Dolansky, Fanny. 2011b. "Honouring the Family Dead on the Parentalia: Ceremony, Spectacle, and Memory." *Phoenix* 65.1–2: 125–57.

Dolansky, Fanny. 2011c. "Reconsidering the Matronalia and Women's Rites." *Classical World* 104: 191–209.

Dolansky, Fanny. 2012. "Playing with Gender: Girls, Dolls, and Adult Ideals in the Roman World." *Classical Antiquity* 31: 256–92.

Donaldson, Ian. 1982. *The Rapes of Lucretia: A Myth and Its Transformations*. Oxford: Oxford University Press.

Doody, Aude. 2010. *Pliny's Encyclopedia: The Reception of the* Natural History. Cambridge: Cambridge University Press.

Dryden, John. 1700. *Fables Ancient and Modern; Translated into Verse, from Homer, Ovid, Boccace, & Chaucer: with Original Poems*. London: Jacob Tonson.

Dubisch, Jill, ed. 1986. *Gender and Power in Rural Greece*. Princeton: Princeton University Press.

DuBois, Page. 1982a. *Centaurs and Amazons: Women and the Prehistory of the Great Chain of Being*. Ann Arbor: University of Michigan Press.

DuBois, Page. 1982b. "On the Invention of Hierarchy." *Arethusa* 15: 203–20.

DuBois, Page. 1988. *Sowing the Body: Psychoanalysis and Ancient Representations of Women*. Chicago: University of Chicago Press.

DuBois, Page. 1995. *Sappho Is Burning*. Chicago: University of Chicago Press.

DuBois, Page. 2001. *Trojan Horses: Saving the Classics from Conservatives*. New York: New York University Press.

DuBois, Page. 2003. *Slaves and Other Objects*. Chicago: University of Chicago Press.

DuBois, Page. 2010. *Out of Athens: The New Ancient Greeks*. Cambridge, MA: Harvard University Press.

Du Boulay, Juliet. 1986. "Women—Images of Their Nature and Destiny in Rural Greece." In *Gender and Power in Rural Greece*, ed. Jill Dubisch, 138–68. Princeton: Princeton University Press.

Dumézil, Georges. 1980. *Camillus*. Berkeley: University of California Press.

Dunbabin, Katherine M. D., and M. W. Dickie. 1983. "*Invidia rumpantur pectora*: The Iconography of Phthonos/Invidia in Graeco-Roman Art." *Jahrbuch für Antike und Christentum* 26: 7–37.

Duncan, Anne. 2006. *Performance and Identity in the Classical World*. Cambridge: Cambridge University Press.

Dupont, Florence. 1985. *L'acteur-roi, ou, Le théâtre dans la Rome antique*. Paris: Société d'Edition "Les belles lettres."

Dutsch, Dorota. 2008. "*Nenia*: Gender, Genre, and Lament in Ancient Rome." In *Lament: Studies in the Ancient Mediterranean and Beyond*, ed. Ann Suter, 258–79. Oxford: Oxford University Press.

Dutsch, Dorota M. 2009. *Feminine Discourse in Roman Comedy: On Echoes and Voices*. Oxford: Oxford University Press.

Echols, Alice. 1983. "The New Feminism of Yin and Yang." In *Powers of Desire*, ed. Ann Snitow, Christine Stansell, and Sharon Thompson, 439–59. New York: Monthly Review Press.

Echols, Alice. 1989. *Daring to Be Bad: Radical Feminism in America 1967–1975*. Minneapolis: University of Minnesota Press.

Eco, Umberto. 1984. "Frames of Comic 'Freedom.'" In *Carnival!*, ed. Thomas A. Sebeok, 1–9. Berlin: Mouton.

Edmondson, Jonathan, and Alison Keith, eds. 2008. *Roman Dress and the Fabrics of Roman Culture*. Toronto: University of Toronto Press.

Edut, Ophira, ed. 1998. *Adiós, Barbie: Young Women Write about Body Image and Identity*. Seattle: Seal Press.

Edwards, Catharine. 1993. *The Politics of Immorality in Ancient Rome*. Cambridge: Cambridge University Press.

Edwards, Catharine. 1997. "Unspeakable Professions: Actors, Gladiators, Prostitutes, and Pimps." In *Roman Sexualities*, ed. Judith P. Hallett and Marilyn Skinner, 66–95. New York: Oxford University Press.

Ehrenreich, Barbara, and Deirdre English. 1973. *Witches, Midwives, and Nurses: A History of Women Healers*. New York: The Feminist Press.

Eilberg-Schwartz, Howard. 1995. "Introduction: The Spectacle of the Female Head." In *Off with Her Head! The Denial of Women's Identity in Myth, Religion, and Culture*, ed. Howard Eilberg-Schwartz and Wendy Doniger, 1–13. Berkeley: University of California Press.

Eller, Cynthia. 2000. *The Myth of Matriarchal Prehistory: Why an Invented Past Won't Give Women a Future*. Boston: Beacon Press.

Ember, Carol R. 1978. "Men's Fear of Sex with Women: A Cross-Culture Study." *Sex Roles* 4: 657–78.

Evans, D. Ellis. 1967. *Gaulish Personal Names: A Study of Some Continental Celtic Formations*. Oxford: Clarendon Press.

Evans, Rhiannon. 1999. "Ethnography's Freak Show: The Grotesques at the Edges of the Roman Earth." *Ramus* 28: 54–73.

Evans Grubbs, Judith. 1993. "Marriage More Shameful than Adultery: Slave-Mistress Relationships, 'Mixed Marriages', and Late Roman Law." *Phoenix* 47: 125–54.

Evans Grubbs, Judith. 2002. *Women and the Law in the Roman Empire: A Sourcebook on Marriage, Divorce and Widowhood*. London: Routledge.

Fantham, Elaine. 1975. "Sex, Status and Survival in Hellenistic Athens: A Study of Women in New Comedy." *Phoenix* 29: 44–74.

Fantham, Elaine. 1983. "Sexual Comedy in Ovid's *Fasti*: Sources and Motivation." *HSCP* 87: 185–216.

Fantham, Elaine. 1991. "*Stuprum*: Public Attitudes and Penalties for Sexual Offences in Republican Rome." *Échos du monde classique / Classical Views* 35, n.s. 10: 267–91.

Fantham, Elaine. 2006. *Julia Augusti, The Emperor's Daughter*. London: Routledge.

Fantham, Elaine. 2008. "Covering the Head at Rome: Ritual and Gender." In *Roman Dress and the Fabrics of Roman Culture*, ed. Jonathan Edmondson and Alison Keith, 158–71. Toronto: University of Toronto Press.

Fantham, Elaine, Helene Peet Foley, Natalie Boymel Kampen, Sarah B. Pomeroy, and H. Alan Shapiro. 1994. *Women in the Classical World*. New York: Oxford University Press.

Faraone, Christopher A. 1992. "Sex and Power: Male-Targeting Aphrodisiacs in the Greek Magical Tradition." *Helios* 19.1–2: 92–103.

Faraone, Christopher A. 2001. *Ancient Greek Love Magic*. Cambridge, MA: Harvard University Press.

Faraone, Christopher A., and Laura K. McClure, eds. 2006. *Prostitutes and Courtesans in the Ancient World*. Madison: University of Wisconsin Press.

Fear, Trevor, ed. 2000. "*Fallax Opus*: Approaches to Reading Roman Elegy." Special issue of *Arethusa* (33.2).

Feltovich, Anne C. 2011. "Women's Social Bonds in Greek and Roman Comedy." Diss. University of Cincinnati.

Ferguson, John. 1970. *The Religions of the Roman Empire*. Ithaca: Cornell University Press.

Ferrill, Arthur. 1980. "Augustus and His Daughter: A Modern Myth." In *Studies in Latin Literature and Roman History*, vol. 2, 332–46. Brussels: Latomus.

Ferris, I. M. 2000. *Enemies of Rome: Barbarians through Roman Eyes*. Phoenix Mill, UK: Sutton.

Fetterley, Judith. 1978. *The Resisting Reader*. Bloomington: Indiana University Press.

Fetterley, Judith. 1986. "Reading about Reading: 'A Jury of Her Peers,' 'The Murders in the Rue Morgue,' and 'The Yellow Wallpaper.'" In *Gender and Reading: Essays on Readers, Texts, and Contexts*, ed. Elizabeth A. Flynn and Patrocinio P. Schweikart, 147–64. Baltimore: Johns Hopkins University Press.

Fine, Gary Alan. 1976. "Obscene Joking across Cultures." *Journal of Communications* 26: 134–40.

Finley, M. I. 1975. "Anthropology and the Classics." In *The Use and Abuse of History*, 102–19. New York: Viking Penguin.

Fischler, Susan. 1994. "Social Stereotypes and Historical Analysis: The Case of the Imperial Women in Rome." In *Women in Ancient Societies*, ed. Léonie J. Archer, Susan Fischler, and Maria Wyke, 115–33. New York: Routledge.

Fisher, Elizabeth A. 1984. "Theodora and Antonina in the *Historia Arcana*: History and/or Fiction?" In *Women in the Ancient World*, ed. John Peradotto and J. P. Sullivan, 287–313. Albany: State University of New York Press.

Fissell, Mary. 2003. "Hairy Women and Naked Truths: Gender and the Politics of Knowledge in *Aristotle's Masterpiece*." *The William and Mary Quarterly* 60: 43–74.

Fitzgerald, William. 1995. *Catullan Provocations: Lyric Poetry and the Drama of Position*. Berkeley: University of California Press.

Flemming, Rebecca. 1999. "*Quae Corpore Quaestum Facit*: The Sexual Economy of Female Prostitution in the Roman Empire." *Journal of Roman Studies* 89: 38–61.

Flemming, Rebecca. 2000. *Medicine and the Making of Roman Women: Gender, Nature, and Authority from Celsus to Galen.* Oxford: Oxford University Press.

Flemming, Rebecca. 2007a. "Festus and Women's Role in Roman Religion." In *Verrius, Festus and Paul,* ed. Fay Glinister and Clare Woods, 87–108. *Bulletin of the Institute of Classical Studies,* Supplement 93. London: Institute of Classical Studies.

Flemming, Rebecca. 2007b. "Women, Writing and Medicine in the Classical World." *Classical Quarterly* 57: 257–79.

Fletcher, John. 1986. "Poetry, Gender, and Primal Fantasy." In *Formations of Fantasy,* ed. Victor Burgin, James Donald, and Cora Kaplan, 109–41. London: Methuen.

Flory, Marleen Boudreau. 1984. "*Sic Exempla Parantur*: Livia's Shrine to Concordia and the Porticus Liviae." *Historia* 33: 309–30.

Flower, Harriet I. 1996. *Ancestor Masks and Aristocratic Power in Roman Culture.* Oxford: Oxford University Press.

Flower, Harriet I. 2002. "Were Women Ever 'Ancestors' in Republican Rome?" In *Images of Ancestors,* ed. Jakob Munk Højte, 159–84. Gylling: Aarhus University Press.

Foley, Helene P., ed. 1981. *Reflections of Women in Antiquity.* New York: Gordon and Breach Science Publishers.

Forbis, Elizabeth P. 1990. "Women's Public Image in Italian Honorary Inscriptions." *American Journal of Philology* 111: 493–512.

Foucault, Michel. 1978. *The History of Sexuality. Vol. 1: An Introduction.* Trans. Robert Hurley. New York: Vintage.

Fredrick, David. 1992. "She's Nothing: Gender and Representation in Catullus and Elegy." Diss. University of Southern California.

Fredrick, David. 1995. "Beyond the Atrium to Ariadne: Erotic Painting and Visual Pleasure in the Roman House." *Classical Antiquity* 14: 266–87.

Fredrick, David. 1997. "Reading Broken Skin: Violence in Roman Elegy." In *Roman Sexualities,* ed. Judith P. Hallett and Marilyn B. Skinner, 172–93. Princeton: Princeton University Press.

Fredrick, David, ed. 2002. *The Roman Gaze: Vision, Power, and the Body.* Baltimore: Johns Hopkins University Press.

French, Roger, and Frank Greenaway, eds. 1986. *Science in the Early Roman Empire: Pliny the Elder, His Sources and His Influence.* Totowa, NJ: Barnes & Noble.

French, Valerie. 1986. "Midwives and Maternity Care in the Greco-Roman World." *Helios* 13.2: 69–84.

French, Valerie. 1987. "The Cult of Mater Matuta." Paper presented at the Berkshire Conference on Women's History.

Fulkerson, Laurel. 2005. *The Ovidian Heroine as Author: Reading, Writing, and Community in the* Heroides. Cambridge: Cambridge University Press.

Gaca, Kathy L. 2003. *The Making of Fornication: Eros, Ethics, and Political Reform in Greek Philosophy and Early Christianity.* Berkeley: University of California Press.

Gaca, Kathy L. 2008. "Reinterpreting the Homeric Simile of *Iliad* 16.7–11: The Girl and Her Mother in Ancient Greek Warfare." *American Journal of Philology* 129: 145–71.

Gaca, Kathy L. 2010. "The Andrapodizing of War Captives in Greek Historical Memory." *Transactions of the American Philological Association* 140: 117–61.

Gaca, Kathy L. 2010–11. "Telling the Girls from the Boys and Children: Interpreting Παῖδες in the Sexual Violence of Populace-Ravaging Ancient Warfare." *Illinois Classical Studies* 35–36: 85–109.

Gaca, Kathy L. 2011. "Girls, Women, and the Significance of Sexual Violence in Ancient Warfare." In *Sexual Violence in Conflict Zones: From the Ancient World to the Era of Human Rights*, ed. Elizabeth D. Heineman, 73–88. Philadelphia: University of Pennsylvania Press.

Gagé, Jean. 1963. *Matronalia: essai sur les dévotions et les organisations culturelles des femmes dans l'ancienne Rome*. Brussels: Collection Latomus (60).

Gagnier, Regenia. 1988. "Between Women: A Cross-class Analysis of Status and Anarchic Humor." *Women's Studies* 15: 135–48.

Gal, Susan. 1991. "Between Speech and Silence: The Problematics of Research on Language and Gender." In *Gender at the Crossroads of Knowledge*, ed. Micaela di Leonardo, 175–203. New York: Routledge.

Galinsky, G. Karl. 1969. *Aeneas, Sicily, and Rome*. Princeton: Princeton University Press.

Galinsky, G. Karl. 1975. *Ovid's* Metamorphoses: *An Introduction to the Basic Aspects*. Berkeley: University of California Press.

Gamel, Mary-Kay. n.d. "The Aesthetics of Dismemberment I: Philomela's Tongue." Unpublished manuscript.

Gamel, Mary-Kay. 1989. "*Non Sine Caede*: Abortion Politics and Poetics in Ovid's *Amores*." *Helios* 16.2: 183–206.

Garber, Marjorie. 1992. *Vested Interests: Cross-dressing & Cultural Anxiety*. New York: HarperCollins.

Gardner, Jane F. 1986. *Women in Roman Law and Society*. Bloomington: Indiana University Press.

Garland, Lynda. 2006. "Street Life in Constantinople: Women and the Carnivalesque." In *Byzantine Women: Varieties of Experience 800–1200*, ed. Lynda Garland, 163–76. Aldershot, UK: Ashgate.

Garlick, Barbara, Suzanne Dixon, and Pauline Allen, eds. 1992. *Stereotypes of Women in Power: Historical Perspectives and Revisionist Views*. New York: Greenwood Press.

Garnsey, Peter. 1967. "Adultery Trials and the Survival of the *Quaestiones* in the Severan Age." *Journal of Roman Studies* 57: 56–60.

Garnsey, Peter. 1970. *Social Status and Legal Privilege in the Roman Empire*. Oxford: Clarendon Press.

Gates, Henry Louis, Jr. 1988. *The Signifying Monkey: A Theory of African-American Literary Criticism*. Oxford: Oxford University Press.

Gauthier, Xavière. 1980 [1974]. "Is there such a thing as women's writing?" In *New French Feminisms: An Anthology*, ed. Elaine Marks and Isabelle de Courtivron, 161–64. Trans. Marilyn A. August. Amherst: University of Massachusetts Press.

Gero, Joan, and Margaret Conkey, eds. 1991. *Engendering Archaeology*. Oxford: Blackwell.

Giacosa, Giorgio. n.d. *Women of the Caesars: Their Lives and Portraits on Coins*. Trans. R. Ross Holloway. Montclair, NJ: Numismatic Fine Arts.

Gilhuly, Kate. 2009. *The Feminine Matrix of Sex and Gender in Classical Athens*. Cambridge: Cambridge University Press.

Gill, Lesley. 1990. "Painted Faces: Conflict and Ambiguity in Domestic Servant-Employer Relations in La Paz, 1930–1988." *Latin American Research Review* 25.1: 119–36.

Gilmore, David D. 1990. *Manhood in the Making*. New Haven, CT: Yale University Press.

Ginsburg, Judith. 2006. *Representing Agrippina: Constructions of Female Power in the Early Roman Empire*. Oxford: Oxford University Press.

Giovannini, Maureen J. 1981. "Woman: A Dominant Symbol within the Cultural System of a Sicilian Town." *Man* n.s. 16: 408–26.

Glazebrook, Allison, and Madeleine M. Henry, eds. 2011. *Greek Prostitution in the Ancient Mediterranean, 800 BCE–200 CE*. Madison, WI: University of Wisconsin Press.

Gleason, Maud W. 1995. *Making Men: Sophists and Self-Presentation in Ancient Rome*. Princeton: Princeton University Press.

Gold, Barbara K. 1993. "'But Ariadne Was Never There in the First Place': Finding the Female in Roman Poetry." In *Feminist Theory and the Classics*, ed. Nancy Sorkin Rabinowitz and Amy Richlin, 75–101. New York: Routledge.

Gold, Barbara K. 1998a. "'The House I Live in Is Not My Own': Women's Bodies in Juvenal's Satires." *Arethusa* 31: 369–86.

Gold, Barbara K. 1998b. "'Vested Interests' in Plautus' *Casina*: Cross-Dressing in Roman Comedy." *Helios* 25: 17–29.

Golden, Mark. 1992. "Continuity, Change and the Study of Ancient Childhood." *Échos du monde classique/ Classical Views* 36, n.s. 11: 7–18.

Goodyear, Dana. 2005. "Quiet Depravity." *The New Yorker*, October 24: http://www.newyorker.com/archive/2005/10/24/051024fa_fact?current.

Goold, G. P. 1983. "The Cause of Ovid's Exile." *Illinois Classical Studies* 8: 94–107.

Gordon, Linda. 1986. "What's New in Women's History?" In *Feminist Studies/ Critical Studies*, ed. Teresa de Lauretis, 20–30. Bloomington: Indiana University Press.

Gordon, Pamela. 2002. "Some Unseen Monster: Rereading Lucretius on Sex." In *The Roman Gaze: Vision, Power, and the Body*, ed. David Fredrick, 86–109. Baltimore: Johns Hopkins University Press.

Gordon, Richard. 1990a. "From Republic to Principate: Priesthood, Religion and Ideology." In *Pagan Priests*, ed. Mary Beard and John North, 177–98. Ithaca: Cornell University Press.

Gordon, Richard. 1990b. "The Veil of Power: Emperors, Sacrificers and Benefactors." In *Pagan Priests*, ed. Mary Beard and John North, 199–232. Ithaca: Cornell University Press.

Gossen, Gary H. 1974. *Chamulas in the World of the Sun: Time and Space in a Maya Oral Tradition*. Cambridge: Harvard University Press.

Gossen, Gary H. 1976. "Verbal Dueling in Chamula." In *Speech Play*, ed. Barbara Kirshenblatt-Gimblett, 121–46. Philadelphia: University of Pennsylvania Press.

Gourevitch, Danielle. 1984. *Le mal d'être femme: La femme et la médecine dans la Rome antique*. Paris: Société d'édition "Les belles lettres."

Gowers, Emily. 1993. *The Loaded Table: Representations of Food in Roman Literature*. Oxford: Clarendon Press.

Grant, Michael. 1975. *Eros in Pompeii*. New York: William Morrow and Company.

Grassmann, Victor. 1966. *Die erotischen Epoden des Horaz*. Munich: Beck.

Green, Carin M. C. 2008. *Roman Religion and the Cult of Diana at Aricia*. Cambridge: Cambridge University Press.

Green, Carin M. C. 2010. "Holding the Line: Women, Ritual, and the Protection of Rome." In *Women and Gender in Ancient Religions: Interdisciplinary Approaches*, ed. Stephen P. Ahearne-Kroll, Paul A. Holloway, and James A. Kelhoffer, 279–95. Tübingen: Mohr Siebeck.

Green, Monica. 1989. "Women's Medical Practice and Health Care in Medieval Europe." *Signs* 14.2: 434–73.

Green, Peter. 1979. "*Ars Gratia Cultus*: Ovid as Beautician." *American Journal of Philology* 100: 381–92.

Green, Peter. 1982. "*Carmen et Error: Prophasis* and *aitia* in the Matter of Ovid's Exile." *Classical Antiquity* 1: 202–20.

Green, Rayna. 1977. "Magnolias Grow in Dirt: The Bawdy Lore of Southern Women." *The Radical Teacher* 6: 26–31.

Greene, Elizabeth M. 2011. "Women and Families in the Auxiliary Military Communities of the Roman West in the First and Second Centuries AD." Diss. University of North Carolina–Chapel Hill.

Greene, Elizabeth M. 2013. "Female Networks in Military Communities in the Roman West: A View from the Vindolanda Tablets." In *Women and the Roman City in the Latin West,* ed. Emily A. Hemelrijk and Greg Woolf, 369–90. Leiden: Brill.

Greene, Ellen. 1998. *The Erotics of Domination: Male Desire and the Mistress in Latin Love Poetry.* Baltimore: Johns Hopkins University Press.

Greenidge, A. H. J. 1894. *Infamia in Roman Law.* Oxford: Clarendon Press.

Griffin, Susan. 1981. *Pornography and Silence: Culture's Revenge Against Nature.* New York: Harper & Row.

Gubar, Susan. 1987. "Representing Pornography: Feminism, Criticism, and Depictions of Female Violation." *Critical Inquiry* 13:4: 712–41.

Gunderson, Erik. 2000. *Staging Masculinity: The Rhetoric of Performance in the Roman World.* Ann Arbor: University of Michigan Press.

Gutzwiller, Kathryn J., and Ann Norris Michelini. 1991. "Women and Other Strangers: Feminist Perspectives in Classical Literature." In *(En)Gendering Knowledge: Feminists in Academe,* ed. Joan E. Hartman and Ellen Messer-Davidow, 66–84. Knoxville: University of Tennessee Press.

Habinek, Thomas N. 2005. *The World of Roman Song: From Ritualized Speech to Social Order.* Berkeley: University of California Press.

Haley, Shelley P. 1993. "Black Feminist Thought and Classics: Re-membering, Reclaiming, Re-empowering." In *Feminist Theory and the Classics,* ed. Nancy Sorkin Rabinowitz and Amy Richlin, 23–43. New York: Routledge.

Hallett, Judith P. 1973. "The Role of Women in Roman Elegy: Counter-cultural Feminism." *Arethusa* 6: 103–24.

Hallett, Judith P. 1977. "*Perusinae Glandes* and the Changing Image of Augustus." *American Journal of Ancient History* 2.2: 151–71.

Hallett, Judith P. 1984. *Fathers and Daughters in Roman Society.* Princeton: Princeton University Press.

Hallett, Judith P. 1985. "Buzzings of a Confirmed Gadfly." *Helios* 12.2: 23–37.

Hallett, Judith P. 1989. "Woman as *Same* and *Other* in the Classical Roman Elite." *Helios* 16.1: 59–78.

Hallett, Judith P. 1992a. "Ancient Greek and Roman Constructions of Sexuality: The State of the Debate." Paper presented at the symposium "Sexualities, Dissidence, and Cultural Change," April 10, University of Maryland at College Park.

Hallett, Judith P. 1992b. "Martial's Sulpicia and Propertius' Cynthia." *Classical World* 86: 99–123.

Hallett, Judith P. 1993. "Feminist Theory, Historical Periods, Literary Canons, and the Study of Greco-Roman Antiquity." In *Feminist Theory and the Classics*, ed. Nancy Sorkin Rabinowitz and Amy Richlin, 44–72. New York: Routledge.

Hallett, Judith P. 1997. "Female Homoeroticism and the Denial of Roman Reality in Latin Literature." In *Roman Sexualities*, ed. Judith P. Hallett and Marilyn B. Skinner, 255–73. Princeton: Princeton University Press.

Hallett, Judith P. 2004. "Matriot Games? Cornelia, Mother of the Gracchi, and the Forging of Family-Oriented Political Values." In *Women's Influence on Classical Civilization*, ed. Fiona McHardy and Eireann Marshall, 26–39. London: Routledge.

Hallett, Judith P. 2006a. "Fulvia, Mother of Iullus Antonius: New Approaches to the Sources on Julia's Adultery at Rome." *Helios* 33.2: 149–64.

Hallett, Judith P. 2006b. "Sulpicia and her *Fama*: An Intertextual Approach to Recovering Her Latin Literary Image." *Classical World* 100: 37–42.

Hallett, Judith P., and Marilyn B. Skinner, eds. 1997. *Roman Sexualities*. Princeton: Princeton University Press.

Hallett, Judith P., and Thomas Van Nortwick, eds. 1997. *Compromising Traditions: The Personal Voice in Classical Scholarship*. London: Routledge.

Halperin, David M., John J. Winkler, and Froma I. Zeitlin, eds. 1990. *Before Sexuality: The Construction of Erotic Experience in the Ancient Greek World*. Princeton: Princeton University Press.

Hamer, Mary. 1988. "Cleopatra: Housewife." *Textual Practice* 2: 159–79.

Hanmer, Jalna. 1981. "Violence and the Social Control of Women." *Feminist Issues* 1: 29–46.

Hanson, Ann Ellis. 1990. "The Medical Writers' Woman." In *Before Sexuality*, ed. David M. Halperin, John J. Winkler, and Froma I. Zeitlin, 309–38. Princeton: Princeton University Press.

Hanson, Ann Ellis. 1992. "Conception, Gestation, and the Origin of Female Nature in the *Corpus Hippocraticum*." *Helios* 19.1–2: 31–71.

Harding, Sandra, ed. 1987. *Feminism and Methodology*. Bloomington: Indiana University Press.

Harding, Sandra. 1991. "Who Knows? Identities and Feminist Epistemology." In *(En)Gendering Knowledge: Feminists in Academe*, ed. Joan E. Hartman and Ellen Messer-Davidow, 100–115. Knoxville: University of Tennessee Press.

Harper, Graeme, ed. 2002. *Comedy, Fantasy, and Colonialism*. London: Continuum.

Harper, Kyle. 2011. *Slavery in the Late Roman World, AD 275–425*. Cambridge: Cambridge University Press.

Harper, Kyle. 2013. *From Shame to Sin: The Christian Transformation of Sexual Morality in Latin Antiquity*. Cambridge, MA: Harvard University Press.

Hartman, Geoffrey H. 1970. "The Voice of the Shuttle." In *Beyond Formalism*, 337–55. New Haven, CT: Yale University Press.

Hartsock, Nancy. 1990. "Foucault on Power: A Theory for Women?" In *Feminism/Postmodernism*, ed. Linda J. Nicholson, 157–75. New York: Routledge.

Havelock, Christine Mitchell. 1982. "Mourners on Greek Vases: Remarks on the Social History of Women." In *Feminism and Art History*, ed. Norma Broude and Mary D. Garrard, 44–61. New York: Harper & Row.

Heath, Jennifer, ed. 2008. *The Veil: Women Writers on Its History, Lore, and Politics*. Berkeley: University of California Press.

Heath, Stephen. 1986. "Joan Rivière and the Masquerade." In *Formations of Fantasy*, ed. Victor Burgin, James Donald, and Cora Kaplan, 45–62. London: Methuen.

Hejduk, Julia D. 2011. "Epic Rapes in the *Fasti*." *Classical Philology* 106: 20–31.

Hemelrijk, Emily A. 1999. *Matrona docta: Educated Women in the Roman Elite from Cornelia to Julia Domna*. London: Routledge.

Hemelrijk, Emily A., and Greg Woolf, eds. 2013. *Women and the Roman City in the Latin West*. Leiden: Brill.

Hemker, Julie. 1985. "Rape and the Founding of Rome." *Helios* 12: 41–47.

Henderson, Jeffrey. 1975. *The Maculate Muse*. New Haven, CT: Yale University Press.

Henderson, John. 1999. *Writing down Rome: Satire, Comedy, and other Offences in Latin Poetry*. Oxford: Clarendon Press.

Henderson, Katherine Usher, and Barbara F. McManus. 1985. *Half Humankind: Contexts and Texts of the Controversy about Women in England, 1540–1640*. Urbana: University of Illinois Press.

Henry, Madeleine M. 1992. "The Edible Woman: Athenaeus's Concept of the Pornographic." In *Pornography and Representation in Greece and Rome*, ed. Amy Richlin, 250–68. Oxford: Oxford University Press.

Herrin, Judith. 1983. "In Search of Byzantine Women: Three Avenues of Approach." In *Images of Women in Antiquity*, ed. Averil Cameron and Amélie Kuhrt, 167–89. Detroit: Wayne State University Press.

Hersch, Karen K. 2010. *The Roman Wedding: Ritual and Meaning in Antiquity*. Cambridge: Cambridge University Press.

Herzfeld, Michael. 1985. *The Poetics of Manhood: Contest and Identity in a Cretan Mountain Village*. Princeton: Princeton University Press.

Highet, Gilbert. 1954. *Juvenal the Satirist*. Oxford: Clarendon Press.

Hinds, Stephen. 1987. "The Poetess and the Reader: Further Steps Toward Sulpicia." *Hermathena* 143: 29–46.

Hinds, Stephen. 2010. "Between Formalism and Historicism." In *The Oxford Handbook of Roman Studies*, ed. Alessandro Barchiesi and Walter Scheidel, 369–85. Oxford: Oxford University Press.

Hirsch, Marianne, and Evelyn Fox Keller, eds. 1990. *Conflicts in Feminism*. New York: Routledge.

Hochschild, Arlie. 1983. *The Managed Heart: Commercialization of Human Feeling*. Berkeley: University of California Press.

Hoffer, Carol P. 1974. "Madam Yoko: Ruler of the Kpa Mende Confederacy." In *Woman, Culture, and Society*, ed. Michelle Zimbalist Rosaldo and Louise Lamphere, 173–87. Stanford: Stanford University Press.

Holland, Lora L. 2008. "*Diana Feminarum Tutela?*: The Case of *Noutrix Paperia*." *Studies in Latin Literature and Roman History*, vol. 14, 95–115. Brussels: Latomus.

Holland, Lora L. 2012. "Women and Roman Religion." In *A Companion to Women in the Ancient World*, ed. Sharon L. James and Sheila Dillon, 204–14. Chichester, UK: Wiley-Blackwell.

Holst-Warhaft, Gail. 1992. *Dangerous Voices: Women's Laments and Greek Literature*. London: Routledge.

Holum, Kenneth G. 1982. *Theodosian Empresses*. Berkeley: University of California Press.

Holzberg, Niklas. 1998–99. "Four Poets and a Poetess or a Portrait of the Poet as a Young Man? Thoughts on Book 3 of the *Corpus Tibullianum*." *Classical Journal* 94.2: 169–91.

Hondagneu-Sotelo, Pierrette. 2007. *Doméstica: Immigrant Workers Cleaning and Caring in the Shadows of Affluence*. Rev. ed. Berkeley: University of California Press.

hooks, bell. 1990. *Yearning: Race, Gender, and Cultural Politics*. Boston: South End Press.

hooks, bell. 1992. "Out of the Academy and into the Streets." *Ms.* 3.1 (July/August): 80–82.

Hopkins, Keith. 1964–65. "The Age of Roman Girls at Marriage." *Population Studies* 18: 309–27.

Hopkins, Keith. 1965. "Contraception in the Roman Empire." *Comparative Studies in Society and History* 8: 124–51.

Horney, Karen. 1932. "The Dread of Woman." *International Journal of Psychoanalysis* 13: 348–60.

Horsfall, Nicholas. 1990. "Eduard Fraenkel." In *Classical Scholarship: A Biographical Encyclopedia*, ed. Ward W. Briggs and William M. Calder III, 61–67. New York: Garland.

Horsfall, Nicholas. 2003 [1996]. *The Culture of the Roman Plebs*. London: Duckworth. Originally published as *La cultura della plebs romana*. Barcelona: University of Barcelona, 1996.

Hubbard, Thomas K. 2004. "The Invention of Sulpicia." *Classical Journal* 100: 177–94.

Hughes, Lisa A. 2007. "Unveiling the Veil: Cultic, Status, and Ethnic Representations of Early Imperial Freedwomen." *Material Religion* 3.2: 218–41.

Humphreys, Sally. 1978. *Anthropology and the Greeks*. London: Routledge and Kegan Paul.

Hunter, Nan D. 1986. "The Pornography Debate in Context: A Chronology." In *Caught Looking*, ed. F.A.C.T. Book Committee, 26–29. New York: Caught Looking Inc.

Isaac, Benjamin. 2004. *The Invention of Racism in Classical Antiquity*. Princeton: Princeton University Press.

Izzet, Vedia. 2012. "Etruscan Women: Towards a Reappraisal." In *A Companion to Women in the Ancient World*, ed. Sharon L. James and Sheila Dillon, 66–77. Chichester, UK: Wiley-Blackwell.

James, Sharon L. 1997. "Slave-Rape and Female Silence in Ovid's Love Poetry." *Helios* 24: 60–76.

James, Sharon L. 1998. "From Boys to Men: Rape and Developing Masculinity in Terence's *Hecyra* and *Eunuchus*." *Helios* 25: 31–47.

James, Sharon L. 2003. *Learned Girls and Male Persuasion: Gender and Reading in Roman Love Elegy*. Berkeley: University of California Press.

James, Sharon L. 2008. "Feminist Pedagogy and Teaching Latin Literature." *Cloelia* 38: 11–14.

James, Sharon L. 2010. "Trafficking Pasicompsa: A Courtesan's Travels and Travails in Plautus' *Mercator*." *New England Classical Journal* 37: 39–50.

James, Sharon L. 2012. "Domestic Female Slaves in Roman Comedy." In *A Companion to Women in the Ancient World*, ed. Sharon L. James and Sheila Dillon, 235–37. Chichester, UK: Wiley-Blackwell.

James, Sharon L. 2014. "Talking Rape in the Classics Classroom." In *From Abortion to Pederasty: Addressing Difficult Topics in the Classics Classroom*, ed. Nancy Sorkin Rabinowitz and Fiona McHardy. Columbus: Ohio State University Press.

James, Sharon L., and Sheila Dillon, eds. 2012. *A Companion to Women in the Ancient World*. Chichester, UK: Wiley-Blackwell.

Jehlen, Myra. 1981. "Archimedes and the Paradox of Feminist Criticism." *Signs* 6: 575–601.

Jenkins, Keith, ed. 1997. *The Postmodern History Reader*. London: Routledge.

Jillette, Penn, and Paul Provenza. 2005. *The Aristocrats*. Directed by Paul Provenza.

Johanson, Christopher. 2011. "A Walk with the Dead: A Funerary Cityscape of Ancient Rome." In *A Companion to Families in the Greek and Roman Worlds*, ed. Beryl Rawson, 408–30. Chichester, UK: Wiley-Blackwell.

Johns, Catherine. 1982. *Sex or Symbol? Erotic Images of Greece and Rome*. Austin: University of Texas Press.

Johnson, Merri Lisa. 2002. *Jane Sexes It Up*. New York: Four Walls Eight Windows.

Johnson, Patricia J. 2008. *Ovid Before Exile: Art and Punishment in the* Metamorphoses. Madison: University of Wisconsin Press.

Johnson, Robbie Davis. 1973. "Folklore and Women: A Social Interactional Analysis of the Folklore of a Texas Madam." *Journal of American Folklore* 86: 211–24.

Johnson, W. R. 1996. "The Rapes of Callisto." *Classical Journal* 92.1: 9–24.

Johnston, Dafydd. 1998. "Erotica and Satire in Medieval Welsh Poetry." In *Obscenity: Social Control and Artistic Creation in the European Middle Ages*, ed. Jan M. Ziokowski, 60–72. Leiden: Brill.

Johnston, Sarah Iles. 1995a. "Defining the Dreadful: Remarks on the Child-Killing Demon." In *Ancient Magic and Ritual Power*, ed. Marvin Meyer and Paul Mirecki, 361–89. Leiden: Brill.

Johnston, Sarah Iles. 1995b. "The Song of the *Iynx*: Magic and Rhetoric in *Pythian* 4." *Transactions of the American Philological Association* 125: 177–206.

Johnston, Sarah Iles. 1999. *The Restless Dead: Encounters between the Living and the Dead in Ancient Greece*. Berkeley: University of California Press.

Jones, A. H. M., J. R. Martindale, and J. Morris, eds. 1971. *The Prosopography of the Later Roman Empire*. Cambridge: Cambridge University Press.

Jones, C. P. 1987. "*Stigma*: Tattooing and Branding in Graeco-Roman Antiquity." *Journal of Roman Studies* 77: 139–55.

Joplin, Patricia Klindienst. 1985. "Epilogue: Philomela's Loom." In *Coming to Light: American Women Poets in the Twentieth Century*, ed. Diane Wood Middlebrook and Marilyn Yalom, 254–67. Ann Arbor: University of Michigan Press. (Longer version: "The Voice of the Shuttle Is Ours," *Stanford Literature Review* 1 [1984]).

Joplin, Patricia Klindienst. 1990. "Ritual Work on Human Flesh: Livy's Lucretia and the Rape of the Body Politic." *Helios* 17: 51–70.

Joshel, Sandra R. 1986. "Nurturing the Master's Child: Slavery and the Roman Child-Nurse." *Signs* 12: 3–22.

Joshel, Sandra R. 1992a. "The Body Female and the Body Politic: Livy's Lucretia and Verginia." In *Pornography and Representation in Greece and Rome*, ed. Amy Richlin, 112–30. New York: Oxford University Press.

Joshel, Sandra R. 1992b. *Work, Identity and Legal Status at Rome: A Study of the Occupational Inscriptions*. Norman: University of Oklahoma Press.

Joshel, Sandra R. 1997. "Female Desire and the Discourse of Empire: Tacitus's Messalina." In *Roman Sexualities*, ed. Judith P. Hallett and Marilyn B. Skinner, 221–54. Princeton: Princeton University Press.

Joshel, Sandra R. 2011. "Slavery and Roman Literary Culture." In *The Cambridge World History of Slavery*, vol. 1, ed. Keith Bradley and Paul Cartledge, 214–40. Cambridge: Cambridge University Press.

Joshel, Sandra R., and Sheila Murnaghan. 1998a. "Introduction: Differential Equations." In *Women and Slaves in Greco-Roman Culture: Differential Equations*, ed. Sandra R. Joshel and Sheila Murnaghan, 1–21. Cambridge: Cambridge University Press.

Joshel, Sandra R., and Sheila Murnaghan, eds. 1998b. *Women and Slaves in Greco-Roman Culture: Differential Equations*. London: Routledge.

Kahn, Madeleine. 2005. *Why Are We Reading Ovid's Handbook on Rape? Teaching and Learning at a Women's College*. Boulder: Paradigm.

Kallendorf, Craig W., ed. 2007. *A Companion to the Classical Tradition*. Chichester, UK: Wiley-Blackwell.

Kamm, Antony. 2008. *The Romans: An Introduction*. 2nd ed. Abingdon, UK: Routledge.

Kampen, Natalie Boymel. 1982. "Social Status and Gender in Roman Art: The Case of the Saleswoman." In *Feminism and Art History*, ed. Norma Broude and Mary D. Garrard, 63–78. New York: Harper & Row.

Kampen, Natalie Boymel. 1985. "Julia Domna and the Program of the Severan Arch at Leptis Magna." Tenney Frank Lecture, University of Kansas, Lawrence.

Kampen, Natalie Boymel. 1991. "Between Public and Private: Women as Historical Subjects in Roman Art." In *Women's History and Ancient History*, ed. Sarah B. Pomeroy, 218–48. Chapel Hill: University of North Carolina Press.

Kampen, Natalie Boymel. 1996. "Omphale and the Instability of Gender." In *Sexuality in Ancient Art*, ed. Natalie Boymel Kampen, 233–46. Cambridge: Cambridge University Press.

Kaplan, E. Ann. 1983. "Is the Gaze Male?" In *Powers of Desire*, ed. Ann Snitow, Christine Stansell, and Sharon Thompson, 309–27. New York: Monthly Review Press.

Kaplan, Cora. 1986. "*The Thorn Birds*: fiction, fantasy, femininity." In *Formations of Fantasy*, ed. Victor Burgin, James Donald, and Cora Kaplan, 142–66. London: Methuen.

Kapparis, Konstantinos. 2002. *Abortion in the Ancient World*. London: Duckworth.

Kappeler, Susanne. 1986. *The Pornography of Representation*. Minneapolis: University of Minnesota Press.

Kaster, Robert. 1980. "Macrobius and Servius: *Verecundia* and the Grammarian's Function." *Harvard Studies in Classical Philology* 84: 219–62.

Keith, Alison. 1997. "*Tandem venit amor*: A Roman Woman Speaks of Love." In *Roman Sexualities*, ed. Judith P. Hallett and Marilyn B. Skinner, 295–310. Princeton: Princeton University Press.

Keith, Alison. 2006. "Critical Trends in Interpreting Sulpicia." *Classical World* 100: 3–10.

Keith, Alison. 2008. "Lament in Lucan's *Bellum Civile*." In *Lament: Studies in the Ancient Mediterranean and Beyond*, ed. Ann Suter, 233–57. Oxford: Oxford University Press.

Keith, Alison. 2009. "Sexuality and Gender." In *A Companion to Ovid*, ed. Peter E. Knox, 355–69. Chichester, UK: Wiley-Blackwell.

Keith, Alison. 2011. "Lycoris Galli/ Volumnia Cytheris: A Greek Courtesan in Rome." *Eugesta* 1: 23–53.

Keltanen, Minerva. 2002. "The Public Image of the Four Empresses: Ideal Wives, Mothers and Regents?" In *Women, Wealth and Power in the Roman Empire*, ed. Päivi Setälä, 105–46. Acta Instituti Romani Finlandiae, vol. 25. Rome: Institutum Romanum Finlandiae.

Kent, Sarah, and Jacqueline Morreau, eds. 1985. *Women's Images of Men*. London and New York: Writers and Readers Publishing.

Keuls, Eva C. 1993. *The Reign of the Phallus: Sexual Politics in Ancient Athens*. 2nd ed. Berkeley: University of California Press.

Kilmer, Martin. 1982. "Genital Phobia and Depilation." *Journal of Hellenic Studies* 72: 104–12.

Kincaid, Jamaica. 1990. *Lucy*. Harmondsworth, UK: Plume/Penguin.

King, Helen. 1994. "Producing Woman: Hippocratic Gynaecology." In *Women in Ancient Societies*, ed. Léonie J. Archer, Susan Fischler, and Maria Wyke, 102–14. New York: Routledge.

King, Helen. 1995. "Self-Help, Self-Knowledge: In Search of the Patient in Hippocratic Gynaecology." In *Women in Antiquity: New Assessments*, ed. Richard Hawley and Barbara Levick, 135–48. New York: Routledge.

King, Helen. 1998. *Hippocrates' Woman: Reading the Female Body in Ancient Greece*. New York: Routledge.

King, Helen. 2011. "Galen and the Widow: Towards a History of Therapeutic Masturbation in Ancient Gynaecology." *Eugesta* 1: 205–35.

Kingston, Maxine Hong. 1976. *The Woman Warrior*. New York: Knopf.

Klapisch-Zuber, Christiane. 1985. *Women, Family, and Ritual in Renaissance Italy*. Trans. Lydia G. Cochrane. Chicago: University of Chicago Press.

Kleiner, Diana E. E. 1978. "The Great Friezes of the Ara Pacis Augustae: Greek Sources, Roman Derivatives, and Augustan Social Policy." *Mélanges de l'École française de Rome—Antiquité* 90: 753–85.

Kleiner, Diana E. E., and Susan B. Matheson, eds. 1996. *I, Claudia: Women in Ancient Rome*. Austin: University of Texas Press.

Kleiner, Diana E. E., and Susan B. Matheson, eds. 2000. *I, Claudia II: Women in Roman Art and Society*. Austin: University of Texas Press.

Knoche, Ulrich. 1975. *Roman Satire*. Trans. Edwin S. Ramage. Bloomington: Indiana University Press.

Kolb, Anne, ed. 2010. *Augustae: Machtbewusste Frauen am römischen Kaiserhof? Herrschaftsstrukturen und Herrschaftspraxis II. Akten der Tagung in Zürich 18.-20.9.2008*. Berlin: Akademie Verlag.

Kolodny, Annette. 1985 [1980]. "A Map for Rereading: Gender and the Interpretation of Literary Texts." In *The New Feminist Criticism*, ed. Elaine Showalter, 46–62. New York: Pantheon.

Konstan, David, and Martha Nussbaum, eds. 1990. "Sexuality in Greek and Roman Society." *differences* 2.1 (special issue).

Kothoff, Helga. 2006. "Gender and Humor: The State of the Art." *Journal of Pragmatics* 38: 4–25.

Kraemer, Ross S[hepard]. 1988 [2004]. *Maenads, Martyrs, Matrons, Monastics*. Philadelphia: Fortress. Revised as *Women's Religions in the Greco-Roman World: A Sourcebook*. Oxford: Oxford University Press, 2004.

Kraemer, Ross Shepard. 1992. *Her Share of the Blessings: Women's Religions Among Pagans, Jews, and Christians in the Greco-Roman World*. New York: Oxford University Press.

Kraemer, Ross Shepard. 2011. *Unreliable Witnesses: Religion, Gender, and History in the Greco-Roman Mediterranean*. Oxford: Oxford University Press.

Kristeva, Julia. 1982. *Powers of Horror: An Essay on Abjection*. Trans. Leon S. Roudiez. New York: Columbia University Press.

Kroll, W. 1931. "Sulpicia 115." In Pauly-Wissowa, *Real-Encyclopädie der classischen Alter-tumswissenschaft* 2.4.880–82.

Lada-Richards, Ismene. 2007. *Silent Eloquence: Lucian and Pantomime Dancing*. London: Duckworth.

Lada-Richards, Ismene. 2013. "*Mutata corpora:* Ovid's Changing Forms and the Metamorphic Bodies of Pantomime Dancing." *TAPA* 143: 105–52.

Lamp, Frederick. 1985. "Cosmos, Cosmetics, and the Spirit of Bondo." *African Arts* 28.3: 28–43, 98–99.

Langlands, Rebecca. 2006. *Sexual Morality in Ancient Rome*. Cambridge: Cambridge University Press.

Langston, Donna. 1990. "Down on the Strike Line with My Children." In *Calling Home: Working-Class Women's Writings*, ed. Janet Zandy, 281. New Brunswick: Rutgers University Press.

La Regina, Adriano. 1976. Report on the Pietrabbondante roof-tile in "Rivista di epigrafia italica." *Studi Etruschi* 44: 284–88.

Larmour, David H. J., Paul Allen Miller, and Charles Platter, eds. 1997. *Rethinking Sexuality: Foucault and Classical Antiquity*. Princeton: Princeton University Press.

Larsen, Anne R., Diana Robin, and Carole Levin, eds. 2007. *Encyclopedia of Women in the Renaissance: Italy, France, and England*. Santa Barbara: ABC-CLIO.

Latte, Kurt. 1967. *Römische Religionsgeschichte*. Munich: C.H. Beck.

Lavin, Suzanne. 2004. *Women and Comedy in Solo Performance: Phyllis Diller, Lily Tomlin, and Roseanne*. London: Routledge.

Leach, Edmund. 1964. "Anthropological Aspects of Language: Animal Categories and Verbal Abuse." In *New Directions in the Study of Language*, ed. Eric H. Lenneberg, 23–63. Cambridge: Harvard University Press.

Lederer, Laura, ed. 1980. *Take Back the Night: Women on Pornography*. New York: William Morrow.

Lee, Rachel. 2004. "'Where's My Parade?': Margaret Cho and the Asian American Body in Space." *The Drama Review* 48: 108–32.

Leeman, A. D. 1963. *Orationis Ratio*. Amsterdam: Hakkert.

Lefkowitz, Mary R. 1981. "Men and Women on Women's Lives." In *Heroines and Hysterics*, 26–31. New York: St. Martin's Press.

Lefkowitz, Mary R., and Maureen B. Fant. 2005. *Women's Life in Greece and Rome: A Source Book in Translation*. 3rd ed. Baltimore: Johns Hopkins University Press.

Le Guin, Ursula K. 1974. *The Dispossessed*. New York: Avon Books.

Le Guin, Ursula K. 1994. "The Rock That Changed Things." In *A Fisherman of the Inland Sea*, 57–67. New York: HarperPrism.

Lerner, Gerda. 1986. *The Creation of Patriarchy*. New York: Oxford University Press.

Levick, B. 1975. "Julians and Claudians." *Greece & Rome* 22: 29–38.

Levin-Richardson, Sarah. 2013. "*Fututa Sum Hic:* Female Subjectivity and Agency in Pompeian Sexual Graffiti." *Classical Journal* 108.3: 319–45.

Levine, Molly Myerowitz. 1995. "The Gendered Grammar of Ancient Mediterranean Hair." In *Off with Her Head! The Denial of Women's Identity in Myth, Religion, and Culture*, ed. Howard Eilberg-Schwartz and Wendy Doniger, 76–130. Berkeley: University of California Press.

Lightman, Marjorie, and William Zeisel. 1977. "*Univira:* An Example of Continuity and Change in Roman Society." *Church History* 46: 19–32.

Lilja, Saara. 1965. *The Roman Elegists' Attitude to Women*. Helsinki: Suomalaisen Tie-deakatemia.

Liveley, Genevieve. 2006. "Surfing the Third Wave? Postfeminism and the Hermeneu-tics of Reception." In *Classics and the Uses of Reception*, ed. Charles Martindale and Richard F. Thomas, 55–66. Oxford: Blackwell.

Liveley, Genevieve. 2011. *Ovid's* Metamorphoses: *A Reader's Guide*. London: Continuum.

Livingston, Jennie, director. 1990. *Paris Is Burning*. Off-White Productions.

Llewellyn-Jones, Lloyd. 2003. *Aphrodite's Tortoise: The Veiled Woman of Ancient Greece*. Swansea: The Classical Press of Wales.

Lloyd, G. E. R. 1979. *Magic, Reason and Experience: Studies in the Origins and Develop-ment of Greek Science*. Cambridge: Cambridge University Press.

Lloyd, G. E. R. 1983. *Science, Folklore and Ideology: Studies in the Life Sciences in Ancient Greece*. Cambridge: Cambridge University Press.

Long, Jacqueline. 2000. "Julia-Jokes at Macrobius's Saturnalia: Subversive Decorum in Late Antique Reception of Augustan Political Humor." *International Journal of the Classical Tradition* 6: 337–55.

Loraux, Nicole. 1990. "Herakles: The Super-Male and the Feminine." In *Before Sexual-ity*, ed. David M. Halperin, John J. Winkler, and Froma I. Zeitlin, 24–52. Princeton: Princeton University Press.

Loraux, Nicole. 1998. *Mothers in Mourning*. Trans. Corinne Pache. Ithaca: Cornell Uni-versity Press.

Loraux, Nicole. 2002. *The Mourning Voice: An Essay on Greek Tragedy*. Trans. Elizabeth Trapnell Rawlings. Ithaca: Cornell University Press.

Lorde, Audre. 1984. "The Master's Tools Will Never Dismantle the Master's House." In *Sister Outsider*, 110–13. Trumansburg, NY: The Crossing Press.

Lowe, N. J. 1988. "Sulpicia's Syntax." *Classical Quarterly* 38: 193–205.

Luck, Georg. 1987. "*AJP* Today." *American Journal of Philology* 108: vii–x.

Lugones, María C. 1991. "On the Logic of Pluralist Feminism." In *Feminist Ethics*, ed. Claudia Card, 35–44. Lawrence: University Press of Kansas.

MacCormack, Sabine G. 1981. *Art and Ceremony in Late Antiquity*. Berkeley: University of California Press.

MacKinnon, Catharine. 1992. "Does Sexuality Have a History?" In *Discourses of Sexual-ity: From Aristotle to AIDS*, ed. Domna C. Stanton, 117–36. Ann Arbor: University of Michigan Press.

MacLachlan, Bonnie, and Judith Fletcher, eds. 2007. *Virginity Revisited: Configurations of the Unpossessed Body*. Toronto: University of Toronto Press.

Maclean, Marie. 1987. "Oppositional Practices in Women's Traditional Narrative." *New Literary History* 19: 37–50.

MacMullen, Ramsay. 1980. "Woman in Public in the Roman Empire." *Historia* 29: 208–18.

Makarius, Laura. 1970. "Ritual Clowns and Symbolic Behaviour." *Diogenes* 69: 44–73.

Marchand, Suzanne L. 1996. *Down from Olympus: Archaeology and Philhellenism in Ger-many, 1750–1970*. Princeton: Princeton University Press.

Marcus, Jane. 1983. "Liberty, Sorority, Misogyny." In *The Representation of Women in Fic-tion: Selected Papers from the English Institute, n.s. 7 (1981)*, ed. Carolyn G. Heilbrun and Margaret R. Higonnet, 60–97. Baltimore: Johns Hopkins University Press.

Marcus, Jane. 1984. "Still Practice, A/Wrested Alphabet: Toward a Feminist Aesthetic." *Tulsa Studies in Women's Literature* 3: 79–97.

Marshall, C. W. 2013. "Sex Slaves in New Comedy." In *Slaves and Slavery in Ancient Greek Comic Drama*, ed. Ben Akrigg and Rob Tordoff, 173–96. Cambridge: Cambridge University Press.

Martindale, Charles, and Richard F. Thomas, eds. 2006. *Classics and the Uses of Reception*. Oxford: Blackwell.

Mascia-Lees, Frances E., Patricia Sharpe, and Colleen Ballerino Cohen. 1989. "The Postmodernist Turn in Anthropology: Cautions from a Feminist Perspective." *Signs* 15: 7–33.

Matthews, John. 1975. *Western Aristocracies and Imperial Court A.D. 364–425*. Oxford: Oxford University Press.

Mayor, John E. B., ed. 1979 [1877]. *Thirteen Satires of Juvenal*. New York: Arno Press. (Originally London: Macmillan).

McCann, Carole R., and Seung-Kyung Kim, eds. 2010. *Feminist Theory Reader: Local and Global Differences*. 2nd ed. New York: Routledge.

McClure, Laura K. 2003. *Courtesans at Table: Gender and Greek Literary Culture in Athenaeus*. New York: Routledge.

McGinn, Thomas A. J. 1991. "Concubinage and the *Lex Julia* on Adultery." *Transactions of the American Philological Association* 121: 335–74.

McGinn, Thomas A. J. 1998a. "*Feminae Probrosae* and the Litter." *Classical Journal* 93.3: 241–50.

McGinn, Thomas A. J. 1998b. *Prostitution, Sexuality, and the Law in Ancient Rome*. New York: Oxford University Press.

McGinn, Thomas A. J. 2002. "The Augustan Marriage Legislation and Social Practice: Elite Endogamy vs. Male 'Marrying Down.'" In *Speculum Iuris: Roman Law as a Reflection of Economic and Social Life*, ed. Jean-Jacques Aubert and Boudewijn Sirks, 46–93. Ann Arbor: University of Michigan Press.

McGinn, Thomas A. J. 2004. *The Economy of Prostitution in the Roman World: A Study of Social History and the Brothel*. Ann Arbor: University of Michigan Press.

McHardy, Fiona, and Eireann Marshall, eds. 2004. *Women's Influence on Classical Civilization*. London: Routledge.

McManus, Barbara F. 1997. *Classics and Feminism: Gendering the Classics*. New York: Twain.

McNamara, Jo Ann. 1984. "Cornelia's Daughters: Paula and Eustochium." *Women's Studies* 11: 9–27.

Merriam, Carol U. 1991. "The Other Sulpicia." *Classical World* 84.4: 303–5.

Meyers, Rachel. 2012. "Female Portraiture and Female Patronage in the High Imperial Period." In *A Companion to Women in the Ancient World*, ed. Sharon L. James and Sheila Dillon, 453–66. Chichester, UK: Wiley-Blackwell.

Miller, B. D. 1997. *The Endangered Sex: Neglect of Female Children in Rural North India*. Oxford: Oxford University Press.

Miller, Paul Allen. 1998. "The Bodily Grotesque in Roman Satire: Images of Sterility." *Arethusa* 31: 257–83.

Milnor, Kristina. 2005. *Gender, Domesticity, and the Age of Augustus: Inventing Private Life*. Oxford: Oxford University Press.

Mitchell, Carol. 1985. "Some Differences in Male and Female Joke-Telling." In *Women's Folklore, Women's Culture*, ed. Rosan A. Jordan and Susan J. Kalčik, 163–86. Philadelphia: University of Pennsylvania Press.

Mitchell, Dolores. 1981. "Humor in California Underground Women's Comix." In *Women's Culture: Renaissance of the Seventies*, ed. Gayle Kimball, 72–90. Metuchen, NJ: Scarecrow.

Mitchell, Juliet. 1966. "Women: The Longest Revolution." *New Left Review* 40: 11–31.

Mittman, Asa Simon, and Peter J. Dendle, eds. 2012. *The Ashgate Research Companion to Monsters and the Monstrous*. Farnham, UK: Ashgate.

Modleski, Tania. 1982. *Loving with a Vengeance*. London: Methuen.

Modleski, Tania. 1991. *Feminism without Women: Culture and Criticism in a "Postfeminist" Age*. New York: Routledge.

Mommsen, Theodor. 1899. *Römisches Strafrecht*. Leipzig: Duncker & Humblot.

Montrose, Louis. 1989. "Professing the Renaissance: The Poetics and Politics of Culture." In *The New Historicism*, ed. H. Aram Veeser, 15–36. New York: Routledge.

Moore, Henrietta L. 1988. *Feminism and Anthropology*. Minneapolis: University of Minnesota Press.

Moore, Stephen D. 1996. *Empire and Apocalypse: Postcolonialism and the New Testament*. Sheffield, UK: Sheffield Phoenix.

Moraga, Cherríe. 1986. "From a Long Line of Vendidas: Chicanas and Feminism." In *Feminist Studies/ Critical Studies*, ed. Teresa de Lauretis, 173–90. Bloomington: Indiana University Press.

Morales, Helen. 1996. "The Torturer's Apprentice: Parrhasius and the Limits of Art." In *Art and Text in the Roman World*, ed. Jaś Elsner, 182–209. Cambridge: Cambridge University Press.

Morel, Willy. 1927. *Fragmenta Poetarum Latinorum Epicorum et Lyricorum praeter Ennium et Lucilium*. Leipzig: Teubner.

Morgan, Sue, ed. 2006. *The Feminist History Reader*. Routledge: London.

Mouritsen, Henrik. 2005. "Freedmen and Decurions: Epitaphs and Social History in Imperial Italy." *Journal of Roman Studies* 95: 38–63.

Mouritsen, Henrik. 2011. *The Freedman in the Roman World*. Cambridge: Cambridge University Press.

Mueller, Hans-Friedrich. 2011. "Spectral Rome from Female Perspective: An Experiment in Recouping Women's Religious Experience (*CIL* 6.18817 = *ILS* 8006 = Orelli 2.4775)." *Classical World* 104: 227–43.

Mulvey, Laura. 1975. "Visual Pleasure and Narrative Cinema." *Screen* 16.3: 6–18.

Mulvey, Laura. 1992. "Pandora: Topographies of the Mask and Curiosity." In *Sexuality & Space*, ed. Beatriz Colomina, 53–71. Princeton: Princeton Architectural Press.

Murphy, Trevor. 2004. *Pliny the Elder's Natural History: The Empire in the Encyclopedia*. Oxford: Oxford University Press.

Myerowitz, Molly. 1985. *Ovid's Games of Love*. Detroit: Wayne State University Press.

Myerowitz, Molly. 1992. "The Domestication of Desire: Ovid's *Parva Tabella* and the Theater of Love." In *Pornography and Representation in Greece and Rome*, ed. Amy Richlin, 111–57. New York: Oxford University Press.

Najmabadi, Afsaneh. 2006. "Beyond the Americas: Are Gender and Sexuality Useful Categories of Historical Analysis?" *Journal of Women's History* 18: 11–21.

Narayan, Uma. 1997. *Dislocating Cultures: Identities, Traditions, and Third World Feminism*. New York: Routledge.

Narayan, Uma. 2000. "Essence of Culture and a Sense of History: A Feminist Critique of Cultural Essentialism." In *Decentering the Center: Philosophy for a Multicultural,*

Postcolonial, and Feminist World, ed. Uma Narayan and Sandra Harding, 80–100. Bloomington: Indiana University Press.

Narayan, Uma, and Sandra Harding, eds. 2000. *Decentering the Center: Philosophy for a Multicultural, Postcolonial, and Feminist World*. Bloomington: Indiana University Press.

NEH Humanities Institute on Women in Classical Antiquity. 1983. *Women in Classical Antiquity: Four Curricular Modules*. New York: Hunter College Department of Classical and Oriental Studies.

Neitz, Mary Jo. 1980. "Humor, Hierarchy, and the Changing Status of Women." *Psychiatry* 43: 211–23.

Newton, Judith. 1988. "History as Usual? Feminism and the 'New Historicism.'" *Cultural Critique* 9: 87–121.

Nicholson, Linda J., ed. 1990. *Feminism/Postmodernism*. New York: Routledge.

Nisbet, R. G. M., ed. 1961. *M. Tulli Ciceronis in L. Calpurnium Pisonem Oratio*. Oxford: Clarendon Press.

Nugent, S. Georgia. 1990. "This Sex Which Is Not One: De-Constructing Ovid's Hermaphrodite." *differences* 2: 160–85.

Nussbaum, Martha C. 1989. "Beyond Obsession and Disgust: Lucretius' Genealogy of Love." *Apeiron* 22.1: 1–59.

Nussbaum, Martha C. 1999. *Sex and Social Justice*. Oxford: Oxford University Press.

Nutton, Vivian. 1986. "The Perils of Patriotism: Pliny and Roman Medicine." In *Science in the Early Roman Empire: Pliny the Elder, His Sources and His Influence*, ed. Roger French and Frank Greenaway, 30–58. Totowa, NJ: Barnes & Noble.

O'Brien, Jay, and William Roseberry. 1991. "Introduction." In *Golden Ages, Dark Ages: Imagining the Past in Anthropology and History*, 2–18. Berkeley: University of California Press.

O'Higgins, Laurie. 2003. *Women and Humor in Classical Greece*. Cambridge: Cambridge University Press.

O'Higgins, D. M. [Laurie]. 2001. "Women's Cultic Joking and Mockery: Some Perspectives." In *Making Silence Speak: Women's Voices in Greek Literature and Society*, ed. André Lardinois and Laura McClure, 137–60. Princeton: Princeton University Press.

Olson, Kelly. 2002. "*Matrona* and Whore: The Clothing of Women in Roman Antiquity." *Fashion Theory* 6.4: 387–420.

Olson, Kelly. 2004–5 [2007]. "*Insignia lugentium*: Female Mourning Garments in Roman Antiquity." *American Journal of Ancient History* 3–4: 89–130.

O'Neill, Peter. 2003. "Going Round in Circles: Popular Speech in Ancient Rome." *Classical Antiquity* 22: 135–76.

Oost, Stewart Irvin. 1968. *Galla Placidia Augusta: A Biographical Essay*. Chicago: University of Chicago Press.

Opelt, Ilona. 1965. *Die lateinischen Schimpfwörter und verwandte sprachliche Erscheinungen: Eine Typologie*. Heidelberg: C. Winter.

Ortner, Sherry B. 1974. "Is Female to Male as Nature Is to Culture?" In *Woman, Culture, and Society*, ed. Michelle Zimbalist Rosaldo and Louise Lamphere, 68–87. Stanford: Stanford University Press.

Ortner, Sherry B. 1978. "The Virgin and the State." *Feminist Studies* 4: 19–35.

Ostriker, Alicia. 1985. "The Thieves of Language." In *The New Feminist Criticism*, ed. Elaine Showalter, 314–38. New York: Pantheon.

Packman, Zola Marie. 1993. "Call It Rape: A Motif in Roman Comedy and Its Suppression in English-Speaking Publications." *Helios* 20: 42–55.

Pally, Marcia. 1984. "'Double' Trouble." *Film Comment* 20: 12–17.

Parca, Maryline. 2012. "The Women of Ptolemaic Egypt: The View from Papyrology." In *A Companion to Women in the Ancient World*, ed. Sharon L. James and Sheila Dillon, 316–28. Chichester, UK: Wiley-Blackwell.

Parca, Maryline, and Angeliki Tzanetou, eds. 2007. *Finding Persephone: Women's Rituals in the Ancient Mediterranean*. Bloomington: Indiana University Press.

Parker, Holt N. 1992a. "Love's Body Anatomized: The Ancient Erotic Handbooks and the Rhetoric of Sexuality." In *Pornography and Representation in Greece and Rome*, ed. Amy Richlin, 90–111. New York: Oxford University Press.

Parker, Holt N. 1992b. "Other Remarks on the Other Sulpicia." *Classical World* 86.2: 89–95.

Parker, Holt N. 1994. "Sulpicia, the *Auctor de Sulpicia*, and the Authorship of 3.9 and 3.11 of the *Corpus Tibullianum*." *Helios* 21: 39–62.

Parker, Holt N. 1997. "The Teratogenic Grid." In *Roman Sexualities*, ed. Judith P. Hallett and Marilyn B. Skinner, 47–65. Princeton: Princeton University Press.

Parker, Holt N. 2004 [2007]. "Why Were the Vestals Virgins? Or, the Chastity of Women and the Safety of the Roman State." *American Journal of Philology* 125: 563–601. Reprinted in *Virginity Revisited: Configurations of the Unpossessed Body*, ed. Bonnie MacLachlan and Judith Fletcher, 66–99. Toronto: University of Toronto Press, 2007.

Parker, Holt N. 2012. "Galen and the Girls: Sources for Women Medical Writers Revisited." *Classical Quarterly* 62: 359–86.

Parker, Holt N. Forthcoming. *Metrodora: The Gynecology. The Earliest Surviving Work by a Woman Doctor and Other Works from the Florentine Manuscript*. Leiden: Brill.

Parker, Holt N., and Susanna Braund. 2012. "Imperial Satire and the Scholars." In *A Companion to Persius and Juvenal*, ed. Susanna Braund and Josiah Osgood, 436–64. Chichester, UK: Wiley-Blackwell.

Parker, Trey, and Matt Stone. 2004. *Team America: World Police*. Dir. Trey Parker.

Partner, Nancy, and Sarah Foot, eds. 2013. *The SAGE Handbook of Historical Theory*. London: SAGE Publications.

Patel, Tulsi, ed. 2007. *Sex-selective Abortion in India: Gender, Society and New Reproductive Technologies*. New Delhi and Thousand Oaks, CA: Sage Publications.

Peiss, Kathy. 1990. "Making Faces: The Cosmetics Industry and the Cultural Construction of Gender, 1890–1930." *Genders* 7: 143–69.

Peradotto, John, and J. P. Sullivan, eds. 1984. *Women in the Ancient World: The Arethusa Papers*. Albany: State University of New York Press.

Peretti, Lisa. 2003. *Women and Laughter in Medieval Comic Literature*. Ann Arbor: University of Michigan Press.

Perianayagam, Arokiasamy, and Srinivas Goli. 2012. "Provisional Results of the 2011 Census of India: Slowdown in Growth, Ascent in Literacy, but More Missing Girls." *International Journal of Social Economics* 39.10: 785–801.

Petersen, Lauren Hackworth. 2006. *The Freedman in Roman Art and Art History*. Cambridge: Cambridge University Press.

Phang, Sara Elise. 2001. *The Marriage of Roman Soldiers (13 BC—AD 235)*. New York: Columbia University Press.

Pierce, Christine. 1991. "Postmodernism and Other Skepticisms." In *Feminist Ethics*, ed. Claudia Card, 60–77. Lawrence: University Press of Kansas.

Pierce, Karen F. 1997. "The Portrayal of Rape in New Comedy." In *Rape in Antiquity*, ed. Susan Deacy and Karen F. Pierce, 163–84. London: Classical Press of Wales/ Duckworth.

Pinault, Jody Rubin. 1992. "The Medical Case for Virginity in the Early Second Century C.E.: Soranus of Ephesus, *Gynecology* 1.32." *Helios* 19.1–2: 123–39.

Plaza, Maria. 2006. *The Function of Humour in Roman Verse Satire: Laughing and Lying*. Oxford: Oxford University Press.

Pollard, Elizabeth Ann. 2008. "Placing Greco-Roman History in World Historical Context." *Classical World* 102: 49–64.

Pollard, Elizabeth Ann. 2009. "Pliny's *Natural History* and the Flavian *Templum Pacis*: Botanical Imperialism in First-Century C.E. Rome." *Journal of World History* 20: 309–38.

Pollard, Elizabeth Ann. 2010. "Rethinking Primary Sources for Cross-Cultural Interaction in World History: 'Standard' Problems and Connected Possibilities." *Social Studies Review* 49: 38–41.

Pollard, Elizabeth Ann. 2013. "Indian Spices and Roman 'Magic' in Imperial and Late Antique Indomediterranea." *Journal of World History* 24.1: 1-23.

Pomeroy, Sarah B. 1975. *Goddesses, Whores, Wives, and Slaves: Women in Classical Antiquity*. New York: Schocken.

Pomeroy, Sarah B. 1976. "The Relationship of the Married Woman to Her Blood Relatives in Rome." *Ancient Society* 7: 215–27.

Pomeroy, Sarah B. 1984. *Women in Hellenistic Egypt*. New York: Schocken.

Pomeroy, Sarah B., ed. and trans. 1994. *Xenophon,* Oeconomicus: *A Social and Historical Commentary*. Oxford: Clarendon Press.

Prager, Emily. 1982. "A Visit from the Footbinder." In *A Visit from the Footbinder and Other Stories*, 13–43. New York: Vintage.

Prum, Michel, Bénédicte Deschamps, and Marie-Claude Barbier, eds. 2007. *Racial, Ethnic, and Homophobic Violence: Killing in the Name of Otherness*. Abingdon, UK: Routledge-Cavendish.

Rabinowitz, Nancy Sorkin. 1992. "Tragedy and the Politics of Containment." In *Pornography and Representation in Greece and Rome*, ed. Amy Richlin, 36–52. New York: Oxford University Press.

Rabinowitz, Nancy Sorkin. 1993. *Anxiety Veiled: Euripides and the Traffic in Women*. Ithaca, NY: Cornell University Press.

Rabinowitz, Nancy Sorkin. 1995. "The Male Actor of Greek Tragedy: Evidence of Misogyny or Gender-Bending?" *Didaskalia* 1.6, Supplement 1: www.didaskalia.net/issues/supplement1/rabinowitz.html.

Rabinowitz, Nancy Sorkin. 1998. "Embodying Tragedy: The Sex of the Actor." *Intertexts* 2: 3–25.

Rabinowitz, Nancy Sorkin. 2001. "Personal Voice/ Feminist Voice." *Arethusa* 34.2: 191–210.

Rabinowitz, Nancy Sorkin, and Amy Richlin, eds. 1993. *Feminist Theory and the Classics*. New York: Routledge.

Rabinowitz, Nancy Sorkin, and Lisa Auanger, eds. 2002. *Among Women: From the Homosocial to the Homoerotic in the Ancient World*. Austin: University of Texas Press.

Rankin, H. D. 1971. *Petronius the Artist: Essays on the* Satyricon *and its Author*. The Hague: Martinus Nijhoff.

Redfield, James. 1991. "Classics and Anthropology." *Arion* (third series) 1.2: 5–23.

Rein, W. 1844. *Das Criminalrecht der Römer*. Leipzig: Köhler.

Reynolds, R. W. 1946. "The Adultery Mime." *Classical Quarterly* 40: 77–84.

Richlin, Amy. 1978. "Sexual Terms and Themes in Roman Satire and Related Genres." Diss. Yale University.

Richlin, Amy. 1981a. "Approaches to the Sources on Adultery at Rome." In *Reflections of Women in Antiquity*, ed. Helene P. Foley, 379–404. New York: Gordon and Breach Science Publishers.

Richlin, Amy. 1981b. "The Meaning of *Irrumare* in Catullus and Martial." *Classical Philology* 76: 40–46.

Richlin, Amy. 1989. "'Is Classics Dead?' The 1988 Women's Classical Caucus Report." In *Classics: A Discipline and Profession in Crisis*, ed. Phyllis Culham, Lowell Edmunds, and Alden Smith, 51–65. Lanham, MD: University Press of America.

Richlin, Amy. 1990. "Hijacking the Palladion." *Helios* 17: 175–85.

Richlin, Amy. 1991. "Zeus and Metis: Foucault, Feminism, Classics." *Helios* 18: 160–80.

Richlin, Amy. 1992. *The Garden of Priapus: Sexuality and Aggression in Roman Humor*. Rev. ed. Oxford: Oxford University Press.

Richlin, Amy. 1993. "Not Before Homosexuality: The Materiality of the *Cinaedus* and the Roman Law against Love between Men." *Journal of the History of Sexuality* 3: 523–72.

Richlin, Amy. 1997a. "Foucault's *History of Sexuality*: A Useful Theory for Women?" In *Rethinking Sexuality: Foucault and Classical Antiquity*, ed. David H. J. Larmour, Paul Allen Miller, and Charles Platter, 138–70. Princeton: Princeton University Press.

Richlin, Amy. 1997b. "Gender and Rhetoric: Producing Manhood in the Schools." In *Roman Eloquence: Rhetoric in Society and Literature*, ed. William J. Dominik, 90–110. London: Routledge.

Richlin, Amy. 1997c. "Towards a History of Body History." In *Inventing Ancient Culture: Historicism, Periodization, and the Ancient World*, edited by Mark Golden and Peter Toohey, 16–35. London: Routledge.

Richlin, Amy. 1999. "Cicero's Head." In *Constructions of the Classical Body*, ed. James I. Porter, 190–211. Ann Arbor: University of Michigan Press.

Richlin, Amy. 2004. Review of *Classics in Progress*, ed. T. P. Wiseman (Oxford: Oxford University Press, 2002). *Classical Review* 54: 12–17.

Richlin, Amy. 2009. "Sex in the *Satyrica*: Outlaws in Literatureland." In *Petronius: A Handbook*, ed. Jonathan Prag and Ian Repath, 82–100. Chichester, UK: Wiley-Blackwell.

Richlin, Amy. 2010. "What We Need to Know Right Now." *Journal of Women's History* 22.4: 268–81.

Richlin, Amy. 2011a. "Old Boys: Teacher-Student Bonding in Roman Oratory." *Classical World* 105.1: 37–53.

Richlin, Amy. 2011b. "Parallel Lives: Domitia Lucilla and Cratia, Fronto and Marcus." *Eugesta* 1: 163–203.

Richlin, Amy. 2013a. "The Fragments of Terentia." In *Roman Literature, Gender, and Reception*, ed. Barbara Gold, Donald Lateiner, and Judith Perkins, 93–118. London: Routledge.

Richlin, Amy. 2013b. "Sexuality and History." In *The SAGE Handbook of Historical Theory*, ed. Nancy Partner and Sarah Foot, 294–310. London: SAGE Publications.

Richlin, Amy. 2014. "Talking to Slaves in the Plautine Audience." *Classical Antiquity* 33: 175–226.

Richlin, Amy. In progress. *Plautine Comedy as Slave Theater.*

Riddle, John M. 1992. *Contraception and Abortion from the Ancient World to the Renaissance.* Cambridge, MA: Harvard University Press.

Riddle, John M., J. Worth Estes, and Josiah C. Russell. 1994. "Birth Control in the Ancient World." *Archaeology* (March/April): 29–35.

Rimell, Victoria. 2005. "Facing Facts: Ovid's *Medicamina* through the Looking Glass." In *Gendered Dynamics in Latin Love Poetry*, ed. Ronnie Ancona and Ellen Greene, 177–205. Baltimore: Johns Hopkins University Press.

Rivière, Joan. 1986. "Womanliness as a Masquerade." In *Formations of Fantasy*, ed. Victor Burgin, James Donald, and Cora Kaplan, 35–44. London: Methuen.

Robbins, Trina, and catherine yronwode. 1985. *Women and the Comics.* Forestville, CA: Eclipse Books.

Roberts, Michael. 1989. *The Jeweled Style: Poetry and Poetics in Late Antiquity.* Ithaca, NY: Cornell University Press.

Robin, Diana. 2007. *Publishing Women: Salons, the Presses, and the Counter-Reformation in Sixteenth-Century Italy.* Chicago: University of Chicago Press.

Rolfe, J. C., trans. 1997. *Suetonius.* 2 vols. Cambridge, MA: Harvard University Press.

Roller, Matthew B. 2003. "Horizontal Women: Posture and Sex in the Roman *Convivium*." *American Journal of Philology* 124: 377–422.

Romano, Allen. 2009. "The Invention of Marriage: Hermaphroditus and Salmacis in Ovid." *Classical Quarterly* 59.2: 543–61.

Rosaldo, Michelle Zimbalist. 1980. "The Use and Abuse of Anthropology: Reflections on Feminism and Cross-Cultural Understanding." *Signs* 5.3: 389–417.

Rosaldo, Michelle Zimbalist, and Louise Lamphere, eds. 1974. *Woman, Culture, and Society.* Stanford: Stanford University Press.

Rosaldo, Renato. 1986. "From the Door of His Tent: The Fieldworker and the Inquisitor." In James Clifford and George E. Marcus, eds., *Writing Culture*, 77–97. Berkeley: University of California Press.

Rose, Peter W. 1993. "The Case for Not Ignoring Marx in the Study of Women in Antiquity." In *Feminist Theory and the Classics*, ed. Nancy Sorkin Rabinowitz and Amy Richlin, 211–37. New York: Routledge.

Rosen, Ralph M. 2007. *Making Mockery: The Poetics of Ancient Satire.* Oxford: Oxford University Press.

Ross, Sarah Gwyneth. 2009. *The Birth of Feminism: Woman as Intellect in Renaissance Italy and England.* Cambridge, MA: Harvard University Press.

Rowe, Kathleen. 1995. *The Unruly Woman: Gender and the Genres of Laughter.* Austin: University of Texas Press.

Rowlandson, Jane, ed. 1998. *Women and Society in Greek and Roman Egypt: A Sourcebook.* Cambridge: Cambridge University Press.

Rüpke, Jörg. 2007a. *Religion of the Romans.* Trans. Richard Gordon. London: Polity. First published 2001 as *Die Religion der Römer*, by C. H. Beck.

Rüpke, Jörg. 2007b. *Römische Priester in der Antike: Ein biographisches Lexikon.* Stuttgart: Franz Steiner Verlag.

Russ, Joanna. 1983. *How to Suppress Women's Writing*. Austin: University of Texas Press.

Russ, Joanna. 1985. *Magic Mommas, Trembling Sisters, Puritans and Perverts*. Trumansburg, New York: The Crossing Press.

Russo, Mary. 1986. "Female Grotesques: Carnival and Theory." In *Feminist Studies/ Critical Studies*, ed. Teresa de Lauretis, 213–29. Bloomington: Indiana University Press.

Russo, Mary. 1994. *The Female Grotesque: Risk, Excess and Modernity*. New York: Routledge.

Saller, Richard P. 1998. "Symbols of Gender and Status Hierarchies in the Roman Household." In *Women and Slaves in Greco-Roman Culture: Differential Equations*, ed. Sandra R. Joshel and Sheila Murnaghan, 85–91. London: Routledge.

Salzman, Michele Renee. 1990. *The Codex-Calendar of 354 and the Rhythms of Urban Life in Late Antiquity*. Berkeley: University of California Press.

Salzman, Michele Renee. 2002. *The Making of a Christian Aristocracy: Social and Religious Change in the Western Roman Empire*. Cambridge, MA: Harvard University Press.

Salzman-Mitchell, Patricia B. 2005. *A Web of Fantasies: Gaze, Image, and Gender in Ovid's* Metamorphoses. Columbus: Ohio State University Press.

Sauer, Eberhard. 1996. "An Inscription from Northern Italy, the Roman Temple Complex in Bath and Minerva as a Healing Goddess in Gallo-Roman Religion." *Oxford Journal of Archaeology* 15: 63–93.

Schade, Kathrin. 2009. "The Female Body in Late Antiquity: Between Virtue, Taboo and Eroticism." In *Bodies and Boundaries in Graeco-Roman Antiquity*, ed. Thorsten Fögen and Mireille M. Lee, 215–36. Berlin: Walter de Gruyter.

Schaps, David M. 1979. *Economic Rights of Women in Ancient Greece*. Edinburgh: Edinburgh University Press.

Scheid, John. 1992. "The Religious Roles of Roman Women." Trans. Arthur Goldhammer. In *A History of Women in the West, vol. 1: From Ancient Goddesses to Christian Saints*, ed. Pauline Schmitt Pantel, 377–408. Cambridge, MA: Harvard University Press.

Scheid, John. 2003. *An Introduction to Roman Religion*. Trans. Janet Lloyd. Bloomington: Indiana University Press. First published 1998 as *La religion des Romans*.

Scheidel, Walter. 1995. "The Most Silent Women of Greece and Rome: Rural Labour and Women's Life in the Ancient World (I)." *Greece & Rome* 2nd series 42.2: 202–17.

Scheidel, Walter. 1996. "The Most Silent Women of Greece and Rome: Rural Labour and Women's Life in the Ancient World (II)." *Greece & Rome* 2nd series 43.1: 1–10.

Scheidel, Walter. 2007. "Roman Funerary Commemoration and the Age at Marriage." *Classical Philology* 102: 389–402.

Schultz, Celia E. 2006. *Women's Religious Activity in the Roman Republic*. Chapel Hill: University of North Carolina Press.

Schultz, Celia E. 2007. "*Sanctissima Femina*: Social Categorization and Women's Religious Experience in the Roman Republic." In *Finding Persephone: Women's Rituals in the Ancient Mediterranean*, ed. Maryline Parca and Angeliki Tzanetou, 92–113. Bloomington: Indiana University Press.

Schüssler Fiorenza, Elisabeth. 1989. *In Memory of Her: A Feminist Theological Reconstruction of Christian Origins*. New York: Garland.

Scott, James C. 1990. *Domination and the Arts of Resistance: Hidden Transcripts*. New Haven, CT: Yale University Press.

Scott, Joan W. 1989. "Gender: A Useful Category of Historical Analysis." In *Coming to Terms: Feminism, Theory, Politics*, ed. Elizabeth Weed, 81–100. New York: Routledge.

Scott, S. P., trans. 1932. *The Civil Law*. Cincinnati: Central Trust Company.

Scullard, H. H. 1981. *Festivals and Ceremonies of the Roman Republic*. Ithaca: Cornell University Press.

Sebesta, Judith Lynn. 1997. "Women's Costume and Feminine Civic Morality in Augustan Rome." *Gender & History* 9: 529–41.

Sebesta, Judith Lynn, and Larissa Bonfante, eds. 1994. *The World of Roman Costume*. Madison: University of Wisconsin Press.

Segal, Charles. 1998. "Ovid's Metamorphic Bodies: Art, Gender, and Violence in the *Metamorphoses*." *Arion* 5.3: 9–41.

Severy-Hoven, Beth A. 2003. *Augustus and the Family at the Birth of the Roman Empire*. New York: Routledge.

Shackleton Bailey, D. R., ed. 1965. *Cicero's Letters to Atticus*. Vol. 1. Cambridge: Cambridge University Press.

Shapiro, Judith. 1981. "Anthropology and the Study of Gender." In *A Feminist Perspective in the Academy*, ed. Elizabeth Langland and Walter Gove, 110–29. Chicago: University of Chicago Press.

Sharp, Margery. 1937. *The Nutmeg Tree*. New York: Grosset & Dunlap.

Sharrock, Alison. 2011. "Womanly Wailing? The Mother of Euryalus and Gendered Reading." *Eugesta* 1: 55–77.

Shaw, Brent. 2002. "'With Whom I Lived': Measuring Roman Marriage." *Ancient Society* 32: 195–242.

Sherwin-White, A. N. 1966. *The Letters of Pliny: A Historical and Social Commentary*. Oxford: Clarendon Press.

Sherwin-White, A. N. 1967. *Racial Prejudice in Imperial Rome*. Cambridge: Cambridge University Press.

Showalter, Elaine, ed. 1985. *The New Feminist Criticism*. New York: Pantheon.

Shumka, Leslie. 2008. "Designing Women: The Representation of Women's Toiletries on Funerary Monuments in Roman Italy." In *Roman Dress and the Fabrics of Roman Culture*, ed. Jonathan Edmondson and Alison Keith, 172–91. Toronto: University of Toronto Press.

Silverblatt, Irene. 1991. "Interpreting Women in States: New Feminist Ethnohistories." In *Gender at the Crossroads of Knowledge*, ed. Micaela di Leonardo, 140–71. Berkeley: University of California Press.

Silverman, Kaja. 1984. "*Histoire d'O*: The Construction of a Female Subject." In *Pleasure and Danger*, ed. Carole S. Vance, 320–49. Boston: Routledge and Kegan Paul.

Silverman, Sarah. 2005. *Jesus Is Magic*. Dir. Liam Lynch.

Sissa, Giulia. 1990. *Greek Virginity*. Trans. Arthur Goldhammer. Cambridge, MA: Harvard University Press.

Sissa, Giulia. 2003 [2008]. *Eros tiranno: Sessualità e sensualità nel mondo antico*. Rome: Laterza. = *Sex and Sensuality in the Ancient World*. Trans. George Staunton. New Haven, CT: Yale University Press, 2008.

Sivan, Hagith. 2011. *Galla Placidia: The Last Roman Empress*. Oxford: Oxford University Press.

Skinner, Marilyn B. 1982a. "The Contents of Caelius' *Pyxis*." *Classical World* 75: 243–45.

Skinner, Marilyn B. 1982b. "Pretty Lesbius." *Transactions of the American Philological Association* 112: 197–208.

Skinner, Marilyn B. 1983a. "Clodia Metelli." *Transactions of the American Philological Association* 113: 273–87.

Skinner, Marilyn B. 1983b. "Corinna of Tanagra and Her Audience." *Tulsa Studies in Women's Literature* 2: 9–20.

Skinner, Marilyn B. 1986. "Classical Studies vs. Women's Studies: *duo moi ta noêmmata.*" *Helios* 12.2: 3–16.

Skinner, Marilyn B. 1987a. "Classical Studies, Patriarchy and Feminism: The View from 1986." *Women's Studies International Forum* 10.2: 181–86.

Skinner, Marilyn B. 1987b. "Rescuing Creusa: New Methodological Approaches to Women in Antiquity." *Helios* 13.2: 1–8. (Editor's introduction to the fall 1986 special issue on women in antiquity, which carries the publication date of 1987.)

Skinner, Marilyn B. 1989. "Sapphic Nossis." *Arethusa* 22.1: 5–18.

Skinner, Marilyn B. 1991. "Nossis *Thêlyglôssos*: The Private Text and the Public Book." In *Women's History and Ancient History*, ed. Sarah B. Pomeroy, 20–47. Chapel Hill: University of North Carolina Press.

Skinner, Marilyn B. 1993. "Woman and Language in Archaic Greece, or, Why Is Sappho a Woman?" In *Feminist Theory and the Classics*, ed. Nancy Sorkin Rabinowitz and Amy Richlin, 125–44. New York: Routledge.

Skinner, Marilyn B. 1996. "Zeus and Leda." *Thamyris* 3.1: 103–23.

Skinner, Marilyn B. 2001. "Ladies' Day at the Art Institute: Theocritus, Herodas, and the Gendered Gaze." In *Making Silence Speak: Women's Voices in Greek Literature and Society*, ed. André Lardinois and Laura McClure, 201–22. Princeton: Princeton University Press.

Skinner, Marilyn B. 2011. *Clodia Metelli: The Tribune's Sister.* Oxford: Oxford University Press.

Skinner, Quentin, ed. 1985. *The Return of Grand Theory in the Human Sciences.* Cambridge: Cambridge University Press.

Skoie, Mathilde. 2002. *Reading Sulpicia: Commentaries, 1475–1990.* Oxford: Oxford University Press.

Skutsch, O. 1905. "Domitius Marsus." *RE* 5.1430–32.

Slater, Philip E. 1968. *The Glory of Hera.* Boston: Beacon Press.

Smith, Christopher. 2000. "Worshipping Mater Matuta: Ritual and Context." In *Religion in Archaic and Republican Rome and Italy: Evidence and Experience*, ed. Edward Bispham and Christopher Smith, 136–55, 171–73. Chicago: Fitzroy Dearborn.

Smith, Martin, ed. 1975. *Petronius* Cena Trimalchionis. Oxford: Clarendon Press.

Snowden, Frank M., Jr. 1970. *Blacks in Antiquity.* Cambridge, MA: Harvard University Press.

Snyder, Jane. 1989. *The Woman and the Lyre.* Carbondale: Southern Illinois University Press.

Soren, David. 1999. "Hecate and the Infant Cemetery at Poggio Gramignano." In *A Roman Villa and Late Roman Infant Cemetery: Excavation at Poggio Gramignano (Lugnano in Teverino)*, ed. David Soren and Noelle Soren, 619–31. Rome: "L'Erma" di Bretschneider.

Soren, David, Todd Fenton, and Walter Birkby. 1999. "The Infant Cemetery at Poggio

Gramignano: Description and Analysis." In *A Roman Villa and Late Roman Infant Cemetery: Excavation at Poggio Gramignano (Lugnano in Teverino)*, ed. David Soren and Noelle Soren, 477–530. Rome: "L'Erma" di Bretschneider.

Spaeth, Barbette Stanley. 1996. *The Roman Goddess Ceres*. Austin: University of Texas Press.

Spelman, Elizabeth V. 1982. "Woman as Body: Ancient and Contemporary Views." *Feminist Studies* 8: 109–31.

Spelman, Elizabeth V. 1988. *Inessential Woman: Problems of Exclusion in Feminist Thought*. Boston: Beacon Press.

Spentzou, Efrossini. 2003. *Readers and Writers in Ovid's* Heroides: *Transgressions of Genre and Gender*. Oxford: Oxford University Press.

Spivak, Gayatri Chakravorty. 1988. "Can the Subaltern Speak?" In *Marxism and the Interpretation of Culture*, ed. Cary Nelson and Lawrence Grossberg, 271–313. Urbana: University of Illinois Press.

Starks, John H., Jr. 2008. "Pantomime Actresses in Latin Inscriptions." In *New Directions in Ancient Pantomime*, ed. Edith Hall and Rosie Wyles, 111–45. Oxford: Oxford University Press.

Starks, John H., Jr. 2010. "*servitus, sudor, sitis*: Syra and Syrian Slave Stereotyping in Plautus' *Mercator*." *New England Classical Journal* 37.1: 51–64.

Starks, John H., Jr. 2011. "Was Black Beautiful in Vandal Africa?" In *African Athena: New Agendas*, ed. Daniel Orrells, Gurminder K. Bhambra, and Tessa Roynton, 239–57. Oxford: Oxford University Press.

Staves, Susan. 2010. *A Literary History of Women's Writing in Britain, 1660–1789*. Cambridge: Cambridge University Press.

Stears, Karen. 1998. "Death Becomes Her: Gender and Athenian Death Ritual." In *The Sacred and the Feminine in Ancient Greece*, ed. Sue Blundell and Margaret Williamson, 113–27. London: Routledge.

Stehle, Eva. 1989. "Venus, Cybele and the Sabine Women: The Roman Construction of Female Sexuality." *Helios* 16: 143–64.

Stehle, Eva. 1990. "Sappho's Gaze: Fantasies of a Goddess and a Young Man." *differences* 2.1: 88–125.

Stephens, Susan A., and Phiroze Vasunia, eds. 2010. *Classics and National Cultures*. Oxford: Oxford University Press.

Šterbenc Erker, Darja. 2011. "Gender and Roman Funeral Ritual." In *Memory and Mourning: Studies on Roman Death*, ed. Valerie M. Hope and Janet Huskinson, 40–60. Oxford: Oxbow Books.

Stevenson, Jane. 2005. *Women Latin Poets: Language, Gender, and Authority, from Antiquity to the Eighteenth Century*. Oxford: Oxford University Press.

Stryker, Susan, and Stephen Whittle, eds. 2006. *The Transgender Studies Reader*. New York: Routledge.

Sullivan, J. P. 1973. "Editorial." *Arethusa* 6.1: 4–5.

Sullivan, J. P. 1991. *Martial: The Unexpected Classic*. Cambridge: Cambridge University Press.

Suter, Ann, ed. 2008. *Lament: Studies in the Ancient Mediterranean and Beyond*. Oxford: Oxford University Press.

Sutherland, C. H. V., and R. A. G. Carson. 1984. *The Roman Imperial Coinage*. Vol. 1 (rev.). London: Spink and Sons.

Sutton, Robert F., Jr. 1992. "Pornography and Persuasion in Attic Pottery." In *Pornography and Representation in Greece and Rome*, ed. Amy Richlin, 3–35. Oxford: Oxford University Press.

Swift, Ellen. 2009. *Style and Function in Roman Decoration: Living with Objects and Interiors*. Burlington, VT: Ashgate.

Takács, Sarolta. 2007. *Vestal Virgins, Sibyls, and Matrons: Women in Roman Religion*. Austin: University of Texas Press.

Talalay, Lauren. 2012. "Case Study I: The Mother Goddess in Prehistory: Debates and Perspectives." In *A Companion to Women in the Ancient World*, ed. Sharon L. James and Sheila Dillon, 7–10. Chichester, UK: Wiley-Blackwell.

Temkin, Owsei, trans. 1991 [1956]. *Soranus' Gynecology*. Baltimore: The Johns Hopkins University Press.

Temporini, H. 1978. *Die Frauen am Hofe Trajans*. Berlin: De Gruyter.

Thakur, Sanjaya. 2014. "Challenges in Teaching Sexual Violence and Rape: A Male Perspective. " In *From Abortion to Pederasty: Addressing Difficult Topics in the Classics Classroom*, ed. Nancy Sorkin Rabinowitz and Fiona McHardy. Columbus: Ohio State University Press.

Theweleit, Klaus. 1987. *Male Fantasies*. Vol. 1: *Women Floods Bodies History*. Trans. Stephen Conway. Minneapolis: University of Minnesota Press.

Thurston, Carol. 1987. *The Romance Revolution: Erotic Novels for Women and the Quest for a New Sexual Identity*. Urbana: University of Illinois Press.

Tong, Rosemarie. 1989. *Feminist Thought: A Comprehensive Introduction*. Boulder: Westview Press.

Toynbee, J. M. C. 1971. *Death and Burial in the Roman World*. Ithaca: Cornell University Press.

Trachtenberg, Joshua. 1961 [1939]. *Jewish Magic and Superstition*. Cleveland: World Publishing.

Treggiari, Susan. 1969. *Roman Freedmen During the Late Republic*. Oxford: Clarendon Press.

Treggiari, Susan. 1976. "Jobs for Women." *American Journal of Ancient History* 1: 76–104.

Treggiari, Susan. 1979. "Questions on Women Domestics in the Roman West." In *Schiavitù, manomissione e classi dipendenti nel mondo antico*. Università degli studi di Padova, Pubblicazioni dell'Istituto di Storia Antica 13: 185–201. Rome: "L'Erma" di Bretschneider.

Treggiari, Susan. 1991. *Roman Marriage: Iusti Coniuges from the Time of Cicero to the Time of Ulpian*. Oxford: Clarendon Press.

Treggiari, Susan. 1998. "Home and Forum: Cicero between 'Public' and 'Private.'" *Transactions of the American Philological Association* 128: 1–23.

Turner, Victor. 1969. *The Ritual Process*. Chicago: Aldine.

Tylawsky, Elizabeth. 2001. "Supplying a Genealogy: Self-promotion by Praising Dead Women." In *Essays in Honor of Gordon Williams*, ed. Elizabeth Tylawsky and Charles Weiss, 283–93. New Haven, CT: Henry R. Schwab.

Upson-Saia, Kristi. 2011. *Early Christian Dress: Gender, Virtue, and Authority*. New York: Routledge.

Uzzi, Jeannine Diddle. Forthcoming. "Ethnicity and Sexuality in Roman Imperial Relief: Reconstructing the Pederastic Gaze." In *Children as Archaeological Enigma*, ed. Peter F. Biehl and Güner Coskunsu. Albany: State University of New York Press.

Van Bremen, Riet. 1983. "Women and Wealth." In *Images of Women in Antiquity*, ed. Averil Cameron and Amélie Kuhrt, 223–42. Detroit: Wayne State University Press.

Van Bremen, Riet. 1996. *The Limits of Participation: Women and Civic Life in the Greek East in the Hellenistic and Roman Periods*. Amsterdam: J. C. Gieben.

Vance, Carole S., ed. 1984. *Pleasure and Danger*. Boston: Routledge and Kegan Paul.

Van Sickle, John. 1987. "The Elogia of the Cornelii Scipiones and the Origin of Epigram at Rome." *American Journal of Philology* 108: 41–55.

Veeser, H. Aram, ed. 1989. *The New Historicism*. New York: Routledge.

Verducci, Florence. 1985. *Ovid's Toyshop of the Heart*. Princeton: Princeton University Press.

Versnel, H. S. 1992. "The Festival for Bona Dea and the Thesmophoria." *Greece & Rome* 39: 31–55.

Vickers, Nancy J. 1981. "Diana Described: Scattered Woman and Scattered Rhyme." *Critical Inquiry* 8: 265–79.

Vickers, Nancy J. 1985. "'This Heraldry in Lucrece' Face.'" In *The Female Body in Western Culture*, ed. Susan Rubin Suleiman, 209–22. Cambridge, MA: Harvard University Press.

Vinson, Martha. 1998. "Gender and Politics in the Post-Iconoclastic Period: The *Lives* of Antony the Younger, the Empress Theodora, and the Patriarch Ignatios." *Byzantion* 68: 469–515.

Vinson, Martha. 2004. "Romance and Reality in the Byzantine Bride Shows." In *Gender in the Early Medieval World*, ed. Leslie Brubaker and Julia M. H. Smith, 102–20. Cambridge: Cambridge University Press.

Vons, Jacqueline. 2000. *L'image de la femme dans l'œuvre de Pline l'Ancien*. Brussels: Latomus.

von Staden, Heinrich. 1991. "*Apud nos foediora verba*: Celsus' Reluctant Construction of the Female Body." In *Le latin médical: La constitution d'un langage scientifique*. Mémoires du Centre Jean Palerne 10, ed. Guy Sabbah, 271–96. Saint-Étienne, France: Publications de l'Université du Saint-Étienne.

von Staden, Heinrich. 1992. "Women and Dirt." *Helios* 19: 7–30.

Walcot, Peter. 1987. "Plato's Mother and Other Terrible Women." *Greece & Rome* 34: 12–31.

Walker, Nancy A. 1988. *A Very Serious Thing: Women's Humor and American Culture*. Minneapolis: University of Minnesota Press.

Wallace-Hadrill, Andrew. 2008. *Rome's Cultural Revolution*. Cambridge: Cambridge University Press.

Walters, Jonathan. 1993. "'No More Than a Boy': The Shifting Construction of Masculinity from Ancient Greece to the Middle Ages." *Gender & History* 5: 20–33.

Ward, Allen M., Fritz M. Heichelheim, and Cedric A. Yeo. 2009. *A History of the Roman People*. Fifth ed. Englewood Cliffs, NJ: Prentice Hall.

Warde Fowler, W. 1916. *The Roman Festivals of the Period of the Republic*. London: Macmillan & Co., Ltd.

Warmington, E. H., ed. and trans. 1961. *Remains of Old Latin*. Vol. 3. Cambridge, MA: Harvard University Press.

Warrior, Valerie. 2006. *Roman Religion*. Cambridge: Cambridge University Press.

Webb, Ronald G. 1981. "Political Uses of Humor." *Et cetera* 38: 35–50.

Weed, Elizabeth, ed. 1989. *Coming to Terms: Feminism, Theory, Politics*. New York: Routledge.

Wegner, Judith Romney. 1991. "The Image and Status of Women in Classical Rabbinic Judaism." In *Jewish Women in Historical Perspective*, ed. Judith R. Baskin, 94–114. Detroit: Wayne State University Press.

Weissler, Chava. 1987. "The Religion of Traditional Ashkenazic Women: Some Methodological Issues." *Association for Jewish Studies Review* 12: 73–94.

Weissler, Chava. 1991. "Prayers in Yiddish and the Religious World of Ashkenazic Women." In *Jewish Women in Historical Perspective*, ed. Judith R. Baskin, 159–81. Detroit: Wayne State University Press.

Weissler, Chava. 1998. *Voices of the Matriarchs: Listening to the Prayers of Early Modern Jewish Women*. Boston: Beacon Press.

Wessner, P. 1928. "Macrobius." *RE* 14.184.

Wilfong, Terry G. 2002. *Women of Jeme: Lives in a Coptic Town in Late Antique Egypt*. Ann Arbor: University of Michigan Press.

Williams, Gordon. 1958. "Some Aspects of Roman Marriage Ceremonies and Ideals." *Journal of Roman Studies* 48: 16–29.

Williams, Gordon. 1962. "Poetry in the Moral Climate of Augustan Rome." *Journal of Roman Studies* 52: 28–46.

Williams, Gordon. 1968. *Tradition and Originality in Roman Poetry*. Oxford: Clarendon Press.

Williams, Gordon. 1978. *Change and Decline*. Berkeley: University of California Press.

Winkler, John J. 1981. "Gardens of Nymphs: Public and Private in Sappho's Lyrics." In *Reflections of Women in Antiquity*, ed. Helene P. Foley, 63–89. New York: Gordon and Breach.

Winkler, John J. 1990a. *The Constraints of Desire: The Anthropology of Sex and Gender in Ancient Greece*. New York: Routledge.

Winkler, John J. 1990b. "The Constraints of Desire: Erotic Magical Spells." In *The Constraints of Desire*, 71–98. New York: Routledge.

Winkler, John J. 1990c. "The Laughter of the Oppressed: Demeter and the Gardens of Adonis." In *The Constraints of Desire*, 188–209. New York: Routledge.

Wittig, Monique. 1981. "One Is Not Born a Woman." *Feminist Issues* 1.2: 47–54.

Wood, Susan. 1999. *Imperial Women: A Study in Public Images, 40 B.C.—A.D. 68*. Leiden: Brill.

Woodhull, Margaret L. 2004. "Matronly Patrons in the Early Roman Empire: The Case of Salvia Postuma." In *Women's Influence on Classical Civilization*, ed. Fiona McHardy and Eireann Marshall, 75–91. London: Routledge.

Woods, Marjorie Curry. 1996. "Rape and the Pedagogical Rhetoric of Sexual Violence." In *Criticism and Dissent in the Middle Ages*, ed. Rita Copeland, 56–86. Cambridge: Cambridge University Press.

Woolf, Virginia. 1957 [1929]. *A Room of One's Own*. New York: Harcourt Brace Jovanovich.

Wyke, Maria. 1994. "Woman in the Mirror: The Rhetoric of Adornment in the Roman World." In *Women in Ancient Societies*, ed. Léonie Archer, Susan Fischler, and Maria Wyke, 134–51. New York: Routledge.

Wyke, Maria. 2002. *The Roman Mistress: Ancient and Modern Representations*. Oxford: Oxford University Press.

Zajko, Vanda. 2009. "'Listening With' Ovid: Intersexuality, Queer Theory, and the Myth of Hermaphroditus and Salmacis." *Helios* 36: 175–202.

Zeitlin, Froma. 1985. "Playing the Other: Theater, Theatricality, and the Feminine in Greek Drama." *Representations* 11: 63–94.

Zijderveld, Anton C. 1968. "Jokes and Their Relation to Social Reality." *Social Research* 35: 286–311.

Zweig, Bella. 1993. "The Primal Mind: Using Native American Models for the Study of Women in Ancient Greece." In *Feminist Theory and the Classics*, ed. Nancy Sorkin Rabinowitz and Amy Richlin, 145–80. New York: Routledge.

Index Locorum

Listings are by common title, except for the works of Cicero, the titles for which are abbreviated as in the *Oxford Latin Dictionary*.

General Index

women's humor, 66–67, 95, 97–100, 113, 128–29, 332n17

women's religion, Roman, 154, 167, 197–240, 306, 309–10, 340–41n2; cult of the emperor's wife, 82, 208; household cult, 199, 206, 230; spirituality, 211, 213, 214

Women's Studies, 3, 12, 35, 200, 289–90, 308

women's work, 25–26, 270–71, 285–88, 315, 344n34, 344n35. *See also* beauticians; Pietrabbondante roof tile; *praefica*; wet-nurses; weaving and spinning; women, Roman, and mourning; women, Roman, as medical practitioners

Woolf, Virginia, 18, 34, 128, 137, 248, 268, 311, 355n16

"wrong because depressing," 296, 303, 304

World History, 34

Wyke, Maria, 19, 168, 331n4, 335n1, 337n1

Year King phenomenon, 33

Zweig, Bella. *See* Vivante, Bella